Lecture Notes in Computer Science 2932

Edited by G. Goos, J. Hartmanis, and J. van Leeuwen

T0240563

Springer
Berlin
Heidelberg
New York
Hong Kong
London
Milan
Paris
Tokyo

Peter Van Emde Boas   Jaroslav Pokorný
Mária Bieliková   Július Štuller (Eds.)

SOFSEM 2004:
Theory and Practice
of Computer Science

30th Conference on Current Trends
in Theory and Practice of Computer Science
Měřín, Czech Republic, January 24-30, 2004
Proceedings

 Springer

Series Editors

Gerhard Goos, Karlsruhe University, Germany
Juris Hartmanis, Cornell University, NY, USA
Jan van Leeuwen, Utrecht University, The Netherlands

Volume Editors

Peter Van Emde Boas
University of Amsterdam, Faculty of Sciences
ILLC - Department of Mathematics and Computer Science
Plantage Muidergracht 24, 1018 TV Amsterdam, The Netherlands
E-mail: peter@science.uva.nl

Jaroslav Pokorný
Charles University, Faculty of Mathematics and Physics
Malostranské nám. 25, 118 00 Prague 1, Czech Republic
E-mail: pokorny@ksi.ms.mff.cuni.cz

Mária Bieliková
Slovak University of Technology
Faculty of Informatics and Information Technologies
Ilkovičova 3, 812 19 Bratislava, Slovak Republic
E-mail: bielik@elf.stuba.sk

Július Štuller
Academy of Sciences of the Czech Republic, Institute of Computer Science
Pod Vodárenskou věží 2, 182 07 Prague 8, Czech Republic
E-mail: stuller@cs.cas.cz

Cataloging-in-Publication Data applied for

A catalog record for this book is available from the Library of Congress.

Bibliographic information published by Die Deutsche Bibliothek
Die Deutsche Bibliothek lists this publication in the Deutsche Nationalbibliografie;
detailed bibliographic data is available in the Internet at <http://dnb.ddb.de>.

CR Subject Classification (1998): F.1, F.2, F.3, H.2, I.2, H.3, H.4, C.2

ISSN 0302-9743
ISBN 3-540-20779-1 Springer-Verlag Berlin Heidelberg New York

Springer-Verlag is a part of Springer Science+Business Media

springeronline.com

© Springer-Verlag Berlin Heidelberg 2004
Printed in Germany

Typesetting: Camera-ready by author, data conversion by PTP-Berlin, Protago-TeX-Production GmbH
Printed on acid-free paper   SPIN: 10979303   06/3142   5 4 3 2 1 0

Preface

The 30th Anniversary Conference on Current Trends in Theory and Practice of Computer Science, **SOFSEM 2004**, took place during January 24–30, 2004, in the Hotel VZ Měřín, located about 60 km south of Prague on the right shore of Slapská přehrada ("Slapy Dam") in the Czech Republic.

Having transformed itself over the years from a local event to a fully international conference, the contemporary SOFSEM tries to keep the best of its winter school aspects (the high number of invited talks) together with multidisciplinarity trends in computer science – this year illustrated by the selection of the following 4 tracks:
- Computer Science Theory (Track Chair: Peter Van Emde Boas)
- Database Technologies (Track Chair: Jaroslav Pokorný)
- Cognitive Technologies (Track Chair: Peter Sinčák)
- Web Technologies (Track Chair: Július Štuller)

Its aim was, as always, to promote cooperation among professionals from academia and industry working in various areas of computer science.

The 17 SOFSEM 2004 Program Committee members coming from 9 countries evaluated a record 136 submissions. After a careful review process (counting usually at least 3 reviews per paper), followed by detailed discussions at the PC meeting held on October 2–3, 2003 in Prague, Czech Republic, 59 papers were selected for presentation at the SOFSEM 2004:
- 22 contributed talks papers selected by the SOFSEM 2004 PC for publication in the Springer-Verlag LNCS proceedings volume (acceptance rate 19%), including the best paper from the Student Research Forum,
- 29 contributed talks papers that will appear in the MatFyzPress Proceedings (acceptance rate 26%),
- 9 student research forum papers (acceptance rate 38%), 8 of which will appear in the MatFyzPress proceedings.

The Springer-Verlag proceedings were completed by the 10 invited talks papers.

SOFSEM 2004 was the result of considerable effort by a number of people. It is our pleasure to express our thanks to:
- the SOFSEM Steering Committee for its general guidance,
- the SOFSEM 2004 Program Committee and additional referees who devoted an extraordinary effort to reviewing a huge number of assigned papers (on average about 24 papers per PC member),
- the Springer-Verlag LNCS Executive Editor Mr. Alfred Hofmann for his continuing trust in SOFSEM,
- Springer-Verlag for publishing the proceedings, and
- the SOFSEM 2004 Organizing Committee for a smooth preparation of the conference.

Special thanks go to:

- Hana Bílková from the Institute of Computer Science (ICS), Prague, who did an excellent job in the completion of the proceedings,
- Michal Bušta and Martin Stareček from ICS for realizing the SOFSEM 2004 web pages and a submission and review system that worked perfectly thus allowing a smooth PC session in Prague.

Finally we highly appreciate the financial support of our sponsors (ERCIM, Microsoft, Deloitte & Touche, SOFTEC Bratislava, Centrum.cz) which assisted with the invited speakers and helped the organizers to offer lower student fees.

November 11, 2003
Peter Van Emde Boas
Jaroslav Pokorný
Mária Bieliková
Július Štuller

▮▬ Advisory Board

Dines Bjørner	Technical University of Denmark, Lyngby, DK
Peter Van Emde Boas	University of Amsterdam, NL
Manfred Broy	Technical University Munich, DE
Michal Chytil	ANIMA Prague, CZ
Georg Gottlob	Vienna University of Technology, AT
Keith G. Jeffery	CLRC RAL, Chilton, Didcot, Oxon, UK
Maria Zemánková	NSF, Washington, DC, USA

▮▬ Steering Committee

Branislav Rovan, *Chair*	Comenius University, Bratislava, SK
Miroslav Bartošek	Masaryk University, Brno, CZ
Mária Bieliková	Slovak University of Technology in Bratislava, SK
Keith G. Jeffery	CLRC RAL, Chilton, Didcot, Oxon, UK
Antonín Kučera	Masaryk University, Brno, CZ
Július Štuller	Institute of Computer Science, Prague, CZ
Gerard Tel	Utrecht University, NL
Petr Tůma	Charles University in Prague, CZ
Jan Staudek, *Observer*	Masaryk University, Brno, CZ
Jiří Wiedermann, *Observer*	Institute of Computer Science, Prague, CZ

▮▬ Program Committee

Peter Van Emde Boas, *Chair*	University of Amsterdam, NL
Jaroslav Pokorný, *Co-chair*	Charles University, Prague, CZ
Peter Sinčák, *Co-chair*	Technical University, Košice, SK
Július Štuller, *Co-chair*	Institute of Computer Science, Prague, CZ
Witold Abramowicz	Poznan University of Economics, PL
Martin Beran	Charles University, Prague, CZ
Mária Bieliková	Slovak University of Technology, Bratislava, SK
Shuji Hashimoto	Waseda University/Humanoid Institute, JP
Juraj Hromkovič	RWTH University, Aachen, D
Leonid Kalinichenko	Institute for Problems of Informatics, RU
Vladimír Kvasnička	Slovak University of Technology, Bratislava, SK
Roman Neruda	Institute of Computer Science, Prague, CZ
Dimitris Plexousakis	University of Crete, GR
Michael Schröder	City University, London, UK
Václav Snášel	VŠB-TU Ostrava, CZ
Gerard Tel	Utrecht University, NL
Bernhard Thalheim	Brandenburg Technical University, Cottbus, D

⁞═ Additional Referees

Eduardo Alonso
Vangelis Angelakis
Grigoris Antoniou
Yannis Askoxylakis
Krzysytof Banaskiewicz
Andrzej Bassara
David Bednárek
Hans-Joachim Boeckenhauer
Hans L. Bodlaender
Dirk Bongartz
Peter A.N. Bosman
Harry M. Buhrman
Lubomír Bulej
Bernadette Charron-Bost
David Coufal
Panos Dafas
Martin Doerr
Gunar Fiedler
Miroslav Galbavý
Christos Georgis
Jurgen Giesl
Jacek Gomoluch
Jurriaan Hage
Pavel Hloušek
Martin Holeňa
Tomasz Kaczmarek
Ivan Kapustik
Stamatis Karvounarakis
George Kokkinidis
Manolis Koubarakis
Marek Kowalkiewicz
Stano Krajčí
Jaroslav Král
Ivan Kramosil
Kiriakos Kritikos

Joachim Kupke
Rasto Lencses
Peter Lennartz
Maarten Marx
Vladimír Mencl
Daniel Moody
Tshiamo Motshegwa
Manfred Nagl
Athanasis Nikolaos
Petr Pajas
Demos Panagopoulos
Nikos Papadopoulos
Štefan Porubský
Jiří Pospíchal
Anthony Savidis
Ralf Schweimeier
Sebastian Seibert
George Serfiotis
Manolis Spanakis
Branislav Steinmuller
Yannis Stylianou
Ioannis Tollis
Vojtěch Toman
Nikolaos M. Tsatsakis
Petr Tůma
Walter Unger
Marinus Veldhorst
Peter Verbaan
Krzysztof Wecel
Marek Wisniewski
Jakub Yaghob
Pawel Zebrowski
Stanislav Žák
Michal Žemlička

⦂▅ Organization

The 30th Anniversary SOFSEM 2004 was organized by

Institute of Computer Science, Academy of Sciences of the Czech Republic, Prague
Charles University, Faculty of Mathematics and Physics, Prague
Faculty of Informatics, Masaryk University, Brno
Institute of Computer Science, Masaryk University, Brno
Czech Society for Computer Science

in co-operation with the Slovak Society for Computer Science

⦂▅ Organizing Committee

Július Štuller, *Chair*	Institute of Computer Science, Prague, CZ
Hana Bílková	Institute of Computer Science, Prague, CZ
Martina Brodská	Action M Agency, Prague, CZ
Michal Bušta	Institute of Computer Science, Prague, CZ
Zuzana Hájková	Action M Agency, Prague, CZ
Martin Stareček	Institute of Computer Science, Prague, CZ
Milena Zeithamlová	Action M Agency, Prague, CZ

⦂▅ Sponsoring Institutions

ERCIM
Microsoft
Deloitte & Touche
SOFTEC Bratislava
Centrum.cz

Table of Contents

Invited Talks

Regular Papers

The Best Student Paper

Games, Theory and Applications

H.J. van den Herik and H.H.L.M. Donkers

Institute for Knowledge and Agent Technology (IKAT),
Department of Computer Science, Universiteit Maastricht
P.O. Box 616, 6200 MD, Maastricht, The Netherlands.
{herik,donkers}@cs.unimaas.nl

Abstract. Computer game-playing is a challenging topic in artificial intelligence. The recent results by the computer programs DEEP BLUE (1996, 1997) and DEEP JUNIOR (2002) against Kasparov show the power of current game-tree search algorithms in Chess. This success is owed to the fruitful combination of the theoretical development of algorithms and their practical application. As an example of the theoretical development we discuss a game-tree algorithm called Opponent-Model search. In contrast to most current algorithms, this algorithm uses an opponent model to predict the opponent's moves and uses these predictions to lure the opponent into uncomfortable positions. We concentrate on the time complexity of two different implementations of the algorithm and show how these are derived. Moreover, we discuss some possible dangers when applying Opponent-Model search in practice.

1 Games

From the very beginning, game-playing has been studied in Artificial Intelligence. In [1] an overview is given showing that research in this domain has led to a variety of successes. Examples of computer programs that defeated the best human players occurred in Chess, Checkers, Draughts, and Othello. Still, there are many additional challenges in this area and in domains of other games. One of them is the application of knowledge of the opponent's strategy.

The idea of anticipating the opponent's strategy is not new. As a simple example (from [2]), we consider playing TicTacToe by the following ordered strategy **S**:

1. If completing three-in-a-row is possible, do so.
2. If the opponent threatens completing three-in-a-row, prevent this.
3. Occupy the central square whenever possible.
4. Occupy a corner square whenever possible.

TicTacToe is known to be drawn, and it might be questioned whether knowledge of one's opponent strategy could improve on this result. Intuitively, it seems clear that **S** should achieve a draw since it correctly evaluates the squares and acts on this evaluation. Yet, a program aware of the opponent's strategy **S** may win. Allow the program the first move as X, the following sequence of moves then causes player X to win, where at move 2 and 4 player O follows **S**.

P. Van Emde Boas et al. (Eds.): SOFSEM 2004, LNCS 2932, pp. 1–8, 2004.
© Springer-Verlag Berlin Heidelberg 2004

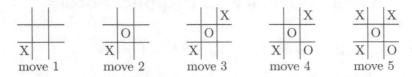

The win by X is due to X's awareness of the opponent's strategy **S**, admittedly non-optimal, or to rephrase this statement, due to X's successful prediction of O's moves.

2   Opponent-Model Search

OM search [3], [4], [5] is a game-tree search algorithm that uses a player's hypothesized model of the opponent in order to exploit weak points in the opponent's search strategy. The opponent model may be correct, but more frequently it may have some small errors. Therefore, it can be a possible help as well as a hindrance in playing the opponent. The OM-search algorithm is based on three strong assumptions concerning the opponent and the player:

1. the opponent (called MIN) uses minimax (or an equivalent algorithm) with an evaluation function (V_{op}), a search depth, and a move ordering that are all three known to the first player (called MAX);
2. MAX uses an evaluation function (V_0) that is *better* than MIN's evaluation function;
3. MAX searches at least as deep as MIN.

Obviously, OM search is still closely related to minimax. In OM search, MAX maximizes at max nodes, and selects at min nodes the moves that MAX thinks MIN would select.

Below we provide a brief technical description of OM search, its notation and the relations between the nodes in the search tree. Moreover, we mention a few enhancements to which adequate references are made. For an extensive description of OM search we refer to [6], [7].

OM search can be described by the following equations, in which $V_0(\cdot), V_{op}(\cdot)$ are the evaluation functions, and $v_0(\cdot), v_{op}(\cdot)$ are the node values. Subscript '0' is used for MAX values (it is not strictly necessary, but used to balance with the subscript 'op'), subscript 'op' is used for MIN values.

$$v_0(P) = \begin{cases} \max_j v_0(P_j) & \text{if } P \text{ is a max node,} \\ v_0(P_j), \quad j = \min \arg_i v_{op}(P_i) & \text{if } P \text{ is a min node,} \\ V_0(P) & \text{if } P \text{ is a leaf node.} \end{cases}$$

$$v_{op}(P) = \begin{cases} \max_j v_{op}(P_j) & \text{if } P \text{ is a max node,} \\ \min_j v_{op}(P_j) & \text{if } P \text{ is a min node,} \\ V_{op}(P) & \text{if } P \text{ is a leaf node.} \end{cases} \tag{1}$$

If P is a min node at a depth larger than the search-tree depth of the opponent, then $v_0(P) = \min_j v_0(P_j)$.

3   Algorithms

The equations (1) in the previous section do not prescribe how Opponent-Model search should be implemented efficiently. An important aspect of game-tree search algorithms is *pruning*, which means that portions of the tree are disregarded because those parts cannot influence the result. The more an algorithm is able to prune from a tree, the faster a tree is searched. β-pruning OM search [4] is an improvement of plain OM search that is able to prune in max nodes (not in min nodes, hence the name 'β'-pruning) and still yields the same result. The pruning is analogous to α-β pruning: when for one of the children P_j of a non-leaf max node P the value of $v_{op}(P_j)$ is higher than the resultant value of the already evaluated siblings of the max node, then the remaining children of the max node can be pruned.

We present in Fig. 1 two implementations of β-pruning OM search: a one-pass version that visits nodes only once (denoted by $OM^{\beta 1p}$) and a version with so-called α-β probes that uses α-β search to predict MIN's moves (denoted by $OM^{\beta Pb}$). For a detailed explanation of these algorithms we refer to [7].

Algorithm $OM^{\beta 1p}(P, \beta)$:	Algorithm $OM^{\beta Pb}(P, \beta)$:
if (P is leaf node) **return** $(V_0(P), V_{op}(P), 0)$	**if** (P is leaf node) **return** $(V_0(P), 0)$
if (P is max node)	**if** (P is max node)
$\quad v_0^* \leftarrow -\infty;\ v_{op}^* \leftarrow -\infty$	$\quad v_0^* \leftarrow -\infty$
$\quad$ **for** (all children P_j of P)	$\quad$ **for** (all children P_j of P)
$\quad\quad$ **if** (P_j is leaf node)	$\quad\quad (v_0, k) \leftarrow OM^{\beta Pb}(P_j, \beta)$
$\quad\quad\quad v_{op} \leftarrow V_{op}(P_j);$ **if** $(v_{op} < \beta)\ v_0 \leftarrow V_0(P_j)$	$\quad\quad$ **if** $(v_0 > v_0^*)\ v_0^* \leftarrow v_0;\ j^* \leftarrow j$
$\quad\quad$ **else** $(v_0, v_{op}, k) \leftarrow OM^{\beta 1p}(P_j, \beta)$	**if** (P is min node)
$\quad\quad$ **if** $(v_0 > v_0^*)\ v_0^* \leftarrow v_0;\ j^* \leftarrow j$	$\quad (v_{op}^*, j^*) \leftarrow \alpha\text{-}\beta \text{ search}(P, -\infty, \beta, V_{op}(\cdot))$
$\quad\quad$ **if** $(v_{op} > v_{op}^*)\ v_{op}^* \leftarrow v_{op}$	$\quad (v_0^*, k) \leftarrow OM^{\beta Pb}(P_{j*}, v_{op}^* + 1)$
$\quad\quad$ **if** $(v_{op}^* \geq \beta)$ **break**	**return** (v_0^*, j^*)
if (P is min node)	
$\quad v_{op}^* \leftarrow \beta$	
$\quad$ **for** (all children P_j of P)	
$\quad\quad$ **if** (P_j is leaf node) $v_{op} \leftarrow V_{op}(P_j)$	
$\quad\quad$ **else** $(v_0, v_{op}, k) \leftarrow OM^{\beta 1p}(P_j, v_{op}^*)$	
$\quad\quad$ **if** $(v_{op} < v_{op}^*)\ v_{op}^* \leftarrow v_{op};\ v_0^* \leftarrow v_0;\ j^* \leftarrow j$	
$\quad$ **if** $(P_{j*}$ is leaf node $\wedge\ v_{op}^* < \beta)\ v_0^* \leftarrow V_0(P_{j*})$	
return (v_0^*, v_{op}^*, j^*)	

F ig.1. Two implementations of β-pruning OM search. The left algorithm is a one-pass version and the right algorithm uses α-β probing

4   Time-Complexity

Below we discuss the best-case behaviour of the one-pass version of β-pruning OM search ($OM^{\beta 1p}$) and of the version with α-β probes ($OM^{\beta Pb}$). Thereafter a comparison is performed.

Best-case analysis of $OM^{\beta 1p}$.   The effect of β-pruning in $OM^{\beta 1p}$ is dependent on the ordering of child nodes with respect to $v_{op}(\cdot)$. In uniform trees, the pruning is maximal if the tree is *well ordered*, which means that the child nodes h_j of all nodes h are sorted on their value of $v_{op}(h_j)$. For max nodes the child nodes must be ordered in decreasing order and for min nodes in increasing order.

Proposition 1. *Any algorithm that implements β-pruning OM search will need at least the number of evaluations on a* well-ordered uniform tree *that $OM^{\beta 1p}$ needs.*

Proof. To prove this proposition, we first determine the minimal number. Then we show that $OM^{\beta 1p}$ uses exactly this number of evaluations in the best case.

Fig. 2 gives a schematic representation of a well-ordered uniform tree to which β-pruning OM search is applied. From this figure we derive a formula in closed form for the number of evaluations at least needed for β-pruning OM search. Assume a uniform tree with branching factor w and depth d. There are w^2 nodes at depth 2 to be expanded in such a search tree, because only branches at max nodes can be pruned and no

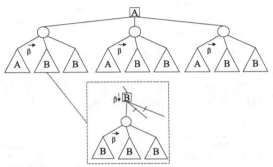

Fig.2. Theoretically best-case tree for β-pruning OM search

pruning takes place at the root. The subtrees at these max nodes are of two different types. The first type of subtrees (type A) are the subtrees on the leftmost branch of every node at depth 1. These subtrees are of the same type as the original tree and their number is w. The other $w(w-1)$ subtrees (type B) only have to be considered for the opponent's evaluation using α-β search with window $[-\infty, \beta]$. In Fig. 2, one of the type-B subtrees is worked out in detail. In this subtree, β pruning takes place directly under the root, so only one min node remains at the first level. Directly below this min node, no α pruning can take place. The subtree at the first max child node of this min node is again of type B. The subtrees at the other max child nodes also are of type B. It is not possible that α pruning takes place in these subtrees because the maximal β pruning at all max nodes prohibits the passing-through of α values.

The minimum number of evaluations C_{OM} (i.e., the best case for any implementation of β-pruning OM search) can now be given in the following recursive expression:

$$C_{OM}(d, w) = w\, C_{OM}(d-2, w) + w(w-1)\, C'_{OM}(d-2, w)$$
$$C_{OM}(1, w) = 2w \; ; \; C_{OM}(2, w) = w(w+1) \tag{2}$$

In these formulae, $C_{OM}(d, w)$ stands for the number of evaluations needed at a subtree of type A, and $C'_{OM}(d, w)$ for a subtree of type B. In the case that the type-A subtree has depth 1, $2w$ evaluations are needed: $v_0(.)$ and $v_{op}(.)$ have to be evaluated for all w leaf min nodes. When it has depth 2, $w(w+1)$ evaluations are needed: for all w^2 leaf max nodes, $v_{op}(.)$ has to be obtained, but only for the most left max node at every min child node, $v_0(.)$ is needed. The value of $C'_{OM}(d, w)$ is given by the next recursive expression:

$$C'_{OM}(d, w) = w\, C'_{OM}(d - 2, w)$$
$$C'_{OM}(1, w) = 1 \; ; \; C'_{OM}(2, w) = w$$
(3)

In the case that the type-B subtree has depth 1, only 1 evaluation is needed in the best case, since the value of $v_{op}(.)$ for the first child will be greater than β. Hence $v_0(.)$ does not have to be obtained. If the type-B subtree has depth 2, w evaluations are needed, one for every grandchild of the first child node. Since all values for $v_{op}(.)$ will be greater than β, no value of $v_0(.)$ has to be obtained. Formula 3 can easily be written in closed form:

$$C'_{OM}(d, w) = w^{\lfloor d/2 \rfloor}$$
(4)

The equation for C_{OM} can also be written in closed form (which can be found by applying repeated substitution):

$$C_{OM}(d, w) = k\, w^{\lceil d/2 \rceil} + (w - 1) \sum_{i=1}^{\lceil d/2 \rceil - 1} w^i \, C'_{OM}(d - 2i, w)$$
(5)

($k = 2$ if d is odd, $k = w + 1$ if d is even.) The validity of the closed form can be proven by complete induction on d. For $d = 1$ and $d = 2$ equation (5) is clearly correct: the summation on the right-hand side is zero in both cases. For $d > 2$ we first write down equation (5) with parameter $d - 2$:

$$C_{OM}(d - 2, w) = k\, w^{\lceil (d-2)/2 \rceil} + (w - 1) \sum_{i=1}^{\lceil (d-2)/2 \rceil - 1} w^i \, C'_{OM}(d - 2 - 2i, w)$$

$$= k\, w^{\lceil d/2 \rceil - 1} + (w - 1) \sum_{i=1}^{\lceil d/2 \rceil - 2} w^i \, C'_{OM}(d - 2 - 2i, w)$$
(6)

$$= k\, w^{\lceil d/2 \rceil - 1} + (w - 1) \sum_{i=2}^{\lceil d/2 \rceil - 1} w^{i-1} \, C'_{OM}(d - 2i, w)$$

Substituting equation (6) into (2) results directly in equation (5), which proves the correctness of the closed form. The closed form of equation (5) can be reduced further by applying equation (4) and canceling out the summation:

$$C_{OM}(d, w) = k\, w^{\lceil d/2 \rceil} + (w - 1) \sum_{i=1}^{\lceil d/2 \rceil - 1} w^i w^{\lfloor (d-2i)/2 \rfloor}$$

$$= k\, w^{\lceil d/2 \rceil} + (w - 1) \sum_{i=1}^{\lceil d/2 \rceil - 1} w^{\lfloor d/2 \rfloor}$$
(7)

$$= k\, w^{\lceil d/2 \rceil} + (w - 1) (\lceil d/2 \rceil - 1)\, w^{\lfloor d/2 \rfloor}$$

The expression $k\,w^{\lceil d/2\rceil}$ can be rewritten to $w^{\lfloor d/2\rfloor+1} + w^{\lceil d/2\rceil}$, which removes the k. This can be used to rewrite the equation to:

$$C_{OM}(d, w) = w^{\lceil d/2\rceil} + w^{\lfloor d/2\rfloor} + (w-1)\lceil d/2\rceil\, w^{\lfloor d/2\rfloor} \tag{8}$$

This concludes the first part of the proof. The number of evaluations in the best case for $OM^{\beta 1p}$ appears to be equal to $C_{OM}(d, w)$. The reasoning is as follows (Fig. 2 can be used to illustrate this reasoning). The type-A subtrees are of the same type as the original tree, just like the theoretical case. This means that the overall formula 5 also holds for $OM^{\beta 1p}$. However, $OM^{\beta 1p}$ does not apply α-β search to the type-B subtrees. Fortunately, in the best case optimal β pruning on all internal max nodes and on all leaf nodes can take place. So no evaluation of V_0 takes place in type-B subtrees. The number of evaluations in these type-B subtrees is given by equation 4. Now the theoretical derivation can be followed. This proves the proposition.   □

Best-case analysis of $OM^{\beta Pb}$.   The number of leaf nodes that are evaluated for MAX's evaluation function in $OM^{\beta Pb}$ depends on the size of the tree, not on the ordering of the nodes. For the moment, the α-β probes can be disregarded. At every max node, all w child nodes are visited and at every min node, exactly 1 child is visited. This means that there are exactly $w^{\lceil d/2\rceil}$ leaf nodes visited and evaluated for MAX.

The number of α-β probes in OM search, too, is only dependent on the size of the tree. At every odd ply $2i-1$ $(i>0)$, exactly w^i probes are performed. The α-β probes at the first odd ply have a β parameter of $+\infty$ and take $C_{\alpha-\beta}(w, d-1)$ evaluations. All other α-β probes have a smaller β parameter. Fig. 3 illustrates the best case for these α-β probes.

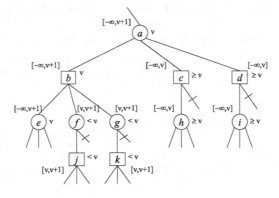

Fig. 3. An example to illustrate the best case for α-β probes. The $[\alpha, \beta]$ windows and the subgame values are given next to the nodes

The best case (i.e., the most pruning) for an α-β probe with $\beta = v+1$ on a min node a occurs when the values of nodes a ... k are as indicated in Fig. 3. A careful inspection of the figure indicates that in the best case, the β parameter $v+1$ does not have influence on the pruning in the tree. The amount of pruning is therefore equal to the best case of α-β search with an open window on the same tree: $w^{\lfloor d/2\rfloor} + w^{\lceil d/2\rceil} - 1$.

As stated above, there are w^i probes at every odd ply $2i-1$ that each cost $C_{\alpha-\beta}(d-2i+1, w)$ evaluations. Together with the $w^{\lceil d/2\rceil}$ evaluations for the max player, β-pruning OM search with α-β probes in the best case costs:

$$C_{OM^{\beta pb}}(d,w) = w^{\lceil d/2\rceil} + \sum_{i=1}^{\lceil d/2\rceil} w^i \, C_{\alpha-\beta}(d-2i+1,w)$$

$$= w^{\lceil d/2\rceil} + \sum_{i=1}^{\lceil d/2\rceil} w^i \left(w^{\lfloor (d-2i+1)/2\rfloor} + w^{\lceil (d-2i+1)/2\rceil} - 1\right) \qquad (9)$$

$$= w^{\lceil d/2\rceil} + \lceil d/2\rceil \left(w^{\lfloor (d+1)/2\rfloor} + w^{\lceil (d+1)/2\rceil}\right) - \frac{w^{\lceil d/2\rceil+1} - w}{w-1}$$

A comparison.   The next formulae summarize the best-case analyses for β-pruning OM search:

$$OM^{\beta 1p}: \qquad w^{\lceil d/2\rceil} + w^{\lfloor d/2\rfloor} + (w-1)\lceil d/2\rceil \, w^{\lfloor d/2\rfloor}$$

$$OM^{\beta Pb}: \quad w^{\lceil d/2\rceil} + \lceil d/2\rceil (w^{\lfloor (d+1)/2\rfloor} + w^{\lceil (d+1)/2\rceil}) - \frac{w^{\lceil d/2\rceil+1}-w}{w-1}$$

Despite the closed forms of the functions, their relation is not immediately clear. In Fig. 4 these functions are plotted next to each other. All four diagrams show the value of the equation above *divided* by the best case of α-β search. In each diagram, the lines give the results for the branching factors 20, 16, 12, 8, and 4 respectively, from top to bottom. Because the behaviour of the functions differs considerably for odd and even search depths (see x-axis), we present separate diagrams for both cases. On the left we show the best-case complexities of $OM^{\beta 1p}$ and $OM^{\beta Pb}$ for even search depths, on the right for odd depths.

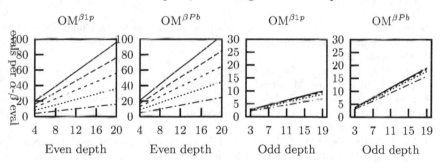

F ig . 4 . Best-case results of $OM^{\beta 1p}$ and $OM^{\beta Pb}$ compared

In all cases the complexity of $OM^{\beta 1p}$ is smaller than the complexity of $OM^{\beta Pb}$. Furthermore, the complexity approximates a linear function of the (odd or even) search depth for both $OM^{\beta 1p}$ and $OM^{\beta Pb}$. It is also approximately linear in the branching factor for both $OM^{\beta 1p}$ and $OM^{\beta Pb}$, but only in the case of even search depths (cf. the different scaling of the y-axis).

In contrast to the expectation, it is shown in [7] that in the average-case $OM^{\beta Pb}$ appears to be the most efficient of the two. Moreover, in practical implementations, this version offers better opportunities for the application of search enhancements which increase the efficiency further.

5   Attractors

The practical application of Opponent-Model search is bound to several forms of risk. Next to the obvious risk, being an ill prediction of the opponent's moves ([7], [8]), there is a subtle risk that is potentially more dangerous. This risk is caused by MAX's overestimation of positions that MIN judges correctly to be favourable for MIN. Such positions can act as an *attractor*: MAX is eager to reach such a position and MIN follows willingly. The larger the overestimation, the more MAX will be attracted to the position and the larger the damage will be. In [7], [9] a condition on the evaluation functions V_0 and V_{op} is formulated, called *admissibility*, that should prevent the occurrence of these attractors. When this risk of OM search is neglected, its application is bound to fail [7].

6   Conclusion

In this paper we presented a best-case complexity analysis of two variants of β-pruning OM search as an example of theoretical research in computer game-playing. The corresponding practical application is described among others in [7]. Surprisingly, practice leads to a different conclusion with respect to the complexities of the best cases. Moreover, practice prominently shows several forms of risk.

References

1. Schaeffer, J., Herik, H. J. van den (eds.): Chips Challenging Champions. Games, Computers and Artificial Intelligence. Elsevier Science Publishers, Amsterdam, The Netherlands (2002)
2. Herik, H.J. van den: Informatica en het menselijk blikveld. Inaugural Address. University of Limburg, Maastricht (in Dutch). (1988)
3. Carmel, D., Markovitch, S.: Learning models of opponent's strategies in game playing. In: Proceedings AAAI Fall Symposion on Games: Planning and Learning, Raleigh, NC (1993) 140–147
4. Iida, H., Uiterwijk, J.W.H.M., Herik, H.J. van den: Opponent-model search. Technical Report CS 93-03, Universiteit Maastricht, Maastricht, The Netherlands (1993)
5. Iida, H., Uiterwijk, J.W.H.M., Herik, H.J. van den, Herschberg, I.S.: Potential applications of opponent-model search. Part 1, the domain of applicability. ICCA Journal 16 (4) (1993) 201–208 Part 2, risks and strategies. ICCA Journal, 17 (1) (1994) 10–14.
6. Carmel, D., Markovitch, S.: Pruning algorithms for multi-model adversary search. Artificial Intelligence 99 (1998) 325–255
7. Donkers, H.H.L.M.: Nosce Hostem – Searching With Opponent Models. PhD thesis, Universieit Maastricht, Maastricht, The Netherlands (2003)
8. Iida, H., Kotani, I., Uiterwijk, J.W.H.M., Herik, H.J. van den: Gains and risks of OM Search. In Herik, H.J. van den, Uiterwijk, J.W.H.M., eds.: Advances in Computer Chess 8, Maastricht, The Netherlands, Universiteit Maastricht (1997) 153–165
9. Donkers, H.H.L.M., Uiterwijk, J.W.H.M., Herik, H.J. van den: Admissibility in opponent-model search. Information Sciences 154 (3–4) (2003) 119–140

Database Research Issues in a WWW and GRIDs World

Keith G. Jeffery

Director, IT and Head, Information Technology Department
CCLRC Rutherford Appleton Laboratory
Chilton, Didcot, OXON OX11 0QX UK
k.g.jeffery@rl.ac.uk
http://www.itd.clrc.ac.uk/Person/K.G.Jeffery

Abstract. The WWW has made information update fast and easy, and (through search engines such as Google) retrieval fast and easy. The emerging GRIDs architecture offers the end-user complete solutions to their simple request involving data and information, computation and processing, display and distribution. By comparison conventional database systems and their user interfaces appear clumsy and difficult. Nonetheless, experience with WWW has taught us that fast and easy can also equate with information that is inaccurate, imprecise, incomplete and irrelevant. To overcome these problems there is intensive research on 'the semantic web' and 'the web of trust'. The GRIDs environment is being developed to include Computer Science fundamentals in handling data, information and knowledge. The key aspects are representativity of the data and information - accuracy, precision, structure (syntax), meaning (semantics) - and expressivity of the languages to represent and manipulate the data, information and knowledge - syntax, semantics. There are related issues of security and trust, of heterogeneity and distribution and of scheduling and performance. The key architectural components arc metadata, agents and brokers. Access to the GRIDs environment will be from ambient computing clients; this raises a host of new problems in security and performance and in information summarisation and presentation. There remains an exciting active research agenda for database technology.

1   Introduction

There is an argument that database R&D (research and development) – or more generally ISE (Information Systems Engineering) R&D - has not kept pace with the user expectations raised by WWW. Tim Berners-Lee threw down the challenge of the semantic web and the web of trust [1]. However, the GRIDs concept [6] placed database R&D (ISE R&D) back in the forefront. The EC (European Commission) has argued for the information society, the knowledge society and the ERA (European Research Area) – all of which are dependent on database R&D in the ISE sense.

It is time for the database community (in the widest sense, i.e. the information systems engineering community) to take stock of the research challenges and plan a campaign to meet them with excellent solutions, not only academically or theoretically correct but also well-engineered for end-user acceptance and use.

P. Van Emde Boas et al. (Eds.): SOFSEM 2004, LNCS 2932, pp. 9–21, 2004.

2   GRIDs

2.1   The Idea

In 1998-1999 the UK Research Council community was proposing future programmes for R&D. The author was asked to propose an integrating IT architecture [6]. The proposal was based on concepts including distributed computing, metacomputing, metadata, middleware, client-server migrating to three-layer architectures and knowledge-based assists. The novelty lay in the integration of various techniques into one architectural framework.

2.2   The Requirement

The UK Research Council community of researchers was facing several IT-based problems. Their ambitions for scientific discovery included post-genomic discoveries, climate change understanding, oceanographic studies, environmental pollution monitoring and modelling, precise materials science, studies of combustion processes, advanced engineering, pharmaceutical design, and particle physics data handling and simulation. They needed more processor power, more data storage capacity, better analysis and visualisation – all supported by easy-to-use tools controlled through an intuitive user interface.

2.3   Architecture Overview

The architecture proposed consists of three layers (Fig. 1). The computation / data grid has supercomputers, large servers, massive data storage facilities and specialised devices and facilities (e.g. for VR (Virtual Reality)) all linked by high-speed networking and forms the lowest layer. The main functions include compute load sharing / algorithm partitioning, resolution of data source addresses, security, replication and message rerouting. The information grid is superimposed on the computation / data grid and resolves homogeneous access to heterogeneous information sources mainly through the use of metadata and middleware. Finally, the uppermost layer is the knowledge grid which utilises knowledge discovery in database technology to generate knowledge and also allows for representation of knowledge through scholarly works, peer-reviewed (publications) and grey literature, the latter especially hyperlinked to information and data to sustain the assertions in the knowledge.

The concept is based on the idea of a uniform landscape within the GRIDs domain, the complexity of which is masked by easy-to-use interfaces. To this facility are connected external appliances – ranging from supercomputers, storage access networks, data storage robots, specialised visualisation and VR systems, data sensors and detectors (e.g. on satellites) to user client devices such as workstations and PDAs (Personal Digital Assistants). The connection between the external appliances and the GRIDs domain is through agents, supported by metadata, representing the appliance

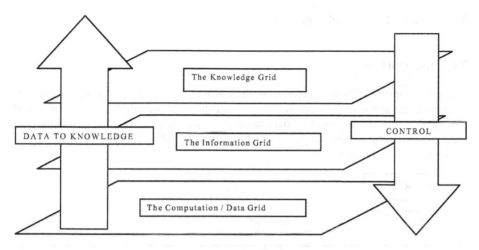

Fig. 1. The 3-Layer GRIDs Architecture

(and thus continuously available to the GRIDs systems).These representative agents handle credentials of the end-user in their current role, appliance characteristics and interaction preferences (for both user client appliances and service appliances), preference profiles and associated organisational information. These agents interact with other agents in the usual way via brokers to locate services and negotiate use. The key aspect is that all the agent interaction is based upon available metadata.

2.4   The GRID

In 1998 – in parallel with the initial UK thinking on GRIDs - Ian Foster and Carl Kesselman published a collection of papers in a book generally known as 'The GRID Bible' [4]. The essential idea is to connect together supercomputers to provide more power – the metacomputing technique. However, the major contribution lies in the systems and protocols for compute resource scheduling. Additionally, the designers of the GRID realised that these linked supercomputers would need fast data feeds so developed GRIDFTP. Finally, basic systems for authentication and authorisation are described. The GRID has encompassed the use of SRB (Storage Request Broker) from SDSC (San Diego Supercomputer Centre) for massive data handling. SRB has its proprietary metadata system to assist in locating relevant data resources. It also uses LDAP as its directory of resources. The GRID corresponds to the lowest grid layer (computation / data layer) of the GRIDs architecture.

3   The GRIDs Architecture

3.1   Introduction

The idea behind GRIDs is to provide an IT environment that interacts with the user to determine the user requirement for service and then satisfies that requirement across a heterogeneous environment of data stores, processing power, special facilities for display and data collection systems thus making the IT environment appear homogeneous to the end-user.

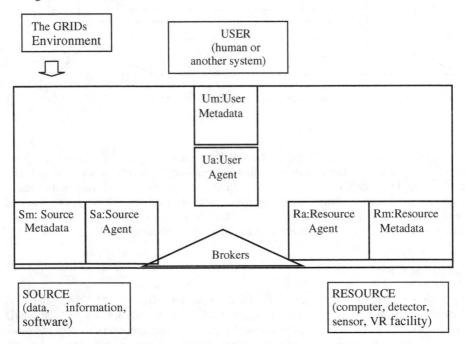

Fig. 2. The GRIDs Components

Referring to Fig. 2, the major components external to the GRIDs environment are:

a)   users: each being a human or another system;
b)   sources: data, information or software
c)   resources: such as computers, sensors, detectors, visualisation or VR (virtual reality) facilities

Each of these three major components is represented continuously and actively within the GRIDs environment by:

1)   metadata: which describes the external component and which is changed with changes in circumstances through events
2)   an agent: which acts on behalf of the external resource representing it within the GRIDs environment.

As a simple example, the agent could be regarded as the answering service of a person's mobile phone and the metadata as the instructions given to the service such as 'divert to service when busy' and / or 'divert to service if unanswered'.

Finally there is a component which acts as a 'go between' between the agents. These are brokers which, as software components, act much in the same way as human brokers by arranging agreements and deals between agents, by acting themselves (or using other agents) to locate sources and resources, to manage data integration, to ensure authentication of external components and authorisation of rights to use by an authenticated component and to monitor the overall system.

From this it is clear that they key components are the metadata, the agents and the brokers.

3.2   Metadata

Metadata is data about data [7]. An example might be a product tag attached to a product (e.g. a tag attached to a piece of clothing) that is available for sale. The metadata on the product tag tells the end-user (human considering purchasing the article of clothing) data about the article itself – such as the fibres from which it is made, the way it should be cleaned, its size (possibly in different classification schemes such as European, British, American) and maybe style, designer and other useful data. The metadata tag may be attached directly to the garment, or it may appear in a catalogue of clothing articles offered for sale (or, more usually, both). The metadata may be used to make a selection of potentially interesting articles of clothing before the actual articles are inspected, thus improving convenience. Today this concept is widely-used. Much e-commerce is based on B2C (Business to Customer) transactions based on an online catalogue (metadata) of goods offered. One well-known example is www.amazon.com.

What is metadata to one application may be data to another. For example, an electronic library catalogue card is metadata to a person searching for a book on a particular topic, but data to the catalogue system of the library which will be grouping books in various ways: by author, classification code, shelf position, title – depending on the purpose required.

It is increasingly accepted that there are several kinds of metadata. The classification proposed (Fig. 3) is gaining wide acceptance and is detailed below.

Schema Metadata. Schema metadata constrains the associated data. It defines the intension whereas instances of data are the extension. From the intension a theoretical universal extension can be created, constrained only by the intension. Conversely, any observed instance should be a subset of the theoretical extension and should obey the constraints defined in the intension (schema). One problem with existing schema metadata (e.g. schemas for relational DBMS) is that they lack certain intensional information that is required [8]. Systems for information retrieval based on, e.g. the SGML (Standard Generalised Markup Language) DTD (Document Type Definition) experience similar problems.

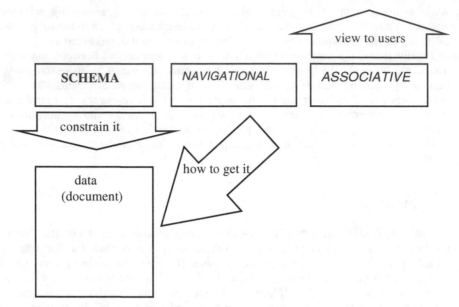

Fig. 3. Metadata Classification

It is noticeable that many ad hoc systems for data exchange between systems send with the data instances a schema that is richer than that in conventional DBMS – to assist the software (and people) handling the exchange to utilise the exchanged data to best advantage.

Navigational Metadata. Navigational metadata provides the pathway or routing to the data described by the schema metadata or associative metadata. In the RDF model it is a URL (universal resource locator), or more accurately, a URI (Universal Resource Identifier). With increasing use of databases to store resources, the most common navigational metadata now is a URL with associated query parameters embedded in the string to be used by CGI (Common Gateway Interface) software or proprietary software for a particular DBMS product or DBMS-Webserver software pairing.

The navigational metadata describes only the physical access path. Naturally, associated with a particular URI are other properties such as:

a)   security and privacy (e.g. a password required to access the target of the URI);
b)   access rights and charges (e.g. does one have to pay to access the resource at the URI target);
c)   constraints over traversing the hyperlink mapped by the URI (e.g. the target of the URI is only available if previously a field on a form has been input with a value between 10 and 20). Another example would be the hypermedia equivalent of referential integrity in a relational database;
d)   semantics describing the hyperlink such as 'the target resource describes the son of the person described in the origin resource'

However, these properties are best described by associative metadata which then allows more convenient co-processing in context of metadata describing both resources and hyperlinks between them and – if appropriate - events.

Associative Metadata. In the data and information domain associative metadata can describe:

a) a set of data (e.g. a database, a relation (table) or a collection of documents or a retrieved subset). An example would be a description of a dataset collected as part of a scientific mission;

b) an individual instance (record, tuple, document). An example would be a library catalogue record describing a book;

c) an attribute (column in a table, field in a set of records, named element in a set of documents). An example would be the accuracy / precision of instances of the attribute in a particular scientific experiment;

d) domain information (e.g. value range) of an attribute. An example would be the range of acceptable values in a numeric field such as the capacity of a car engine or the list of valid values in an enumerated list such as the list of names of car manufacturers;

e) a record / field intersection unique value (i.e. value of one attribute in one instance) This would be used to explain an apparently anomalous value.

In the relationship domain, associative metadata can describe relationships between sets of data e.g. hyperlinks. Associative metadata can – with more flexibility and expressivity than available in e.g. relational database technology or hypermedia document system technology – describe the semantics of a relationship, the constraints, the roles of the entities (objects) involved and additional constraints.

In the process domain, associative metadata can describe (among other things) the functionality of the process, its external interface characteristics, restrictions on utilisation of the process and its performance requirements / characteristics.

In the event domain, associative metadata can describe the event, the temporal constraints associated with it, the other constraints associated with it and actions arising from the event occurring.

Associative metadata can also be personalised: given clear relationships between them that can be resolved automatically and unambiguously, different metadata describing the same base data may be used by different users.

Taking an orthogonal view over these different kinds of information system objects to be described, associative metadata may be classified as follows:

1) descriptive: provides additional information about the object to assist in understanding and using it;

2) restrictive: provides additional information about the object to restrict access to authorised users and is related to security, privacy, access rights, copyright and IPR (Intellectual Property Rights);

3) supportive: a separate and general information resource that can be cross-linked to an individual object to provide additional information e.g. translation to a different language, super- or sub-terms to improve a query – the kind of support provided by a thesaurus or domain ontology;

Most examples of metadata in use today include some components of most of these kinds but neither structured formally nor specified formally so that the metadata tends to be of limited use for automated operations – particularly interoperation – thus requiring additional human interpretation.

3.3   Agents

Agents operate continuously and autonomously and act on behalf of the external component they represent. They interact with other agents via brokers, whose task it is to locate suitable agents for the requested purpose. An agent's actions are controlled to a large extent by the associated metadata which should include either instructions, or constraints, such that the agent can act directly or deduce what action is to be taken. Each agent is waiting to be 'woken up' by some kind of event; on receipt of a message the agent interprets the message and – using the metadata as parametric control – executes the appropriate action, either communicating with the external component (user, source or resource) or with brokers as a conduit to other agents representing other external components.

An agent representing an end-user accepts a request from the end-user and interacts with the end-user to refine the request (clarification and precision), first based on the user metadata and then based on the results of a first attempt to locate (via brokers and other agents) appropriate sources and resources to satisfy the request. The proposed activity within GRIDs for that request is presented to the end-user as a 'deal' with any costs, restrictions on rights of use etc. Assuming the user accepts the offered deal, the GRIDs environment then satisfies it using appropriate resources and sources and finally sends the result back to the user agent where – again using metadata – end-user presentation is determined and executed.

An agent representing a source will – with the associated metadata – respond to requests (via brokers) from other agents concerning the data or information stored, or the properties of the software stored. Assuming the deal with the end-user is accepted, the agent performs the retrieval of data requested, or supply of software requested.

An agent representing a resource – with the associated metadata – responds to requests for utilisation of the resource with details of any costs, restrictions and relevant capabilities. Assuming the deal with the end-user is accepted the resource agent then schedules its contribution to providing the result to the end-user.

3.4   Brokers

Brokers act as 'go betweens' between agents. Their task is to accept messages from an agent which request some external component (source, resource or user), identify an external component that can satisfy the request by its agent working with its associated metadata and either put the two agents in direct contact or continue to act as an intermediary, possibly invoking other brokers (and possibly agents) to handle, for example, measurement unit conversion or textual word translation.

Other brokers perform system monitoring functions including overseeing performance (and if necessary requesting more resources to contribute to the overall system e.g. more networking bandwidth or more compute power). They may also monitor usage of external components both for statistical purposes and possibly for any charging scheme.

3.5   The Components Working Together

Now let us consider how the components interact. An agent representing a user may request a broker to find an agent representing another external component such as a source or a resource. The broker will usually consult a directory service (itself controlled by an agent) to locate potential agents representing suitable sources or resources. The information will be returned to the requesting (user) agent, probably with recommendations as to order of preference based on criteria concerning the offered services. The user agent matches these against preferences expressed in the metadata associated with the user and makes a choice. The user agent then makes the appropriate recommendation to the end-user who in turn decides to 'accept the deal' or not.

4   Ambient Computing

The concept of ambient computing implies that the computing environment is always present and available in an even manner. The concept of pervasive computing implies that the computing environment is available everywhere and is 'into everything'. The concept of mobile computing implies that the end-user device may be connected even when on the move. In general usage of the term, ambient computing implies both pervasive and mobile computing.

The idea, then, is that an end-user may find herself connected (or connectable – she may choose to be disconnected) to the computing environment all the time. The computing environment may involve information provision (access to database and web facilities), office functions (calendar, email, directory), desktop functions (word processing, spreadsheet, presentation editor), perhaps project management software and systems specialised for her application needs – accessed from her end-user device connected back to 'home base' so that her view of the world is as if at her desk. In addition entertainment subsystems (video, audio, games) should be available.

A typical configuration might comprise:

a)   a headset with earphone(s) and microphone for audio communication, connected by bluetooth wireless local connection to

b)   a PDA (personal digital assistant) with small screen, numeric/text keyboard (like a telephone), GSM/GPRS (mobile phone) connections for voice and data, wireless LAN connectivity and ports for connecting sensor devices (to measure anything close to the end-user) in turn connected by bluetooth to

c)   an optional notebook computer carried in a backpack (but taken out for use in a suitable environment) with conventional screen, keyboard, large hard disk and connectivity through GSM/GPRS, wireless LAN, cable LAN and dial-up telephone.

The end-user would perhaps use only (a) and (b) (or maybe (b) alone using the built in speaker and microphone) in a social or professional context as mobile phone and 'filofax', and as entertainment centre, with or without connectivity to 'home base' servers and IT environment.   For more traditional working requiring keyboard and screen the notebook computer would be used, probably without the PDA. The two might be used together with data collection validation / calibration software on the notebook computer and sensors attached to the PDA.

The balance between that (data, software) which is on servers accessed over the network and that which is on (one of) the end-user device(s) depends on the mode of work, speed of required response and likelihood of interrupted connections. Clearly the GRIDs environment is ideal for such a user to be connected.

Such a configuration is clearly useful for a 'road warrior' (travelling salesman), for emergency services such as firefighters or paramedics, for businessmen, for production industry managers, for the distribution / logistics industry (warehousing, transport, delivery), for scientists in the field.... and also for leisure activities such as mountain walking, visiting an art gallery, locating a restaurant or visiting an archaeological site.

5   The Challenges

Such an IT architectural environment inevitably poses challenging research issues. The major ones are:

5.1   Metadata

Since metadata is critically important for interoperation and semantic understanding, there is a requirement for precise and formal representation of metadata to allow automated processing. Research is required into the metadata representation language expressivity in order to represent the entities user, source, resource. For example, the existing Dublin Core Metadata standard [11] is machine-readable but not machine-understandable, and furthermore mixes navigational, associative descriptive and associative restrictive metadata. A formal version has been proposed [2].

5.2   Agents

There is an interesting research area concerning the generality or specificity of agents. Agents could be specialised for a particular task or generalised and configured dynamically for the task by metadata. Furthermore, agents may well need to be reactive and dynamically reconfigured by events / messages. This would cause a designer to lean towards general agents with dynamic configuration, but there are performance, reliability and security issues. In addition there are research issues concerning the syntax and semantics of messages passed between agents and brokers to ensure optimal representation with appropriate performance and security.

5.3   Brokers

A similar research question is posed for brokers – are they generalised and dynamic or specific? However, brokers have not just representational functions, they have also to negotiate. The degree of autonomy becomes the key research issue: can the broker decide by itself or does it solicit input from the external entity (user, source, resource) via its agent and metadata? The broker will need general strategic knowledge (negotiation techniques) but the way a broker uses the additional information supplied by the agents representing the entities could be a differentiating factor and therefore a potential business benefit. In addition there are research issues concerning the syntax and semantics of messages passed between brokers to ensure optimal representation with appropriate performance and security.

5.4   Security

Security is an issue in any system, and particularly in a distributed system. It becomes even more important if the system is a common marketplace with great heterogeneity of purpose and intent. The security takes the forms:

a) prevention of unauthorised access: this requires authentication of the user, authorisation of the user to access or use a source or resource and provision or denial of that access. The current heterogeneity of authentication and authorisation mechanisms provides many opportunities for deliberate or unwitting security exposure;

b) ensuring availability of the source or resource: this requires techniques such as replication, mirroring and hot or warm failover. There are deep research issues in transactions and rollback/recovery and optimisation;

c) ensuring continuity of service: this relates to (b) but includes additional fallback procedures and facilities and there are research issues concerning the optimal (cost-effective) assurance of continuity.

In the case of interrupted communication there is a requirement for synchronisation of the end-user's view of the system between that which is required on the PDA and / or laptop and the servers.

There are particular problems with wireless communications because of interception. Encryption of sensitive transmissions is available but there remain research issues concerning security assurance.

5.5   Privacy

The privacy issues concern essentially the tradeoff of personal information provision for intelligent system reaction. There are research issues on the optimal balance for particular end-user requirements. Furthermore, data protection legislation in countries varies and there are research issues concerning the requirement to provide data or to conceal data.

5.6   Trust

When any end-user purchases online (e.g. a book from www.amazon.com) there is a trust that the supplier will deliver the goods and that the purchaser's credit card information is valid. This concept requires much extension in the case of contracts for supply of engineered components for assembly into e.g. a car. The provision of an e-marketplace brings with it the need for e-tendering, e-contracts, e-payments, e-guarantees as well s opportunities to re-engineer the business process for effectiveness and efficiency. This is currently a very hot research topic since it requires the representation in an IT system of artefacts (documents) associated with business transactions.

5.7   Interoperability

There is a clear need to provide the end-user with homogeneous access to heterogeneous information sources. His involves schema reconciliation / mapping and associated transformations. Associated with this topic are requirements for languages that are more representative (of the entities / objects in the real world) and more expressive (in expressing the transformations or operations). Recent R&D [10], [9] has indicated that graphs provide a neutral basis for the syntax with added value in graph properties such that structural properties may be used.

5.8   Data Quality

The purpose of data, especially when structured in context as information, is to represent the world of interest. There are real research issues in ensuring this is true – especially when the data is incomplete or uncertain, when the data is subject to certain precision, accuracy and associated calibration constraints or when only by knowing its provenance can a user utilise it confidently.

5.9   Performance

The architecture opens the possibility of, knowing the characteristics of data / information, software and processing power on each node, generating optimal execution plans. Refinements involve data movement (expensive if the volumes are large) or program code movement (security implications) to appropriate nodes.

6   Conclusion

The GRIDs architecture will provide an IT infrastructure to revolutionise and expedite the way in which we do business and achieve leisure. The Ambient Computing architecture will revolutionise the way in which the IT infrastructure intersects with our lives, both professional and social. The two architectures in combination will provide the springboard for the greatest advances yet in Information Technology. This can only be achieved by excellent R&D leading to commercial take-up and development of suitable products, to agreed standards, ideally within an environment such as W3C (the World Wide Web Consortium). The current efforts in GRID computing have moved some way away from metacomputing and towards the architecture described here with the adoption of OGSA (Open Grids Services Architecture). However, there is a general feeling that Next Generation GRID requires an architecture rather like that described here, as reported in the Report of the EC Expert Group on the subject [3].

Acknowledgements. Some of the material presented here has appeared in previous papers by the author. Although the author remains responsible for the content, many of the ideas have come from fruitful discussions not only with the author's own team at CCLRC-RAL but also with many members of the UK science community (requirements) and the UK Computer Science / Information systems community. The author has also benefited from discussions in the contexts of ERCIM (www.ercim.org) and W3C (www.w3.org).

References

1. Berners-Lee,T; Weaving the Web 256 pp Harper, San Francisco September 1999 ISBN 0062515861
2. http://purl.oclc.org/dc/
3. www.cordis.lu/ist/grids/index.htm
4. Foster, I., Kesselman, C. (eds): The Grid: Blueprint for a New Computing Infrastructure. Morgan-Kauffman (1998)
5. Jeffery, K G: An Architecture for Grey Literature in a R&D Context. Proceedings GL'99 (Grey Literature) Conference Washington DC October 1999
6. http://www.konbib.nl/greynet/frame4.htm
7. Original Paper on GRIDs, unpublished, available from the author
8. Jeffery, K.G.: Metadata. In Brinkkemper,J; Lindencrona,E; Solvberg,A (eds): Information Systems Engineering' Springer Verlag, London (2000), ISBN 1-85233-317-0.
9. Jeffery, K.G., Hutchinson, E.K., Kalmus, J.R., Wilson, M.D., Behrendt, W., Macnee, C.A.: A Model for Heterogeneous Distributed Databases. Proceedings BNCOD12 July 1994; LNCS 826 Springer-Verlag (1994) 221-234
10. Kohoutkova, J; Structured Interfaces for Information Presentation. PhD Thesis, Masaryk University, Brno, Czech Republic
11. Skoupy,K; Kohoutkova,J; Benesovsky,M; Jeffery,K G: Hypermedata Approach: A Way to Systems Integration' Proceedings Third East European Conference, ADBIS'99, Maribor, Slovenia, September 13-16, 1999, Published: Institute of Informatics, Faculty of Electrical Engineering and Computer Science, Smetanova 17, IS-2000 Maribor, Slovenia,1999, ISBN 86-435-0285-5, 9-15
12. http://www.dublincore.org/

Integration, Diffusion, and Merging in Information Management Discipline

Vijay Kumar

SCE, Computer Networking, University of Missouri-Kansas City
5100 Rockhill, Kansas City, MO 64110, USA
kumarv@umkc.edu

Abstract. We observe that information is the life force through which we interact with our environment. The dynamic state of the world is maintained by information management. These observations motivated us to develop the concept of *fully connected information space* which we introduce in this paper. We discuss its structure and properties and present our research work and contributions for its maintenance. We also speculate the future of this information space and our mode of interaction with it.

1   Introduction

The dynamic state of the world is managed by the laws of the nature, which we cannot alter or mess around with. The only way to maintain our lives in this dynamic environment is to synchronize our activities with the activities of nature. For example, we must learn about natural disasters in an appropriate time and plan our activities accordingly. In many situations activities are time bound and therefore, we must define *time constraints* (TC) for our approach to handle such activities. For example, we retrieve/acquire information about a possible earthquake from multiple sources. We integrate relevant pieces of information for making some sense and then we decide to take some safety measure. We would like to describe the entire process in three simple steps, which we refer to as *Pull-Process-Push* (PPP). In Pull step information is retrieved from the *global information space*, in Process step the retrieved and integrated information is manipulated and finally in Push step the result and modified information is thrown back to the information space. Unfortunately these steps are not that easy to perform. Each defines a large research domain, which is increasing continuously as our interaction with information change and with our new requirements. It is important to note that the research activities in these domains are interdisciplinary with a high degree of cooperation among majority of technical disciplines. We confine our discussion to information management discipline.

To achieve these PPP successfully the information management discipline, initially, worked in a modular fashion with little integration. Thus, data processing, networking, telecommunication, etc., evolved in a modular fashion and appeared to be remotely complementary to each other. Our ever growing need of new technology for managing information either motivated us or forced us to discover interrelationship

P. Van Emde Boas et al. (Eds.): SOFSEM 2004, LNCS 2932, pp. 22–40, 2004.
© Springer-Verlag Berlin Heidelberg 2004

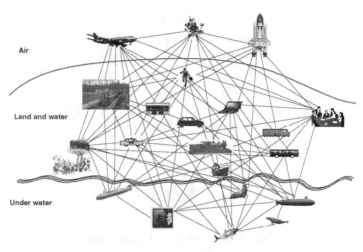

Fig. 1. A Fully Connected Information Space

among these disciplines. Our investigation reveled that they are not only complementary but highly dependent on each other and essential to build the fully connected information space we deserve.

Figure 1 illustrates the fully connected information space we require. A node of this space which can be any real world object that has some functionality is fully and continuously connected with all other objects. Nearly all these connections are duplex where any two parties can exchange *consistent* information without any temporal and spatial constraints. This will create a very high degree of concurrent traffic and if updates are allowed - which must be - then there will be an extremely high degree of data and resource (CPU, I/O, etc.) contention. At present there is no concurrency control and scheduling mechanisms which can satisfactorily managed such traffic. The information space will inherit not only the problem of concurrency but all other information management problems – system and application - and each one will require an innovative solution. We will have to deal with information space recovery, database distribution, and so on, in a very different way. These are some of the problems we present in this paper and provide our solutions to the basic problems.

2   Application Domain

There will be millions of application level problems. A user will retrieve information from a large number of sources, which must be integrated to make some sense out of that. No information integration scheme is capable to handle such varied formats. It is so frustrating to deal with state tax form format, federal tax form format, admission forms format, and so on. Some ask First name, Middle initial, Last name, in this order where as some other forms ask for them in reverse order. It is obvious that such diversity is likely to increase significantly in the globally shared information space and to improve quality of service and user comfort some information integration interface is highly desirable. Figure 2 presents a possible scenario of information integration.

Fig. 2. Information integration scenario

2.1 Medical Informatics

Let us consider highly heterogeneous medical informatics domain. Current health care infrastructure and the services it provides are highly federated. Patients are seen in emergency departments, specialized clinics, physician's offices, and inpatient hospital environments. Prescriptions are filled in pharmacies, and laboratory and radiographic information is captured in yet another environment. From data format viewpoint information from each device including human is represented in a specialized format usually not compatible to each other. The physician reviews each data separately and discovers compatibility in an ad hoc manner which is good enough for a correct diagnosis. This is not only time consuming but primitive from current information management viewpoint.

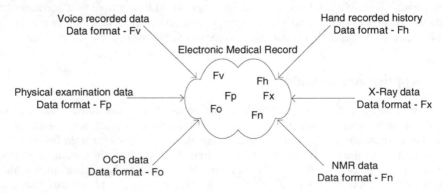

Fig. 3. Heterogeneous medical data repository

Figure 3 visualizes the current scenario in practice. A number of data sources such as X-Ray, OCR, etc., have their own specific format suitable for recording the results of a patient. A data format such as Fv is usually not compatible; semantically and syntactically with other format. The data compatibility problem gets worse because of synonyms and homonyms which may be present in all or some of the formats. Then there is a question of false data redundancy which may not be easily recognizable. For example two different patients with the same name may be examined by two different caregivers and one is subjected to OCR and another to X-Ray. If not careful these two records may falsely taken as duplication which may lead to incorrect billing or diagnosis. A significant challenge lies in the fact that medical information is related to people, and people are inherently difficult to uniquely identify. There are a finite number of combinations of first and surnames. This leads to significant real-world duplication of partial or entire names. Presenting further difficulties is the fact that many people are actually identified by more than one name, often using a nickname or preferring the use of a middle name rather than their given first name. Government or corporate identifiers such as SSN (*Social Security Number*), or medical record number do not exist for all people; additional differentiators which are inherent to all persons such as DOB (*Date of Birth*), gender, race are limited in their ability to uniquely identifier an individual again by the finite set of combinations. A positive DNA identification of individual patients is not practicable in most locations. Sequencing technology is currently limited and expensive, and the resultant data is large, in the order of 3×10^9 base pairs or 1GB per patient. This is clearly too large to be a suitable primary key even if all participating component systems could access this data.

Positive identification of an entity (e.g., patient, department, equipment, etc.) within a single well-regulated database system is relatively simple and is a foundation of relational databases. In a relational model the instance of an entity is represented by a row and a *primary key* is used to uniquely identify the entity. Other related relations are linked together using the concept of *foreign key*. This scheme however only enforces *tuple* uniqueness and does not guarantee that a real world entity is not duplicated within the *base* relation. For example, multiple instances of Thomas Smith may occur in a table each with an internally unique identifier as a result of treatments at multiple locations, which may not be related. This is desirable if indeed more than one real patient is named Thomas Smith. At the architecture level this demonstrates the significance of choosing appropriate *candidate keys*. Identification and duplication prevention of entities can be regulated through intelligent applications such as good Human Computer Interface (HCI) for data entry and creation of patients through the Admission, Discharge, and Transfer (ADT) software. A human operator can make decisions regarding the uniqueness of a real patient and distinguish between the requirement to create a new patient database instance or the selection of an existing record. Significant challenges are introduced however when an automation of this process is to be achieved; as in the case of entity resolution across a federation or batch import processes.

Integration of distributed data sources does not guarantee unique instances of real-world entities. The component systems of a federation or data feeds into a repository may use different *candidate keys* for the *base* entity relations. Several approaches have been developed to address this problem ranging from probabilistic key matching, to pre-hoc user-defined mapping [1]. In addition to this integration issue, another major problem which frequently occurs and has not been addressed satisfactorily is the correctness of data. They assume that accessed or data read by any equipment is correct. Often potential key elements are inconsistent or incomplete due to the data acquisition method or clinical environment. For example OCR (*Optical Character Recognition*) scanners are prone to character misrecognition. Clinically induced ambiguity can result from the chaos of acquiring data in emergent situations or lack of enforcement of standard operation procedures. Often a physician's initials or only last name are collected, or non-standard clinical abbreviations are used.

The variety of data acquisition methods involved in the collection of medical information increases the difficulty of assimilating these facts into a comprehensive patient history. A majority of relevant medical history is still hand-written into patient charts. Often this information is difficult or impossible to acquire electronically. Data is frequently collected in an urgent or emergent clinical setting where it is impracticable to interact directly with an online data acquisition tool. The non-prompted and non-validated nature of this data collection often leads to incomplete information, and data acquired in this manner is difficult to later merge to an electronic system. Snapshot digital images of the paper charts can be linked to patient database records; however this increases the storage requirements of the system without significant analytical benefit. Images are not easily analyzed programmatically. Physician dictation is also not easily captured. Voice recognition technologies are in their infancy, and libraries to address the specialized vocabulary of the medical domain are even less developed. Transcription remains the primary method of electronically acquiring dictation; and even then this information is in *natural-language* syntax rather than an easily analyzable format. Some attempt has been made to facilitate directed point of care data entry by physicians through mobile online systems such as Pen & Pad which prompt the user to build statements which are valid in predefined meta-knowledge syntax [2]. However, in practice point of care data collection is largely performed on paper forms, which are converted to electronic format by means of OCR scanners. This acquisition method is prone to character misrecognition and form alignment issues.

Thus, from administrative as well as from treatment viewpoints a correct and consistent maintenance of EMR (*Electronic Medical Record*) is highly desirable. This kind of maintenance must not undermine the security and efficiency in data access and management. In this paper we do not address security, which is a highly complex problem to solve in its own right.

To express the entire patient experience in an EMR or assemble a comprehensive *continuum of care* has become extremely complex but these have to be resolved efficiently for accurately identifying and treating patients across systems. If the specialized component systems are to be expressed through a federated schema or contribute to a data warehouse, an automated mechanism must be built to facilitate this entity resolution.

Due to limitations of the Human Computer Interface (HCI) in HIMS, the data collection process especially at point of care is prone to error. This error however, once quantified can be exploited to provide an information gain. Our work in progress explores using contextually implied keys and probabilistic adjustments to enhance a traditional key equivalence approach for solving some of the medical data management problems.

We observe that data produced by a source acquires some characteristics of the source. Thus, an instrument that measures blood pressure or heart beat leaves its mark on the result. We argue that a reverse process can be applied which will allow us to identify the source of data by examining the data value. Thus, by looking at a patient's history it would be possible to identify what medical instruments were used to collect health data for diagnosis. This will also provide us a reasonable amount of data accuracy and some motivation for further examination.

2.2   World Wide Web (Web)

The advent of *World Wide Web* (Web) presented a global sharable repository. Any user could surf the web anytime without being aware of the physical location of the repository. However, it did little to create a unified information space which is being experimented by the *Grid* infrastructure. However, in spite of a number of limitations the web has turned out to be an excellent platform for e-commerce and m-commerce. Organizations no longer want to limit the scope of the web to a repository and a showcase; rather they want to use it as a powerful communication tool to disseminate latest information on all kinds of things. They find web systems more suitable in every respect than legacy systems for managing their activities because of its flexibility and universality. As a result of this, all information storage and access activities are migrating to web. In our work we are experimenting with web services to provide desired information and services to static as well as mobile users.

Web Bazzar: A Web-Based System for Service Discovery. There have been increasing demands from mobile users (M-users) to access location-based information (locations of restaurant, movie theatres, etc.) and desired services (ticket booking, buying pizzas, etc.) at any time and from anywhere through mobile devices using *Location Dependent Query* (LDQ). The significant advances in mobile technology can easily incorporate this facility into the existing mobile infrastructure. The idea of providing services and information through web is not new and currently there are a few middleware-based solutions for accessing location-based information are available [1], [2], [3], [5], [8], [9], [16] but they are limited in scope. Their limitation is mainly due to a tight integration between *Content Providers* (CP) and *Service Providers* (SP), which makes dynamic configuration becomes harder to develop and expensive to process.

Service Provider (SP)   Content Provider (CP)

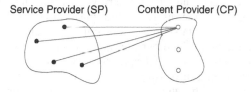

Fig. 4. Location based information scheme

Figure 1 illustrates the current scheme. Each CP provides specific information (i.e., weather, hotel, etc.) and supports specific format. A SP or a number of CPs has to individually register with a SP for satisfying the needs of a mobile user. In this tight integration or mapping, the user may have to content with fixed information format and if the user wants information on a particular topic his SP may not be able to provide it because the SP may not be able to register with the desired CP dynamically. In order to overcome these problems and efficiently satisfy all users' (static or mobile) demands, we propose to use Web service as an interface (middleware) between the CPs and SPs. Thus, a SP will interact with *Universal Description, Discovery & Integration* (UDDI), which in turn will reach relevant web service to get the answer.

Web Service-based middleware does provide a standard way to communicate among heterogonous applications and it is highly flexible and scalable but at present it is not well equipped to provide location-based services because (a) it uses centralized repository (e.g., UDDI) for publishing Web services, (b) it has limited keyword-based search facility for services and (c) it lacks appropriate semantics for discovering location based services. We propose to overcome these limitations in our architectural framework, referred to as "Web Bazzar", of middleware approach which will make it possible to discover location-based web services easily and cheaply through the location-aware UDDI. We present a couple of simple examples to show the usefulness of our proposal.

Example 1. *User subscribes to SP for service by giving payment information and preference profile. The user during his trip to Kansas City wants to go to a coffee shop. He enters the request (using some location dependent query language), gets the list of coffee shops (identified using his personal profile), selects the shop which gives discount on coffee, clicks the link and pays for the item. In return he gets a transaction id, goes to the shop, enters the id and gets his coffee. The user profiles can be maintained and the information can be given to the user proactively.*

Example 2. *User wants to eat special pizza. He selects pizza store using mobile device after getting store's information from Web Bazzar. The service selects the right kinds of pizzas using information from profile. The pizza order is given to the shop and when it is ready the GPS service is used to get user's location. User location is dispatched to map web service to obtain route for delivery.*

Issues in the Design and Development of Web Bazaar. M-commerce application architecture framework can be broadly classified in to two models: Push Model and Pull Model [4], [5]. In the pull model user requests a transaction, server looks for appropriate service, contacts the CP and retrieves the information, process data and gives the results back to the user. In the push model the server collects the information from different data sources according to the current location of the user and pushes it to mobile unit. Since our aim is to develop a proactive architecture for m-commerce applications push model is more suited to our requirements. Proactive architecture requires caching of possible user required context services on the mobile unit which greatly reduces the query processing time as the upward communication from the mobile unit to the middleware is greatly reduced. So the major requirements in mobile middleware are (a) *semantic* profile driven cache management (b) *semantic* web services description, (c) *semantic* web services discovery protocol, (d) proposing a structure of UDDI, which can search, based location context of the user, and (e) broadcasting of web services information. Figure 5 shows the components of the proposed middleware.

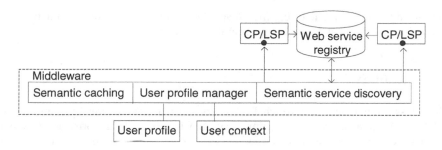

Fig. 5. A reference structure of Web Bazaar

Semantic profile driven caching component. Traditional caching uses spatial locality of data, but semantic caching considers the semantic relation of data. In our case we relate data with respect to the location and data related to the same location is cached. For example all the restaurants are related with location. So all the restaurants at a particular location are cached rather than the restaurants stored physically next to each other in the database. Semantic caching is required in our architecture to minimize communication overhead and retrieval time.

Semantic Caching for Location Dependent Data (LDD). When the user is on the move, data of the current location is cached in the MU. Data that is cached is based on the preferences specified by the user in his profile. Also as user moves out of the current location data stored in the MU becomes invalid. Mechanisms have been specified in [13] on cache replacement of location dependent data. For LDD cache replacement should be a balance between how frequently the location data is cached and the proximity of the current user location to the location data stored on the MU. The aim here is to optimize the tradeoff between the number of cache refreshes, which are triggered by the change in user location and validity of the LDD stored on the MU. Schemes like [14] assume that the speed and direction of the MU is available so the future location of the MU is predicted and the location data is cached accordingly which further reduces the number of cache refreshes. The information about user movement (direction, speed, etc.) can be obtained and we plan to use this in the development of Web Bazzar.

We also have to deal with user connectivity problem. If the user is continuously connected to the wireless network then the cached data can be refreshed as soon as user moves to a different location. But if the user is not continuously connected then data-recharging scheme [11] needs to be used. Whenever the user connects to the network, cache is recharged with the data depending on the current location, his future plans and the preferences user specifies in the profile.

Thus, in the information management discipline the integration, diffusion, and merging of web, data warehousing, business processes, mobility, networking, etc., become seamless. Now a days it is very common to hear mobile web mining, web mining, web caching, mobile database systems, mobile federated systems, and so on, and the state of the research and development in this integrated area. It is, therefore, not acceptable to say that one is doing research in mobile web caching but is not knowledgeable in mobile discipline. Researchers as well as the research activities are integrated, diffused and merged in a seamless manner.

3 Mobility

Wireless communication through PCS (Personal Communication Systems) or GSM (Global System for Mobile Communications) has become a norm of present day society. Cell phones are more common than watches and in addition to being portable communication tools, they have become web-browsing platforms. Telecommunication companies are continuously improving the communication qualities, security, availability and reliability of cell phones and trying to enhance its scope by adding data management capabilities, which is highly desirable. Motivated by such growing demand, we envision an information processing system based on PCS or GSM architecture, which we refer to as the *Mobile Database System* (MDS). It is essentially a distributed client/server system where clients can move around freely while performing their data processing activities in *connected*, *disconnected* or *intermittent* connected mode. The MDS that we present here is a ubiquitous database system where unlike conventional systems the processing unit could also reach data location for processing. Thus, it can process debit/credit transactions, pay utility bills, make airline reservations, and other transactions without being subject to any geographical constraints. Since there is no MDS type of system available, it is difficult to identify the transaction volume at mobile units, however, the present information processing needs and trends in e-commerce indicate that transaction workload at each mobile unit could be high and MDS would be a useful resource to organizations and individuals alike.

Although MDS is a distributed system based on client server paradigm, it functions differently than conventional centralized or distributed systems and supports diverse applications and system functionalities. It achieves such diverse functionalities by imposing comparatively more constraints and demands on MDS infrastructure. To manage system-level functions, MDS may require different transaction management schemes (concurrency control, database recovery, query processing, etc.), different logging scheme, different caching schemes, and so on. The topic of this paper is log management for application recovery through the use of mobile agents.

3.1 Reference Architecture of Mobile Database System

Figure 6 illustrates our reference architecture of Mobile Database System (MDS). It is a distributed multidatabase client/server system based on cellular infrastructure. We have added a number of DBSs (database Servers) to incorporate data processing capability without affecting any aspect of the generic mobile network [3].

A set of general purpose computers (PCs, workstations, etc.) are interconnected through a high-speed wired network, which are categorized into Fixed Hosts (FH) and Base Stations (BS) or mobile support stations (MSS). One or more BSs are connected with a BS Controller or Cell Site Controller (BSC) [9], which coordinates the operation of BSs using its own stored software program when commanded by the MSC (Mobile Switching Center). We also incorporate some additional simple data processing capability in BSs to handle the coordination of transaction processing.

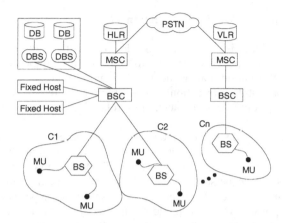

Fig. 6. A reference architecture of Mobile Database System (MDS)

Unrestricted mobility in PCS and GSM is supported by wireless link between BS and mobile units such as PDA (Personal Digital Assistants), laptop, cell phones, etc. We refer to these as Mobile Hosts (MH) or Mobile Units (MU) [9], [12], which communicate with BSs using wireless channels [9]. The power of a BS defines its communication region, which we refer to as a *cell*. The size of a *cell* depends upon the power of its BS and also restricted by the limited bandwidth of wireless communication channels. Thus, the number of BSs in MDS defines the number of cells. In reality a high power BS is not used because of a number of factors [9], [12] rather a number of low power BSs are deployed for managing movement of MUs. A MU may be in powered off or in idle state (doze mode) or it may be actively processing data and can freely move from one cell to another. When a MU crosses a cell boundary, it is disconnected from its last BS and gets connected to the BS of the cell it enters. In such inter-cell movement the *handoff* mechanism makes sure that the boundary crossing is seamless and data processing is not affected.

A DBS provides full database services and it communicates with MUs only through a BS. DBSs can either be installed at BSs or can be a part of FHs or can be independent to BS or FH. A MU is unable to provide reliable storage as provided by conventional clients and for this reason it usually relies on the static nodes (FH or BS) to save its data. This is especially true for activities such as recovery, logging, concurrency control, data caching, etc. It is possible to install DBS at BSs, however, we argue against this approach. Note that BS is a switch and it has specific tasks to perform, which does not include database functionality. To work as a database server the entire architecture of a BS (hardware and software) may have to be revised, which would be unacceptable from mobile communication viewpoint. We argue that mobile database functionality and wireless communication should be modular with minimum degree of overlap on their functionality. For these reasons and for the reason of scalability, we created DBSs as separate nodes on the wired network, which could be reached by any BS at anytime.

3.2   Mobilaction: A Mobile Transaction Model

Transaction concept is essential for dealing with any type of information management. It is especially true in MDS because it imposes a number of new constraints in information management. Motivated by unique requirements of MDS, we developed a mobile transaction model which we refer to as *"Mobilaction"* [20]. We present here some data characteristics related to mobility before we introduce *Mobilaction*.

Conventional data do not change their values based on the mode of the query (when and where the query originated). Consider for example, the "SSN", "mother's maiden name", "city of birth", "mother tongue", etc., of a person. Any enquiry about these attributes of the person either from any where in the world will provide an identical response. On the other hand, there are some data types that generate different but correct responses when the mode of the query on them changes (for example, room rent of a hotel, sales tax, city tax, etc). If an enquiry on the tax rate is made about Kansas City and then at Dallas, then there would be two different but correct answers. Thus the same query on this data from a moving object with a changing query location could have different correct answers. We refer to the first type of data as "location free data" and to the second type as "Location Dependent Data (LDD)".

LDD gives rise to Location Dependent Query (LDQ) and Location Aware Query (LAQ). The answer of a LDQ depends on the geographical origin of the query. For example the answer to a query *"What is the distance of the airport"* is strongly tied to the geographical origin of this query. Now let us introduce mobility in query processing. Let us consider, for example, a person who is traveling by car on a business trip from Boston, first to Kansas City and then to Dallas. While on the road the traveler continues to ask *"What is the distance of the airport"* after every few minutes. The system will generate multiple correct answers to this query and each answer will be strongly related with the geographical origin of the query. Thus from these reasoning we came to the conclusion that like ACID (Atomicity, Consistency, Isolation, and Durability) property, location mapping has to be a basic property of *Mobilaction* which we incorporate. We now formally define our *Mobilaction* model.

An Execution Fragment e_{ij} is a partial order $e_{ij} = \{\sigma_j, \leq_j\}$ where

- $\sigma_j = OS_j \cup \{N_j\}$ *where* $OS_j = \cup_k O_{jk}$, $O_{jk} \in \{read, write\}$, *and* $N_j \in \{abort_L,$ *commit$_L\}$. Here these are location dependent commit and abort.*

- *For any O_{jk} and O_{jl} where $O_{jk} = R(x)$ and $O_{jl} = W(x)$ for a data object x, then either $O_{jk} \leq_j O_{jl}$ or $O_{jl} \leq_j O_{jk}$*

- $\forall O_{jk} \in OS_j, OS_j \leq_j N_j$

A Mobile Transaction T_i is a triple $<F_i, L_i, FLM_i>$ where $F_i = \{e_{i1}, e_{i2}..., e_{in}\}$ is a set of execution fragments, $L_i = \{l_{i1}, l_{i2}, ..., l_{in}\}$ is a set of locations, and $FLM_i = \{flm_{i1}, flm_{i2}, ..., flm_{in}\}$ is a set of fragment location mappings where $\forall_j, flm_{i1}(e_{ij}) = l_{ij}$.

3.3 Mobilaction: Execution and Commitment

Although MDS is a distributed system based on client server paradigm, it functions differently than conventional centralized or distributed systems and supports diverse applications and system functionalities. It achieves such diverse functionalities by imposing comparatively more constraints and demands on MDS infrastructure. To manage system-level functions, MDS may require different transaction management schemes (concurrency control, database recovery, query processing, etc.), different logging scheme, different caching schemes, and so on. We describe one way of execution *Mobilaction* on MDS and present a commit protocol.

A *Mobilaction* may run on multiple nodes which could be located anywhere in the network. Each e_i represents a subset of the total T_i processing. A T_i is requested at a MU, it is fragmented [20], and are executed at the MU and at a set of DBSs. Note that no fragment of a *Ti* is sent to another MU for execution. This is because in MDS, a MU is a personal unit and its use is controlled by its owner who can switch it off or disconnect it from the network at any time. This could force the *Ti* to fail unnecessary. Furthermore, other MUs may not have necessary data to process the fragment generated by another MU, in which case the fragment will end up at a DBS. Also transfer of e_i's to other MUs will incur wireless communication overhead which could be prohibitive.

In MDS, like conventional distributed database systems, a coordinator (CO) is required to manage the commit of T_i [20] and its role can be illustrated with the execution of a T_i. A T_i originates at MU and its BS is identified as the holder of the CO of T_i. The MU fragments *Ti* extracts its e_i, sends $T_i - e_i$ to the CO and begins processing e_i. The MU may move to other cell during the execution of e_i, which must be logged for recovery. At the end of the execution of e_i, the MU updates its cache copy of the database, composes update shipment and sends it to the CO. CO logs the updates from the MU.

Upon receipt of $T_i - e_i$ from MU, the CO splits $T_i - e_i$ into e_j's $(i \neq j)$ and sends them to a set of relevant DBSs for execution. Note that the presence of handoff may delay the execution and commit of a T_i. In this situation even a *small* T_i may appear as a *long-running* T_i. Thus, the meaning of *long-running* T_i on MDS could be (a) a *small* T_i (such as debit/credit) may take long time to run because of frequent handoffs and (b) the T_i does access a large number of data items, such as the preparation of bank customer monthly statements, and takes long time to execute in the absence of any handoff. It is, however, meaningless to run statement preparation transactions on MU and long-running transaction in our case will be mostly of (a) type.

It is obvious that a conventional two-phase or three-phase commit protocol [10] would not work satisfactorily in MDS. It will generate excessive overhead, which could not be handled by MDS. We have developed a commit protocol, which we refer to as TCOT (Transaction Commit on Timeout) which meets the following objectives:

- Uses minimum number of wireless messages.
- MU and DBS involved in Ti processing have independent decision making capability and
- It is non-blocking.

TCOT is based on *timeout* concept. *Timeouts* are usually used to identify a failure situation. For example, in messaging systems the sender waits for the acknowledgement of a message receipt for a timeout period before resending or not sending the message at all. In distributed database systems the use of timeout is necessary for developing a "non-blocking" transaction commit protocol [10], [11], [12]. We propose the use of timeout for our commit protocol. We assume that instead of failure the end of timeout period indicates a success. Thus, at the end of the timeout it is *expected* that the receiver has received the message sent by the sender. This is the basis of defining the completion of transaction commit in TCOT.

TCOT strives to limit the number of messages (especially uplink) needed to commit a T_i. It does so by assuming that all members of a commit set successfully commit their fragments within the defined timeout leading to commit of T_i. Unlike 2PC or 3PC [10], [11], [12], no further communications between the CO and participants take place for keeping track of the progress of fragments. However, the failure situation is immediately communicated to CO to make a final decision about commit.

It is well known that finding the most appropriate value of a timeout is not always easy because it depends on a number of system variables, which could be difficult to quantify [10]. However, it is usually possible to define a value for timeout, which performs well in all cases. It should be noted that an imprecise value of timeout does not affect the correctness but affects the performance of an algorithm. We, therefore, assume that timeout value can be defined with some degree of accuracy satisfactory to TCOT. We discuss in detail the behavior and performance of TCOT in our paper [13].

3.4   Application Recovery in Mobile Database System

An efficient scheme for application is required for MDS. We are not concerned about the database recovery because that is taken care by the underlying database recovery mechanisms. We have developed an efficient recovery protocol which uses mobile agents to recover from any kind of failure.

Application recovery, unlike database recovery, enhances application availability by recovering the execution state of applications. This process is relatively more complex than database recovery because (a) there are a large numbers of applications required to manage database processing (b) presence of multiple application states, and (c) the absence of the notion of the "last consistent state". This gets more complex in MDS because of (a) unique processing demands of mobile units, (b) the existence of random handoffs, and (c) the presence of operations in connected, disconnected, and intermittent connected modes.

The log management is the main component of any recovery scheme. We present here our mobile agent based recovery approach. We argue that for MDS the use of conventional approaches for managing log, even with modifications, would impose unmanageable burden on the limited channel capacity and, therefore, reject their use.

An efficient recovery scheme requires that the log management must consume minimum system resources and recreate the execution environment as soon as possible after MU reboots. For application recovery the MU and the server must build a log of the events that change the execution states of T_i. In conventional distributed systems, log management is straightforward since no mobility is involved and a single stable storage area is available for storing log. In MDS a MU cannot be relied upon and, therefore, it is necessary to store the log information at some stable place that can survive MU failure. Schemes that provide recovery in PCS failure use the BS where the MU currently resides for storing the log. Note that managing log for PCS failure is relatively easy because it does not support T_i processing.

Our objective is to utilize the unique processing capability of mobile agents in managing application log for efficient application recovery, which will conform to MDS limitations and mobile discipline constraints. We aim to achieve this conformity and desired efficiency by incorporating the following properties in our scheme: (a) communication overhead (wired/wireless) should be low, (b) recovery time should be minimal, and (c) easy deployment of recovery schemes in the network.

A *mobile agent* is an autonomous program that can move from machine to machine in heterogeneous network under its own control [14]. It can suspend its execution at any point, transport itself to a new machine, and resume execution from the point it stopped execution. An agent carries both the code and the application state. Actually mobile agent paradigm is an extension of the client/server architecture with code mobility. Some of the advantages of mobile which we exploit are:

a. **Protocol Encapsulation:** Mobile agents can incorporate their own protocols in their code instead of depending on the legacy code provided by the hosts.

b. **Robustness and fault-tolerance:** When failures are detected, host systems can easily dispatch agents to other hosts. This ability makes the agents fault-tolerant.

c. **Asynchronous and autonomous execution:** Once the agents are dispatched from a host, they can make decisions independently and autonomously.

Our idea was to delegate all operations that involved mobility to mobile agents. We created a number of agents for creating, identifying, and writing log records. Thus, one agent was responsible for writing local log records, one was responsible for dispatching the local log records to a stable storage (at the base station), one was responsible for identifying mobile unit failure and log unification, and one was responsible for making log available to mobile unit for recovery. We developed two recovery protocols under a scheme which is referred to as "Forward Strategy". Under this scheme we developed two recovery protocols which are called (a) Forward Log Unification Scheme and (b) Forward Notification Scheme. To establish the superiority of our schemes we compared its performance with three other schemes. We showed that our schemes gave better performance in most of the recovery situations.

4   Sensor Technology

All pervading aspect of information space introduced earlier was a very useful property but at the same time it created a serious problem related to the capture of information from difficult to reach geographical locations not easily reachable by humans such as ocean bed, enemy territories, deep space, and so on. The medical field also has similar difficulty, how to collect data of internal live organs such as liver, heart, etc. Such requirements gave rise to sensor technology where minute device called "sensor" is utilized for data collection, validation, processing, and storing. A sensor is a programmable, low-cost, low-power, multi-functional device. One of its multi-functional properties is its capability of continuously gathering desired information about the location of its deployment. For medical field two types of sensor (a) immersive and (b) non-immersive were developed. Immersive sensors were planted inside human body and non-immersive sensors remained outside the body.

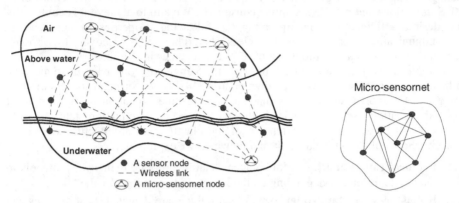

Fig. 7. An ESN with Micro-sensornet   A Micro-sensor net

We define the concept of "Embedded Sensor Space (ESS)", which is a countably infinite set of uniquely programmed sensors. Thus, $ESS = s_1, s_2, \ldots, s_\infty$ where s_i $(i = 1, 2, \ldots, \infty)$ is a programmed sensor. A node in the embedded sensor net captures data of its environment and dispatches it to other sensors through routers. There are quite a few unsolved problems related to network management and routing. From ESN viewpoint s_i and s_j $(i \neq j)$ are fully connected and have direct communication facility.

We are working on a complex sensor network which is illustrated in Figure 7. The Embeded sensor net is composed of individual sensors and *micro-sensor* net. A *micro-sensor* net is a set of small number of specialized sensors fully connected together. One of the nodes in a micro-sensor net is responsible for coordinating the activities of other sensors in the set. This gives rise to the problem of *leader election* problem, which we do not discuss in this paper.

The unique properties of sensors allowed us to link them in all kinds of topology. Thus, it is possible to build a globally connected infrastructure where uniquely programmed sensors are embedded at desired places. For example, programmed sensors may be embedded at various points in all cars of a family, in the house, in the office, in children's school bags, in parents' briefcases, etc. Each sensor will capture data and communicate with other sensors, which will help the parents to be aware of and be fully connected with everyday activities of each family member. At the time of need any family members can be reached instantly. On a large scale we can visualize sensor deployment at various places (buildings, malls, factories, etc.) of a city for continuous monitoring of events for managing security. Similarly to protect water supply, gas pipelines, and so on, programmed sensors can be deployed at strategic locations.

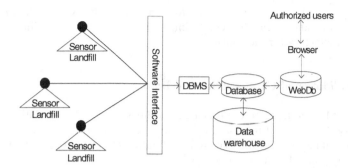

Fig. 8. Data capture, Validation, Analysis, Formatting and storage

Figure 8 illustrates an example of sensor network deployment to monitor gas emission at various landfills and send information to the DBMS for further processing and dissemination. The reference sensor network architecture we envision will be very large and highly data intensive since sensors will be capturing data continuously. The emission of gases and their volume are not predictable so these sensors will have to be active continuously and there must also have a fail-safe scheme, which would ensure that any sensor failure or malfunctioning is promptly propagated to the servers for immediate action to minimize the damage. This implies that they will be sending different types of data with different constraints associated with them. Some data will be temporal in nature with limited validity. These must be processed in real-time and decision, if any, must be propagated to target sensors for changing or altering their functionality. The diversity of data category, their real-time characteristics, propagation of results to target sensors present a number of complex data management problems.

We identify the following data management tasks, which must be performed efficiently for managing the entire network and dissemination of right information to right destination (people and institutions). Each of these steps are elaborated below and our research approach for their management is described

- Stream data capture from specific sensors.
- Validation of captured streams data.
- Analyzing, formatting, and verifying real-time processing of stream data.
- Storing of formatted data in the database and updating the data warehouse.
- Posting necessary information on the web.

4.1   Stream Data Capture from Specific Sensors

A sensor can send data in any form, i.e., pulses, packets, sound, etc. There are a large number of data capture schemes are available [15], [18], [19]. We are in the process of developing, which will take into consideration energy conservation aspect. This stream data must be converted before it can be stored and processed. Since sensors in our network could be location specific we propose to program the L/L information in the sensor, which will be appended to each dispatch from that sensor. We agree that this will increase the cost but the benefit will outweigh the cost. This conversion can be easily done by a simple mapping function, since the type of the dispatch from a sensor will be known in advance. A simple conversion table, residing in the interface, will be satisfactory for the conversion.

4.2   Validation of Captured Streams Data

Data must be validated before it is accepted for storage. The validation will require to (a) verify the source of the data, which must be the right sensor and (b) check that the captured data is not corrupt. We are investigating the use a directory, which will store the mapping of L/L with sensor.

4.3   Posting Necessary Information on the Web

Many organizations (private and government) will share the captured and processed stream data results. We propose to make them available through secured web. The web will be accessed through static and mobile clients. We have done significant amount of work on mobility [13], [19], [22], [23] and we will use one of the existing techniques for managing mobile data access and query. In addition to this, we will implement an automatic message delivery system where all the mobile clients will be informed through e-mail the arrival of any crucial or pre-selected type of data from any of the sensors.

In dealing with ESS, we regard a sensor as a data with some semantics, which is provided to it by its unique programmed state. In a massive ESN, therefore, it becomes necessary to identify or trace individual sensor for whatever reason. This requirement creates a situation, which is very similar to data mining in conventional information space. In conventional approach for mining data with fuzzy information "a large person with red shirt", mining techniques are used to find the correct data. It is also necessary to mine sensor in ESN when fuzzy information such as "find sensor which captures temperature of high rise building" is used.

Sensors in a sensornet are insecure repositories and routers of data. There are many applications where sensors are deployed in hazardous environments in which they are subject to failure or destruction under attack by a malicious adversary. For example, consider seismic sensor networks in earthquake or rubble zones or sensors in military battlegrounds under enemy threat. Wireless sensor networks are also extremely vulnerable to data loss under denial of service (DoS) attacks. Nodes use wireless communication because the network's large scale, ad-hoc deployment and limited energy resources makes wired or satellite communication impractical. Jamming a transmitting nodes frequency makes its data unavailable. Thus, any model for ensuring effective query reporting and collaborative mining in sensor networks, while incorporating the constraints of energy efficiency and distributed decision-making, should simultaneously take sensor failure and security considerations into account. This will require the development of specific algorithms to ensure that the tasks of (a) data storage and content in distributed repositories (which could be special sensor nodes within the network) and (b) data retrieval are not affected by the inhospitable environment.

5   Conclusions and Future Direction

In this paper we presented the role of information and its management for synchronizing our activities with the dynamic state of the environment around us. We identified essential activities which are continuously being imposed on the information we desire. We introduced the concept of *fully connected information space* to illustrate the nature and instances of these activities. We recognized the significance of advances in wired and wireless technologies and discussed their effect on information management schemes. We presented our research work and contributions in this area for wired and wireless platforms. In particular we addressed the problems of information integration, medical informatics, e-commerce, m-commerce, static and mobile web, and sensor technology.

The future of information management is quite bright. Significant changes will occur in the way we interact with the information space and state of the art gadget we will use. Wireless world will dominate and continuous connectivity will persist. Information processing will pervade every object of this world and fancy gadgets will rule our lives. Let us hope that we still drive these gadgets not the other way round.

Acknowledgement. Thanks to Kelly Kern for his help in preparing medical informatics part on and to Raj Kannan for his support in the presentation of sensor technology material. Julius Stuller's input on web technology was highly useful

References

1. Ee-Peng, L., Srivastava, J., Prabhakar, S., Richardson J.: Entity Identification in Database Integration. Information Sciences, Vol. 89. No. 1, (1996) 1–38
2. Goeble, C.A., Glowinski, A., Crowther P.: Semantic Constraints in a Medical Information System
3. Jin, L., Miyazawa, T.: MRM Server: A Context-aware and Location-based Mobile E-Commerce Server. In: Proceeding of Workshop WMC '02
4. Varshney, U.: Location Management Support for Mobile Commerce Applications. In: Proceeding of Workshop WMC '02
5. Munson, J.P., Gupta, V.K.: Location-Based Notification as a General-Purpose Service. In: Proceeding of Workshop WMC '02
6. Jung , I.-D., You, Y.-H., Lee, J.-H., Kim, K.: Broadcasting and Caching Policies for Location-Dependent Queries in Urban Areas
7. Sivashanmugam, K., Verma, K., Mulye, R., Zhong, Z.: Speed-R:Semantic P2P Environment for Diverse web service Registries
8. Chakraborty, D., Perich, F., Avancha, S., Joshi, A.: DReggie: Semantic Service Discovery for M-Commerce Applications
9. Pilioura, T., Tsalgatidou, A., Hadjiefthymiades, S.: Scenarios of using Web Services in M-Commerce. ACM SIGecom Exchanges, Vol. 3, No. 4, January 2003, 28–36
10. Bernstein, P.A., Hadzilacos, V., Goodman, N.: Concurrency Control and Recovery in Database Systems. Addision Wesley (1987)
11. Kumar, V., Son, S.H.:Database Recovery. Kluwer International
12. Kumar, V., Hsu, M.: Recovery in Mechanisms in Database Systems. Prentice Hall, (1998)

13. Kumar, V., Prabhu, N., Dunham, M., Seydim, Y.A.: TCOT – A Timeout-based Mobile Transaction Commitment Protocol. Special issue of IEEE Transaction on Computers, Vol. 51, No. 10, Oct. 2002, 1212–1218
14. Kotz, D., Gray, R., Nog, S., Rus, D., Chawla, S., Cybenko, G.: AgentTCL: Targeting the needs of Mobile Computers. IEEE Internet Computing, Vol. 1, No. 4 (1997)
15. www.dpye.iimas.unam.mx/mocap/MocapSystem.html
16. Dunham, M.H., Kumar, V.: Location Dependent Data and its Management in Mobile Databases. Proc. of the Ninth Workshop of Database and Expert Systems Applications DEXA'98, Vienna, Austria, August 26–28, 1998
17. Dunham, M., Kumar, V.: Impact of Mobility on Transaction Management. Int. Workshop on Data Engineering for Wireless and Mobile Access (MobiDE99), Seattle, Washington, August 20, 1999
18. http://64.38.123.238/flash/professional/projects/glove.htm
19. Lindsey, S., Raghvendra, C., Sivalingam, K.: Data Gathering Algorithms in Sensor Networks Using Energy Metrics. IEEE Transactions on Parrallel and Distributed Systems, Vol. 13, No. 9, September 2002
20. Ren, Q., Dunham, M., Kumar, V.: Semantic Caching and Query Processing. IEEE Transactions on Knowledge and Data Engineering, to appear
21. Samtani, S., Mohania, M., Kumar, V., Kambayashi, Y.: Recent Advances and Research Problems in Data Warehousing Inernational. Workshop on Data Warehousing and Data Mining (ER '98), November 1998, 81–92
22. Samtani, S., Kumar, V., Mohania, M.: Self Maintenance of Multiple Views in Data Warehousing. 8th International Conference on Information and Knowledge Management (CIKM '99), Kansas City, MO, November 2-6, 1999, 292–299
23. Seyedim, A., Dunham, M., Kumar, V.:An Architecture for Location Dependent Query Processing. 4th International Workshop on Mobility in Databases and Distributed Systems, Technical University of Munich, Germany, September 3–7, 2001
24. Seydim, Y., Dunham, M., Kumar, V.: Location Dependent Query Processing. 2nd ACM Int. Workshop on Data Engineering for Wireless and Mobile Access (MOBIDE01), Santa Barbara, pp: 47–53, May 20, 2001

Flexibility through Multiagent Systems:
Solution or Illusion?

Peter C. Lockemann and Jens Nimis

Fakultät für Informatik, Universität Karlsruhe
Postfach 6980, 76128 Karlsruhe, Germany
{lockeman, nimis}@ipd.uka.de

Abstract. Multiagent software systems are known to exhibit a system-level behavior that rarely can be predicted from the description of individual agents but must be observed in simulation or real-life. On the other hand there are indications that agent technology is superior in situations that are non-deterministic or so ill-structured as to appear non-deterministic. This paper examines whether one can give a more precise characterization of those situations where multiagent systems hold great promise, and to test the corresponding hypothesis by simulating a real-world production scenario. After refining the hypothesis the paper examines whether one can guarantee the reliability of the agents in the presence of disturbances, because otherwise the flexibility of the multiagent system could become uncontrollable. After examining various transactional approaches that all pose major challenges the paper concludes that to go beyond an illusion still requires intensive research.

1 The Need for Multiagent Software Systems

1.1 A Minimalist View of Agents

Multiagent systems are an extremely active area of computer science research [1]. What, then, is a multiagent system? Or, for that matter, an agent? Surprisingly, there is no universally accepted definition of the notion of "agent", rather there is still a good deal of ongoing debate on this subject [2]. One begins to wonder: How can there be so much activity, such high expectations in a technology if there is not even agreement on its basic concepts? Or from an application view: How can we judge the practical benefits of this technology if we do not clearly understand it?

The reason for the debate may simply be that agents are too many things to too many people. On the one hand take engineers. For example, some ten years ago pieces of mobile but otherwise ordinary program code that was called agents was used to overcome the interruptions in telecommunications networks or to avoid large transmission volumes, and were sent to other nodes to perform computations [3], [4]. Today the idea lives on in Java applets or in peer-to-peer mobile systems. More ambitiously, in today's global networks where the nodes are expected to provide useful services the nodes must necessarily act with a certain degree of autonomy. Consequently, any one node has only limited influence over how another node

P. Van Emde Boas et al. (Eds.): SOFSEM 2004, LNCS 2932, pp. 41–56, 2004.
© Springer-Verlag Berlin Heidelberg 2004

responds to its requests so that some people refer to the systems in the nodes as agents even though these systems are just ordinary programs with a deterministic, externally specified behavior.

At the other end of the spectrum, take distributed artificial intelligence where agents are often adorned with almost human-like capabilities. They are autonomous in their decisions, reactive and proactive in line with the goals they pursue, they can learn from the past, reason, and communicate with others, and they may even have social ability. Such agents may replace humans under certain circumstances, e.g., when too many factors influence a decision that has to be taken in split seconds but the decision itself requires a certain degree of "intelligence", or when the human person cannot be physically present.

Engineers dislike independent and unpredictable system behavior whereas AI scientists view such behavior as one of the advantages of agent technology. But wouldn't even practical systems have something to gain from a more independent behavior? Take the success of agents that predict stock quotations even though they have few of the AI capabilities. And indeed, there seems to be agreement on the basic essentials. Agents are *autonomous*, computational entities that are *situated* in some environment and to some extent have control over their behavior so that they can act without the intervention of humans and other systems. They are intelligent in the sense that they operate *flexibly* and *rationally* in a variety of environmental situations, given the information they have and their perceptual and effectual capabilities (see Prolog to [1] and also [4]).

1.2   Multiagent Systems

To be intelligent – even in the limited sense of above – requires specialization. To observe a complex environment in its entirety in order to reach a given goal or to execute a given task requires a set of specializations. Hence, an agent must have its own *specialized competence*, and several of them need to collaborate. As a consequence, as another essential agents are *interacting*. Hence, they may be affected by other agents in pursuing their goals and executing their tasks, either indirectly by observing one another through the environment or directly through a shared language.

Systems of interacting agents are referred to as multiagent systems (MAS). Our interest is in MAS that can be engineered, i.e., systems that have no "soft" properties. Hence we define a *multiagent system as a system of autonomous, interacting, specialized agents that act flexibly depending on the situation*.

Note that nothing in this definition says that multiagent systems must necessarily be distributed systems. Any system with decentralized control and asynchronous communication meets the test.

1.3   Multiagent Software Systems

We know that larger software is organized into modules. In modern software systems the modules have the properties of objects. Objects seem a natural foundation for agents. All one has to do to turn it into a multiagent systems is to write code for them that entails the minimal properties of autonomy, flexibility and interactivity.

But let's be careful. Do we always need autonomy, flexibility and interactivity? After all, multiagent systems come at a price. The system-level behavior often cannot be predicted analytically from the description of individual agents but must be observed in simulation or real-life. Consequently, the detailed behavior of an implemented system may not be known in advance [5]. Hence, we should restrict multiagent software systems to situations where we are reasonably sure that we gain more than we pay for. There is agreement that MAS are at their best, i.e., fully play out their strengths in environments, e.g., the real-world processes to be supported, that are *non-deterministic* or so complex or ill-structured as to appear non-deterministic [2].

Now, what is a non-deterministic behavior? Or how non-deterministic should the environment become so that the price is worth the additional flexibility? It seems doubtful that one can come up with a metric to find an unambiguous answer, and even less one that would be general enough to apply to each and every environment. Instead, we will propose a methodical approach to find an answer for a given. We base the approach on a qualitative hypothesis [6]:

Hypothesis: Multiagent systems offer an advantage if
- *the range of environmental situations (the problem space) is too large to be enumerated and dealt with by conventional means,*
- *the problem space can be divided into sets of simpler tasks, each requiring specialized competence,*
- *the simpler tasks can be dealt with autonomously by individual agents,*
- *the overall situation can only be solved by cooperation among the agents.*

Given such an approach we would have to perform a whole set of experiments on a wide spectrum of software applications to gain credible empirical evidence for or against the hypothesis. This clearly is beyond the means of a single group of researchers. Rather we pursue the more modest goal of developing a first approach for a real-world scenario of a production facility.

Suppose we are able to show that MAS have their applications. The autonomy and flexibility of agents can only go so far before the common orientation gets lost and turns into chaos. Hence, flexibility itself must be in some sense reliable or predictable. Therefore, we examine in a second step how agents and agent communication can be made robust in the presence of technical disturbances.

2   Testing the Need for Flexibility

2.1   Scenario

We choose a shop floor scenario, in this case for the assembly of circuit breakers [7]. Shop floors are of particular interest for our purpose because on the one hand the incoming orders are the result of centralized production planning and control, on the other hand it is the shop floor that has to cope with short-term disturbances like machine failures or priority jobs. Moreover, the shop floor is made up of several larger sections (Figure 1), along which we consider the Unit Assembly Area in more detail. It consists of 13 assembly lines where 6 different component families and 4 subcomponent families are assembled.

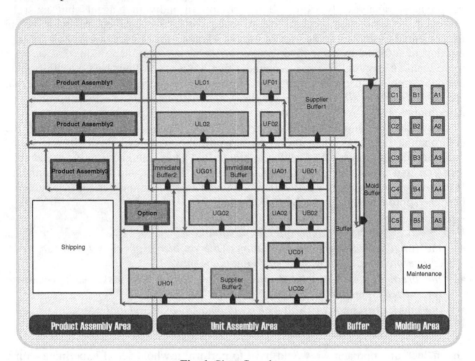

Fig. 1. Shop floor layout

This is a scenario that comes close to the conditions under which we believe MAS offer benefits: There is a good number of stations which offer the potential for local, decentralized decisions, and the overall situation space has a good starting size. However, to test our hypothesis it should be much larger. Of particular interest to production practice is an increase in the space by subjecting each assembly station to machine disturbances or – particularly feared – depletion of stock.

2.2   Experiments

To test the hypothesis we have to devise two sets of experiments. For one we have to prove that in a large situation space a multi-agent systems (MAS) offers some advantages. More precisely, we examine whether MAS demonstrate improved performance in the presence of machine disturbances. Second, we have to show that in smaller situation spaces no benefits accrue from MAS. Here, we examine the behavior of MAS in the absence of disturbances. In fact, both experiments can be rolled into one by varying the level of disturbances.

What is the basis for comparison (the benchmark)? We know that classical centralized planning (production planning and control, PPC) allows long-term optimization of production schedules provided the possibility of disturbances can be excluded. The latter, if they occur, are left to the shop floor to deal with them. Specifically, we choose "Job-shop", a mixed-model sequencing problem line-balancing algorithm with a longer-term horizon.

We also have to settle for a suitable MAS architecture. Unfortunately, there is a large spectrum of possible architectures, and it is not known how different architectures influence the outcome of the experiments. We choose an architecture that seems a natural counterpart of the production scenario. We distinguish two kinds of agents, machine agents representing a production facility, and order agents. For the protocol governing the interaction within the MAS we investigated two algorithms that differed in their planning horizons. It turned out that the more potent one was an exclusively reactive algorithm in which a machine agent asks for new orders as soon as it finished the current order (Figure 2). The algorithm, therefore, has no planning horizon whatsoever. Communication among the agents follows a protocol similar to the ContractNet protocol [8].

We note that the experiment could have considerable practical value. Suppose that assembly follows a Kanban system, that is, a pull-oriented production system that follows decentralized, self-controlling control cycles with the main goal of minimizing of the internal buffer stock. Then if MAS show superior results in the presence of disturbances, the local control cycles – and hence the Kanban system itself – could be made more sturdy by realizing them via MAS.

Since for obvious reasons nobody can interrupt production to experiment with various control schemes, the experiments had to be done by simulation. Details can be found in [7].

2.3   Benchmarking Results

To verify or falsify the hypothesis we have to determine the parameters that are to be varied over the course of the experiments. These were the master data with the bill of materials and the operation list for each product, the number of machines and their assignment to operations, the list of customer orders, the lot size which affects the number of partial orders generated from a single customer order, the production order generated by the PPC, and the disturbance profile (disruption interval and duration) for each machine. By varying the master data, the list of customer orders, the lot sizes and the disturbance profiles we can influence the size of the situation space.

Output variables for benchmarking that express the salient features of a production facility is the throughput. Both the average and the standard deviation are determined, the latter because it shows whether large variations occur – something that we would hope MAS would be able to reduce.

The more than 1000 simulation runs proceeded as follows. Among the input parameters varying combinations of two parameters were fixed and the others were varied. For each combination the results were compressed into two-dimensional area diagrams that indicate the number of scenarios where MAS perform better, where the Job-shop algorithm performs better, and where results are indifferent. For a detailed description and discussion see [7].

We summarize the results of the experiments. One would expect that with little complexity of the planning task MAS are inferior to the Job-shop algorithm, something that was indeed borne out by the experiments. However, the first big

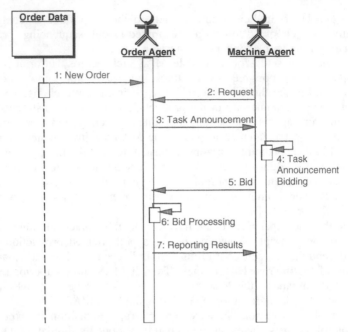

Fig. 2. AUML diagram of a reactive MAS approach solving a Mixed-model Assembly Line Balancing Problem

surprise was that even when raising the complexity of the planning task by increasing the number of assembly operations for a product and by raising the level of disturbances, MAS still remained inferior to the Job-shop algorithm. At least this was true for the average, whereas MAS indeed reduced the standard deviation, i.e., MAS produced almost constant throughput times. Closer inspection revealed that MAS had little chance to play out their strengths because the assembly lines ran close to capacity. Apparently, MAS need some slack to have a positive effect. The next surprise came when additional production facilities were introduced to provide some slack, but MAS became barely better by comparison. The reason now found was that all machines followed the same disturbance profile. Only after introducing large variations in the profile did MAS become significantly superior. And only then did increases in the other factors that influence the complexity of the planning task demonstrate the benefits of MAS as well, although to varying degrees.

To quote from [7]: "Two key features [..] explain the superiority of MAS in a turbulent production environment [..]. First of all, MAS have the ability to follow good results. Due to the short planning horizon, the machine agents are able to consider time-dependent planning variables for their ratings, which leads to more precise results. On the other hand, the waiting queues of the lines are handled more efficiently when disturbances occur. [..] the medium throughput times and its standard deviations are smaller. The second factor is important with respect to the predictability of the results."

2.4 Refining the Hypothesis

The lesson drawn from the experiments is that a large situation space is a necessary but not sufficient condition for the utility of MAS. It seems that if there is no decision space commensurate with the situation space there is too little discriminative power for a MAS to become effective. Hence we refine the first part of our hypothesis:

Hypothesis: Multiagent systems offer an advantage if
- *the range of environmental situations (the problem space) is too large to be enumerated and dealt with by conventional means,*
- **the range of decisions (the solution space) for responding is commensurate in size with the problem space,**
- *the problem space can be divided into sets of simpler tasks, each requiring specialized competence,*
- *the simpler tasks can be dealt with autonomously by individual agents,*
- *the overall situation can only be solved by cooperation among the agents.*

Note that the experiment used the last three parts of the hypothesis as a premise rather than testing it. Note also that the hypothesis is fairly abstract. It says little about what the problem and solutions spaces are in a specific application scenario, nor what would be large and commensurate sizes. Consequently, the hypothesis allows little more than a first estimate on whether to consider a MAS as a reasonable alternative. As this chapter has shown, a closer inspection by means of a simulation model should precede the commitment to a MAS solution, at least for bigger, more costly systems.

3 Making Flexibility Reliable

3.1 Behavioral Abstraction

Our next objective is to make autonomy and flexibility itself reliable in the sense that it never goes out of the given bounds. Even if implemented according to specification agents may be subjected to technical disturbances that may cause them to enter forbidden behavioral territory. Therefore, we examine how agents can be made robust in the presence of technical disturbances.

But even if all agents in a MAS can be made robust the MAS as a whole may still misbehave if the communication between agents is disrupted or corrupted. If we assume that the collaboration between agents follows a script or protocol that reflects a specific task – referred to as a conversation –, robustness must be extended beyond the individual agents to the conversation.

Probably the best-known behavioral abstraction that includes robustness is the transaction. Autonomous and situated behavior is unthinkable without keeping an internal model of the environment and perhaps of the past history, i.e., agents must maintain and update an internal state. Hence, the basis for any robustness is non-volatility of the internal state. Therefore, agents will carry their own database. For robustness purposes the behavioral abstraction is the database transaction [9]. In its purest form the transaction has the ACID properties: It is atomic, i.e., is executed completely or not at all; it is consistent, i.e., if executed to completion it performs a legitimate state transition; it is isolated, i.e., remains unaffected by any parallel transactions; and it is durable, i.e., the state reached can only explicitly be changed. Transaction systems are mechanistic systems that guarantee these properties even in the presence of failures, and do so without any knowledge of the algorithms underlying the transactions.

The behavioral abstraction for the conversation is the distributed transaction, i.e., a transaction that coordinates the transactions in the individual nodes in such a way that certain overall properties are guaranteed, also again in the presence of failures which may now include networks failures. ACID properties are difficult to maintain even under modest degrees of autonomy and hence are usually relaxed [9]. Consequently, it seems that to make conversations robust even under strong autonomy of individual agents requires a type of distributed transaction where guarantees are weak and the agents may themselves have to take corrective action.

3.2   Agents

A possible solution for the agents is taken from [10], [11]. To obtain the necessary autonomy and flexibility in reacting to the situation at hand and taking decisions, an architecture based on the BDI theory is chosen [12], [13]. The architecture is organized into three layers. The lowest layer is responsible for the reactive behavior and communicates with the environment including the other agents. The middle layer does the planning and accounts for deliberations on how to respond to perceived events in the environment. The uppermost layer takes the widest context into account and plans the cooperation with other agents. Accordingly, the agent database is hierarchically structured into corresponding models: the world model, the mental model, and the cooperation model (Figure 3).

If control flow were purely sequential, starting with sensor input on the lowest level and, if need be, progressing upwards to the deliberation layer or even to the cooperation layer, a flat ACID transaction would suffice. But flexibility demands more complicated dynamics. A decision may very well be taken locally on the reaction layer, resulting in some change to the database. The planning layer may recognize the change as affecting its own behavior, and may initiate a process local to this layer. The effect may continue into the cooperation layer. The upper layers may in turn initiate actions on the next lower levels.

As a consequence, the robustness properties of the agents must be modeled as something more complicated than flat transactions. First, the behavioral abstraction should reflect the fact that an external event may spawn several actions that are on different layers but nonetheless interrelated. If we model each action as a transaction then their interrelationship is most naturally modeled as a nested transaction. Under a nested transaction model, a transaction can launch any number of subtransactions, thus forming a transaction tree (Figure 4). In its strictest form, a transaction cannot commit unless all its children are terminated. On the other hand, if one of the children fails, the parent has the choice between aborting the subtransaction, retrying it or launching another compensating subtransaction. However, no matter what happens each transaction in the tree is guaranteed to execute atomically.

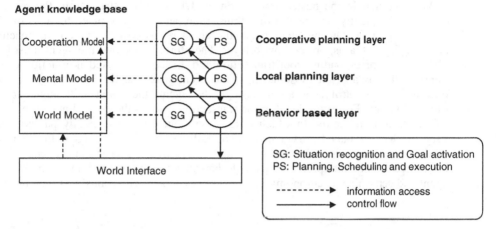

Fig. 3. INTERRAP architecture

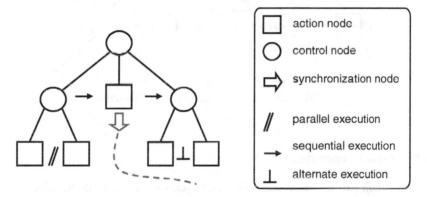

Fig. 4. Nested agent transaction

There are two kinds of nested transactions. In closed nested transactions a subtransaction leaves its changes to the database invisible to all but the parent and the siblings. This allows a committed subtransaction to be invalidated if its parent fails. This is too restrictive a property considering the flexibility of spawning new transactions as we move up or down the layers. Hence we choose as the behavioral abstraction the open nested transaction model. In it a committed subtransaction makes its results available to all other subtransactions as soon as it commits. This leaves compensation as the only way to mitigate its effects if a parent fails.

Agents are supposed to act flexibly. Clearly then, the fixed regime of a classical transaction would be counterproductive. Instead, the nested transactions should evolve dynamically as control progresses through the agent. Consequently, we employ a restricted form of nested transaction (Figure 4): Actions take exclusively place in the leaves, whereas intermediate nodes just control the execution within their subtrees whose subtransactions may execute sequentially, in parallel or alternatively.

We note that in the nested transaction model execution starts from the root on down. Consequently, we need a root transaction, and the only place for it is on the cooperation layer. On the other hand, the agent receives its input on the reactive behavior layer, that is, on the lowest layer. Therefore, to respond the agent must first identify the corresponding root transaction and, hence, the nested transaction itself. Suppose that as a result of some input the agent starts the left-hand transaction of Figure 5. As control progresses through the agent, the agent will augment the transaction tree. For example, after the transaction reaches the control node the agent augments it by a subtree to which transaction control is subsequently passed. This very mechanism may be used in case of failures, because the agent may simply modify the tree to include compensating subtransactions. In summary, the set of initial trees can be interpreted as a set of plans that define the possible behavior of an agent and determine its autonomy and flexibility coupled with robustness guarantees.

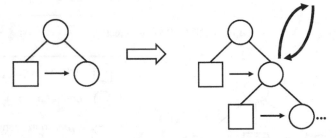

Fig. 5. Evolution of a nested agent transaction

3.3   Agent Cooperation

An important part of our hypothesis is that agents must cooperate to solve an overall situation. Cooperation should follow some protocol. Execution of the protocol is itself subject to technical disturbances. We have experimented with several approaches to make cooperation robust.

Agent synchronization. A seemingly simple approach starts from the premise that nested agent transactions should suffice to guarantee reliability, provided we can augment them such that they can also deal with failures during the communication with other agents. To do so they must be able to exert some control over the communication. Such a control regime is commonly referred to as synchronization. Figure 6 illustrates the principle.

To enable such a controlled synchronization, the nested transaction for an individual agent is augmented by special synchronization nodes. Figure 4 shows such a node (indicated by the arrow).

Figure 7 illustrates the synchronization for two separate transactions. M_{11} does not only start subtransactions M_{111} and M_{112} but also wakes up subtransaction S_{11}. In turn, M_{112} cannot continue until S_{11} has finished and S_1 has regained control. For a full compensation support, two further pairs of synchronization nodes are needed. Pair (3) prevents the termination of the slave transaction tree before the termination of the master transaction tree and pair (4) causes the compensation of the slave subtree S_i in the case M_{11} fails. More common, however, will be simpler master-slave situations.

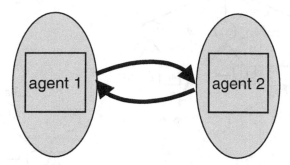

Fig. 6. Synchronization of nested agent transactions

In a physically centralized environment it makes sense to base the synchronization, like the nested transactions, on a common database. A well-known technique to deal with asynchronous events in databases are Event-Condition-Action rules (ECA rules). Database systems with this capability are known as active database systems [14]. This is a very powerful mechanism and allows for a broad variety of cooperation schemes over and above the task delegation in Figure 7. A serious drawback of the approach, though, lies in the need for handling the ECA rules explicitly in the agent behavior. In combination with the evolutionary character of the nested transactions including the frequent need for compensating subtractions the complexity of nested agent transactions may become unmanageably high.

Transactional conversations. The difficulties of the previous approach suggest another approach where the cooperation (like the one of Figure 2) is concentrated within a separate protocol and is protected as an own – now distributed – transaction. We refer to such a protocol as a conversation, and since it is protected by a transaction, as a transactional conversation. Figure 8 illustrates the principle.
Clearly, there are action nodes that participate in both the nested agent transaction and in the transactional conversation. While this may conceptually be in order, technically the transactions need to be separate. Their interrelation can only be via a common database structure. In order to gain a measure of control we restrict the (conceptual) intersection of the transactions to the leaf nodes. As a consequence, though, transactional conversation must be ACID.

Figure 9 outlines our technical solution [15]. Conversations are handled transparently by wrapping the tasks that handle the protocol execution within the communicating agents by transactional tasks (ta-tasks) that observe this execution and the occurrence of local state changes. Consequently, conversations that represent instantiations of such protocols are mapped to distributed transactions. As a result, the changes in the states of the communicating agents now are synchronized via the success or failure of the overall distributed transaction. The transaction manager is integrated in the multiagent platform so that as usual, depending on the success or failure of the interrelated user-tasks, a global commit or rollback can be initiated.

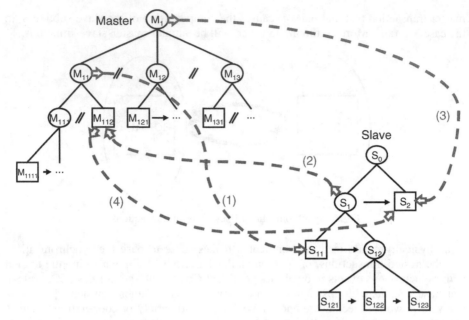

Fig. 7. Two synchronized agent transactions

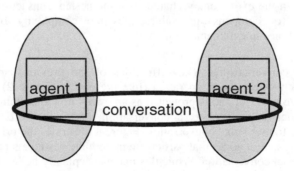

Fig. 8. Transactional conversation

There is also a drawback to this approach. ACID imposes a rigidity that stands in drastic contrast to the desired flexibility of MAS as it manifests itself in the evolutionary nested transactions. On the other hand, it does not seem advisable to do away with the ACID properties for conversations in order for the system to remain manageable. In addition it seems a bit unnatural to place cooperation in the leaf nodes rather than in the root nodes.

Messaging. The stand high-level solution for asynchronous communication are message queuing systems. There is a growing tendency for making these queues persistent and base them on database technology [16]. Persistent message queues (or message-oriented middleware, MOM, as it is often referred to) give certain guarantees regarding safe transmission, and one may request further guarantees such as notification, reproducibility of message exchange, and non-repudiation. Based on these properties one may develop cooperation protocols that may even evolve dynamically.

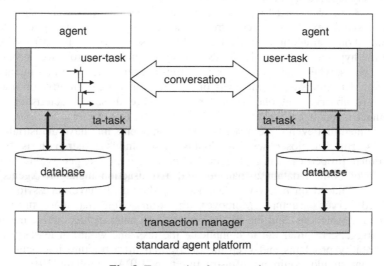

Fig. 9. Transactional conversations

We have done first experiments with this third approach. Conversations, and hence protocols, are composed of so-called speech acts for which a formal semantics exists. For each message a speech act keyword, like e.g. "confirm" or "propose", defines the impact of the message content to the states of the sender and the receiver [17]. The meaning of the keywords is presented by a pair of precondition and postcondition, both specified in a first order modal logic [18]. In our current work, we investigate what impact a commit and a rollback according to the speech act semantics should have and especially how to exploit the speech act preconditions for the necessary compensation actions in case of limited isolation.

The local portions of the protocol can easily be integrated with the nested transaction trees. Each portion consists of speech acts that can be arranged in tree form. Evolving transaction trees may thus be augmented by the protocol trees which then can be subjected to the local transaction regime. Hence, each single message within the conversation rather than the whole conversation is now considered atomic. Transaction trees now include the control flow within the protocols and between different protocols, while the submission of a single message is treated as an action with ACID properties and, consequently, must be mapped to a leaf node.

4   Conclusion

Are multiagent systems a panacea, a cure-all for all problems that require flexible software? As discussed in Section 1, multiagent systems exact a heavy price in that system-level behavior often cannot be predicted analytically from the description of individual agents but must be observed in simulation or real-life. Hence, one should be extremely restrictive when it comes to deciding on the application of a multiagent software system. We started from a hypothesis on the qualitative characteristics that a situation should exhibit in order to treat multiagent software as a candidate solution. We reported on a simulation study for a production scenario which confirmed but also refined the hypothesis. Basically, MAS can be recommended for large problem and solution spaces, where the problem space is non-deterministic or so ill-structured as to appear non-deterministic. As members of a national research initiative on multiagent systems we observe that one particular area where these characteristics seem to predominate is health care.

We claimed that even these benefits depend on agents that have industrial-strength properties. But on closer scrutiny doubts arise. Industrial-strength is based on transactional properties. These require an extensive and expensive infrastructure consisting of both, a database manager and a transaction manager. Agents should therefore be placed on heavy-weight nodes or should all have access to the same centralized server structure. Moreover, the transaction managers must support distributed transactions, and the database managers must include active mechanisms such as triggers. In order not to complicate the task one would at least try to avoid interoperability problems and keep the distributed infrastructure homogeneous. For example, one should require all infrastructure to be FIPA compliant [19].

The nested transaction model raises additional problems of a semantic nature. The set of initial transaction trees is related to the plans of an agent, and the evolution of a tree to the reactive behavior of an agent. Consequently, as opposed to traditional database transactions, agent transactions cannot be imposed orthogonally but become part of the agent design proper. Further, it proved extremely complex to extend the reliability to the cooperation between agents. Either the transaction trees have to be made even more complicated by including synchronization or messaging mechanisms in the tree, or the cooperation protocols are concentrated in transactional conversations that impose a certain rigidity through their ACID properties. Robustness of agents still seems to pose considerable research challenges.

To separate the issues of normal agent behavior and agent robustness we have experimented with splitting the agent into two – albeit interrelated – parts, a regular domain agent responsible for, among others, planning of the transactions, and a transaction agent (Figure 10).

Another challenge has to do with the details of a transaction tree. It should be possible to generate it from a more abstract description by the software engineer of the behavior, desired autonomy and flexibility of an agent, somewhat similar to the descriptive query languages for database access that just describe the properties of the desired result. Indeed, if according to the hypothesis the problem space is too large to be enumerated and may not even be completely known at system development time, an abstract characterization is the only viable alternative. Examples are predicative expressions or sets of production rules. We refer to such characterizations as *descriptive characterizations.* Since we expect decision spaces of a similar size, these will also have to be characterized descriptively.

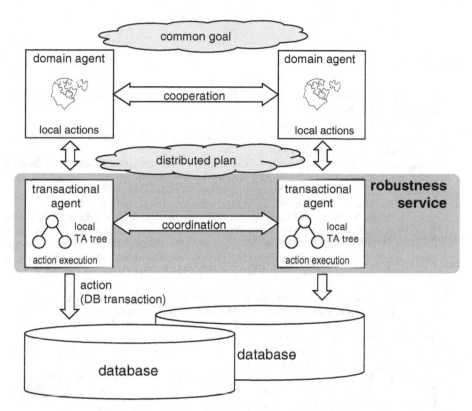

Fig. 10. Semi-orthogonal organization of agent software

Descriptive characterizations of agents is nothing new to the MAS community. Indeed, agents in artificial intelligence follow fairly complicated descriptions, often on the basis of complex architectures such as the BDI (belief-desire-intention) architecture. But since we pursue the more modest goal of making software systems more flexible, we should insist on simpler description techniques that are acceptable to the practitioner, for example because it relates to the application domain. In our shop floor scenario priority rule-based machine scheduling methods assign a certain value to the different production tasks that compete for the same machine (or other resource). This value is directly derived from characteristic value ratios and forms the basis for the construction of the execution sequence of the tasks. Already in the mid-seventies more than one hundred priority rules were systemized and described in literature [20]. An open research issue for agent technology would then be the mapping from the global priority rules to the local agent behavior.

Acknowledgement. Part of this research was funded by Deutsche Forchungsgemeinschaft contract no. Lo 296/17-2 within the National Research Initiative 1083.

References

1. Weiss, G. (ed): Multiagent Systems – A Modern Approach to Distributed Artificial Intelligence. MIT Press (1999)
2. Wooldridge, M.: Intelligent Agents. In [1], 27–7
3. White, J.E.: Telescript Technology: The Foundation for the Electronic Marketplace. General Magic White Paper (1994)
4. Lange, D. B., Oshima, M.: Agents in E-commerce – Seven Good Reasons for Mobile Agents. Communications of the ACM 42:3, ACM (1999) 88-91
5. Parunak, H.V.D.: Industrial and Practical Applications of DAI. In [1], 377–421
6. Durfee, E.H.: Distributed Problem Solving and Planning. In [1], 121–164
7. Frey, D., Nimis, J., Wörn, H., Lockemann, P.C.: Benchmarking and Robust Multi-Agent Based Production Planning and Control. Engineering Appl. of Artificial Intelligence **16** 4 Elsevier (2003) 307–320
8. Smith, R.G.: The Contract Net Protocol: High-Level Communication and Control in a Distributed Problem Solver. IEEE Transactions on Computers **29** 12 IEEE (1980) 1104–1113
9. Weikum, G., Vossen, G.: Transactional Information Systems. Morgan Kaufmann (2002)
10. Nagi, K., Lockemann, P.: Implementation Model for Agents with Layered Architectures in a Transactional Database Environment. Proc. 1st Int. Bi-Conf. Workshop on Agent-Oriented Information Systems (AOIS'99). (1999)
11. Nagi, K.: Transactional Agents – Towards a Robust Multi-Agent System. Lect. Notes in Computer Science, Vol. 2249. Springer (2001)
12. Bratman, M.: Intentions, Plans and Practical Reason. Harvard University Press (1987)
13. Mueller, J.: The Design of Intelligent Agents: A Layered Approach. Lect. Notes on Artificial Intelligence, Vol. 1177. Springer (1996)
14. Widom, J., Ceri, S. (eds.): Active Database Systems. Morgan Kaufmann (1996)
15. Vogt, R.: Einbettung eines transaktionsgestützten Robusheitsdienstes in das FIPA-Agentenrahmenwerk. Diploma thesis at Universität Karlsruhe (TH). Karlsruhe (2001)
16. Lockemann, P.C., Dittrich, K.R.: Architecture of Database Systems. dpunkt.verlag (2004) (in German)
17. Foundation for Intelligent Physical Agents: FIPA Communicative Act Library Specification. (2000)
18. Sadek, M. D.: Attitudes Mentales et Interaction Rationnelle: Vers une Théorie Formelle de la Communication. Thèse de Doctorat Informatique, Université de Rennes I, France. (1991)
19. Foundation for Intelligent Physical Agents: Specification Repository. Available at http://www.fipa.org/repository/index.html (11-05-2003)
20. Panwalkar, S. S., Iskander, W.: A Survey of Scheduling Rules. Operations Research **25**,1 (1977)

World Wide Web Challenges:
Supporting Users in Search and Navigation

Natasa Milic-Frayling

Microsoft Research Ltd, Roger Needham Building, 7 J J Thomson Avenue
Cambridge CB3 0FB, United Kingdom
natasamf@microsoft.com

Abstract. World Wide Web poses many challenges for designing effective information services and applications. Addressing these challenges requires good understanding of Web characteristics and their implications. In this presentation we focus on selected aspects of the Web that affect searching and navigation by the users. We offer our insights into the issues and present our preferred strategies for addressing them. We demonstrate prototype systems that illustrate our solutions and discuss system evaluations that we have conducted.

1   Introduction

World Wide Web is a highly distributed and dynamic information environment. Users access information through a variety of devices, performing a wide spectrum of user tasks. This poses many challenges for designing effective information services and applications. Addressing these challenges requires a good understanding of Web characteristics and their implications on the design and usability of services and applications.

Here we focus on three aspects of the Web that impact the user's experience during search and navigation [1]: (a) separation of search and document delivery, (b) separation of document authoring and creation of metadata that is required by services and applications, and (c) lack of a generic publishing format that supports flexible viewing of the Web content on a variety of devices. We briefly state the problems and describe our recommendations and prototypes that illustrate the possible solutions.

2   Separation of Search and Document Delivery

With regards to the Web information seeking, it is important to note that processing of users' requests for information and delivery of documents in response to these requests are typically two disjoint processes. Indeed, services like Web search and online directories typically provide the user with URLs of information sources rather than the documents themselves. Documents are hosted on Web site servers, out of

P. Van Emde Boas et al. (Eds.): SOFSEM 2004, LNCS 2932, pp. 57–59, 2004.

control of the service itself. This separation places a particular importance on the design of the user interface for accessing the Web, the Web browser.

Indeed, the browser is the *first layer interface*, hosted on the client side, which exposes the *second layer interface*, the Web pages of the service, e.g., a search page, that is designed and managed by the service team. In the search scenario, for example, the user enters the query into the search box and sends it for processing to a search engine. The browser then displays the search results and delivers the document for the URL selected by the user. Thus, the browser is involved in all essential stages and should provide bridges between them by creating and maintaining a rich context of the user's activities.

As an illustration of this recommendation we designed and implemented a prototype system, MS Read [2] that captures and applies the search context. It captures the user's queries, creates a representation of the search topic through linguistic analysis of the query or subsequent refinement by the user, and provides visual feedback on the matches between the topic and the delivered documents through term highlighting. The user's topic is also used to analyze the text of the linked documents for the currently viewed page. Essentially, the browser has been extended with natural language processing capabilities and indexing of viewed or linked pages. These added facilities provide foundations for rich client side processing. With visual features, such as thumbnails of full pages and term highlights, the enhanced browser provides more effective support for searching and browsing.

3   Separation of Document Authoring and Metadata Creation

Web services that involve a representation of the entire or a large portion of the Web often resort to Web crawling and centralized processing of the collected content. They create metadata, such as searchable indices, that are then used to facilitate the service. However, as the authors continue to update their Web sites, this metadata quickly becomes out of sync with the source documents. Thus, centralized Web services essentially work with the data representations that are out of date.

Furthermore, because of the sheer scale of the Web and the need for fast and frequent crawling, Web services can apply only relatively simplistic content analyses. As a consequence, information they provide to the users about the content and structure of the Web sites is typically suboptimal.

We thus promote the idea of generating information about the Web site and page structures at the authoring or publishing stage, and providing that information to applications and services upon request. This will potentially eliminate the need for collecting the Web documents (they are not delivered to the user except when cached pages are made available). The services would crawl the Web for metadata instead.

An immediate benefit of this distributed metadata creation model is the ability to generate and supply more sophisticated content and structure analyses. Furthermore, if a mechanism is provided for sites to 'push' their indices onto the services right upon authoring or updating, this helps with the issue of outdated indices.

In support to this idea we present the MIDAS framework [3] (Meta-Information Delivery and Annotation Services) which we implemented to enable creation, distribution, and utilization of metadata about the structure and content of Web sites and pages. We illustrate how MIDAS can be used to enhance the user's experience during search and navigation and highlight the way it complements the Semantic Web effort.

4   Flexible Viewing of Web Content across Devices

Use of Web on mobile devices, e.g., Personal Digital Assistants (PDAs) and Internet enabled mobile phones, poses further challenges. Viewing Web pages of complex layout structure is incompatible with the restricted screen space. Such pages assume a fix standard size of the browser display and are not automatically modified to fit the size of devices with small screens. As a result, viewing such pages requires extensive horizontal and vertical scrolling. This can lead to disorientation while reading and cause difficulty with identifying relevant parts of the page during search.

We describe and demonstrate SmartView [4] and SearchMobil [5], two applications that support browsing, reading, and searching of Web documents on small devices. They involve analyses of HTML pages and their decomposition into logical units that could be selected for individual viewing. The user can choose to view a graphical overview of the page in the form of a thumbnail image, indicating the partition into page segments. As the user selects a segment for viewing, the corresponding content is automatically reformatted to support reading with no horizontal scrolling. In the search context, SearchMobil provides highlighting of hits and assessment of individual page segments for their relevance to the user's topic.

We discuss the usability studies performed with the implemented systems [6] and discuss how mobile device applications in general could be effectively supported by the MIDAS framework.

References

1. Milic-Frayling, N., Sommerer, R.: Enhanced Web Publishing: Towards Integration of Search and Navigation. In the Proceedings of Libraries in the Digital Age (LIDA) Conference (2003)
2. Milic-Frayling, N., Sommerer, R.: MS Read: Context Sensitive Document Analysis in the WWW Environment, Microsoft Technical Report, MSR-TR-2001-63 (2001)
3. Milic-Frayling, N., Sommerer, R., Smyth, G.: MIDAS: Towards Rich Site Structure and Content Metadata. Poster, On-line Proceedings of the 12the World Wide Web Conference, Budapest (2003)
4. Milic-Frayling, N., Sommerer, R.: SmartView: Flexible Viewing of Web Page Contents. Poster. On-line Proceedings of the 11th World Wide Web Conference (2002)
5. Milic-Frayling, N., Sommerer, R., Rodden, K., Blackwell, A.: SearchMobil. Web Viewing and Search for Mobile Devices. Poster, On-line Proceedings of the 12 the World Wide Web Conference, Budapest (2003)
6. Rodden, K., Milic-Frayling, N., Sommerer, R., Blackwell, A.: Effective Web Searching on Mobile Devices. In the Proceedings of HCI 2003, Bath, United Kingdom (2003).

Querying and Viewing the Semantic Web:
An RDF-Based Perspective

Dimitris Plexousakis

Department of Computer Science, University of Crete, and
Institute of Computer Science, Foundation for Research and Technology Hellas
dp@ics.forth.gr

Abstract. Real-scale Semantic Web applications, such as Knowledge Portals and E-Marketplaces, require the management of voluminous repositories of resource metadata. At the same time, personalized access and content syndication involving diverse conceptual representations of information resources are key challenges for such applications. The Resource Description Framework (RDF) enables the creation and exchange of metadata as any other Web data and constitutes nowadays the core language for creating and exchanging resource descriptions worldwide. Although large volumes of RDF descriptions are already appearing, sufficiently expressive declarative query languages for RDF and full-fledged view definition languages are still missing.

We present RQL, a new query language adopting the functionality of semistructured or XML query languages to the peculiarities of RDF, but also extending this functionality in order to uniformly query both RDF descriptions and schemas. RQL is a typed language, following a functional approach and relies on a formal graph model that permits the interpretation of superimposed resource descriptions created using one or more schemas. We illustrate the syntax, semantics and type systems of RQL and report on the performance of RSSDB, our persistent RDF Store, for storing and querying voluminous RDF metadata. RQL and RSSDB are part of RDFSuite, a set of scalable tools developed at ICS FORTH for managing voluminous RDF/S description bases and schemas.

We also propose RVL, a view definition language capable of creating not only virtual resource descriptions, but also virtual RDF/S schemas from (meta-) classes, properties, as well as, resource descriptions available on the Semantic Web. RVL exploits the functional nature and type system of the RQL query language in order to navigate, filter and restructure complex RDF/S schema and resource description graphs. Last, but not least, we address the problem of integrating legacy data sources using SWIM, a Datalog-based framework for mediating high-level queries to relational and/or XML sources using ontologies expressed in RDF/S.

P. Van Emde Boas et al. (Eds.): SOFSEM 2004, LNCS 2932, pp. 60–61, 2004.
© Springer-Verlag Berlin Heidelberg 2004

References

1. Alexaki, S., Christophides, V., Karvounarakis, G., Plexousakis, D., Tolle, K.: On Storing Voluminous RDF Descriptions: The case of Web Portal Catalogs. In: Proceedings of the 4th International Workshop on the Web and Databases (WebDB), Santa Barbara, CA. (2001)
2. Alexaki, S., Christophides, V., Karvounarakis, G., Plexousakis, D., Tolle, K.: The ICS-FORTH RDF Suite: Managing Voluminous RDF Description Bases. In: Proceedings of the 2nd International Workshop on the Semantic Web, Hong-Kong, (May 2001) 1–13
3. Karvounarakis, G., Alexaki, S., Christophides, V., Plexousakis, D., Scholl, M.: RQL: A Declarative Query Language for RDF. In: Proceedings of the 11th International Conference on the WWW, Hawaii (2002) 592–603
4. Karvounarakis, G., Maganaraki, A., Alexaki, S., Christophides, V., Plexousakis, D., Scholl, M., Tolle, K.: Querying the Semantic Web with RQL. In: the Computer Networks Journal **42**, (2003) 617–640
5. Maganaraki, A., Tannen, V., Christophides, V., Plexousakis, D.: Viewing the Semantic Web through RVL Lenses. In: Proceedings of the 2nd International Conference on the Semantic Web, Sanibel Island, Florida, (October 2003) 96–112
6. Tannen, V., Christophides, V., Karvounarakis, G., Koffina, I., Kokkinidis, G., Maganaraki, A., Plexousakis, D., Serfiotis, G.: The ICS-FORTH SWIM: a Powerful Semantic Web Integration Middleware. In: Proceedings of the Workshop on the Semantic Web and Databases, VLDB Conference, Berlin, September 2003

Knowledge Acquisition and Processing:
New Methods for Neuro-Fuzzy Systems

Danuta Rutkowska

Department of Computer Engineering, Technical University of Czestochowa,
Armii Krajowej 36, 42-200 Czestochowa, Poland,
drutko@kik.pcz.czest.pl,
Department of Artificial Intelligence, WSHE University in Lodz,
Rewolucji 1905, 52, 90-213 Lodz, Poland

A bstract. The paper presents some new methods of knowledge acquisition and processing with regard to neuro-fuzzy systems. Various connectionist architectures that reflect fuzzy IF-THEN rules are considered.
The so-called flexible neuro-fuzzy systems are described, as well as relational systems and probabilistic neural networks. Other connectionist
systems, such hierarchical neuro-fuzzy systems, type 2 systems, and hybrid rough-neuro-fuzzy systems are mentioned. Finally, the perception-
based approach, which refers to computing with words and perceptions,
is briefly outlined. Within this framework, a multi-stage classification
algorithm and a multi-expert classifier are proposed.

1   Introduction

Various combinations of fuzzy systems and neural networks create neuro-fuzzy
systems [65]. When fuzzy systems are represented in the form multi-layer architectures, similar to neural networks, we have connectionist neuro-fuzzy systems [30]. Different architectures of such systems can be considered, and a general
form that includes many special cases is presented in Section 3.

When systems of this kind solve a problem, they perform according to fuzzy
IF-THEN rules, which constitute a knowledge base. The knowledge acquisition
realized by intelligent systems is very important from application point of view,
and this ability is a feature of intelligence.

This paper, as mentioned in the abstract, concerns various methods of knowledge acquisition and processing in neuro-fuzzy systems. Connectionist architectures of the systems are considered. Apart from the general architecture, flexible
neuro-fuzzy systems are described in Section 4, relational systems in Section 5,
and probabilistic neural networks in Section 6. Other systems, such hierarchical neuro-fuzzy systems, type 2 systems, and hybrid rough-neuro-fuzzy systems,
are mentioned in Section 7. The perception-based approach, which incorporates
the computing with words and perceptions, introduced by Zadeh [43], is briefly
outlined in Section 8. A multi-stage classification algorithm and a multi-expert
classifier are proposed with regard to this approach.

P. Van Emde Boas et al. (Eds.): SOFSEM 2004, LNCS 2932, pp. 62–81, 2004.

The methods proposed in this paper are soft computing methods [71], which can be used in computational intelligence (and artificial intelligence) [1], in order to construct intelligent systems. They are related to cognitive technologies, since intelligent systems try to imitate the cognitive behaviour, like neural networks do, with inductive learning.

2 Cognition and Neuro-Fuzzy Systems

Knowledge acquisition and processing with regard to neuro-fuzzy systems can be viewed within the framework of cognitive technologies. Cognitive sciences concern thinking, perception, reasoning, creation of meaning, and other functions of a human mind. The word "cognition" comes from the latin word "cognitio", which means "knowledge". Rule-based systems are knowledge-based systems, where the knowledge is represented by the rules. Connectionist architectures of neuro-fuzzy systems reflect fuzzy IF-THEN rules, which are contained in the rule base.

The aim of artificial intelligence is to develop paradigms or algorithms that allow machines to perform tasks that involve cognition when performed by humans [55]. It is probably an axiom of artificial intelligence, and modern psychology, that intelligent behavior is rule-governed [10]. One of the most significant results demonstrated by Newell and Simon was that much of human problem solving or cognition could be expressed by IF-THEN type production rules. The Newell and Simon model of human problem solving in terms of long-term memory (rules), short-term memory (working memory), and a cognitive processor (inference engine), is the basis of modern rule-based expert systems [9].

Machine learning research has the potential to make a profound contribution to the theory and practice of expert systems, as well as to other areas of artificial intelligence. Its application to the problem of deriving rule sets from examples is already helping to circumvent the knowledge acquisition bottleneck [10].

Learning by examples is one of the simplest cognitive capabilities of a young child. Artificial neural networks with an inductive, supervised learning algorithm, imitate the cognitive behaviour. The most common form of supervised learning task is called induction. An inductive learning program is one which is capable of learning from examples by a process of generalization [10].

Perception is very important in human cognition. The systems that incorporate perceptions expressed by words are fuzzy systems, introduced by Zadeh [68], [69]. Fuzzy systems are rule-based systems (knowledge-based systems) that can be viewed as perception-based systems. The rule base of a fuzzy system is composed of fuzzy IF-THEN rules that are similar to rules used by humans in their reasoning.

Symbolic models of reasoning, e.g. expert systems in AI, have nothing to do with neurobiology, and are not appropriate for pattern recognition, associations, and knowledge generalization. Artificial neural networks do not perform logical inference, and employ associative way of reasoning.

Hybrid systems, such as fuzzy and neural expert systems, as well as connectionist neuro-fuzzy systems are created as intelligent systems that posses features of rule-based reasoning and learning ability. Evolutionary algorithms [15] can also be incorporated into the hybrid intelligent systems.

It seems obvious that artificial neural networks, which try to imitate networks of biological neurons in a human brain, and perception-based fuzzy systems, which perform reasoning based on fuzzy IF-THEN rules, should be combined to create main components of intelligent systems that try to imitate human intelligence.

Various neuro-fuzzy systems can be constructed by combination of neural networks and fuzzy systems. The so-called connectionist networks are viewed as representations of fuzzy systems in the form of connectionist nets, which are similar to neural networks. The systems of this kind can automaticaly create fuzzy IF-THEN rules based on examples, such as elements of a learning sequence presented to neural networks. In this way, the neuro-fuzzy systems get knowledge, avoiding to formulate the rules by human experts. Architectures of the connectionist neuro-fuzzy systems reflect the rules. The connectionist architectures are multi-layer architectures, like neural networks. Thus, the neuro-fuzzy systems can be trained in the similar way as neural networks [73], [30].

The relation between neuro-fuzzy systems and cognitive technologies, explained above, was a part of the plenary lecture, entitled "Cognition, perception, and rule-based systems", presented by the author during the conference on cognitive sciences and computational intelligence, in Stara Lesna, Slovakia, May 14-16, 2003.

3   General Form of Fuzzy Inference Neural Network

The dominant feature of fuzzy systems is an inference process, which is based on fuzzy logic [68], [69]. Two main approaches to the inference of fuzzy (or neuro-fuzzy) systems are distinguished: the best known as well as mostly applied Mamdani approach [13], and later developed — the logical approach [67], [6], [30]. Neuro-fuzzy systems based on both approaches are included into the general multi-layer architecture of the so-called fuzzy inference neural network, which is illustrated in Fig. 1.

The difference between the Mamdani and logical approaches concerns the inference and aggregation layers shown in Fig. 1. The antecedent and defuzzification layers are the same in both cases. The form of this neuro-fuzzy connectionist architecture is explained in detail in [41], [30]. Now, let us briefly present the most important information about this network.

At first, we should notice that the name *fuzzy inference neural network* suggests that this means a neural network architecture that performs a fuzzy inference. As a matter of fact, this connectionist network is similar to the multi-layer perceptron, which is the most popular artificial neural network (see e.g. [73], [30]). However, the elements (nodes) of the fuzzy inference neural network differ from neurons of the multi-layer perceptron. Only two elements in the

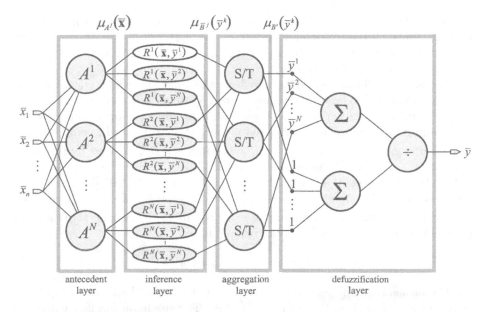

$$\mu_{A^j}(\bar{\mathbf{x}}) \qquad\qquad \mu_{\bar{B}^j}(\bar{y}^k) \qquad \mu_{B'}(\bar{y}^k)$$

F ig.1. General architecture of fuzzy inference neural network

defuzzification layer, in Fig. 1, in fact, are linear neurons, almost the same as those applied in neural networks. Other elements realize different functions, e.g. the third node in the last layer performs the division operation.

It should be emphasized that the network portrayed in Fig. 1 is not a fuzzy neural network (see [37], [30]), because the input/output signals at each layer and the connection weights are not fuzzy. On the other hand, there are connectionist neuro fuzzy systems based on the generic fuzzy perceptron [18], which is a fuzzy neural network. Examples of such systems are the NEFCON, NEFCLASS, and NEFPROX, presented in [19]. An equivalence between these neuro-fuzzy systems and a special case of the fuzzy inference neural network illustrated in Fig. 1, i.e. the RBF-like system, can be shown [31]. Thus, the more general name *neuro-fuzzy inference system* may be used instead of the *fuzzy inference neural network*. However the word *network* informs about the connectionist form of the system. Therefore, connectionist neuro-fuzzy systems are often called *neuro-fuzzy networks*.

The first layer of the network portrayed in Fig. 1 is the same in the RBF-like system, when the nodes realize the Gaussian radial basis functions [30]. Functional equivalence between RBF neural networks and fuzzy inference systems is shown in [11]. The nodes of the antecedent layer, in Fig. 1, perform the membership functions of the fuzzy sets in the antecedent part of the fuzzy IF-THEN rules, which are formulated as follows

$$R^{(k)} : \textbf{IF } \mathbf{x} \text{ is } A^k \textbf{ THEN } y \text{ is } B^k \tag{1}$$

where $\mathbf{x} = [x_1, \ldots, x_n]^T \in \mathbf{X} \subset R^n$, and $y \in Y \subset \mathbf{R}$, are linguistic variables corresponding to the input and output of the system, $A^k = A_1^k \times \cdots \times A_n^k$ and B^k are fuzzy sets characterized by the membership functions $\mu_{A^k}(\mathbf{x})$ and $\mu_{B^k}(y)$, respectively, for $k = 1, \ldots, N$.

The network illustrated in Fig. 1 reflects the rules (1), which constitute the rule base (knowledge base) of the neuro-fuzzy system. The second layer of this network (inference layer) contains elements performing the operation which is most important from the inference point of view. According to the compositional rule of inference, introduced by Zadeh [69], fuzzy set $\overline{B}^k$, inferred by the fuzzy relation $A^k \to B^k$, which corresponds to the IF-THEN rule $R^{(k)}$, is a composition of the input fuzzy set A' and the relation, i.e. $A' \circ (A^k \to B^k)$. If the input fuzzy set A' is the singleton, which means that the singleton fuzzifier is applied, then the membership function of the fuzzy set $\overline{B}^k$ equals to the membership function of the fuzzy set which represents the fuzzy relation

$$\mu_{\overline{B}^k}(y) = \mu_{A^k \to B^k}(\overline{\mathbf{x}}, y) \tag{2}$$

The elements of the inference layer, in Fig. 1, realize the membership functions given by Equation (2), for $k = 1, \ldots, N$. The singleton fuzzifier is characterized by the following membership function

$$\mu_{A'}(\mathbf{x}) = \begin{cases} 1 & \text{if} \quad \mathbf{x} = \overline{\mathbf{x}} \\ 0 & \text{if} \quad \mathbf{x} \neq \overline{\mathbf{x}} \end{cases} \tag{3}$$

where the input vector, $\overline{\mathbf{x}} = [\overline{x}_1, \ldots, \overline{x}_n]^T$, is a crisp point in $\mathbf{X} = X_1 \times \cdots \times X_n$. More details can be found in [30].

The difference between the systems based on the Mamdani and logical approach is visible in the inference layer, as well as the aggregation layer, of the network. With regard to the inference, different membership functions $\mu_{A^k \to B^k}(\overline{\mathbf{x}}, y)$ are employed. In the Mamdani approach, the fuzzy relation $A^k \to B^k$ is represented by the membership functions defined by use of the minimum or product operation, i.e.

$$\mu_{A^k \to B^k}(\mathbf{x}, y) = \min\{\mu_{A^k}(\mathbf{x}), \mu_{B^k}(y)\} = \mu_{A^k}(\mathbf{x}) \wedge \mu_{B^k}(y) \tag{4}$$

or

$$\mu_{A^k \to B^k}(\mathbf{x}, y) = \mu_{A^k}(\mathbf{x}) \mu_{B^k}(y) \tag{5}$$

It should be emphasized that the fuzzy relation $R^{(k)}$ characterized by the membership functions given by Equations (4) and (5) is not a fuzzy implication, although it represents a rule of type IF-THEN. Therefore, the relations of this kind are called *engineering implications* [14].

The logical approach to fuzzy inference employs genuine implications instead of the engineering implications. Thus, the following membership functions, characterizing the fuzzy relation $R^{(k)}$, may be applied

$$\mu_{A^k \to B^k}(\mathbf{x}, y) = \max(1 - \mu_{A^k}(\mathbf{x}), \mu_{B^k}(y)) \tag{6}$$

if the Kleene-Dienes implication is used, or

$$\mu_{A^k \to B^k}(\mathbf{x}, y) = \min(1, 1 - \mu_{A^k}(\mathbf{x}) + \mu_{B^k}(y)) \tag{7}$$

if the Łukasiewicz implication is chosen. Other genuine implications are considered in in [30].

Different special cases of the connectionist architecture portrayed in Fig. 1 are obtained depending on the fuzzy implication employed. Some examples can also be found in [38], [39], [40], [22], [42]. The name *constructive* and *destructive*, for the Mamdani and logical approach, respectively, have been introduced in the literature [67], but not often used. The implication-based fuzzy systems have been studied in [8], [3].

The Mamdani and logical approaches differ also with regard to the aggregation layer (Fig. 1). For the Mamdani approach, the elements of this layer realize the (*S-norm*) operation, but for the logical approach — the *T-norm*; see [30] for details. The minimum and product are examples of the *T-norm*, while the maximum — of the *T-conorm*. The *T-norm* or *T-conorm*, respectively, are used in order to aggregate the rules, and get an overall output fuzzy set B' which is expressed as the union of the fuzzy sets $\overline{B}^k$, for $k = 1, \ldots, N$, when the Mamdani approach is employed, and the intersection of the fuzzy sets $\overline{B}^k$, when the logical approach is applied.

The defuzzification layer, in Fig. 1, is composed of the three elements, mentioned earlier, and this layer performs according to the method used in order to obtain a crisp (not fuzzy) output value, $\overline{y}$. In this case, the following defuzzification method is employed

$$\overline{y} = \frac{\sum_{k=1}^{N} \overline{y}^k \, \mu_{B'}(\overline{y}^k)}{\sum_{k=1}^{N} \mu_{B'}(\overline{y}^k)} \tag{8}$$

where $\mu_{B'}(y)$ is a membership function of the output fuzzy set B', and $\overline{y}^k$, for $k = 1, \ldots, N$, are discrete points in Y, which satisfy the condition

$$\mu_{B^k}(\overline{y}^k) = \max_y \{\mu_{B^k}(y)\} \tag{9}$$

Equation (8) expresses a discrete version of the *center of area* defuzzification method [7], [30]. It is easy to notice that the defuzzification layer, in Fig. 1, exactly corresponds to the formula (8).

The connectionist neuro-fuzzy network illustrated in Fig. 1 is described as follows by the mathematical expression

$$\overline{y} = \frac{\sum_{k=1}^{N} \overline{y}^k \, \lambda_k}{\sum_{k=1}^{N} \lambda_k} \tag{10}$$

where

$$\lambda_k = \begin{cases} \underset{j=1}{\overset{N}{\mathbf{S}}} \mu_{A^j \to B^j} \left(\overline{\mathbf{x}}, \overline{y}^k\right) & \text{for the Mamdani approach} \\ \underset{j=1}{\overset{N}{\mathbf{T}}} \mu_{A^j \to B^j} \left(\overline{\mathbf{x}}, \overline{y}^k\right) & \text{for the logical approach} \end{cases} \tag{11}$$

where $\mathbf{S}$ and $\mathbf{T}$ denote the *T-conorm* and *T-norm*, respectively, extended through associativity to more than two arguments. For details about *T-norm* and *T-conorm* functions, see [30], as well as [12].

Let us notice that, for the Mamdani approach, the membership functions $\mu_{A^j \to B^j}$, in Equation (11), for $j = 1, \ldots, N$, are defined according to formulas (4) or (5), respectively, by use of the minimum or product operation, which are examples of the *T-norm*. Other *T-norm* functions may also be used, e.g. the bounded *T-norm* [30], [44]. Thus, for the Mamdani approach, from Equation (11), we have

$$\lambda_k = \underset{j=1}{\overset{N}{\mathbf{S}}} T \left\{ \mu_{A^j} \left(\overline{\mathbf{x}}\right), \mu_{B^j} \left(\overline{y}^k\right) \right\} \tag{12}$$

For the logical approach, the membership functions $\mu_{A^j \to B^j}$, in Equation (11), for $j = 1, \ldots, N$, are defined according to Equations (6), (7) or other formulas that express genuine implications. Let us denote the genuine implication by the letter I. Thus, we can rewrite Equation (11), for the logical approach, as follows

$$\lambda_k = \underset{j=1}{\overset{N}{\mathbf{T}}} I \left\{ \mu_{A^j} \left(\overline{\mathbf{x}}\right), \mu_{B^j} \left(\overline{y}^k\right) \right\} \tag{13}$$

The membership functions $\mu_{A^k} (\mathbf{x})$, for $k = 1, \ldots, N$, are defined by use of the *T-norm*, for both Mamdani and logical approaches. The minimum or product operation is usually chosen as the *T-norm*, which in this case performs the Cartesian product

$$A^k = A_1^k \times \cdots \times A_n^k \tag{14}$$

where A_i^k, for $i = 1, \ldots, n$, and $k = 1, \ldots, N$, are antecedent fuzzy sets in the rules of the following form

$$R^{(k)} : \textbf{IF } x_1 \text{ is } A_1^k \textbf{ AND } x_2 \text{ is } A_2^k \textbf{ AND } \ldots \textbf{ AND } x_n \text{ is } A_n^k \textbf{ THEN } y \text{ is } B^k \tag{15}$$

which is equivalent to the rule base (1).

Thus, the membership functions $\mu_{A^k} (\mathbf{x})$, for $k = 1, \ldots, N$, are expressed as follows

$$\mu_{A^k} (\mathbf{x}) = \underset{i=1}{\overset{n}{\mathbf{T}}} \left\{ \mu_{A_i^k} (x_i) \right\} \tag{16}$$

where the extended *T-norm* is the minimum or product.

The membership functions $\mu_{A^k} (\mathbf{x})$, for $k = 1, \ldots, N$, defined by Equation (16), are realized by elements of the first layer of the network illustrated in Fig. 1. For the crisp input vector $\overline{\mathbf{x}} = [\overline{x}_1, \ldots, \overline{x}_n]^T$, the output values of this layer, $\mu_{A^k}(\overline{\mathbf{x}})$, for $k = 1, \ldots, N$, represent the degree of rule activation (firing strength)

$$\tau_k = \mu_{A^k}(\overline{\mathbf{x}}) = \mathop{\mathbf{T}}_{i=1}^{n} \mu_{A_i^k}(\overline{x}_i) \tag{17}$$

From formulas (2), (10), and (11), we conclude that the output values of the second (inference) layer of the network portrayed in Fig. 1 equal to

$$\mu_{\overline{B}^j}(\overline{y}^k) = \mu_{A^j \to B^j}(\overline{\mathbf{x}}, \overline{y}^k) = R^j(\overline{\mathbf{x}}, \overline{y}^k) \tag{18}$$

for $j = 1, \ldots, N$, where

$$R^j(\overline{\mathbf{x}}, \overline{y}^k) = \begin{cases} T\{\mu_{A^j}(\overline{\mathbf{x}}), \mu_{B^j}(\overline{y}^k)\} & \text{for the Mamdani approach} \\ I\{\mu_{A^j}(\overline{\mathbf{x}}), \mu_{B^j}(\overline{y}^k)\} & \text{for the logical approach} \end{cases} \tag{19}$$

Comparing formulas (8) and (10), we see that output values of the third (aggregation) layer of the network presented in Fig. 1 are

$$\lambda_k = \mu_{B'}(\overline{y}^k) \tag{20}$$

for $k = 1, \ldots, N$, and from Equations (12), (13), and (19), we have

$$\lambda_k = \begin{cases} \mathop{\mathbf{S}}_{j=1}^{N} R^j(\overline{\mathbf{x}}, \overline{y}^k) & \text{for the Mamdani approach} \\ \mathop{\mathbf{T}}_{j=1}^{N} R^j(\overline{\mathbf{x}}, \overline{y}^k) & \text{for the logical approach} \end{cases} \tag{21}$$

which can be called the aggregated value.

The connection weights of the first linear neuron in the last (defuzzification) layer of the network shown in Fig. 1 equal to $\overline{y}^k$, for $k = 1, \ldots, N$. Thus, this layer carries out the crisp output value, $\overline{y}$, according to Equation (10).

As mentioned earlier, the multi-layer architecture of the network illustrated in Fig. 1 resembles the multi-layer perceptron neural network. Therefore it is possible to train the neuro-fuzzy connectionist network, in the similar way as neural networks are trained. As a result of the learnig process, parameters of the membership functions $\mu_{A_i^k}(x_i)$, and $\mu_{B^k}(y)$, for $i = 1, \ldots, n$, and $k = 1, \ldots, N$, such as centers and widths, for example $\overline{y}^k$ which is the center of $\mu_{B^k}(y)$, are optimally adjusted. For details, see e.g. [30].

4 Flexible Neuro-Fuzzy Systems

In Section 3, the Mamdani and logical approaches to fuzzy inference are considered with regard to the general architecture of the connectionist neuro-fuzzy systems. Despite the same general network, shown in Fig. 1, both systems (based on the Mamdani or logical approach) are treated separately, as special cases of this connectionist architecture. This means that at first we have to choose either the architecture of the network based on the Mamdani approach or the network for the logical approach. If the network is chosen it can be trained (like neural networks) in order to find optimal values of parameters of the membership functions which characterize fuzzy sets in the rule base. In this way, the system gathers knowledge represented in the form of the fuzzy IF-THEN rules.

The so-called *flexible neuro-fuzzy systems* were recently introduced and developed [47], [4], [5], [48], [49], [50], [51], [52]. The systems of this kind are represented by the same general architecture like that illustrated in Fig. 1, but the idea of flexibility, which allows to switch smoothly from the Mamdani type of inference to the logical approach, is incorporated into the network. The system automatically, during a learning process, decides whether it should be more Mamdani or logical type. Thus, the system is able to gather more knowledge, not only about the rules, but also concerning the type of inference.

The combination of both types of inference, in the way described above, is possible by means of the so-called *compromise operator*, defined as follows [52]: A function

$$\widetilde{N}_\nu : [0,1] \to [0,1] \tag{22}$$

given by

$$\widetilde{N}_\nu (a) = (1 - \nu) N (a) + \nu N (N (a)) = (1 - \nu) N (a) + \nu a \tag{23}$$

is called a compromise operator, where $\nu \in [0,1]$ and $N (a) = \widetilde{N}_0 (a) = 1 - a$.

The following theorem is formulated and proven in the literature, cited above.

Theorem 1. *Let* T *and* S *be dual tringular norms. The function H mapping*

$$H : [0,1]^n \to [0,1] \tag{24}$$

and defined by

$$H (\mathbf{a}; \nu) = \widetilde{N}_\nu \left(\overset{n}{\underset{i=1}{S}} \left\{ \widetilde{N}_\nu (a_i) \right\} \right) = \widetilde{N}_{1-\nu} \left(\overset{n}{\underset{i=1}{T}} \left\{ \widetilde{N}_{1-\nu} (a_i) \right\} \right) \tag{25}$$

varies between the T*-norm and* T*-conorm as* ν *increases from 0 to 1.*

Observe that the H-function, $\mathbf{T}$-norm and $\mathbf{T}$-conorm are related to each other in the following way

$$H (\mathbf{a}; \nu) = \begin{cases} \mathbf{T} \{\mathbf{a}\} \text{ for } \nu = 0 \\ 0.5 \quad \text{ for } \nu = 0.5 \\ \mathbf{S} \{\mathbf{a}\} \text{ for } \nu = 1 \end{cases} \tag{26}$$

where $\mathbf{a} = (a_1, \dots, a_n)$, and $\mathbf{T} \{\mathbf{a}\} = \overset{n}{\underset{i=1}{\mathbf{T}}} \{a_1, \dots, a_n\}$.

It is easy to notice that, for $0 < \nu < 0.5$, the H-function resembles a $\mathbf{T}$-norm and for $0.5 < \nu < 1$ the H-function resembles a $\mathbf{T}$-conorm.

We apply Theorem 1 in order to illustrate (for $n = 2$) how to switch between the product T-norm

$$T\{a_1, a_2\} = H(a_1, a_2; 0) = a_1, a_2 \tag{27}$$

and the corresponding T-conorm

$$S\{a_1, a_2\} = H(a_1, a_2; 1) = a_1 + a_2 - a_1 a_2 \tag{28}$$

Following Theorem 1, the H-function generated by Equation (27) or (28) is given by

$$H(a_1, a_2; \nu) = \tilde{N}_{1-\nu}\left(\tilde{N}_{1-\nu}(a_1)\,\tilde{N}_{1-\nu}(a_2)\right) \tag{29}$$
$$= \tilde{N}_{\nu}\left(1 - \left(1 - \tilde{N}_{\nu}(a_1)\right)\left(1 - \tilde{N}_{\nu}(a_2)\right)\right)$$

and varies from (27) to (28) as ν increases from 0 to 1.

Now, let us present another theorem formulated and proven in the cited literature.

Theorem 2. *Let T and S be dual tringular norms. Then*

$$I_{flex}(a, b; \nu) = H\left(\tilde{N}_{1-\nu}(a), b; \nu\right) \tag{30}$$

switches between an "engineering implication"

$$I_{eng}(a, b) = I_{flex}(a, b; 0) = T\{a, b\} \tag{31}$$

and an S-implication

$$I_{fuzzy}(a, b) = I_{flex}(a, b; 1) = S\{1 - a, b\} \tag{32}$$

The following example of the H-implication generated by the product T-norm illustrates this theorem.

Let

$$I_{eng}(a, b) = H(a, b; 0) = T\{a, b\} = ab \tag{33}$$

and

$$I_{fuzzy}(a, b) = H\left(\tilde{N}_0(a), b; 1\right) = S\{N(a), b\} = 1 - a + ab \tag{34}$$

then (30) varies between (33) and (34) as ν increases from 0 to 1.

The flexible neuro-fuzzy system is described as follows

$$\tau_k(\overline{\mathbf{x}}) = H\left(\mu_{A_1^k}(\overline{x}_1), ..., \mu_{A_n^k}(\overline{x}_n); 0\right) \tag{35}$$

$$R^k(\overline{\mathbf{x}}, \overline{y}^j) = H\left(\tilde{N}_{1-\nu}(\tau_k(\overline{\mathbf{x}})), \mu_{B^k}(\overline{y}^j); \nu\right) \tag{36}$$

$$\lambda_k \left(\overline{\mathbf{x}}, \overline{y}^k\right) = H \left(R^1 \left(\overline{\mathbf{x}}, \overline{y}^k\right), ..., R^N \left(\overline{\mathbf{x}}, \overline{y}^k\right); 1 - \nu\right) \tag{37}$$

$$\overline{y} = \frac{\sum_{k=1}^{N} \overline{y}^k \, \lambda_k \left(\overline{\mathbf{x}}, \overline{y}^k\right)}{\sum_{k=1}^{N} \lambda_k \left(\overline{\mathbf{x}}, \overline{y}^k\right)} \tag{38}$$

for $k, j = 1, \ldots, N$.

Let us notice that from Equation (26), τ_k expressed by formulas (17) and (35) are the same. In addition, it is easy to show that the implication, I, in Equation (19) can be expressed as follows

$$I \left\{\mu_{A^j} \left(\overline{\mathbf{x}}\right), \mu_{B^j} \left(\overline{y}^k\right)\right\} = S \left\{N \left(\mu_{A^j} \left(\overline{\mathbf{x}}\right), \mu_{B^j} \left(\overline{y}^k\right)\right)\right\}$$
$$= S \left\{N \left(\tau_k \left(\overline{\mathbf{x}}\right), \mu_{B^j} \left(\overline{y}^k\right)\right)\right\} \tag{39}$$

where N is the negation operation; see Equations (6), (7), and compare with the appropriate S-norm. Thus, Equation (36) equals to Equation (19) if $\nu = 0$ and $\nu = 1$, respectively, for the Mamdani and logical approaches. We can also conclude that if $\nu = 0$ then Equation (37) is equal to (21) for the logical approach, as well as for the Mamdani approach if $\nu = 1$.

Thus, the architecture of the system described by Equation (38) is the same as that illustrated in Fig. 1, but this neuro-fuzzy system is flexible, which means that it varies between the Mamdani type of inference ($\nu = 0$) and the logical type of inference ($\nu = 1$), as ν increases from 0 to 1. The parameter ν is called the compromise parameter, and can be determined by a learning process.

5   Neuro-Fuzzy Relational Systems

In this section, the so-called relational neuro-fuzzy systems are presented. They differ from the rule-based systems, described in Sections 3 and 4. Fuzzy relational systems store associations between input and output fuzzy sets in a discrete fuzzy relation [29]. The systems of this kind may be applied to control [2] or classification problems [56], like the systems considered in the previous sections. However, relational systems are more convenient from the viewpoint of adjusting parameters, which is realized by changing elements of the relation. Neuro-fuzzy relational systems are developed in [57], [58], [59], [60].

Like in the previous sections, assume that $\mathbf{x} = [x_1, \ldots, x_n]^T \in \mathbf{X} \subset \mathbf{R}^n$, and $y \in Y \subset \mathbf{R}$, which means n-dimensional input, $\mathbf{x}$, and scalar output, y, that is the MISO fuzzy system. Let A and B denote collections of linguistic terms A^k and B^m, respectively

$$A = \left\{A^1, A^2, ..., A^K\right\} \tag{40}$$

characterized by membership functions $\mu_{A^k} \left(\mathbf{x}\right)$, for $k = 1, ..., K$, and

$$B = \left\{ B^1, B^2, ..., B^M \right\} \tag{41}$$

characterized by membership functions $\mu_{B^m}(y)$, for $m = 1, ..., M$.

Sets (40) and (41) are related to each other with a certain degree by a $K \times M$ relation matrix $\overline{\mathbf{R}}$

$$\overline{\mathbf{R}} = \begin{bmatrix} r_{11} & r_{12} & \cdots & r_{1M} \\ r_{21} & r_{22} & \cdots & r_{2M} \\ \vdots & \vdots & r_{km} & \vdots \\ r_{K1} & r_{K2} & \cdots & r_{KM} \end{bmatrix} \tag{42}$$

where $r_{km} \in [0, 1]$, and $k = 1, ..., K$, $m = 1, ..., M$.

The relation $\overline{\mathbf{R}}$, defined by Equation (42), represents a mapping $A \to B$.

Let $\overline{\mathbf{x}} = [\overline{x}_1, ..., \overline{x}_n]^T$ is a crisp input vector. Given a vector $\overline{A}$ of K membership values $\mu_{A^k}(\overline{\mathbf{x}})$, for a crisp observed input value $\overline{\mathbf{x}}$, we can obtain vector $\overline{B}$ of M crisp membership values μ_m, using the fuzzy relational composition

$$\overline{B} = \overline{A} \circ \overline{\mathbf{R}} \tag{43}$$

implemented element-wise by a generalized form of the $\sup - \min$ composition, that is the $S - T$ composition

$$\mu_m = \mathbf{S}_{k=1}^K \left[T \left(\mu_{A^k}(\overline{\mathbf{x}}), r_{km} \right) \right]$$

The crisp output of the relational system is determined by the weighted mean

$$\overline{y} = \frac{\sum_{m=1}^M \left\{ \overline{y}^m \mathbf{S}_{k=1}^K \left[T \left(\mu_{A^k}(\overline{\mathbf{x}}), r_{km} \right) \right] \right\}}{\sum_{m=1}^M \mathbf{S}_{k=1}^K \left[T \left(\mu_{A^k}(\overline{\mathbf{x}}), r_{km} \right) \right]} \tag{44}$$

where $\overline{y}^m$ is the centre of gravity (centroid) of the fuzzy set B^m.

The system described by Equation (44) can be represented in the form of the connectionist neuro-fuzzy network, illustrated in Fig. 1. The first (antecedent) layer is the same, but it contains K nodes realizing membership functions μ_{A^k}. The last (defuzzification) layer is also the same, but the first linear neuron has M inputs, and the connection weights equal to $\overline{y}^m$. The third (aggregation) layer is includes K nodes performing the $\mathbf{S}$ operation (T-conorm) or the soft OWA S-norm [59]. The second (inference) layer is composed of T-norm elements and r_{km} inputs to these nodes.

In [59], [60] a new relational system with fuzzy antecedent certainty factors is considered. In this case, the relational matrix contains fuzzy sets C_{km} defined on the unitary interval

$$\overline{\mathbf{R}} = \begin{bmatrix} C_{11} & C_{12} & \cdots & C_{1M} \\ C_{21} & C_{22} & \cdots & C_{2M} \\ \vdots & \vdots & C_{km} & \vdots \\ C_{K1} & C_{K2} & \cdots & C_{KM} \end{bmatrix} \tag{45}$$

These fuzzy sets represent linguistic values, which can express an uncertainty concerning antecedent terms. In SISO or MISO systems, with multidimensional antecedent fuzzy sets, an expert may define rules which are similar to the following exemplary ones

$$R^1 : \text{IF } \mathbf{x} \text{ is exactly } A^1 \text{ THEN } y \text{ is } B^1 \tag{46}$$
$$R^2 : \text{IF } \mathbf{x} \text{ is more or less } A^1 \text{ THEN } y \text{ is } B^2$$
$$R^3 : \text{IF } \mathbf{x} \text{ is roughly } A^1 \text{ THEN } y \text{ is } B^3$$

The system description by a mathematical formula, similar to Equation (44), and the connectionist architecture of the system, are presented in [60].

Knowledge acquisition in neuro-fuzzy relational systems is performed by the learning process that includes a clustering algorithm, fine-tuning by the back-propagation method, and computing the fuzzy relation based on the training data using relational equations [58].

6   Probabilistic Neural Networks

Another kind of connectionist networks are probabilistic neural networks, which are equivalent to the inference neural networks. Probabilistic neural networks are studied in [61], [28], [16], and also in [45], [46], [53], [24], where the equivalence, mentioned above, is shown.

Based on te sample sequence $\left\{ (\mathbf{X}, Y), (\mathbf{X}^1, Y^1), ..., (\mathbf{X}^N, Y^N) \right\}$ of i.i.d. random variables, in order to estimate the regression function

$$R(\mathbf{x}) = E[Y \mid \mathbf{X} = \mathbf{x}] \tag{47}$$

the following estimator is proposed in the cited literature

$$\widehat{R}_N(\mathbf{x}) = \frac{\sum_{k=1}^{N} Y^k G\left(\frac{\mathbf{x} - \mathbf{X}^k}{\sigma_N}\right)}{\sum_{i=1}^{n} G\left(\frac{\mathbf{x} - \mathbf{X}^k}{\sigma_N}\right)} \tag{48}$$

Applying the following kernel function

$$G(\mathbf{x}) = (2\pi)^{-\frac{1}{2}n} e^{-\frac{1}{2}\|x\|^2} \tag{49}$$

to Equation (48), we obtain

$$\widehat{R}_N(\mathbf{x}) = \frac{\sum_{k=1}^{N} Y^k \prod_{i=1}^{n} \exp\left[-\frac{1}{2}\left(\frac{x_i - X_i^k}{\sigma_N}\right)^2\right]}{\sum_{k=1}^{N} \prod_{i=1}^{n} \exp\left[-\frac{1}{2}\left(\frac{x_i - X_i^k}{\sigma_N}\right)^2\right]} \tag{50}$$

It is easy to notice that the form of the Equation (50) is the same as the following description of the Mamdani type neuro-fuzzy network

$$\overline{y} = \frac{\sum\limits_{k=1}^{N} \overline{y}^k \prod\limits_{i=1}^{n} \exp\left[-\left(\frac{\overline{x}_i - \overline{x}_i^k}{\sigma_N}\right)^2\right]}{\sum\limits_{k=1}^{N} \prod\limits_{i=1}^{n} \exp\left[-\left(\frac{\overline{x}_i - \overline{x}_i^k}{\sigma_N}\right)^2\right]} \tag{51}$$

The network described by Equation (51) is a special case of the connectionist neuro-fuzzy network portrayed in Fig. 1, where the elements of the first layer realize the Gaussian membership functions

$$\mu_{A_i^k}(\overline{x}_i) = \exp\left[-\left(\frac{\overline{x}_i - \overline{x}_i^k}{\sigma_i^k}\right)^2\right] \tag{52}$$

This neuro-fuzzy network is proposed in [66], and developed in [30]. This network is illustrated in Fig. 2 and equivalent to that shown in Fig. 3

$$\mu_{A^k}(\overline{\mathbf{x}}) = \prod\limits_{i=1}^{n} \exp\left[-\left(\frac{\overline{x}_i - \overline{x}_i^k}{\sigma_i^k}\right)^2\right] \tag{53}$$

where $\overline{x}_i^k$ and σ_i^k are parameters (centers and widths, respectively) of the Gaussian membership functions; $i = 1, \ldots, n$, and $k = 1, \ldots, N$.

The parameters of the membership functions are adjusted during the learning process. In this way, the system gathers knowledge about the shapes of the fuzzy sets in the antecedent part of the rules. The most popular learning method employed in the neuro-fuzzy system of this kind is the gradient method (based on the steepest descent optimization procedure) which is similar to the back-propagation algorithm [73]. Apart from this method, a genetic (evolutionary) algorithm [15] can be applied. For details, see [30], as well as e.g. [20], [21].

The architecture of the neuro-fuzzy connectionist system shown in Fig. 3 is the same as the normalized RBF neural network, introduced in [17]; see e.g. [30].

7 Other Connectionist Neuro-Fuzzy Systems

Based on the systems presented in the previous sections, many different neuro-fuzzy networks can be used. Various fuzzy inference neural networks may be created as special cases of the general architecture portrayed in Fig. 1. Apart from the systems described in Sections 4 and 5, more complex — hierarchical connectionist neuro-fuzzy systems can be constructed [25], [26], [27], as well as the systems that incorporate membership functions of type 2 fuzzy sets [54], [62], [63], [64], and the hybrid rough-neuro-fuzzy systems [23].

When a classification task is considered, the connectionist architecture may be even simpler. In this case, it is not necessary to apply the defuzzification layer, so with regard to the network shown in Fig. 3 only the first layer is sufficient,

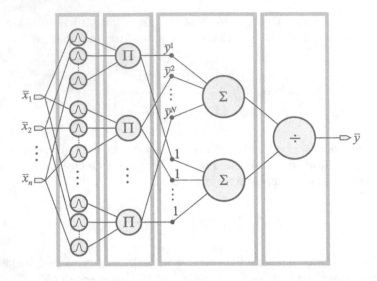

F ig.2. Basic architecture of the connectionist neuro-fuzzy system

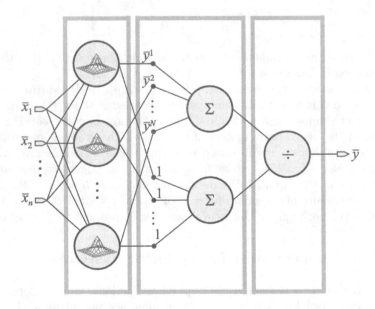

F ig.3. Basic architecture of fuzzy inference neural network based on Mamdani approach

and for the equivalent network portrayed in Fig. 2 we need the first two layers of this network. Such a simple classification network is portrayed in Fig. 4. The input values represent the attribute values which characterize the object to be classified. The output values correspond to the classes to which the object can belong. The nodes that realize membership functions can perform other functions than Gaussian, e.g. triangular, trapezoidal, etc., as well as type 2 membership functions, and input values do not need to be only numerical (crisp), in a more general case, when the network is considered as a fuzzy network.

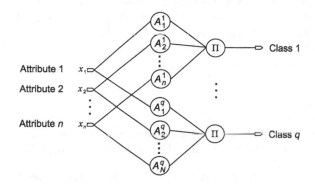

F ig.4. Simple classification neuro-fuzzy network

The network shown in Fig. 4 is very simple, but if it is necessary, more complex architectures may be employed, e.g. hierarchical or multi-segment connectionist systems that use this network as components.

8   Perception-Based Classification Systems

Perception-based intelligent systems that imitate the way of reasoning performed by humans may be created in the form of the neuro-fuzzy network, portrayed in Fig. 4, with applications to classification problems. Examples are presented in [32], [33]. The systems analyze data and generate fuzzy IF-THEN rules, employing the fuzzy granulation [70]. The granules obtained are labeled by words that express perceptions concerning the attributes characterizing the objects to be classified. The reasoning based on these rules refers to the computing with words and perceptions [72], [34].

Fuzzy sets of type 2 can be used in order to represent an uncertainty with regard to the membership functions applied in such systems [32].

The main advantage of the multi-stage classification algorithm [36], which employs the perception-based approach, is the elimination of misclassifications. This is especially important in medical applications [33]. If it is not possible to classify every input data without misclassifications, the multi-stage perception-based algorithm can be combined with other classification methods, in the multi-expert system [35].

9 Conclusions

Neuro-fuzzy systems are soft computing methods utilizing artificial neural networks and fuzzy systems. Various connectionist architectures of neuro-fuzzy systems can be constructed. The knowledge acquisition concerns fuzzy IF-THEN rules, and is performed by a learning process. The systems realize an inference (fuzzy reasoning) based on these rules. Different applications of the systems can be distinguished, such as classification, control, function approximation, prediction. The systems can be viewed as intelligent systems, and considered with regard to artificial intelligence and cognitive sciences.

References

1. Bezdek, J.C.: What is computational intelligence? In: Żurada J.M., Marks II R.J., Robinson C.J. (Eds.): Computational Intelligence: Imitating Life. IEEE Press. New York (1994) 1–12
2. Branco, P.J.C., Dente, J.A.: A Fuzzy Relational Identification Algorithm and its Application to Predict the Behaviour of a Motor Drive System. Fuzzy Sets and Systems. 109 (2000) 343–354
3. Cordòn, O., Herrera, F., Peregrin, A.: T-norms vs. Implication Functions as Implication Operators in Fuzzy Control. Proc. 6th International Fuzzy Systems Association World Congress (IFSA'95). Sao Paulo. Brazil (1995) 501–504
4. Cpałka, K., Rutkowski, L.: Soft Neuro-Fuzzy Systems. Proc. Fifth Conference Neural Networks and Soft Computing. Zakopane. Poland (2000) 296–301
5. Cpałka, K., Rutkowski, L.: Compromise Neuro-Fuzzy System. Proc. Fourth International Conference on Parallel Processing and Applied Mathematics. Częstochowa Poland (2001) 33–40
6. Czogała, E., Leski, J.: Fuzzy and Neuro-Fuzzy Intelligent Systems. Physica-Verlag. A Springer-Verlag Company. Heidelberg New York (2000)
7. Driankov, D., Hellendoorn, H., Reinfrank, M.: An Introduction to Fuzzy Control. Springer-Verlag. Berlin, Heidelberg (1993)
8. Dubois, D., Prade, H.: Fuzzy Sets in Approximate Reasoning. Part I: Inference with possibility distribution. Fuzzy Sets and Systems 40 (1991) 143–202
9. Giorratano, J., Riley, G.: Expert Systems: Principles and Programming. PWS Publishing Company Boston MA (1998)
10. Jackson, P.: Introduction to Expert Systems. Addison Wesley (1999)
11. Jang, J.-S.R., Sun, C.-T.: Fuctional Equivalence between Radial Basis Function Networks and Fuzzy Inference Systems. IEEE Trans. Neural Networks 4 1 (1993) 156–159
12. Klement, E.P., Mesiar, R., Pap, E.: Triangular Norms. Kluwer Academic Publishers Dordrecht Boston London (2000)
13. Mamdani, E.H., Assilian, S.: An Experiment in Linguistic Synthesis with a Fuzzy Logic Controller. International Journal of Man-Machine Studies 7 (1975) 1-13
14. Mendel, J.M.: Uncertain Rule-Based Fuzzy Logic Systems: Introduction and New Directions. Prentice Hall Upper Saddle River N.J. (2001)
15. Michalewicz, Z.: Genetic Algorithms + Data Structures = Evolution Programs. Springer-Verlag Berlin. Heidelberg. New York (1992)
16. Montana, D.J.: A Weighted Probabilistic Neural Network. Advances in Neural Information Processing Systems 4 (1992) 1110-1117

17. Moody, J., Darken, C.: Learning with Localized Receptive Fields. In: Touretzky, D., Hinton, G., Sejnowski, T. (eds.): 1988 Connectionist Models Summer School, Pittsburgh Morgan Kaufmann Publishers San Mateo CA USA (1989) 133–143
18. Nauck, D.: A Fuzzy Perceptron as a Generic Model for Neuro-Fuzzy Approaches. Proc. Conference: Fuzzy-Systeme'94, Munich (1994)
19. Nauck, D., Klawonn, F., Kruse, R.: Foundations of Neuro-Fuzzy Systems. John Wiley & Sons (1997)
20. Nomura, H., Hayashi, I., Wakami, N.: A Self-Tuning Method of Fuzzy Control by Descent Method. Proc. 4th International Fuzzy Systems Association World Congress, IFSA'91 Brussels Belgium (1991) 155–158
21. Nomura, H., Hayashi, I., Wakami, N.: A Self-Tuning Method of Fuzzy Reasoning by Genetic Algorithm. Proceedings of the 1992 International Fuzzy Systems and Intelligent Control Conference, Louisville KY USA (1992) 236–245
22. Nowicki, R., Rutkowska, D.: Neuro-Fuzzy Architectures Based on Yager Implication. Proc. 5th Conference on Neural Networks and Soft Computing, Zakopane Poland (2000) 353–360
23. Nowicki, R., Rutkowski, L.: Rough-Neuro-Fuzzy System for Classification. Proc. 9th International Conference on Neural Information Processing, ICONIP'02 Orchid Country Club Singapore (2002)
24. Nowicki, R., Rutkowski, L.: Soft Techniques for Bayesian Classification. In: Rutkowski, L., Kacprzyk, J. (eds.): Neural Networks and Soft Computing, Physica-Verlag, A Springer-Verlag Company Heidelberg New York (2003) 537–544
25. Nowicki, R., Scherer, R., Rutkowski, L.: A Neuro-Fuzzy System Based on the Hierarchical Prioritized Structure. Proc. 10th Zittau Fuzzy Colloquium, Zittau Germany (2002) 192–198
26. Nowicki, R., Scherer, R., Rutkowski, L.: A Method for Learning of Hierarchical Fuzzy Systems. Proc. 2nd Euro-International Symposium on Computational Intelligence 76 Kosice Slovakia (2002) 124–129
27. Nowicki, R., Scherer, R. , Rutkowski, L.: A Hierarchical Neuro-Fuzzy System Based on s-Implication. IJCNN-2003 Proc. International Joint Conference on Neural Networks, Portland Oregon (2003) 321–325
28. Patterson, D.W.: Artificial Neural Networks: Therory and Applications. Prentice Hall Singapore (1996)
29. Pedrycz, W.: Fuzzy Control and Fuzzy Systems. Research Studies Press London (1989)
30. Rutkowska, D.: Neuro-Fuzzy Architectures and Hybrid Learning. Physica-Verlag, A Springer-Verlag Company Heidelberg New York (2002)
31. Rutkowska, D.: Type 2 Fuzzy Neural Networks: an Interpretation Based on Fuzzy Inference Neural Networks with Fuzzy Parameters. Proc. 2002 IEEE Congress on Computational Intelligence, FUZZ-IEEE'02, Honolulu Hawaii (2002) 1180–1185
32. Rutkowska, D.: A Perception-Based Classification System. Proc. CIMCA 2003 Conference, Vienna Austria (2003) 52–61
33. Rutkowska, D.: Perception-Based Systems for Medical Diagnosis. Proc. Third EUSFLAT 2003, Zittau Germany (2003) 741–746
34. Rutkowska, D.: Perception-Based Reasoning: Evaluation Systems. International Journal Task Quarterly, 7 1 (2003) 131–145
35. Rutkowska, D.: Multi-Expert Systems. Proc. 5th International Conference: Parallel Processing and Applied Mathematics. Częstochowa Poland (2003)
36. Rutkowska, D.: Perception-Based Expert Systems. Soft Computing Journal (2003) submitted

37. Rutkowska, D., Hayashi, Y.: Neuro-Fuzzy Systems Approaches. Journal of Advanced Computational Intelligence. 3 3 (1999) 177-185
38. Rutkowska, D., Nowicki, R.: Fuzzy Inference Neural Networks Based on Destructive and Constructive Approaches and Their Application to Classification. Proc. 4th Conference on Neural Networks and Their Applications, Zakopane Poland (1999) 294-301
39. Rutkowska, D., Nowicki, R.: Constructive and Destructive Approach to Neuro-Fuzzy Systems. Proc. EUROFUSE-SIC'99, Budapest Hungary (1999) 100–105
40. Rutkowska, D., Nowicki, R.: Neuro-Fuzzy Architectures Based on Fodor Implication. Proc. 8th Zittau Fuzzy Colloquium, Zittau Germany (2000) 230–237
41. Rutkowska, D., Nowicki, R.: Implication-Based Neuro-Fuzzy Architectures. International Journal of Applied Mathematics and Computer Science 10 4 (2000) 675–701
42. Rutkowska, D., Nowicki, R.: Neuro-Fuzzy Systems: Destructive Approach. In: Chojcan, J., Łeski, J. (eds.): Fuzzy Sets and Their Applications, Silesian University Press Gliwice Poland (2001) 285–292
43. Rutkowska, D., Kacprzyk, J., Zadeh, L.A. (eds.): Computing with Words and Perceptions. International Journal of Applied Mathematics and Computer Science 12 3 (2002)
44. Rutkowska, D., Rutkowski, L., Nowicki, R.: Neuro-Fuzzy System with Inference Based on Bounded Product. In: Mastorakis, N. (ed.): Advances in Neural Networks and Applications, World Scientific and Engineering Society Press (2001) 104–109
45. Rutkowski, L.: Identification of MISO Nonlinear Regressions in the Presence of a Wide Class of Disturbances. IEEE Trans. Information Theory IT-37 (1991) 214–216
46. Rutkowski, L.: Multiple Fourier Series Procedures for Extraction of Nonlinear Regressions from Noisy Data. IEEE Trans. Signal Processing 41 10 (1993) 3062–3065
47. Rutkowski, L., Cpałka, K.: Flexible Structures of Neuro-Fuzzy Systems. Quo Vadis Computational Intelligence, Studies in Fuzziness and Soft Computing, Springer 54 (2000) 479-484
48. Rutkowski, L., Cpałka, K.: A General Approach to Neuro-Fuzzy Systems. Proc. 10th IEEE International Conference on Fuzzy Systems, Melbourne Australia (2001)
49. Rutkowski, L., Cpałka, K.: A Neuro-Fuzzy Controller with a Compromise Fuzzy Reasoning. Control and Cybernetics 31 2 (2002) 297-308
50. Rutkowski, L., Cpałka, K.: Compromise Approach to Neuro-Fuzzy Systems. Proc. 2nd Euro-International Symposium on Computational Intelligence 76 Kosice Slovakia (2002) 85–90
51. Rutkowski, L., Cpałka, K.: Flexible Weighted Neuro-Fuzzy Systems. Proc. 9th International Conference on Neural Information Processing, ICONIP'02, Orchid Country Club Singapore (2002)
52. Rutkowski, L., Cpałka, K.: Flexible Neuro-Fuzzy Systems. IEEE Trans. Neural Networks 14 (2003) 554-574
53. Rutkowski, L., Gałkowski, T.: On Pattern Classification and System Identification by Probabilistic Neural Networks. Applied Mathematics and Computer Science 4 3 (1994) 413–422
54. Rutkowski, L., Starczewski, J.: From Type-1 to Type-2 Fuzzy Interference Systems – Part 1, Part 2. Proc. Fifth Conference on Neural Networks and Soft Computing, Zakopane Poland (2000) 46–51, 52–65
55. Sage, A.P. (ed.): Coincise Encyclopedia of Information Processing in Systems and Organization. Pergamon Press New York (1990)

56. Setness, M., Babuska, R.: Fuzzy Relational Classifier Trained by Fuzzy Clustering. IEEE Trans. Systems, Man and Cybernetics – Part B: Cybernetics 29 5 (1999) 619–625

57. Scherer, R., Rutkowski, L.: A Neuro-Fuzzy Relational System. Proc. Fourth International Conference on Parallel Processing and Applied Mathematics, Częstochowa Poland (2001) 131–135

58. Scherer, R., Rutkowski, L.: Relational Equations Initializing Neuro-Fuzzy System. Proc. 10th Zittau Fuzzy Colloquium, Zittau Germany (2002) 212–217

59. Scherer, R., Rutkowski, L.: Neuro-Fuzzy Relational Systems. Proc. 9th International Conference on Neural Information Processing, ICONIP'02, Orchid Country Club Singapore (2002)

60. Scherer, R., Rutkowski, L.: A Fuzzy Relational System with Linguistic Antecedent Certainty Factors. In: Rutkowski, L., Kacprzyk, J. (eds.): Neural Networks and Soft Computing, Physica-Verlag, A Springer-Verlag Company Heidelberg New York. (2003) 563-569

61. Specht, D.: Probabilistic Neural Networks. Neural Networks 3 1 (1990) 109-118

62. Starczewski, J., Rutkowski, L.: Connectionist Structures of Type 2 Fuzzy Inference Systems. Lecture Notes in Computer Science 2328 (2001) 634-642

63. Starczewski, J., Rutkowski, L.: Neuro-Fuzzy Inference Systems of Type 2. Proc. 9th International Conference on Neural Information Processing, ICONIP'02, Orchid Country Club Singapore (2002)

64. Starczewski, J., Rutkowski, L.: Interval Type 2 Neuro-Fuzzy Systems Based on Interval Consequents. In: Rutkowski, L., Kacprzyk, J. (eds.): Neural Networks and Soft Computing, Physica-Verlag, A Springer-Verlag Company Heidelberg New York (2003) 570-577

65. Takagi, H.: Fusion Technology of Neural Networks and Fuzzy Systems: A Chronicled Progression from the Laboratory to Our Daily Lives.International Journal of Applied Mathematics and Computer Science 10 4 (2000) 647-673

66. Wang, L.-X.: Adaptive Fuzzy Systems and Control. PTR Prentice Hall Englewood Cliffs New Jersey (1994)

67. Yager, R.R., Filev, D.P.: Essentials of Fuzzy Modeling and Control. John Wiley & Sons (1994)

68. Zadeh, L.A.: Towards a Theory of Fuzzy Systems. In: Kalman, R.E., DeClaris, N. (eds.): Aspects of Network and System Theory, Holt. Rinehart and Winston New York (1971)

69. Zadeh, L.A.: Outline of a New Approach to the Analysis of Complex Systems and Decision Processes. IEEE Trans. Systems, Man, and Cybernetics SMC-3 1 (1973) 28–44

70. Zadeh, L.A.: Fuzzy Sets and Information Granularity. In: Gupta, M., Ragade, R., Yager, R. (eds.): Advances in Fuzzy Set Theory and Applications, North Holland Amsterdam (1979) 3–18

71. Zadeh, L.A.: Fuzzy Logic, Neural Networks and Soft Computing. Communications of the ACM 37 3 (1994) 77–84

72. Zadeh, L.A.: From Computing with Numbers to Computing with Words – from Manipulation of Measurements to Manipulation of Perceptions. IEEE Trans. Circuits and Systems – I: Fundamental Theory and Applications 45 1 (1999) 105–119

73. Żurada, J.M.: Introduction to Artificial Neural Systems. West Publishing Company (1992)

Algorithms for Scalable Storage Servers*

Peter Sanders

Max Planck Institut für Informatik
Saarbrücken, Germany
sanders@mpi-sb.mpg.de

Abstract. We survey a set of algorithmic techniques that make it possible to build a high performance storage server from a network of cheap components. Such a storage server offers a very simple programming model. To the clients it looks like a single very large disk that can handle many requests in parallel with minimal interference between the requests. The algorithms use randomization, redundant storage, and sophisticated scheduling strategies to achieve this goal. The focus is on algorithmic techniques and open questions. The paper summarizes several previous papers and presents a new strategy for handling heterogeneous disks.

1 Introduction

It is said that our society is an information society, i.e., efficiently storing and retrieving a vast amount of information has become a driving force of our economy and society. Most of this information is stored on hard disks — many hard disks actually. Some applications (e.g., geographical information systems, satellite image libraries, climate simulation, particle physics) already measure their data bases in petabytes (10^{15} bytes). Currently, the largest of these applications use huge tape libraries, but hard disks can now store the same data for a similar price offering much higher performance [13]. To store such amounts of data one would need about 10 000 disks. Systems with thousands of disks have already been build and there are projects for "mid-range" systems that would scale to 12 000 disks.

This paper discusses algorithmic challenges resulting from the goal to operate large collections of hard disks in an efficient, reliable, flexible, and user-friendly way. Some of these questions are already relevant if you put four disks in your PC. But things get really interesting (also from a theoretical point of view) if we talk about up to 1024 disks in a traditional monolithic storage server (e.g. http://www.hds.com/products/systems/9900v/), or even heterogeneous networks of workstations, servers, parallel computers, and many many disks. In this paper all of this is viewed as a storage server.

We concentrate on a simple model that already addresses the requirement of user-friendliness to a large extent. Essentially, the entire storage server is

---

* Partially supported by the Future and Emerging Technologies programme of the EU under contract number IST-1999-14186 (ALCOM-FT).

P. Van Emde Boas et al. (Eds.): SOFSEM 2004, LNCS 2932, pp. 82–101, 2004.
© Springer-Verlag Berlin Heidelberg 2004

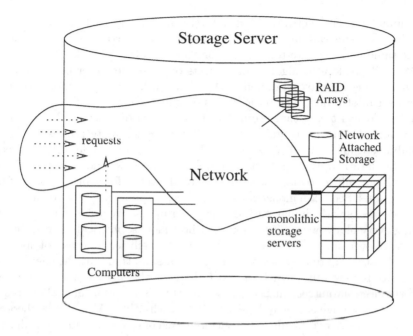

Fig. 1. A storage server appears to the outside world like a huge disk accepting many parallel request from inside and outside the system

presented to the operating system of the computers that run the applications (*clients*) as a single very large disk (see Fig. 1): There is a single *logical* address space, i.e., an array of bytes $A[0..N-1]$.[1] N is essentially the total cumulative usable capacity of all disks. The clients can submit *requests* for bytes $A[a..b]$ to the storage server. There will be some delay (some milliseconds as in a physical disk) and then data is delivered at a high rate (currently up to 50 MByte/s from a single disk). Otherwise, the clients can behave completely naively: In particular, requests should be handled in parallel with minimal additional delays. Large requests (many megabytes) should be handled by many disks in parallel. If any single component of the system fails, no data should be lost and the effect on performance should be minimal. If the system is upgraded with additional disks, usually larger than those previously present, the logical address space should be extended accordingly and future requests should profit from the the increased cumulative data rate of the system.

The storage server can be implemented as part of the operating software of a monolithic system or as a distributed program with processes on the client computers and possibly on dedicated server machines or *network attached storage*, i.e., disks that are directly connected to the computer. All these components

---

[1] We use $a..b$ as a shorthand for the range $a, \ldots , b$ and $A[a..b]$ stands for the subarray $\langle A[a], \ldots , A[b] \rangle$.

communicate over a network. Higher level functionality such as file systems or data base systems can be implemented on top of our virtual address space much in the same way they are today build on top of a physical disk.

We will develop the algorithmic aspects of a storage server in a step by step manner giving intuitive arguments why they work but citing more specialized papers for most proofs. The basic idea is to split the logical address space A into fixed size logical *blocks* that are mapped to *random* disks. Sect. 3 explains that this is already enough to guarantee low latencies for write requests with high probability using a small write buffer. To get basic fault tolerance we need to store the data *redundantly*. Sect. 4 shows that two independently placed copies of each block suffice to also guarantee low read latency for arbitrary sets of block read requests. Sect. 5 demonstrates how we can support accesses to variable size pieces of blocks with similar performance guarantees. We are also not stuck with storing every block twice. Sect. 6 explains how more sophisticated encoding gives us control over different tradeoffs with respect to efficiency, waste of space, and fault tolerance. Up to that point we make the assumption that the clients submit batches of requests in a synchronized fashion — this allows us to give rigorous performance guarantees. In Sect. 7 we lift this assumption and allow requests to enter the storage server independently of each other. Although a theoretical treatment gets more difficult, the basic approach of random redundant allocation still works and we get simple algorithms that can be implemented in a distributed fashion. The algorithms described in Sect. 8 *use* the redundant storage when a disk or other components of the system fails. It turns out that the clients see almost nothing of the fault not even in terms of performance. Furthermore, after a very short time, the system is again in a safe state where further component failures can be tolerated. Sect. 3 assumes that a write operation can return as soon as there is enough space to keep it in RAM memory. In Sect. 9 we explain what can be done if this is not acceptable because a loss of power could erase the RAM. For simplicity of exposition we assume most of the time that the system consists of D identical disks but Sect. 10 generalizes to the case of different capacity disks that can be added incrementally.

2   Related Work

A widely used approach to storage servers is RAID [27] (Redundant Arrays of Independent Disks). Different RAID levels (0–5) offer different combinations of two basic techniques: In *mirroring* (RAID Level 1), each disk has a mirror disk storing the same data. This is similar to the random duplicate allocation (RDA) introduced in Sect. 4 only that the latter stores each block independently on different disks. We will see that this leads to better performance in several respects. *Striping* (RAID Level 0) [31] is a simple and elegant way to exploit disk parallelism: Logical blocks are split into D equal sized pieces and each piece is stored on a different disk. This way, accesses to logical blocks are always balanced over all disks. This works well for small D, but for large D, we would get a huge logical block size that is problematic for applications that need fine grained access. Fault tolerance can be achieved at low cost by splitting logical blocks into $D - 1$ pieces and storing the bit-wise xor of these pieces in a *parity block* (RAID Levels 3, 5).

Larger storage servers are usually operated in such a way that files or partitions are manually assigned to small subsets of disks that are operated like a RAID array. The point of view taken in this paper is that this management effort is often avoidable without a performance penalty. In applications where the space and bandwidth requirement are highly dynamic, automatic methods may even outperform the most careful manual assignment of data to disks.

Load balancing by random placement of data is a well known technique (e.g., [7], [23]). Combining random placement and redundancy has first been considered in parallel computing for PRAM emulation [18] and online load balancing [6]. For scheduling disk accesses, these techniques have been used for multimedia applications [39], [40], [19], [24], [8], [35]. The methods described here are mostly a summary of four papers [34], [33], [32], [16]. Sect. 10 describes new results.

There are many algorithms explicitly designed to work efficiently with coarse-grained block-wise access. Most use the model by Vitter and Shriver [42] that allows identical parallel disks and a fixed block size. Vitter [41] has written a good overview article. More overviews and several introductory articles are collected in an LNCS Tutorial [22].

3   Write Buffering

3.1   Greedy Writing

Consider the implementation of an operation $write(a, B, i)$ that writes a client array $a[0..B - 1]$ to the logical address space $A[i..i+B-1]$. The main observation exploited in this section is that *write* can in principle be implemented to return almost immediately: Just copy the data to a buffer space.[2] The matching read operation $read(B, i)$ returns the cached data without a disk access.

An obvious limitation of this buffering strategy is that we will eventually run out of buffer space without a good strategy for actually *outputting* the data to the disks. We postpone the question how data is mapped to the disks until Sect. 3.2 because the following *greedy writing* algorithm works for any given assignment of data to the disks. We maintain

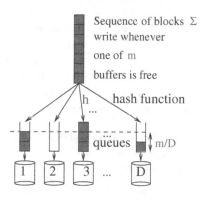

Fig. 2. Optimal Writing

---

[2] We can even do without a copy if we "steal" a from the client and only release it when the data is finally copied or output.

a queue of output requests for each disk. Whenever a disk falls idle, one request from this queue is submitted to the disk. Fig. 2 illustrates this strategy. In some sense, greedy writing is optimal:

Theorem 1 ([16]). *Consider the I/O model of Vitter and Shriver [42] (fixed block size, fixed output cost). Assume some sequence of block writes is to be performed in that logical order and at most m blocks can be buffered by the storage server. Then greedy writing minimizes the number of I/O steps needed if the disk queues are managed in a FIFO (first in first out) manner.*

Proof. (Outline) An induction proof shows that greedy writing is optimal among all output strategies that maintain queues in a FIFO manner. Another simple lemma shows that any schedule can be transformed into a FIFO schedule without increasing the I/O time or the memory requirement.   ∎

Things get more complicated for more realistic I/O models that take into account that I/O times depend on the time to move the disk head between the position of two blocks.

Open Problem: 1 *Can you find (approximately) optimal writing algorithms for the case that I/O costs depend on the position of blocks on the disks? Even for fixed block size[3] and cost estimates only dependent on seek time little is known if the buffer size is limited.[4]*

3.2   Random Allocation

Theorem 1 is a bit hollow because performance can still be very bad if all blocks we need to write have to go to the same disk. We would like to have an allocation strategy that avoids such cases. But this seems impossible — for any given mapping of the address space to the disks, there will be sets of requests that all go to the same disk. Randomization offers a way out of this dilemma. We allocate logical blocks to random disks for some fixed (large) block size B. (Sect. 10 discusses details how this mapping should actually be implemented.) Random mapping makes it very unlikely that a particular set of blocks requested by the clients reside on the same disk. More generally, we get the following performance guarantee for arbitrary sequences of *write* requests:

Theorem 2 ([34], [16]). *Consider the I/O model of Vitter and Shriver [42] (D disks, fixed block size, fixed output cost). Assume some sequence of n randomly mapped different blocks are to be written and at most m blocks can be buffered by*

---

[3] Variable block sizes open another can of worms. One immediately gets NP-hard problems. But allowing a small amount of additional memory removes most complications in that respect.

[4] For infinite buffer size, the problem is easy if we look at seek times only (just sort by track) or rotational delays only [38]. For both types of delays together we have an NP-hard variant of the traveling salesman problem with polynomial time solutions in some special cases [5].

the storage server. Then greedy writing accepts the last block after an expected number of $(1 + \mathcal{O}(D/m))\frac{n}{D}$ *output steps. After the last block has been accepted, the longest queue has length* $\mathcal{O}\left(\frac{m}{D}\log D\right)$.

It can also be shown that longer execution times only happen with very small probability.

Proof. (Outline) The optimal greedy writing algorithm dominates a "throttled" algorithm where in each I/O step $(1 - D/m)D$ blocks are written. The effect of the throttled algorithm on a single disk can be analyzed using methods from queuing theory if the buffer size is unlimited. The average queue length turns out to be bounded by $m/2D$ and hence the expected sum of all queue lengths is bounded by $m/2$. More complicated arguments establish that large deviations from this sum are unlikely and hence the influence of situations where the buffer overflows is negligible.   ∎

Open Problem: 2 *The number of steps needed to write n blocks and flush all buffers should be a decreasing function of the buffer size m. Prove such a monotonic bound that is at least as good as Theorem 1 both for large and small n.*

3.3   Distributed Implementation

We now explain how the abstract algorithms described above can be implemented in a real system. We will assume that one or several disks are connected to a computer where one ore several processors share a memory. Several computers are connected by a communication network to form the storage server. Disks directly attached to the network are viewed as small computers with a single disk attached to them. The client applications either run on the same system or send requests to the storage server via the network. Let us consider the possible routes of data in the first case: When a *write* operation for an array s is called, the data is located in the client memory on computer S. Array s contains data from one or several randomly mapped blocks of data. Let us focus on the data destined for one of the target disks t that is attached to a server machine T. The ideal situation would be that disk t is currently idle and the data is shipped to the network interface card of T which directly forwards it to disk t, bypassing the processor and main memory of T. Since this is difficult to do in a portable way and since t may be busy anyway, the more likely alternative is that S contacts T and asks it to reserve space to put s into the queue of t. If this is impossible, the execution of the *write* operation blocks until space is available or S tries to buffer s locally. Eventually, the data is transferred to the main memory of T. When the request gets its turn, it is transmitted to the disk t which means that it ends up in the local cache of this disk and is then written.

This scenario deviates in several points from the theoretical analysis:

- The nice performance bounds only hold when all disks share the same *global* pool of buffers whereas the implementation makes use only of the local memories of the computer hosting the target disk t. It can be shown that this makes little difference if the local memories are large compared to $\log D$ blocks. Otherwise, one could consider shipping the data to third parties when neither S nor T have enough local memory. But this only makes sense if the the network is very fast.

– Theorem 2 assumes that all written blocks are different. Overwriting a block that is still buffered will save us an output. But it can happen that overwriting blocks that have recently been output can cause additional delays [34]. Again, this can be shown to be unproblematic if the local memory is large compared to $\log D$ blocks. Otherwise dynamically remapping data can help.

– The logical blocks used for random mapping should be fairly large (currently megabytes) in order to allow accesses close to the peak performance of the disks. This can cause a problem for applications that less rely on high throughput for consecutive accesses than on low latency for many parallel fine grained accesses. In that case many consecutive small blocks can lie on the same disk which then becomes a bottleneck. In this case it might make sense to use a separate address space with small logical blocks for fine grained accesses.

4   Random Duplicate Allocation

In the previous section we have seen that random allocation and some buffering allow us to write with high throughput and low latency. The same strategy seems promising for reading data. Randomization ensures that data is spread uniformly over the disks and buffer space can be used for *prefetching* data so that it is available when needed. Indeed, there is a far reaching analogy between reading and writing [16]: When we run a writing algorithm "backwards" we get a reading algorithm. In particular, Theorem 1 transfers. However this reversal of time implies that we need to know the future accesses in advance and we pay the $\mathcal{O}(m \log(D)/D)$ steps for the maximum queue length *up front*.

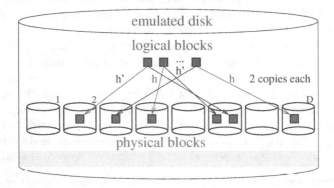

Fig. 3. The concept of (R)andom (D)uplicate (A)llocation

Therefore, we now bring in an additional ingredient: Each logical block is stored redundantly. Figure 3 illustrates this concept. For now we concentrate on the simple case that each block is allocated to two randomly chosen disks. Sect. 6 discusses generalizations. Redundancy gives us flexibility in choosing from where to read the data and this allows us to reduce read latencies dramatically. By choosing two *different* disks for the copies we get the additional benefit that no data is lost when a disk fails.

We begin with two algorithms for scheduling a batch of n requested blocks of fixed size that have been analyzed very accurately: The *shortest queue* algorithm allocates the requests in a greedy fashion. Consider a block e with copies on disks d and d' and let $\ell(d)$ and $\ell(d')$ denote the number of blocks already planned for disks d and d' respectively. Then the shortest queue algorithm plans e for the disk with smaller load. Ties are broken arbitrarily. It can be shown that this algorithm produces a schedule that needs

$$k = \frac{n}{D} + \log \ln D + \Theta(1)$$

expected I/O steps [9]. This is very good for large n but has an additive term that grows with the system size.

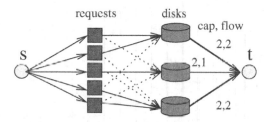

Fig. 4. A flow network showing how five requests are allocated to three disks. The flow defined by the solid lines proves that the requests can be retrieved in two I/O steps

We will see that *optimal* schedules do not have this problem — we can do better by not committing our choices before we have seen all the requests. Optimal schedules can be found in polynomial time [12]: Suppose we want to find out whether k steps suffice to retrieve all requests. Consider a flow network [2] that consists of four layers: A source node in the first layer is connected to each of n request nodes. Each request node is connected to two out of D disk nodes — one edge for each disk that holds a copy of the requested block. The disk nodes are connected to a sink node t. The edges between disk nodes and t have capacity k. All other nodes have capacity 1. Now it is easy to see that a flow saturating all edges leaving the source node exists if and only if k steps are sufficient. A schedule can be derived from an integral maximum flow by reading request r from disk d if and only if the edge (r, d) carries flow. Figure 4 gives an example. The correct value for k can be found by trial and error. First try

$k = \lceil n/D \rceil$ then $k = \lceil n/D \rceil + 1, \dots$, until a solution is found. Korst [19] gives a different flow formulation that uses only D nodes and demonstrates that the problem can be solved in time $\mathcal{O}(n + D^3)$. If $n = \mathcal{O}(D)$ it can be shown that the problem can be solved in time $\mathcal{O}(n \log n)$ with high probability [34].

Theorem 3. *[34] Consider a batch of n randomly and duplicately allocated blocks to be read from D disks. The optimal algorithm needs at most*

$$\left\lceil \frac{n}{D} \right\rceil + 1 \text{ steps with probability at least } 1 - \mathcal{O}(1/D)^{\lceil n/D \rceil + 1} \ .$$

Proof. (Outline) Using a graph theoretical model of the problem, it can be shown that the requests can be retrieved in k steps if and *only if* there is no subset Δ of disks such that more than $|\Delta|k$ requested blocks have both their copies allocated to a disk in Δ [37]. Hence, it suffices to show that it is unlikely that such an *overloaded subset* exists. This is a tractable problem mostly because the number of blocks allocated to Δ is binomially distributed. ∎

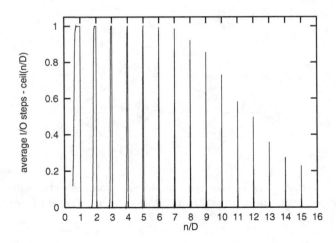

Fig. 5. The number of I/O steps (minus the lower bound $\lceil n/D \rceil$) needed by optimal scheduling when scheduling $n \in 256..4096$ blocks on $D = 256$ disks

Figure 5 shows the performance of the optimal scheduling algorithm. We only give the data for $D = 256$ because this curve is almost independent of the number of disks. We see that the performance is even better than predicted by Theorem 3: We can expect to get schedules that need only $\lceil n/D \rceil$ steps except if n is a multiple of D or slightly below. For example, when $n = 3.84D$, we almost always get a schedule with 4 steps, i.e., we are within 4 % of the best possible performance. We also see that for large n we can even get perfect balance when n is a multiple of D.

Open Problem: 3 *Is there a threshold constant c such that for $n > cD \log D$, optimal scheduling finds a schedule with $\lceil n/D \rceil$ I/O steps even if n is a multiple of D?*

4.1   The Selfless Algorithm

One problem with optimal scheduling is that we do not have good performance guarantees for scheduling large sets of blocks efficiently. Therefore it makes sense to look for fast algorithms that are close to optimal. Here we describe a linear time algorithm that produces very close to optimal solutions [11].

The *selfless algorithm* distinguishes between *committed* and uncommitted requests. Uncommitted requests still have a choice between two disks. Committed requests have decided for one of the two choices. Initially, all requests are uncommitted. A disk d is called committed if there are no uncommitted requests that have d as a choice. Let the *load* $\ell(d)$ of disk d denote twice the number of requests that have committed to d plus the number of uncommitted requests that have d as an option. The selfless algorithm is based on two simple rules:

1. If there is an uncommitted disk with at most $\lceil n/D \rceil$ remaining incident requests (committed or uncommitted), we commit all of them to this disk.
2. Otherwise, we choose an uncommitted disk d with minimum load, choose an uncommitted request with d as an option, and commit it to d.

This algorithm can be implemented to run in linear time using fairly standard data structures: Disks are viewed as nodes of a graph. Uncommitted requests are edges. Using an appropriate graph representation, edges can be removed in constant time (e.g., [21]). When a disk becomes a candidate for Rule 1, we remember it on a stack. The remaining nodes are kept in a priority queue ordered by their load. Insert, decrement-priority and delete-minimum can be implemented to run in amortized constant time using a slight variant of a bucket priority queue [14].

If we would plot the performance of the selfless algorithm in the same way as in Figure 5, it would be impossible to see a difference, i.e., with large probability, the selfless algorithm finds an optimal schedule. This empirical observation will be complemented by an analytical treatment in an upcoming paper [11] using differential equation methods that have previously been used for the mathematically closely related problem of *cores* of random graphs [28].

5   Variable Size Requests

We now drop the assumption that we are dealing with fixed size jobs that take unit time to retrieve. Instead, let $\ell_i \leq 1$ denote the time needed to retrieve request i. This generalization can be used to model several aspects of storage servers:

– We might want to retrieve just parts of a logical block

- Disks are divided into *zones* [30] of different data density and correspondingly different data rate — blocks on the outer zones are faster to retrieve than blocks on the inner zones. We assume here that both copies of a block are stored on the same zone.

The bad news is that it is strongly NP-hard to assign requests to disks so that the I/O time is minimized [1]. The good news is that optimal scheduling is still possible if we allow request to be split, i.e., we are allowed to combine a request from pieces read from both copies. We make the simplifying assumption here that a request of size $\ell = \ell_1 + \ell_2$ stored on disks d_1 and d_2 can be retrieved by spending time ℓ_1 on disk d_1 and time ℓ_2 on disk d_2. This is approximately true if requests are large.

Even the performance guarantees for random duplicate allocation transfer. We report a simplified version of a result from [32] that has the *same* form as Theorem 3 for unit size requests:

Theorem 4. *Consider a set R of request with total size $n = \sum_{r \in R} \ell_r$ of randomly and duplicately allocated requests to be read from D disks. The optimal algorithm computes a schedule with I/O time at most*

$$\left\lceil \frac{n}{D} \right\rceil + 1 \text{ with probability at least } 1 - \mathcal{O}(1/D)^{\lceil n/D \rceil + 1}$$

The proofs and the algorithms are completely analogous. The only difference is that the maximum flows will now not be integral and hence require splitting of requests. Splitting can also have a positive effect for unit size requests since it eliminates threshold effects such es the spikes visible in Fig. 5. A more detailed analysis indicates that the retrieval time becomes a monotonic function of the number of requests [32].

In a sense, Theorem 4 is much more important than Theorem 3. For unit size requests, we can relatively easily establish the expected performance of an algorithm by simulating all interesting cases a sufficient number of times. Here, this is not possible since Theorem 4 holds for a vast space of possible inputs (uncountably big and still exponential if we discretize the piece sizes).

6   Reducing Redundancy

Instead of simply replicating logical blocks, we can more generally encode a logical block which has r times the size of a physical block into w physical blocks such that reading any r out of the w blocks suffices to reconstruct the logical block. Perhaps the most important case is $w = r + 1$. Using *parity-encoding*, r of the blocks are simply pieces of the logical block and the last block is the exclusive-or of the other blocks. A missing block can then be reconstructed by taking the exclusive-or of the blocks read. Parity encoding is the easiest way to reduce redundancy compared to RDA while maintaining some flexibility in scheduling. Its main drawback is that the physical blocks being read are a factor r smaller than the logical blocks so that high bandwidth can only be expected if the logical blocks are fairly large. The special case $r = D - 1, W = D$ yields the coding scheme used for RAID levels 3 and 5.

Choosing $w > r + 1$ can be useful if more than one disk failure is to be tolerated (see Sect. 8) or if we additionally want to reduce output latencies (see Sect. 9). A disadvantage of codes with $w > r+1$ is that they are computationally more expensive than parity-encoding [20], [15], [29], [10], [4], [8].

Most of the scheduling algorithms for RDA we have discussed are easy to generalize for more general coding schemes. Only optimal scheduling needs some additional consideration. A formulation that is a generalization of bipartite matching [33] yields a polynomial time algorithm however.

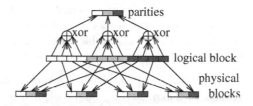

Fig. 6. Encoding of a logical block of size 12 into 4 physical blocks and one parity block of size 3 such that aligned logical requests of size $4s$, $s \in \{1, 2, 3\}$ can be fulfilled by retrieving any 4 out of 5 physical blocks of size s

A small trick also allows us to use general coding schemes for arbitrary request sizes: As before, data is allocated for large logical blocks whereas actual requests may retrieve parts of these blocks. But the coding is done in very small pieces (say sectors of size 512) and the encoded pieces are stored in the physical blocks in an interleaved fashion. Figure 6 gives an example.

7   Asynchronous Access

In Sect. 3.3 we have already explained how writing can be implemented in an asynchronous, distributed way by providing one thread for each disk. We now explain how this can be generalized for read accesses in the presence of redundant allocation. Client requests for a block of data arrive individually in an asynchronous fashion. The clients want to have these requests answered quickly, i.e., they want small delays. The algorithms described in Sect. 4 can be generalized for this purpose [33]. For example, the shortest queue algorithm would commit the request to the disk that can serve it fastest.

However, we loose most of the performance guarantees. For example, it is easy to develop an algorithm that minimizes the maximum delay among all *known* requests but it is not clear how to *anticipate* the impact of these decisions on requests arriving in the future.

Open Problem: 4 *Give theoretical bounds for the expected latency of any of the asynchronous scheduling algorithms discussed in [33] as a function of D* *and ϵ in the following model: A block access on any of the D disks takes unit time. A request for a block arrives every $(1+\epsilon)/D$ time units. For non-redundant random allocation it can be shown that the expected delay is $\Theta(1/\epsilon)$. Experiments and heuristic considerations suggest that time $\mathcal{O}(\log(1/\epsilon))$ is achievable using redundancy.*

Asynchrony also introduces a new algorithmic concept that we want to discuss in more detail: *Lazy decisions*. The simplest lazy algorithm — *lazy queuing* — queues a request readable on disks d and d' in queues for *both* d and d'. The decision which disk actually fetches the block is postponed until the last possible moment. When a disk d falls idle, the thread responsible for this disk inspects its queue and removes one request r queued there. Then it communicates with the thread responsible for the other copy of r to make sure that r is not fetched twice. Lazy queuing has the interesting property that it is equivalent to an "omniscient" shortest queue algorithm, i.e., it achieves the same performance even if it does not know how long it takes to retrieve a request.

Theorem 5. *Given an arbitrary request stream where a disk d needs $t(d,r)$ time units to serve request r. Then the lazy queue algorithm produces the same schedule as a shortest queue algorithm which exactly computes disk loads by summing the $t(d,r)$-values of the scheduled requests.*

The only possible disadvantage of lazy algorithms compared to "eager" algorithms such as shortest queue is that a simple implementation can incur additional communication delays at the performance critical moment when a disk is ready to retrieve the next request (asking another thread and waiting for a reply). This problem can be mitigated by trying to agree on a *primary* copy of a request r before the previous request finishes. The disk holding the primary copy can then immediately fetch r and in parallel it can send a confirmation to the thread with the other copy.

Figure 7 shows that RDA significantly outperforms traditional output schemes. Even mirroring that has the same amount of redundancy produces much larger degrees when the storage server approaches its limits. Measurements not shown here indicate that the gap is much larger when we are interesting in the largest delays that are encountered sufficiently often to be significant for real time applications such as video streaming.

It can also be shown that fluctuations in the arrival rate of requests have little impact on performance if the the number of requests arriving over the time interval of an average delay is not too big. Furthermore, the scheduling algorithms can be adapted in such a way that applications that need high throughput even at the price of large delays can coexist with applications that rely on small delays [33].

8   Fault Tolerance

When a disk fails, the peak system throughput decreases by a small factor of $1/D$. Furthermore, requests which have a copy on the faulty disks lose their

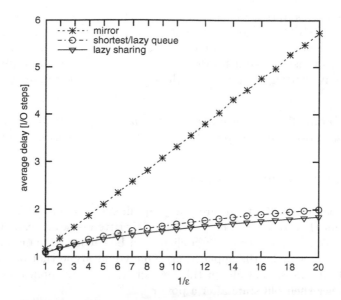

Fig. 7. Average delays for 10^7 requests to $D = 64$ disks arriving at time intervals of $(1+\epsilon)/D$. The mirror algorithm uses random allocation to a RAID-1 array. Lazy sharing is a refinement of lazy queue — an idle disk d leaves a request r to the alternative disk $d'(r)$ if the queue of d' is shorter than the queue of d

scheduling flexibility. Since only few requests are affected, load balancing still works well [32]. In addition, there are now logical blocks that have less redundancy than the others so that additional disk failures could now lead to a loss of data. To get out of this dangerous situation, the lost redundancy has to be reestablished. This can be achieved without exchanging any hardware by dispersing these blocks over unused space of the other disks. This can be done very quickly because the data read and written for this purpose is uniformly distributed over all disks. If we are willing to invest a fraction of ϵ of the peak performance of the system, the reconstruction can finish in a fraction of about $1/\epsilon(D-1)$ of the time needed to read and write one disk. For example, in a large system with 10 000 disks with 100GByte each and a disk I/O rate of 50MByte/s we could in principle reconstruct a failed disk in as little as ten seconds investing 4 % of our peak I/O rate. Section 10 will explain how a random mapping of the data is maintained in this situation.

Failures of disk controllers or entire machines can be handled in a similar manner if the random duplicate allocation is modified in such a way that different copies are allocated to different pieces of hardware. The ultimate realization of this strategy divides the storage server into halves that are physically so far apart that even a fire or another catastrophe is unlikely to destroy both halves at the same time. The limiting factor here are the costs of a high speed interconnection between the halves so that for such systems one may consider to have more than two copies of each block and to send data to the remote half only occasionally.

A major challenge in practical fault tolerance is that it is very difficult to test the behavior of distributed software under faults. Since the data losses can be really expensive, storage servers might therefore be a prime candidate for formal verification:

Open Problem: 5 *Define a useful abstract model of a storage server and its software and prove that it operates correctly under disk failures, power loss, ...*

9   Reducing Write Latency

Somewhat paradoxically, there are many applications where *writes* are much more frequent than *reads*, i.e., much of what is written is never read. The reason is that a lot of the data needed by a client can be cached in main memory (by the storage server or by the application). One could argue that one would not have to output this data at all but this neglects that many applications must be able to recover their old state after a power loss.

There are several ways to handle this situation. One would be to make sure that write buffers are in memory with enough battery backup that they can be flushed to disk at a power loss. The next step on the safety ladder makes sure that the data is buffered in *two* processors with independent power supply before a *write* operation returns. But some applications will still prefer to wait until the data is actually output. In this situation, the strategy from Section 3 leads to fairly long waiting time under high load.

In this situation, the generalized coding schemes outlined in Sect. 6 can be used. If a logical block can be reconstructed from any r out of w pieces, we can return from a *write* operation after r' pieces are output $(r \leq r' \leq w)$ and we get a flexible tradeoff between write latency and fault tolerance. For example, for $r = 1$ and $w = 3$ we could return already when two copies have been written. Which copies are written can be decided using any of the scheduling algorithms discussed above, for example the lazy queuing algorithm from Sect. 7. The remaining copy is not written at all or only with reduced priority so that it cannot delay other time critical disk accesses.

10   Inhomogeneous Dynamically Evolving Storage Servers

A storage server that operates reliably 24h a day 365 days a year should allow us to add disks dynamically when the demands for capacity or bandwidth increase. Since technology is continuously advancing, we would like to add new disks with higher capacity and bandwidth than the existing disks. Even if we would be willing to settle for the old type, this becomes infeasible after a few years when the old type is no longer for sale. In Sect. 8 we have already said that we want to be able to remove failed disks from the system without replacing them by new disks. The main algorithmic challenge in such systems is to maintain our concept of load balancing by randomly mapping logical blocks to disks. We first explain how a single random mapping from the virtual address space to the disks is obtained.

Inhomogeneity can be accommodated by mapping a block not directly to the D inhomogeneous disks but first to D' *volumes* that accommodate $N/D'B$ blocks each. The volumes are then mapped to the disks in such a way that the ratio $r(d) = c(d)/v(d)$ between the capacity $c(d)$ of a disk d and the number of volumes $v(d)$ allocated to it is about the same everywhere. More precisely, when a volume is allocated, it is greedily moved to the disk that maximizes $r(d)$. If $D'/D \gg D \max c(d)/\sum_d c(d)$, we will achieve a good utilization of disk capacity.[5]

When a disk fails, the volumes previously allocated to it will be distributed over the remaining disks. This is safe as long as $\min_d r(d)$ exceeds N/D'. When a new disk d' is added, volumes from the disks with smallest $r(d)$ are moved to the new disk until $r(d')$ would become minimal. In order to move or reconstruct volumes, only the data in the affected volumes needs to be touched whereas all the remaining volumes remain untouched.

It remains to define a random mapping of blocks to volumes. We present a pragmatic solution that outperforms a true random mapping in certain aspects but where an accurate analysis of the scheduling algorithms remains an open question. We achieve a perfectly balanced allocation of blocks to volumes, by *striping* blocks over the volumes, i.e., blocks $iD'..(i+1)D' - 1$ are mapped in such a way that each volume receives one block. To achieve randomness, block $iD' + j$, $0 \le j < D$, is mapped via a (pseudo)random permutation π_i to volume $\pi_i(j)$. Figure 8 summarizes the translation of logical addresses into block offsets, disk IDs, and positions on the disk.

In order to find out which blocks need to be moved or reconstructed when a disk is added or replaced, we would like to have permutations that are easy to invert. *Feistel* permutations [25] are one way to achieve that: Assume for now that $\sqrt{D'}$ is an integer and represent j as $j = j_a + j_b\sqrt{D'}$. Now consider the mapping

$$\pi_{i,1}((j_a, j_b)) = (j_b, j_a + f_{i,1}(j_b) \bmod \sqrt{D'})$$

where $f_{i,1}$ is some (pseudo)random function. If we iterate such mappings two to four times using pseudo-random functions $f_{i,1}, \dots, f_{i,4}$ we get something "pretty random". Indeed, such permutations can be shown to be random in some precise sense that is useful for cryptology [25]. A Feistel permutation is easy to invert.

$$\pi_{i,k}^{-1}((a, b)) = (b - f_{i,k}(a) \bmod \sqrt{D'}, a)$$

We assume that the functions $f_{i,k}$ are represented in some compact way, e.g., using any kind of ordinary pseudo-random hash function h that maps triples

---

[5] If disk bandwidth is more of an issue than disk capacity, we can also balance according to the data rate a disk can support. But even without that, the lazy scheduling algorithms from Sect. 7 will automatically direct some traffic away from the overloaded disks.

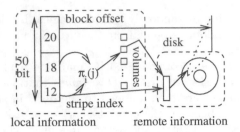

local information   remote information

Fig. 8. How a logical address is mapped to a physical block. The numbers give an example with one Petabyte of address space, $B = 2^{20}$, and $D' = 2^{18}$ that would currently require about 10 000 disks of 100 GByte each

(i, j, k) to values in $0..D' - 1$. In order to find out to which disk a block is mapped, the only additional data structure we need is a lookup table of size D'. This data structure is easy to replicate to the local memory of all processors. For example, even in a large system with $D = 10000$, with disk capacities varying by a factor of four, $D' = 2^{18}$ would already achieve quite good load balance. To achieve fault tolerance, this lookup table and the parameters of the hash function h should be stored redundantly at a predefined place. But even if the table gets lost, it can be reconstructed as long as the capacity of the disks and the order in which they were added or removed is known — we only need to make sure that the algorithms for mapping volumes to disks are deterministic.

Redundant Allocation

In order to use the above scheme in the context of duplicate allocation, we partition the storage server into two partitions whose total storage capacity is about equal. The volumes are mapped to *both* partitions and we have two sets of random permutations — one for each partition. More generally, if we use a coding scheme that writes w physical blocks for each logical block, we need w partitions. To achieve good fault tolerance, components in different partitions should share as few common points of failure as possible (controllers, processors, power supplies, ...). Therefore, the disks will not be assigned to the partitions one by one but in coarse grained units like controllers or even entire machines.

Although this partitioning problem is NP-hard, there are good approximation algorithms [3]. In particular, since we are dealing with a small constant number of partitions, fully polynomial time approximation schemes can be developed using standard techniques [43].

Maintaining reasonably balanced partitions while components enter (new hardware) or leave (failures) the system in an online fashion is a more complicated problem. In general, we will have to move components but these changes in configuration should only affect a small number of components with total capacity proportional to added or removed capacity. At least it is easy to maintain the invariant that the difference between the capacities of the smallest and largest partition is bounded by the maximum component capacity.

11   Discussion

We have introduced some of the algorithmic backbone of scalable storage servers. We have neglected many important aspects because we believe that they are orthogonal to the concepts introduced here, i.e., their implementation does not much affect the decisions for the aspects discussed here: We need an infrastructure that allows reliable high bandwidth communication between arbitrary processors in the network. Although random allocation helps by automatically avoiding hot spots, good routing strategies can be challenging in inhomogeneous dynamically changing networks.

Caching can make actual disk accesses superfluous. This is a well understood topic for centralized memory [17], [26] but distributed caching faces interesting tradeoffs between communication overhead and cache hit rate.

There are further important issues with a different flavor such as locking mechanisms to coordinate concurrent accesses, file systems, real time issues, . . .

In addition, there are interesting aspects that are less well understood yet and pose interesting questions for future work. For example, we have treated all data equal. But in reality, some data is accessed more frequently than other data. Besides the short term measure of caching, this leads to the question of *data migration* (e.g. [36]). Important data should be spread evenly over the disks, it should be allocated to the fastest zones of the disks, and it could be stored with higher redundancy. The bulk of the data that is accessed rarely, could be stored on cheaper disks or even on disks that are powered down for saving energy. Such **Massive Arrays of Idle Disks** [13] are a candidate for replacing tape libraries and could scale to 10s of thousands of disks.

Acknowledgements. In the last years I had many interesting discussions about algorithms for storage servers. Here is a partial list of people who have helped me to form a coherent picture of this complex issue between algorithmics, probability, coding, operating systems, data bases, computer architecture, market mechanisms, patents, . . . : Joep Aerts, Eitan Bachmat, Petra Berenbrink, Andre Brinkmann, Sebastian Egner, Harald Hüls, David Irwin, Mahesh Kallahalla, Jan Korst, Jan Marien, Kurt Mehlhorn, Kay Salzwedel, Christian Scheideler, Martin Skutella, Peter Varman, Jeff Vitter, Gerhard Weikum, Winfried Wilcke, Gerhard Woeginger.

References

1. Aerts, J., Korst, J., Verhaegh, W.: Complexity of Retrieval Problems. Technical Report NL-MS-20.899, Philips Research Laboratories (2000)
2. Ahuja, R.K., Magnanti, R.L., Orlin, J.B.: *Network Flows*. Prentice Hall (1993)
3. Alon, N., Azar, Y., Woeginger, G.J., Yadid, T.: Approximation Schemes for Scheduling. In: SODA (1997) 493–500

4. Alvarez, G.A., Burkhard, W.A., Cristian, F.: Tolerating Multiple Failures in RAID Architectures with Optimal Storage and Uniform Declustering. In: Proceedings of the 24th Annual International Symposium on Computer Architecture (ISCA-97), volume 25,2 of Computer Architecture News New York ACM Press, June 2–4 1997 62–72

5. Andrews, M., Bender, M.A., Zhang, L.: New Algorithms for the Disk Scheduling Problem. In: IEEE, editor, 37th Annual Symposium on Foundations of Computer Science, IEEE Computer Society Press (1996) 550–559

6. Azar, Y., Broder, A.Z., Karlin, A.R., Upfal, E.:   Balanced Allocations.   In: 26th ACM Symposium on the Theory of Computing (1994) 593–602

7. Barve, R.D., Grove, E.F., Vitter, J.S.: Simple Randomized Mergesort on Parallel Disks. Parallel Computing, **23** 4 (1997) 601–631

8. Berenbrink, P., Brinkmann, A., Scheideler, C.: Design of the PRESTO Multimedia Storage Network. In: International Workshop on Communication and Data Management in Large Networks, Paderborn Germany, October 5 1999, 2–12

9. Berenbrink, P., Czumaj, A., Steger, A., Vöcking, B.: Balanced Allocations: The Heavily Loaded Case. In: 32th Annual ACM Symposium on Theory of Computing, (2000) 745–754

10. Blaum, M., Brady, J., Bruck, J., Menon, J.: EVENODD: An Optimal Scheme for Tolerating Double Disk Failures in RAID Architectures. In: Proceedings of the 21st Annual International Symposium on Computer Architecture (1994) 245–254

11. Cain, J., Sanders, P., Wormald, N.: A Random Multigraph Process for Linear Time RDA Disk Scheduling. Manuscript in preparation (2003)

12. Chen, L.T., Rotem, D.: Optimal Response Time Retrieval of Replicated Data (Extended abstract). In: 13th ACM Symposium on Principles of Database Systems, ACM Press **13** (1994) 36–44

13. Colarelli, D., Grunwald, D.: Massive Arrays of Idle Disks for Storage Archives. In: SC'2002 Conference CD, IEEE/ACM SIGARCH, Baltimore, MD, November 2002

14. Dial, R.B.: Algorithm 360: Shortest-Path Forest with Topological Ordering. Communications of the ACM **12** 11 (1969) 632–633

15. Gibson, G.A., Hellerstein, L., Karp, R.M., Katz, R.H., Patterson, D.A.: Coding Techniques for Handling Failures in Large Disk Arrays, CSD-88-477. Technical report, U. C. Berkley (1988)

16. Hutchinson, D.A., Sanders, P., Vitter, J.S.: Duality between Prefetching and Queued Writing with Parallel Disks. In: 9th European Symposium on Algorithms (ESA), LNCS, Vol. 2161. Springer (2001) 62–73

17. Irani, S.: Competetive Analysis of Paging. In: Online Algorithms — The State of the Art, LNCS, Vol. 1442. Springer (1998) 52–73

18. Karp, R.M., Luby, M., Meyer auf der Heide, F.: Efficient PRAM Simulation on a Distributed Memory Machine. In: 24th ACM Symp. on Theory of Computing, May 1992 318–326

19. Korst, J.: Random Duplicate Assignment: An Alternative to Striping in Video Servers. In: ACM Multimedia, Seattle (1997) 219–226

20. MacWilliams, F.J., Sloane, N.J.A.: Theory of Error-Correcting Codes. North-Holland (1988)

21. Mehlhorn, K., Näher, S.: The LEDA Platform of Combinatorial and Geometric Computing. Cambridge University Press (1999)

22. Meyer, U., Sanders, P., Sibeyn, J. (eds): Algorithms for Memory Hierarchies, LNCS Tutorial, Vol. 2625. Springer (2003)

23. Miller E.L., Katz, R.H.: RAMA: An Easy-to-Use, High-Performance Parallel File System. Parallel Computing **23** (1997) 419–446

24. Muntz, R., Santos, J.R., Berson, S.: A Parallel Disk Storage System for Real-Time Multimedia Applications. International Journal of Intelligent Systems **13** (1998) 1137–1174

25. Naor, M., Reingold, O.: On the Construction of Pseudorandom Permutations: Luby-Rackoff Revisited. Journal of Cryptology: the Journal of the International Association for Cryptologic Research **12** 1 (1999) 29–66

26. O'Neil, O'Neil, Weikum: An Optimality Proof of the LRU-K Page Replacement Algorithm. JACM: Journal of the ACM **46** 1999

27. Patterson, D., Gibson, G., Katz, R.: A Case for Redundant Arrays of Inexpensive Disks (RAID). Proceedings of ACM SIGMOD'88 (1988) 109–116

28. Pittel, B., Spencer, J., Wormald, N.: Sudden Emergence of a Giant k-Core in Random Graph. J. Combinatorial Theory, Series B, **67** (1996) 111–151

29. Rabin, M.O.: Efficient Dispersal of Information for Security, Load Balancing and Fault Tolerance. Journal of the ACM, **36** 2 (1989) 335–348

30. Ruemmler, C., Wilkes, J.: An Introduction to Disk Drive Modeling. IEEE Computer, **27** 3 March 1994 17–28

31. Salem, K., Garcia-Molina, H.: Disk Striping. Proceedings of Data Engineering'86 (1986)

32. Sanders, P.: Reconciling Simplicity and Realism in Parallel Disk Models. Parallel Computing, **28** 5 (2002) 705–723. Short version in 12th SODA, (2001) 67–76

33. Sanders, P.: Asynchronous Scheduling of Redundant Disk Arrays. IEEE Transactions on Computers **52** 9 (2003) 1170-1184. Short version in 12th ACM Symposium on Parallel Algorithms and Architectures (2000) 89–98

34. Sanders, P., Egner, S., Korst, J.: Fast Concurrent Access to Parallel Disks. Algorithmica **35** 1 (2003) 21–55. Short version in 11th SODA (2000) 849–858

35. Santos, J.R., Muntz, R.R., Ribeiro-Neto, B.: Comparing Random Data Allocation and Data Striping in Multimedia Servers. In: ACM SIGMETRICS (2000) 44–55

36. Scheuermann, P., Weikum, G., Zabback, P.: Data Partitioning and Load Balancing in Parallel Disk Systems. VLDB Journal: Very Large Data Bases, **7** 1 (1998) 48–66

37. Schoenmakers, L.A.M.: A New Algorithm for the Recognition of Series Parallel Graphs. Technical Report CS-R9504, CWI – Centrum voor Wiskunde en Informatica, January 31, 1995

38. Stone, H.S., Fuller, S.F.: On the Near-Optimality of the Shortest-Access-Time-First Drum Scheduling Discipline. Communications of the ACM **16** 6 (1973) 352–353. Also published in/as: Technical Note No.12, DSL

39. Tetzlaff, W., Flynn, R.: Block Allocation in Video Servers for Availability and Throughput. Proceedings Multimedia Computing and Networking (1996)

40. Tewari, R., Mukherjee, R., Dias, D.M., Vin, H.M.: Design and Performance Trade-offs in Clustered Video Servers. Proceedings of the International Conference on Multimedia Computing and Systems (1996) 144–150

41. Vitter, J.S.: External Memory Algorithms and Data Structures: Dealing with Massive Data. ACM Computing Surveys **33** 2 (2001) 209–271

42. Vitter, J.S., Shriver, E.A.M.: Algorithms for Parallel Memory, I: Two Level Memories. Algorithmica **12** 2/3 (1994) 110–147

43. Woeginger, G.J.: When Does a Dynamic Programming Formulation Guarantee the Existence of a Fully Polynomial Time Approximation Scheme (fptas). INFORMS Journal on Computing **12** (2000) 57–75

Fuzzy Unification and Argumentation for Well-Founded Semantics

Ralf Schweimeier[1] and Michael Schroeder[1,2]

[1] Department of Computing, City University
Northampton Square, London EC1V 0HB, UK
{ralf,msch}@soi.city.ac.uk
[2] Department of Computer Science, Technische Universität Dresden
01062 Dresden, Germany

Abstract. Argumentation as metaphor for logic programming semantics is a sound basis to define negotiating agents. If such agents operate in an open system, they have to be able to negotiate and argue efficiently in a goal-directed fashion and they have to deal with uncertain and vague knowledge. In this paper, we define an argumentation framework with fuzzy unification and reasoning for the well-founded semantics to handle uncertainty. In particular, we address three main problems: how to define a goal-directed top-down proof procedure for justified arguments, which is important for agents which have to respond in real-time; how to provide expressive knowledge representation including default and explicit negation and uncertainty, which is among others part of agent communication languages such as FIPA or KQML; how to deal with reasoning in open agent systems, where agents should be able to reason despite misunderstandings.

To deal with these problems, we introduce a basic argumentation framework and extend it to cope with fuzzy reasoning and fuzzy unification. For the latter case, we develop a corresponding sound and complete top-down proof procedure.

1 Introduction

Argumentation has been widely studied as the basis for the semantics of logic programs [1], [2], [3], [4]. Basically, the execution of a logic program can be described as a dialogue of a proponent defending a goal and an opponent attacking it. Recently, argumentation has been applied to describe and define negotiation of agents [5], [6], [7], [8], [9], [10], [11]. In contrast to negotiation by auctions e.g., argumentation is a natural mechanism to negotiate about multiple criteria and to establish joint beliefs. Initial work in this area [5], [6], [7], [8] gave a proof-of-concept for arguing agents. In this paper, we want to build on this work and go a step further and address problems, which arise when trying to move from a proof-of-concept to an efficient implementation. To this end, there are three main problems, which need to be addressed:

- **Expressive knowledge representation:** At the centre of most agents is a knowledge system with an inference mechanism. This can range from a simple database to a fuzzy factbase [12], [13]. A factbase has tables to store positive and negative knowledge and as a consequence comprises two kinds of negation, explicit and default

P. Van Emde Boas et al. (Eds.): SOFSEM 2004, LNCS 2932, pp. 102–121, 2004.

negation [12]. Such expressiveness is often needed. The widely used KQML [14] for example, distinguishes $untell(A)$ from $tell(\neg A)$. To implement this KQML feature one has to represent positive and explicitly negative facts separately. Furthermore, one requires two types of negation: explicit negation to state that something is in the negative table and default negation to state that something is not in the positive table. As a result, agents compliant with this KQML-feature have to be capable to deal with a three-valued logic (true, false, unknown).

Furthermore, the agents beliefs may be fuzzy. Such a concept of uncertainty is e.g. built into FIPA ACL [15] in the form of an uncertainty operator. Since agents operate in uncertain environments and encounter fuzzy concepts, they have to be able to represent such uncertainty and fuzziness and reason about it. This applies to argumentation in particular, where the attacking arguments, which the agents exchange, may be qualified. This poses a particular problem if combined with a rich knowledge representation for positive and negative knowledge, so that explicit and default negation need to be defined for fuzzy reasoning.

- **Mismatches in open systems:** Many arguing agents will operate in open systems. This means that their knowledge and ontologies are defined by different people and will not necessarily match, leading to misunderstandings. It is doubtful [16], whether the general ontology problem of how to integrate different ontologies will be solved in the near future. Nonetheless one can aim to facilitate agent communication despite missing parameters and mismatches in the predicate and parameter names. This is especially a problem when agents interact across system boundaries or with humans.
- **Goal-directed, top-down proof procedures for justified arguments:** Previous work on arguing agents [5,6,7,8] defines justified arguments as a fixpoint of acceptable arguments. Such a definition is elegant and well-suited to define a *declarative* semantics, but it does not lend itself well for an efficient implementation needed for agents, which have to react in real-time. The reason is that the above fixpoint is computed bottom-up, which requires an agent to compute *all* justified arguments – a heavy burden when the negotiation is only about a single predicate. Agents, which are to perform in real-time, require an efficient proof-procedure. A goal-directed top-down proof procedure, which allows the agent to determine for an individual argument whether it is justified or not, satisfies this need.

In this paper, we will address these three problems by extending established approaches of unification and of well-founded semantics for extended logic programming (ELP) into two directions:

- Fuzzy Reasoning: To tackle the problem of expressive knowledge representation for argumentation, we will develop a framework for fuzzy argumentation, which comprises two kinds of negation. We have to take important decisions on how to interpret fuzziness and negation. Since we place emphasis on extending previous work, our main goal is to conservatively extend an existing semantics, namely WFSX [17], to define a *fuzzy* bottom-up argumentation semantics. Finally, we will solve the first problem of efficient computation. We will reap the benefits of using WFSX as a base semantics. In contrast to stable models [18], WFSX provides both a bottom-up fixpoint semantics and a goal-directed top-down proof procedure [17]. Therefore we are able to complement our declarative bottom-up argumentation semantics with an efficiently computable top-down proof-procedure for fuzzy argumentation.

- Fuzzy Unification: We will introduce fuzzy unification to tackle the problem of missing parameters and mismatching predicates and parameters in agent communication languages in general. While classical unification either unifies two predicates or it does not, fuzzy unification qualifies the degree of match. Our fuzzy unification is based on edit distance [19], which compares strings. To use it for unification, we will show how to normalise it and adapt it to tree structures of strings. We will extend edit distance accordingly and will prove as a general result that our fuzzy unification is a conservative extension of classical unification. Therefore it lends itself to integration for a wide variety of agent systems, which incorporate the notion of unification. As a particular instance, we will show how to embed fuzzy unification into the proof procedure and semantics for extended logic programs.

The rest of the paper is structured as follows: We will give an overview over extended logic programming, well-founded semantics, and argumentation. Next, we will extend ELP to facilitate fuzzy reasoning in section 3. Independently, we will show in section 4 how to define fuzzy unification and incorporate it into the well-founded semantics. We will conclude with a comparison to other work.

2   Background and Definitions

2.1   Knowledge Systems

Knowledge representation and logic programming can seen in the broader context of knowledge systems [12], which are based on relational databases [20]. Wagner structures the extensions of relational databases along three axes: *deduction* to cater for recursion, *negation* to capture explicitly false statements, and *fuzziness* to model vagueness [12], [21].

- **Deduction.** The standard query language for relational databases, SQL, is not Turing-complete. In particular, it lacks recursion, and therefore concepts like the transitive closure of a relation cannot be expressed in SQL. For this reason, relational databases are usually embedded in a 3-tier architecture with some high-level, Turing-complete programming language on top of SQL on the database-tier. In deductive databases, the Turing-completeness is achieved more elegantly by adding rules and deduction, which cater for recursion.
- **Negative information.** Relational databases come with a principle of "negation by default" whereby a fact is assumed to be false if it is not contained in the database. In many circumstances, however, it is desirable to state negative facts explicitly. A database with explicit negative information, also called a *factbase* [12], consists of two databases: one for positive information, and one for negative information. This modification gives rise to two concepts absent in relational databases:
  - *Undefinedness.* A fact may not be contained in either the positive or the negative database. It is then considered *unknown*, or *undefined*.

- *Inconsistency.* A fact may be contained in both the positive and the negative database, i.e. the database is inconsistent. In this case, one may be interested in methods of regaining consistency by dropping either the positive or the negative assumption.

A coherence principle may be imposed to relate explicit negation and negation by default: if a fact is explicitly false, then it is also false by default.

- **Fuzziness.** In many cases, information is not clearly defined as simply true or false. Fuzzy logic deals with this kind of imprecise information. There are two important cases of unclear information:

  - *Uncertain information.* For some concepts whose truth value is *crisp*, i.e. either true or false, there may only be uncertain, or statistical, or probabilistic evidence as to whether they are true or not. For example, a weather forecast might make a statement "there is a 70% chance of rain tomorrow"; the statement whether there is rain tomorrow is either true or false (tomorrow), but today there is no certain evidence for the truth of the statement.

  - *Fuzzy concepts.* Some concepts, such as "tall", or "cheap", are inherently fuzzy; for instance, while 7' would be "tall" for an adult male, and 5' would not, 6' might be considered "tall" to some degree.

These dimensions of knowledge systems have been examined in [12]. The aim of this article is to provide a framework for knowledge representation and reasoning encompassing these dimensions, i.e. a *fuzzy deductive factbase*, while bearing in mind the following requirements:

- It should be characterised by a declarative fixpoint argumentation semantics.
- There should be an efficient, goal-driven, top-down proof procedure.
- It should handle both fuzzy reasoning and fuzzy unification.

We will build on extended logic programming [22], [17] which combines deduction with the ability to model negative information, and extend it by fuzziness. There is already an argumentation semantics for the well-founded semantics with explicit negation, WFSX [23], as well as an efficient proof procedure [17]. Before we proceed, we will review the syntax and argumentation semantics for extended logic programs.

2.2   Extended Logic Programming and Argumentation

Prolog [24] is the language of choice for logic programming. But many knowledge representation problems require a richer language capable of expressing explicitly false statements. An example of such an extension are extended logic programs, which provide two kinds of negation: Explicit negation, which denoted by $\neg$ and default negation, which is denoted by *not*.

Definition 1. *(Extended logic program) An* objective literal *is an atom A or its explicit negation* $\neg A$. *We define* $\neg\neg L = L$. *A* default literal *is of the form* not *L where L is an objective literal. A* literal *is either an objective or a default literal.*
An extended logic program *is a (possibly infinite) set of rules of the form*

$L_0 \leftarrow L_1, \ldots, L_m, not \ L_{m+1}, \ldots, not \ L_{m+n} (m, n \geq 0),$

where each L_i is an objective literal ($0 \leq i \leq m + n$). For such a rule r, we call L_0 the head *of the rule, $head(r)$, and $L_1, \ldots, not \ L_{m+n}$ the* body *of the rule, $body(r)$. A rule with an empty body is called a* fact, *and we often write L_0 or $L_0 \leftarrow true$ instead of $L_0 \leftarrow$.*

Example 1. Consider an information agent, which can subscribe to and unsubscribe mailing lists on behalf of its user. The agent holds a list of topics interesting or uninteresting to the user. The user is not interested in anything outside computer science. Within computing, he or she likes agents and logic. The user is also not interested if the list contains any spam.

$$P = \left\{ \begin{array}{ll} int(agents) & \\ \neg int(X) \leftarrow not \ partOf(X, cs) & sub(X) \leftarrow int(X) \\ \neg int(X) \leftarrow spam(X) & \neg sub(X) \leftarrow not \ int(X) \end{array} \right.$$

Initially, well-founded models [25], [17] and stable models [18] have been put forward as a semantics that can deal with implicit and explicit negation. Later it turned out that the metaphor of argumentation [8], [5], [1], [26] is an elegant approach to capture the semantics of extended logic programs intuitively [1], [3].

In general, an argument A is a proof which may use a set of defeasible assumptions. Another argument B may have a conclusion which contradicts the assumptions or the conclusions of A, and thereby B *attacks* A.

Given a logic program we can define an argumentation semantics by iteratively collecting those arguments which are acceptable to a proponent, i.e. they can be defended against all opponent attacks. In fact, such a notion of acceptability can be defined in a number of ways depending on which attacks we allow the proponent and opponent to use.

In extended logic programs [22], [17], there exist a variety of notions of attack [23] and consequently a variety of argumentation semantics. We define a general framework first, and later use the semantics which is equivalent to the well-founded semantics with explicit negation, WFSX [17], because there is an efficient proof procedure for it [17].

Our actual definition of an argument for an extended logic program is based on [4]. Essentially, an argument is a partial proof, resting on a number of *assumptions*, i.e. a set of default literals.

Definition 2. *(Argument) Let P be an extended logic program. An* argument *for P is a finite sequence $A = [r_1, \ldots r_n]$ of ground instances of rules $r_i \in P$ such that*

- *for every $1 \leq i \leq n$, for every objective literal L_j in the body of r_i there is a $k > i$ such that $head(r_k) = L_j$.*

The head of a rule in A is called a conclusion *of A, and a default literal $not \ L$ in the body of a rule of A is called an* assumption *of A. Given an extended logic program P, we denote the set of arguments for P by $Args_P$.*

Example 2. (cont.) Consider the program P as defined above. Then

$$A_1 = [partOf(agents, cs)]$$
$$A_2 = [\neg int(agents) \leftarrow not\ partOf(agents, cs)]$$
$$A_3 = [int(agents)]$$
$$A_4 = [\neg sub(agents) \leftarrow not\ int(agents)]$$

are arguments.

There are two fundamental notions of attack: *undercut*, which invalidates an assumption of an argument, and *rebut*, which contradicts a conclusion of an argument [2], [4].

Definition 3. *(Notions of Attack) Let A_1 and A_2 be arguments. Then a notion of attack is a binary relation between arguments. We will consider the following notions of attack.*

1. *A_1 undercuts A_2 if there is an objective literal L such that L is a conclusion of A_1 and not L is an assumption of A_2. The binary relation of undercuts is denoted by* u.
2. *A_1 rebuts A_2 if there is an objective literal L such that L is a conclusion of A_1 and $\neg L$ is a conclusion of A_2.*
3. *A_1 attacks A_2 if A_1 undercuts A_2 or if A_1 rebuts A_2. The binary relation of attacks is denoted by* a.

Example 3. (cont.) Consider the arguments A_1, A_2, A_3, A_4 as defined above. Then A_1 undercuts A_2, A_2 rebuts A_3 and vice versa (as rebuts are symmetric), and A_3 undercuts A_4.

Given the above notions of attack, we define acceptability of an argument. Basically, an argument is acceptable if it can be defended against any attack. Depending on which particular notion of attack we use as defence and which for the opponent's attacks, we obtain a host of acceptability notions.

Acceptability forms the basis for our argumentation semantics, which is defined as the least fixpoint of a function, which collects all acceptable arguments. The *least* fixpoint is of particular interest [4], [2], because it provides a canonical fixpoint semantics and it can be constructed inductively.

Definition 4. *(Acceptability) Let x and y be notions of attack. Let A be an argument, and S a set of arguments. Then A is x/y-acceptable wrt. S if for every argument B such that $(B, A) \in x$ there exists an argument $C \in S$ such that $(C, B) \in y$.*

Based on the notion of acceptability, we can then define a fixpoint semantics for arguments.

Definition 5. *(Justified Arguments) Let x and y be notions of attack, and P an extended logic program. The operator $F_{P,x/y} : \mathcal{P}(Args_P) \to \mathcal{P}(Args_P)$ is defined as*

$$F_{P,x/y}(S) = \{A \mid A\ is\ x/y\text{-}acceptable\ wrt.\ S\}$$

We denote the least fixpoint of $F_{P,x/y}$ by $J_{P,x/y}$. If the program P is clear from the context, we omit the subscript P. An argument A is called x/y-justified if $A \in J_{x/y}$; an argument is called x/y-overruled if it is attacked by an x/y-justified argument; and an argument is called x/y-defensible if it is neither x/y-justified nor x/y-overruled.

Proposition 1. *For any program P, the least fixpoint exists by the Knaster-Tarski fixpoint theorem [27], [28], because $F_{P,x/y}$ is monotone. It can be constructed by transfinite induction as follows:*

$$J^0_{x/y} = \emptyset$$
$$J^{\alpha+1}_{x/y} = F_{P,x/y}(J^\alpha_{x/y}) \text{ for } \alpha + 1 \text{ a successor ordinal}$$
$$J^\lambda_{x/y} = \bigcup_{\alpha < \lambda} J^\alpha_{x/y} \quad \text{for } \lambda \text{ a limit ordinal}$$

Then there exists a least ordinal λ_0 such that $F_{x/y}(J^{\lambda_0}_{x/y}) = J^{\lambda_0}_{x/y} = J_{x/y}$.

Example 4. (cont.) Consider the arguments A_1, A_2, A_3, A_4 as defined above. Then

$$J^0_{u/a} = \emptyset$$
$$J^1_{u/a} = \{A_1, A_3\}$$
$$J^2_{u/a} = \{A_1, A_3\}$$

Thus $A_1 = [partOf(agents, cs)]$ and $A_3 = [int(agents)]$ are justified. Since they attack $A_2 = [\neg int(agents) \leftarrow not\ partOf(agents, cs)]$ and $A_4 = [\neg sub(agents) \leftarrow not\ int(agents)]$, these two are overruled.

It is shown in [23] that the argumentation semantics $J_{u/a}$ (where an argument is acceptable if every undercut can be attacked) is equivalent to the well-founded semantics with explicit negation, WFSX [17]. This is of particular importance, because an efficient, goal-directed, top-down proof procedure, SLX [29], exists for WFSX. Because of the equivalence of WFSX and our argumentation semantics, this proof procedure can be used to compute justified arguments. When we extend our argumentation framework with fuzziness, we will build on SLX to obtain sound and complete proof procedures.

3   Fuzzy Reasoning

We will now define a logic programming language suitable for implementing a fuzzy deductive factbase, i.e. given a deductive factbase as sketched in the previous section, we extend it and move to a fuzzy deductive factbase. It has two kinds of negation, explicit negation for specifying falsity of a fact explicitly, and implicit negation for deriving information under the assumption of falsity of a fact. Uncertain information may be specified by assigning a fuzzy truth value to a fact. In accordance with the database view, we do not allow rules to have a fuzzy truth value.

Definition 6. *(Strength of a fact) Let P be an extended logic program and $L \leftarrow true$ a fact in P. Then $str(L \leftarrow true)$ denotes the fuzzy truth value of the fact L, where $0 \leq str(L \leftarrow true) \leq 1$. For convenience, we will sometimes also write $L : V$, where $V = str(L \leftarrow true)$. A fact with a fuzzy truth value is also called a fuzzy fact.*

Example 5. (Cont.) The user qualifies his or her interest in agents to be 80% relevant. Also the topic agents is not solely part of computer science and the uncertainty of spam is 20%:

$$int(agents) : 80\%$$
$$partOf(agents, cs) : 70\%$$
$$spam(agents) : 20\%$$

When defining fuzzy extended logic programming, there are three main issues:

- How is the fuzzy truth value of negated literals defined?
- How can the fuzzy truth value of a justified conclusion be derived in a goal-driven, top-down manner?
- How can backward compatibility to existing approaches be maintained?

Starting with the last requirement, we take the important decision to use WFSX as a base semantics for fuzzy argumentation, as WFSX is established and as there is a proof procedure for WFSX. As we shall see this decision has important implications for the interpretation of fuzziness and negation.

3.1 Fuzzy Negation

In a fuzzy version of extended logic programming, literals are assigned truth values in the interval $[0, 1]$, rather than simply *true* (1) or *false* (0). To define conjunction and disjunction, we use the standard fuzzy definitions via minimum and maximum, respectively. The main problem is then to find a suitable fuzzy semantics for the two kinds of negation. The standard definition of fuzzy negation according to Zadeh [30] is given by

$$A : V \text{ implies } \neg A : 1 - V \tag{1}$$

In our setting this does not work: WFSX is para-consistent, i.e. positive and negative information is independent of each other. When arguing there can be both evidence for and against A. Thus, it does not make sense to define the truth value of an explicit negation $\neg A$ by the truth value of A, as it would mean that positive information takes precedence over negative information. In fact, in the WFSX semantics, the only connection between an explicit negation $\neg A$ and A is indirect via the coherence principle, relating explicit and implicit negation.

$$\neg A \text{ implies } not\ A \tag{2}$$

3.2 Coherence Principle

The coherence principle of WFSX states that if there is evidence that A does not hold, then it should also be assumed by default that A does not hold.

In a fuzzy setting, where formulas have truth values in $[0, 1]$, there are various ways of stating the coherence principle, depending on what is understood by the statement "A holds". If by "A holds", we mean that A has a truth value greater than 0, then the coherence principle can be generally stated as

$$\neg A : V, V > 0 \text{ implies } not\ A : V', V' \geq V \tag{3}$$

This version of the coherence principle does not yet provide a definition of the truth value of an implicit negation $not\ A$ from the truth value of the explicit negation $\neg A$; there are two extreme cases of such a definition which comply with the fuzzy coherence principle (3).

$$\neg A : V, V > 0 \text{ implies } not\ A : 1 \tag{4}$$

This version states that implicit negation is always the extreme case of explicit negation: as long as there is any explicit evidence that A does not hold, then A does *definitely* not hold by default.

$$\neg A : V, V > 0 \text{ implies } not\ A : V \tag{5}$$

This version states a weak connection between explicit and implicit negation: if there is some explicit evidence that A does not hold, then A does not hold by default, with the same degree of evidence.

All of the above three interpretations are valid in principle. However, there are arguments in favour of equation (4). The reason is that default negation is defined indirectly. Without explicit negation, positive information is given precedence over default negation, i.e. if there is the slightest evidence for L ($L : V, V > 0$) then *not* L should not hold (*not* $L : 0$). Applying this principle to explicit negation one arrives at equation (4), i.e. the slightest evidence for $\neg L$ ($\neg L : V, V > 0$) then *not* L should hold (*not* $L : 1$). The interpretation is in line with [21] and we will use it to define the argumentation semantics and proof procedure. But we will also indicate how to realise equation (5).

Example 6. (Cont.) Since $spam(agents) : 20\%$, the agent can derive $\neg int(agents) : 20\%$, despite the fact that $int(agents) : 70\%$. Which conclusion should be drawn *not* $int(agents)$ and subsequently $\neg sub(agents)$? As explained above, explicitly negative information takes precedence over positive information, hence avoiding spam gets highest priority. Following equation (4), *not* $int(agents) : 1$ and subsequently $\neg sub(agents) : 1$ is concluded, whereas equation (5), leads to *not* $int(agents) : 20\%$ and subsequently $\neg sub(agents) : 20\%$.

3.3 Fuzzy Argumentation

Having made these decisions on how to interpret fuzzy negation, it is now easy to extend the argumentation framework with fuzzy reasoning. The existing definitions of arguments do not have to be adapted, we only add on top of them a definition of strength, which extends the fuzzy truth values given for facts to rules and arguments.

Definition 7. *(Strength) Let P be an extended logic program, let $str(L \leftarrow true)$ be the strength of fuzzy facts $L \leftarrow true \in P$, and let A be an argument. Then the strength $str(r, A)$ of a rule r in A is defined inductively as:*

- *Fact: $str(r, A) = str(L \leftarrow true)$, if $r = L \leftarrow true$ is a fuzzy fact*
- *Rule: $str(r, A) = min\{str(r_{i_1}, A), \ldots, str(r_{i_n}, A)\}$, if*

$$r = L \leftarrow L_1, \ldots, L_n, not\ L_{n+1}, \ldots, not\ L_{n+m}$$

is a rule, where r_{i_k} is the rule in A with conclusion L_k.

Based on the strength of a rule, we define:

- *Argument: The strength $str(A)$ of a non-empty argument $A = [r_1, \ldots, r_n]$ is defined as $str(A) = str(r_1, A)$.*

– *Conclusion: The strength $str(L)$ of an objective literal L is defined as the maximum strength of all justified argument for L, i.e.*

$$str(L) = max\{str(A) \mid A \text{ is a justified argument for } L\}$$

The strength of a default literal is 1 if L is not justified or equal to the maximum strength of any justified argument for $\neg L$, i.e.

$$str(not\ L) = \begin{cases} 1 \text{ if } L \text{ is not justified} \\ max\{str(A) \mid A \text{ is a justified argument for } \neg L\} \text{ else} \end{cases}$$

Example 7. (Cont.) With the above definitions, we can compute the strength of justified arguments (a stands for $agents$). For example:

$$str(\neg sub(a)) = max\{str([\neg sub(a) \leftarrow not\ int(a)])\} = 1$$

$$str(\neg int(a)) = max\{str([\neg int(a) \leftarrow spam(a); spam(a) : 20\%])\} = 20\%$$

As argued above the definition of strength implements the interpretation of fuzzy negation put forward in equation (4). To implement equation (5) instead one needs to consider the minimal strength of all body literals of a rule.

In this setting, fuzzy truth values are simply a layer on top of the existing non-fuzzy reasoning process. It is therefore straightforward to extend the proof procedure for WFSX [29] to compute the strength of an argument. We omit it here, and instead present the slightly more involved proof procedure for fuzzy unification and argumentation in detail.

4 Fuzzy Unification

Fuzzy reasoning is important to reason about vague and uncertain concepts and information. However, in open systems there is an additional problem of misunderstandings between agents: predicates and terms may be missing or mismatch. Fuzzy unification addresses this problem by introducing a degree of unification ranging from a full match to a complete mismatch. As such, it is a concept of value for any agent architecture resting on a knowledge system and communication. It can readily be integrated into any system which deploys for example KQML or FIPA ACL. To use our fuzzy unification, an agent system only needs a knowledge system, which caters for fuzziness. To show how this can in principle be done, we develop this concept and embed our fuzzy unification in the argumentation framework introduced in section 2, which in turn is an example of a negotiation mechanism as specified in e.g. FIPA ACL call-for-proposals speech act.

Earlier we defined the syntax of extended logic programs resting on the notion of atoms. To define fuzzy unification we have to define what an atom is.

Definition 8. *(String) Symbols are strings, where a string is either the empty string ϵ or a string $a.A$, where a is a character and A is a string. $|A|$ denotes the length of A.*

Definition 9. *(Atom) Let V be a set of variable names, F a set of function symbols and P a set of predicate symbols. Both F and P include a unique empty function/predicate symbol ϵ.*

The set of terms is defined inductively. Every variable $x \in V$ is a term. Let $f \in F$ be a function symbol of arity n (if $n = 0$, f is also called a constant) and $t_1, \ldots, t_n$ terms, then $f(t_1, \ldots, t_n)$ is a term. Nothing else is a term. Let $p \in P$ be a predicate symbol of arity n and $t_1, \ldots, t_n$ terms, then $p(t_1, \ldots, t_n)$ is an atom.

Note that our definition of an atom differs from the standard definition in that we include an empty function and predicate symbol. Thus there exists a empty term ϵ. We treat $\epsilon(f(a))$ as equivalent to $f(a)$.

Definition 10. *(Unifier [31]) A substitution is a replacement of variables by terms. A substitution sub is a unifier of two literals L, L' if $L sub = L' sub$. A unifier sub of L, L' is the most general unifier (MGU) of L, L' if for every other unifier sub' of L, L' there is a substitution s, such that $sub' = sub\ s$.*

The MGU can be computed using Robinson's unification algorithm [31].

Example 8. The predicates $subscribe(x)$ and $subscribe(agents)$ unify and the MGU is $[x/agents]$. For various reasons all of the following predicates do not unify:

- $subscribe(x)$ and $subscribe(f(x))$, because x occurs in $f(x)$, which would lead to a circular substitution;
- $subscribe(agents)$ and $subscribe(agents, digest)$ as the predicates do not have the same number of parameters;
- $subscribe(agents)$ and $subskribes(agents)$ as the predicate names slightly mismatch;
- $subscribe(agents)$ and $subscribe(agent)$ as the terms slightly mismatch.

In classical unification predicates unify or they do not; we introduce a degree of unification ranging from a complete match (degree 0) as in classical unification to a complete mismatch (degree 1). Previous work by Arcelli, Formato, and Gerla developed a general abstract framework for fuzzy unification, quotient unification, and unification as negotiation [32]. In this paper, we use an alternative approach for fuzzy unification based on edit distance [33]. The concept of edit distance has a well established history dating back to the 60s and 70s [19] and is still widely used, for example, in bioinformatics to compare genomic sequences. The edit distance between two strings A and B is defined as the minimal number of delete, add, and replace operations to convert A into B. The basic principle of edit distance is well-understood, but to employ it for fuzzy unification there are three requirements:

First, a normalisation is required to be able to compare strings independent of their size. A few mismatches of short strings can be worse than some mismatches of two long strings. Second, the definition of edit distance has to be extended to deal with general tree structures representing the predicates and terms to be compared. Third, for compatibility reasons fuzzy unification should be an extension of classical unification.

4.1 Edit Distance

In this section, we set out to broaden the principles of unification to encompass fuzzy matches of predicate and function symbols and to deal with mismatching arguments. We need a comparison measure to define how similar two symbols are. As argued above, edit distance is a suitable basis for this purpose. Alternatively to defining edit distance as the minimal number of add, delete, and replace operations to transform one string into another, one can define it recursively comparing two strings by either dropping one of the two or both first characters of the strings at a penalty of 1 or to drop the two with no penalty if they match.

Definition 11. *(Edit Distance) Let A, B be strings and a, b characters, then*

$$e(A, \epsilon) = e(\epsilon, A) \ = \ |A|$$
$$e(a.A, b.B) = min\{e(A, b.B) + 1, \quad e(a.A, B) + 1,$$
$$e(A, B) + 1, \quad e(A, B) \ if \ a = b \ \}$$

Example 9. $e(subscribe, subskribes) = 2$ and $e(sub, abb) = 2$.

Although the first example has seven letters in common and the second only one, both edit distances amount to 2. Therefore, there is a need to normalise edit distance to judge the penalties for mismatches relative to the size of the strings. Such a normalised edit distance should range between 0 (no matches) to 1 (no mismatches).

Definition 12. *(Normalised Edit Distance) Let A, B be strings and at least one of them non-empty, then*

$$ne(A, B) = \frac{e(A, B)}{max(|A|, |B|)}$$

is the normalised edit distance.

Example 10. With normalisation, we obtain

$$ne(subscribe, subskribes) = \frac{2}{10} = 0.2 \text{ and } ne(sub, abb) = \frac{2}{3} = 0.\bar{6}$$

4.2 Fuzzy Unification

While normalised edit distance is well suited to compare symbols, we want to deal with predicates and terms, which have a tree structure. Therefore, we have to extend our definition. It is very important that for the purpose of comparison there is no difference between a tree structure of a predicate and of terms. Hence, we do not distinguish between predicate and function symbols, and in the remainder t often denotes both a predicate or a term. Please note also that we include the empty symbol ϵ as predicate or function symbol and we do not distinguish between $\epsilon(t)$ and t for a term t.

To define fuzzy unification, we have to recursively traverse the tree representing the predicates and terms. In Definition 13 of edit distance over trees et, the first returned parameter is the number of mismatches, the penalty; the second is the accumulated substitution; the third is a factor for normalisation: the sum of the maximal nodes of the pairwise node comparisons in the recursive traversal. But let us consider this recursive definition in detail: Any term perfectly mismatches the empty symbol, which is penalised with the maximum value - the size of the term. Two variables as well as a variable and a term perfectly match, which is captured by a fuzzy factor of 0 and the corresponding substitutions. Note that for the latter an occurs check is performed. Predicate or function symbols do not contain any further structure and therefore their fuzzy unification factor is given by the edit distance e. For the purpose of normalisation we use here the maximum length of the two symbols. In the core of the definition, we reduce two predicates or terms t, t' and call the edit distance over trees recursively. To the edit distance of the leading predicate or function symbol we add the minimum distance after dropping the first term(s) and adding the penalty of the dropped term(s). Thus, the definition compares terms from left to right dropping terms of either t, t', or both t and t'. The result of this decompositions are added up using $\oplus$, which adds numbers and concatenates substitutions.

Definition 13. *(Fuzzy Unification) Let $t = f(t_1, \ldots, t_n)$ and $t' = f'(t'_1, \ldots, t'_m)$ be two terms or predicates, and let $x, y \in V$ be variables. The size of a term or predicate is defined as: $size(x) = size(\epsilon) = 0$, $size(f) = |f|$, and $size(f(t_1, \ldots, t_n)) = |f| + \sum_{i=1,\ldots,n} size(t_i)$.*

The edit distance over trees et maps two terms or predicate to a tuple of the number of mismatches, a unifier, and a normalisation factor

$$et(t, \epsilon) = (size(t), [], size(t))$$
$$et(x, y) = (0, [x/y], 0)$$
$$et(x, t) = (0, [x/t], 0) \text{ if } x \text{ not in } t \text{ and } t \notin V$$
$$et(f, f') = (e(f, f'), [], max\{|f|, |f'|\})$$
$$et(t, t') = et(f, f') \oplus min_v\{$$
$$et((t_2, \ldots, t_n), (t'_1, \ldots, t'_m)) \oplus et(t_1, \epsilon),$$
$$et((t_1, \ldots, t_n), (t'_2, \ldots, t'_m)) \oplus et(t'_1, \epsilon),$$
$$et((t_2, \ldots, t_n), (t'_2, \ldots, t'_m)) \oplus et(t_1, t'_1)\}$$

where $(u, s, n) \oplus (u', s', n') = (u + u', s\,s', n + n')$ and min_u returns the triple with minimal first component.
et is called edit distance over trees. The normalised edit distance over trees $net(t, t') = (\frac{u}{n}, s)$ with $(u, s, n) = et(t, t')$ is called fuzzy unification. For convenience, we often use net to refer only to its first component.

Example 11. Consider example 8, where unification failed because of mismatching predicate and function symbols or missing parameters. With fuzzy unification, we obtain

$$net(\,subscribe(agents),\ subscribe(agents, digest)\,) = \frac{6}{9 + 6 + 6} = \frac{2}{7} = 0.29$$

as the argument $digest$ cannot be matched,

$$net(\,subscribe(agents),\ subskribes(agents)\,) = \frac{2}{10 + 6} = \frac{1}{8} = 0.125$$

as the predicate names mismatch;

$$net(\ subscribe(agents), subscribe(agent)\ ) = \frac{1}{9+6} = 0.0\bar{6}$$

as the terms slightly mismatch.

Fuzzy unification lifts the normalisation by maximum size of the compared strings as introduced for the simple edit distance to the level of terms and predicates with a tree representation. An alternative to adding all mismatches and then normalising by the pairwise maximum length of the compared nodes is a direct normalisation of compared nodes using ne and then redefining $\oplus$ to take the average. This has however the disadvantage of favouring short mismatches of parameters (see e.g. example 9, 10), which our above definition does not suffer from.

With the definition of net in place we can prove some of its properties.

Theorem 1. *Fuzzy unification is a conservative extension of unification, i.e. if s is an MGU for literals L, L', then $(0, s)$ is a fuzzy unifier for L, L'.*

Proof (Sketch). Literals L and L' unify iff all predicate and function symbols all variables in L and L' respectively have edit distance 0.

4.3 Fuzzy Unification and Argumentation

To embed fuzzy unification into our argumentation framework we have to replace unification by fuzzy unification. Unification appears at two stages: once when rules are "chained" together to form an argument and once when arguments attack each other. Let us consider this in detail.

- Arguments as introduced in Definition 2 are partial proofs, where for every objective literal L in the body of a rule r_i there is a $k > i$ such that $L = head(r_k)$. This unification of L and the head of r_k needs to be replaced by fuzzy unification.
- Attacks between arguments require the literals involved to unify. We will relax this requirement to fuzzy unification.

Definition 14. *(Fuzzily Unified Argument) Let P be an extended logic program, and $0 < U \leq 1$ a maximum unification value, which needs to be met for two literals to unify ($U = 0$ is a complete match, $U = 1$ a complete mismatch). A fuzzily unifying argument for P of maximum unification value U is a finite sequence $A = [r_1, \ldots r_n]$ of ground instances of rules $r_i \in P$ such that*

- *for every $1 \leq i \leq n$, for every objective literal L in the body of r_i there is a $k > i$ such that $net(L, head(r_k)) \leq U$.*

We say that A's unification value is U', where $U' \leq U$ is the minimal maximal unification value for which A still fuzzily unifies.

Example 12. (Cont.) Consider the program

$$subscribe(agent) \leftarrow interest(agents). \qquad\qquad interesting(agents).$$

Let the maximal unification value be $U = 0.01$, then there is no fuzzily unifying argument. If we increase this value to $U = 0.2$ e.g., then

$$A = [subscribe(agent) \leftarrow interest(agents); interesting(agents)]$$

is a fuzzily unifying argument. Indeed, A has unification value $U' = 0.177$.

Since the only difference between an argument as defined in Definition 2 and a fuzzily unified argument is the replacement of unification by fuzzy unification, we will use the two terms interchangeably. This applies in particular to all definitions of section 2 using arguments. Next, we have to adapt the notions of attack.

Definition 15. *(Fuzzily Unifying Attacks) Let P be an extended logic program, and $0 < U \leq 1$ a unification value. Let A_1 and A_2 be arguments, then*

- *A_1 fu-undercuts A_2 iff A_1 has a consequent L and A_2 has an assumption not L', and $net(L, L') \leq U$. The binary relation of fu-undercuts is denoted by* fu-u.
- *A_1 fu-rebuts A_2 iff A_1 has a consequence L and A_2 has a consequence $\neg L'$, and $net(L, L') \leq U$.*
- *A_1 fu-attacks A_2 iff A_1 fu-undercuts or fu-rebuts A_2. The binary relation of fu-attacks is denoted by* fu-a.

Example 13. Let $U = 0.1$ be a unification value, then argument
$A = [subscribe(agents) \leftarrow interest(agents), not\ spam(agents); interest(agents)]$
is fu-undercut by the argument $B = [spam(agent)]$, since

$$net(spam(agents), spam(agent)) = \frac{1}{4 + 6} = 0.1$$

If U is lowered to, say, 0.01, the undercut does not apply any longer.

With the definition of arguments and notions of attack adapted to fuzzy unification all other definitions (acceptability, justified argument) stay the same. Thus we have a declarative definition for an argumentation process with fuzzy unification. In the next section we adapt the proof procedure accordingly.

4.4 Proof Procedure

We modify the proof procedure for WFSX [29], [17] to compute fu-u/fu-a-justified arguments. The proof procedures is based on trees: in a T-tree a literal is proved *true*, while in a TU-tree a literal is proved *not false*. The modified T/TU-trees need to capture the fuzzy unification of literals. We achieve this by labelling nodes with pairs of literals (L, L'), where L is the literal we are seeking to expand and L' is a suitable matching literal, so that the fuzzy unification of L and L' is less than the required maximum.

Definition 16. *(Fuzzily Unifying T-tree, TU-tree) Let P be a ground extended logic program and $0 < U \leq 1$ a unification value. A fuzzily unifying T-tree (resp. TU-tree) of maximum unification value U for a literal L is an and-tree whose nodes are labelled by pairs of literals (L', L''), where L'' is undefined if the node is a leaf; the first component of the label of the root is L. Fuzzily Unifying T-trees (resp. TU-trees) are constructed top-down starting from the root by successively expanding new nodes using the following rules:*

1. *If n is a node whose first label is an objective literal L, then*
   - *if there is a rule $L' \leftarrow L_1, \ldots, L_m, \text{not } L_{m+1}, \ldots, \text{not } L_n$ in P such that $net(L, L') \leq U$, then*
     - *n is labelled (L, L') and*
     - *the successors of n are nodes with first label $(L_1, \ldots, L_m, \text{not } L_{m+1}, \ldots, \text{not } L_n)$ in a fuzzily unifying T-tree,*
     - *while in a fuzzily unifying TU-tree there are, additionally, the successor nodes with first label $(\text{not } \neg L_1, \ldots, \text{not } \neg L_m)$*
   - *If no rule for L' with $net(L, L') \leq U$ exists, then n is a leaf, with the second label undefined.*
2. *Nodes whose first labels are default literals are leaves, and their second label is undefined.*

Definition 17. *(Successful or failed tree) A fuzzily unifying T- or TU-tree with maximum unification value $0 < U \leq 1$ is either successful with unification value $U < U'$, or it fails. All infinite trees are failed. A tree is successful with unification value U' (resp. failed) if its root is successful with unification value U' (resp. failed). Nodes are marked as follows:*

1. *A leaf whose first label is an objective literal, and whose second label is undefined is failed.*
2. *A leaf labelled with a default literal not L is successful with unification value 0 in a fuzzily unifying T-tree (TU-tree) if*
   a) *all fuzzily unifying TU-trees (T-trees) for L are failed, or*
   b) *if there is a successful fuzzily unifying T-tree for $\neg L$.*
   Otherwise it is labelled as failed.
3. *An intermediate node n of a fuzzily unifying T-tree (TU-tree) is successful with unification value U' if its children $t_1, \ldots, t_m$ are successful with unification values $U'_1, \ldots, U'_m$, and $U' = max\{U'_1, \ldots, U'_m\}$. It is failed otherwise.*

All remaining nodes are labelled failed in fuzzily unifying T-trees and successful with unification value 0 in fuzzily unifying TU-trees.

The following theorem states that the proof procedure is sound and complete.

Theorem 2. *T/TU-trees and justified arguments. Let $0 < U \leq 1$, P a ground, possibly infinite, extended logic program, and L an objective literal. Then*

- *There exists a successful fuzzily unifying T-tree for L with maximal unification value U iff there exists a justified fuzzily unifying argument for L with maximal unification value U.*

- *There exists a successful fuzzily unifying TU-tree for L with maximal unification value U iff there exists a fuzzily unifying argument for L with maximal unification value U, which is not overruled.*

Proof (Sketch). First, note that fuzzily unifying T-trees with root labelled L are in one-to-one correspondence with arguments for L; fuzzily unifying TU-trees for L are in one-to-one correspondence with arguments for L, where in each rule each body literal L' is complemented by $not \neg L'$. For successful trees, the unification value of the tree is equal to the unification value a justified argument.

We define the *rank* of a fuzzily unifying T/TU-tree as the number of alterations between T-trees and TU-trees in an attempt to show that the tree is successful. Similarly, we define two kinds of rank for arguments: the *T-rank* of an argument is defined as the number of undercuts and counter-attacks in establishing that an argument is justified. The *TU-rank* of an argument is defined as the number of attacks and counter-undercuts in establishing that an argument is defensible. Note that ranks of trees and arguments may be infinite.

The proof is then by induction on the rank of a tree, showing that successful fuzzily unifying T-trees of rank n correspond to justified arguments of T-rank n, and successful TU-trees of rank n correspond to arguments of TU-rank n which are not overruled.

A successful fuzzily unifying T-tree of rank n depends on the failure of fuzzily unifying TU-trees of rank $< n$; these correspond exactly to the undercuts (of rank $< n$) to the corresponding argument (of rank n); this is equivalent to saying that all undercuts are overruled (by induction hypothesis), i.e. the argument is justified.

Similarly, a successful fuzzily unifying TU-tree of rank n depends on the failure of fuzzily unifying T-trees of rank $< n$, corresponding exactly to undercuts *and* rebuts (of rank $< n$); this is equivalent to saying that no attack is justified (by induction hypothesis), i.e. the argument is not overruled.

Having established the relationship between the declarative argumentation semantics and the operational characterisation by proof trees, we can now turn to the important result that both are conservative extensions of th well-founded semantics for extended logic programs [17]:

Theorem 3. *There exists a successful T-tree (TU-tree) for L iff there exists a successful fuzzily unifying T-tree (TU-tree) for L of maximal unification value $U = 0$.*

Proof. Follows immediately from the definition of justified arguments with fuzzy unification, and from Theorem 1.

5   Comparison

We have presented a framework for fuzzy unification and argumentation, which caters for both a declarative and an operational semantics, which provides expressive knowledge representation with explicit negative information and fuzzy values, and which uses the latter to cope with mismatches of parameters and missing parameters, which is vital for open agent systems. Our argumentation framework relates to two strands of research, namely argumentation as a paradigm for logic programming semantics and argumentation as a paradigm for negotiating agents.

Argumentation and logic programming: Regarding logic programming our approach is based on earlier work by Bondarenko et. al. [1], Dung [2], Prakken and Sartor [4], and Pereira et. al. [17]. A variety of argumentation semantics for logic programming with default negation was proposed by [1] and related to existing semantics. This work was applied to extended logic programming by [2], [4]. In [23], a general hierarchy of different argumentation semantics for extended logic programming is presented, and a particular argumentation semantics equivalent to WFSX [17] is identified. It is this semantics which we base the present work on, mainly because there exists an efficient proof procedure for WFSX [29].

Fuzzy unification: Our fuzzy unification is closely related to Arcelli, Formato, Gerla [32], who develop an abstract framework for fuzzy unification and resolution. There are important differences: First, [32] does not allow unification of predicates of different arity, which is however a problem often occurring in Prolog programming [34]. Second, [32] is not an extension of classical unification, which is important for compatibility reasons. Third, our work is based on a specific similarity measure, namely edit distance [19]. For our interpreter we need a normalised edit distance over trees. Although there has been some work on normalised edit distance [35], we had to modify this work because it does not deal with tree structures.

Argumentation for negotiating agents: A number of authors [5], [6], [7], [8], [9], [10], [11] work on argumentation for negotiating agents. In line with [9] and unlike [6], [7], [8] we base our work on logic programming. A particular aim of our work is to show how to define arguing agents with a rich knowledge representation language and still be able to define goal-directed, top-down proof procedures. This is vital when implementing systems, which need to react in real-time and therefore cannot afford to compute *all* justified arguments, as would be required when a bottom-up argumentation semantics would be used.

As in [11], our fuzzy argumentation framework can be extended to reasoning with multiple agents by introducing multiple contexts.

6 Conclusion

To summarise, the main contributions of this paper are as follows:

- We designed a fuzzy argumentation framework which caters for an expressive knowledge representation including explicit and default negation and fuzzy truth values. We discussed the problem of defining fuzzy truth values in the light of negation and chose an interpretation, which allowed us to conservatively extend WFSX. As argued in the introduction, explicit negation is e.g. required in KQML and the ability to deal with uncertainty in FIPA. Thus our framework is a good basis for agent communication languages.
- We developed fuzzy unification to deal with a problem in open systems: how to interact in the light of missing parameters and mismatches in parameters and predicates. We realised fuzzy unification as normalised edit-distance over trees. Our approach is a conservative extension of classical unification and thus lends itself to

be easily incorporated into any open agent system, which uses unification. As an example, we showed how to incorporate it into the above argumentation framework, by conservatively extending WFSX.
- Our argumentation frameworks provides both a sound theoretical basis and an efficient implementation. The former is achieved through a declarative bottom-up fixpoint semantics, the latter through a goal-directed, top-down proof procedure.

Acknowledgment. We would like to thank David Gilbert for discussion on fuzzy unification.

References

1. Bondarenko, A., Dung, P., Kowalski, R., Toni, F.: An Abstract, Argumentation-Theoretic Approach to Default Reasoning. Artificial Intelligence **93** (1997) 63–101
2. Dung, P.M.: An Argumentation Semantics for Logic Programming with Explicit Negation. In: Proc. of the 10th International Conference on Logic Programming, MIT Press (1993) 616–630
3. Dung, P.M.: On the Acceptability of Arguments and Its Fundamental Role in Nonmonotonic Reasoning, Logic Programming and n-Person Games. Artificial Intelligence **77** (1995) 321–357
4. Prakken, H., Sartor, G.: Argument-Based Extended Logic Programming with Defeasible Priorities. Journal of Applied Non-Classical Logics **7** (1997) 25–75
5. Kraus, S., Sycara, K., Evenchik, A.: Reaching Agreements through Argumentation: A Logical Model and Implementation. Artificial Intelligence **104** (1998) 1-69
6. Parsons, S., Jennings, N.: Negotiation through Argumentation-a Preliminary Report. In: Proc. Second Int. Conf. on Multi-Agent Systems, Kyoto, Japan (1996) 267–274
7. Sierra, C., Jennings, N., Noriega, P., Parsons, S.: A Framework for Argumentation-Based Negotiation. In: Proc. Fourth Int. Workshop on Agent Theories, Architectures and Languages (ATAL-97), Springer-Verlag (1997) 167–182
8. Parsons, S., Sierra, C., Jennings, N.: Agents that Reason and Negotiate by Arguing. Journal of Logic and Computation **8** (1998) 261–292
9. Sadri, F., Toni, F., Torroni, P.: Logic Agents, Dialogue, Negotiation - An Abductive Approach. In: Proceedings of the AISB Symposium on Information Agents for E-commerce (2001)
10. Torroni, P.: A Study on the Termination of Negotiation Dialogues. In: Proceedings of Autonomous Agents and Multi Agent Systems 2002, ACM Press (2002) 1223–1230
11. Schroeder, M.: An Efficient Argumentation Framework for Negotiating Autonomous Agents. In: Proceedings of Modelling Autonomous Agents in a Multi-Agent World MAAMAW99, LNAI 1647, Springer-Verlag (1999)
12. Wagner, G.: Foundations of Knowledge Systems with Applications to Databases and Agents. Kluwer Academic Publishers (1998)
13. Schroeder, M., Wagner, G.: Vivid Agents: Theory, Architecture, and Applications. Journal of Applied Artificial Intelligence **14** (2000) 64-5-676
14. Finin, T., Fritzson, R., McKay, D., e, R.M.: KQML as an Agent Communication Lanugage. In: Proceedings of the Third International Conference on Informati on and Knowledge Management (CIKM'94), ACM Press (1994) 456–463
15. Chiariglione, L., et al.: Specification Version 2.0. Technical Report, Foundations of Intelligent Physical Agents (1997) http://www.fipa.org

16. Nwana, H., Ndumu, D.: A Perspective on Software Agents Research. The Knowledge Engineering Review **14** (1999) 125–142
17. Alferes, J.J., Pereira, L.M.: Reasoning with Logic Programming. (LNAI 1111), Springer-Verlag (1996)
18. Gelfond, M., Lifschitz, V.: The Stable Model Semantics for Logic Programming. In: Kowalski, R.A., Bowen, K.A. (eds.): 5th International Conference on Logic Programming. MIT Press (1988) 1070–1080
19. Levenshtein, V.: Binary Codes Capable of Correcting Deletions, Insertions, and Reversals. Doklady Akademii nauk SSSR (in Russian) **163** (1965) 845–848 Also in Cybernetics and Control Theory **10** 8 (1996) 707–710
20. Codd, E.F.: A Relational Model of Data for Large Shared Data Banks. Communications of the ACM **13** (1970) 377–387
21. Wagner, G.: Negation in Fuzzy and Possibilistic Logic Programs. In: Logic Programming and Soft Computing. Research Studies Press (1998)
22. Gelfond, M., Lifschitz, V.: Logic Programs with Classical Negation. In: Proc. of ICLP90, MIT Press (1990) 579–597
23. Schweimeier, R., Schroeder, M.: A Parametrised Hierarchy of Argumentation Semantics for Extended Logic Programming and Its Application to the Well-Founded Semantics. Theory and Practice of Logic Programming (2004) To appear.
24. Sterling, L., Shapiro, E.: The Art of Prolog. MIT Press (1986)
25. van Gelder, A., Ross, K.A., Schlipf, J.S.: The Well-Founded Semantics for General Logic Programs. Journal of the ACM **38** (1991) 620–650
26. Chesñevar, C.I., Maguitman, A.G., Loui, R.P.: Logical Models of Argument. ACM Computing Surveys **32** (2000) 337–383
27. Tarski, A.: A Lattice-Theoretical Fixpoint Theorem and Its Applications. Pacific Journal of Mathematics **5** (1955) 285–309
28. Birkhoff, G.: Lattice Theory. 3rd edn. American Mathematical Society (1967)
29. Alferes, J.J., Damásio, C.V., Pereira, L.M.: A Logic Programming System for Non-Monotonic Reasoning. Journal of Automated Reasoning **14** (1995) 93–147
30. Zadeh, L.: A Theory of Approximate Reasoning. Machine Intelligence **9** (1979) 149 194
31. Robinson, J.A.: A Machine Oriented Logic Based on the Resolution Principle. Journal of the ACM **12** (1965) 23–42
32. Fontana, F.A., Formato, F., Gerla, G.: Fuzzy Unification as a Foundation of Fuzzy Logic Programming. In: Logic Programming and Soft Computing. Research Studies Press (1998) 51–68
33. Gilbert, D., Schroeder, M.: FURY: Fuzzy Unification and Resolution Based on Edit Distance. In: Proc. 1st International Symposium on Bioinformatics and Biomedical Engineering (2000) 330–336
34. Fung, P., Brayshaw, M., du Boulay, B., Elsom-Cook, M.: Towards a Taxonomy of Misconceptions of the Prolog Interpreter. In: Brna, P., du Boulay, B., Pain, H. (eds.): Learning to Build and Comprehend Complex Information Structures: Prolog as a Case Study. Ablex (1999)
35. Vidal, E., Marzal, A., Aibar, P.: Fast Computation of Normalized Edit Distances. IEEE Transactions on Pattern Analysis and Machine Intelligence **17** (1995) 899–902

Tree Signatures and Unordered XML Pattern Matching

Pavel Zezula[1], Federica Mandreoli[2], and Riccardo Martoglia[2]

[1] Masaryk University, Brno, Czech Republic
zezula@fi.muni.cz
[2] University of Modena and Reggio Emilia, Modena, Italy
{mandreoli.federica, martoglia.riccardo}@unimo.it

Abstract. We propose an efficient approach for finding relevant XML data twigs defined by unordered query tree specifications. We use the tree signatures as the index structure and find qualifying patterns through integration of structurally consistent query path qualifications. An efficient algorithm is proposed and its implementation tested on real-life data collections.

1 Introduction

With the rapidly increasing popularity of XML for data representation, there is a lot of interest in query processing over data that conform to the *labelled-tree* data model. The idea behind evaluating tree pattern queries, sometimes called the *twig queries*, is to find all existing ways of embedding the pattern in the data. Since XML data collections can be very large, efficient evaluation techniques for tree pattern matching are needed.

From the formal point of view, XML data objects can be seen as ordered labelled trees. Following this model, previous approaches considered also the query trees ordered, so the problem can be characterized as the *ordered tree pattern matching*. Though there are certainly situations where the ordered tree pattern matching perfectly reflects the information needs of users, there are many other that would prefer to consider query trees as unordered. For example, when searching for a twig of the element person with the subelements first name and last name (possibly with specific values), ordered matching would not consider the case where the order of the first name and the last name is reversed. However, this could exactly be the person we are searching for. The way to solve this problem is to consider the query twig as an unordered tree in which each node has a label and where only the *ancestor-descendant* relationships are important – the *preceding-following* relationships are unimportant.

In general, the process of unordered tree matching is difficult and time consuming. For example, the *edit distance* on unordered trees was found in [5] NP hard. To improve efficiency, an approximate searching for nearest neighbors, called ATreeGrep, was proposed in [3]. However, the problem of unordered twig pattern matching in XML data collections has not been studied, to the best of our knowledge.

In this paper we propose an efficient evaluation of the unordered tree matching. We use the tree signature approach [4], which has originally been proposed for the ordered tree matching. In principle, we decompose the query tree into a collection of root to leaf paths and search for their embedding in the data trees. Then we join the *structurally consistent* path qualifications to find unordered query tree inclusions in the data.

P. Van Emde Boas et al. (Eds.): SOFSEM 2004, LNCS 2932, pp. 122–139, 2004.

The rest of the paper is organized as follows. In Section 2, we summarize the concepts of tree signatures and define their properties that are relevant towards our objectives. In Section 3, we analyze the problem of unordered tree matching, and in Section 4 we propose an efficient algorithm to compute the query answer set. Performance evaluations are presented in Section 5. Final conclusions are in Section 6.

2   Tree Signatures

The idea of *tree signatures* proposed in [4] is to maintain a small but sufficient representation of the tree structures able to decide the ordered tree inclusion problem for the XML data processing. As a coding schema, the *preorder* and *postorder* ranks [1] are used. In this way, tree structures are linearized, and extended string processing algorithms are applied to identify the tree inclusion.

An ordered tree T is a rooted tree in which the children of each node are ordered. If a node $v \in T$ has k children then the children are uniquely identified, left to right, as $i_1, i_2, \ldots, i_k$. A labelled tree T associates a label (name) $t_v \in \Sigma$ (the domain of tree node labels) with each node $v \in T$. If the path from the root to v has length n, we say that the node v is on the level n, i.e. $level(v) = n$. Finally, $size(v)$ denotes the number of nodes rooted at v – the size of any leaf node is zero. In this section, we consider ordered labelled trees.

The preorder and postorder sequences are ordered lists of all nodes of a given tree T. In a preorder sequence, a tree node v is traversed and assigned its (increasing) preorder rank, $pre(v)$, before its children are recursively traversed from left to right. In the postorder sequence, a tree node v is traversed and assigned its (increasing) postorder rank, $post(v)$, after its children are recursively traversed from left to right. For illustration, see the preorder and postorder sequences of our sample tree in Fig. 1 – the node's position in the sequence is its preorder/postorder rank, respectively.

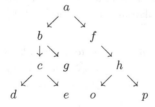

$$pre: a\ b\ c\ d\ e\ g\ f\ h\ o\ p$$
$$post: d\ e\ c\ g\ b\ o\ p\ h\ f\ a$$
$$rank: 1\ 2\ 3\ 4\ 5\ 6\ 7\ 8\ 9\ 10$$

Fig. 1. Preorder and postorder sequences of a tree

Given a node $v \in T$ with $pre(v)$ and $post(v)$ ranks, the following properties are important towards our objectives:

- all nodes x with $pre(x) < pre(v)$ are the *ancestors* or *preceding* nodes of v;
- all nodes x with $pre(x) > pre(v)$ are the *descendants* or *following* nodes of v;
- all nodes x with $post(x) < post(v)$ are the *descendants* or *preceding* nodes of v;
- all nodes x with $post(x) > post(v)$ are the *ancestors* or *following* nodes of v;
- for any $v \in T$, we have $pre(v) - post(v) + size(v) = level(v)$;
- if $pre(v) = 1$, v is the root, if $pre(v) = n$, v is a leaf. For all the other neighboring nodes v_i and v_{i+1} in the preorder sequence, if $post(v_{i+1}) > post(v_i)$, v_i is a leaf.

As proposed in [2], such properties can be summarized in a two dimensional diagram. See Fig. 2 for illustration, where the *ancestor* (A), *descendant* (D), *preceding* (P), and *following* (F) nodes of v are strictly located in the proper regions. Notice that in the preorder sequence all descendant nodes (if they exist) form a continuous sequence, which is constrained on the left by the reference node v and on the right by the first following node of v (or by the end of the sequence). The parent node of the reference is the ancestor with the highest preorder rank, i.e. the closest ancestor of the reference.

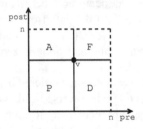

Fig. 2. Properties of the preorder and postorder ranks

2.1   The Signature

The tree signature is a list of entries for all nodes sorted in acceding preorder. In addition to the node name, each entry also contains the node's position in the postorder sequence.

Definition 1. *Let T be an ordered labelled tree. The signature of T is a sequence, $sig(T) = \langle t_1, post(t_1); t_2, post(t_2); \ldots t_n, post(t_n) \rangle$, of $n = |T|$ entries, where t_i is a name of the node with $pre(t_i) = i$. The $post(t_i)$ value is the postorder value of the node named t_i.*

Observe that the index i in the signature sequence is the preorder rank of t_i, so the value of i serves actually two purposes. In the following, we use the term preorder if we mean the rank of the node. When we consider the position of the node's entry in the signature sequence, we use the term index. For example, $\langle a, 10; b, 5; c, 3; d, 1; e, 2; g, 4; f, 9; h, 8; o, 6; p, 7 \rangle$ is the signature of the tree from Fig. 1. The first signature element a is the tree root. Leaf nodes in signatures are all nodes with postorder smaller than the postorder of the following node in the signature sequence, that is nodes d, e, g, o – the last node, in our example it is the node p, is always a leaf. We can also easily determine the level of leaf nodes, because the $size(t_i) = 0$ for all leaves t_i, thus $level(t_i) = i - post(t_i)$.

Extended Signatures. By extending entries of tree signatures with two preorder numbers representing pointers to the *first following*, ff, and the *first ancestor*, fa, nodes, the *extended signatures* are also defined in [4]. The generic entry of the i-th extended signature is $\langle t_i, post(t_i), ff_i, fa_i \rangle$. Such version of the tree signatures makes possible to compute levels for any node as $level(t_i) = ff_i - post(t_i) - 1$, because the cardinality of the descendant node set can be computed as: $size(t_i) = ff_i - i - 1$. For the tree in Fig. 1, the extended signature is: $sig(T) = \langle a, 10, 11, 0; b, 5, 7, 1; c, 3, 6, 2; d, 1, 5, 3;$ $e, 2, 6, 3; g, 4, 7, 2; f, 9, 11, 1; h, 8, 11, 7; o, 6, 10, 8; p, 7, 11, 8 \rangle$.

Sub-Signatures. A sub-signature $sub\_sig_S(T)$ is a specialized (restricted) view of T through signatures, which retains the original hierarchical relationships of elements in T. Specifically, $sub\_sig_S(T) = \langle t_{s_1}, post(t_{s_1}); t_{s_2}, post(t_{s_2}); \ldots t_{s_n}, post(t_{s_n}) \rangle$ is a sub-sequence of $sig(T)$, defined by the ordered set $S = \{s_1, s_2, \ldots s_k\}$ of indexes (preorder values) in $sig(T)$, such that $1 \leq s_1 < s_2 < \ldots < s_k \leq n$. Naturally, the set operations of the union and the intersection can be applied on sub-signatures provided the sub-signatures are derived from the same signatures and the results are kept sorted. For example, consider two sub-signatures of the signature representing the tree in Fig. 1, defined by ordered sets $S_1 = \{2, 3, 4\}$ and $S_2 = \{2, 3, 5, 6\}$. The union of S_1 and S_2 is the set $\{2, 3, 4, 5, 6\}$, that is the sub-signature representing the subtree rooted at the node b of our sample tree.

2.2   Ordered Tree Inclusion Evaluation

Let D and Q be ordered labelled trees. The tree Q is included in D, if D contains all elements (nodes) of Q and when the *sibling* and *ancestor* relationships of the nodes in D are the same as in Q. Using the concept of signatures, we can formally define the ordered tree inclusion problem as follows. Suppose the data tree D and the query tree Q specified by signatures

$$sig(D) = \langle d_1, post(d_1); d_2, post(d_2); \ldots d_m, post(d_m) \rangle,$$

$$sig(Q) = \langle q_1, post(q_1); q_2, post(q_2); \ldots q_n, post(q_n) \rangle.$$

Let $sub\_sig_S(D)$ be the *sub-signature* (i.e. a subsequence) of $sig(D)$ induced by a name sequence-inclusion of $sig(Q)$ in $sig(D)$ – a specific query signature can determine zero or more data sub-signatures. Regarding the node names, any $sub\_sig_S(D) \equiv sig(Q)$, because $q_i = d_{s_i}$ for all i, but the corresponding entries can have different postorder values. The following lemma defines the necessary constraints for qualification.

Lemma 1. *The query tree Q is included in the data tree D if the following two conditions are satisfied: (1) on the level of node names, $sig(Q)$ is sequence-included in $sig(D)$ determining $sub\_sig_S(D)$ through the ordered set of indexes $S = \{s_1, \ldots, s_n\}$, (2) for all pairs of entries i and j in $sig(Q)$ and $sub\_sig_S(D)$, $i, j = 1, 2, \ldots |Q| - 1$ and $i + j \leq |Q|$, $post(q_{i+j}) > post(q_i)$ implies $post(d_{s_{i+j}}) > post(d_{s_i})$ and $post(q_{i+j}) < post(q_i)$ implies $post(d_{s_{i+j}}) < post(d_{s_i})$.*

Proof. Because the index i increases according to the preorder sequence, node $i+j$ must be either the descendant or the following node of i. If $post(q_{i+j}) < post(q_i)$, the node $i+j$ in the query is a descendant of the node i, thus also $post(d_{s_{i+j}}) < post(d_{s_i})$ is required. By analogy, if $post(q_{i+j}) > post(q_i)$, the node $i+j$ in the query is a following node of i, thus also $post(d_{s_{i+j}}) > post(d_{s_i})$ must hold.

Observe that Lemma 1 defines a *weak inclusion* of the query tree in the data tree, meaning that the parent-child relationships of the query are implicitly reflected in the data tree as only the ancestor-descendant. However, due to the properties of preorder and postorder ranks, such constraints can easily be strengthened, if required.

For example, consider the data tree D in Fig. 1 and the query tree Q in Fig. 3. Such

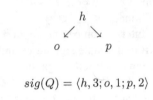

$$sig(Q) = \langle h, 3; o, 1; p, 2 \rangle$$

Fig. 3. Sample query tree Q

query qualifies in D: $sig(Q) = \langle h, 3; o, 1; p, 2 \rangle$ determines $sub\_sig_S(T) = \langle h, 8; o, 6; p, 7 \rangle$ through the ordered set $S = \{8, 9, 10\}$ because (1) $q_1 = d_8, q_2 = d_9$, and $q_3 = d_{10}$, (2) the postorder of node h is higher than the postorder of nodes o and p, and the postorder of node o is smaller than the postorder of node p (both in the $sig(Q)$ and $sub\_sig_S(T)$). If we change in our query tree Q the label h for f, we get $sig(Q) = \langle f, 3; o, 1; p, 2 \rangle$. Such modified query tree is also included in D, because Lemma 1 does not insist on the strict parent-child relationships, and implicitly considers all such relationships as ancestor-descendant. However, the query tree with the root g, resulting in $sig(Q) = \langle g, 3; o, 1; p, 2 \rangle$, does not qualify, even though it is also sequence-included (on the level of names) as the sub-signature $sub\_sig_S(D) = \langle g, 4; o, 6; p, 7 \rangle | S = \{6, 9, 10\}$. The reason is that the query requires the postorder to go down from g to o (from 3 to 1), while in the sub-signature it actually goes up (from 4 to 6). That means that o is not a descendant node of g, as required by the query, which can be verified in Fig. 1.

Multiple nodes with common names may result in multiple tree inclusions. As demonstrated in [4], the tree signatures can easily deal with such situations just by simply distinguishing between node names and their unique occurrences.

3   Unordered Tree Pattern Matching

In this section, we propose an approach to the unordered tree pattern matching using the tree signatures. The following definition specifies the notion of the unordered tree inclusion.

Definition 2 (Unordered Tree Inclusion). *Given a query twig pattern Q and an XML tree D, an unordered tree inclusion of Q in D is identified by a total mapping from nodes in Q to some nodes in D, such that only the ancestor-descendant structural relationships between nodes in Q are satisfied by the corresponding nodes in D.*

The unordered tree inclusion evaluation essentially searches for a node mapping keeping the ancestor-descendant relationships of the query nodes in the target data nodes. Potentially, tree signatures are suitable for such a task, because they rely on a numbering scheme allowing a unique identification of nodes in the tree and also retaining the ancestor-descendant relationships between them. However, signatures assume (data and query) trees always ordered, so the serialization of trees based on the preorder and postorder ranks does not only capture the ancestor-descendant but also the sibling relationships. For this reason, the unordered tree inclusion can not be evaluated by directly checking inclusion properties of the query in the data tree signature. More formally, using the concept of tree signatures, the unordered query tree Q is included in the data tree D if at least one qualifying index set exists.

Lemma 2. *Suppose the data tree D and the query tree Q to be specified by signatures*

$$sig(D) = \langle d_1, post(d_1); d_2, post(d_2); \ldots d_m, post(d_m) \rangle$$

$$sig(Q) = \langle q_1, post(q_1); q_2, post(q_2); \ldots q_n, post(q_n) \rangle$$

The unordered query tree Q is included in the data tree D if the following two conditions are satisfied: (1) on the level of node names, an ordered set of indexes $S = \{s_1, s_2, \ldots s_n\}$ exists, $1 \leq s_i \leq n$ for $i = 1, \ldots, n$, such that $d_{s_i} = q_i$, (2) for all pairs of entries i and j, $i, j = 1, 2, \ldots |Q| - 1$ and $i + j \leq |Q|$, if $post(q_{i+j}) < post(q_i)$ then $post(d_{s_{i+j}}) < post(d_{s_i}) \wedge s_{i+j} > s_i$.

Observe that the order of entries in the index set S is determined by the name equality of condition (1). But unlike for the ordered inclusion, given by Lemma 1, values of indexes s_i are not necessarily increasing with growing i. Since the query signature is a sequence of nodes in increasing preorder, ancestor-descendant relationships in condition (2) are simply recognized by a test of postorders for all pairs of entries $post(q_{i+j}) < post(q_i)$, and whenever the entry with higher preorder, i.e. $i + j$, has a smaller postorder, the required relationship is found. However, to check the same ancestor-descendant relationships in the data sub-signature, we must not only test the postorders of the corresponding pair of entries in the sub-signature, $post(d_{s_{i+j}}) < post(d_{s_i})$, but also their preorders, $s_{i+j} > s_i$, because the correct location of a relationship is a two-dimensional problem. If required, any S satisfying the properties specified in Lemma 2 can always undergo a sorting process in order to determine the corresponding sub-signature of $sig(D)$ qualifying the unordered tree inclusion of Q in D.

Example 1. Consider the query Q and the data tree D in Fig. 4 where the double arrow represents an ancestor-descendant edge. The only sub-signature qualifying the unordered tree inclusion of Q in D is defined by the index set $\{1, 5, 3\}$ and the corresponding sub-signature is $sub\_sig_{\{1,3,5\}}(D) = \langle a, 5; b, 1; f, 4 \rangle$.

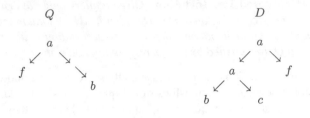

$$sig(Q) = \langle a, 3, 4, 0; f, 1, 3, 1; b, 2, 4, 1 \rangle \quad sig(D) = \langle a, 5; a, 3; b, 1; c, 2; f, 4 \rangle$$

Fig. 4. Sample of query evaluation

The solution we propose basically employs tree signatures to represent data trees. Then we transform the query tree into multiple (partial) queries and evaluate the ordered inclusion of such multiple queries to obtain an answer to the unordered tree inclusion. Suppose the data tree D specified by signature $sig(D)$ and the query tree Q specified by signature $sig(Q)$, the unordered tree inclusion can be evaluated in the following two alternative ways:

- Consider all and only such permutations Q_i of the query Q satisfying its ancestor-descendant relationships and compute the answers to the ordered inclusion of the corresponding signatures $sig(Q_i)$ in the data signature $sig(D)$. The union of the partial answers is the result of the unordered inclusion of Q in D. Indeed, the signature of any Q_i maintains all the ancestor-descendant relationships of Q and a specific form of the sibling relationships – the ordered tree inclusion evaluation checks both types of relationships.
- Decompose the query tree Q into a set of root-to-leaf paths P_i and evaluate the inclusion of the corresponding signatures $sig(P_i)$ in the data signature $sig(D)$. Any path P_i represents all (and only) the ancestor-descendant relationships between the involved nodes. Thus, an ordered inclusion of $sig(P_i)$ in $sig(D)$ states that a mapping, keeping the ancestor-descendant relationships, exists from the nodes in P_i to some nodes in D. If there are structurally consistent answers to the ordered inclusion of all the paths P_i in D, the unordered tree inclusion of Q in D is found.

In the following, we first analyze the second approach, and then we experimentally compare it with the first one. In principle, the decomposition approach consists of the following three steps:

1. decomposition of the query Q into a set of paths P_i;
2. evaluation of the inclusion of the corresponding signatures $sig(P_i)$ in the data signature $sig(D)$;
3. identification of the set of answers to the unordered inclusion of Q in D.

Input: query Q represented by the extended signature
$sig(Q) = \langle t_1, post(t_1), ff_1, fa_1; \dots ; t_n, post(t_n), ff_n, fa_n \rangle$
Output: the ordered set $rew(Q)$ of paths of $sig(Q)$ defined by the index sets P_j
Algorithm:

```
(1)  for j from 1 to n do
(2)      if (ffⱼ = (j + 1))
(3)         i = j;
(4)         Pⱼ = {i};
(5)         while(faᵢ <> 0)
(6)             Pⱼ = Pⱼ ∪ {faᵢ};
(7)             i = faᵢ;
(8)         push(rew(Q), Pⱼ);
(9)  sort(rew(Q));
```

Fig. 5. The query decomposition algorithm

3.1 Query Decomposition

The query decomposition process transforms a query twig into a set of root-to-leaf paths so that the ordered tree inclusion can be safely applied. For efficiency reasons, we sort the paths on the basis of their selectivity, so that in the next phase, the more selective paths are evaluated before the less selective ones. Fig. 5 shows an algorithm based on the above assumption for the detection of all the root-to-leaf paths of a query Q represented by the extended signature $sig(Q) = \langle t_1, post(t_1), ff_1, fa_1; \dots ; t_n, post(t_n), ff_n, fa_n \rangle$. Firstly, it identifies all the root-to-leaf paths and then sorts them assuming a predefined policy. The outcome is an ordered set $rew(Q)$ of the sub-signatures $sub\_sig_{P_j}(Q)$ defined by the index sets P_j, for each leaf j. It sequentially scans the signature $sig(Q)$ (line 1) and, whenever it finds a leaf (line 2) j, it follows the path connecting j with the tree root (lines 3-7). The nodes found in the path constitute the set of indexes P_j. Finally, in line 9, it sorts the sets of indexes on the basis of their selectivity. As statistics about the selectivity of paths are lacking, we suppose that the longer the path, the more selective it is. Recall that the length of any path corresponds to the level of the path's leaf node. In this case, as shown in Sec. 2, the level of any leaf j can be easily computed from the extended signature $sig(Q)$ and paths can be sorted according to the leaf node level in descending order. The outcome is an ordered set of root-to-leaf paths covering the overall query Q and arranged according to the selectivity.

Example 2. Let us consider the query tree in Fig. 6. The algorithm sequentially scans the signature $sig(Q)$ up to $j = 4$ since $ff_4 = 5$ (no descendant nodes), so the 4-th node is a leaf defining $P_4 = \{1, 2, 3, 4\}$. Then the algorithm iterates by starting from $j = 5$. Assuming that the paths are ordered on the basis of their lengths, the final outcome is $rew(Q) = \{P_4, P_5, P_7, P_8\}$ such that $P_5 = \{1, 2, 5\}$, $P_7 = \{1, 6, 7\}$, and $P_8 = \{1, 6, 8\}$. Notice that, as $rew(Q)$ is an ordered set, paths will be evaluated in the same order as they appear in $rew(Q)$.

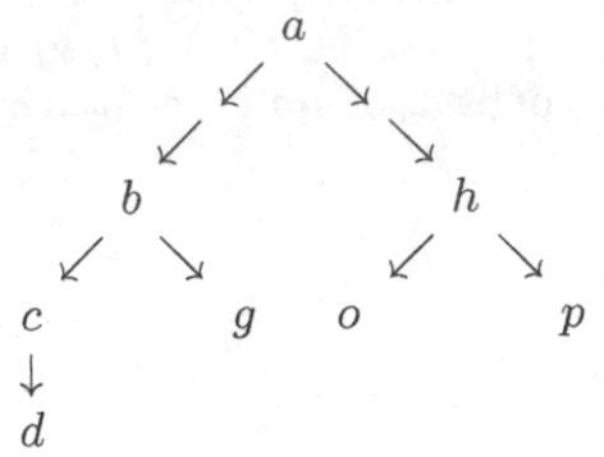

$$sig(Q) = \langle a, 8, 9, 0; \ b, 4, 6, 1; \ c, 2, 5, 2; \ d, 1, 5, 3; \ g, 3, 6, 2; \ h, 7, 9, 1; \ o, 5, 8, 6; \ p, 6, 9, 6 \rangle$$

Fig. 6. Sample query tree

3.2 Path Inclusion Evaluation

After the query has been decomposed into a sequence of paths, it has to be evaluated against the data signature. The answers to the unordered tree inclusion of Q in D are computed by joining the solutions to the individual paths of $rew(Q)$. As far as the evaluation of each individual path $P \in rew(Q)$ with respect to a data tree D is concerned, it can be performed in an ordered fashion – for path queries, the ordered evaluation coincides with the unordered one. As each $P \in rew(Q)$ identifies a path of Q, we know that each node is the descendant of the nodes appearing before the node in P. Following the numbering scheme of the sub-signature $sub\_sig_{S=P}(Q) = \langle t_{s_1}, post(t_{s_1}), ff_{s_1}, fa_{s_1}; \dots, t_{s_h}, post(t_{s_h}), ff_{s_h}, fa_{s_h} \rangle$ defined by $S = \{s_1 = p_1, \dots, s_h = p_1\}$, the postorder values of subsequent entries i and $i+j$ ($i, j = 1, 2, \dots h-1$ and $i + j \leq h$) always satisfy the inequality $post(q_{s_i}) < post(q_{s_{i+j}})$. The lemma below easily follows from the above observation and from the fact that inequalities are transitive.

Lemma 3. *A path $P \in rew(Q)$ is included in the data tree D, in the sense of Definition 2, if the following two conditions are satisfied: (1) on the level of node names, $sub\_sig_P(Q)$ is sequence-included in $sig(D)$ determining $sub\_sig_S(D)$ through the ordered set of indexes $S = \{s_1, \dots, s_h\}$, (2) for each $i \in [1, n-1]$: $post(d_{s_i}) < post(d_{s_{i+1}})$.*

For each path query $P \in rew(Q)$, we are thus able to compute the answer set $ans_P(D) = \{S \mid sub\_sig_S(D) \text{ qualifies the inclusion of } P \text{ in } D\}$. Such evaluation is simpler than the ordered tree inclusion evaluation of Lemma 1, because the path relationships are strictly of the ancestor-descendant type. Since the relationship, expressed by the inequality $<$, is transitive, we can simply check inequalities between postorder values of adjacent entries, and limit the verification to $h-1$ checks, provided the length of the path P is h. Notice that, as in the ordered tree inclusion evaluation case, all hierarchical relationships in the query tree are implicitly considered as the ancestor-descendant, rather than the parent-child relationships. In case the parent-child relationships are strictly required, an additional simple control through the first ancestor pointer is necessary.

3.3   Identification of the Answer Set

The answer set $ans_Q(D)$ of the unordered inclusion of Q in D can be determined by joining compatible answer sets $ans_P(D)$, for all $P \in rew(Q)$. The main problem is to establish how to join the answers for the paths in $rew(Q)$ to get the answers of the unordered inclusion of Q in D. Not all pairs of answers of two distinct sets are necessarily "joinable". The condition is that any pair of paths P_i and P_j share a common sub-path (at least the root) and differ in the other nodes (at least the leaves). Such *commonalities* and *differences* must meet a correspondence in any pair of index sets $S_i \in ans_{P_i}(D)$ and $S_j \in ans_{P_j}(D)$, respectively, in order that they are joinable. In this case, we state that $S_i \in ans_{P_i}(D)$ and $S_j \in ans_{P_j}(D)$ are structurally consistent.

Example 3 (cont. Ex. 1). Consider again the query Q and the data tree D in Fig. 4. Notice that the index set $\{1, 5, 3\}$ satisfies both conditions of Lemma 2 whereas the index set $\{2, 5, 3\}$ only matches at the level of node names but it is not a qualifying one. The rewriting of Q gives rise to the following paths $rew(Q) = \{P_2, P_3\}$, where $P_2 = \{1, 2\}$ and $P_3 = \{1, 3\}$, and the outcome of their evaluation is $ans_{P_2} = \{\{1, 5\}\}$ and $ans_{P_3} = \{\{1, 3\}, \{2, 3\}\}$. The common sub-path between P_2 and P_3 is $P_2 \cap P_3 = \{1\}$. The index 1 occurs in the first position both in P_2 and P_3. From the cartesian product of $ans_{P_2}(D)$ and $ans_{P_3}(D)$ it follows that the index sets $\{1, 5\} \in ans_{P_2}(D)$ and $\{1, 3\} \in ans_{P_3}(D)$ are structurally consistent as they share the same value in the first position and have different values in the second position, whereas $\{1, 5\} \in ans_{P_2}(D)$ and $\{2, 3\} \in ans_{P_3}(D)$ are not structurally compatible and thus are not joinable.

The following definition states the meaning of structural consistency for two generic subtrees T_i and T_j of Q – paths P_i and P_j are particular instances of T_i and T_j.

Definition 3 (Structural consistency). *Let Q be a query twig, D a data tree, $T_i = \{t_i^1, \ldots, t_i^n\}$ and $T_j = \{t_j^1, \ldots, t_j^m\}$ two ordered sets of indexes determining $sub\_sig_{T_i}(Q)$ and $sub\_sig_{T_j}(Q)$, respectively, $ans_{T_i}(D)$ and $ans_{T_j}(D)$ the answers of the unordered inclusion of T_i and T_j in D, respectively. $S_i = \{s_i^1, \ldots, s_i^n\} \in ans_{T_i}(D)$ and $S_j = \{s_j^1, \ldots, s_j^m\} \in ans_{T_j}(D)$ are structurally consistent if:*

– *for each pair of common indexes $t_i^h = t_j^k$, $s_i^h = s_j^k$;*
– *for each pair of different indexes $t_i^h \neq t_j^k$, $s_i^h \neq s_j^k$.*

Definition 4 (Join of answers). *Given two structurally consistent answers $S_i \in ans_{T_i}(D)$ and $S_j \in ans_{T_j}(D)$, where $T_i = \{t_i^1, \ldots, t_i^n\}$, $T_j = \{t_j^1, \ldots, t_j^m\}$, $S_i = \{s_i^1, \ldots, s_i^n\}$ and $S_j = \{s_j^1, \ldots, s_j^m\}$, the join of S_i and S_j, $S_i \bowtie S_j$, is defined on the ordered set $T_i \cup T_j = \{t^1, \ldots, t^k\}$ as the index set $\{s^1, \ldots, s^k\}$ where:*

– *for each $h = 1, \ldots, n, l \in \{1, \ldots, k\}$ exists such that $t_i^h = t^l$ and $s_i^h = s^l$;*
– *for each $h = 1, \ldots, m, l \in \{1, \ldots, k\}$ exists such that $t_j^h = t^l$ and $s_j^h = s^l$.*

Any answer to the unordered inclusion of Q in D is the result of a sequence of joins of structurally consistent answers, one for each $P \in rew(Q)$, identifying distinct paths in $sig(D)$. The answer set $ans_Q(D)$ can thus be computed by sequentially joining the sets of answers of the evaluation of the path queries. We denote such operation as the *structural join*.

$ans_{P_2}(D)$: $\mathbf{P_2}$ $\begin{array}{|c|c|} \hline 1 & 2 \\ \hline 1 & 5 \\ \hline \end{array}$ $ans_{P_3}(D)$: $\mathbf{P_3}$ $\begin{array}{|c|c|} \hline 1 & 3 \\ \hline 1 & 3 \\ \hline 2 & 3 \\ \hline \end{array}$ $sj(ans_{P_2}, ans_{P_3})$: $\mathbf{P_2 \cup P_3}$ $\begin{array}{|c|c|c|} \hline 1 & 2 & 3 \\ \hline 1 & 5 & 3 \\ \hline \end{array}$

Fig. 7. Structural join of Ex.1

Definition 5 (Structural join). *Let Q be a query twig, D a data tree, T_i and T_j two ordered sets of indexes determining $sub\_sig_{T_i}(Q)$ and $sub\_sig_{T_j}(Q)$, respectively, $ans_{T_i}(D)$ and $ans_{T_j}(D)$ the answers of the unordered inclusions of T_i and T_j in D, respectively.*

The structural join $sj(ans_{T_i}(D), ans_{T_j}(D))$ between the two sets $ans_{T_i}(D)$ and $ans_{T_j}(D)$ is the set $ans_T(D)$ where:

- *$T = \{t^1, \ldots, t^k\}$ is the ordered set obtained by the union $T_i \cup T_j$ of the ordered sets T_i and T_j;*
- *$ans_T(D)$ contains the join $S_i \bowtie S_j$ of each pair of structurally consistent answers $(S_i \in ans_{T_i}(D), S_j \in ans_{T_j}(D))$.*

The structural join $sj(ans_{T_i}(D), ans_{T_j}(D))$ thus returns an answer set defined on the union of two sub-queries T_i and T_j as the join of the structurally consistent answers of $ans_{T_i}(D)$ and $ans_{T_j}(D)$. Starting from the set of answers $\{ans_{P_{x_1}}(D), \ldots, ans_{P_{x_k}}(D)\}$ for paths in $rew(Q)$, we get the answer set $ans_Q(D)$ identifying the unordered inclusion of Q in D by incrementally merging the answer sets by means of the structural join. Since the structural join operator is associative and symmetric, we can compute $ans_Q(D)$ as:

$$ans_Q(D) = sj(ans_{P_{x_1}}(D), \ldots, ans_{P_{x_k}}(D)) \tag{1}$$

where $rew(Q) = \{P_{x_1}, \ldots, P_{x_k}\}$.

Example 4. The answer set $ans_Q(D)$ of Example 1 is the outcome of the structural join $sj(ans_{P_2}(D), ans_{P_3}(D)) = ans_{P_2 \cup P_3}(D)$ where $P_2 \cup P_3 = \{1, 2\} \cup \{1, 3\}$ is the ordered set $\{1, 2, 3\}$. The answers to the individual paths and the final answers are shown in Fig. 7 (the first line of each table represents the query). It joins the only pair of structurally consistent answers: $\{1, 5\} \in ans_{P_2}(D)$ and $\{1, 3\} \in ans_{P_3}(D)$.

Example 5. Given the query Q in Fig. 8, in this example we show the evaluation of the unordered tree inclusion of Q in the data tree D from Fig. 4. It can be easily verified that there is no qualifying sub-signature since at most two of the three paths find a correspondence in the data tree.

The rewriting phase produces the set $rew(Q) = \{P_2, P_3, P_4\}$ where $P_2 = \{1, 2\}$, $P_3 = \{1, 3\}$, and $P_4 = \{1, 4\}$. The final result $ans_Q(D)$ is the outcome of the structural join:

$$sj(ans_{P_2}(D), ans_{P_3}(D), ans_{P_4}(D)) = sj(sj(ans_{P_2}(D), ans_{P_3}(D)), ans_{P_4}(D)) = \emptyset$$

The answer sets of the separate paths and of $sj(ans_{P_2}(D), ans_{P_3}(D))$ are shown in Fig. 9. The final result is empty since the only pair of joinable answers $\{1, 5, 3\} \in$

$$a$$

$$\swarrow \quad \downarrow \quad \searrow$$

$$f \qquad \downarrow \qquad f$$

$$b$$

$$sig(Q) = \langle a, 4, 5, 0; f, 1, 3, 1; b, 2, 4, 1; f, 3, 5, 1 \rangle$$

Fig. 8. Sample of query

$ans_{P_2}(D)$: $\mathbf{P_2}$ | 1 | 2 |
|---|---|
| 1 | 5 |

$ans_{P_3}(D)$: $\mathbf{P_3}$ | 1 | 3 |
|---|---|
| 1 | 3 |
| 2 | 3 |

$ans_{P_4}(D)$: $\mathbf{P_4}$ | 1 | 4 |
|---|---|
| 1 | 5 |

$sj(ans_{P_2}(D), ans_{P_3}(D))$: $\mathbf{P_2} \cup \mathbf{P_3}$ | 1 | 2 | 3 |
|---|---|---|
| 1 | 5 | 3 |

Fig. 9. Structural join from Example 5

$sj(ans_{P_2}(D), ans_{P_3}(D))$ and $\{1,5\} \in ans_{P_4}(D)$ is not structurally consistent: the two different query nodes $2 \in P_2 \cup P_3$ and $4 \in P_4$ correspond to the same data node 5. It means that there are not as many data tree paths as query tree paths.

Theorem 1. *Given a query twig Q and a data tree D, the answer set $ans_Q(D)$ as defined by Eq. 1 contains all and only the index sets S qualifying the unordered inclusion of Q in D according to Lemma 2.*

4   Efficient Computation of the Answer Set

Till now, we have studied how tree signatures can be employed to support unordered tree pattern matching. However, XML data trees can have many nodes and the tree signatures, linearly proportional to the number of nodes, can be very large, so the performance aspects of such operation becomes a matter of concern. In the previous section, we have specified two distinct phases for unordered tree pattern matching: the computation of the answer set for each root-to-leaf path of the query and the structural join of such sets. The main drawback of this approach is that many intermediate results may not be part of any final answer. In the following, we show how these two phases can be merged into one to avoid unnecessary computations. The basic idea is to evaluate at each step the most selective path among the available ones and to directly combine the partial results computed with structurally consistent answers of the paths.

The full algorithm is depicted in Fig. 10. It makes use of the pop operation which extracts the next element from the ordered set of paths $rew(Q)$. The algorithm essentially computes the answer set by incrementally joining the partial answers collected up to that moment with the answer set of the next path P in $rew(Q)$. As paths are sorted by their selectivity, P is the most selective path among those which have not been evaluated

Input: the paths of the rewriting phase $rew(Q)$
Output: $ans_Q(D)$
Algorithm:

```
(1)  P = pop(rew(Q));
(2)  pQ = P;
(3)  evaluate ans_pQ(D);
(4)  while((rew(Q) not empty) AND (ans_pQ(D) not empty))
(5)      P = pop(rew(Q));
(6)      pP = P \ (P ∩ pQ);
(7)      t^k is the parent of pP, k is the position in pQ;
(8)      PAns = ∅;
(9)      for each answer S in ans_pQ(D)
(10)         evaluate ans_pP(sub_sig_{s_k+1,...,ffs_k-1}(D));
(11)         if(ans_pP(sub_sig_{s_k+1,...,ffs_k-1}(D)) not empty)
(12)             add sj({S}, ans_pP(sub_sig_{s_k+1,...,ffs_k-1}(D))) to PAns;
(13)      pQ = pQ ∪ P;
(14)      ans_pQ(D)=PAns;}
```

Fig. 10. The unordered tree pattern evaluation algorithm

yet. In particular, from step 1 to step 3, the algorithm initializes the partial query pQ evaluated up to moment to the most selective path P and stores in the partial answer set $ans_{pQ}(D)$ the evaluation of the inclusion of pQ in D. From step 4 to step 12, it iterates the process by joining the partial answer set $ans_{pQ}(D)$ with the answer set $ans_P(D)$ of the next path P of $rew(Q)$. Notice that, at each step, it does not properly compute first the answer set $ans_P(D)$ and the structural join $sj(ans_{pQ}(D), ans_P(D))$ as shown in Eq. 1, but it rather applies a sort of nested loop algorithm in order to perform the two phases in one shot. As each pair of index sets must be structurally consistent in order to be joinable, we compute only such answers in $ans_P(Q)$, which are structurally consistent with some of the answers in $ans_{pQ}(D)$. As a matter of fact, only such answers may be part of the answers to Q. In order to do it, the algorithm tries to extend each answer in $ans_{pQ}(D)$ to the answers to $pQ \cup P$ by only evaluating such sub-path of P which has not been evaluated in pQ. In particular, step 6 stores in the sub-path pP such part of the path P to be evaluated which is not in common with the query pQ evaluated up to that moment: $P \setminus (P \cap pQ)$. Step 7 identifies t^k as the parent of the partial path pP where k is its position in pQ. For instance, by considering Example 3, the two paths P_2 and P_3 of the query Q are depicted in Fig. 4a. If $rew(Q) = \{P_2, P_3\}$, then at step 5 $pQ = P_2$ and, as the part of the path P_3 corresponding to the query node a has already been evaluated while evaluating P_2, the partial path pP to be evaluated and the parent t^k of pP are depicted in Fig. 4b.

For each index set $S \in ans_{pQ}(D)$, each index set in $ans_P(Q)$, which is structurally consistent with S, must share the same values in the positions corresponding to the common sub-path $P \cap pQ$. In other words, we assume that the part of the path P which is common to pQ has already been evaluated and that the indexes of the data nodes

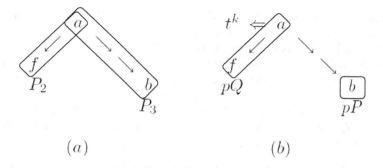

(a) (b)

Fig. 11. Evaluation of paths in Algorithm of Fig. 10: an example

matching $P \cap pQ$ are contained in S. In particular, the index s^k in S actually represents the entry of the data node matching the query node corresponding to t^k. Thus, in order to compute the answers in $ans_P(D)$ that are structurally consistent with S and, then, join with S, the algorithm extends S to the answers to $P \cup pQ$ by only evaluating in the "right" sub-tree of the data tree the inclusion of the part pP of the path P which has not been evaluated yet (step 10). As the path P has been split into two branches $P \cap pQ$ and pP, where t^k is the parent of pP and S contains a set of indexes matching $P \cap pQ$, the evaluation of pP must be limited to the descendants of the data node d_{s^k} which in the tree signature corresponds to the sequence of nodes having preorder values from $s_k + 1$ up to $ff_{s_k} - 1$. Then it joins S with such answer set by only checking that different query entries correspond to different data entries (step 12). Notice that, in step 10, by shrinking the index interval to a limited portion of the data signature, we are able to reduce the computing time for the sequence inclusion evaluation.

The algorithm ends when we have evaluated all the paths in $rew(Q)$ or when the partial answer set collected up to that moment $ans_{pQ}(D)$ becomes empty. The latter case occurs when we evaluate a path P having no answer which is structurally consistent with those in $ans_{pQ}(D)$: $sj(ans_{pQ}(D), ans_P(D)) = \emptyset$. In this case, for each answer S in $ans_{pQ}(D)$ two alternatives exists. Either the evaluation of the partial path pP fails (line 11), which means that none of the answers in $ans_P(D)$ share the same values of S in the positions corresponding to the common sub-path $P \cap pQ$, or the structural join between S and the answers to pP fails (line 12), which means that some of the answers in $ans_P(D)$ share the same values of S in positions corresponding to different indexes in P and pQ.

Example 6. Let us apply the algorithm described in Fig. 10 to Example 3 where the signatures involved are $sig(Q) = \langle a, 3, 4, 0; f, 1, 3, 1; b, 2, 4, 1 \rangle$ and $sig(D) = \langle a, 5; a, 3; b, 1; c, 2; f, 4 \rangle$. Since the two paths are of the same length, we start from $P_2 = \{1, 2\}$ whose answer set is $ans_{P_2}(D) = \{\{1, 5\}\}$. Then, the algorithm essentially deals with the next path, e.g. $P_3 = \{1, 3\}$, in the way shown in Fig. 4. It computes $P_2 \cap P_3 = \{1\}$, $t^k = 1$ where $k = 1$, and $pP = \{3\}$. It then considers the only index set $S = \{1, 5\}$ in $ans_{P_2}(D)$ and stores in $ans_{pP}(D)$ the index sets qualifying the inclusion of the query $sub\_sig_{\{3\}}(Q) = \langle b, 2, 4, 1 \rangle$ on the sub-tree rooted by the data node labelled with a and having index $s^1 = 1$ that is in the signature $sub\_sig_{\{2,3,4,5\}}(D) = \langle a, 3; b, 1; c, 2; f, 4 \rangle$.

The outcome is thus $ans_{pP}(D) = \{\{3\}\}$ and $ans_Q(D) = \{\{1, 5, 3\}\}$. Being P_2 and P_3 of the same length, we can also start from $ans_{P_3}(D) = \{\{1, 3\}, \{2, 3\}\}$. In this case $pP = \{2\}$ while, as in the previous case, $t^k = 1$ where $k = 1$. We then consider the first index set $\{1, 3\}$ and evaluate $ans_{pP}(D)$ on the descendants of the data node having index $s^1 = 1$. The answer $ans_{pP}(sub\_sig_{\{2,3,4\}}(D)$ to the inclusion of $sub\_sig_{\{pP\}}(Q) = \langle f, 1, 3, 1; \rangle$ in $sub\_sig_{\{2,3,4,5\}}(D) = \langle a, 3; b, 1; c, 2; f, 4 \rangle$ is $\{\{5\}\}$. Thus $ans_Q(D) = \{\{1, 5, 3\}\}$. For the next index set $\{2, 3\}$, it is required to evaluate $sub\_sig_{\{pP\}}(Q)$ on the sub-tree rooted by $s^1 = 2$ that is $sub\_sig_{\{3,4\}}(D) = \langle b, 1; c, 2 \rangle$ and the answer set $ans_{pP}(D)$ is empty.

In summary, the proposed solution performs a small number of additional operations on the paths of the query twig Q, but dramatically reduces the number of operations on the data trees by avoiding the computation of useless path answers. In this way, we remarkably reduce computing efforts. Indeed, while query twigs are usually very small and have a limited number of paths, XML data trees can have many nodes and tree signatures can be very large.

Table 1. DBLP Test-Collection Statistics

Middle-level		Leaf-level	
Element name	**Occs**	**Element name**	**Occs**
inproceedings	241244	author	823369
article	129468	title	376737
proceedings	3820	year	376709
incollection	1079	url	375192
book	1010	pages	361989
phdthesis	72	booktitle	245795
mastersthesis	5	ee	143068
		crossref	141681
		editor	8032
		publisher	5093
		isbn	4450
		school	77
Summary			
Total number of elements			3814975
Total number of values			3438237
Maximum tree height			3

5 Performance Evaluation

In this section we evaluate the performance of our unordered tree inclusion technique. We measure the time needed to process different query twigs using the paths decomposition approach, deeply described in this paper, and compare the obtained results with the query processing performance of the permutation approach.

All algorithms are implemented in Java JDK 1.4.2 and the experiments are executed on a Pentium 4 2.5Ghz Windows XP Professional workstation, equipped with 512MB RAM and a RAID0 cluster of 2 80GB EIDE disks with NT file system (NTFS).

Since synthetic data sets are not significant enough to show the performance of real-life XML query scenarios, we performed our experiments on a real data set, specifically the complete DBLP Computer Science Bibliography archive as of April 2003. Table 1 shows more details about this XML archive. Notice that the file consists of over 3.8 Millions of elements, where over 3.4 Millions of them have associated values. The size of the XML file is 156MB.

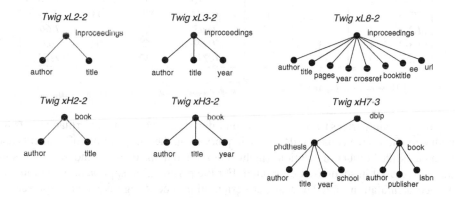

Fig. 12. The query twigs templates used in the performance tests

We tested the performance of our approach for queries derived from six query twig templates (see Fig. 12). Such templates present different *element name selectivity*, i.e. the number of elements having a given element name, different *branching factors*, i.e. the maximum number of sibling elements, and different *tree heights*. We refer to the templates as "*xSb-h*", where S stands for element name selectivity and can be H(igh) or L(ow), b is the branching factor, and h the tree height. To understand the element name selectivity, refer to Table 1, showing the number of occurrences of each name in the DBLP data set. In particular, we used `inproceedings` for the low selectivity and `book` and `phdthesis` for the high selectivity.

We have conducted experiments by using not only queries defined by the plain templates (designated as "*NSb-h*") which only contain tree structural relationships, but also queries (designated as "*VSb-h*"), where the templates are extended by predicates on the author name. Value accesses are supported by a content index. We have chosen the highly content-selective predicates, because we believe that this kind of queries is especially significant for highly selective fields, such as the author name. On the other hand, the performance of queries with low selectivity fields should be very close to the corresponding templates. In this way, we measure the response time of twelve queries, half of which contain predicates.

Table 2. Performance comparison of the two unordered tree inclusion alternatives

Query			Evaluation			
Twig	elements	predicates	solutions	Decomposition	Permutation		
	#	#	#	(sec)	N	mean (sec)	total (sec)
NH2-2	3	0	1343	0.016	2	0.014	0.028
NH3-2	4	0	1343	0.016	6	0.015	0.105
NH7-3	10	0	90720	1.1	288	0.9	259.2
NL2-2	3	0	559209	2.2	2	2.28	4.56
NL3-2	4	0	559209	4.2	6	2.49	14.94
NL8-2	9	0	149700	7.7	40320	4.8	193536
VH2-2	3	1	1	0.015	2	0.014	0.028
VH3-2	4	1	1	0.016	6	0.016	0.096
VH7-3	10	2	1	0.031	288	0.03	8.64
VL2-2	3	1	39	0.65	2	0.832	1.664
VL3-2	4	1	36	0.69	6	1.1	6.6
VL8-2	9	1	29	0.718	40320	2.3	92736

Table 2 summarizes the results of the unordered tree inclusion performance tests for both approaches we considered. For each query twig, the total number of elements and predicates, the number of solutions (inclusions) found in the data set, and the processing time, expressed in seconds, are reported. For the permutation approach, the number of needed permutations and the mean per-permutation processing time are also presented. It is evident that the decomposition approach is superior and scores a lower time in every respect. In particular, with low branching factors (i.e. 2), such approach is twice as faster for both selectivity settings. With high branching factors (i.e. 3, 8) the speed increment becomes larger and larger – the number of permutations required in the alternative approach grows factorially: for queries NL8-2 and VL8-2 the decomposition method is more than 25,000 times faster. The decomposition approach is particularly fast with the high selectivity queries. Even for greater heights (i.e. in VH7-3), the processing time remains in milliseconds.

For the decomposition method, as we do not have statistics on the path selectivity at our disposal, we measured the time needed to solve each query for each of the possible order of path evaluation and reported only the lower one. As we expected, we found that starting with the most highly selective paths always increases the query evaluation efficiency. In particular, the time spent is nearly proportional to the number of occurrences of such path in the data. Evaluating query NL2-2 starting with the title path produces a response time of 2.2 seconds, while starting with the less selective author path, the time would nearly double (3.9 sec.). This holds for all the query twigs as well – for NL8-2, the time ranges from 7.7 sec (crossref path) up to 15.7 sec (author path). Of course, for the predicate queries the best time is obtained by starting the evaluation from the value-enabled paths.

Finally, notice that the permutation approach also requires an initial "startup" phase where all the different permutation twigs are generated; the time used to generate such permutations is not taken into account.

6 Conclusions

In this paper, we have studied the problem of efficient evaluation of unordered query trees in XML tree structured data collections. As the underlying concept, we have used the tree signatures, which have proved to be useful structure for an efficient tree navigation and ordered tree matching, see [4]. We have identified two evaluation strategies, where the first strategy is based on multiple evaluation of all query tree structure permutations and the second on decomposing a query tree into a collection of all root-to leaf paths.

We have deeply studied the decomposition approach and established rules for decomposition as well as strategies for integration of partial, structurally consistent, results through structural joins. Based on the developed theoretical grounds, an efficient implementation algorithm is proposed.

The permutation and decomposition approaches to the unordered tree matching have been tested on the DBLP data set for various types of queries. The experiments demonstrate a clear superiority of the decomposition approach, which is especially advantages for the large query trees, and for trees with highly selective predicates.

Experiments also confirmed the expected fact that the order in which the paths are evaluated in the decomposition approach can have significant effects on the overall performance. Though the proposed strategy of starting with the longest path seems to work quite well, we plan to work on this aspect more deeply in the near future.

References

1. Dietz, P.F.: Maintaining Order in a Linked List. In: Proceedings of STOC, 14th Annual ACM Symposium on Theory of Computing, May 1982, San Francisco, CA, 1982 122-127
2. Grust, T.: Accelerating XPath Location Steps. In: Proceedings of the 2002 ACM SIGMOD International Conference on Management of Data, Madison, Wisconsin (2002) 109-120
3. Shasha, D., Wang, J.T.L., Shan, H., Zhang, K.: ATreeGrep: Approximate Searching in Unordered Trees. Proceedings of the 14th International Conference on Scientific and Statistical Database Management, July 24-26, 2002, Edinburgh Scotland UK 89-98
4. Zezula, P., Amato, G., Debole, F., Rabitti, F.: Tree Signatures for XML Querying and Navigation. In: Proceedings of the XML Database Symposium, XSym 2003, Berlin, September 2003, LNCS 2824, Springer 149-163
5. Zhang, K., Statman, R., Shasha, D.: On the Edit Distance between Unordered Labeled Trees. Information Processing Letters **42** (1992) 133-139

Quantum Query Complexity for Some Graph Problems*

Aija Berzina, Andrej Dubrovsky, Rusins Freivalds, Lelde Lace, and
Oksana Scegulnaja

Institute of Mathematics and Computer Science, University of Latvia, Raina bulv.
29, Riga, Latvia
aija.berzina@tietoenator.com, a.dubrovskis@alise.lv,
{Rusins.Freivalds,Lelde.Lace}@mii.lu.lv, oksana.s@liis.lv

Abstract. The paper [4] by H. Buhrman and R. de Wolf contains
an impressive survey of solved and open problems in quantum query
complexity, including many graph problems. We use recent results by
A.Ambainis [1] to prove higher lower bounds for some of these problems.
Some of our new lower bounds do not close the gap between the best
upper and lower bounds. We prove in these cases that it is impossible to
provide a better application of Ambainis' technique for these problems.

1   Introduction

Recently it has become clear that a quantum computer could, in principle, solve
certain problems faster than a conventional computer. A quantum computer is
a device, which takes full advantage of quantum mechanical superposition and
interference. Building an actual quantum computer is probably far off in the
future.

Boolean decision trees model is the most simple model to compute Boolean
functions. In this model the primitive operation made by an algorithm is evaluating an input Boolean variable. The cost of a (deterministic) algorithm is the
number of variables it evaluates on a worst case input. It is easy to find the
deterministic complexity of all explicit Boolean functions (for most functions it
is equal to the number of variables).

The *black-box* model of computation arises when one is given a black-box
containing an N-tuple of Boolean variables $X = (x_0, x_1, ..., x_{N-1}.)$. The box
is equipped to output x_i on input i. We wish to determine some property of
X,accessing the x_i only through the black box. Such a black-box access is called
a *query*. A property of X is any Boolean function that depends on X, i.e. a
property is function $f : \{0,1\}^N \rightarrow \{0,1\}$. We want to compute such properties
using as few queries as possible.

Consider, for example, the case where the goal is to determine whether or
not X contains at least one 1, so we want to compute the property $OR(X) =$

---

* Research supported by Grant No.01.0354 from the Latvian Council of Science

$x_0 \vee \ldots \vee x_{N-1}$. It is well known that the number of queries required to compute OR by any *classical* (deterministic or probabilistic) algorithm is $O(N)$.

Grover [6] discovered a remarkable *quantum* algorithm that, making queries in superposition, can be used to compute OR with small error probability using only $O(\sqrt{N})$ queries.

On the other hand, quantum algorithms are in a sense more restricted. For instance, only unitary transformations are allowed for state transitions. Hence rather often a problem arises whether or not the needed quantum automaton exists. In such a situation lower bounds of complexity are considered. It is proved in [3] that Grover database search algorithm is the best possible. It is proved in [3] that no quantum query algorithm exists for PARITY with $\Omega(N)$ queries.

We use a result by A.Ambainis [1] to prove lower complexity bounds for quantum query algorithms. Currently, this is the most powerful method to prove lower bounds of complexity for quantum query algorithms. In some cases there still remains a gap between the upper and the lower bounds of the complexity. In these cases we prove additionally that Ambainis' method cannot provide a better lower bound for this problem.

2   Definitions

2.1   Quantum Computing

We introduce the basic model of quantum computing. For more details, see textbooks by Gruska [7] and Nielsen and Chuang [8].

Quantum states: We consider finite dimensional quantum systems. An n-dimensional pure state is a vector $|\psi\rangle \in C^n$ of norm 1. Let $|1\rangle, |2\rangle, \ldots, |n-1\rangle$ be an orthonormal basis for C^n. Then, any state can be expressed as $|\psi\rangle = \sum_{i=0}^{n-1} a_i |i\rangle$ for some $a_0 \in C, a_1 \in C, \ldots, a_{n-1} \in C$. Since the norm of $|\psi\rangle$ is 1, $|a_i|^2 = 1$. We call the states $|1\rangle, |2\rangle, \ldots, |n-1\rangle$ *basic states*. Any state of the form $\sum_{i=0}^{n-1} a_i |i\rangle$ is called a *superposition* of $|1\rangle, |2\rangle, \ldots, |n-1\rangle$. The coefficient a_i is called *amplitude* of $|i\rangle$.

A quantum system can undergo two basic operations: an unitary evolution and a measurement.

Unitary evolution: A *unitary transformation* U is a linear transformation on C^k that preserves the l_2 norm (i.e., maps vectors of unit norm to vectors of unit norm). If, before applying U, the system was in a state $|\psi\rangle$, then the state after the transformation is $U|\psi\rangle$.

Measurements: In this survey, we just use the simplest case of quantum measurement. It is the full measurement in the computation basis. Performing this measurement on a state $|\psi\rangle = a_1|0\rangle + \ldots a_k|k\rangle$ gives the outcome i with probability $|a_i|^2$. The measurement changes the state of the system to $|i\rangle$. Notice that the measurement destroys the original state $|\psi\rangle$ and repeating the measurement gives the same i with probability 1 (because the state after the first measurement is $|i\rangle$.

More general classes of measurements are general von Neumann and POVM measurements [8].

2.2 Query Model

In the query model, the input $x_1, \ldots, x_N$ is contained in a black box and can be accessed by queries to the black box. In each query, we give i to the black box and the black box outputs x_i. The goal is to solve the problem with the minimum number of queries. The classical version of this model is known as *decision trees* [4].

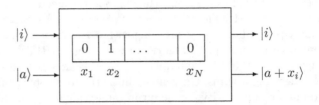

Fig. 1. *Quantum black box*

There are two ways how to define the query box in the quantum model. The first is the extension of the classical query (Figure 1). It has two inputs: i, consisting of $\lceil \log N \rceil$ bits and b consisting of 1 bit. If the input to the query box is a basic state $|i\rangle|b\rangle$, the output is $|i\rangle|b \oplus x_i\rangle$. If the input is a superposition $\sum_{i,b} a_{i,b}|i\rangle|b\rangle$, the output is $\sum_{i,b} a_{i,b}|i\rangle|b \oplus x_i\rangle$. Notice that this definition applies both to case when x_i are binary and to the case when they are k-valued. In the k-valued case, we just make b to consist of $\lceil \log_2 k \rceil$ bits and take $b \oplus x_i$ to be bitwise XOR of b and x_i.

In the second form of quantum query (which only applies to problems with $\{0,1\}$-valued x_i), the black box has just one input i. If the input is a state $\sum_i a_i|i\rangle$, the output is $\sum_i (-1)^{x_i} a_i|i\rangle$. While this form is less intuitive, it is very convenient for the use in quantum algorithms, including Grover's search algorithm [6]. A query of second type can be simulated by a query of first type [6].

A quantum query algorithm with T queries is just a sequence of unitary transformations

$$U_0 \to O \to U_1 \to O \to \ldots \to U_{T-1} \to O \to U_T$$

on some finite- dimensional space C^k. $U_0, U_1, \ldots, U_T$ can be any unitary transformations that do not depend on the bits $x_1, \ldots, x_N$ inside the black box. O are query transformations that consist of applying the query box to the first $\log N + 1$ bits of the state. That is, we represent basic states of C^k as $|i, b, z\rangle$. Then, O maps $|i, b, z\rangle$ to $|i, b \oplus x_i, z\rangle$. We use O_x to denote the query transformation corresponding to an input $x = (x_1, \ldots x_N)$.

The computation starts with state $|0\rangle$. Then, we apply $U_0, O_x, \ldots, O_x, U_T$ and measure the final state. The result of the computation is the rightmost bit of the state obtained by the measurement (or several bits if we are considering a problem where the answer has more than 2 values).

The quantum algorithm computes a function $f(x_1, \ldots, x_N)$ if, for every $x = (x_1, \ldots, x_N)$ for which f is defined, the probability that the rightmost bit of $U_T O_x U_{T-1} \ldots O_x U_0 |0\rangle$ equals $f(x_1, \ldots, x_N)$ is at least $1 - \epsilon < \frac{1}{2}$.

The query complexity of f is the smallest number of queries used by a quantum algorithm that computes f. We denote it $Q(f)$.

Our proofs use the following results by A.Ambainis.

Theorem 1. *[1] Let $A \subset \{0,1\}^n$, $B \subset \{0,1\}^n$ be such that $f(A)=1$, $f(B)=0$ and*

- *for every $x = (x_1..x_n) \in A$, there are at least m values $i \in \{1,\ldots,n\}$ such that $(x_1,\ldots,x_{i-1}, 1 - x_i, x_{i+1},\ldots,x_n) \in B$,*
- *for every $x = (x_1..x_n) \in B$, there are at least m' values $i \in \{1,\ldots,n\}$ such that $(x_1,\ldots,x_{i-1}, 1 - x_i, x_{i+1},\ldots,x_n) \in A$.*

Then, $Q(f) = \Omega(\sqrt{mm'})$.

Theorem 2. *[1] Let $f(x_1, x_2, \ldots, x_n)$ be a function of n $\{0,1\}$ - valued variables and X, Y be two sets of inputs such that $f(x) \neq f(y)$ if $x \in X$ and $y \in Y$. Let $R \subset X * Y$ be such that*

- *for every $x \in X$ there exist at least m different $y \in Y$ such that $(x,y) \in R$,*
- *for every $y \in Y$ there exist at least m' different $x \in X$ such that $(x,y) \in R$,*
- *for every $x \in X$ and $i \in \{1,\ldots,n\}$ there are at most l_i different $y \in Y$ such that $(x,y) \in R$ and $x_i \neq y_i$,*
- *for every $y \in Y$ and $i \in \{1,\ldots,n\}$ there are at most l'_i different $x \in X$ such that $(x,y) \in R$ and $x_i \neq y_i$.*

Then, any quantum algorithm computing f uses $\Omega(\sqrt{\frac{mm'}{max(l_i * l'_i)}})$ queries.

Definition 1. *For any Boolean function $f : \{0,1\}^N \to \{0,1\}$ and any $x = (x_1 \ldots x_n)$, $ND(f,x)$ is the number of queries needed by nondeterministic algorithms on the values $x = (x_1 \ldots x_n)$.*

Definition 2. *For any Boolean function $f : \{0,1\}^N \to \{0,1\}$: $ND_0(f) = \max_{f(x)=0} ND(f,x)$ and $ND_1(f) = \max_{f(x)=1} ND(f,x)$. $ND_0(f) = \sum$*

Theorem 3. *[2] Whatever the sets A and B, Theorem 1 cannot prove a better lower bound for the query complexity $Q(f)$ than $\sqrt{ND_0(f) * ND_1(f)}$.*

We consider the following graph problems in our paper.

Problems

Problem 1. Partition into cliques
INSTANCE: Graph G=(V,E), with $|V| = qk$ for fixed integer $q > 1$ and some integer k.
QUESTION: Can the vertices of G be partitioned into k disjoints sets $V_1, V_2, \ldots,$ V_k such that, for $1 \leq i \leq k$, the subgraph induced by V_i is a complete graph and $|V_i| = q$?

Problem 2. Partition into triangles
INSTANCE: Graph G=(V,E), with $|V| = 3k$ for some integer k.
QUESTION: Can the vertices of G be partitioned into q disjoint sets $V_1, V_2, \ldots,$

V_k, each containing exactly 3 vertices, such that for each $V_i = \{u_i, v_i, w_i\}$, $1 \leq i \leq k$, all three of the edges $\{u_i, v_i\}, \{u_i, w_i\}, \{v_i, w_i\}$ belong to E?

Problem 3. Matching
INSTANCE: Graph G=(V,E), $|V| = n$.
QUESTION: Can the vertices of G be partitioned into n/2 disjoints pairs $P_1, P_2, \ldots, P_{n/2}$ such that for each $P_i = \{u_i, v_i\}$, $1 \leq i \leq n/2$, edge $\{u_i, v_i\}$ belong to E?

Problem 4. Parity
INSTANCE: Matrix M $2n \times 2n$, $M_{ij} \in \{0, 1\}$.
QUESTION: $\sum_{i=1,2n} PARITY(M_i) = n$?

Problem 5. Hamiltonian circuit
INSTANCE: Graph G=(V,E).
QUESTION: Does G contain Hamiltonian circuit?

Problem 6. Directed Hamiltonian circuit
INSTANCE: Directed graph G=(V,A).
QUESTION: Does G contain directed Hamiltonian circuit?

Problem 7. Hamiltonian path
INSTANCE: Graph G=(V,E).
QUESTION: Does G contain Hamiltonian path?

Problem 8. Travelling salesman
INSTANCE: Set C of m cities, distance $d(c_i, c_j) \in Z^+$ for each pair of cities, $c_i c_j \in C$, positive integer B.
QUESTION: Is there a tour of C having length B or less, i.e. a permutation $\langle c_{\pi(1)}, c_{\pi(2)}, \ldots, c_{\pi(m)} \rangle$ of C such that $(\sum_{i=1}^{m} d(c_{\pi(i)}, c_{\pi(i+1)})) + d(c_{\pi(m)}, c_{\pi(1)}) \leq B$?

Problem 9. Dominating set for trees
INSTANCE: Tree G=(V, E), positive integer $K \leq |V|$.
QUESTION: Is there a dominating set of size K or less for G,i.e. a subset $V' \subseteq V$ with $|V'| \leq K$ such that for all $u \in V - V'$ there is a $v \in V'$ for which $\{u, v\} \in E$?

Problem 10. Dominating set
INSTANCE: Graph G=(V, E), positive integer $K \leq |V|$.
QUESTION: Is there a dominating set of size K or less for G,i.e. a subset $V' \subseteq V$ with $|V'| \leq K$ such that for all $u \in V - V'$ there is a $v \in V'$ for which $\{u, v\} \in E$?

We use incidence matrix representation of graphs.

3   Main Results

Lemma 1. *If there are k+1 not connected points in the graph G=(V,E), $|V| = kq$, then* **Partition into cliques** *problem is not solvable.*

Proof. If there is a solution for **Partition into cliques**, we get k disjoints sets. Since there is k+1 mutually not connected vertices, there is at least one subset containing two mutually not connected vertices and **Partition into cliques** problem is not solvable.

Lemma 2. *If graph G=(V,E), $|V| = kq$, satisfies the following requirements:*

- *there are $k/2$ mutually not connected (red) vertices,*
- *there are k green vertices not connected with red ones, green vertices are grouped in pairs and each pair is connected by edge,*
- *subgraph induced by all the rest vertices (black) is a complete graph and all black vertices are connected to all red and green vertices,*

then **Partition into cliques** *problem is solvable.*

Proof. Vertices are grouped in subsets in accordance with the following:

- each red vertex is put in a separate subset ($k/2$ subsets),
- each pair of green vertices is put in a separate subset ($k/2$ subsets),
- black vertices are added as follows: q 1 to red and q-2 to green vertices.

Such a distribution satisfies **Partition into cliques** problem.

Lemma 3. *If graph G=(V,E), $|V| = kq$, satisfies the following requirements:*

- *there are $k/2 + 2$ mutually not connected (red) vertices,*
- *there are k-2 green vertices not connected with red ones, green vertices are grouped in pairs and each pair is connected by edge,*
- *subgraph induced by all the rest vertices (black) is a complete graph and all black vertices are connected to all red and green vertices,*

then **Partition into cliques** *problem is not solvable*

Proof. If we take red vertices and one from each pair of green vertices then we get $k/2 + 2 + (k - 2)/2 = k + 1$ vertices. These vertices are not mutually connected. The Partition into cliques problem is not solvable because the set of selected vertices satisfies the requirements of Lemma 1.

Theorem 4. Partition into cliques *requires $\Omega(n^{1.5})$ quantum queries.*

Proof. We construct the sets A and B for the usage of Theorem 1. The set A consists of all graphs G satisfying the requirements of Lemma 2. The value of the function corresponding to the **Partition into cliques** problem is 1. (This follows from Lemma 2.) The set B consists of all graphs G satisfying the requirements of Lemma 3. The value of the function corresponding the **Partition into cliques** problem is 0. (This follows from Lemma 3.)

From each graph $G \in A$, we can obtain $G' \in B$ by disconnecting any one of the edges, which connect the green vertices. Hence $m = k/2 = O(k)$. From each graph $G' \in B$, we can obtain $G \in A$ by connecting any two red vertices. Hence $m' = (k/2 + 2)(k/2 + 1)/2 = O(k^2)$.

Since q is fixed, it follows that $k = O(n)$. By Theorem 10, the quantum query complexity is $\Omega\sqrt{n * n^2} = \Omega(n^{1.5})$.

The same idea proves the following two theorems.

Theorem 5. Matching *requires $\Omega(n^{1.5})$ quantum queries.*

Theorem 6. Partition into triangles *requires $\Omega(n^{1.5})$ quantum queries.*

Theorem 7. *The lower bound for Partition into cliques cannot be improved by Ambainis' method*

Proof. We use Theorem 3. Let the Boolean function f describe **Partition into cliques.** $ND_1(f) = O(n)$, because it suffices to ask the edges for all the guessed subsets of vertices; all the subsets are of constant size. $ND_0(f) = O(n^2)$, because it suffices to exhibit a subset of $k + 1$ vertices connected by no edges. Since $k = O(n)$, $(k-1)k/2 = O(n^2)$.
    Hence $\sqrt{ND_1(f) * ND_0(f)} = O(n^{1.5})$.

Theorem 8. Parity *problem requires $\Omega(n^2)$ quantum queries.*

Proof. We construct the sets A and B for the usage of Theorem 1. The set A consists of all matrices M with n rows containing n symbols "v1" per row plus n rows containing n+1 symbols "1" per row. The set B consists of all matrices M with n-1 rows containing n symbols "1" per row plus n+1 rows containing n+1 symbols "12 per row.
    Every matrix $M \in A$ can be transformed into a matrix $M' \in B$ by taking an arbitrary row with n symbols "1" and transforming an arbitrary "0" into "1". Hence $m = n^2$. Every matrix $M' \in B$ can be transformed into a matrix $M \in A$ by taking an arbitrary row with n+1 symbols "1" and transforming an arbitrary symbol "1" into "0". Hence $m' = n^2$.
    By Theorem 1, the quantum query complexity is $\Omega\sqrt{n^2 * n^2} = \Omega(n^2)$. This is the maximum possible lower bound.

Lemma 4. *If a graph G=(V,E), $|V| = 5n$, satisfies the following requirements:*

- *there are n mutually not connected (red) vertices,*
- *there are 2n green vertices not connected with red ones,green vertices are grouped in pairs and each pair is connected by edge,*
- *subgraph induced by the rest 2n vertices (black) is a complete graph and all black vertices are connected to all red and green vertices,*

then **Hamiltonian circuit** *problem is solvable.*

Proof. We denote black vertices m_1 to m_{2n}. Red vertices are denoted k_1 to k_n, pairs of green with k_{n+1} to k_{2n}. Sequence $m_1 k_1 \ldots m_n k_n m_{n+1} k_{n+1} \ldots m_{2n} k_{2n} m_1$ (i.e. black, red,... black, red, black, green, green,...,black, green, green, black) satisfies **Hamiltonian circuit** problem.

Lemma 5. *If graph G=(V,E), $|V| = 5n$, satisfies the following requirements:*
- *there are n+2 mutually not connected (red) vertices,*

- *there are 2n-2 green vertices not connected with red ones, green vertices are grouped in pairs and each pair is connected by edge,*
- *subgraph induced by the rest 2n vertices (black) is a complete graph and all black vertices are connected to all red and green vertices,*

then **Hamiltonian circuit** *problem is not solvable.*

Proof. The red vertices and the pairs of green vertices are mutually not connected. The only way to get from one red vertex to another (or from one green pair to another) is through some black vertex. There are $2n$ black in the graph, but $n + 2$ red vertices, and $n - 1$ green pair makes altogether $2n + 1$. So at least one of the black vertices will be used twice, which is not allowed in Hamiltonian circuit.

Theorem 9. *Hamiltonian circuit problem requires $\Omega(n^{1.5})$ quantum queries.*

Proof. We construct the sets A and B for the usage of Theorem 1. The set A consists of all graphs G satisfying the requirements of Lemma 4. The value of the function corresponding to the **Hamiltonian circuit** problem is 1. (This follows from Lemma 4.) The set B consists of all graphs G satisfying the requirements of Lemma 5. The value of the function corresponding the **Hamiltonian circuit** problem is 0. (This follows from Lemma 5.)

From each graph $G \in A$, we can obtain $G' \in B$ by disconnecting any one of the edges, which connect the green vertices. Hence $m = n = O(n)$. From each graph $G' \in B$, we can obtain $G \in A$ by connecting any two red vertices. Hence $m' = (n + 2)(n + 1) = O(n^2)$.

By Theorem 1, the quantum query complexity is $\Omega\sqrt{n * n^2} = \Omega(n^{1.5})$.

The same idea proves Theorem 10.

Theorem 10. Directed Hamiltonian circuit *requires $Omega(n^{1.5})$ quantum queries.*

Lemma 6. *If graph $G=(V,E)$, $|V| = 5n$, satisfies the requirements of Lemma 5, then* **Hamiltonian path** *problem is solvable.*

Proof. We denote black vertices m_1 to m_{2n}. Red vertices are denoted k_1 to k_{n+2}, pairs of green with k_{n+3} to k_{2n+1}. Sequence $k_1 m_1 \ldots k_{n+2} m_{n+2} k_{n+3} m_{n+3} \ldots m_{2n} k_{2n+1}$ (i.e. red, black, ... red, black, green, green, black, ...,black, green, green) satisfies **Hamiltonian path** problem.

Lemma 7. *If graph $G=(V,E)$, $|V| = 5n$, satisfies the following requirements:*
- *there are $n+4$ mutually not connected (red) vertices,*
- *there are $2n-4$ green vertices not connected with red ones, green vertices are grouped in pairs and each pair is connected by edge,*
- *subgraph induced by the rest 2n vertices (black) is a complete graph and all black vertices are connected to all red and green vertices,*

then **Hamiltonian path** *problem is not solvable.*

Proof. The proof is analogical to that of Lemma 5.

Theorem 11. Hamiltonian path *requires* $Omega(n^{1.5})$ *quantum queries.*

Proof. We construct the sets A and B for the usage of Theorem 1. The set A consists of all graphs G satisfying the requirements of Lemma 6. The value of the function corresponding to the **Hamiltonian path** problem is 1. The set B consists of all graphs G satisfying the requirements of Lemma 7. The value of the function corresponding the **Hamiltonian path** problem is 0.

From each graph $G \in A$, we can obtain $G' \in B$ by disconnecting any one of the edges, which connect the green vertices. Hence $m = n - 1 = O(n)$. From each graph $G' \in B$, we can obtain $G \in A$ by connecting any two red vertices. Hence $m' = (n + 4)(n + 3) = O(n^2)$.

By Theorem 1, the quantum query complexity is $\Omega\sqrt{n * n^2} = \Omega(n^{1.5})$.

Theorem 12. Travelling salesman *problem requires* $Omega(n^{1.5})$ *quantum queries.*

Proof. **Travelling salesman** problem can be easily reduced to **Hamiltonian circuit** problem, by taking all the distances equal to 1 and B equal to number of cities.

Theorem 13. *The lower bound for* **Hamiltonian circuit** *cannot be improved by Ambainis' method.*

Proof. We use Theorem 3. Let the Boolean function f describe **Hamiltonian circuit**. $ND_1(f) = O(n)$, because it suffices to guess the sequence of vertices and ask the edge for every pair of subsequent vertices. $ND_0(f) = O(n^2)$, because it suffices to check that a graph satisfies conditions of Lemma 5.
Hence $= \sqrt{ND_1(f) * ND_0(f)} = O(n^{1.5})$.

Lemma 8. *If tree $G=(V,E)$, $|V| = 3n + 1$, $K=n$, satisfies the following requirements:*

- *root vertex is connected to n red vertices,*
- *each of n red vertices is connected to exactly one green vertex,*
- *each of n black vertices is connected to exactly one red vertex, but any red vertex can be connected to any number of black vertices,*

then **Dominating set** *problem is solvable.*

Proof. We have a tree with three layers: root layer, red vertices layer and green and black vertices layer. Middle layer, which consists of n red vertices, satisfies **Dominating set** problem.

Lemma 9. *If tree $G=(V,E)$, $|V| = 3n + 1$, $K=n$, satisfies the following requirements:*
- *root vertex is connected to n red vertices,*
- *each of n red vertices is connected to exactly one green vertex,*

- *each of n-1 black vertices is connected to exactly one red vertex, and there is one black vertex that is connected to another black vertex,*

then **Dominating set** *problem is not solvable*

Proof. We have a tree with four layers: root layer, red vertices layer and green and black vertices layer, and the fourth is the layer with only one black vertex. That means that we need at least one more vertex in Dominating set in addition to middle layer, which gives us n+1 vertices.

Theorem 14. Dominating set *problem for trees requires $Omega(n^{1.5})$ quantum queries.*

Proof. We construct the sets X and Y for the usage of Theorem 2. The set X consists of all graphs G satisfying the requirements of Lemma 8. The set Y consists of all graphs G satisfying the requirements of Lemma 9.

From each graph $G \in X$, we can obtain $G' \in Y$ by removing any one of the edges, which connect the black and the red vertex (there are n ways we can do it) and connecting that black vertex to any other black vertex (n ways to do it). Hence m= $O(n^2)$. From each graph $G' \in Y$, we can obtain $G \in X$ by removing the edge connecting two black vertices (1 way to do it) and connecting the free black vertex to any red one (n ways to do it). Hence $m' = O(n)$.

Now we'll find $\max(l_i * l'_i)$. For any edge connecting black and red vertices $l_i = n$, because when we remove black – red edge, we can do that in n combinations of remove-and-create operations, and $l'_i = 1$, because we can build black-red edge using only one combination; for any edge connecting two black vertices $l_i = 1$ and $l'_i = n$ with the same idea. Thus $\max(l_i * l'_i) = n$.

By Theorem 2, the quantum query complexity is $\Omega\sqrt{\frac{n*n^2}{n}} = \Omega(n)$.

Theorem 15. *The lower bound for* **Dominating set** *for trees cannot be improved by Ambainis' method.*

Proof. We use Theorem 3. Let the Boolean function f describe **Dominating set** for trees. $ND_1(f) = O(n)$, because it suffices to guess dominating set of vertices and the connections to it from other vertices. $ND_0(f) = O(n)$, supposing that tree is given with adjacency list, because there are only n-1 edges in the tree.
Hence $= \sqrt{ND_1(f) * ND_0(f)} = O(n)$.

Lemma 10. *If graph $G=(V,E)$, $|V| = n$, $K=3n/4-1$, satisfies the following requirements:*

- *there are $n/2 + 2$ red vertices, pairwisely connected,*
- *there are $n/2 - 2$ black vertices, not mutually connected,*

then **Dominating set** *problem is solvable.*

Proof. n/2+2 red vertices make n/4+1 dominating vertices, adding n/2-2 black vertices gives 3n/4-1 dominating vertices, which satisfies Dominating set problem.

Lemma 11. *If graph G=(V,E), $|V| = n$, K=3n/4-1, satisfies the following requirements:*

- *there are n/2 red vertices, pairwisely connected,*
- *there are n/2 black vertices, not mutually connected,*

then **Dominating set** *problem is not solvable.*

Proof. n/2 red vertices make n/4 dominating vertices, adding n/2 black vertices gives 3n/4 dominating vertices, which is more than K and doesn't satisfy **Dominating set** problem.

Theorem 16. *Dominating set problem requires $\Omega(n^{1.5})$ quantum queries.*

Proof. We construct the sets A and B for the usage of Theorem 1. The set A consists of all graphs G satisfying the requirements of Lemma 10. The set B consists of all graphs G satisfying the requirements of Lemma 11.

From each graph $G \in A$, we can obtain $G' \in B$ by removing any one of the edges, which connect red vertices. Hence $m = (n/4 + 1) = O(n)$. From each graph $G' \in B$, we can obtain $G \in A$ by connecting any two black vertices. Hence m'=$(n/2)(n/2 - 1) = O(n^2)$.

By Theorem 1, the quantum query complexity is $\Omega\sqrt{n * n^2} = \Omega(n^{1.5})$.

Theorem 17. *The lower bound for* **Dominating set** *cannot be improved by Ambainis' method.*

Proof. We use Theorem 3. Let the Boolean function f describe Dominating set. $ND_1(f) = O(n)$, because it suffices to guess dominating set of vertices and the connections to it from other vertices. $ND_0(f) = O(n^2)$, because it suffices to read all edges and run deterministic algorithm.

Hence $= \sqrt{ND_1(f) * ND_0(f)} = O(n^{1.5})$.

References

1. Ambainis, A.: Quantum Lower Bounds by Quantum Arguments. Journal of Computer and System Sciences, **64** (2002) 750–767
2. Ambainis, A.: Personal communication (2003)
3. Bennett, C.H., Bernstein, E., Brassard, G., Vazirani, U.V.: Strengths and Weaknesses of Quantum Computing. SIAM Journal on Computing, **26** (1997) 1510–1523
4. Buhrman, H., de Wolf, R.: Complexity Measures and Decision Tree Complexity: A Survey. Theoretical Computer Science, **288** 1 (2002) 21–43
5. Freivalds, R., Winter, A.: Quantum Finite State Transducers. In: SOFSEM 2001 (2001) 233–242
6. Grover, L.: A Fast Quantum Mechanical Algorithm for Database Search. Proceedings of the 28th ACM symposium on Theory of Computing (1996) 212–219
7. Gruska, J.: Quantum Computing. McGraw-Hill (1999)
8. Nielsen, M., Chuang, I.: Quantum Computation and Quantum Information. Cambridge University Press (2000)

A Model of Versioned Web Sites*

Mária Bieliková and Ivan Noris

Faculty of Informatics and Information Technologies, Slovak University of Technology
Ilkovičova 3, 812 19 Bratislava, Slovakia
bielik@fiit.stuba.sk
http://www.fiit.stuba.sk/~bielik

Abstract. In this paper we present a model of versioned web sites which
is aimed at building a web site configuration. The web site configuration
is a consistent version of the web site and serves for navigation purposes.
We exploit the fact that the versioning of web sites is in many aspects
similar to versioning of software systems (and their components). On
the other hand, specific characteristics related to the web environment
and web sites in particular are considered. The web site is modelled by
an AND/OR type graph. The model serves as a useful abstraction simplifying the process of configuration building. Being essentially a graph
search, it is inevitable to have a method for selecting a proper version.
Presented approach is best suited for web sites where several variants
of web pages exist. It is advantageous for example for presentation of
multilingual web sites. We briefly discuss developed software tool for
versioning and navigation on the multilingual web site which is based on
proposed model of versioned web site.

1 Introduction

Web sites evolve by changing their content and structure over time. Change
is inevitable. However, the web today as a rule supports only one version of
a document – the current one. Requirement to store and access previous versions of the web content, retrieve the history of the content, annotate revisions
with comments about the changes, or navigate through a versioned web site is
explicitly noted already in [2]. This requirement follows the evolution in the area
of hypermedia research, where version control has been identified as a critically
important task [8].

The literature lists many reasons for saving the history of an object (be
it software component, hypermedia node, or web page), including distributed
and collaborative development, keeping old versions for later use, assuring the
safety of recent work against various kinds of accidents, preserving cited work in
the original state. The purpose of document versions is not only a change. For

---

* This work has been supported by the Grant Agency of Slovak Republic grant No.
VG1/ 0162/03 "Collaborative accessing, analysis and presentation of documents in
internet environment using modern software tools".

example, to be accessible to a large audience web sites often contain information written in more than one language – each can be considered as a version.

Evolution of information presented on the web and related problems are discussed in several works [18], [14], [4], [17]. Content management systems often provide versioning in the sense of software systems versioning [6]. A user – content manager – can store snapshots of his work (revisions) and come back to them later, or develop the web site by collaboration in a distributed team. Such scheme can be sufficient from a developer point of view, but not from a user (reader) point of view, who stands in a need of navigation through versioned web site.

In this paper we address the problem of computer support for navigation within a versioned web site. We have proposed a model of versioned web site which is simple, but still sufficiently rich to reflect the principal relations and properties which are decisive in the web site configuration building. The web site configuration is a consistent version of the web site that serves for navigation purposes. We have adopted the AND/OR graph model formalized for software systems in [3]. Semantics of the model is specified according to specific properties of web sites.

Central notions of proposed model include following: web pages are characterized by properties defined at three levels: family level, variant level and revision level; links are established with respect to a family of target page rather than the pages themselves; page to page connections are established at time of a configuration building; several revisions (of different page variants) can be included in the configuration.

2   Modelling a Web Site

A model is used to express a web site structure, respecting in our case the point of view of navigation of the versioned web site (i.e. building its configuration). The web site configuration can be used for off-line browsing within selected version of the versioned web site.

2.1   Elements of the Model

A web site consists of several independent parts (nodes) interconnected by *links*. Each node – a *web page* – primarily comprises the content going to be presented. Obviously, there exists a mechanism for presentation layout definition (either embedded in each node or represented separately in one place for several nodes, or the whole web site). The web page often comprises both the content in the form of a text or other media and chunks of programming source code which provide dynamic content.

We consider two scenarios for a web page version creation [5], [6], [18]. First, versions are created to represent alternate forms of a page. Such 'parallel' versions, or *variants*, are frequently results of alternative realizations of the same concept (e.g., multilingual variants). The variants can evolve independently. Second, versions are created to represent improvements of previous ones, or as modifications caused by an error correction, content enhancement, and/or adaptation to changes in the environment. Such 'serial' versions, or *revisions*, are frequently results of modifications of the same variant. A *family* of web pages comprises all web pages which are versions of one another. Note that the concept of parallel versions induces an equivalence relation within the set of web pages. We shall use the term *version* in cases where both variants or revisions can be considered.

Let us formulate the notions more formally now. Let P_S be a set of web pages of a web site S. Then a binary relation $is\_version_S \subseteq P_S \times P_S$ is given as the reflexive and transitive closure of another binary relation which is defined by elementary transformations describing such modifications of web pages that they can still be considered to be expressing essentially the same content. Relation $is\_version_S$ is reflexive, symmetric and transitive.

A set of all equivalence classes induced by the $is\_version_S$ relation is denoted F_S and called a set of families of web pages of the web site S. An element of F_S is called a family of web sites. In other words, a family consists of web pages which are related by relation $is\_version$. Usually such web pages are presented by means of the relation $is\_developed\_from$ as so called version graph [11], [10], [6]. Nodes denote various versions as they are created; an arrow from version A to version B indicates that B was created from A. All the web pages included in the version graph form a family of web pages.

We define for each versioned web page a set of properties (using attribute-value pairs) and its content (usually a HTML text, scripts, and embedded media). Based on that, we consider *variants* as sets of those web pages which share certain properties. This conceptual design choice does not impose any serious limitations in most cases. On the contrary, it provides a considerable flexibility to the specification of versioned web site navigation. It offers a useful abstraction that should simplify the process of navigation. In order to describe variants, we define a binary relation $is\_variant$ which determines a set of web pages with the same subset of properties within a given family. The binary relation $is\_variant_S \subseteq P_S \times P_S$ is defined by:

$$x \; is\_variant_S \; y \Leftrightarrow x \; is\_version_S \; y \wedge x.VariantAttr = y.VariantAttr$$

Variants are important to simplify management of web page versions when selecting a revision of some page, or during an automatic navigation within the versioned web site. We can treat a whole group of web pages in a uniform way due to the fact that all of them have the relevant properties defined as equal (e.g., the content is written in English).

One consequence of our design decision of taking variants to be sets of web pages is that from the two kinds of versions of web pages, only revisions are left to represent actual single web pages. Figure 1 depicts the above defined relationships.

The distribution of web pages to variants depends on a decision which properties are considered as variant properties and which are considered as revision

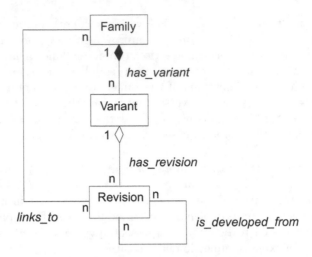

Fig. 1. Family-Variant-Revision relationships

properties, i.e. unique properties of the actual web page. Decision about distributing attributes is left open for a developer in our approach because it depends on the project, its size, problem domain, etc. Typical recommendations applicable in many cases are to consider as variant attributes specific characteristics of the user knowledge (e.g., novice, intermediate, advances), characteristics of a developer environment (e.g., HTML version), or characteristics of a user environment (e.g., browser used). This means that a change of these properties leads to a new variant. Properties related to the development process such as state, change description, author, date, time are often considered as revision attributes, i.e. their change leads to a new revision.

2.2   Model Formulation

The concepts introduced above allow us to formulate a model of a versioned web site which would support a navigation. Determining versions for navigation resembles a configuration building in software configuration management. From the point of view of a family, a model should involve families and variants included in them. Links from a family to all its variants are defined by the relation $has\_variant_S \subseteq F_S \times V_S : x \; has\_variant_S \; y \Leftrightarrow y \subseteq x$.

From the point of view of a variant, the model should represent links to all those families which are referred to in revisions of that variant. When building a configuration, for each family already included in a configuration there must be selected at least one variant. For each variant already included in a configuration, there must be included precisely one revision. For all selected revisions, all the families related by links to that revision must be included. A configuration comprising more than one variant of the web page is inevitable for example in case of building the configuration of a multilingual web site with specific requirements for English and Slovak language pages.

Our method of modelling a web site S is to describe it by an oriented graph, with nodes representing families and revisions in such a way that these two kinds of nodes alternate on every path. Let F_S be a set of families of web pages, P_S be a set of web page revisions of a web site S. Let FN be a set of names and $f\_name_S : F_S \rightarrow FN$ an injective function which assigns a unique name to each family of a web site S. Let $A \subseteq P_S \times FN$ be a binary relation defined as:

$e_1 \; A \; e_2 \Leftrightarrow \exists r(r \in e_1.Link \wedge r.FamilyId = e_2)$

Let $O \subseteq FN \times P_S$ be a binary relation defined as:

$e_1 \; O \; e_2 \Leftrightarrow e_2 \in f\_name_S^{-1}(e_1)$.

We define a model of a web site S to be an oriented graph $M_S = (N, E)$, where $N = FN_S \cup P_S$ is a set of nodes with $FN_S = \{\, x \mid x \in FN \wedge f\_name_S^{-1}(x) \in F_S \}$, and $E = A \cup O$ is a set of edges such that every maximal connected subgraph has at least one root.

We remark that the binary relation A stands for hyperlinks (relating revisions to families) and the relation O mirrors *has_revision* relation. Such A/O graph model refers for the previously introduced notions (revision, variant, family). Variants are covered in the model implicitly through sets of A-nodes which represent revisions.

The usual interpretation is that A-nodes are origins of edges leading to nodes, all of which must be considered provided the A-node is under consideration (logical AND). Similarly, O-nodes are origins of edges leading to nodes, from among which exactly one must be considered provided the O-node is under consideration (logical OR).

The example of a web site model is depicted in Figure 2. For the sake of clarity we depict also variants and relation *has_variant*. One possible configuration for the content written in Slovak language is highlighted (bold).

Proposed model is a version–family kind of model (an analogy of intertwined model known in software engineering [6]). The navigation relations are defined for each revision and the revisions are connected to the web page families only. Therefore, when a new version of target of a relation is created, the relation itself is not affected, so there is no need to create new version of the source component. Definition of links within revisions and families compromises the complexity of the model and subsequent support for navigation, and its flexibility.

If all links were defined on the variant level (all revisions within a variant share the same links), we would be able to exploit the model on several levels of abstraction: as an abstract model containing families and variants; a generic configuration containing selected variants, and bound configuration containing interconnected revisions. However, requirement for links definition on the variant level is in many cases too limiting. It can be successfully used for multilingual sites with only several revisions.

3   Navigation and Configuration Building

Process of navigation within a versioned web site is based on determining a target of the selected link. The navigation procedure is defined as a graph search,

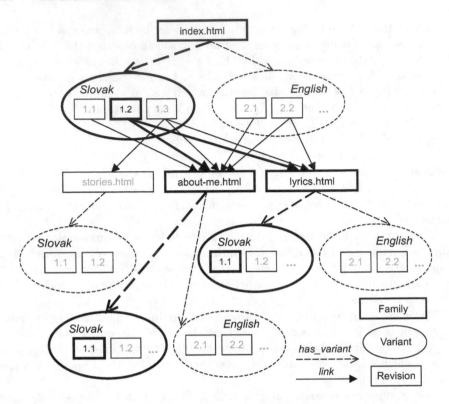

Fig. 2. Example model of a web site

where the graph constitutes model of the versioned web site. We use the version selection filters which are conditions applied to all versions of appropriate families of the web pages [13].

Any version can have its own and independent attribute structure, so it can be modified without affecting other versions. This makes the attribute structure sufficiently flexible. On the other hand, some attributes (e.g., Language, Browser) are supposed to be shared between several revisions of the web page (or web page families). Several types of attributes are defined (e.g., string, number, time, list, set). A set of system attributes further improves the management of meta-data related to the versioning. The system attributes are automatically set by a tool providing the model of versioned web site. We distinguish several types of system attributes:

Read-only system attributes: their values are set only once after creating a new revision (e.g., InsertTime, InsertUser). The values cannot be changed.

Auto-updating system attributes: their values are updated automatically after each version significant change (e.g., ChangeTime, ChangeUser).

Default-value system attributes: they have some predefined values, but can be changed later (e.g., VersionCodename, Owners, Author, Keywords).

In the proposed model we use variant attributes to distinguish between revisions of various variant sets. Each variant wires revisions with the same values of the variant attributes. In the course of version selection process the variant attributes are evaluated first. Any attribute may be flagged as the variant attribute. The revisions are grouped into variants considering their properties.

The version selection is a two-step process: first, the corresponding variant and then the revision is selected. Thus, the variants exist only on a "logical level". Version selection is described and formalized in [12]. We concentrate in this paper on specific features applicable for version selection of web pages.

3.1   Version Selection Filters

Version of a web page is selected using a set of selection filters. Selection filter is represented by a logical expression which operates on version properties.

Limitation of the proposed approach is that selection filters need not guarantee that exactly one version is selected. If the sequence of filters is too strict, none of the versions would match. On the other hand, more than one version could match loose filters. To avoid such cases, an implementation of the proposed approach should allow to refine (add, modify or even remove) the filter, at least as a user-initiated action. Also internal restrictions based on e.g., last modification time, can be implemented to filter out all but one matching version.

Version selection filters can be of two kinds: user-defined filters, and default filters. The option to save a sequence of filters as a "named configuration specification" makes the version selection mechanism more flexible and allows its reuse.

User-defined filters. The user-defined filters can be entered by any visitor of the versioned web site. The filters are defined explicitly on the user request. The number of filters is not limited in our proposal, however, some implementation limitations are expected to occur. The user-defined filters can be defined for any attribute and any required values.

Default filters. Default filters are defined by the web page author and are automatically applied when accessing a versioned web page. The need for default filters is based on the fact that a version-unaware users could easily visit the web site. Such users are not expected to be concerned with version control and may feel confused when dealing with the attributes and configuration specifications. On the other hand, it may be useful for the content author to guide the visitors in some way.

We distinguish static and dynamic default filters. A static default filter specifies a version in such a way that its evaluation will lead always to the same version. The dynamic default filters allow the author to set conditions which will automatically apply when the version within the family should be selected. The simplest dynamic filter selects the last inserted revision.

The dynamic default filters are flexible and allow the author to write conditions which ensure a version selection according to the current browsing session. The browser type, preferred language, client's top-level domain etc. can be used to determine user's requirements. The dynamic default filters can also be used to distinguish local and remote users. They are evaluated automatically, if the filter trigger has been activated. The trigger's actual value is compared with the author-supplied value. If the values match, the trigger is activated and the filter based on the trigger would apply. If more filters use the same trigger, they are defined separately. In developed software tool (see next section) we have used environment variables as filter triggers (e.g., HTTP_USER_AGENT variable stores identification of the current client; HTTP_ACCEPT_LANGUAGE contains accept language codes sorted by client's preference). These variables are set automatically by the web server.

Specified sequence of default selection filters can be set at the logon time for certain users or groups of users. Presentation of a versioned web site using described mechanisms becomes adaptive.

We have also proposed a mechanism for accession alternatives of currently displayed page. This is accomplished by conditions for alternatives. The alternative versions have different values for combinations of the specified attributes. Conditions for alternatives together with displaying mechanism allow a user to see links to the corresponding versions with the alternative content (e.g. written in different language) on each visited page.

On a user request the value of selected attribute in selected filter changes and the alternative version is provided. In developed software tool, we use only one attribute for updating the conditions (the *ContentLanguage* attribute). This simplification is partially based on the purpose of the developed tool (to provide a support for multilingual sites). However, the greater number of attributes implies the greater number of possible combinations of their values produced, i.e. the number of alternate contents would grow exponentially.

3.2   Configuration Building

A configuration building is the process of selection appropriate revisions for all web pages families to be included in the configuration. The configuration can be built for off-line content reading or by actual browsing through the versioned web site. This process consists of four basic steps:

1. Select a starting family f of web pages (the O-node in the model); obviously the starting family is the root of the web site model.
2. Select appropriate revision v of the web page (one of the A-nodes connected to the family f by *has_revision* relation); this step is based on specified version selection filters; at first variant is selected and then revision within this variant [13], [12].
3. Provide attached elements for revision v, provide versions of attached elements.
4. IF the stop condition is false THEN select next web page to be included in the configuration (all those families which are referred to in the revision v are considered) and go to the step 2.

If the configuration is created in a browser, the family considered in the next cycle (step 4) is determined by a visitor by clicking on a link. Otherwise, next family for processing is selected according the search strategy adopted (e.g., depth-search or breath-search strategy).

4   An Application of the Model

We developed a software tool called *DiVer* for support of the navigation on versioned web sites [13]. DiVer implements described model for web pages written in HTML. Its primary purpose was presentation of multilingual web sites. We considered following requirements while developing a prototype of versioned web site navigation tool:

1. URLs pointed to the web page from the external (unversioned) space should remain working;
2. a reader should understand that he is viewing a versioned page; he should be able to access different versions of the displayed page;
3. there must be a mechanism for navigation within versioned space (method for web site configuration presented in the previous section is exploited); this mechanism should mimic standard web navigating (as without versions);
4. web pages with alternative content (written for example in different languages) should be easily accessible.

DiVer tool similarly to the V-Web tool [14] adds to the top of a web page a frame containing a textual depiction of the web page's version information together with possibility to select a version, define selection filters or see alternative versions. Original HTML page is replaced by a new HTML composite page which comprises menu and the content of the selected version from an archive of versions (see Figure 3).

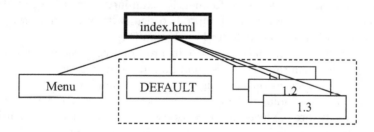

Fig. 3. Versioned web page

The version control related attributes are defined only for versions (variants, revisions) of the HTML-elements. In our opinion, there is no need to define attributes of other elements, e.g., images, because the images are included in the composite HTML elements and not selected into configurations separately. This simplification significantly influences the data that have to be stored and processed. Of course, the attached components are also versioned and can be identified and accessed by the version number. Therefore, only HTML-elements are represented in the model. When the HTML-element revision is selected, appropriate revisions of all attached elements are selected. The information about attached elements and their versions is stored in the attribute structure of the HTML-element revision.

Our software tool uses RCS [15] as a revision control back end on the server side. The graphical front end on the client side is developed in Perl language. The archive library is used to save and restore version attributes which are stored separately in XML archives. Version attribute structure is used to select appropriate version while creating the configuration. "Cookie" mechanism is used to transfer the selection filters. RCS uses a check-in/check-out paradigm to create revisions. It organizes the revisions into an ancestral graph and stores them in a file called an archive. We suppose that a tool which implements proposed model will rest the version control responsibility for the files with a revision control system such as RCS, while responsibility for maintaining the relations between the files will reside with the tool.

The DiVer tool conforms WebDAV protocol (Distributed Authoring and Versioning over the Web) [1] and its DeltaV extension (Web Versioning and Configuration Management) [11] (however, it was not developed with assumption of a web server supporting such extended HTTP protocol because of non availability of the WebDAV web server support in time of the tool development). The tool for navigation in versioned web space built on our model should be responsible for substituting the family URL (the same as for unversioned page) by the DeltaV stable URL.

5   Related Work

In the hypermedia field, the problems connected to version control and configuration management have been frequently examined and discussed [16]. Also a wide variety of research has attempted to deal with versioning issues on the web. Example of this work include [14], [1], [2], [11], [17].

Two basic version models are used in area of hypermedia [7]: state-based versioning which maintains the version of an individual resource, and task-based versioning which focuses on tracking versions of complex systems as a whole. These concepts are similar to those of state-based and change-based versioning as known in software engineering [6]. Proposed model is oriented towards state-based versioning. While it does not support the tracking of a set of changes, it enables effective and efficient realization within web environment.

Several hypermedia systems define links on the level of particular pages (nodes) (see a comparison of hypermedia data models presented in [19]). In our model links are defined on the version—family level. This means that the link points to the family of web pages and is resolved on time of a configuration building (or navigating the web site). Linking on the level of page versions can lead into many broken links when versioned items are deleted from the public web repository (even if this is not consistent with the idea behind versioning –

to preserve all states of an entity – deleting some versions from the web public presentation is prevalent).

Important issue while discussing versioning of web documents (or hypermedia in general) is that of links versioning. Several different solutions are described in [16]. There is no consensus on the issue whether links should be modelled (and represented) separately from the content. We can find approaches where links are embedded in the content; or links are represented separately; or some links are local and modelled within the content (their change causes creation of the new version) and some links are external (represented separately, their change does not cause creation of a new version). Although at present, linking on the web consists in primarily of tags embedded in HTML, XLink proposal provides for storing links between XML documents externally to the documents they reference (see `http://www.w3c.org/XML/Linking`). Realization of our model does not restrict in any way the representation of versioned entities. Defining version—family model covers the structure versioning, i.e. within each revision relationships are maintained.

We do not introduce a new hypermedia model. But we build on the Dexter hypermedia model [0] and propose its specialisation with the aim of allowing efficient navigation within versioned web site.

6   Conclusions

Versioned web site offers significant advantages to the content developers and readers. It provides mechanisms to allow version-dependent navigation through the site. Content developers can concentrate on the content and relationships between versioned families of web pages. They do not have to deal with complexities of versioning and versioned navigation implementation.

We have proposed a model for versioned web site which aims at computer support of the process of the web site configuration building. We have concentrated in this paper on modelling presentation space (on the contrary of many existing approaches which stress on the development space). In fact, both spaces can exploit devised model. Basic distinction would be in granularity of versioning. A limitation of our approach is that the model does not provide substantive web site structure modelling. However, there is no model which suits all purposes.

The advantages of our proposal include:
- the model is simple and effective (version-family links present the main advantage of the model which produces also above mentioned limitation),
- the model can be used in web site design on several levels of abstraction,
- navigation within versioned site is intuitive,
- the model is ready for using with current web technologies (as demonstrated by the DiVer software tool).

Dynamic approach to resolving links improves the maintenance of the web site integrity. If a user has stored a bookmark to the particular version, it points to the page family with version selection data. In the case of missing version (or no version satisfying the selection filter) the user has still an option to select different version.

The model can serve also during the web site design (its structure and navigation). Several models on various level of abstraction can be constructed. Levels of abstraction regard to hierarchy of composite elements (web site versus web page) and to interconnections (explicit versus implicit links).

References

1. IETF WEBDAV working group. www.ics.uci.edu/pub/ietf/webdav
2. Berners-Lee, T.: Versioning, 1990. A web page that is part of the original design notes for the WWW, available at www.w3.org/DesignIssues/Versioning.html
3. Bieliková, M., Návrat, P.: Modelling Software Systems in Configuration Management. Applied Mathematics and Computer Science **5** 4 (1995) 751–764
4. Bieliková, M., Návrat, P.: Modelling Versioned Hypertext Documents. In: Magnusson, B. (ed.): System Configuration Management, ECOOP'98 SCM-8 Symposium, Brussels, Belgium. LNCS 1439. Springer-Verlag (1998) 188–197
5. Bieliková, M., Návrat, P.: An Approach to Automated Building of Software System Configurations. International Journal of Software Engineering and Knowledge Engineering, **9** 1 (1999) 73–95
6. Conradi, R., Westfechtel, B.: Version Models for Software Configuration Management. ACM Computing Surveys, **30** 2 (1998) 232–282
7. Haake, A., Hicks, D.: VerSE: Towards Hypertext Versioning Styles. In: Proc. of the 7th ACM Conf. on Hypertext, Washington DC, USA, March 1996, 224–234. Available at www.cs.unc.edu/~barman/HT96/
8. Halasz, F.G.: Reflections on Notecards: Seven Issues for the Next Generation of Hypermedia Systems. Communications of the ACM, **31** 7 (1988) 836–852
9. Halasz, F.G., Schwartz, M.: The Dexter Hypertext Reference Model. Communications of the ACM, **37** 2 (1994) 30–39
10. Hicks, D.L., Leggett, J.J., Nurnberg, P.J., Svhnase, J.L.: A hypermedia Version Control Framework. ACM Transactions on Information Systems, **16** 2 (1998) 127–160
11. Hunt, J.J., Reuter, J.: Using the Web for Document Versioning: An Implementation Report for DeltaV. In: Proc. of the 23rd Int. Conf. on Software Engineering, Toronto, May 2001. IEEE Press, 507–513
12. Návrat, P., Bieliková, M.: Knowledge Controlled Version Selection in Software Configuration Management. *Software – Concepts and Tools* **17** (1996) 40–48
13. Noris, I.: Building a Configuration of Hypertext Documents. Master's Thesis, Department of Computer Science and Engineering, Slovak University of Technology (2000), (supervised by Mária Bieliková)
14. Sommerville, I., Rodden, T., Rayson, P., Kirby, A., Dix, A.: Supporting Information Evolution on the WWW. *World Wide Web*, **1** 1 January 1998, 45–54
15. Tichy, W.F.: RCS – a System for Version Control. Software-Practice and Experience, **15** 7 (1985) 637-654
16. Vitali, F.: Versioning Hypermedia. ACM Computing Surveys, **31** (4es) (1999)
17. Vitali, F., Durand, D.G.: Using Versioning to Support Collaboration on the WWW. In: Proc. of 4th World Wide Web Conference (1995). Available at www.w3.org/pub/Conferences/WWW4
18. Whitehead, E.J.: An Analysis of the Hypertext Versioning Domain. PhD Thesis, University of California, Irvine (2000)
19. Whitehead, E.J.: Uniform Comparison of Data Models Using Containment Modeling. In: Proc. of ACM Conf. on Hypertext – HT'02, ACM, June 2002 182-191

Design of Secure Multicast Models for Mobile Services

Elijah Blessing, R.* and Rhymend Uthariaraj, V.

Ramanujan Computing Centre, Anna University, Chennai, India
elijahblessing@yahoo.com, rhymend@annauniv.edu

Abstract. Mobile multicast service is an emerging technology in this decade. Incorporating security features in multicast services gives rise to overheads and computational complexities. The secure movement of members between areas gives rise to additional overheads with reduced throughput and increased complexities at the server. Designing an efficient and secure multicast model for mobile services is a challenging area for the researchers. In this paper, two models has been designed and proposed. The algorithms for these models have been experimentally simulated, tested, analyzed and compared with the already existing models. The experimental results prove that the proposed Enhanced LeaSel model has increased throughput with complexity $O(1)$, when compared to existing models whose complexity is $O(N_A +1 +2n)$.

Keywords. Multicast, mobile, security, complexity, encryptions, key distribution, Basic simple model, Enhanced LeaSel.

1   Introduction

Mobile multicast service is an efficient means of distributing data to a group of participants. With the widespread use of internet, securing data transmission is an important requirement for many mobile services. The data is secured by encrypting it with the group key, which is shared by all the members of the mobile group. To achieve backward confidentiality and forward confidentiality [11], the group key should be changed whenever a member join or leave during the course of a multicast service. When there are large mobile groups with members joining, leaving and moving frequently, secure mobile multicast services gives rise to additional computational complexity with poor throughput.

Many literatures are available for wired secure multicast services [1], [7], [8], [6], [10] and research works are in progress for mobile multicast services. In this paper, two different secure mobile multicast models viz, Basic simple model and Enhanced LeaSel model are designed and proposed. The algorithms of these models are simulated, tested and analyzed for all the mobile multicast events. They are also compared with the existing models. It is found that the Enhanced LeaSel model is best suited for mobile services whose members highly move between areas. The experimental results prove that when members move between areas, the Enhanced LeaSel model has increased throughput with complexity $O(1)$.

---

* Research Scholar Under FIP from Karunya Institute of Technology, India

P. Van Emde Boas et al. (Eds.): SOFSEM 2004, LNCS 2932, pp. 163–173, 2004.
© Springer-Verlag Berlin Heidelberg 2004

The remainder of the section is organized as follows. The section 2 briefly lists out the multicast events for mobile services. The section 3 presents the objectives in designing the secure mobile multicast models. The section 4 gives a review of mobile multicast models. The section 5 explains in detail, the proposed multicast models and its algorithms for mobile services. The section 6 shows the experimental results and finally section 7 concludes.

2   Mobile Multicast Events

The following are the events for the mobile multicast services.

Member JOIN: The authorized members join the mobile service by sending JOIN request.

Member LEAVE: A member leaving the mobile multicast service can be voluntary or compelled. In Voluntary LEAVE, the authorized member sends a LEAVE request to the area controller. In Compelled LEAVE, if the member is not authorized to continue in the mobile service, the area controller expels the member by sending EXPEL message.

Member TRANSFER: Due to mobility, the member moves from one mobile area to another mobile area.[4], [5].

3   Design Objectives

The following are the objectives while designing an efficient multicast model for mobile services.

Forward Confidentiality: If the members LEAVE the mobile multicast service, the encryption key should be updated for every LEAVE operation to prevent the former member accessing the future communications. This property is termed as Forward Confidentiality. [11], [12].

Backward Confidentiality: If the members JOIN the mobile multicast service, the encryption key should be updated for every JOIN operation to prevent the new member accessing the past communications. This is termed as Backward confidentiality. [11], [12].

Mobility: Mobility affects performance only when members cross the areas. The rate at which the members cross the areas is defined as mobility transfer factor. Even if the mobile members are highly dynamic with large mobility transfer factor, the model should be efficient with increased throughput.

Computational efficiency: The computational complexity is determined based on the number of encryptions the server performs for key distribution and the total number of rekey distribution messages the server unicasts or multicasts. The secure multicast model for mobile service is said to be highly efficient only when it has less computational complexity at the server for all mobile multicast events.

4   Review of Secure Multicast Models

In this section, the algorithms proposed by B.Decleene et.al [4] is studied and evaluated for all mobile multicast events. In this algorithm [4], the *Domain Key Distributor (DKD)* generates the data key and uses it for encrypting the data. Whenever a new member joins a current session or an existing member leaves a session, a new data key [4] is generated and distributed to ensure both forward and backward confidentiality. The domain is further divided into areas and the *Area Key Distributor (AKD)* is responsible for distributing the data key to members within that area.

When a member joins, the total number of key generation is 2. Therefore the key generation cost is O (2). For key distribution, the encryption complexity is O(n+2) where n is the number of AKD's in the domain. The rekey message distribution complexity is O (n+2). When a member leaves, the total number of key generation is also 2 and the key generation cost is O(2). For key distribution, the encryption complexity is $O(N_A - 1 + n)$, where N_A is the number of members in the area. The rekey message distribution complexity is $O(N_A - 1 + n)$. For member transfer the algorithms proposed by B.Decleene were

a)   Baseline rekeying[4] : Here the total number of key generations is 4. Therefore the key generation cost is O(4). The encryption complexity is $O(N_A+1+ 2n)$. The rekey message distribution complexity is $O(N_A +1+2n)$.

b)   Immediate rekeying[4]: The total number of key generations is 2. Therefore the key generation cost is O(2). The encryption complexity is $O(N_A +1)$. The rekey message distribution complexity is $O(N_A + 1)$.

5   Proposed Secure Multicast Models for Mobile Services

In this section, the algorithms of the proposed secure multicast models for mobile services are described. There are two types of specialized controllers that control, manage, generate and distribute the keys. They are Domain Controller and Area Controller. All the members in the service belong to the domain controlled by a Domain controller. Based on the administrative regions, the domain is divided into areas. Each area is controlled and managed by area controller. The models consists of three different keys viz. member private key(k), domain key(DK), area key (AK). The domain key is shared between domain controller and area controller. The area key is shared between area controller and all the members. Let there be nine members in the mobile multicast service MMS with individual keys $k_1,k_2,...k_9$ respectively. Let there be three areas A_1, A_2 and A_3 controlled by area controllers AC_1, AC_2, and AC_3 respectively. Let N_A be the number of members in the area. Assume that A_3 contains member's m_7, m_8, m_9 and the area controller generates AK_3. Throughout this section the notation [y]x represents y is encrypted by x.

Group creation: When the member registers to participate in the mobile service, the DC distributes the member private key(k) to all the registered members of the group securely. Then the DC prepares the access Control List (ACL) and distributes (multicasts) it to all the AC. The information in the ACL includes the session for which the member is authorized to receive the mobile multicast data.

Initial Group:

MMS = { $m_1, m_2, m_3, m_4, m_5, m_6, m_7, m_8, m_9$ }
A_1 = { m_1, m_2, m_3 }; All members of A_1 know area key AK_1
A_2 = { m_4, m_5, m_6 }; All members of A_2 know area key AK_2
A_3 = { m_7, m_8, m_9 }; All members of A_3 know area key AK_3

5.1   Basic Simple Model

This model is well suited for multicast services whose members rarely move between areas.

Member JOIN: When a new member joins, the area controller verifies and authorizes it. The Area controller then changes the area key AK to AK' to ensure backward confidentiality. To accomplish this task, the area controller sends the KEYUPDATE_JOIN message in encrypted form to the current members and the joining member.

Member LEAVE: When a member voluntarily leaves the multicast service or when deputy controller expels a member, the Area Controller changes AK' to ensure forward confidentiality and distributes it to all the members securely.

Member TRANSFER: The member transfer is considered as member leaving one area and joining another area. This is achieved by sending leave message to its local area controller. The data transmission stops and the local area controller updates the area key for the remaining members and securely distributes it. Now the data transmission resumes. Meanwhile the transferring member informs the other area that it wishes to join. The area controller stops data transmission, verifies the transferring member authentication and if approved it generates new area key and distributes it to the present members and the transferring member.

Member JOIN Algorithm

Let A_3 = { m_7, m_8, m_9 } and member m_{10} joins A_3
Step 1: m_{10} sends JOIN message to AC_3
Step 2: AC_3 verifies with ACL_3 and if approves go to step 3 else do not authenticate m_{10}.
Step 3: AC_3 sends an approval message to m_{10} and generates new area Key AK_3'
Step 4: AC_3 stops data transmission
Step 5: AC_3 distributes area key AK_3' as follows:

   $AC_3 \rightarrow m_7, m_8, m_9 : [AK_3']\ AK_3$ (multicast)
   $AC_3 \rightarrow m_{10}: [AK_3']\ k_{10}$ (unicast)
Step 6: AC_3 resumes data transmission as follows:

   MMS $\rightarrow AC_1, AC_2, AC_3:$ [Data] DK (multicast)
   $AC_3 \rightarrow A_3 :$ [Data] AK_3' (multicast)
And now A_3 = { m_7, m_8, m_9, m_{10} }.

For member JOIN, it is obvious that the encryption complexity for key distribution is O(2) and the rekey message distribution complexity is also O(2).

Member LEAVE Algorithm

Let A_3 = { m_7, m_8, m_9, m_{10} } and member m_{10} LEAVE A_3

Step 1: a) m_{10} sends LEAVE message to AC_3 or b) AC_3 sends EXPEL message to m_{10} if it is not authorized for the new session.
Step 2: AC_3 generates new area Key AK_3'
Step 3: AC_3 stops data transmission
Step 4: AC_3 distributes area key AK_3' as follows:

$$AC_3 \rightarrow m_7: [AK_3'] \, k_7 \quad \text{(unicast)}$$
$$AC_3 \rightarrow m_8: [AK_3'] \, k_8 \quad \text{(unicast)}$$
$$AC_3 \rightarrow m_9: [AK_3'] \, k_9 \quad \text{(unicast)}$$

Step 5: AC_3 resumes data transmission as follows:

$$MMS \rightarrow AC_1, AC_2, AC_3: [Data] \, DK \text{ (multicast)}$$
$$AC_3 \rightarrow A_3 : [Data] \, AK_3' \text{(multicast)}$$

and now $A_3 = \{m_7, m_8, m_9\}$.
For member LEAVE, it is obvious that the encryption complexity for key distribution is $O(N_A -1)$ and the rekey message distribution complexity is also $O(N_A-1)$.

Member TRANSFER Algorithm

Let member m_{10} TRANSFER from A_3 to A_2.
Member transfer is considered as member leave from A_3 and member join in A_2.
$A_3 = \{m_7, m_8, m_9, m_{10}\}$
Step 1: m_{10} sends LEAVE message to AC_3
Step 2: AC_3 sends an approval message to m_{10} and generates new area Key AK_3'
Step 3: AC_3 stops data transmission
Step 4: AC_3 distributes area key AK_3' as follows:

$$AC_3 \rightarrow m_7: [AK_3'] \, k_7 \quad \text{(unicast)}$$
$$AC_3 \rightarrow m_8: [AK_3'] \, k_8 \quad \text{(unicast)}$$
$$AC_3 \rightarrow m_9: [AK_3'] \, k_9 \quad \text{(unicast)}$$

Step 5: AC_3 resumes data transmission as follows:

$$MMS \rightarrow AC_1, AC_2, AC_3: [Data] \, DK \text{ (multicast)}$$
$$AC_3 \rightarrow A_3: [Data] \, AK_3' \text{(multicast)}$$

and now $A_3 = \{m_7, m_8, m_9\}$.
$A_2 = \{m_4, m_5, m_6\}$ and member m_{10} joins A_2
Step 6: m_{10} sends JOIN message to AC_2
Step 7: AC_2 Verifies with ACL_2 and if approves go to step 8 else do not authenticate m_{10}.
Step 8: AC_2 sends an approval message to m_{10} and generates new area Key AK_2'
Step 9: AC_2 stops data transmission.
Step 10: AC_2 distributes area key AK_2' as follows:

$$AC_2 \rightarrow m_4, m_5, m_6 : [AK_2'] \, AK_2 \text{ (multicast)}$$
$$AC_2 \rightarrow m_{10}: [AK_2'] \, k_{10} \text{ (unicast)}$$

Step 11: AC_2 resumes data transmission as follows:

$$MMS \rightarrow AC_1, AC_2, AC_3: [Data] \, DK \text{ (multicast)}$$
$$AC_2 \rightarrow A_2 : [Data] \, AK_2 \text{ (multicast)}$$

and now $A_2 = \{m_4, m_5, m_6, m_{10}\}$.
For member transfer, it is obvious that the encryption complexity is $O(N_A +1)$, if there are equal number of members in each area and the rekey message distribution complexity is also $O(N_A +1)$.

5.2   Enhanced LeaSel Model

The LeaSel model was proved to be a highly secure [7], [9], fault tolerant [13] multicast model for wired multicast services. It was also proved that it is highly efficient [2] in terms of computational complexities. In this model, the group key generation and distribution is performed by the leader and it is completely hidden from the members of the group. The mathematical and experimental evaluations has proved [7], [9] the fact that it is very difficult to break the multicast service. To support mobility between areas, the Area controller in addition to access control list it also maintains Area Key holders list (AKHL). The AKHL contains those active members who are not in its area but present in the multicast service but hold the current area key. The AKHL helps unnecessary stoppage of data transmission and also reduce the computational complexities and overheads at the area controller while transfer. Every member possesses a member area key list (MAKL) and the key ID identifies its keys. When a member wants to transfer from one area A_1 to another area A_2, it sends a MEMBER_TRANSFER message to both the area A_1, A_2. The A_2 on receiving the MEMBER_TRANSFER message checks its AKHL to find whether the member possess the valid area key. If it does not possess the valid area key, it transmits the recent area key encrypted with the member's individual key. On the other hand, A_1 updates its AKHL and will not change the area key.

Member JOIN Algorithm
Let $A_3 = \{m_7, m_8, m_9\}$ and member m_{10} joins A_3
Step 1: m_{10} sends JOIN message to AC_3
Step 2: AC_3 verifies with ACL_3 and if approves go to step 3 else do not authenticate $m_{10.}$
Step 3: AC_3 sends an approval message to m_{10} and triggers KGM module of the area leader.
Step 4: L_3 generates new area Key AK_3'
Step 5: L_3 stops data transmission
Step 6: L_3 distributes area key AK_3' as follows:
$\quad\quad L_3 \rightarrow m_7, m_8, m_9 : [AK_3']\ AK_3$ (multicast)
$\quad\quad L_3 \rightarrow m_{10}: [AK_3']\ k_{10}$ (unicast)
Step 7: Data transmission resumes as follows:
$\quad\quad MMS \rightarrow AC_1, AC_2, AC_3: [Data]\ DK$ (multicast)
$\quad\quad AC_3 \rightarrow L_3: [Data]\ DK$ (unicast)
$\quad\quad L_3 \rightarrow A_3 : [Data]\ AK_3'$ (multicast)
And now $A_3 = \{m_7, m_8, m_9, m_{10}\}$.
For member JOIN, it is obvious that the encryption complexity for key distribution is $O(2)$ and the rekey message distribution complexity is also $O(2)$.

Member LEAVE Algorithm
Let $A_3 = \{m_7, m_8, m_9, m_{10}\}$ and member m_{10} LEAVE A_3
Step 1: a) m_{10} sends LEAVE message to AC_3 or b) AC_3 sends EXPEL message to m_{10} if it is not authorized for the new session.
Step 2: AC_3 forwards it to L_3 and L_3 removes m_{10} from $AKHL_3$ and generates new area Key AK_3'

Step 3: L_3 stops data transmission

Step 4: L_3 distributes area key AK_3' as follows:

$$L_3 \rightarrow m_7: [AK_3'] \, k_7 \quad \text{(unicast)}$$
$$L_3 \rightarrow m_8: [AK_3'] \, k_8 \quad \text{(unicast)}$$
$$L_3 \rightarrow m_9: [AK_3'] \, k_9 \quad \text{(unicast)}$$

Step 5: The data transmission resumes as follows:

$$MMS \rightarrow AC_1, AC_2, AC_3: [Data] \, DK \, \text{(multicast)}$$
$$AC_3 \rightarrow L_3 : [Data] \, AK_3 \quad \text{(unicast)}$$
$$L_3 \rightarrow A_3 : [Data] \, AK_3 \quad \text{(multicast)}$$

and now $A_3 = \{m_7, m_8, m_9\}$.

For member LEAVE, it is obvious that the encryption complexity for key distribution is $O(N_A - 1)$ and the rekey message distribution complexity is also $O(N_A - 1)$.

Member TRANSFER Algorithm

Consider m_{10} transferring from A_2 to A_3.

Step 1: m_{10} sends MEMBER_TRANSFER message to A_2 and A_3.

Step 2: A_2 and A_3 forward it to L_2 and L_3 respectively.

Step 3: L_2 updates its $AKHL_2$ by including the transferring member into its list. The data transmission continues uninterrupted

$$AC_2 \rightarrow L_2: [Data] \, DK \, \text{(unicast)}$$
$$L_2 \rightarrow A_2 : [Data] \, AK_2 \, \text{(multicast)}$$

Step 4: L_3 checks $AKHL_3$ and verifies whether it possess current area key. If No go to step 5 else go to step7.

Step 5: The data transmission stops.

Step 6: L_3 distributes the current area key to m_{10} as follows:

$$L_3 \rightarrow m_{10}: [AK_3] \, k_{10} \, \text{(unicast) and go to step 8.}$$

Step 7: The data is distributed and the member uses the area key available in the member area key list (MAKL).

Step 8: The data transmission resumes

$$AC_3 \rightarrow L_3 : [Data] \, AK_3 \, \text{(unicast)}$$
$$L_3 \rightarrow A_3 : [Data] \, AK_3 \quad \text{(multicast)}$$

If the transferring member possesses the current area key, then there are no encryptions for key distribution and there are no key distribution messages. If it is not so, then the encryption complexity for key distribution and the key distribution complexity is $O(1)$.

6   Results and Discussion

The multicast models for the mobile service are simulated and run with all nodes moving at medium speed. The codes are written in JAVA. For different mobile multicast events, the number of encryptions for key distribution and the number of key distribution messages are experimentally determined. Further, all the algorithms are evaluated for different mobile environments with different mobility transfer factors. For the experimental setup, it is assumed that the members of the mobile multicast service are equally divided into 14 areas each controlled by its area controller. In the graphs, the Basic simple model is represented as BS and the Enhanced LeaSel model is represented as EN_LEA.

Experiment 1: A member was allowed to join the area A_1 by sending the JOIN request to its area controller AC_1. For different members in the area, the total number of encryptions for distributing the key and the number of rekey distribution messages due to member JOIN were determined and its results are shown in Fig. 1(a) and Fig. 1(b) respectively.

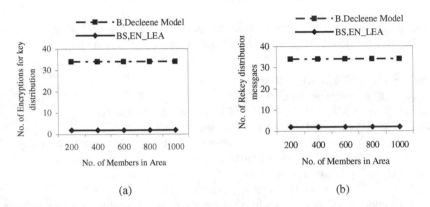

(a)   (b)

Fig. 1. Member JOIN a) Number of Encryptions vs. Number of Members b) key distribution messages vs. Number of Members

Experiment 2: From the area A_1, a member was allowed to leave the service by sending LEAVE request to its area controller. The total number of encryptions for distributing the key and the number of rekey distribution messages due to member LEAVE were determined and its results are shown in Fig. 2(a) and Fig. 2(b) respectively.

Experiment 3: For different number of members in the mobile service, the member transfer algorithm for the models are run and the total number of control messages when the mobility transfer factor is set to 10 % and 20% is determined and its results are shown in Fig. 3(a) and Fig. 3(b) respectively.

Experiment 4: For different number of members in the mobile service, the models are run and the number of rekey messages distributed when the mobility transfer factor is set to 10 % and 30% were determined and its results are shown in Fig. 4(a) and Fig. 4(b) respectively.

Experiment 5: The performance of the mobile service for all the models are evaluated by determining the number of times the sender stops and resumes the data transmission i.e., interruption of data transmission, for different number of member transitions. The results are shown in Fig. 5(a).

Experiment 6: The multicast models are run with all nodes moving at medium speed with 20% mobility transfer factor. Each area is flooded with packets such that the congestion level in each area is 10%. For different number of members in the mobile service, the time required to successfully transmit 50 packets of data is determined and the results are shown in Fig. 5(b).

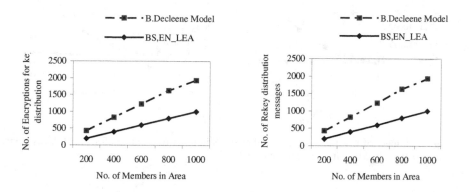

Fig. 2. Member LEAVE a) Number of Encryptions vs. Number of Members b) Rekey distribution messages vs. Number of Members

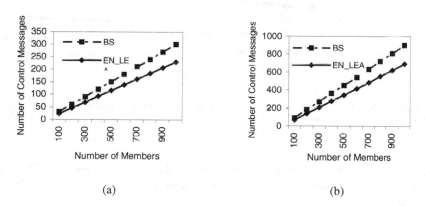

(a)   (b)

Fig. 3. Number of control messages VS Number of members a) For mobility transfer factor = 10% b) For mobility transfer factor = 20%

It is obvious from the Fig. 1, Fig. 2 that the proposed models have less encryption cost with reduced overheads. Also it is obvious from Fig. 3 that the Enhanced LeaSel model shows better result compared to Basic simple model. The Fig. 4 proves that Enhanced LeaSel model is best suited for mobile multicast services whose members dynamically move between areas and also suited for mobile service which has large number of members. The Fig. 5(a) shows that for Enhanced LeaSel model, there

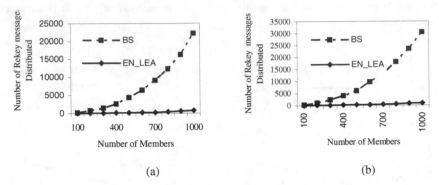

(a)   (b)

Fig. 4. Number of rekey messages distributed VS number of members for (a) Mobility transfer factor = 10% (b) Mobility transfer factor = 30%

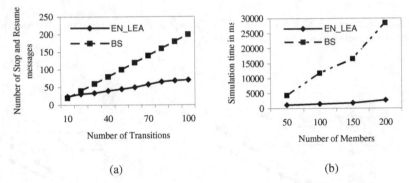

(a)   (b)

Fig. 5. a) Number of stop and resume messages VS Number of transitions b) Simulation time VS Number of members.

is very less interruption of data transmission. The Fig. 5(b) shows that Basic simple model has poor throughput whereas Enhanced LeaSel model has relatively good throughput.

7   Conclusion

In this paper, two different secure mobile multicast models are designed, simulated, tested and analyzed for all the mobile multicast events and it is compared with the existing models. It is proved that Enhanced LeaSel model has better performance in terms of complexity, overheads and throughput.

References

1. Wong, C, Gouda, M, Lam, S.S.: Secure Group Communication Using Key Ggraphs. IEEE/ACM Transaction on Networking, Vol. 8. no.1, (2000) 16–30
2. Elijah Blessing, R, Rhymend Uthariaraj, V.: Evaluation and Analysis of Computational Complexity for Secure Multicast Models. In: Kumar. V et al. (eds.): Computational Science and Its Applications. Lecture Notes in Computer Science, Vol. 2668. Springer-Verlag, Berlin Heidelberg New York (2003) 684–694
3. Gong, G, Shacham, N.: Multicast Security and Its Extension to Mobile Environment. Wireless Networks, (1995) 281–295
4. Decleene, D, Dondeti, L et al.: Secure Group Communications for Wireless Networks. Proceedings of INFOCOM (2001)
5. Bhargava, B et al.: Fault Tolerant Authentication and Group Key Management in Mobile Computing. CERIAS Technical Report (2000)
6. Berkovits, S.: How to Broadcast a Secret. In: Davis. D.W (ed): Advances in Cryptology. Lecture Notes in Computer Science, Vol. 547. Springer-Verlag, Berlin Heidelberg New York (1991) 535–541
7. Elijah Blessing, R, Rhymend Uthariaraj, V.: Secure and Efficient Scalable Multicast Model for Online Network Games. Proceedings of International Conference ADCOG (2003) 8–15
8. Fiat, A, Naor, M.: Broadcast Encryption. In: Stinson. D.R (ed): Advances in Cryptology. Lecture Notes in Computer Science, Vol. 773. Springer-Verlag, Berlin Heidelberg New York (1994) 480–491
9. Elijah Blessing, R, Rhymend Uthariaraj, V.: LeaSel: An Efficient Key Management Model for Scalable Secure Multicast System. Proceedings of International Conference ICORD (2002)
10. Wallner, D.M, Harder, E.J., Agee. R.C.: Key Management for Multicast: Issues and Architectures. RFC 2627 (July 1997)
11. Mittra, S.: Iolus: A framework for Scalable Secure Multicasting. Proceedings of ACM SIGCOMM (1997) 277–288
12. Harney, H, Muckenhim, C.: Group Key Management Protocol (GKMP) Architecture. RFC 2094 (July 1997)
13. Elijah Blessing, R, Rhymend Uthariaraj, V.: Fault Tolerant Analysis of Secure Multicast Models. Accepted for Presentation in International IEEE Conference ICICS-PCM (2003)

Some Notes on the Complexity of Protein Similarity Search under mRNA Structure Constraints

Dirk Bongartz

Lehrstuhl für Informatik I, RWTH Aachen
Ahornstraße 55, 52074 Aachen, Germany
bongartz@cs.rwth-aachen.de

Abstract. In [2], Backofen et al. propose the MRSO problem, that is to compute an mRNA sequence of maximal similarity to a given mRNA and a given protein, that additionally satisfies some secondary structure constraints. The study of this problem is motivated by an application in the area of protein engineering. Modeled in a mathematical framework, we would like to compute a string $s \in \{a, b, \overline{a}, \overline{b}\}^{3n}$ which maximizes the sum of the values of n functions, which are blockwise applied to triples of s, and additionally satisfies some complementary constraints on the characters of s given in terms of position pairs. While the decision version of this problem is known to be NP-complete (see [2]), we prove here the APX-hardness of the general as well as of a restricted version of the problem. Moreover, we attack the problem by proposing a 4-approximation algorithm.

1 Introduction

Before we describe the MRSO problem, which we will consider throughout this paper, in a mathematical framework, we first give a rough idea of the biological background by which the problem is motivated.

The fundamental process in molecular biology and although in biology itself is the transformation of hereditary information coded in DNA into proteins. DNA as well as proteins are long chains of smaller molecular entities, so called nucleotides and amino acids, respectively. In nature, we distinguish four different types of nucleotides and about twenty amino acids. Thus, we can view these molecules as strings over the corresponding alphabet of nucleotides or amino acids. Furthermore, certain types of nucleotides can establish bonds to each other which results in the possibility of the connection of two DNA single strands to one double strand, which is actually the conformation DNA occurs in nature. A rather similar molecule, called RNA, also consists of nucleotides but appears as a single strand and thus, has the probability to establish bonds between nucleotides of the same strand, resulting in the so called secondary structure of the RNA. This secondary structure is usually described by a set of index pairs, representing the positions of nucleotides in the string establishing a bond. Some examples of these secondary structures are visualized in Figure 1.

P. Van Emde Boas et al. (Eds.): SOFSEM 2004, LNCS 2932, pp. 174–183, 2004.
© Springer-Verlag Berlin Heidelberg 2004

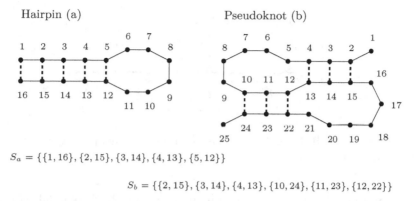

$$S_a = \{\{1,16\}, \{2,15\}, \{3,14\}, \{4,13\}, \{5,12\}\}$$

$$S_b = \{\{2,15\}, \{3,14\}, \{4,13\}, \{10,24\}, \{11,23\}, \{12,22\}\}$$

Fig. 1. Two types of secondary structure elements occurring in RNA

The transformation of DNA into proteins is now divided into two subprocesses. In the first step a copy of the DNA is constructed in a process called transcription providing a special kind of RNA molecule, denoted as messenger RNA, mRNA for short. In the second step, the translation, this mRNA is transfered into an amino acid sequence by reading triples of nucleotides in a blockwise fashion, each coding for one specific amino acid. This process is universal for all living creatures. Biologists found out that according to the secondary structure of the mRNA a certain triple of nucleotides might encode for different things. In particular, in the investigated case a triple might code for a STOP (terminating the construction of the amino acid sequence) or, if followed by a special secondary structure known as hairpin loop (see Figure 1(a)), for the amino acid selenocysteine which enhances the function of the resulting protein [5].

Due to the enhancing effect of this mechanism it would be useful to utilize this knowledge in the context of protein engineering. Thus we try to determine for a given mRNA and a protein, a sequence of nucleotides which has maximal similarity to the given mRNA as well as its induced protein sequence is maximally similar to the given protein, and additionally obeys some specified secondary structure constrains.

In [2] Backofen, Narayanaswamy, and Swidan modeled this problem in terms of an optimization problem called MRSO (MRna Structure Optimization [1]) whose complexity we will investigate in the sequel of this paper.

To describe the idea of the problem formulation, let $r = r_1 \ldots r_{3n}$ be a string over an alphabet Σ and $p = p_1 \ldots p_n$ a string over an alphabet Σ' representing the given mRNA and the given protein, respectively. Thus, we look for a string $s = s_1 \ldots s_{3n}$, which is most similar to r and p as suggested by Figure 2, with the additional requirement that s satisfies certain secondary structure constraints.

In Figure 2 the string p' represents the amino acid sequence inferred from s by blockwise translation of triples of nucleotides into one amino acid. By $\sim$ we visualize the similarity between the given nucleotides from r and s, $(r_j \sim s_j)$, and the given amino acids from p and the inferred amino acids from p', $(p_j \sim p'_j)$.

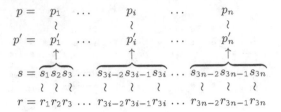

Fig. 2. Idea of the MRSO-problem. (This picture stems from [2], except for a slightly differing notation)

We will introduce this model more formally in Section 2, where we also formalize the similarity and the structure constraints.

For the MRSO problem it has been shown in [2] that there exists a linear time algorithm if the considered secondary structure corresponds to an outerplanar graph. For the general case, an NP-completeness result has been obtained for the decision version of the problem, and a 2-approximation algorithm has been proposed.

After presenting some preliminaries in Section 2, we will improve the hardness results of [2] by giving two APX-hardness proofs including explicit lower bounds. Moreover, in Section 4, we present a 4-approximation algorithm based on a greedy approach. Finally, in Section 5, we propose to attack the problem applying the concept of parameterized complexity.

2   Preliminaries

Let us now consider Figure 2 again. Let $r = r_1 \ldots r_{3n}$ be a string over an alphabet $\Sigma = \{a, b, \overline{a}, \overline{b}\}$ of size four, where a and $\overline{a}$ as well as b and $\overline{b}$ denote complementary nucleotides, between which bonds can be established according to a certain secondary structure.[1] Any other pairing is not allowed. Moreover it is usually assumed that bonds can only occur between complementary nucleotides which are at least 4 positions apart. Let $p = p_1 \ldots p_n$ be a string over an alphabet Σ' representing a protein.[2]

To fix the similarities $s_j \sim r_j$ and $p_j \sim p'_j$, we can provide a set of functions f_i, for $1 \leq i \leq n$, which assign a value to the triple $(s_{3i-2}s_{3i-1}s_{3i})$ according to the similarity of this triple to $(r_{3i-2}, r_{3i-1}, r_{3i})$ and p_i.

Our goal is to compute a string s such that the sum of these function values is maximized under the constraints given by the secondary structure. For this problem, it should be clear that it is sufficient to know the set of functions, knowing the strings r and p is not necessary.

---

[1] In a biological setting it is more usual to use the alphabet $\{A, C, G, U\}$ denoting the four types of nucleotides occurring in RNA (adenine, cytosine, guanine, and uracil). Bonds may establish between A and U, and C and G.

[2] In biology one considers an alphabet of size 20 corresponding to the standard amino acids.

Moreover, instead of providing a set of pairs of positions we can represent the secondary structure constraints in terms of an undirected graph.

Thus our constraints can be given in terms of the following *structure graph*.

Definition 1. *(similar to [2]) Let* $S = \{\{i,j\} \mid 1 \leq i < j \leq 3n\}$ *represent a secondary structure of an mRNA of length* $3n$. *Then the* structure graph $G = (V, E)$ *is defined by* $V := \{1, \ldots, 3n\}$, $E := S$.

In the sequel, we will always think of structure graphs in a way such that the vertices are laid out on a line in increasing order. In Figure 3 we depict the structure graphs corresponding to the secondary structures given in Figure 1 represented in this style.

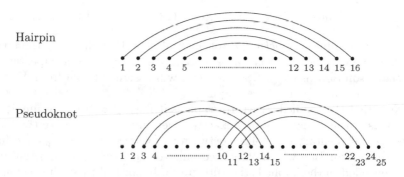

Fig. 3. Structure graphs for hairpin and pseudoknot secondary structures, where vertices are laid out on a line.

Next we give the formal definition of the MRSO problem in terms of an optimization problem.

Definition 2. *MRSO denotes the following maximization problem.*

Input: *A structure graph* $G = (V, E)$, *with* $V = \{1, \ldots, 3n\}$, *and* n *functions* $f_i : \Sigma^3 \to \mathbb{Q}^{\geq 0}$ *for* $1 \leq i \leq n$, *where* $\Sigma = \{a, b, \overline{a}, \overline{b}\}$.
Constraint: *For all inputs* $x = (G, f_1, \ldots, f_n)$, *the set of feasible solutions is defined by:*

$$\mathcal{M}(x) = \{s = s_1 \ldots s_{3n} \in \Sigma^{3n} \mid \{i, j\} \in E \text{ implies } s_i = \overline{s_j}\},$$

where $\overline{\overline{a}} = a$ *and* $\overline{\overline{b}} = b$. *(We call this the* complementary constraint.)
Costs: *For all inputs* $x = (G, f_1, \ldots, f_n)$ *and feasible solutions* $s = s_1 \ldots s_{3n} \in \mathcal{M}(x)$,

$$cost(s, x) = \sum_{i=1}^{n} f_i(s_{3i-2}, s_{3i-1}, s_{3i}).$$

Goal: *Maximization.*

Note that a feasible solution of MRSO may also be viewed as an assignment of labels from Σ to the vertices from G, such that the complementary constraint is satisfied.

Sometimes we will prefer a representation where we focus on the amino acid level instead of the nucleotide level. Therefore we introduce the definition of the so called *implied structure graph*.

Definition 3. *(similar to [2]) Let* $S = \{\{i, j\} \mid 1 \leq i < j \leq 3n\}$ *represent a secondary structure of an mRNA of length $3n$. Then the* implied structure graph $G_{\text{impl}} = (V, E)$ *is defined by*

$$V := \{1, \ldots, n\},$$
$$E := \{\{x, y\} \mid there\ exists\ a\ pair\ \{i, j\} \in S,$$
$$such\ that\ i \in \{3x - 2, 3x - 1, 3x\}\ and\ j \in \{3y - 2, 3y - 1, 3y\}\}.$$

Thus the implied structure graph may also be thought of as the structure graph where we blockwise join three consecutive vertices to one supervertex and a feasible solution of the MRSO problem will assign a triple from Σ^3 to each vertex of the implied structure graph.

Note that the implied structure graph as defined here does not mimic all implications of the structure graph exactly. There might be multiple (but at most three) complementary constraints between two vertices from G_{impl}, and furthermore the information which pairs according to the structure graph that will be, is not encoded in the implied structure graph. In spite of these shortcomings the notation of the implied structure graph will turn out to be sufficient and helpful for some observations in the rest of this paper.

In the next section we will prove that MRSO is APX-hard, i.e. there exists a constant c such that it is NP-hard to approximate the problem by a factor smaller than c. For a general overview on the concept of approximation algorithms we refer the reader to [6].

3   APX-Hardness and Lower Bounds for MRSO

First, we consider the MRSO in its general form, i.e. as given by Definition 2. Here we consider the case that vertices in the structure graph may have arbitrary degree. This does not really correlate to the biological motivation, since usually each nucleotide can pair with at most another one, hence implying a maximum degree of one. This restricted version of the problem will be considered later in this paper.

We will show now that MRSO is a generalization of the MaxE3SAT problem and thus, it is APX-hard and not approximable within a factor of $\frac{8}{7} - \varepsilon$, for arbitrary small $\varepsilon > 0$. Therefore, we first define the MaxE3SAT problem formally.

Definition 4. MaxE3SAT *is defined as the following maximization problem. Given a boolean formula* $\Phi = C_1 \wedge \cdots \wedge C_m$ *in 3-CNF over a set of variables*

$X = \{x_1, \ldots, x_n\}$, where each clause $C_i = c_{i_1} \vee c_{i_2} \vee c_{i_3}$ consists of exactly three literals.

Compute an assignment $\varphi : X \to \{0,1\}$ such that the number of satisfied clauses is maximized.

Theorem 1. *The MRSO is a generalization of the MaxE3SAT problem.*

Proof. The idea to prove this result is to use the characters of the searched string s of MRSO as boolean values and the structure graph to encode the valid assignments.

Let $\Phi = C_1 \wedge \cdots \wedge C_m$ be a boolean formula in 3-CNF over variables $\{x_1, \ldots, x_n\}$, where $C_i = c_{i_1} \vee c_{i_2} \vee c_{i_3}$. We assume that each variable occurs at least once positively and at least once negatively in this formula. Otherwise it could be directly simplified by removing all clauses in which these variables occur, since we clearly are able to satisfy those clauses by an appropriate assignment of the variables. The corresponding input for the MRSO problem is given by

- $G := (V, E)$, where $V := \{1, \ldots, 3m\}$, and
  $E := \{\{i, j\} \mid$ there exist integers g, h, k, l, such that
    $i = 3(g-1) + h, j = 3(k-1) + l$, and $c_{g_h} = \overline{c_{k_l}}\}$.

  Thus, the vertices in G correspond to the occurrences of literals in the clauses of Φ and the edges in G correspond to pairs of literals where the same variable occurs positively and negatively.
- For all i, $1 \leq i \leq m$, we define the function f_i by the same function f:

$$f(t_1, t_2, t_3) = \begin{cases} 0 & \text{if } (t_1, t_2, t_3) \notin \{a, \bar{a}\}^3 \\ 1 - \prod_{i=1}^{3}(1 - \varphi(t_i)) & \text{otherwise} \end{cases},$$

where $\varphi(a) = 1$ and $\varphi(\bar{a}) = 0$. Thus, f computes for each clause its boolean evaluation given an assignment of the variables in which we interpret a as the boolean value 1 and $\bar{a}$ as the boolean value 0.

By the definition of G the above reduction guarantees that all assignments corresponding to a solution of the MRSO are well defined, i.e. that no variable is assigned to different boolean values in different clauses. Moreover the function f restricts useful solutions of the MRSO to those which only include characters a and $\bar{a}$,[3] and additionally counts the number of satisfied clauses by increasing the cost of the solution for the MRSO. Hence, a feasible solution $s = s_1 \ldots s_{3n}$ with cost k for the MRSO directly corresponds to an assignment for Φ that satisfies k clauses. $\square$

By applying the inapproximability result for MaxE3SAT from [4] we can directly infer the following from Theorem 1.

---

[3] This is a convenient but not necessary restriction, since we could also extend the interpretation to the whole alphabet Σ by defining $\varphi(b) = 1$ and $\varphi(\bar{b}) = 0$.

Theorem 2. *The problem MRSO is APX-hard and not approximable within* $\frac{8}{7} - \varepsilon$, *for an arbitrary* $\varepsilon > 0$.   □

While this result holds for the general version of the MRSO-problem, we have to admit that it does not fit the biological motivation exactly, since we allow vertices to have degree higher than one, which corresponds to bonds between more than two nucleotides in the secondary structure of an RNA molecule. Although there are some reports in the literature about the possibility of bonds between more than two nucleotides, e.g. bonds between triples of nucleotides [8], this is a rather rare phenomenon, and hence it is useful to assume only *pairs* of nucleotides, which is also the case in most models concerning RNA secondary structure (see, for instance, [7], [8]). Therefore, we will now consider a restricted version of MRSO, where the input instances are restricted to graphs that does not contain vertices of degree higher than one. We will denote this modified problem by *MRSO-d1*.

In what follows we show that also for MRSO-d1, we can obtain an APX-hardness result as well as an explicit lower bound on the approximability. For this we consider the Max Independent Set problem for graphs where the degree is upper-bounded by three (MaxIS-3) and show that MRSO-d1 is a generalization of MaxIS-3.

Definition 5. MaxIS-3 *is the following maximization problem. Given a graph* $G = (V, E)$ *with maximum degree 3. Compute a subset* I *of* V, *such that every pair of vertices* $(x, y) \in I^2$ *implies* $\{x, y\} \notin E$, *and* $|I|$ *is maximized.*

Theorem 3. *The MRSO-d1 is a generalization of MaxIS-3.*

Proof. In order to prove this theorem, we will compute for a given instance of MaxIS-3 an instance of MRSO-d1 such that the cost achieved by an optimal solution for MRSO-d1 matches the size of the maximum independent set.

Let $G = (V, E)$ be an instance of MaxIS-3. We construct the following instance of the MRSO-d1 in terms of the representation on implied structure graphs, that is, we consider blocks of three consecutive vertices of a structure graph as one supervertex.

- $G_{\text{impl}} = G$.
- For all i, $1 \le i \le |V|$, define the function f_i by the same function f:

$$f(t_1, t_2, t_3) = \begin{cases} 1 & \text{, if } t_1 t_2 t_3 = aaa \\ 0 & \text{, otherwise} \end{cases}$$

The idea of this reduction is simply to identify the set of vertices which are assigned to aaa in an optimal solution for MRSO-d1 with a maximum independent set.

To verify this we have to prove the following two claims:

(i) Every feasible solution for MRSO-d1 corresponds to an independent set (of the same cost).

(ii) Every feasible solution for MaxIS-3 corresponds to an feasible solution for MRSO-d1 (of the same cost).

If a vertex $v \in G_{\text{impl}}$ is assigned to aaa by a feasible solution of MRSO-d1, due to the complementary constraints no neighbor u of v in G_{impl} could be assigned to aaa, too. Thus, Claim (i) follows immediately.

To prove Claim (ii), we have to be careful that every independent set could be transformed into an assignment to the vertices of G_{impl} without violating the complementary constraints. Note that although we are considering the implied structure graph the complementary constraints are on the nucleotide level, hence assigning aaa to a vertex of G_{impl} does not enforce the assignment $\overline{a}\,\overline{a}\,\overline{a}$ to all its neighbors, but only implies that the neighbors must be from the set $\{\overline{a}t_2t_3, t_1\overline{a}t_3, t_1t_2\overline{a} \mid t_1, t_2, t_3 \in \{a, b, \overline{a}, \overline{b}\}\}$.

For each independent set I let us assign the vertices in I to aaa. This does no harm since they are not connected by any edge. We are able to label each end point of the edges incident to any vertex $v \in G_{\text{impl}}$ injectively by one of the numbers from $\{1, 2, 3\}$. Note that this labeling is no edge coloring but only a labeling of the end points of the edges specifically for each vertex.[4] Now, an end point labeled i enforces complementarity according to the ith character t_i represented by the vertex v. Since this labeling is injective and we restrict ourselves to graphs with maximal degree 3, we can assign the other vertices obeying the complementary constraints.

According to our choice of the functions f_i for $1 \leq i \leq |V|$, the cost of a computed solution for MRSO-d1 corresponds to the size of an independent set and vice versa. Thus, the theorem is proved.   □

From the proof of Theorem 3 it became clear that we need the restriction to graphs of maximal degree three and cannot extend the same (or similar) reduction to arbitrary instances of MaxIS.

Together with the inapproximability result from [3], Theorem 3 infers the following.

Theorem 4. *The problem MRSO-d1 is APX-hard and not approximable within $\frac{1676}{1675} - \varepsilon$, for an arbitrary $\varepsilon > 0$.*   □

It is worth to note that, as we have seen from the proofs of Theorem 1 and Theorem 3, the APX-hardness results already hold for alphabets of size two.

4   Approximation Algorithm for MRSO

In this section we will investigate a simple greedy approach for the MRSO-d1 problem which will turn out to be a 4-approximation algorithm. As described already in Section 2, we will view the problem as to assign characters from the set $\{a, b, \overline{a}, \overline{b}\}$ to the vertices of the structure graph.

---

[4] Thus each edge has two labels according to its incident vertices.

Algorithm 1 Greedy-MRSO-d1

Input: *An instance of the MRSO-d1 problem, i.e. a graph $G = (V, E)$, where $V = \{1, \ldots, 3n\}$, each vertex in G has at most degree one, and n functions $f_i : \{a, b, \overline{a}, \overline{b}\}^3 \to \mathbb{Q}^{\geq 0}$ for $1 \leq i \leq n$.*

Step 1: *Find a pair $((t_{3i-2}, t_{3i-1}, t_{3i}), f_i)$, where $t_{3i-2}, t_{3i-1}, t_{3i} \in \{a, b, \overline{a}, \overline{b}\}$, such that the function $f_i(t_{3i-2}, t_{3i-1}, t_{3i})$ achieves the maximum value over all possibilities, where already fixed assignments remain unchanged.[5] (Ties are broken arbitrarily.)*

Step 2: *According to the pair $((t_{3i-2}, t_{3i-1}, t_{3i}), f_i)$ found in Step 1, assign t_{3i-2} to vertex $3i - 2$, t_{3i-1} to vertex $3i - 1$, and t_{3i} to vertex $3i$. Moreover, assign $\overline{t_j}$ to vertex k, if there exists an edge $\{j, k\} \in E$ for $j \in \{3i - 2, 3i - 1, 3i\}$.*

Step 3: *Iterate Step 1 and Step 2 until all vertices are assigned to a character from $\{a, b, \overline{a}, \overline{b}\}$.*

Output: *The assignment $t_1, \ldots, t_{3n}$ to the vertices from V.*

Next we argue that Algorithm 1 guarantees a 4-approximation.

Theorem 5. *Algorithm Greedy-MRSO-d1 is a polynomial-time 4-approximation algorithm for MRSO-d1.*

Proof. Let G and $f_1, \ldots, f_n$ as considered in algorithm Greedy-MRSO-d1. In Step 2 of the algorithm we do not only perform the assignment of characters to vertices that maximize the value of all possible functions as found in Step 1, but also assign the complementary characters to their neighbors according to the given graph. Since each vertex in G has degree at most one, the constructed assignment is a feasible solution for the MRSO-d1.

Now consider an optimal assignment $\alpha = (\alpha_1, \ldots, \alpha_n)$ for each consecutive triple of positions in $\{1, \ldots, 3n\}$, i.e. α_i denotes an element from $\{a, b, \overline{a}, \overline{b}\}^3$. Moreover let $\beta = (\beta_1, \ldots, \beta_n)$, with $\beta_i \in \{a, b, \overline{a}, \overline{b}\}^3$ for $1 \leq i \leq n$, be the corresponding assignment computed by the algorithm, i.e. $\beta_i = t_{3i-2}t_{3i-1}t_{3i}$.

If two assignments α_i and β_i differ, i.e. $\alpha_i \neq \beta_i$, the assignment β_i executed by Algorithm 1 can prevent at most *three* other assignments of α from being performed, since in G each vertex has at most degree one. Due to the greedy behavior of the algorithm the achieved cost $f_i(\beta_i)$ is not lower as any other possible cost. Thus, even if the three prevented assignments of the optimal solution contribute to the solution of the algorithm only cost 0, but in the optimal solution all contribute also $f_i(\beta_i)$, the cost achieved by the greedy approach is at least $\frac{1}{4}$ of the cost of the optimal solution for this situation. Since this situation only affects these four assignments, it does not influence the other ones, and this allows us to generalize this analysis to the whole problem.

By this it has been shown that the cost achieved by Algorithm 1 is at least a fraction $\frac{1}{4}$ of the cost of the optimal solution.

Concerning the running time, an implementation that computes the optimal assignments for each block needs time in $O(n)$ for this step. To sort the blocks

---

[5] Note that complementary constraints are forbidden inside a triple, since this would require a too sharp folding of the corresponding molecule.

according to their assigned costs will take another $O(n \log n)$ time. After fixing one assignment in Step 2 of the algorithm will require an update of the sorted list. This could be done in time $O(\log n)$ by deletion and reinsertion of the at most three blocks that obtain a new score due to the assignment by using binary search. Altogether this will result in a running time in $O(n \log n)$. $\qquad\square$

Although this algorithm does not outperform the 2-approximation algorithm given in [2] with respect to the approximation ratio, it is conceptually simpler and therefore a possible alternative.

5   Parameterized Complexity

Finally, we would like to propose the possibility to attack the MRSO-d1 problem using the concept of parameterized complexity. Therefore, decompose the implied structure graph into its connected components and solve these by intelligent total search strategies. Since we can consider the assignments of the connected components independently, because they do not influence each other, we will obtain an optimal solution. It is clear, that such an approach consumes exponential running time only in terms of the size of the largest component.

Thus, this approach would be helpful for input instances that only have small components, which might be the case for some practical cases. Furthermore it might be worth to investigate other parameters, as for instance the number of crossing edges in the representation of the structure graph shown in Figure 3.

Acknowledgments. I would like to thank Hans-Joachim Böckenhauer, Juraj Hromkovič, Joachim Kupke, and Walter Unger for discussions and their helpful comments on previous versions of this paper.

References

1. Backofen, R.: Personal communication
2. Backofen, R., Narayanaswamy, N.S., Swidan, F.: On the Complexity of Protein Similarity Search under mRNA Structure Constraints. STACS 2002, LNCS 2285, Springer (2002) 274–286
3. Berman, P., Karpinski, M.: On Some Tighter Inapproximability Results. ECCC Report TR98-029 (1998) www.eccc.uni-trier.de/eccc/
4. Håstad, J.: Some Optimal Inapproximability Results. STOC (1997) ACM, 1–10
5. Hazebrouck, S., Camoin, L., Faltin, Z., Strosberg, A.D., Eshdat, Y.: Substituting Selenocysteine for Catalytic Cysteine 41 Enhances Enzymatic Activity of Plant Phospholipid Hydroperoxide Glutathione Peroxidase Expressed in Escherichia coli. Journal of Biological Chemistry **275** 37 (2000) 28715–28721
6. Hromkovič, J.: Algorithmics for Hard Problems. Springer (2003), 2nd edition
7. Setubal, J., Meidanis, J.: Introduction to Computational Molecular Biology. PWS Publishing Company (1997)
8. Wang, Z., Zhang, K.: RNA Secondary Structure Prediction. In: Jiang, T., Xu, Y., Zhang, M.Q. (eds.): Current Topics in Computational Molecular Biology. MIT Press (2002) 345–363

Measures of Intrinsic Hardness for Constraint Satisfaction Problem Instances

George Boukeas, Constantinos Halatsis,
Vassilis Zissimopoulos, and Panagiotis Stamatopoulos

Department of Informatics and Telecommunications, University of Athens

Abstract. Our aim is to investigate the factors which determine the intrinsic hardness of constructing a solution to any particular constraint satisfaction problem instance, regardless of the algorithm employed. The line of reasoning is roughly the following: There exists a set of distinct, possibly overlapping, trajectories through the states of the search space, which start at the unique initial state and terminate at complete feasible assignments. These trajectories are named solution paths. The entropy of the distribution of solution paths among the states of each level of the search space provides a measure of the amount of choice available for selecting a solution path at that level. This measure of choice is named solution path diversity. Intrinsic instance hardness is identified with the deficit in solution path diversity and is shown to be linked to the distribution of instance solutions as well as constrainedness, an established hardness measure.

1 Introduction

A constraint satisfaction problem consists of a set of variables and a set of constraints. A variable which has been given a value is said to be *instantiated*. A set of instantiations to i distinct variables is an *assignment* α_i of size i. If the size of an assignment α_n equals the number of problem variables n then it is a *complete assignment*. A complete assignment which satisfies all problem constraints is a feasible *solution*. The set of solutions to a problem instance is denoted by S. Given a constraint satisfaction problem instance, the goal is to find a feasible solution or to prove that none exists. In order to accomplish this, *constructive search methods* start from the empty assignment and iteratively extend partial assignments until a feasible solution is found. Therefore, the complete search space comprises all distinct assignments of all sizes, partitioned into disjoint levels according to size. An extensive presentation can be found in [1]. In contrast, *repair search methods* iteratively transform complete assignments until a feasible solution is found. Therefore, the complete search space comprises only complete assignments.

This research aims at investigating the factors which determine the *intrinsic hardness* of constructing a solution to any particular constraint satisfaction problem instance. Other than the assumption that a constructive algorithm is employed, instance hardness is treated in a manner independent of the particular

P. Van Emde Boas et al. (Eds.): SOFSEM 2004, LNCS 2932, pp. 184–195, 2004.

tree-search method used, hence the use of the term "intrinsic". In line with [1], as well as [2], [3], our viewpoint focuses on the structure of the induced search space, which allows an abstraction away from problem-specific properties.

The line of reasoning is roughly the following: There exists a set of distinct, possibly overlapping, trajectories through the states of the search space, which start at the unique initial state (the empty assignment containing no instantiations) and terminate at complete feasible assignments. These trajectories are named *solution paths*. See Fig. 1 for an illustration of the search space and solution paths. The entropy of a distribution is a measure of *choice* in selecting

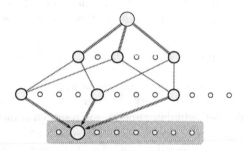

Fig. 1. The search space of a constructive method for instances with $n = 3$ binary variables. The search space is partitioned into disjoint levels, with each level i containing the $2^i C(n, i)$ possible instantiations of size i. The $n!$ possible paths to a particular complete assignment are also depicted. The search space for a repair method comprises the complete assignments in the shaded rectangle

an event [4]. The entropy of the distribution of solution paths among the states of each level of the search space provides a measure of the amount of choice available for selecting a solution path at that level. This measure of choice is named *solution path diversity*. Intrinsic instance hardness is identified with the *deficit* in solution path diversity: the lower the amount of choice available to any algorithm for selecting a solution path, the higher the intrinsic instance hardness. Choice is inherent in the search space of the problem instance and thus independent of the algorithm used to traverse it. In this work, the focus lies on investigating the choices offered by the search space of instances, not on how particular algorithms may make use of such choices. Therefore, throughout the presentation, the reader should bear in mind that the notion of intrinsic instance hardness is not to be confused with computational cost. The former is invariant for a problem instance and manifests itself through the latter, the exact value of which depends on the particular algorithm employed.

To our knowledge, the application of such reasoning in order to characterize intrinsic instance hardness is novel. Moreover, it uncovers a remarkable link between intrinsic instance hardness and *constrainedness* [2]. The latter has been successfully introduced as an estimator of solution cost for problem ensembles but its justification as *average information content per variable* in [5] is intuitive rather than theoretical, especially since it provides no link between constrained-ness and computational cost. Here, it is shown that the constrainedness of an instance can be regarded as *deficit in the total amount of choice available for selecting a solution path, averaged over all levels of the search tree.*

There is substantial relevance between the object of this work and research in phase transitions as well as other areas. Similarities and deviations are elaborated upon in Sect. 2. Apart from that, measures of choice are discussed in Sect. 3, leading to measures of intrinsic instance hardness in Sect. 4. The presentation is concluded in Sect. 5 which underlines the contributions of this work. The majority of the propositions to be found herein have short proofs, mostly involving algebraic manipulations, and have been omitted due to space restrictions.

2   Related Research

Research in *phase transitions* investigates how problem structure affects the average computational cost [6]. Although such work deals with *ensembles of instances* rather than individual instances, our research is intimately linked to [2] and [1]. In the former, the *number* of feasible solutions is used in the definition of *constrainedness*, an established predictor of computational cost. In the latter, the *number* of partial consistent assignments (goods) at each level of the search space is also employed. Refining these approaches, we use information-theoretic measures, similar to those found in [7], to quantify the *distribution* of solutions and, consequently, partial consistent assignments. This uncovers an interesting link between the measures proposed here and constrainedness. There is also a close connection between our work and [8], which investigates the relationship between algorithmic complexity and computational cost.

3   Measures of Choice

3.1   Solution Path Diversity

There are $n!$ paths towards any solution $\alpha_n \in \mathcal{S}$, corresponding to the $n!$ distinct orderings of the instantiations in α_n. The total number of paths towards the solutions in $\mathcal{S}$ is thus $n!|\mathcal{S}|$. The subset of these solution paths containing a particular assignment α_i is $i!(n-i)!\rho_\mathcal{S}(\alpha_i)$, where $\rho_\mathcal{S}(\alpha_i)$ is the number of complete assignments which are solutions of $\mathcal{S}$ and are reachable from α_i. Consequently, the fraction $\wp(\alpha_i)$ of solution paths containing partial assignment α_i is:

$$\wp(\alpha_i) = \frac{\rho_\mathcal{S}(\alpha_i)}{|\mathcal{S}|C(n,i)}$$

where $C(n,i) = n!/(i!(n-i)!)$. These fractions are not probabilities, although they can be interpreted as such. Essentially, the fractions $\wp(\alpha_i)$ define the *distribution* of solution paths among the assignments of level i. Apparently, the *entropy* of this distribution provides a measure of choice in selecting a solution path at level i.

Definition 1 ($\mathcal{D}_i$). *The entropy of the distribution of solution paths among the assignments of level i, as defined by the fractions $\wp(\alpha_i)$, is called* solution path diversity *at level i:*

$$\mathcal{D}_i = -\sum_{\alpha_i} \wp(\alpha_i) \log \wp(\alpha_i)$$

Solution path diversity is a concise quantitative measure of the amount of choice available to any constructive algorithm for selecting a solution path at level i. It is measured in *bits* (assuming the logarithm is base 2). A more refined measure of choice can be obtained through the fraction $\wp(\alpha_{i-1} \cdot \alpha_i)$ of solution paths containing consecutive assignments α_{i-1} and α_i, which can be shown to be:

$$\wp(\alpha_{i-1} \cdot \alpha_i) = \frac{\sigma(\alpha_{i-1}, \alpha_i)\rho_S(\alpha_i)}{i|S|\,C(n,i)}$$

The fractions $\wp(\alpha_{i-1} \cdot \alpha_i)$ define the distribution of solution paths among the instantiations leading to level i.

Definition 2 ($\Delta\mathcal{D}_i$). *The conditional entropy of the distribution of solution paths among the instantiations leading to level i, as defined by the fractions $\wp(\alpha_{i-1} \cdot \alpha_i)$, is called* conditional solution path diversity *at level i:*

$$\Delta\mathcal{D}_i = -\sum_{\alpha_{i-1}}\sum_{\alpha_i} \wp(\alpha_{i-1} \cdot \alpha_i) \log \frac{\wp(\alpha_{i-1} \cdot \alpha_i)}{\wp(\alpha_{i-1})}$$

Conditional solution path diversity is a measure of the amount of choice available to any constructive algorithm for selecting a solution path at level i, having reached level $i-1$. It is a monotonic decreasing function with respect to i and is measured in *bits per level*. Figure 2 depicts the search spaces for two constraint satisfaction problem instances with three binary variables and two solutions, along with the distribution of solution paths. It is straightforward to show that the two forms of solution path diversity are connected in the following manner:

$$\Delta\mathcal{D}_i = \mathcal{D}_i - \mathcal{D}_{i-1} + \log i \tag{1}$$

Recall that the search space involves all possible partial assignments and therefore (implicitly) all possible variable orderings for constructing these assignments. It can be shown that this is the reason for the appearance of the $\log i$ term.

3.2   The Distribution of Solutions

Assume the n problem variables are all binary. There exist 2^n distinct complete assignments which correspond to the 2^n vertices of a n-dimensional hypercube. Let the vertices which correspond to solutions be colored black and let the rest of the vertices be colored white. This coloring, which essentially reflects the placement of solutions on the vertices of the hypercube, is the *distribution of*

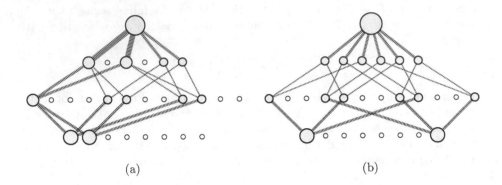

(a)   (b)

Fig. 2. The search space and solution paths for instances with $n = 3$ binary variables and $|\mathcal{S}| = 2$ solutions, with the distance between the solutions being (a) minimal: one instantiation and (b) maximal: n instantiations. Circle area and line thickness reflect the distribution of solution paths among assignments and instantiations

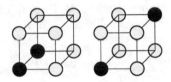

Fig. 3. The distribution of solutions for two non-isomorphic instances of three binary variables and two solutions. The instances correspond to the search spaces of Fig. 2

solutions. As an example, Fig. 3 contains the distribution of solutions for two problem instances with three binary variables and two solutions.

Problem instances are *isomorphic* if the corresponding distributions of solutions (colored hypercubes) are isomorphic. If the solution sets $\mathcal{S}$ and $\mathcal{T}$ of two distinct instances of n variables are isomorphic, then for every level i of the search space, it holds that:

$$\mathcal{D}_i^{\mathcal{S}} = \mathcal{D}_i^{\mathcal{T}}$$

There is currently no available proof for the inverse (that equal entropy implies isomorphism) although it is our strong belief that it is also true. This entails that solution path diversity $\mathcal{D}_i$ directly reflects the distribution of solutions and is both necessary and sufficient for discriminating between instances with non-isomorphic solution sets. It is not uncommon for entropy to be an invariant of isomorphic structures (see [9]).

3.3   The Sum Property

An accumulated measure of choice is obtained by summing (1) over all levels i of the search space. This is acceptable since the conditional solution path diversity $\Delta\mathcal{D}_i$ pertains exclusively to level i of the search space.

Proposition 1 ($\mathbf{D}^n$). *The sum of the conditional solution path diversities $\Delta\mathcal{D}_i$ over all levels i of the search space is the* total solution path diversity $\mathbf{D}^n$ *and is identical among all problem instances with the same number of variables n and the same number of solutions $|\mathcal{S}|$.*

$$\mathbf{D}^n(\mathcal{S}) = \sum_{i=1}^{n} \Delta\mathcal{D}_i = \log(n!|\mathcal{S}|)$$

Not surprisingly, $\mathbf{D}^n(\mathcal{S})$ depends upon $n!|\mathcal{S}|$, the number of solution paths. Proposition 1 holds even though the individual $\Delta\mathcal{D}_i$'s which make up $\mathbf{D}^n$ need not be identical among all such instances. This will be referred to as *the sum property*.

3.4   General Path Diversity

Solution path diversity cannot, by itself, serve as a measure of hardness because it is a *relevant* quantity. It measures the amount of choice available in selecting a solution path and therefore becomes meaningful only when compared to the total amount of choice available in selecting *any* path. This is computed using the entropy of the uniform distribution of all possible paths among all possible assignments. For the sake of simplicity, it will be assumed that variables are binary.

Definition 3 ($\mathcal{G}_i$). *The entropy of the uniform distribution of the $n!2^n$ distinct possible paths among the $2^i C(n,i)$ distinct possible assignments of level i is called* general path diversity *at level i:*

$$\mathcal{G}_i = \log\left[2^i C(n,i)\right] = i + \log C(n,i)$$

General path diversity is a measure of the amount of choice available in selecting any path at level i. It essentially reflects the size of the search space.

Definition 4 ($\Delta\mathcal{G}_i$). *The conditional entropy of the uniform distribution of the $n!2^n$ distinct possible paths among the $C(n,i)2^i i$ distinct possible instantiations leading to level i is called* conditional general path diversity *at level i.*

$$\Delta\mathcal{G}_i = \mathcal{G}_i - \mathcal{G}_{i-1} + \log i = 1 + \log(n - i + 1)$$

Conditional general path diversity is a measure of the amount of choice available in selecting any path at level i, having reached level $i - 1$. It is a monotonic decreasing function with respect to i.

In a sense, the (conditional) general path diversity defines the *maximal attainable value* for the (conditional) solution path diversity. If all paths of a search space were solution paths, then the solution path diversity would be equal to the general path diversity.

Proposition 2 ($\mathbf{G}^n$). *The sum of the conditional general path diversities $\Delta\mathcal{G}_i$ over all levels i of the search space is the* total general path diversity $\mathbf{G}^n$ *and is identical among all problem instances with the same number of variables n.*

$$\mathbf{G}^n = \sum_{i=1}^{n} \Delta\mathcal{G}_i = \log(n!2^n)$$

4   Measures of Intrinsic Hardness

The easiest possible problem instance arises when all assignments are feasible and every path is thus a solution path. In this case, the solution path diversity $\mathcal{D}_i$ is maximized and equal to the general path diversity $\mathcal{G}_i$ at every level i. In every other case, there is a *deficit* in the amount of choice available for selecting a solution path. The magnitude of this deficit identifies intrinsic instance hardness.

Definition 5 ($\mathcal{H}_i$). *The difference between the general path diversity $\mathcal{G}_i$ and the solution path diversity $\mathcal{D}_i$ is called the* intrinsic instance hardness *at level i.*

$$\mathcal{H}_i = \mathcal{G}_i - \mathcal{D}_i$$

Definition 6 ($\Delta\mathcal{H}_i$). *The difference between the conditional general path diversity $\Delta\mathcal{G}_i$ and the conditional solution path diversity $\Delta\mathcal{D}_i$ is called the* conditional intrinsic instance hardness *at level i:*

$$\Delta\mathcal{H}_i = \Delta\mathcal{G}_i - \Delta\mathcal{D}_i = \mathcal{H}_i - \mathcal{H}_{i-1}$$

The intrinsic instance hardness $\mathcal{H}_i$ and $\Delta\mathcal{H}_i$ rises as the solution path diversity $\mathcal{D}_i$ and $\Delta\mathcal{D}_i$ drops. It is maximal when there are no solutions and minimal when there are no infeasible assignments. It also rises along with the size of the search space, which manifests itself through the general path diversity $\mathcal{G}_i$ and $\Delta\mathcal{G}_i$. An illustration can be found in Fig. 4.

Both forms $\mathcal{H}_i$ and $\Delta\mathcal{H}_i$ of intrinsic instance hardness are monotonic increasing functions with respect to the search level i, which is due to the fact that solution paths tend to spread at deeper levels of the search space. This is not in conflict with the intuition that subproblems encountered by search algorithms become easier as the search progresses into deeper levels. Both $\mathcal{H}_i$ and $\Delta\mathcal{H}_i$ involve *averages* over all the assignments or instantiations of a level and thus contain no information about the hardness of the subproblems that may be encountered *during search* by a particular search algorithm (a subject of vast practical significance discussed in [10], [5]).

4.1   The Sum Property and Constrainedness

Using Props. 1 and 2, it follows that the sum property also holds for the total intrinsic instance hardness:

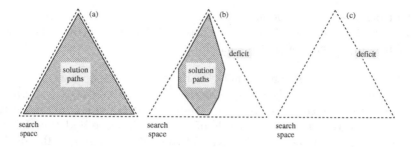

Fig. 4. (a) Hardness is eradicated when the entire search space consists of solution paths: $\mathcal{G}_i = \mathcal{D}_i$. (b) Hardness arises as the deficit in the solution path diversity: $\mathcal{H}_i = \mathcal{G}_i - \mathcal{D}_i$. (c) Hardness is maximized when no solution paths exist: $\mathcal{H}_i = \mathcal{G}_i$. In all cases, the entire search space is taken into account when computing $\mathcal{G}_i$, i.e. there is no pruning of nogoods

Proposition 3 ($\mathbf{H}^n$). *The sum of the conditional intrinsic instance hardness $\Delta\mathcal{H}_i$ over all levels i of the search space is the* total *intrinsic instance hardness $\mathbf{H}^n$ and is identical among all problem instances with the same number of variables n and the same number of solutions $|\mathcal{S}|$.*

$$\mathbf{H}^n(\mathcal{S}) = \mathbf{G}^n(\mathcal{S}) - \mathbf{D}^n(\mathcal{S}) = \sum_{i=1}^{n} \Delta\mathcal{H}_i = n - \log|\mathcal{S}|$$

This is especially intriguing. According to Proposition 3, all instances with the same number of variables n and the same number of solutions $|\mathcal{S}|$ have the same amount of total intrinsic hardness $\mathbf{H}^n$. However, bear in mind that the individual $\Delta\mathcal{H}_i$'s which make up $\mathbf{H}^n$ are not necessarily identical for all such instances (only isomorphic instances have equal $\Delta\mathcal{H}_i$'s for all levels). What this essentially entails is that, among instances with equal n and $|\mathcal{S}|$, the equal total intrinsic hardness $\mathbf{H}^n$ is expended at different levels of the search space. A relevant discussion in Sect. 4.2 will show that instances with a uniform distribution of solutions have low $\Delta\mathcal{H}_i$ for low values of i. On the other hand, instances with clustered solutions have a uniform distribution of the intrinsic hardness $\Delta\mathcal{H}_i$ among all levels of the search space.

Proposition 3 also serves to obviate the intimate connection between the total intrinsic instance hardness $\mathbf{H}^n$ and the constrainedness κ of a single instance:

$$\kappa = 1 - \frac{\log|\mathcal{S}|}{n} = \frac{\mathbf{H}^n(\mathcal{S})}{n} \tag{2}$$

Under this light, κ can be understood as the *average instance hardness over all levels of the search space* or, alternatively, as average deficit in the amount of choice available for selecting a solution path, throughout the search space. This development provides well-founded justification for the establishment of κ as a hardness predictor and verifies the following claim from [2]:

Our definition of κ generalizes a number of parameters introduced in a variety of problem classes. This suggests that constrainedness is a fundamental property of problem ensembles.

Unfortunately, both $\mathbf{H}^n$ and κ suffer from the same deficiency in characterizing instance hardness: they *fail to discriminate between instances with non-isomorphic solution sets*. This is due to the fact that $\mathbf{H}^n$ and κ are, respectively, a sum and an average over the levels of the search space and thus fail to retain any information about the behavior of the individual $\Delta\mathcal{H}_i$'s. Recall that in Sect. 3.2 it was argued that the individual $\Delta\mathcal{H}_i$'s directly reflect the distribution of solutions and that they are necessary and sufficient for discriminating between non-isomorphic solution sets.

This provides an additional explanation as to the reason why there is significant variance in computational cost among problem instances belonging to the same ensemble: since κ depends only upon the number of solutions $|\mathcal{S}|$ and not their distribution, it is possible for non-isomorphic instances with different intrinsic instance hardness $\Delta\mathcal{H}_i$ per level to belong to the same ensemble.

The question then naturally arises: which hardness measure is not so crude as to be able to discriminate between instances with non-isomorphic solution sets? It can be argued, along the lines of [7], that a quantity such as the sum of $\mathcal{H}_i$'s can be employed in order to capture additional information about problem instances. In such a case, drawing from Sect. 4.2, the most difficult instances (among all instances with the same number of solutions $|\mathcal{S}|$) are the ones in which the solutions are *clustered*. This is in complete accordance with [11], [3] but further exploration is required. Note that *approximate entropy*, another information theoretic measure, is applied on problem structure in [12] in order to distinguish among ensemble instances with different distributions of solutions.

4.2   Bounds

The upper bound for solution path diversity $\mathcal{D}_i$ corresponds to the case when the solution paths are uniformly distributed among the assignments of level i. The lower bound corresponds to the case when the solutions form a cluster of diameter c, thereby resulting in the greatest possible non-uniformity in the distribution of solution paths among the assignments of level i. The derivation of the lower bound is somewhat involved.

Proposition 4 ($\mathcal{D}_i$ Bounds). *If $|\mathcal{S}|=2^c$, $0 \leq c \leq n$, then the following holds for solution path diversity $\mathcal{D}_i$ at level i:*

$$\frac{ci}{n} + \log C(n, i) \leq \mathcal{D}_i \leq \min\{i, c\} + \log C(n, i)$$

Using Proposition 4 and Defs. 5 and 6 it is trivial to compute bounds for the intrinsic instance hardness $\mathcal{H}_i$ and $\Delta\mathcal{H}_i$.

Proposition 5 ($\mathcal{H}_i$, $\Delta\mathcal{H}_i$ Bounds). *If $|\mathcal{S}|=2^c$, $0 \le c \le n$, then the following holds for $\mathcal{H}_i$ and $\Delta\mathcal{H}_i$ at level i:*

$$\max\{0, i - c\} \le \mathcal{H}_i \le \left(\frac{n-c}{n}\right) i$$

$$0 \le \Delta\mathcal{H}_i \le 1$$

Note that both bounds pertain exclusively to instances with non-empty solution sets and no pruning of nogoods. The case when the solution set is empty is trivial: intrinsic hardness $\mathcal{H}_i$ coincides with the general path diversity $\mathcal{G}_i$. Illustrations are to be found in Fig. 5 for problem instances with 10 variables and 2^4 solutions.

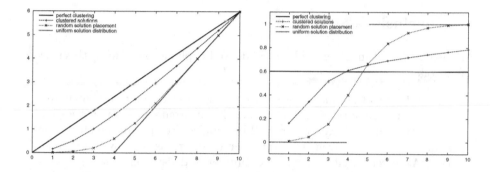

Fig. 5. Intrinsic instance hardness $\mathcal{H}_i$ bounds and conditional intrinsic instance hardness $\Delta\mathcal{H}_i$ bounds vs. search level i, for problem instances with 10 variables and 2^4 solutions. Additional values for $\mathcal{H}_i$ and $\Delta\mathcal{H}_i$ computed for two specific instances are included

The bound for $\Delta\mathcal{H}_i$ reveals how informative a quantity it is and how it conveys information by mere inspection. Notice also how $\Delta\mathcal{H}_i$ remains constant at all levels in the case when the solutions are organized in a single cluster. Bearing in mind that $\Delta\mathcal{H}_i$ reflects an average over the instantiations of level i, this entails that the subproblems encountered throughout the search space are *persistently versatile*: there is ample margin for both error and success and algorithmic choices play the decisive part. On the other hand, when the solutions are as far apart as possible, there is such uniformity in the distribution of solution paths that the hardness $\Delta\mathcal{H}_i$ remains zero up to level c: algorithmic choices are inconsequential since all choices to be made are equally beneficial. However, the hardness $\Delta\mathcal{H}_i$ reaches its maximum beyond level c, with all choices being equally critical because of the spread and scarcity of solution paths.

Approximating Instance Hardness. The form of $\mathcal{H}_i$ and $\Delta\mathcal{H}_i$ for specific instances (as depicted in Fig. 5) is especially intriguing. It becomes apparent that these quantities can be approximated by simple functions involving a control parameter μ, which characterizes the uniformity of solution distribution in the set $\mathcal{S}$. This behavior is due to the direct association between the distribution of solution paths among consecutive levels and is also in accordance with very similar observations made in [7]. An initial attempt was to employ the sigmoid:

$$\Delta\mathcal{H}_i \approx \frac{1}{1 + (\frac{c}{n-c})2^{-\mu(i-c)}}$$

For values $\mu \to 0$ (uniform solution distribution) and $\mu \to \infty$ (perfect clustering), the approximation coincides with the derived bounds. Unfortunately, for $0 < \mu < 1$, the approximation is unsatisfactory. This remains a stimulating open issue.

5   Conclusions

An insightful hint in [13] provides a condensed explanation of what this research has to offer:

> In addition to the *number of solutions*, their clustering also contributes to the variance in the search cost. [...] It thus remains an open question whether additional parameters will be required to specify the clustering sufficiently tightly even if the number of solutions were well specified. [...] A better specification of the number and location of solutions requires more information about the structure of the problems, but is independent of the search method used. However, search methods themselves can differ in how well they avoid unproductive choices [...].

This is exactly the gap that is now bridged by intrinsic instance hardness. It is an intuitively appealing, algorithm-independent measure of instance hardness which directly reflects the clustering of solutions. At the same time, it justifies and supersedes constrainedness, which ignores the distribution of solutions and pertains only to their number. Novel issues are raised regarding constructive search and the constituents of hardness, especially with the bounds and rudimentary approximation results of section 4.2 in mind.

References

1. Williams, C., Hogg, T.: Exploiting the Deep Structure of Constraint Problems. Artificial Intelligence **70** (1994) 73–117
2. Gent, I.P., MacIntyre, E., Prosser, P., Walsh, T.: The Constrainedness of Search. In: AAAI/IAAI. Volume 1. (1996) 246–252
3. Parkes, A.J.: Clustering at the Phase Transition. In: AAAI/IAAI. (1997) 340–345
4. Shannon, C.E.: A Mathematical Theory of Communication. The Bell Systems Technical Journal **27** (1948) Reprinted with corrections
5. Slaney, J.: Is there a Constrainedness Knife-Edge? In: Proceedings of the 14th European Conference on Artificial Intelligence. (2000) 614–618

6. Hogg, T., Huberman, B., Williams, C.: Phase Transitions and the Search Problem. Artificial Intelligence **81** (1996) 1–15
7. Crutchfield, J., Feldman, D.: Regularities Unseen, Randomness Observed: Levels of Entropy Convergence. Chaos **13** (2003) 25–54
8. Vlasie, D.: The Very Particular Structure of the Very Hard Instances. In: AAAI/IAAI. Volume 1. (1996) 266–270
9. Ornstein, D.: Bernoulli Shifts with the Same Entropy are Isomorphic. Adv. in Math. **4** (1970) 337–352
10. Walsh, T.: The Constrainedness Knife-Edge. In: AAAI/IAAI. (1998) 406–411
11. Mezard, M., Ricci-Tersenghi, F., Zecchina, R.: Alternative Solutions to Diluted p-Spin Models and Xorsat Problems. Journal of Statistical Physics (2002)
12. Hogg, T.: Which Search Problems are Random? In: Proceedings of AAAI98. (1998)
13. Hogg, T.: Refining the Phase Transitions in Combinatorial Search. Artificial Intelligence **81** (1996) 127–154

Validity Conditions in Agreement Problems and Time Complexity

Bernadette Charron-Bost[1] and Fabrice Le Fessant[2]

[1] STIX, École Polytechnique, 91128 Palaiseau Cedex, France
[2] Microsoft Research Lab, 7 JJ Thomson Avenue, CB3 0FD, Cambridge, UK

Abstract. We first introduce a new class of distributed agreement problems, ranging from Uniform Consensus to Non-Blocking Atomic Commitment, by varying the validity condition in the specification. We then provide an early deciding algorithm to solve each problem of this class in the synchronous model with crash failures. Our algorithm achieves the previously established lower bounds for time complexity showing that these lower bounds are tight.

Keywords. Distributed Algorithms, Complexity.

1 Introduction

Reaching agreement in a distributed system is a fundamental problem which arises in numerous guises. In all versions of agreement problems, each process starts with an initial value from some fixed set V. At some point in the computation, correct processes must irrevocably decide on some values in V. The specification of an agreement problem includes two safety conditions which fundamentally depend on the failure model that is considered [10]. In this paper, we suppose that processes can fail only by crashing; for this failure model, all the agreement problems share the same safety condition, called *agreement*, which specifies that no two processes may decide differently. Another safety condition, called *validity*, describes the decision values that are permitted. The validity condition varies according to the particular version of the agreement problem. For instance, Fischer, Lynch, and Paterson [5] consider a weak form of validity, called *non-triviality*, which only specifies that there exist at least two runs with two different decision values. For the crash failure model, the validity condition of the *Consensus* problem, which we call *integrity*, requires every process's decision value to be the inital value of some process. Integrity is inappropriate as a validity condition for the transaction commitment problem where the initial votes of all processes influence the decision. Indeed, the validity condition of the *non-blocking atomic commitment* (*NB-AC*, for short) is *unanimity*: decide 1 (commit) only if every process's initial value is 1 (yes), and decide 0 (abort) if some process starts with 0 (no) or a failure occurs.

In this paper, we investigate the relationships between different agreement problems. Indeed, slight modifications in the validity condition may yield considerable discrepancy between agreement problems. For instance, Dwork and

P. Van Emde Boas et al. (Eds.): SOFSEM 2004, LNCS 2932, pp. 196–207, 2004.
© Springer-Verlag Berlin Heidelberg 2004

Moses [4] show that, in synchronous systems, two rounds are always sufficient for solving the agreement problem of [5] with the non-triviality condition, while any Consensus algorithm tolerating t failures requires $t + 1$ rounds. In asynchronous systems Charron-Bost and Toueg [2] show that Consensus and NB-AC are incomparable in almost all environments: NB-AC is never reducible to Consensus, and Consensus is not reducible to NB-AC, except when at most one process may fail. However, we observe that increasing the synchrony degree allows us to compare these two problems, and makes them closer and closer: In each of the partially synchronous models described in [3], NB-AC is harder than Consensus; indeed if a majority of processes is correct, then Consensus is solvable but not NB-AC. Moreover, in synchronous systems Consensus and NB-AC are both solvable no matter how many processes fail, and so are equivalent in terms of solvability. Actually they are equivalent in a stronger sense: in the presence of up to t failures, $t + 1$ rounds are necessary and sufficient in the worst case execution to solve as well Consensus as NB-AC [10]. One can refine this comparison by discriminating runs according to the number of failures f that actually occur. Charron-Bost and Schiper [1] and subsequently Keidar and Rajsbaum [6] proved that both Consensus and NB-AC require at least $f + 2$ rounds if $f < t - 1$, and only $f + 1$ rounds if $t - 1 \leq f \leq t$ (where t is the maximum number of failures).

One may wonder whether these lower bounds for early deciding in Consensus and NB-AC algorithms are tight. An algorithm for Consensus is presented in [1] that achieves these lower bounds. Unfortunately, this algorithm cannot be easily adapted for the NB-AC problem. As noticed by Lamport in [8], "a [popular] belief is that a three-phase commit protocol à la Skeen [12] is needed" for solving NB-AC. It is not exactly clear what that means, but it seems to imply that at least three rounds are required in failure-free runs for deciding. The $f + 2$ lower bound would be therefore weak in the case of NB-AC.

In this paper, we show that this intuition is incorrect: we devise an algorithm for NB-AC that achieves the general lower bounds for early deciding of [1]. This proves that even when refining the comparison in this way (i.e., considering the actual number of failures f instead of the worst case t), Consensus and NB-AC remain two equivalent problems.

Another contribution of the paper is to introduce a natural extension of the NB-AC problem, which we call the k-Threshold Agreement problem. It turns out that this problem is also a generalization of Consensus. In this way, we connect Consensus and NB-AC from the strict view point of problem specification. Actually, our algorithm for NB-AC is general enough to work for any k-Threshold Agreement problem. Therefore all these agreement problems for various values of k, which can be proved incomparable in asynchronous systems [2], are equivalent in synchronous systems in the strong sense that a common optimal algorithm solves them.

2 Preliminaries

2.1 The Model

In this paper, we consider the synchronous model for distributed systems described in [10], which we review briefly.

Let Π be a fully connected graph with n nodes. We consider some fixed message alphabet M, and we let null be a placeholder indicating the absence of message.

A *synchronous algorithm* A is a collection of n *processes*, one for each node of Π. Each process $p_i \in \Pi$, is defined by four components: a set of states $states_i$, a subset $start_i \subseteq states_i$ of initial states, a message-generation function $msgs_i$ mapping $states_i \times \Pi$ to a unique (possibly null) message, and a state transition function $trans_i$ mapping $states_i$ and vectors of messages indexed by Π to $states_i$.

An execution of the algorithm A begins with each process in an arbitrary initial state. Then each process p_i, in lock-step, repeatedly performs the following three steps: (1) apply $msgs_i$ to the current state to determine the messages to be sent and send these messages, (2) receive *all* the messages which are sent to p_i during the previous step, and (3) apply $trans_i$ to the current state and the just received messages to obtain the new state. The combination of these three steps is called a *round* of A.

A *run* of A models an execution of the entire system: it is defined by the collection of the initial states of processes, and the infinite sequence of rounds of A that are executed. The *time complexity* of a synchronous algorithm is measured in terms of the number of rounds until all the required outputs are produced.

We assume that links are reliable but we allow processes to fail by crashing, i.e., by stopping somewhere in the middle of their execution. A process may crash before or during some instance of the steps described above. In particular, a process may succeed in sending only a subset of the messages specified to be sent. After crashing at a round, a process does not send any message during subsequent rounds. A process is said to be *correct* in a run if it does not crash; otherwise it is said to be *faulty*. In the following, we assume that at least one process is correct.

2.2 Agreement Problems

We now focus on the two well-known agreement problems: Consensus and Non-Blocking Atomic Commitment. The *Consensus* problem considers a fixed collection of processes which have each an initial value drawn from some domain V. Processes must eventually decide on the same value; moreover, the decision value must be the initial value of some process. The *Non-Blocking Atomic Commitment* *(NB-AC)* problem arises in distributed database systems to ensure the consistent termination of transactions. Each process that participates in a database transaction arrives at an initial opinion about whether to commit the transaction or abort it, and votes yes or no accordingly. Processes must eventually reach a common decision (commit or abort). The decision to commit may be reached only if all processes initially vote **yes**. In this case, **commit** must be decided if there is no failure.

When identifying **yes** and **commit** with 1, and **no** and **abort** with 0, it appears that binary Consensus ($V = \{0, 1\}$) and NB-AC are two very similar problems. They share the following two conditions:

Agreement: No two processes (whether correct or faulty) decide differently.
Termination: All correct processes eventually decide.

Binary Consensus and NB-AC only differ in their *validity conditions*, i.e., the conditions describing the decision values that are permitted: in the Consensus problem, the possible decision values are related only to the initial values, contrary to the NB-AC problem for which the decision values depend on both input values *and* failure pattern. More precisely, the validity condition of Consensus is as follows:

Integrity: Any decision value for any process is the initial value of some process.

Note that, for binary Consensus, Integrity can be equivalently formulated as follows:

Binary Integrity: If all processes start with the same value v, then v is the only possible decision value.

The validity condition of NB-AC is:

Unanimity:
1. If any process starts with 0, then 0 is the only possible decision value.
2. If all processes start with 1 and there is no failure, then 1 is the only possible decision value.

At this point, it is relevant to consider the *weak validity condition* introduced in [7]:

Weak Validity: If there is no failure, then any decision value is the initial value of some process.

Obviously, the weak validity condition is weaker than the validity conditions of both Consensus and Atomic Commitment, but it is stronger than the one in [5] which only precludes the trivial protocols that always decide the same value. This latter condition, that we call *non-triviality*, is as follows:

Non-Triviality: For each value $v \in \{0, 1\}$, there is an execution in which some process decides v.

Binary Consensus and NB-AC specifications are clearly not comparable because of their incomparable validity conditions.[1] However, it is possible to link

---

[1] Furthermore, Charron-Bost and Toueg [2] showed that these two problems are also incomparable from an algorithmic point of view: NB-AC is not reducible to binary Consensus, and *vice-versa* (except when the maximum number of failures is 1).

up these two problems from a syntactic standpoint. For that, we introduce the
k-Threshold Agreement problem (the *k-TAg* problem, for short) that is para-
metrized by some integer $k \in \{1, \cdots, n\}$. The termination and agreement conditions of k-TAg are the same as those of Consensus and NB-AC, and its validity
condition is as follows:

k-Validity:
1. If at least k processes start with 0, then 0 is the only possible decision
   value.
2. If all processes start with 1 and at most $k - 1$ failures occur, then 1 is
   the only possible decision value.

This new problem is a natural generalization of the Atomic Commitment problem (1-TAg is exactly NB-AC), but turns out to be also a generalization of
Consensus; Indeed, n-TAg actually corresponds to binary Consensus, since at
most $n - 1$ processes are faulty. We have thereby defined a chain of problems
which interpolates between NB-AC and binary Consensus. The original motivation for this generalization is purely theoretical: it is interesting to connect two
incomparable problems by exploiting differences in validity conditions. But it is
easy to imagine actual situations in which such a generalization could be natural:
for example, it might be desirable for processes to enforce them to decide abort
only if a majority of processes initially vote no, but to require that they commit
if all of them initially vote yes as soon as a minority of processes are faulty.

2.3   Lower Bounds for Time Complexity

A fundamental result in synchronous systems [11] is that if $n \geq t + 2$, then
any Consensus algorithm that tolerates t crashes must run $t + 1$ rounds in some
execution before all processes have decided. As noticed by Lynch [10], the proof
of this result still works if one weakens the validity condition to the weak validity
condition. So the $t+1$ lower bound also holds for NB-AC and more generally, for
all the k-TAg problems. However, it no longer holds if one weakens validity to the
non-triviality condition. Indeed, Dwork and Moses [4] devised a simple algorithm
achieving non-triviality, agreement, and termination in only two rounds.

   These remarks, which concern the generalization of the worst case time complexity of Consensus to other agreement problems, also apply when one refines
the analysis of time complexity by discriminating runs according to the number
of failures that *actually* occurs. More precisely, Charron-Bost and Schiper [1]
show the following lower bounds:

Theorem 1. *Let A be a Consensus algorithm which tolerates t process crashes.
For each f, $0 \leq f \leq t$, there exists a run of A with at most f crashes in which
at least one process decides not earlier than during round $f + 2$ if $f \leq t - 2$, and
not earlier than during round $f + 1$ otherwise.*

Afterwards, Keidar and Rajsbaum [6] showed the same lower bounds by an
alternative method. The two proofs use different techniques but both clearly

extend to the weak validity condition. As a consequence, this shows that each k-TAg problem, and in particular NB-AC, requires at least $f + 2$ rounds to decide if $0 \leq f \leq t - 2$ and $f + 1$ rounds if $t - 1 \leq f \leq t$.

---

states$_i$

   $rounds \in N$, initially 0
   $W \in (V \cup \{\bot\})^n$, initially $(\bot, \cdots, v, \cdots, \bot)$ where v is p_i's initial value
   $ready, halt$, Booleans, initially `false`
   $Rec\_Failed, Failed \subseteq \Pi$, initially $\emptyset$
   $decision \in V \cup \{\text{unknown}\}$, initially `unknown`

msgs$_i$

   if $\neg halt$ then
       if $\neg ready$ then send $W[i]$ to all processes
       else send $(ready, W[i])$ to all processes

trans$_i$

   if $\neg halt$ then
       $rounds := rounds + 1$
       let w_j be the value sent by p_j, for each p_j from which a message arrives
       if a message has arrived from p_j then $W[j] := w_j$
       else $W[j] := \bot$
       if $ready$ then
           if $rounds \leq t$ then $decision := W[i]$
           $halt := \text{true}$
       else if some message $(ready, w)$ arrives then
               $W[i] := w$
               $ready := \text{true}$
           else $Rec\_Failed := Failed$
               $Failed := \{p_j : \text{no message arrives from } p_j \text{ in the current round}\}$
               $W[i] := \Phi(rounds, W)$
               if $Rec\_Failed = Failed$ then $ready := \text{true}$
           if $ready$ and $rounds \geq t$ then $decision := W[i]$

Fig. 1. A General Algorithm for Early Deciding

3   A General Early Deciding Algorithm

We now describe a general algorithm for the k-TAg problem that tolerates t crashes and achieves the lower bounds of Theorem 1 for early deciding.

   Our algorithm is based on a strategy borrowed from [9] for determining the time of decisions: each process p_i maintains a variable $Failed$ containing the set of processes that p_i detects to have crashed. During a round, p_i learns that p_j

has crashed if p_i receives no message from p_j in this round. At the end of every round, each process p_i updates its variable $Failed$. If $Failed$ remains unchanged during some round, namely if p_i detects no new crash failure, then p_i becomes ready to decide. Any process which becomes ready at round r is permitted to decide at round $r+1$ if $r \leq t-1$ or as early as round r if $r = t$ or $r = t+1$; furthermore, it broadcasts a $ready$ message at round $r+1$ both to inform other processes that it is ready to decide and to force the other processes to become ready too.

To determine its decision value, each process maintains a vector W of size n. Initially, every process sets its own component of W to its initial value, and the other components to $\perp$. At each round $r \geq 1$, every process p_i broadcasts its own component $W[i]$. Then it collects all the values it has just received into W; if p_i does not receive a value from p_j, it simply sets $W[j] := \perp$. Finally, p_i sets its own component to a new value which depends on the round number r and the values p_i has received, that is $W[i] = \Phi(r, W)$ where Φ is an arbitrary function [2] mapping $\{1, \cdots, t+1\} \times (V \cup \{\perp\})^n$ to V. A simple induction on the round number r shows that no process will ever compute the value of Φ on elements of $\{1, \cdots, t+1\} \times (\{\perp\})^n$. The formal code of the algorithm is given in Figure 1.

In this section, we first prove that if all the processes invoke the same function Φ to adjust their own components in W, then agreement is guaranteed. This common function is then determined according to the validity condition to satisfy: in particular, we specify a function Φ that guarantees the k-validity property.

3.1   Correctness Proof

Theorem 2. *For any mapping $\Phi : \{1, \cdots, t+1\} \times (V \cup \{\perp\})^n \to V$, the algorithm in Figure 1 satisfies the termination and agreement properties in a synchronous system with at most t faulty processes. Moreover, the algorithm achieves the lower bounds of Theorem 1 for early deciding.*

Proof. To prove this theorem, we use the following notation and terminology. The value of any variable x at process p_i just at the end of round r is denoted by $x_i^{(r)}$. By extension, $x_i^{(0)}$ denotes the initial value of x_i. A round r is *quiescent with regard to* process p_i, also noted i-*quiescent*, if p_i detects no additional failure during round r.

For termination, consider a run of the algorithm in which exactly f processes crash $(0 \leq f \leq t)$. Every correct process p_i detects f crashes in this run, and so there is at least one round r_i with $1 \leq r_i \leq f+1$ which is i-quiescent, i.e., $Rec\_Failed_i^{(r_i)} = Failed_i^{(r_i)}$. Suppose p_i has not yet decided at the end of round $r_i - 1$; then we have $halt_i^{(r_i-1)} = \texttt{false}$. There are two cases to consider:

---

[2] V may be an arbitrary non-empty set when examining termination and agreement (Theorem 3.1), but must be instantiated to $\{0, 1\}$ for the k-validity (Theorem 3.2).

1. Process p_i is not ready at the end of round $r_i - 1$, that is $ready_i^{(r_i-1)} =$ false. Since round r_i is i-quiescent, p_i necessarily becomes ready at round r_i, and so p_i decides at the end of round $r_i + 1$ if $r_i \leq t - 1$ and at the end of round r_i if $r_i \geq t$.

2. Process p_i is ready at the end of round $r_i - 1$. In this case, the algorithm forces p_i to decide the current value of $W_i[i]$ at the end of round r_i.

In any case, p_i decides by the end of round $f + 2$ if $0 \leq f < t - 1$ and by the end of round $f + 1$ if $t - 1 \leq f \leq t$. This proves that the algorithm meets the lower bounds of Theorem 1, and subsequently the termination property.

For agreement, we first give a lemma which establishes a weak form of agreement among the processes that are ready. More precisely, the lemma states that two *ready* messages sent at the same round carry the same value.

Lemma 1. *If two messages $(ready, v)$ and $(ready, v')$ are sent at the same round $r \geq 2$, then $v = v'$.*

Proof. The proof is by induction on r. Let p_i and p_j be the senders of $(ready, v)$ and $(ready, v')$, respectively; from the algorithm, p_i and p_j have not yet halted but have both become ready at the end of round $r - 1$.

Basis: $r = 2$. Processes p_i and p_j can send a *ready* message at round 2 only if the first round is i and j-quiescent. In other words, both p_i and p_j receive the same vector W of n initial values at round 1, and so $W_i[i]^{(1)} = W_j[j]^{(1)} = \Phi(1, W)$. From the code of the algorithm, p_i and p_j send *ready* messages at round 2 which are tagged by $W_i[i]^{(1)}$ and $W_j[j]^{(1)}$, respectively. Therefore, we have $v = v'$.

Inductive step: Assume $r > 2$, and suppose the lemma holds at any round r' with $2 \leq r' < r$. There are three cases to consider:

1. Processes p_i and p_j both receive some *ready* messages at round $r - 1$. From the inductive hypothesis, all these *ready* messages are tagged by the same value ν. Upon receiving $(ready, \nu)$ at round $r - 1$, p_i and p_j set $W_i[i] := \nu$ and $W_j[j] := \nu$, respectively. At round r, p_i and p_j both broadcast *ready* messages which carry the current value of $W_i[i]$ and $W_j[j]$, i.e., the value ν. Therefore, we have $v = \nu = v'$.

2. Exactly one of the two processes, say p_i, receives some *ready* messages at round $r - 1$; the same argument as before shows that each message is tagged with value ν. Let p be the sender of such a message; process p is obviously alive at the very beginning of round $r - 2$. On the other hand, since p_j becomes ready at round $r - 1$ without receiving a *ready* message, it follows that round $r-1$ is j-quiescent. At round $r-1$, process p_j thus detects no new failure and so receives a message from p. This message is equal to $(ready, \nu)$ since p sends the same message to all processes. This contradicts that only p_i receives a *ready* message at round $r - 1$, and so this case cannot occur.

3. Neither p_i nor p_j receives *ready* messages at round $r-1$. From the algorithm, it follows that round $r-1$ is both i and j-quiescent. Then p_i and p_j receive the same information at this round, and so the W_i and W_j vectors are equal just

after the receive phase of round $r-1$. Let W denote this vector. Since neither p_i nor p_j receive a *ready* message at round $r-1$, both p_i and p_j set their own component to $\Phi(r-1, W)$, that is $W_i[i]^{(r)} = W_j[j]^{(r)} = \Phi(r-1, W)$. Then p_i and p_j tag the *ready* messages that they send at round r with the current values of $W_i[i]$ and $W_j[j]$, respectively. Therefore, we have $v = W_i[i]^{(r-1)}$, $v' = W_j[j]^{(r-1)}$, and so $v = v'$ as needed.

$$\square_{Lemma\ 1}$$

Now we prove that the algorithm in Figure 1 satisfies agreement. Let r be the first round in which some process decides. Let p_i denote this process and v its decision value. Let p_j be a process that decides v' at round r'. Thus, we have $r' \geq r$. We consider two cases:

1. Process p_i is ready at the end of round $r-1$, and so sends a *ready* message at round r. From the algorithm, this message is tagged by $W_i[i]^{(r-1)}$. Afterwards, p_i does not modify the value of $W_i[i]$, and so decides $v = W_i[i]^{(r-1)}$. The $(ready, v)$ message from p_i is received by p_j since p_j is still alive at the end of round r', and $r' \geq r$.

   a) If p_j is also ready at the end of round $r-1$, then it sends a *ready* message at round r. Therefore, $r = r'$ and the *ready* message from p_j is tagged by the current value of $W_j[j]^{(r-1)}$. Following the same argument as for p_i, process p_j decides value $v' = W_j[j]^{(r-1)}$. Lemma 1 shows that $W_i[i]^{(r-1)} = W_j[j]^{(r-1)}$, and so $v = v'$.

   b) Otherwise, p_j receives some *ready* messages at round r, and by Lemma 1 all these messages are tagged by v. From the algorithm, p_j must set $W_j[j]$ to v and becomes ready at the end of round r. Then p_j decides the current value of $W_j[j]$ at round r or $r+1$. This implies that $v' = v$, as needed.

2. Process p_i is not ready at the end of round $r-1$. This may happen only if $r \geq t$, i.e., $r = t$ or $r = t+1$. Moreover, we can assume that p_j is also not ready at the end of round $r-1$ (otherwise, we have $r' = r$ and then we go back to the first case by exchanging the roles of p_i and p_j). Therefore, none of the rounds $1, \cdots, r-1$ are i or j-quiescent. There are two sub-cases to consider:

   a) Process p_i receives some *ready* messages at round r. Then all these messages are tagged by the decision value v of p_i. Let p_k be the sender of such a message.

      i. Assume process p_j also receives $(ready, v)$ from p_k at round r; then p_j becomes ready and sets $W_j[j]$ to v. Since $r \geq t$, process p_j decides at the end of round r and its decision value is the current value of $W_j[j]$, i.e., $W_j[j]^{(r)} = v$. This proves that $v' = v$.

      ii. Otherwise process p_j receives no message from p_k at round r. Since p_k sends a message to p_i at this round, it necessarily succeeded in sending a message to p_j at the previous round $r-1$. Therefore, round r is not j-quiescent, and so p_j does not decide at round r. Moreover, p_j has detected at least r crashes at the end of round r. Since $r \geq t$, no additional failure can occur later. This shows that process p_i (that is still alive at the end of round r) is actually correct, and that it succeeds in sending $(ready, v)$ to p_j at round $r+1$. It follows that p_j decides the value $v' = v$ at round $r+1$.

b) Process p_i receives no $ready$ message at round r. From the algorithm, it follows that round r is i-quiescent.

    i. If process p_j receives a $ready$ message at round r, then p_j becomes ready and since $r \geq t$, it decides at round r. We get $r' = r$, and by exchanging the roles of p_i and p_j we go back to the previous sub-case 2(a)ii.

    ii. Otherwise process p_j receives no $ready$ message at round r. At this point there are two possible cases:

        A. Round r is also j-quiescent. According to the algorithm, p_j decides at round r, and so $r' = r$. The fact that round r is both i and j-quiescent ensures that p_i and p_j receive the same information at this round, and so vectors W_i and W_j are equal just after the receive phase of round r. Let W denote this vector. Since neither p_i nor p_j receive a $ready$ message at round r, both p_i and p_j set their own component to $\Phi(r, W)$, that is $W_i[i]^{(r)} = W_j[j]^{(r)} = \Phi(r, W)$. Then p_i and p_j decide on $v = W_i[i]^{(r)}$ and $v' = W_j[j]^{(r)}$, respectively. This ensures that $v = v'$.

        B. Otherwise, p_j detects a new crash at round r. Therefore, p_j has detected at least r crashes at the end of round r. We then argue as in a previous case (2(a)ii). Since $r \geq t$, no additional failure can occur later. This shows that process p_i which is still alive at the end of round r, is actually correct, and that it succeeds in sending $(ready, v)$ to p_j at round $r+1$. It follows that p_j decides the value $v' = v$ at round $r+1$.

$$\square_{Theorem\ 2}$$

We now address k-validity (and so, $V = \{0, 1\}$). For that, we constrain the set to which Φ belongs. More precisely, for each $k \in \{1, \cdots, n\}$ we restrict ourselves to functions Φ that satisfy the following condition $\mathcal{C}_k$:

(1) $\Phi(r, W) = 0$ if $r = 1$ and $|\{i : W[i] \in \{0, \bot\}\}| \geq k$;

(2) $\Phi(r, W) \in \{W[i] : W[i] \neq \bot\}$ otherwise, when moreover $W \neq (\bot, \cdots, \bot)$

Note that for every $k \in \{1, \cdots, n\}$, there exist functions satisfying $\mathcal{C}_k$. Moreover, part (2) in $\mathcal{C}_k$ is natural since Φ is never applied to $(\bot, \cdots, \bot)$ during the algorithm (cf. Section 3).

We now prove that condition $\mathcal{C}_k$ for function Φ in Figure 1 shows an algorithm which solves the k-TAg problem.

Theorem 3. *For any function $\Phi : \{1, \cdots, t+1\} \times (V \cup \{\bot\})^n \to V$ satisfying $\mathcal{C}_k$, the algorithm in Figure 1 satisfies the k-validity property.*

Proof. First suppose that at least k processes start with the initial value 0. Let p_i be any process. Process p_i receives value 0 or no message at the first round from at least k processes. From the definition of $\Phi_k(1, -)$, it follows that $W_i[i]^{(1)} = 0$. By the algorithm, any component $W_j[j]$ remains equal to 0 in the subsequent rounds. So, 0 is the only possible decision value.

On the other hand, consider a run of the algorithm in which every process starts with 1, and with at most $k - 1$ failures. In the first round, every process p_i receives at least $n - k + 1$ messages with value 1, and so $W_i[i]^{(1)} = 1$ (if p_i is still alive at the end of round 1). A simple induction on r shows that for any r, we have $W_i[i]^{(r)} = 1$ because of the definition of $\Phi_k(r, -)$ for $r \geq 2$. Therefore, the only possible decision value in this run is 1.

$$\square_{Theorem\ 3}$$

For $k = n$, the algorithm in Figure 1 thereby solves binary Consensus. Obviously, this algorithm can be generalized for an arbitrary value set V.

Part (2) of $\mathcal{C}_k$ allows flexibility in the choice of Φ. For instance, $\min, \max$, and $W[i]$ where $i = \min\{j : W[j] \neq \perp\}$ all yield correct solutions of the k-TAg problems. In the Non-Blocking Atomic Commitment case, this flexibility can be used to tune the frequency of commit decisions. Indeed, setting $\Phi(r, W) = \max_i W[i]$ in part (2) of $\mathcal{C}_k$ allows processes to commit more often: if all processes initially vote yes, then the decision is commit as soon as at least one correct process has received yes from all processes in the first round no matter whether failures occur. This is clearly a desirable feature of any database transaction system.

Conclusion

In this paper, we introduced a new class of distributed agreement problems, ranging from Consensus to Non-Blocking Atomic Commitment, by varying the validity condition in the specification. We also provided an early deciding algorithm to solve each problem of this class in the synchronous model with crash failures.

Lower bounds on time-complexity have already been established for early deciding algorithms for both Consensus and Non-Blocking Atomic Commitment, and can be easily extended to any k-TAg problem. In this paper, we proved that our algorithm meets these lower bounds, so showing that these lower bounds are tight.

These results show that Consensus and Non-Blocking Atomic Commitment, two incomparable agreement problems in asynchronous systems, can be solved by the same optimal algorithm in synchronous systems. Consequently, the common belief that Non-Blocking Atomic Commitment requires a three-phase commit protocol "*à la Skeen*" is false.

Acknowledgments. We are grateful to Leslie Lamport and James Leifer for their very constructive and helpful comments.

References

1. Charron-Bost, B., Schiper, A.: Uniform Consensus is Harder than Consensus. Technical Report DSC/2000/028, Département Systèmes de Communication, EPFL, May 2000. To appear in Journal of Algorithms
2. Charron-Bost, B., Toueg, S.: Comparing the Atomic Commitment and Consensus Problems. In preparation (2001)
3. Dwork, C., Lynch, N.A., Stockmeyer, L.: Consensus in the Presence of Partial Synchrony. Journal of the ACM **35** 2 (1988) 288–323
4. Dwork, C., Moses, Y.: Knowledge and Common Knowledge in a Byzantine Environment: Crash Failures. Information and Computation **88** 2 (1990) 156–186
5. Fischer, M.J., Lynch, N.A., Paterson, M.S.: Impossibility of Distributed Consensus with One Faulty Process. Journal of the ACM, **32** 2 (1985) 374–382
6. Keidar, I., Rajsbaum, S.: A Simple Proof of the Uniform Consensus Synchronous Lower Bound. Information Processing Letters, **85** 1 (2003) 47–52
7. Lamport, L.: The Weak Byzantine Generals Problem. Journal of the ACM **30** 3 (1983) 668–676
8. Lamport, L.: Lower Bounds on Consensus. Unpublished note, March 2000
9. Lamport, L., Fischer, M.: Byzantine Generals and Transaction Commit Protocols. Technical Report 62, SRI International, April 1982
10. Lynch, N.A.: Distributed Algorithms. Morgan Kaufmann (1996)
11. Merritt, M.J.: Unpublished Notes (1985)
12. Skeen, D.: Nonblocking Commit Protocols. In: Proceedings of the ACM SIGMOD Conf. on Management of Data, ACM, June 1982, 133–147

Supporting Evolution in Workflow Definition Languages

Sérgio Miguel Fernandes, João Cachopo, and António Rito Silva

INESC-ID/Technical University of Lisbon
Rua Alves Redol n° 9, 1000-029 Lisboa, Portugal
{Sergio.Fernandes, Joao.Cachopo, Rito.Silva}@inesc-id.pt
http://www.esw.inesc-id.pt

Abstract. Workflow definition languages are evolving rapidly. However, there is not any agreed-upon standard for such languages. In this paper we address the problem of how to develop a workflow system that is able to cope with the constant changes in these languages. We address the definition aspect of workflow systems by distinguishing between frontend and backend languages. This way, a workflow system can be developed based on the backend language whereas the frontend language can change.

1 Introduction

In its simplest form, a *Workflow System* (WfS) allows its users to describe and execute a workflow. The language used to describe a workflow is a *Workflow Definition Language* (WfDL).

In this paper we address a software engineering problem: The problem of developing a WfS that supports changes in the WfDL. Moreover, it should be able to support more than one WfDL simultaneously. The solution we propose is to split the WfS into two layers: (1) a layer implementing a *Workflow Virtual Machine*, which is responsible for most of the WfS activities; and (2) a layer where the different WfDLs are handled, which is responsible for making the mapping between each WfDL and the Workflow Virtual Machine.

In the next section, we give some motivation for this work and discuss some of the problems that a WfS faces when it is not built with WfDL change in mind. In Sect. 3 we describe our proposal of creating a Workflow Virtual Machine to support different WfDLs, and in Sect. 4 we describe the object-oriented framework we implemented using this approach. Then, in Sect. 5 we discuss some related work and open issues. Finally, in Sect. 6 we conclude the paper.

2 Motivation

There are many WfSs available, each one of them with its own WfDL – different from all the others. Actually, despite the efforts of the Workflow Management Coalition [5], different languages give different names to the same concept (e.g.

P. Van Emde Boas et al. (Eds.): SOFSEM 2004, LNCS 2932, pp. 208–217, 2004.

some call "Activity" to what others call "Step"). The lack of a common language to describe workflows makes impossible the easy migration from one WfS to another. This is a problem for users – those that want to model and execute workflows.

Some authors have already recognised this problem [9] and presented a critical evaluation of some of these languages. This problem would be solved if we had a standard WfDL that all systems supported. As a matter of fact, different groups presented their proposals for such a standard [2], [3]. Yet, so far, the workflow community has not reached an agreement on which language to adopt.[1]

This proliferation of languages has disadvantages also for the developers of WfSs. It poses the question of which language to support in the system under development. If the chosen language becomes the standard, fine, but what if the chosen language is abandoned?

Even if a consensus was reached, the agreed upon language would be changing over time, as the specifications themselves are not yet stable, containing many open issues, as their own creators acknowledge [3], [2].

The WfS exists to support the execution of workflows, which are described by a WfDL. That WfDL has a certain set of concepts and constructs. Naturally, the WfS has to deal with those concepts and constructs to perform its tasks (such as the execution of a workflow). If the WfDL changes significantly (e.g., because it was abandoned and replaced by another), the WfS developers may have to rewrite a significant part of the system. Therefore, a major concern for the WfS developers is how to make it able to cope with changes in the WfDL, with the minimum impact in the rest of the system.

3   The Workflow Virtual Machine

To isolate the core of the WfS from changes to the WfDL, we propose the creation of a *Workflow Virtual Machine* (WfVM).

Although there are many workflow definition languages, they all share a common subset of concepts such as "activities," "activity sequencing," "data handling," and "invoking domain-specific logic" [5]. The idea of the WfVM is that it should support these core concepts, allowing the definition and the execution of workflows described in a simple language that uses those concepts. We call this language the *backend language*. This is not the language that WfS users use to describe their workflows. That language – the WfDL we have been talking about – is what we call the *frontend language*.

With a WfVM in place, the description of a workflow in the frontend language is compiled into a workflow described in the backend language and then executed. This way, the core of the WfS does not depend on the frontend language, which can change freely – provided that it can always be compiled to an appropriate backend description.

---

[1] Unfortunately, we cannot foresee in a near future such an agreement.

This separation between frontend and backend languages has two additional benefits. First, we can have different frontend languages simultaneously very easily. A universal WfDL that suits all users is not feasible. For particular domains, some constructs related to the domain can simplify greatly the modelling task. Of course, different domains have different needs. So, being able to support different frontend languages is an important requirement for a successful WfS.

Second, the existence of two distinct languages solves the conflict between the two forces that guide the specification of a WfDL: From the standpoint of a WfS user, the language should be easy to use (i.e., user-friendly), preferably supported by modelling tools, containing many constructs to help on the modelling process, and designed to help the user to avoid making errors. On the other hand, we have the WfS developers, who are concerned with qualities such as extensibility, maintainability and simplicity of implementation – therefore, the language should be minimal, with no redundancy in it. The backend language is not to be used by humans, so it does not have the user-friendliness requirements; it can meet the requirements of the WfS developers. The language to be used by humans (the frontend language), is not to be operated by the WfS (apart from the compilation process); it can be as large and user-friendly as we want.

To conclude this section, note that there are some important requirements for the backend language: it needs to be expressive enough to support different frontend languages, and it needs to be flexible enough to adapt smoothly to new concepts that may be expressed in future frontend languages. We will not examine in detail these requirements in the paper but we will discuss them briefly in Sect. 5.

4   Workflow Framework Implementation

We developed an object-oriented workflow framework using the approach proposed in this paper: The core of the framework implements a Workflow Virtual Machine, supporting the execution of workflows defined in a backend language we designed. The framework also supports a frontend language – based on the work of Manolescu [7] – which is compiled to the backend language. We will not describe the framework in detail but we will discuss some of its aspects to illustrate our approach.

The core of the framework presented in Fig. 1 is composed of two modules: the Definition Module, and the Execution Module. The former is responsible for managing workflow definitions whereas the latter is responsible for managing the execution of instances of the stored definitions.[2]

In the next section, we present the backend language, and in Sect. 4.2 we describe how a workflow is executed. This gives an operational semantic to the

---

[2] This framework was developed with modularity in mind. Only the core aspects of workflow management are implemented at the kernel. Extended functionality (such as monitoring, persistence, access control, and dynamic modification of the workflow definitions) is implemented as separate modules. These modules can be composed as needed, thus making the framework lighter and easier to extend.

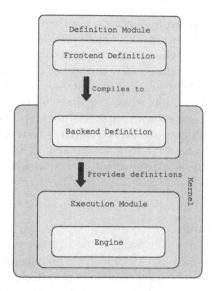

Fig. 1. The framework's core architecture

backend language. Next, in Sect. 4.3 we present the frontend language we referred to above. Finally, Sect. 4.4 shows a mapping from the frontend language to the backend language.

4.1 Backend Definition

The basic structure for the backend workflow definition is a directed graph. In the graph, the nodes represent activity steps, and the transitions between nodes represent the flow. The flow can be either control or data. Control flow establishes the order in which the graph should be navigated to execute its nodes. Data flow defines what data is passed from one activity to another. In this paper we will focus on the control flow aspects only.

Every graph should have exactly one start node and one end node. A node represents a *step*. Every step has a *service object* associated which contains the node's domain-specific behaviour. The service object is invoked every time the step is scheduled for execution by the engine. When this invocation returns, the engine assumes that the domain-specific operations for this step have been completed and graph navigation can proceed.[3]

Control flows link steps. A control flow is a directed edge in a graph from one node to another. The direction specifies the order in which the two steps will be performed. The source step must have ended before the target begins execution. Every control flow has a *transition condition*, which indicates whether the flow of control can proceed through that transition to the target step.

---

[3] Service objects may be empty, not doing anything.

Concurrency is supported by having more than one control flow originating from the same step, thus creating two or more parallel flows. Concurrent work can be *synchronised* later by having more than one control flow targeting the same step. Steps have *synchronisation rules*. Currently, there are two rules available: the *OR-rule* and the *AND-rule*. A step that has an OR synchronisation rule will be scheduled for execution when the first control flow reaches that step (a control flow reaches a step when a preceding step ends and the transition condition of the connecting control flow evaluates to true). When the following control flows reach the same step, they are ignored. A join step that has an AND synchronisation rule will be scheduled for execution when all preceding control flows reach that step.

4.2 Execution Module

The execution module contains the life-cycle-management operations for the workflow instances. The execution module is responsible for reading the shared workflow definitions from the definition module and for managing each workflow instance in a separate execution context. This way, the framework can concurrently execute multiple workflows sharing the same definition. For each *execute* operation, the engine creates an object – the *executor* – responsible for holding all the information relevant for executing a single workflow instance, as well as carrying out the graph navigation algorithm. The following summarises the executor algorithm:

1. The execution starts on the graph's start node: A node instance representing the execution of the start node is placed on the execution queue. From here on, the navigation takes place whenever a step finishes its execution and returns control to its executor.
2. When a step finishes, the outgoing control flows from its node are iterated. For each control flow evaluate its transition condition. If it is false, ignore the control flow. If it is true, traverse to the target node and check if the node can be scheduled for execution. If the target node has a single incoming control flow, then it can be scheduled; otherwise:
   a) If the target node is an AND-node then all its incoming control flows must have been traversed already in order to proceed (i.e., the last transition to the node has just been made).
   b) If the target node is an OR-node then execution will not proceed, unless this is the first transition to the node – this causes all other transitions to the target node to have no effect and allows execution to proceed immediately.
3. When the next node is ready to be executed, a node instance is placed on the execution queue.
4. The workflow execution ends when a node finishes its execution, there are no control flows to apply, and there are no other nodes still in execution.

4.3   Frontend Definition

The choice of a frontend language is like the choice of a high-level, structured programming language, whereas the choice of a backend language is more like the choice of a low-level, unstructured byte-code language. At the frontend we rather have some modelling rules enforced, to get a more understandable and structured model. The backend language described in the Sect. 4.1 is a graph-based representation of a workflow, which therefore allows for the creation of unstructured workflow models (e.g., jumps in and out of loop's bodies, splitting with inconsistent merging, etc). This freedom and expressiveness is required to support the different frontend languages available. The frontend language we implemented is a subset of the typical workflow definition languages, that supports only commonly used structured workflow patterns [10].

The frontend language we describe here is based on the work by Manolescu, in his PhD Thesis [7]. The key abstraction of this particular frontend language is the *Procedure*. A tree of hierarchically composed procedures defines a workflow. Manolescu proposes control structures for procedures which are similar to those available in structured programming languages.

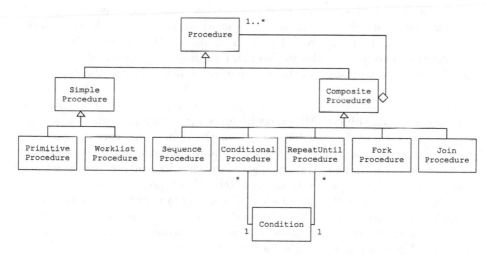

Fig. 2. Meta-model of the frontend definition

Procedures are built using the Composite [4] design pattern to abstract the concrete type of the procedures that constitute the workflow definition, thus allowing the easy extension of the framework with new procedures. The diagram in Fig. 2 shows the complete hierarchy. We will discuss some of them. There are two main sub-types of procedure: *Simple Procedures* and *Composite Procedures*.

Simple procedures are leaf nodes in the tree of procedures that constitute the workflow definition. These procedures are associated with domain-specific tasks performed outside the framework, i.e., they represent workflow steps which must be delegated for execution by the domain workers (either applications or humans).

Composite procedures are used to represent the structures that manage the flow of control (such as sequencing, and branching). We defined five types of composite procedures:

- *Sequence Procedures,* which represent the execution of all their children procedures in the sequential order in which they are stored;
- *Conditional Procedures,* which enable the control flow to change by having a condition that specifies one of two mutually exclusive paths to take;
- *Fork Procedures,* which spawn the parallel execution of all their children and wait for the first to finish;
- *Join Procedures,* which, like the previous one, spawn the parallel execution of all their children, but wait for all of them to complete execution before completing;
- *RepeatUntil Procedures,* which hold one procedure as their body and cyclically execute it until a given condition is achieved.

4.4   Mapping the Frontend to the Backend

In this section we describe some of the transformation rules used to generate the backend definition from the frontend based on procedures. The compilation starts in the root of the tree of procedures and is defined recursively: Each composite procedure compiles its children (which generates part of the backend graph), and then links some of the resulting nodes, depending on the procedure's semantics.

The compilation of a leaf procedure produces only one node, containing the appropriate service object. All composite procedures are represented by, at least, two graph nodes containing between them the nodes that correspond to the compiled children procedures. By default, transition conditions always evaluate to **true**, meaning that the transition should always be made to the target node (the exceptions are the Conditional and RepeatUntil procedures).

The entire compilation process is quite straightforward, but its details are outside the scope of this paper. To illustrate the compilation method, Fig. 3 shows some examples of workflows represented in procedure-like fashion and its corresponding compilation to the backend language.

The top three workflows (from left to right) illustrate the compilation of: (1) a sequence with three steps; (2) a conditional choice between two steps; (3) the concurrent execution of two steps. In the first case, the steps are simply linked sequentially. In the second case, there are two mutually exclusive paths, created using opposite transition conditions. In the third case, after steps 1 and 2 are placed in concurrent execution, they must both finish, in order for the workflow to finish, due to the AND synchronisation rule (&). Finally, the workflow in the bottom, depicts a sequence where the second step is a composite step, that is executed repeatedly until the guard is true, hence the compilation produces two conditional transitions, with one of them being a backward ("loop") transition in the graph.

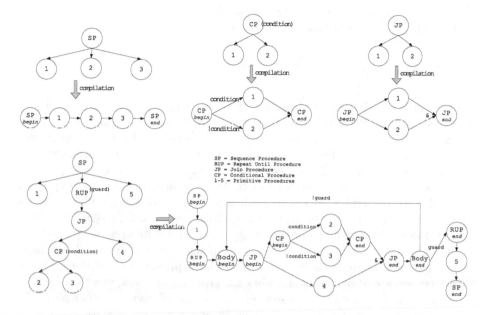

Fig. 3. Frontend representations and the respective compilations to the backend

5 Discussion

Some previous work approached, already, the construction of object-oriented WfSs. For instance, [7] proposes a new workflow architecture for software developers that focuses on customising the workflow features and composing them; and in [8] a lightweight workflow kernel is proposed, with some emphasis on distributed execution capabilities. However, none of this work approaches the architectural issue of supporting different languages for representing workflows. Therefore, all of them are limited on the workflow languages they support. To the extent of our knowledge, there is no other WfS that follows our approach.

On the other hand, our workflow framework implementation raises some interesting questions. For instance, is the backend language we designed expressive enough? We took a pragmatic approach in our development: We chose to incrementally and iteratively develop the language. We began by identifying the core/common workflow concerns expressed in most languages and defined a language to support that. Later, if the need arises, the backend language can be extended or reviewed.

Recently, some authors performed a very complete study on the expressiveness of workflow languages and its application to typical workflow patterns [6], [10]. One result of this study was the proposal of a workflow language [1] with a representation based on Petri nets. Despite its high expressiveness, we do not consider it adequate as a frontend language. For many users it is far more complex than what they need. However, it could be used as the backend language in our approach. A drawback is that this language is very complex, which may difficult its implementation in a WfS.

6   Conclusion

We presented a technique for dealing with the variations in workflow languages, which consists in separating the language used to model workflows from the language used by the workflow system to execute them. With this separation, the core system behaves like a workflow virtual machine. This technique was applied to the development of an object-oriented workflow framework that provides workflow concepts to software developers. We consider that this technique can be applied to the development of any workflow system to increase its reusability when dealing with changes in the workflow languages. It also presents a solution for developers that intend to provide support for more than one language.

It would be interesting to exercise the compilation of more frontend languages to our backend language, as a way to test the expressiveness of the backend. Currently, we are also undergoing work for creating modular functional extensions to our framework (e.g. monitoring, access control, dynamic changes of the workflows). These modules will allow us to assess the savings we can obtain by developing code for the backend that will automatically provide the same functionality to many frontend languages.

Acknowledgements. The work presented in this paper is partially being developed in the context of the ACE-GIS project (project funded by the V Framework Programme IST-2001-37724). For more information see http://www.acegis.net.

References

1. van der Aalst, W.M.P., ter Hofstede, A.H.M.: Yawl: Yet Another Workflow Language. Technical Report FIT-TR-2002-06, Queensland University of Technology (2002)
2. Assaf Arkin: Business Process Modelling Language, November 2002
3. Curbera, F., Goland, Y., Klein, J., Leymann, F., Roller, D., Thatte, S., Weerawarana, S.: Business Process Execution Language for Web Services.
4. Gamma, E., Helm, R., Johnson, R., Vlissides, J.: Design Patterns: Elements of Reusable Object-Oriented Software. Addison-Wesley (1995)
5. Hollingsworth, D.: The Workflow Reference Model. Workflow Management Coalition, Jan 1995. Document Number TC-00-1003.
6. Kiepuszewski, B.: Expressiveness and Suitability of Languages for Control Flow Modelling in Workflows. PhD thesis, Queensland University of Technology, Brisbane, Australia (2002)
7. Manolescu, D.-A.: Micro-Workflow: A Workflow Architecture Supporting Compositional Object-Oriented Software Development. PhD thesis, University of Illinois at Urbana-Champaign (2001)

8. Muth, P., Weissenfels, J., Gillmann, M., Weikum, G.: Mentor-Lite: Integrating Light-Weight Workflow Management Systems within Existing Business Environments (extended abstract) (1998)

9. van der Aalst, W.: Don't Go with the Flow: Web Services Composition Standards Exposed (2003)

10. van der Aalst, W.M.P., ter Hofstede, A.H.M., Kiepuszewski, B., Barros, A.P.: Workflow Patterns. QUT Technical report, FIT-TR-2002-02, Queensland University of Technology, Brisbane (2002). (Also see http://www.tm.tue.nl/it/research/patterns).

Clustered Level Planarity*

Michael Forster and Christian Bachmaier

University of Passau, 94030 Passau, Germany
{forster,bachmaier}@fmi.uni-passau.de

Abstract. Planarity is an important concept in graph drawing. It is generally accepted that planar drawings are well understandable. Recently, several variations of planarity have been studied for advanced graph concepts such as k-level graphs [16], [15], [13], [14], [11], [12], [10], [6] and clustered graphs [7], [5]. In k-level graphs, the vertices are partitioned into k levels and the vertices of one level are drawn on a horizontal line. In clustered graphs, there is a recursive clustering of the vertices according to a given nesting relation. In this paper we combine the concepts of level planarity and clustering and introduce clustered k-level graphs. For connected clustered level graphs we show that clustered k-level planarity can be tested in $\mathcal{O}(k|V|)$ time.

1 Introduction

Many structures in real life applications cannot be represented appropriately by standard graphs. In biochemical pathways, for example, substances and reactions can be modelled as vertices and (hyper) edges. But often it is also desirable to visualise the cell compartments containing distinct substances and reactions. These compartments define different components (clusters) of the graph and are recursively nested. This leads to an extended graph model: A *clustered graph* $G = (V, E, \Gamma)$ is a directed or undirected graph with an additional recursive nesting relation $\Gamma = (V_\Gamma, E_\Gamma)$ with $V_\Gamma = C \cup V$. Γ is a rooted tree of the clusters C as inner nodes and the leaves V. Each cluster $c \in C$ represents a subgraph $G_c = (V_c, E_c)$ of G induced by its descendant leaves V_c. It can be assumed that each cluster has at least two children. Thus the number of clusters $|C|$ is linear. Clustered graphs are drawn such that the clusters are simple closed curves that define closed regions of the plane. The region of each cluster contains exactly the clustered drawing of the subgraph induced by its vertices. Regions are nested recursively according to Γ. A clustered graph is *c-planar* if it has a drawing without edge crossings, region intersections, or crossings between an edge and a region. An edge crosses a region if it crosses its border at least twice. It is an open problem, see e.g. [7], [5], [9], whether c-planarity can be tested efficiently. Here connectivity plays a crucial role. It can be done in linear time if the clustered graph is *c-connected*, i.e., if each subgraph induced by a cluster is connected, see [7], [5].

---

* This research has been supported in part by the Deutsche Forschungsgemeinschaft, grant BR 835/9-1.

For drawing clustered graphs there are different approaches. See [2] for an overview. If the underlying graph is directed, then Sander's extension of the Sugiyama algorithm [18], [17], [19] can be used. The first step of this algorithm is to distribute the vertices to k levels. Then it uses heuristics to reduce the number of edge crossings, see also [8], because the minimisation problem is NP-hard. It does not even guarantee a planar drawing if one is possible. Since in this case it is especially desirable to avoid crossings we analyse this problem called clustered level planarity. This is the combination of c-planarity and level planarity.

A *k-level graph* $G = (V, E, \phi)$ is a directed or undirected graph with a level assignment $\phi\colon V \to \{1, 2, \ldots, k\}$, $1 \leq k \leq |V|$, that partitions the vertex set into $V = V^1 \dot\cup V^2 \dot\cup \cdots \dot\cup V^k$, $V^i = \phi^{-1}(i)$, $1 \leq i \leq k$, such that $\phi(u) \neq \phi(v)$ for each edge $(u, v) \in E$. A k-level graph G is k-level planar if it is possible to draw it in the Cartesian plane such that all vertices $v \in V^i$ of the i-th level are placed on a single horizontal line $l_i = \{(x, i) \mid x \in \mathbb{R}\}$ and the edges are drawn as vertically strictly monotone curves without crossings. A *clustered k-level graph* $G = (V, E, \Gamma, \phi)$, or short *cl-graph*, is a k-level graph with a recursive clustering. For every cluster $c \in C$ denote the minimum and maximum levels with vertices in c by $\phi_{\min}(c)$ and $\phi_{\max}(c)$. A clustered k-level graph G is *clustered k-level planar* or short *cl-planar* if it has a level planar embedding in the plane such that the following restrictions are satisfied:

R1 Each intersection of a level line and a cluster region is a single interval, i.e., the vertices on each level that belong to the same cluster are placed next to each other with no other vertices in between.

R2 Clusters do not cross each other, i.e., the relative position of two clusters is the same on all levels.

R3 Edges do not cross clusters, i.e., no edge intersects the border of a cluster region twice.

See Fig. 1 for a visualisation of R1–R3. These restrictions ensure that any cl-planar graph can be drawn without crossings such that all cluster regions are convex. They can even be drawn as rectangles by using Sander's algorithm.

Lemma 1. *If $G = (V, E, \Gamma, \phi)$ is a clustered k-level graph, then obviously*

1. *G is cl-planar $\Rightarrow (V, E, \phi)$ is level planar $\Rightarrow (V, E)$ is planar.*
2. *G is cl-planar $\Rightarrow (V, E, \Gamma)$ is c-planar $\Rightarrow (V, E)$ is planar.*

Note that a level planar and c-planar cl-graph is not necessarily cl-planar. Figure 2 is a counter-example. Without loss of generality we consider only simple graphs without self loops and parallel edges. Because of Lemma 1 a simple input graph with $|E| > 3|V| - 6$ is rejected as not cl-planar and we can assume that the number of edges is linear in the number of vertices.

We give an $\mathcal{O}(k|V|)$ time algorithm based on the previous work of Di Battista and Nardelli [6]. It solves cl-planarity for cl-graphs that are proper, level connected, and hierarchies: A *hierarchy* is a level graph with a single *source* and an

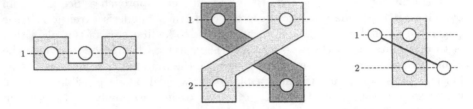

Fig. 1. Violations of the cl-planarity restrictions

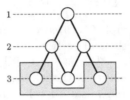

Fig. 2. A cl-graph that is level planar and c-planar but not cl-planar

arbitrary number of *sinks*, where a source is a vertex having only edges to a higher level and a sink is defined analogously. Note that hierarchies should not be confused with the hierarchical clustering Γ. A (clustered) k-level graph is *proper* if $|\phi(u) - \phi(v)| = 1$ for each edge $(u, v) \in E$. A clustered level graph is *level connected* if any two consecutive levels of the same cluster are spanned by an edge of the cluster, i.e., if $\forall c \in C: \forall i \in \{\phi_{\min}(c), \ldots, \phi_{\max}(c) - 1\}: \exists (u, v) \in E_c: \phi(u) \leq i \wedge \phi(v) \geq i + 1$. Level connectivity follows directly from c-connectivity.

2   Related Work

There are several algorithms for level planarity testing. The first is from Di Battista and Nardelli [6]. It is restricted to hierarchies and runs in linear time. Chandramouli and Diwan [3] present a linear time algorithm for triconnected DAGs. Leipert et al. [16], [15], [13], [14], based on the work of Heath and Pemmaraju [11], [12], finally come up with a linear time algorithm for general level graphs. Their algorithm is based on [6] and it is also able to compute a level planar embedding. Since this algorithm is rather complex there is a simpler approach of Healy and Kuusik which runs in $\mathcal{O}(|V|^2)$ time on proper graphs and computes an embedding in $\mathcal{O}(|V|^3)$ time. Since our algorithm extends the algorithm of [6] we have to recall some details which are necessary to understand our extensions. We use a simplified notation.

The basic idea of the algorithm is to perform a top down sweep, processing the levels in order $1, 2, \ldots, k$ and for every level V^i compute a set of permutations of V^i that appear in some level planar embedding of G^i. G^i is the subgraph induced by $V^1 \cup V^2 \cup \cdots \cup V^i$. G is level planar if and only if the set of permutations of $G^k = G$ is not empty.

In order to represent and store sets of vertex permutations efficiently, a data structure called PQ-tree, introduced by Booth and Lueker [1], is used. A PQ-tree represents the permutations of a finite set S in which the members of specified subsets of S occur consecutively. It is a rooted and ordered tree with leaves and two types of inner nodes, P- and Q-nodes. In the context of this paper the term vertex denotes an element of a graph and the term node denotes an element of a PQ-tree or of a cluster tree. The leaves correspond to the elements of S and the possible permutations are encoded by the combination of the two types of inner nodes. The children of a P-node can be permuted arbitrarily, whereas the children of a Q-node are ordered and this order can only be reversed. If PQ-trees are used in planarity tests, a P-node always represents a cut vertex and a Q-node represents a biconnected component of a graph. The leaves represent edges to the not yet processed part of the graph. If there are no permutations with the given restrictions, the PQ-tree is empty. The most important operation on PQ-trees is REDUCE. It restricts the encoded set of permutations such that all elements of a given set $S' \subseteq S$ are consecutive in all remaining permutations. During the reduce phase, PQ-leaves representing elements of S' are called *pertinent*. The minimum subtree containing all pertinent leaves is called the *pertinent subtree*. All its nodes are said to be pertinent, too. Its root is called *pert-root*.

Algorithm 1 describes the LEVEL-PLANARITY-TEST for hierarchies where $T(G^i)$ is a PQ-tree representing the set of admissible permutations of the vertices in V^i that appear in some level planar embedding of G^i. The procedure CHECK-LEVEL realises a sweep over a single level i. All operations are performed in $T(G^i)$. Define H^i to be the *extended form* of G^i. It consists of G^i plus some new *virtual vertices* and *virtual edges*. For every edge (u, v) with $u \subset V^i$ and $v \in V^{i+1}$, a new virtual vertex with label v and a virtual edge connecting it to u is introduced in H^i. Note that there may be several virtual vertices with the same label but each with exactly one entering edge. The extension of $T(G^i)$ to $T(H^i)$ is accomplished by a PQ-tree operation called RE-PLACE_PERT. Since all PQ-leaves with the same label appear consecutively after the PQ-tree operation REDUCE in every admissible permutation, each

---

Algorithm 1: LEVEL-PLANARITY-TEST

Input: A level graph $G = (V^1 \cup V^2 \cup \ldots \cup V^k, E, \phi)$

Output: boolean value indicating whether G is level planar

Initialise $T(G^1)$

for $i \leftarrow 1$ **to** $k - 1$ **do**
  $\mid$ $T(G^{i+1}) \leftarrow$ CHECK-LEVEL($T(G^i)$, V^{i+1})
  $\mid$ **if** $T(G^{i+1}) = \emptyset$ **then return false**
end

return true

---

consecutive set of PQ-leaves is replaced with REPLACE_PERT by a P-node. This is the parent of new leaves representing the adjacent vertices of v in V^{i+1}. Afterwards all PQ-leaves representing vertices in V^{i+1} with the same label are reduced to appear as a consecutive sequence in any permutation stored in the PQ-tree. R^i denotes this *reduced extended form* of H^i. Finally in a new sweep over this level all PQ-leaves representing sinks v in V^{i+1} are deleted from the PQ-tree reconstructing it such that it obeys the properties of a valid PQ-tree again. See [1], [16], [15], [13], [14], [11], [12] for details on these operations.

3   Algorithm

3.1   Idea

Our algorithm for testing cl-planarity of proper and level connected hierarchies is based on the PQ-tree method for level planarity testing of hierarchies of [6]. This method already ensures that the calculated embedding is level planar. It remains to show how the additional properties R1–R3 for cl-planar embeddings can be maintained. We will see later that R2 and R3 are automatically satisfied if the graph is level connected, while an extension is necessary for R1.

An analysis of R1 reveals a similarity to the ordering constraints of PQ-trees because the vertices of one cluster have to be placed next to each other. This corresponds directly to the semantics of the REDUCE operation which restricts the set of admissible permutations to those where the PQ-leaves given as an argument appear consecutively. We obtain the following idea: The level by level sweep of the level planarity testing algorithm remains the same. The admissible permutations are stored in a PQ-tree T. We ensure R1 by additional applications of REDUCE. This is done by an extension of CHECK-LEVEL, see Algorithm 2. On each level a new method REDUCE-CLUSTERS is called, which ensures that the interior of each cluster is consecutive.

Algorithm 2: CHECK-LEVEL

Input: PQ-tree $T(G^i)$ of the current level, Vertices V^{i+1} of the next level

Output: PQ-tree $T(G^{i+1})$ of the next level

extend $T(G^i)$ to $T(H^i)$
reduce $T(H^i)$ to $T(R^i)$
if $T(R^i) = \emptyset$ **then return** $T(G^{i+1}) \leftarrow \emptyset$
REDUCE-CLUSTERS($T(R^i)$, V^{i+1})   *// NEW*
remove sinks from $T(R^i)$
return $T(G^{i+1}) \leftarrow T(R^i)$

3.2   Efficient Cluster Reduction

A straightforward implementation of the REDUCE-CLUSTERS method is to call REDUCE for the PQ-leaves of each cluster. This leads to a running time of $\mathcal{O}(k|C||V|)$, i.e., up to $\mathcal{O}(k|V|^2)$, since for each of the k levels and for each of the —C— clusters the whole PQ-tree of size $\mathcal{O}(|V|)$ must be traversed. With the following approach this can be improved to $\mathcal{O}(k|V|)$ time.

First consider only two clusters c_1 and c_2 on the same level. There are two cases how c_1 and c_2 can interact, either they are disjoint or they are nested. In the first case c_1 and c_2 can be reduced independently. For each cluster only a subtree of the PQ-tree has to be considered. Because these subtrees are disjoint, in the worst case the whole PQ-tree has to be traversed once per level. In the second case suppose that c_2 is nested in c_1. Then all descendants of c_2 are descendants of c_1 and the result of reducing c_2 can be used for reducing c_1. It is not necessary to traverse the corresponding PQ-subtree again but we can start the second REDUCE at the pert-root of c_2.

This result can be generalised to the whole cluster tree by using a simultaneous bottom up traversal of the cluster tree Γ and the PQ-tree $T(R^i)$. After a cluster c has been reduced, all PQ-leaves representing vertices contained in c are consecutive in any permutation stored in $T(R^i)$. They are exactly the leaves of a pertinent subtree. Pert-root of this subtree can be a single node or a consecutive part of a Q-node. Therefore we temporarily replace the pertinent subtree(s) by a new PQ-leaf X_c with label c. This avoids calling REDUCE for inner PQ-nodes which may not be supported by existing PQ-tree implementations. It is important that the replaced subtrees are reinserted later in the same order as they had before their removal. For this, reversions of their parent Q-node and other modifications have to be respected. Fortunately this can be done easily by remembering which sibling pointer of X_c represents the direction, w.l.o.g. the first stored pointer. This is similar to the *direction indicators* of [4].

Algorithm 3 shows the method REDUCE-CLUSTERS. The cluster tree Γ is traversed in a similar way as the REDUCE method traverses a PQ-tree. The cluster nodes are processed bottom up using a queue to ensure that nodes cannot be processed before their children on the same level have been processed. This can be tested by comparing the number of processed children with $child\_count(c, i + 1)$, the number of children of c on level $i + 1$.

3.3   Correctness

Theorem 1. *Algorithm 1 with the extended CHECK-LEVEL method shown in Algorithm 2 returns true if and only if the graph is cl-planar.*

Proof. "$\Rightarrow$": Since our algorithm does not modify the level planarity test part, a positive result ensures that G is level planar. Thus it remains to be shown that the restrictions R1–R3 imposed by the definition of cl-planarity are satisfied. The semantics of R1 for the intersection of a cluster $c \in C$ and a level line i are exactly the same as the semantics of a REDUCE operation applied to the

---

Algorithm 3: REDUCE-CLUSTERS

Input: PQ-tree $T(R^i)$, Vertices V^{i+1} of the next level

Output: PQ-tree $T(R^i)'$ with reduced clusters

foreach $c \in C \cup V$ **do** $children\_leaves[c] \leftarrow \emptyset$

Initialise Queue Q with V^{i+1}

while Q *not empty* **do**

$\quad c' \leftarrow delete\_first(Q)$

$\quad c \leftarrow parent(c')$ $\qquad\qquad$ // *parent in* Γ

$\quad$ // *make cluster vertices consecutive*

$\quad T(R^i) \leftarrow$ REDUCE$(T(R^i), children\_leaves[c'])$

$\quad$ **if** $T(R^i) = \emptyset$ **then**

$\quad\quad |$ **return** $T(R^i)' \leftarrow \emptyset$

$\quad$ **end**

$\quad$ // *expand children*

$\quad$ **foreach** $Y \in children\_leaves[c']$ **do**

$\quad\quad |$ replace Y by $subtrees[Y]$

$\quad$ **end**

$\quad$ // *contract pertinent subtree(s)*

$\quad X_{c'} \leftarrow$ new PQ-leaf with label c'

$\quad$ **if** *pert-root has only pertinent children* **then**

$\quad\quad |$ $subtrees[X_{c'}] \leftarrow \{pert\text{-}root\}$

$\quad$ **else**

$\quad\quad |$ $subtrees[X_{c'}] \leftarrow$ pertinent children of *pert-root*

$\quad$ **end**

$\quad$ REPLACE_PERT$(T(R^i), X_{c'})$

$\quad insert(children\_leaves[c], X_{c'})$

$\quad$ // *ensure correct processing order*

$\quad$ **if** $|children\_leaves[c]| = child\_count(c, i+1)$ **then**

$\quad\quad |$ $insert(Q, c)$

$\quad$ **end**

end

return $T(R^i)' \leftarrow T(R^i)$

---

children of c on level i. Since our algorithm explicitly calls REDUCE for every cluster on every level it is clear that R1 is satisfied. R2 is trivially satisfied for level connected graphs, because crossing clusters would imply crossing edges which are prohibited by the level planarity test. See Fig. 3(a). The same is true for R3. The graph is proper and thus the crossing edge connects two adjacent levels. Between these two levels there is an edge in the cluster because of the level connectivity of the graph. Any intersection between these two edges is prohibited by level planarity. See Fig. 3(b).

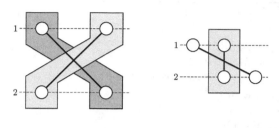

(a) Violation of R2 is   (b) Violation of R3 is
not possible   not possible

Fig. 3. Correctness of the algorithm

"$\Leftarrow$": Given a cl-planar graph we have to show that our algorithm returns true. Suppose the algorithm returns false. This means that a call of REDUCE failed, either in the level planarity test part or in REDUCE-CLUSTERS. In the former case the graph is not level planar. In the latter case there is no level planar permutation respecting R1. In any case this contradicts the assumption. □

3.4 Complexity

The complexity of Algorithm 3 depends also on the complexity of the *child_count* operation returning the number of cluster children on a given level. We assume that the used data structure for clustered level graphs provides $\mathcal{O}(1)$ time access to this information. If this is not true, an additional $\mathcal{O}(k|V|)$ size data structure can be pre-computed in $\mathcal{O}(k|V|)$ time. We use a two dimensional matrix $M_{ci} = child\_count(c, i)$ with $c \in C \cup V$ and $i \in \{1, \ldots, k\}$ as indices. M_{ci} is filled as shown in Algorithm 4 which traverses the cluster tree Γ in a similar way as Algorithm 3. Having this efficient *child_count* operation, the complexity of REDUCE-CLUSTERS derives as follows:

Lemma 2. *The time complexity of REDUCE-CLUSTERS described in Algorithm 3 is $\mathcal{O}(|V|)$.*

Proof. In REDUCE-CLUSTERS every cluster is considered exactly once. Since Γ is of linear size this can be done in $\mathcal{O}(|V|)$ time. Additionally every node of the PQ-tree is considered only once such that the time complexity of the REDUCE operations sum up to $\mathcal{O}(|V|)$. □

Theorem 2. *There is an $\mathcal{O}(k|V|)$ time algorithm for testing cl-planarity of a level connected and proper hierarchy.*

Algorithm 4: CHILD-COUNT

> **Input:** $G = (V, E, \Gamma, \phi)$
> **Output:** M_{ci}
>
> Initialise M_{ci} with zeros
> **foreach** $v \in V$ **do** $M_{v,\phi(v)} \leftarrow 1$
> **foreach** $c \in C$ **do** $processed\_children[c] \leftarrow 0$
>
> Initialise Queue Q with V
> **while** Q *not empty* **do**
> > $c' \leftarrow delete\_first(Q)$
> > $c \leftarrow parent(c')$ // *parent in Γ*
> >
> > **for** $i \leftarrow 1$ **to** k **do**
> > > **if** $M_{c'i} > 0$ **then** $M_{ci} \leftarrow M_{ci} + 1$
> >
> > **end**
> >
> > $processed\_children[c] \leftarrow processed\_children[c] + 1$
> > **if** $processed\_children[c] = |children(c)|$ **then**
> > > $insert(Q, c)$
> >
> > **end**
>
> **end**
> **foreach** $v \in V$ **do** $M_{v,\phi(v)} \leftarrow 0$
>
> **return** M_{ci}

4   Discussion

The given algorithm solves the cl-planarity problem only for a subclass of cl-graphs. It is desirable to extend it to general cl-graphs, but a straightforward extension is difficult.

Level planarity testing has been extended to non-hierarchical graphs in [16], [15], [13], [14], [11], [12]. This is realised by the utilisation of multiple PQ-trees, one for each connected component of G^i. If a vertex is common to more than one PQ-tree, these are merged into one. In a straightforward extension of our algorithm clusters can span multiple PQ-trees. This means that REDUCE-CLUSTERS cannot be applied directly. A possible solution would be to additionally merge the PQ-trees according to the contained clusters. It is not clear, however, how this could be done because in contrast to vertex merges there is no distinct position in the higher PQ-tree where the smaller one is to be inserted.

An application of our algorithm to non-proper graphs leads to problems as well. A priori it is not clear whether long span edges entering or leaving a cluster have to be routed within or outside of the cluster. In Fig. 4 is not clear whether the reduction of the cluster nodes on level 2 has to include the dotted edge. When processing level 3 it becomes clear that this edge has to be routed within the cluster, but this is too late. On level 2 both routing alternatives would have to be stored in the PQ-tree. This is not possible, however, without major extensions of the data structure.

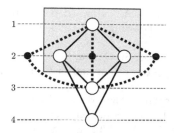

Fig. 4. Problems with long span edges

The third remaining restriction of our algorithm is the needed level connectivity. A straightforward idea to extend it to cl-graphs that are not level connected would be to insert level connecting dummy edges for each cluster. It is difficult, however, to find the correct places for insertion without violating cl-planarity. The same problem occurs with c-planarity. There are some advances like in [9] but the general problem is unsolved. Apparently the connectivity of the graph plays a major role for the detection of c-planarity and cl-planarity.

5   Conclusion

We have presented an algorithm for detecting clustered k-level planarity of a level connected proper hierarchy in $\mathcal{O}(k|V|)$ time. For this we have enhanced the linear time algorithm for level planarity detection of [6], [11], [12], [13], [15], [14], [16].

The presented extension to level planarity testing can also be used to extend the level planar embedding algorithm of Sect. 2 to calculate a cl-planar embedding without any major modifications. Such an embedding can be used as a basis for generating a drawing using for example the algorithm of Sander [18], [17], [19]. This algorithm draws the clusters as nested rectangles, i.e., as convex regions.

It is open, whether our algorithm can be improved to linear time. This would probably be the case if the nesting relations Γ_i of each level i can be computed in linear time, such that each Γ_i only contains the vertices of level i and clusters with at least two children in Γ_i. Further investigations are desired for level graphs which are not necessarily proper and level connected hierarchies. It is not clear if this problems can be solved in polynomial time.

References

1. Booth, K.S., Lueker, G.S.: Testing for the Consecutive Ones Property, Interval Graphs, and Graph Planarity Using PQ-Tree Algorithms. Journal of Computer and System Sciences **13** (1976) 335–379
2. Brockenauer, R., Cornelsen, S.: Drawing Clusters and Hierarchies. In: Kaufmann, M., Wagner, D. (eds): Drawing Graphs. LNCS, Vol. 2025, chapter 8. Springer (2001) 193–227

3. Chandramouli, M., Diwan, A.A.: Upward Numbering Testing for Triconnected Graphs. In: Proc. Graph Drawing, GD 1995, LNCS, Vol. 1027. Springer (1996) 140–151

4. Chiba, N., Nishizeki, T., Abe, S., Ozawa, T.: A Linear Algorithm for Embedding Planar Graphs Using PQ-Trees. Journal of Computer and System Sciences, **30** (1985) 54–76

5. Dahlhaus, E.: A Linear Time Algorithm to Recognize Clustered Planar Graphs and Its Parallelization. In: Lucchesi, C.,L. (ed.): 3rd Latin American Symposium on Theoretical Informatics, LATIN '98. LNCS, Vol. 1380. Springer (1998) 239–248

6. Di Battista, G., Nardelli, E.: Hierarchies and Planarity Theory. IEEE Transactions on Systems, Man, and Cybernetics, **18** 6 (1988) 1035–1046

7. Feng, Q.-W., Cohen, R.F., Eades, P.: Planarity for Clustered Graphs (Extended abstract). In: European Symposium on Algorithms, ESA '95. LNCS, Vol. 979. Springer (1995) 213–226

8. Forster, M.: Applying Crossing Reduction Strategies to Layered Compound Graphs. In: Proc. Graph Drawing, GD 2002. LNCS, Vol. 2528. Springer (2002) 276–284

9. Gutwenger, C., Jünger, M., Leipert, S., Mutzel, P., Percan, M., Weiskircher, R.: Advances in c-Planarity Testing of Clustered Graphs. In: Goodrich, M., Kobourov, S. (eds): Proc. Graph Drawing, GD 2002. LNCS, Vol. 2528. Springer (2002) 220–235

10. Healy, P., Kuusik, A.: The Vertex-Exchange Graph: A New Concept for Multi-Level Crossing Minimisation. In: Proc. Graph Drawing, GD 1999. LNCS, Vol. 1731. Springer (1999) 205-216

11. Heath, L.S., Pemmaraju, S.V.: Recognizing Leveled-Planar Dags in Linear Time. In: Proc. Graph Drawing, GD 1995. LNCS, Vol. 1027. Springer (1996) 300-311

12. Heath, L.S., Pemmaraju, S.V.: Stack and Queue Layouts of Directed Acyclic Graphs: Part II. SIAM Journal on Computing **28** 5 (1999) 1588–1626

13. Jünger, M., Leipert, S.: Level Planar Embedding in Linear Time. In: Proc. Graph Drawing, GD 1999. LNCS, Vol. 1731. Springer (1999) 72–81

14. Jünger, M., Leipert, S.: Level Planar Embedding in Linear Time. Journal of Graph Algorithms and Applications **6** 1 (2002) 67–113

15. Jünger, M., Leipert, S., Mutzel, P.: Level Planarity Testing in Linear Time. In: Proc. Graph Drawing, GD 1998. LNCS, Vol. 1547. Springer (1998) 224–237

16. Leipert, S.: Level Planarity Testing and Embedding in Linear Time. Dissertation, Mathematisch-Naturwissenschaftliche Fakultät der Universität zu Köln (1998)

17. Sander, G.: Layout of Compound Directed Graphs. Technical Report A/03/96, Universität Saarbrücken (1996)

18. Sander, G.: Visualisierungstechniken für den Compilerbau. PhD thesis, Universität Saarbrücken (1996)

19. Sander, G.: Graph Layout for Applications in Compiler Construction. Theoretical Computer Science **217** (1999) 175–214

Artificial Perception: Auditory Decomposition of Mixtures of Environmental Sounds – Combining Information Theoretical and Supervised Pattern Recognition Approaches

Ladislava Janku

Department of Cybernetics, Faculty of Electrical Engineering
Czech Technical University in Prague, Czech Republic
janku@ieee.org

Abstract. This paper deals with the new algorithm for the general audio classification which explores auditory scene analysis approach and has been inspired by the recent results in cognitive psychology and audition. This algorithm combines an information theoretical approach with the supervised pattern recognition models of environmental sounds, namely Hidden Markov Models; and with modern missing feature techniques. The investigated algorithm has been tested on the set of environmental sounds; increase in the classification accuracy of the selected environmental sound source in the mixtures of sounds corrupted by noise or by mixing process has been shown.

1 Introduction

A fundamental characteristics of human hearing is the ability of the selective listening. Listening to the composite signal originating from the different sound sources, humans are able to separate and identify different sound sources without apparent effort. First who described this problem was Cherry [1]; he used a term of a "cocktail party problem" to denote this human auditory system capability. Humans are able to separate sound sources - as Mellinger [2] states, "...despite the fact that many different processes interact to produce the sound signal reaching the ears and that the acoustic events produced by different sources may overlap in time, in frequency or in other characteristics." Till now, this process of auditory system has not been fully discovered, although many attempts have been done. An overview of experimental evidence on the heuristics principles used by the brain to organize auditory input was in comprehensive and exhaustive form given by Bregman [3], who investigated that our auditory system solves the problem in two ways by the use of primitive processes of auditory grouping and by governing the listening process by schemas that incorporate our knowledge of familiar sounds. In this context, cognitive psychologists [4] speak about top-down and bottom-top approaches to the scene analysis problem. Bregman's research is related mostly to the primitive processes of scene analysis; the higher processes are unfortunately very poorly understood.

P. Van Emde Boas et al. (Eds.): SOFSEM 2004, LNCS 2932, pp. 229–240, 2004.
© Springer-Verlag Berlin Heidelberg 2004

Computational systems inspired by the human auditory system capability of scene analysis can be divided into three main groups: computational auditory scene analysis (CASA) approaches, blind signal separation (BSS) or extraction (BSE) approaches, sometimes called also multi-channel methods, and neural models of known parts of auditory pathways and central auditory system. Notice, that this classification is only vague and that the groups can overlap. CASA approaches usually combine modelling of stages of auditory signal processing with some artificial intelligence oriented approaches, as knowledge-based systems or multi-agent solutions [5], [6], [7], [8], [9]. Some of them attempt to include also prediction [10], [11], but in fact these systems don't rich high accuracy or efficiency, particularly in comparison to their complexity. Also attempts to apply Mixtures of HMM have been done [12]. Modern techniques, known as blind signal processing (or blind signal separation) techniques [13], have no knowledge of the environment (hence the term blind), and only use the statistics of the recordings to make their estimation. The only assumptions made are that different sources are not dependent to each other; by trying to construct an unmixing matrix that produces maximally independent outputs it is possible to obtain the original sources. Although there are many ways to attack this problem when armed with this assumption, the most relevant to our work is the application of Independent Component Analysis (ICA) methods [14], [15], [16].

Empirical results in cognitive psychology proved existence of both the bottom-up and top-down mechanisms of perception [17]. Although many researchers still support only one of these theories (bottom-up or top-down theory), it is much more than probable that perceptual system uses both ways of percept processing. These two ways have to be viewed as complementary, instead of exclusive [4]. This leads back to the problem of application of the ICA techniques in auditory scene analysis - it results in systems processing information only in one way.

In this paper, we investigated a new algorithm, which combines both the principles of primitive grouping processes performing redundancy reduction and knowledge- and attention-driven perceptual mechanisms.

2 Problem Formulation

This paper is addressed to the problem of sound source identification in a complex, composite signal that reaches one microphone. We also focus mostly on the environmental sounds (natural sounds produced by environmental sound sources).

First, we meet the problem of sound source definition. In hearing literature, there is a lack of precious, accurate definition of sound source; understanding of this term is more intuitive than rigorously defined. Most definitions of sound source are related to perception - sound source is defined as a perceptual whole recognized by human listeners as one sound stream. The problem consists in a fact, that this process is not unique and differ for the listeners in accordance to their previous knowledge and sound scene analysis mechanisms development [3], [18]. It makes this definition in its general form unusable for most rigorous computational systems. Despite of this fact, till now implemented CASA methods have usually followed this intuitive definition, which - together with the requirement be general as much as possible - seems to be the reason for low efficiency and success rate of these systems. In opposite to CASA, blind signal separation techniques use the formal apparatus of the theory of signal processing and define sound source in a mixture of sounds as a signal, which is statistically independent on the other sound sources - signals - forming the scene.

In our work, we address this problem by using terms of *sound source* and *independent component*. Sound source $s(t)$ is a signal $s(t)$, which is recognized by a control group of human listeners as a separable sound source at some level of resolution. Each sound source may consists of one or more statistically independent components (in other words be a mixture of statistically independent components). Notice, that grouping independent components in sound sources needs previous knowledge about sound source structure.

Let have a sound scene

$$S = s(t) = \{(s_1(t), ...s_M(t))^T; t = (0..k)\} , \tag{1}$$

where $s_i(t)$ represents an i-th sound source and M denotes number of sound sources forming the scene S. Each sound source $s_i(t)$ can be a linear mixture of independent components $r(t)$. Using a mixing matrix B_i, we can write:

$$s_i(t) = B_i r(t) . \tag{2}$$

We cannot observe directly the sound sources $s_i(t)$ forming the scene; instead of that, we can observe only a mixture

$$x(t) = As(t) \tag{3}$$

of the sound sources acquired by one microphone. This equation describes instantaneous linear mixing of sound sources $s(t)$, where A denotes the mixing matrix. We assume linear mixing process, so this equation can be rewritten in the following way

$$x(t) = Cr(t) , \tag{4}$$

where C represents a mixing matrix depending on matrices B and A.

The aim of our work is extraction, reconstruction and classification of particular sound sources on assumption, that these sound sources are statistically independent. We also assume that the scene is formed only from environmental sounds and eventually noise. Next, we assume that the number of classes C of environmental sounds is a finite number N_C. Mathematically, we want to find the sources $(s_1'(t), ...s_M'(t))$

$$S' = \{(s_1'(t), ...s_M'(t))^T; t = (0..k)\} , \tag{5}$$

which are the best estimation of the sources forming the analyzed scene

$$S = \{(s_1(t), ...s_M(t))^T; t = (0..k)\} , \tag{6}$$

represented by the observed mixture $x(t)$ of the sound sources; a mixture acquired by one microphone.

3   Method Description

Our approach is based on the following assumptions:

- *Perceptual processes* can be viewed as *processes exploiting redundancy*, at least at the lower level; and they can be modelled by *application of information theory*. This assumption arises from work of Attneave [19] and more recently Attick [20], who have used information theory for description of perceptual processes . Recent results came from Olshausen and Field [21], Bell and Sejnowski [22], [23], and Hyvorinen and Hoyer [16], who have used modern information theory optimization algorithms to analyze natural images. They obtained decompositions which were very similar to the reception fields, which human visual system uses.
- Although the *Independent Component Analysis (ICA)* has been developed to analyze mixtures of signals acquired from the different sensors, it *can be applied to any multi-channel representation*, if we assume that these channels contain signals, which have been derived from the mixture of statistically independent sources. So, ICA algorithm can be applied to analyze time-frequency signal representations, e.g. time frequency representation acquired by application of FFT or cochleogram.
- *All primitive auditory grouping rules explored by Bregman [3] can be expressed in terms of information theory by the mutual information maximization*. Consequently, ICA algorithm, which uses mutual information minimization approach, can be applied to find mixture decomposition; similarly to the direct application of grouping rules. Recently, Smaragdis [24] investigated information theoretical interpretation of the primitive auditory grouping rules and explored application of ICA algorithm to sound scene decomposition.
- *There are two mechanisms, which influence auditory grouping*: primitive auditory grouping processes at lower level and higher grouping mechanisms as attention or previous knowledge exploration at higher level. Both mechanisms work complementary. In our work, ICA represents primitive, low-level grouping principles, which uses only environmental information to perform grouping. Attenion-driven grouping and source restoration are based on previous knowledge; they represents high-level grouping principles. Notice, that notations "low-level grouping" or "high-level grouping" are not accurate, because they implicitly suggest existence of hierarchical structure with one-way information flow (bottom-up approach);instead of that, the grouping mechanisms are complementary and information flows in both ways. More accurate expressions can be "primitive grouping" and "attention&knowledge-driven grouping".
- *Higher grouping principles*, as attention or previous knowledge exploration operates at higher level; they *can influence primitive grouping processes only in indirect way*; they are not used directly to perform grouping at lower level. Generally, attention or knowledge exploration can influence grouping in many ways; in this work, we assume only focusing on the particular sound source and attention-driven missing feature reconstruction

– Similarly to speech, *environmental sounds can be modelled using Hidden Markov Models*. Recent work on the neurocognitive processing of environmental sound [25], [26], [27], [28] have provided new insights about the cognitive processing of environmental sounds especially when a sound is very identifiable. The general finding of these studies is that meaningful sounds are processed in the brain like meaningful words. That is, the brain areas activated and the time course of this activation are very similar for meaningful sounds and words.

Our approach tries to combine bottom-up and top-down approach to sound scene analysis. The algorithm works as follows:

1. We compute the time-frequency representation F of the frame of the input signal $x(t)$ of length of U seconds by the application of some short-time transform. U can be from the interval of (0.5 to 5 s).
2. We apply the Principal Component Analysis (PCA) decomposition to suppress correlation among the frequency channels. Then, we apply Independent Component Analysis (ICA) to the uncorrelated frequency channels; we compute independent components forming the sound scene.
3. We reconstruct the time-frequency representation of the selected independent component or components.
4. Coefficients of the reconstructed time-frequency representation are used as input features for classifier based on the HMM models of environmental sounds. Before classification, we search for the starting and ending points of the particular sound; only the time-frequency representation between these two points is used as a ground for feature vectors derivation.
5. HMM model representing class, in which the sound source has been classified, is used for the missing features reconstruction. This missing feature reconstruction process is applied to the time-frequency representation of the signal $x(t)$. Similarly to human perceptual processes based on attention, we can focus only on one sound source and reconstruct unreliable features in the input time-frequency representation (only features related to this sound source). We call this method attention-driven missing feature reconstruction, because it is driven by focalization to one sound source and explores preliminary knowledge accumulated in the model of this sound source.

The training phase consists in computation of independent components and reconstructed spectra for the particular environmental sound sources, feature vector computation and training HMM models on them.

4 Method Exploration

4.1 Time-Frequency Representation Computation: Gamma-Tone Filter Bank

In our work, we computed time-frequency representation using a filter bank of narrow-band gamma-tone filters; and not the Short-Time Fourier Transform

(STFT), although in the absence of extensive and reliable biological data, the STFT has been viewed as valuable model of the early stage of the hearing process, for a long time. The analysis filters in the cochlea of the ear are not uniformly spaced, by rather logaritmically; and they are also not of equal bandwidth; instead, they have approximately constant tuning factor [18], [29]. The set of cochlear filters have been described by Patterson [30], who derived their shapes. Cochlear filter bank can be modelled as a bank of narrow-band bandpass gamma-tone filters [29], [30], where the impulse response of one gamma-tone filter is described by:

$$g(t) = t^{N-1}exp(-bt)cos(\omega.t + \phi) , \qquad (7)$$

where parameters b and ω define filter center frequency and bandwidth.

The discrete representation of this continuous gamma-tone filter can be derived in many ways; usually we select such a transformation, which assures the best approximation of some selected continuous filter characteristic, e.g. amplitude or frequency response. In our work we used an effective computational algorithm derived by Slaney [31]. Recent speech processing systems used more physiologically plausible input transformations as Wavelet Transform , Perceptual Linear Prediction (PLP) or Mel-Frequency Cepstral Coefficients (MFCC) [32].

Last step describes time-frequency representation of the observed mixture $x(t)$. We assume that this signal has been windowed by the overlapping windows of length of 30 ms each 10 ms and time-frequency representation has been computed for each windowed segment of the input signal. After application of the selected time-frequency transform, we obtain a set of vectors $f(i)$, $i = 1..n$, representing time-frequency spectrum at the time point i. We can construct a matrix F, which describes evolving of the time-frequency representation components through time.

4.2   Finding Independent Components and Forming Auditory Objects

We apply PCA to the matrix F representing time-frequency representation of sound scene S.

$$Y_{PCA} = T_{PCA}F , \qquad (8)$$

where Y_{PCA} denotes a matrix derived from F, which has uncorrelated rows and T_{PCA} denotes a transformation matrix of the PCA transform. F can be computed using matrix T_{PCA}^{-1}. To reduce dimension, we use only several first rows of matrix T_{PCA} , we obtain a submatrix T_{PCA}^*, because we don't need an accurate reconstruction. Then, we apply ICA transform to the matrix Y_{PCA} computed by application of PCA transform to F. We receive equation

$$Y_{ICA} = T_{ICA}Y_{PCA} = T_{ICA}T_{PCA}^{(*)}F = TF , \qquad (9)$$

where Y_{ICA} denotes a matrix derived by application of ICA and T_{ICA} represents a transformation matrix of ICA transform. The matrix F' a reconstructed matrix F can be

$$F' = T^{-1}Y_{ICA} \; . \tag{10}$$

If we wanted to obtain a time-frequency representation reconstruction using only one component, we could write:

$$G_{(i)} = T_{(i)}^{-1}Y_{ICA,(i)} \; , \tag{11}$$

where the subscript on the right hand matrices selects the i-th column of T and i-th row of Y_{ICA}, e.g. other matrix elements are equal to zero. In other words, we are able to reconstruct time-frequency representation of each independent component. If we used reduced transformation matrix to compute Y_{PCA}, the reconstruction is limited in its accuracy.

Auditory object can be formed from more than one independent components. If we are able to recognize all these components, we can reconstruct time-frequency representation of the auditory object using particular columns and rows of matrices T and Y_{ICA}. We denote it $G_{(s)}$:

$$G_{(s)} = T_{(s)}^{-1}Y_{ICA,(s)} \; . \tag{12}$$

Notice, that the decision which independent components belong to one sound source cannot be done without any previous knowledge about the sound source, e.g. a model of sound source must be available.

4.3   Modelling Environmental Sounds: Hidden Markov Models

Hidden Markov Models (HMM) form a large class of stochastic processes important in wide range of areas, foremost in speech recognition [32], [33], molecular biology and biomedicine, econometrics and many others. First experiments on application of HMM to modelling environmental sounds can be found in [34].

Let X_n, n is a natural number, be a homogenous discrete Markov chain on a finite state space Q, which is not observable, and let $\{Y_n\}$ be a probabilistic function of $\{X_n\}$. The pair of processes $\{X_n\}$ and $\{Y_n\}$ form the HMM model. For detailed definition, see [12], [32]. HMM models are characterized by three parameters: number of hidden states, transition matrix and state likelihood representation. In recent years, many methods have been developed to estimate these parameters [32], [35]. Reyens-Gomez and Ellis [36] compared clustering & Expectation Maximization (EM) algorithm [3] approach to GMM-EM algorithm with different optimization criteria - Low Entropy Criterion, Low State Occupancy Criterion and Bayesian Information Criterion for general audio.

The feature vectors are formed through the columns of the matrix of reconstructed time-frequency representation, e.g F' during the training phase and $G_{(i)}$ or $G_{(s)}$ during the testing phase. When we use $G_{(i)}$ or $G_{(s)}$, we speak about attention-driven recognition, because we work with one sound source/ independent component and model the mechanism of selective perception known from the cognitive psychology [4]. However, we can simultaneously analyze and classify all the independent components.

In our research, we combined clustering, namely K-variable K-means algorithm, and well-known EM algorithm to find different clusters with similar acoustic properties between the files on the same class, and to compute state likelihoods and transition probabilities. Each cluster corresponds to one state, but we have not any prior knowledge on the number of clusters in each class. To assure clustering algorithm convergence, we used a minimization of the criterion of within cluster variance.

Table 1. The number of mixture components

Feature vectors per cluster	Number of components
0-40	1
41-80	2
81-120	3
121-160	4
161 and more	5

To model state likelihoods, we used triangular mixtures. The number of triangular mixture components depends on the number of feature vectors in each cluster in accordance to the Table 1. The parameters of the mixtures have been computed by the EM algorithm. The transition probabilities have been computed in accordance to the following equation:

$$P(i,j) = k_{i,j}/k_i \, , \tag{13}$$

where $k_{i,j}$ denotes a number of transitions from the state i to the state j and k_i denotes a number of transitions from state i to all other states.

Notice again, that the model have operated on the feature vectors acquired from the reconstructed time-frequency representation of independent components or sound sources.

4.4   Modelling Attention: Reconstruction and Attention-Driven Missing Feature Approach

First step in modelling attention is the sound source selection and classification among other sound sources forming the audio scene. But this principle of selective perception can be explored for the reconstruction of the missing data for the particular sound source.

Classical missing feature approaches comprise one family of noise compensation algorithms that have shown an ability to provide highly robust recognition in the presence of high level of noise. In these methods, noise-corrupted regions of a spectrographic representation of the speech signal are identified and treated like unreliable. Recognition is performed with remaining reliable regions. The unreliable features can be replaced by the estimated components. In literature, two main groups of missing feature approaches have been described feature-compensation methods and classifier-compensation methods. All these methods estimate the reliability of the signal from the context or use statistical properties of speech, but they don't operate with preliminary knowledge.

In our work, we used attention- and knowledge-driven missing feature approach: by application of the HMM model of the selected sound source, next frame of the time-frequency representation of input signal F has been transformed to F_{REC}, which is further processed by the PCA and ICA and mehod described above. The selection of sound source (attention focusing) has been done manually. These technique results in source classification improvement, if the input signal is damaged by noise or some information is missing because of mixing process.

5   Experimental Results

The model described above has been used for content-based audio classification for mixtures of sounds. The the database of environmental sounds have been divided into two sets. Notice, that environmental sounds formed by one independent component have been used in experiments. The training set was used to estimate the class models. The testing set was used for classification; audio scenes - mixtures of sounds - used for testing have been created in different ways. The first group of mixtures included linear mixtures of two or more (maximally five) sounds both from the training and testing set. The second group included mixtures of sounds from the testing set. The third group included linear mixtures of sounds from the testing set and unknown sounds or noise. Table 2 defines classes for the environmental sounds database. All sounds have been sampled with the sample frequency of 22 kHz. The last group of experiments have been focused on sound scenes damaged by noise.

Table 2. Environmental sounds database and number of states of HMM for each class

Class	A Number of Sound Samples in Class	Number of the States
Bells	7	4
Ocean	6	10
Rain	6	8
Photocopier	7	7
Jet Engines	22	8
Automotive Machines	20	8
Insect	14	6
Wind	14	10
Doggies	8	7
Percussion	22	24

First, we evaluated the classification accuracy in classification of single sound sources, which depends highly on quality of HMM. Each example has been classify according to the model using Viterbi algorithm. In the next step, we evaluated classification accuracy of the sound source in a mixture of sounds. Mixtures were constructed from the sounds of similar intensities.

Table 3. Classification Accuracy Overview: Test 1: Single sound source classification, Test 2: Sound source in mixture classification (mixtures created from sounds from both the training and the testing set, Test 3: Sound source in mixture classification (mixtures created from sounds from the testing set, Test 4: Sound source in mixture classification (mixtures created from sounds from the testing set and unknown sounds, Test 5: Sound source in corrupted mixture classification (without attention-driven missing feature reconstruction), Test 6: Sound source in corrupted mixture classification (with attention-driven missing feature reconstruction)

Test	Classification accuracy	Notice
Test 1	89%	
Test 2	82%	
Test 3	80%	
Test 4	80%	Classification was evaluated only for the known sounds
Test 5	62%	
Test 6	82%	

6   Conclusion and Future Work

A new algorithm combining information theoretical approach to perception with HMM models has been presented. In comparison to current blind signal techniques, which require sensor arrays (more sensors than independent sources), we elaborated ICA technique on the time-frequency signal representation. We also elaborated incorporation of previous knowledge into model using HMM models. Our approach to auditory scene analysis can be viewed as an attempt to combine redundancy reduction at lower level and higher grouping mechanisms as attention or previous knowledge exploration at higher level. Both mechanisms work complementary. In our work, ICA represents primitive, low-level grouping principles, which uses only environmental information to perform grouping. Attention-driven grouping and source restoration are based on previous knowledge; they represent high-level grouping principles. Described experimental results are for environmental sounds formed by one independent component.

References

1. Cherry, E.C.: Some Experiments on the Recognition of Speech, with One and Two Ears. J. Acoustic Soc. Am. **25** (1953) 975–979
2. Mellinger, D.K., Mont-Reynaud, B.R.: Scene Analysis. In: Hawkins et al.(eds): Auditory Computation, Springer-Verlag (1995)
3. Bregman, A.S.: Auditory Scene Analysis: the Perceptual Organization of Sound. MIT Press, Cambridge, Massachusetts (1990)
4. Sternberg, R.J.: Cognitive Psychology. Harcourt Inc. (1996)
5. Kashino, K., Murase, H.: Sound Source Identification for Ensemble Music Based on the Music Stream Extraction. In: Proc. IJCAI'97, Workshop on Computational Auditory Scene Analysis (1997)

6. Cooke, M.P.: Modelling Auditory Processing and Organization: Distinguished Dissertations in Computer Science Series. Cambridge University Press, Cambridge (1993)

7. Nakatani, O., Kawabata, Okuno, H.G.: A Computational Model of Sound Stream Segregation. Proc. ICASSP'95 (1995)

8. Nakatani, O. Kawabata, T., Okuno, H.G.: Residue-driven Architecture for Computational Auditory Scene Analysis. Proc. IJCAI'95 (1995)

9. Nawab, S.H., Espy-Wilson, C.Y., Mani, R., Bitar, N.N.: Knowledge-based Analysis of Speech Mixed with Sporadic Environmental Sounds. In: Rosenthal, D.F., Okuno, E.G. (eds.): Readings in Computational Auditory Scene Analysis. Mahweh NJ: Lawrence Erlbaum (1998)

10. Ellis, D.P.W.: Prediction-Driven Computational Auditory Scene Analysis. Ph.D. Thesis, MIT Dept. of Electrical Engineering and Computer Science, Cambridge, Massachusetts (1996)

11. Ellis, D.P.W., Rosenthal, D.F.: Mid-level Representations for Computational Auditory Scene Analysis: The Weft Element. In: Rosenthal, D.F., Okuno, E.G. (eds.): Readings in Computational Auditory Scene Analysis. Mahweh NJ: Lawrence Erlbaum (1998)

12. Couvreur, C.: Hidden Markov Models and their Mixtures. Habilitation Thesis, Catholic University of Louvan (1996)

13. Cichocki, A., Amari, S.: Adaptive Blind Signal and Image Processing. John Willey & Sons, New York (2002)

14. Common, P.: Independent Component Analysis – a New Concept? Signal Processing **36** (1997) 287-314

15. Herault, J., Jutten, C.: Blind Separation of Sources – Part I: An Adaptive Algorithm Based on Neuromimetic Architecture. Signal Processing **24** (1991)

16. Hyvorinen, A.: Fast and Robust Fixed-Point Algorithms for Independent Component Analysis, IEEE Trans. Neural Networks **10** 3 (1999)

17. Palmer, S.E.: Modern Theories of Gestalt Perception. In: Understanding Vision: An Interdisciplinary Perspective: Readings in Mind and Language, Oxford, England, Blaskwell (1992)

18. Moore, B.C.J.: Hearing. Handbook of Perception and Cognition Series, Academic Press (1995)

19. Attneave, F.: Informational Aspects of Visual Perception. Psychological Review **61** (1954) 183-193

20. Atick, J.J., Redlich, A.N.: Towards a Theory of Early Visual Processing. In: Neural Computation 2, MIT Press, Cambridge, Massachusetts (1990)

21. Olshausen, B.A., Field, D.J.: Emergence of Simple-Cell Receptive Field Properties by Learning a Sparse Code for Natural Images. Nature **381** (1996) 607–609

22. Bell A.J., Sejnowski, T.J.: Learning the Higher-order Structure of a Natural Sound. Network. Computation in Neural Systems **7** (1996)

23. Bell, A.J, Sejnowski, T.J.: The 'Independent Components' of Natural Scenes are Edge Filters. Vision Research, **37** 23 (1997) 3327–3338

24. Smaragdis, P.: Redundancy Reduction for Computational Audition – an Unifying Approach. Ph.D. Thesis, MIT, Massachusetts (2001)

25. Marcell, M.E., Borella, D., Greene, M.: Confrontation Naming of Environmental Sounds. Journal of Clinical and Experimental neurophysiology **22** (6) (2000) 830-864

26. Mecklinger, A., Opitz, B., Friederici, A.D.: Semantic Aspects of Novelty Detection in Humans. Neuroscience Letters **235** (1-2) (1997) 65-68

27. Lebrun, N., et al.: An ERD Mapping Study of the Neurocognitive Processes Involved in the Perceptual and Semantic Analysis of Environmental Sounds and Words. Cognitive Brain Research **11** 2 (2001) 235–248
28. Cycowicz, Y.M., Friedman, D.: Effect of Sound Familiarity on the Event-related Potentials Elicited by Novel Environmental Sounds. Journal of the Brain and Cognition **36** 1 (1998) 30–51
29. Gold, B., Morgan, N.: Speech and Audio Signal Processing. John Willey & Sons (2000)
30. Patterson, R.D., Moore, B.C.J.: Auditory Filters and Excitation Patterns as Representation of Frequency Resolution. In: Moore, B.C.J. (ed.): Hearing, Academic Press, London (1996)
31. Slaney, M.: Auditory Toolbox. Apple Computer, Inc., Technical Report #45, Cupertino, California (1994)
32. Huang X., Acero, A., Hisao-Wuen, H.: Spoken Language Processing. Prentice Hall (2001)
33. Rabiner, L.R.: A Tutorial on Hidden Markov Models and Selected Applications in Speech Recognition. Proc. IEEE **77** (1989)
34. Gaunard, P.: Automatic Classification of Environmental Noise Events by Hidden Markov Models. Proc. ICASSP, Seattle (1998)
35. Mitchell, T.: Machine Learning. MIT Press, Cambridge, Massachusetts (1999)
36. Reyes-Gomez, M., Ellis, D.E.: Selection, Parameter Estimation, and Discriminative Training of Hidden Markov Models for General Audio Modelling. Proc. ICME (2003)

Features of Neighbors Spaces[*]

Marcel Jirina[1] and Marcel Jirina, Jr.[2]

[1] Institute of Computer Science, Academy of Sciences of the Czech Republic
Pod Vodárenskou věží 2, 182 07 Prague 8 - Libeň, Czech Republic
marcel@cs.cas.cz,
[2] Center of Applied Cybernetics, Faculty of Electrical Engineering,
Czech Technical University in Prague
Technická 2, 166 27 Prague 6 - Dejvice, Czech Republic
jirina@fel.cvut.cz

Abstract. Distances of the nearest neighbor or several nearest neighbors are essential in probability density estimate by the method of k nearest neighbors or in problems of searching in large databases. A typical task of the probability density estimate using several nearest neighbors is the Bayes's classifier. The task of searching in large databases is looking for other nearest neighbor queries. In this paper it is shown that for a uniform distribution of points in an n-dimensional Euclidean space the distribution of the distance of the i-th nearest neighbor to the n-power has Erlang distribution. The power approximation of the newly introduced probability distribution mapping function of distances of nearest neighbors in the form of suitable power of the distance is presented. A way to state distribution mapping exponent q for a probability density estimation including boundary effect in high dimensions is shown.

1   Introduction

In a probability density estimate by the method of k nearest neighbors [5], [7] or in problems of searching in large databases [1], [2], [3], distances of the nearest neighbor or several nearest neighbors are essential.

The rather strange behavior of the nearest neighbors in high dimensional spaces was accoutered. For the problem of searching the nearest neighbor in large databases the boundary phenomenon was studied in [1] using approximation by so called bucketing algorithm and l_{max} metrics. In [10] the problem of finding k nearest neighbors was studied in general metric spaces and in [11] the so-called concentration phenomenon was described. In [2] and in [11] it was found that as dimensionality increases, the distance to the nearest data point approaches the distance to the farthest data point of the learning set.

For probability density estimation by the k-nearest-neighbor method, the best value of k must be carefully tuned to find optimal results. Let there be

---

[*] This work was supported by the Ministry of Education of the Czech Republic under project No. LN00B096.

P. Van Emde Boas et al. (Eds.): SOFSEM 2004, LNCS 2932, pp. 241–248, 2004.

a ball with its center in x and containing k points. Let the volume of the ball be V_k and total number of points m_T. Then for the probability density estimate in point x (a query point [3]) it holds [5]

$$p_k(x) = \frac{k/m_T}{V_k}. \tag{1}$$

It will be shown that starting from some k the value of $p_k(x)$ is not constant for larger k, as it should be, but lessens. It is caused by the "boundary effect".

The goal of this study is to analyze the distances of the nearest neighbors from the query point x and the distances between two of these neighbors, the i-th and $(i-1)$-st in the space of randomly distributed points without and with boundary effect consideration. We introduce the probability distribution mapping function, and the distribution density mapping function which maps probability density distribution of points in E_n to a similar distribution in the space of distances, which is one-dimensional, i.e. E_1. The power approximation of the probability distribution mapping function in the form of $(\text{distance})^q$ is introduced and a way to choose distribution mapping exponent q for a probability density estimation including the boundary effect in high dimensions is shown.

2 Probability Density Estimate Based on Powers of Distances

The nearest-neighbor-based methods usually use (1) for a probability density estimate and are based on the distances of neighbors from a given (unknown) point, i.e. on a simple transformation $E_n \to E_1$.

The idea of most nearest-neighbors-based methods as well as kernel methods [7] does not reflect the boundary effects. That means that for any point x, the statistical distribution of the data points x_i surrounding it is supposed to be independent of the location of the neighbor points and their distances x_i from point x. This assumption is often not met, especially for small data sets and higher dimensions.

To illustrate this, let us consider points uniformly distributed in a cube and a ball inserted tightly into the cube. The higher space dimension the smaller amount of the cube is occupied by the ball. In other words, the majority of points lie outside the ball somewhere "in the corner" of the cube (the boundary effect [1]). It seems that in farther places from the origin, the space is less dense than near the origin.

Let us look at function $f(i) = r_i^n$, where r_i is the mean distance of the i-th neighbor from point x. The function should grow linearly with index i in the case of uniform distribution without the boundary effect mentioned. In the other case this function grows faster than linearly and therefore we suggest choosing function $f(i) = r_i^q$, where $q \leq n$ is a suitable power discussed later.

3   Uniform Distribution without Boundary Effects

Let us assume random and uniform distribution of points in some subspace S of E_n. Further suppose that point x is inside S in the following sense: For each neighbor y considered the ball with its center at x and radius equal to $\|x - y\|$ lies inside S. This is the case where the boundary effects do not take place.

In this Chapter one-dimensional case is studied, the multidimensional case is subject of the next Chapter.

Points spread on a line randomly and uniformly. In this case the distance Δ between two neighbor points is a random variable with exponential distribution function $P(\Delta) = 1 - e^{-\lambda\Delta}$ and probability density $p(\Delta) = e^{-\lambda\Delta}$ [4], [6]. For this distribution the mean is $E\{\Delta\} = 1/\lambda = d$ and it is the mean distance between two neighbor points.

Randomly chosen point on a line with randomly and uniformly spread points. It can be simply derived that the distance Δ between this point and the nearest of two its neighbor points is a random variable with exponential distribution function which differs from the previous case by $\lambda = 2/d$.

The second, third, etc. nearest neighbor. Let us sort consecutive nearest neighbors from point x in an ascending order. The mean distance between two successive points is $d/2$. It is the same situation as in the previous case. From it it follows that the distance between two successive points has the exponential distribution with $\lambda = 2/d$. $1/\lambda$ corresponds to one half of the mean distance of the neighbor points on the line.

Composed Distribution
Let the true distance of the i-th neighbor be denoted x_i. Let the difference in the distances of two successive neighbors, the $(k\text{-}1)$-st and the k-th be denoted $x_{k-1,k}$. Then it holds

$$x_i = x_1 + \sum_{k=2}^{i} x_{k-1,k}$$

because the distance is simply a sum of all successive differences and it is a sum of independent exponentially distributed random variables. The probability density of the sum of independent random variables is given by convolution of the probability densities of these variables. Assuming exponential distribution of individual random variables then the composed distribution has gamma or Erlang distribution $\mathrm{Erl}(i, \lambda)$.

For statistical distribution of distances of the first, the second, the third, ..., the i-th nearest point from point x with $\lambda = 2/d$ it holds $\mathrm{Erl}(1,\lambda) = \mathrm{Exp}(\lambda)$, $\mathrm{Erl}(2,\lambda) = \lambda^2 x e^{-\lambda x}$, etc.

4   Probability Distribution Mapping Function

To study a probability distribution of points in the neighborhood of a query point x let us construct individual balls around point x embedded one into another like peels of onion. Radii of individual balls can be expressed by formula $r_i = const.^n \sqrt{V_i}$. A mapping between the mean density in an i-th peel ρ_i and its radius r_i is $\rho_i = p(r_i).p(r_i)$ is the mean probability density in the i-th ball peel with radius r_i. The probability distribution of points in the neighborhood of a query point x is thus simplified to a function of a scalar variable. We call this function a probability distribution mapping function $D(x, r)$ and its partial derivation according to r the distribution density mapping function $d(x, r)$. Functions $D(x, r)$ and $d(x, r)$ for x fixed are one-dimensional analogs to the probability distribution function and the probability density, respectively.

4.1   Nearest Neighbors in E_n

A number of points in a ball neighborhood with a center in the query point x and the probability distribution mapping function $D(x, r)$ grow with the n-th power of distance from the query point. Let us denote this n-th power of distance from the query point $d_{(n)}$. Let a, b be distances of two points from a query point x in E_n. Then it holds $d_{(n)} = |a^n - b^n|$. Using $d_{(n)}$ instead of r, both the number of points and the $D(x, r)$ grow linearly with r^n. The distribution density mapping function $d(x, r^n)$ taken as $\frac{\partial}{\partial (r^n)} D(x, r^n)$ is constant.

It can be easily seen that $d_{(n)}$ of successive neighbors is a random variable with exponential distribution function. The $d_{(n)}$ of the i-th nearest neighbor from the query point is given by the sum of $d_{(n)}$ between the successive neighbors. Then, it is a random variable with Erlang distribution Erl(i,λ), $\lambda = 1/\bar{d}_{(n)}$, where $\bar{d}_{(n)}$ is mean $d_{(n)}$ between the successive neighbors. The only difference is that instead of distance r the n-th power of distance is used in an n-dimensional Euclidean space and then $d_{(n)} = r_i^n - r_{i-1}^n, r_0^n = 0$.

Example of a Uniform Ball. Let us suppose a ball in an n-dimensional space containing uniformly distributed points over its volume. Let us divide the ball on concentric "peels" of the same volume. Using the formula $r_i = S(n)/2^n.^n \sqrt{V_i}$ we obtain a quite interesting succession of radii corresponding to the individual volumes. The symbol $S(n)$ denotes the volume of a ball with unit radius in E_n; note $S(3) = {}^4/_3\pi$. The higher space dimension is considered the more similar values of the radii approaching the outer ball radius are obtained. The inner part of the ball is thus nearly empty. The $d_{(n)}$ or radius to the n-th power correspond much better to the probability distribution mapping function $D(x, r) = const.r^n$. The radii of balls to the n-th power grow thus linearly. Differences are then constant, which well corresponds to uniformity of the distribution.

4.2   Influence of a Dimensionality and a Total Number of Points

Distances, as well as $d_{(n)}$, of several nearest neighbors depend on probability distribution $p(z)$ of points in the neighborhood of a query point x and also on true density of points in this neighborhood.

Example of normal distribution. Let us consider a distribution of m_T samples with distribution density mapping function $d(x.r^n) = 2N(0,1)|_{r^N \geq 0} = 2\frac{1}{\sqrt{2\pi}}e^{-\frac{1}{2}r^{2n}}$ in E_n. Coefficient 2 was introduced to get $D(x, r_n) \to 1$ for $r_n \to \infty$. Thus $D(x, r_n)$ can be considered as a probability distribution function. For the mean r_i^n of r^n for the i-th nearest neighbor of the query point x it holds that $r_i^n = N^{-1}(0.5 + 0.5i/m_T)$.

Fig. 1 shows distances r_i^n of the first several nearest neighbors for different space dimensions n. Fig. 2 shows distances r_i^n for different numbers of points (samples in the set) for different space dimensions n.

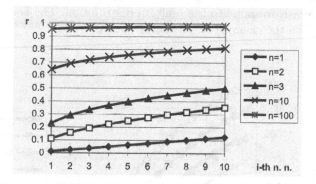

Fig. 1. Distances r_i^n of the first several nearest neighbors for different space dimensions n

5   Influence of Boundary Effects

The problem of boundary effects was studied in [1] in $l_{\max}$ metric and for different problems of searching the nearest neighbor in large databases. Taking the boundary effects into account, the estimation of the searching time was lesser than if no boundary effect is considered and is closer to reality.

5.1   Boundary Effect Phenomenon

Let the boundary effect be understood as a phenomenon such that within a given spherical neighborhood with radius r the probability density is a (not strictly)

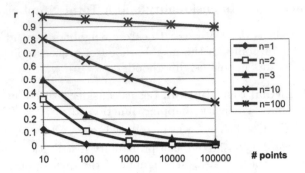

Fig. 2. Distances r_i^n for different numbers of points for different space dimensions n

decreasing function and decreases starting from some point. Moreover, this fact influences the mean distances of neighbors of the query point so that these distances do not correspond to the uniform distribution. The boundary effect is demonstrated on the example of a uniform cube in Fig. 3.

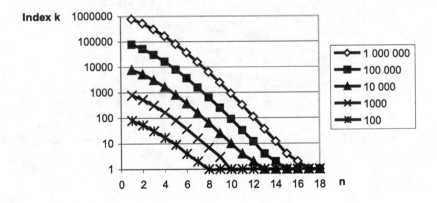

Fig. 3. Index k of the k-th nearest neighbor for which the boundary effect arises for different dimensionalities n and for $m_T = 100$ till 1,000,000 points (a unit cube with uniform distribution and the query point x in the origin)

5.2   Power Approximation of the Probability Distribution Mapping Function

A course of the probability distribution mapping function is often not known and it is not easy to derive it analytically. Therefore, we suggest using power approximation r_q of the probability distribution mapping function $D(x, r_n)$ such that $\frac{D(x,r^n)}{r^q} \to const$ for $r \to 0+$.

The exponent q is the distribution mapping exponent. The variable $\alpha = q/n$ we call the distribution mapping ratio. Using the approximation of the probability distribution mapping function by $D(x, r^n) = const.(r^n)^\alpha$, the distribution mapping exponent is $q = n\alpha$.

An example of values of the distribution mapping exponent is shown in Fig. 4.

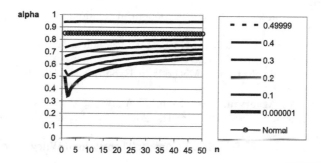

Fig. 4. Distribution mapping ratio α as a function of dimension n for normal distribution and for the uniform unit cube, with the query point in the distance $l(0 < l < 0.5,$ see legend) from the center of the cube to the center of one of its walls.

6   Conclusion

By using a notion of distance, i.e. a simple transformation $E_n \to E_1$, the problems with dimensionality are easily eliminated at a loss of information on the true distribution of points in the neighborhood of the query point. It is known [1], [3] that for larger dimensions something like local approximation of real distribution by uniform distribution does not exist. But the assumption of at least local uniformity in the neighborhood of a query point is usually inherent in methods based on the distances of neighbors. This problem is solved by introduction of a power approximation of the probability distribution mapping function here. An essential variable of this approximation is the distribution mapping exponent. By using this exponent the real distribution is transformed to be uniform. It is possible to do it either locally or globally. In essence, there are two ways in estimating the distribution mapping exponent. One of them is to estimate this exponent globally for the whole data set and rely on not too large local differences. The other way is to estimate the distribution mapping exponent locally, i.e. for each query point anew. A disadvantage of this approach is a large possible error in the distribution mapping exponent when a small number of neighbor points is used. Processing of a larger number of points, on the other hand, makes estimation closer to global estimation especially for small data sets.

References

1. Arya, S., Mount, D.M., Narayan, O.: Accounting for Boundary Effects in Nearest Neighbor Searching. Discrete and Computational Geometry, Vol. **16** (1996) 155–176
2. Beyer, K. et al.: When is "Nearest Neighbor" Meaningful? Proc. of the 7th International Conference on Database Theory. Jerusalem, Israel (1999) 217–235
3. Burton, B.G.: The Poisson distribution and the Poisson process. http://www.zoo.cam.ac.uk/zoostaff/laughlin/brian/minireviews/poisson/poisson.pdf
4. Demaret, J.C., Gareet, A.: Sum of Exponential Random Variables. AEÜ, Vol. **31**, No. 11 (1977) 445–448
5. Duda, R.O., Hart, P.E., Stork, D.G.: Pattern Classification. Second Edition. John Wiley and Sons, Inc., New York (2000)
6. Eadie, Wt.T. et al.: Statistical Methods in Experimental Physics. North-Holland (1982)
7. Hinnenburg, A., Aggarwal, C.C., Keim, D.A.: What is the Nearest Neighbor in High Dimensional Spaces? Proc. of the 26th VLDB Conf., Cairo, Egypt (2000) 506–515
8. Kleinrock, L.: Queueing Systems. Volume I: Theory. John Wiley & Sons, New York (1975)
9. Silverman, B.W.: Density Estimation for Statistics and Data Analysis. Chapman and Hall, London (1986)
10. Chávez, E., Figueroa, K., Navarro, G.: A Fast Algorithm for the All k Nearest Neighbors Problem in General Metric Spaces. http://citeseer.nj.nec.com/correct/462760
11. Pestov, V.: On the Geometry of Similarity Search: Dimensionality Curse and Concentration of Measure. Information Processing Letters, Vol. **73**, No. 1–2, 31 January 2000, 47–51

Discovery of Lexical Entries for Non-taxonomic Relations in Ontology Learning

Martin Kavalec[1], Alexander Maedche[2], and Vojtěch Svátek[1]

[1] Department of Information and Knowledge Engineering,
University of Economics, Prague, W. Churchill Sq. 4, 130 67 Praha 3, Czech Republic
{kavalec,svatek}@vse.cz
[2] Robert Bosch GmbH, Borsigstrasse 14, 70469 Stuttgart-Feuerbach, Germany
Alexander.Maedche@de.bosch.com

Abstract. Ontology learning from texts has recently been proposed as a new technology helping ontology designers in the modelling process. Discovery of non–taxonomic relations is understood as the least tackled problem therein. We propose a technique for extraction of lexical entries that may give cue in assigning semantic labels to otherwise 'anonymous' relations. The technique has been implemented as extension to the existing *Text-to-Onto* tool, and tested on a collection of texts describing worldwide geographic locations from a tour–planning viewpoint.

1 Introduction

Ontologies are the backbone of the prospective semantic web as well as of a growing number of knowledge management systems. The difficulty of their manual development is however a significant drawback. Recently, *ontology learning* (OL) from text has been suggested as promising technology for building lightweighted ontologies with limited effort. It relies on combination of shallow text analysis, data mining and knowledge modelling. In [9], three core subtasks of OL have systematically been examined: lexical entry extraction (also used for concept extraction), taxonomy extraction, and *non–taxonomic relation[1] extraction* (NTRE), considered as most difficult. The NTRE technique [10] embedded in the *Text-to-Onto* tool [11] of the KAON system[2] produces, based on a corpus of documents, an ordered set of binary relations between concepts. The relations are *labelled* by a human designer and become part of an ontology. Empirical studies [9] however suggest that designers may not always appropriately label a relation between two general concepts (e.g. 'Company' and 'Product'). First, various relations among instances of the same general concepts are possible; for example, a company may not only *produce* but also *sell*, *consume* or *propagate* a product. Second, it is often hard to guess which among synonymous labels

---

[1] Although it might be useful to distinguish the terms 'relation' and 'relationship' (set of tuples vs. high–level association between concepts), we mostly speak about 'relations' since this term is systematically used in the ontology engineering community.
[2] Karlsruhe Ontology infrastructure, http://kaon.semanticweb.org.

P. Van Emde Boas et al. (Eds.): SOFSEM 2004, LNCS 2932, pp. 249–256, 2004.

(e.g. 'produce', 'manufacture', 'make'...) is preferred by the community. *Lexical entries* picked up from domain–specific texts thus may give an important cue.

The paper is organised as follows. Section 2 describes the principles of our method. Section 3 presents and discusses the results of an experiment in the tour–planning domain. Section 4 compares our approach with related research. Finally, section 5 summarises the paper and outlines directions for future work.

2   Seeking Labels for Relations in *Text-to-Onto*

2.1   Method Description

The standard approach to *relation discovery* in text corpus is derived from *association rule learning* [1]. Two (or more) lexical items are understood as belonging to a *transaction* if they occur together in a document or other predefined unit of text; frequent transactions are output as *associations* among their items. *Text–to–Onto*, however, discovers binary relations not only for lexical items but also for ontological concepts [10]. This presumes existence of a *lexicon* (mapping lexical entries to underlying concepts) and preferably a *concept taxonomy*.

Modification of the method, which is the subject of this paper, relies on an extended notion of transaction. Following up with our prior work on lexical entry extraction from business websites [7], we hypothesised that the 'predicate' of a non–taxonomic relation can be characterised by *verbs* frequently occurring in the neighbourhood of pairs of lexical entries corresponding to associated concepts.

Definition 1. *VCC(n)–transaction holds among a verb v, concept c_1 and concept c_2 iff c_1 and c_2 both occur within n words from an occurrence of v.*

Good candidates for labelling a non–taxonomic relation between two concepts are the verbs frequently occurring in VCC(n) transactions with these concepts, for some 'reasonable' n. Very simple measure of association between a verb and a concept pair are conditional frequencies (empirical probabilities)

$$P(c_1 \wedge c_2/v) = \frac{|\{t_i|v, c_1, c_2 \in t_i\}|}{|\{t_i|v \in t_i\}|} \tag{1}$$

$$P(v/c_1 \wedge c_2) = \frac{|\{t_i|v, c_1, c_2 \in t_i\}|}{|\{t_i|c_1, c_2 \in t_i\}|} \tag{2}$$

where $|.|$ denotes set cardinality, and t_i are the VCC(n)–transactions. The first one helps to find concept pairs possibly associated with a given verb; the second one helps to find verbs possibly associated with a given concept pair.

However, conditional frequency of a pair of concepts given a verb (or vice versa) is not the same as conditional frequency of a *relation* between concepts given a verb (or vice versa). A verb may occur frequently with each of the concepts, and still have nothing to do with any of their mutual relationships. For example, in our experimental domain, lexical entries corresponding to the concept 'city' often occur together with the verb 'to reach', and the same holds for lexical entries corresponding to the concept 'island', since both types of location can typically be reached from different directions. Therefore, conditional frequencies $P(City \wedge Island/'reach')$ and $P('reach'/City \wedge Island)$ will be relatively high, and might even dominate those of verbs expressing a true semantic relation between the concepts, such as 'located' (a city is located on an island).

To tackle this problem, we need a measure expressing the increase of conditional frequency, as defined in (1) and (2), compared to frequency expected under assumption of *independence* of associations of each of the concepts with the verb. Our heuristic 'above expectation' (AE) measure thus is, respectively:

$$AE(c_1 \wedge c_2/v) = \frac{P(c_1 \wedge c_2/v)}{P(c_1/v).P(c_2/v)} \tag{3}$$

$$AE(v/c_1 \wedge c_2) = \frac{P(v/c_1 \wedge c_2)}{P(v/c_1).P(v/c_2)} \tag{4}$$

(the meaning of $P(c_1/v)$ etc. being obvious). This measure resembles the 'interest' measure (of implication) suggested by Kodratoff [8] as operator for knowledge discovery in text[3]. The 'interest' however merely compares the relative frequency of a pattern (in data) conditioned with another pattern, with its unconditioned relative frequency. Our AE measures, in turn, compare a conditional frequency with the product of two 'simpler' conditional frequencies.

2.2   Implementation

The computation of $VCC(n)$ transactions and associated frequency measures has been implemented as a new module of *Text–to–Onto tool*. Resulting concept–concept–verb triples are shown in a separate window popping up from its parent window of 'bare' relation extractor, upon choosing one or more among the relations. A screenshot of KAON environment is at Fig. 1; note the list of verbs potentially associated with relations between 'Country' and 'City', in the front window. In addition, complete results are output into a textual protocol.

3   Experiments

3.1   Problem Setting

For experiments, we selected the popular domain of tourism. Our text corpus contained web pages from the Lonely Planet website[4]: 1800 short documents in English, about 5 MB overall. These are free–text descriptions of various world locations encompassing geography, history and available leisure activities; there is no systematic information about hotel infrastructure. Our goal was to verify

---

[3] There is also some similarity with statistical measures such as χ^2. These however involve applicability conditions that are hard to meet in OL, where a high number of relatively infrequent features have to be examined.

[4] http://www.lonelyplanet.com/destinations/

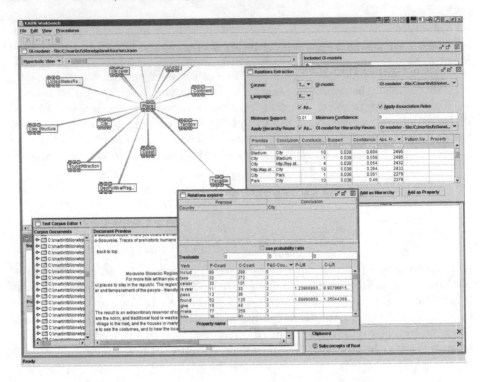

Fig. 1. KAON environment with interface for non–taxonomic relation discovery

to what extent such a text collection can be used as support for discovering and *labelling* non–taxonomic relations for an ontology of the domain. Such an ontology could be used for diverse purposes, from ad–hoc question answering (about world geography), to serious tour recommendation applications.

NTRE is a task typically superposed over several other tasks, which can be carried out via manual modelling or OL: lexical entry extraction, mapping of lexical entries to concepts, and taxonomy building:

- In *Text-to-Onto*, *lexical entry extraction* has previously been used for discovery of potential *concept* labels, based on the well–known TFIDF (information retrieval) measure, in the whole document collection. In contrast, our goal was *relation* labelling, which is also a form of lexical entry extraction but requires a more focused approach. Since our hypothesis was that 'relational' information is most often conveyed by verbs, we embedded a *part-of-speech* (POS) tagger into the process of frequent transaction discovery.
- Mapping *lexical entries to concepts* can hardly be accomplished automatically. We adopted portions of the *TAP knowledge base*[5] recently developed at Stanford: a large repository of lexical entries—proper names of places,

---

[5] http://tap.stanford.edu

companies, people and the like. It has previously been used for automated annotation of web pages [4] but its use as 'lexicon for OL' was novel.
- TAP includes a simple *taxonomy*, which is however not compatible with standard upper–level ontologies and contains ontologically unsound constructs. We therefore combined the TAP taxonomy with our small hand–made tourism ontology, and slightly 'tweaked' it where needed. Although *Text–to–Onto* also contains an automatic taxonomy–building tool, we did not use it to prevent error chaining from one OL task to another.

3.2   Analysis and Its Results

The whole analysis consisted of several phases, in which we used different components of *Text–to–Onto*. The output of earlier phases was stored and subsequently used for multiple (incl. debugging) runs of the last phase.

1. First, locations of ontology concepts (i.e. lexicon entries) were found in text and stored in an index. There were about 9300 such entries.
2. Next, we used the POS tagger to identify the locations of verb forms in the text; they were stored in another index.
3. We post–processed the POS tags to couple verbs such as 'to be' or 'to have' with their presumed syntactical objects, to obtain more usable verb constructs (these were subsequently handled in the same way as generic verbs).
4. Finally, we compared the indices from step 1 and 2, recorded the $VCC(n)$–transactions for $n = 8$, and aggregated them by triples. This last phase took about 45 seconds on a 1.8GHz Athlon XP computer.

Table 1 lists the 24 concept–concept–verb triples with $AE(c_1 \wedge c_2/v)$ higher than 100% (ordered by this value); triples with occurrence lower than 3, for which the relative frequencies do not make much sense, have been eliminated[6].

We can see that roughly the first half of triples (even those with low absolute frequencies, 4 or 5) corresponds to meaningful semantic relations, mostly topo–mereological ones: an island or a country is located in a world–geographical region (wg_region), a country 'is a country' of a particular continent and may be located on an island or consist of several islands[7], a city may be home of a famous museum etc. However, with $AE(c_1 \wedge c_2/v)$ dropping to about 150 %, the verbs cease to pertain to a relation. This leads us to the heuristics that triples below this value should probably not be presented to the ontology designer.

Note that the table suggests which pairs of concepts should certain verbs be assigned to, as lexical entries for non–taxonomic relations. We could also reorder the triples by an alternative measure, $AE(v/c_1 \wedge c_2)$: this would yield (also quite useful) information on which verbs most typically occur with a certain relation.

The results do not seem too impressive given the amount of underlying material. This however reflect many circumstances independent of the method itself:

---

[6] Since some of required filtering options were not yet available through the window environment at the moment of performing the experiments, the results were partly obtained via offline analysis of textual protocol produced by *Text–to–Onto*.
[7] Example of *multiple relations* between the same concepts, cf. end of section 1.

Table 1. Final results of label extraction

c_1	c_2	v	$|\{t_i|v, c_1, c_2 \in t_i\}|$	$P(c_1 \wedge c_2/v)$	$AE(c_1 \wedge c_2/v)$
island	wg_region	locate	3	0.95%	750.00%
country	wg_region	locate	10	3.17%	744.68%
continent	country	is_country	26	10.12%	431.10%
us_city	wg_region	locate	4	1.27%	350.00%
country	island	made	5	1.68%	270.42%
country	island	locate	5	1.59%	239.36%
country	island	consist	10	7.41%	234.78%
museum	us_city	is_home	3	1.74%	234.55%
country	island	comprise	6	5.56%	200.62%
country	tourist	enter	6	2.79%	176.95%
country	island	divide	5	3.88%	172.46%
island	us_city	locate	3	0.95%	168.75%
city	stadium	known	9	1.25%	165.69%
city	country	allow	24	13.71%	152.89%
city	tourist	is_city	9	1.74%	151.61%
country	us_city	locate	9	2.86%	150.80%
city	country	is_settlement	6	16.22%	148.00%
island	us_city	connect	3	2.86%	140.00%
country	island	populate	5	6.02%	139.73%
city	island	locate	8	2.54%	131.39%
city	country	reflect	5	8.06%	117.42%
city	country	grant	4	12.90%	105.98%
city	park	is_city	11	2.13%	104.23%
city	country	stand	8	5.06%	104.03%

- *Richness and relevance of concept taxonomy.* The TAP–based taxonomy was not a true ontology of the domain, and was rather sparse. Construction of a good taxonomy is a demanding task; by complex study in [9], however, it is not as big a challenge as the invention of plausible non–taxonomic relations.
- *Richness and relevance of lexicon.* The lexicon only covered a part of the relevant lexical space. It listed many names of places (most however only appeared in a single document) but few names of activities for tourists or art objects (reusable across many documents). Better coverage would require either comprehensive lexicons (some can also be found on the web) or heavy–weighted linguistic techniques such as anaphora resolution.
- *Style of underlying text.* The Lonely Planet documents are written in a quite free, expressive style. The same relation is often expressed by different verbs, which decreases the chance of detecting a single, most characteristic one.
- *Performance of POS tagger.* Sometimes, the tagger does not properly categorise a lexical entry. For example, a verb associated with concept *Country* was 'cross'; some of its alleged occurrences however seemed to be adverbs.

4   Related Work

Our work differs from existing research on 'relation discovery' in a subtle but important aspect: in other projects, the notion of 'relation' is typically used for relation *instances*, i.e. statements about concrete pairs of entities: labels are directly assigned to such pairs. Rather than OL in the proper sense (since instances are usually not expected to be part of an ontology), this research should be viewed as *information extraction* (IE). In contrast, we focus on *proper relations*[8], which *possibly* hold among (various instances of) certain ontology concepts. The design of proper relations is a creative task: it *can* and *should* be accomplished by a human, for whom we only want to offer partial support.

Yet, many partial techniques are similar. Finkelstein&Morin [6] combine 'supervised' and 'unsupervised' extraction of relationships between terms; the latter (with unspecified underlying relations) relies on 'default' labels, under assumption that e.g. the relation between a Company and a Product is always 'produce'. Byrd&Ravin [3] assign the label to a relation (instance) via specially–built finite state automata operating over sentence patterns. Some automata yield a pre–defined relation (e.g. *location* relation for the '–based' construction) while other pick up a promising word from the sentence itself. Labelling of proper relations is however not addressed, and even the 'concepts' are a mixture of proper concepts and instances. The *Adaptiva* system [2], allows the user to choose a relation from the ontology and interactively learns its recognition patterns. Although the goal is to *recognise* relation instances in text, the interaction with the user may also give rise to new proper relations. Such massive interaction however does not pay off if the goal is merely to *find* important domain–specific relations to which the texts refer, as in our case. The *Asium* system [5] synergistically builds two hierarchies: that of concepts and that of verb subcategorisation frames (an implicit 'relation taxonomy'), based on co–occurrence in text . There is however no direct support for conceptual 'leap' from a 'bag of verbs' to a named relation.

Another stream, more firmly grounded in ontology engineering, systematically seeks new *unnamed* relations in text. Co–occurrence analysis (with little attention to sentence structure) is used, and the results filtered via frequency measures, as in our approach. In prior work on the *Text–to–Onto* project [10], the labelling problem was left upon the ontology designer. In the *OntoLearn* project [12], WordNet mapping was used to automatically assign relations from a small predefined set (such as 'similar' or 'instrument').

5   Conclusions and Future Work

Our experiment suggests that ontology learning from text may be used not only for discovering ('anonymous') relations between pairs of concepts, but also for providing lexical entries as potential *labels* for these relations. Verbs, identified merely by POS tagger (i.e. without structural analysis of the sentence) can be viewed as first, rough, approximation of the desired category of such entries.

---

[8] The notion of *categorical relationship* is also used, in contrast to *factual relationship*.

Most imminent future work concerns the possibility to immediately verify the semantics of discovered concept–concept–verb triples, via return to the original text. Sometimes the ontology designer might wonder (e.g. assuming a 'borderline' AE measure) whether a verb really pertains to the relation in text or the result arose just by some strange incidence. For example, looking at our result table, s/he might ask if it is really typical (and thus worth modelling) for cities *to be known* for their museums. Display of the underlying text fragments (which are not overwhelmingly numerous in our case) would be of much help.

Acknowledgements. The work was partly carried out during M. Kavalec's stay at *Forschungszentrum Informatik* (FZI) Karlsruhe, Germany, supported by Marie Curie Fellowship, Semantic Web Center of Excellence, IST, MCFH-2001-00435. A. Maedche participated in the project during his appointment as Head of the Knowledge Management Group at FZI Karlsruhe. M. Kavalec and V. Svátek are partially supported by grant no.201/03/1318 of the Grant Agency of the Czech Republic.

References

1. Agrawal, R., Imielinski, T., Swami, A.: Mining Association Rules between Sets of Items in Large Databases. In: Proc. ACM SIGMOD Conference on Management of Data (1993) 207–216
2. Brewster, C., Ciravegna, F., Wilks, Y.: User-Centred Ontology Learning for Knowledge Management. In: 7th Int'l Conf. Applications of Natural Language to Information Systems, Stockholm, LNAI, Springer (2002)
3. Byrd, R., Ravin, Y.: Identifying and Extracting Relations in Text. In: Proceedings of NLDB 99, Klagenfurt, Austria (1999)
4. Dill, S., et al.: SemTag and Seeker: Bootstrapping the Semantic Web via Automated Semantic Annotation. In: Proc. WWW2003, Budapest (2003)
5. Faure, D., Nédellec, C.: ASIUM: Learning Subcategorization Frames and Restrictions of Selection. In: ECML'98, Workshop on Text Mining (1998)
6. Finkelstein-Landau, M., Morin, E.: Extracting Semantic Relationships between Terms: Supervised vs. Unsupervised Methods. In: Int'l Workshop on Ontological Engineering on the Global Information Infrastructure, Dagstuhl (1999)
7. Kavalec, M., Svátek, V.: Information Extraction and Ontology Learning Guided by Web Directory. In: ECAI Workshop on NLP and ML for ontology engineering. Lyon (2002)
8. Kodratoff, Y.: Comparing Machine Learning and Knowledge Discovery in DataBases: An Application to Knowledge Discovery in Texts. In: ECCAI Summer Course, Crete July 1999, LNAI, Springer (2000)
9. Maedche, A.: Ontology Learning for the Semantic Web. Kluwer (2002)
10. Maedche, A., Staab, S.: Mining Ontologies from Text. In: EKAW'2000, Juan-les-Pins, Springer (2000)
11. Maedche, A., Volz, R.: The Text-To-Onto Ontology Extraction and Maintenance System. In: ICDM-Workshop on Integrating Data Mining and Knowledge Management, San Jose, California, USA (2001)
12. Missikoff, M., Navigli, R., Velardi, P.: Integrated Approach for Web Ontology Learning and Engineering. IEEE Computer, November (2002)

Approaches Based on Markovian Architectural Bias in Recurrent Neural Networks

Matej Makula[1], Michal Čerňanský[1], and Ľubica Beňušková[2]

[1] Faculty of Informatics and Information Technologies,
Slovak University of Technology,
Ilkovičova 3, 812 19 Bratislava, Slovakia
{makula, cernans}@fiit.stuba.sk
http://www.fiit.stuba.sk
[2] Institute of Informatics, Comenius University,
Mlynská dolina, 842 48 Bratislava, Slovakia
benus@ii.fmph.uniba.sk

Abstract. Recent studies show that state-space dynamics of randomly initialized recurrent neural network (RNN) has interesting and potentially useful properties even without training. More precisely, when initializing RNN with small weights, recurrent unit activities reflect history of inputs presented to the network according to the Markovian scheme. This property of RNN is called Markovian architectural bias. Our work focuses on various techniques that make use of architectural bias. The first technique is based on the substitution of RNN output layer with prediction model, resulting in capabilities to exploit interesting state representation. The second approach, known as echo state networks (ESNs), is based on large untrained randomly interconnected hidden layer, which serves as reservoir of interesting behavior. We have investigated both approaches and their combination and performed simulations to demonstrate their usefulness.

1 Introduction

The key part of recurrent neural networks (RNNs) performance is encoded in activities of recurrent units (network state) and their variations in time (network dynamics). It is well-known fact that recurrent neural networks have universal approximation capability, although development of desired dynamics in training might be sometimes difficult or even unfeasible task. Classical gradient-based training methods face severe problems such as information latching problem [4]. This problem arises because gradient of the error function tends to vanish in time, thus it is impossible for RNNs to catch the long time dependencies in the input sequence. Several approaches have been developed in order to at least partially overcome this problem [5], [1]. But recent studies show that sometimes instead of complicated RNN weights adaptation, it might be beneficial to leave network dynamics randomly initialized.

P. Van Emde Boas et al. (Eds.): SOFSEM 2004, LNCS 2932, pp. 257–264, 2004.

It has been known for some time that when RNN is used to process symbolic sequences, activations of recurrent units show considerable amount of information about input sequence prior to training [2], [9], [10]. It was experimentally shown that RNNs initialized with small weights are inherently biased towards Markov models [11], [12]. This phenomenom is refered as Markovian architectural bias of RNNs. When dealing with problems, where this Markovian representation is useful, initial network dynamics can be leaved unchanged and only transformation of state to desired output has to be carried out. This can be performed either by simple neural network layer or by other advanced method, e.g. by prediction model.

Major advantage of this 'unusual' approach is the elimination of the recursive dependencies between weights in adjustment process, i.e. problem when even small 'positive' weight change in one step can have huge impact on network activities in other steps. Thus, instead of complicated training of whole network, only output layer (or prediction model) is adjusted to produce desired output from the inherent 'Markovian' dynamics.

2   Alternative Training Approaches

Typical example of 'classical' approach in recurrent network community is the first-order Elman simple recurrent network (SRN) [3], trained by various gradient-based techniques. Recently a novel approach based on architectural bias called echo state networks (ESNs) has been introduced [6].

Layer interconnections and units used in ESN are mostly equal to SRN architecture[1], but the main difference is in the size of recurrent layer and in the training process. ESNs use large randomly initialized recurrent layer, called dynamical reservoir, to obtain massive response to the input signal. In training, output weights are adjusted to use this response to 'reconstruct' desired output. Essential condition for the ESN approach is that dynamical reservoir must produce meaningful response, i.e. network state must be an 'echo' of input signal. This is achieved by rescaling network weights to small values, which is apparently equivalent to architectural bias condition, i.e. *initialization with 'small' weights*. Thus, ESNs can be viewed as 'architectural bias' based counterparts of classical RNNs.

As it was mentioned earlier, once we skip recurrent weights training, the output weights can be calculated effectively by linear regression. In ESNs it is usually done offline by calculation of pseudoinverse matrix, but also other online algorithms, such as least mean squares (LSM) or recursive least squares (RLS), can be used. It is important to notice that before training suitable memory capacity of ESN can be set up by rescaling weights in dynamical reservoir [7]. More detailed description of ESN approach can be found in [8].

Another widely used technique is to extract finite state representation from trained recurrent networks. By clusterization of recurrent units activities, com-

---

[1] ESN approach allows also additional input-output and output-hidden layer interconnection, but we did not use them in our experiments.

Table 1. Differences between 'classical' approaches and approaches based on 'architectural bias'

	SRN	NPM	ESN	untrained NPM
approach	classical		based on architectural bias	
output layer	neural network	prediction model	neural network	prediction model
output	symbols and real values	only symbols	symbols and real values	only symbols
hidden layer	small ≈ 10 units	small ≈ 10 units	large $\approx 10^2$ units	small ≈ 10 units
network dynamics	adjusted	adjusted	random - Markovian	random - Markovian
adjustment	both network dynamics and state-output mapping	same as SRN + prediction model building	only state-output mapping	only prediction model building
training algorithm	gradient based [14], extended Kalman filter	same as SRN + model adjustment	linear regression	only model adjustment

plex network dynamics can be easily substituted with more useful finite state representation. This kind of state representation is used in simple modification of RNN called neural prediction machine (NPM) [12], where network output layer is replaced with prediction model. NPM seeks state clusters in network state space and associates them with conditional probabilities for the next symbol prediction. Conditional probabilities are determined by counting of *(state cluster, output symbol)* occurrences in training sequence. Because NPM can be also built from an untrained network, this approach can be used to exploit Markovian state representation in untrained network.

Architectures described in previous chapters are summarized in the Table. 1. The first two columns describe architectures where both input-state and state-output mapping is adjusted in training. The approaches based on architectural bias are in the third and fourth column.

3 Experiments and Results

In the following subsections we describe our experiments, data sets, and training parameters. The first experiment is comparison of SRN and ESN approach on problem of periodic sequence prediction task. The second problem is the prediction of symbolic sequence obtained by quantization of chaotic laser activity, where we compared performance of NPMs built on recurrent layer of trained and untrained recurrent network.

3.1   Periodic Sequence Prediction Task

In this experiment we studied how the desired solution is achieved by both classical SRN and novel ESN approach. Original experiment was based on problem of stable generation of periodic sequence by ESN [6]. We simplified original problem to next value prediction task and evaluated SRN and ESN with various numbers of hidden units.

Input sequence was the melody "The House of the Rising Sun" transformed to numerical values to fit interval [-0.05,0.5] (Fig. 1). Multiple melody samples were concatenated together to form the target sequence of period 48.

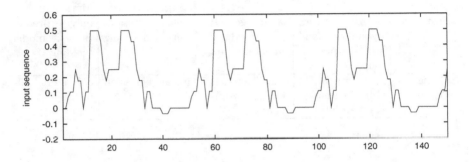

Fig. 1. Input sequence was created by concatenation of multiple samples from melody "The House of the Rising Sun"

ESN input weights were selected randomly from uniform distribution [-2, 2]. Recurrent weights were set to values +0.4, -0.4 and then scaled down to obtain $\lambda_{max} = 0.908$. The connectivity of recurrent layer was sparse with ratio 1.25 %. Since we were not concerned about stable melody generation, we did not incorporate noise into the training data. Both training and testing sequence had 1500 input symbols, where first 500 inputs were used for initialization. Output weights were calculated offline with linear regression.

All weights in SRN were selected randomly from uniform distribution [-0.1,0.1]. Training was performed by extended Kalman filter method (EKF). Error covariance matrix was initialized $\mathbf{P} = 1000 \cdot \mathbf{I}$, measurement noise matrix was set to $\mathbf{R} = 100 \cdot \mathbf{I}$ and output noise matrix was set to $\mathbf{Q} = 10^{-4} \cdot \mathbf{I}$, where $\mathbf{I}$ is the identity matrix. Weights derivatives were calculated by back-propagation through time (BPTT) method [13] with window size 30. Both training and testing sequence had 10000 input symbols, where first 500 inputs were used for initialization.

We use bipolar ($tanh$) activation function for both ESN and SRN units. All values presented in figure Fig. 2 are the averages of mean square error (MSE) with standard deviations from 10 runs of ESN and SRN network training.

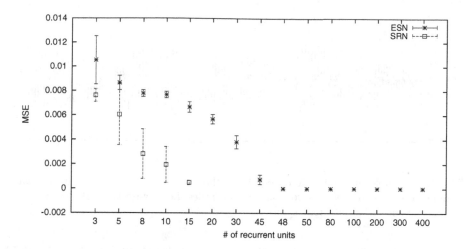

Fig. 2. Mean square error (MSE) for SRN and ESN after training. MSE was calculated for networks with different number of hidden units. We can see that SRN with the same number of hidden units outperforms ESN, although MSE for larger ESNs is almost zero (MSE $\approx 10^{-30}$ - limited by computer decimal number precision)

3.2 Chaotic Sequence Prediction Task

In this experiment we focus on the second approach based on architectural bias, i.e. NPM built on untrained RNN. Performance of NPMs built on untrained network was compared with performance of NPMs built on recurrent layer of trained SRN. We have used networks with various numbers of hidden units.

As a training sequence for this experiment we chose a long symbolic sequence of quantized activity changes of laser in chaotic regime. Data set includes various levels of memory structures, i.e. relatively predictable subsequences followed by global, harder to predict events, that require a deeper memory (Fig. 3).

Whole sequence[2], i.e. 10 000 differences Δ_t between two subsequent activations, was quantized into a symbolic stream of four symbols from the alphabet $\{a, b, c, d\}$, corresponding to low / high and positive / negative activity changes. Entire sequence was divided into the training sequence (the first 8000 symbols) and the test sequence (the last 2000 symbols). Symbols were encoded using one-hot-encoding.

As activation function we use unipolar sigmoid $1/(1 + c^x)$. Training of SRN was performed by EKF in 10 epochs. First 50 symbols were used for initialization. Other SRN parameters were the same as in the previous experiment. For NPMs built form untrained network underlying dynamics was produced by dynamical reservoir of ESN initialized identically with the previous experiment.

Finally, state space of both trained and untrained network was clustered by K-means algorithm with 250 clusters and NPM was built. Performance of

---

[2] Taken from http://www-psych.stanford.edu/~andreas/Time-Series/SantaFe.html

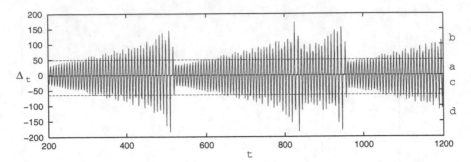

Fig. 3. Example of 1000 differences Δ_t of the laser activations. Dotted horizontal lines corresponds to 10% and 90% sample quantiles. Letters on the right vertical axis indicate quantization into four symbols

NPMs was evaluated by means of the normalized negative log-likelihood (NNL) (Fig. 4). NNL can be viewed as inverse compression ratio, i.e. NNL=0.5 means that sequence can be compressed to half of its original size. Ideal NNL value is 0, NNL = 1 corresponds to random guessing.

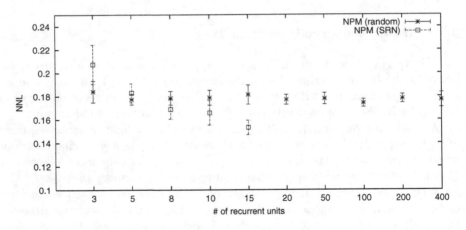

Fig. 4. Normalized negative log-likelihood (NNL) for NPMs build from trained SRN and untrained ESN reservoir

4   Discussion

First task is a straightforward demonstration of difference between the classical and novel approach. Once a periodic signal is presented to the untrained RNN, its state moves on periodic orbit in the state space. Classical approach performs training by reshaping state trajectory and simultaneous adaptation of state-output mapping. When sufficient number of recurrent units is used and network has enough state space dimensions to examine, desired dynamics emerges and the next value can be successfully predicted (Fig. 2, for SRN with 15 hidden units MSE $\approx 1.7 \cdot 10^{-4}$).

The way in which ESN produces desired solution is different. Initial network dynamics behave similarly with SRN, i.e. network state jumps between 48 different clusters in the state space. In training, output weights are used to fit desired output from network state. When dimension of state space is small, i.e. small number of recurrent units, network output cannot be precisely reconstructed. Once output weights have enough state space dimension to explore, linear combination of state vector components can produce desired periodic output signal with almost zero precision (MSE $\approx 10^{-30}$). It might seem that great number of units in ESN recurrent layer is not necessary, but in original experiment this additional dimensions were used by ESN to stably reproduce original periodic sequence [6].

Results of our second experiment confirm that the prediction of chaotic laser sequence is rather difficult task due to long time dependency problem. Training of recurrent network by extended Kalman filter slightly improve state representation, which is clearly visible when sufficient number of hidden units is used (Fig. 4). However, NPM built on hidden layer of untrained network can provide comparable results. Interestingly, in this case larger number of hidden units did not help to improve NPM performance.

5   Conclusion

In this paper we presented approaches based on architectural bias. These approaches leave randomly initialized network dynamics unchanged and adjust only state to output transformation. On selected experiments we evaluate their performance and compared obtained results with classical approaches.

Results show that SRN can produce desired solution with smaller number of recurrent units, although it requires much more computationally expensive training. On the other hand, nature of approaches based on architectural bias allows to increase the number of recurrent units without significant increasing of training complexicity. ESN can use this high dimensional state space to fit desired output accurately. In the second experiment simple prediction model - NPM, built on untrained network with 5 recurrent units, produced little worse results than NPM built on much larger network trained by computationally demanding EKF technique.

Acknowledgments. This work was supported by the VEGA grant 1/9046/02.

References

1. Bengio, Y., Simard, P., Frasconi, P.: Learning Long-Term Dependencies with Gradient Descent is Difficult. IEEE Transactions on Neural Networks, **5** 2 (1994) 157–166

2. Christiansen, M.H., Chater, N.: Toward a Connectionist Model of Recursion in Human Linguistic Performance. Cognitive Science **23** (1999) 417–437
3. Elman, J.L.: Finding Structure in Time. Cognitive Science **14** (1990) 179–211
4. Hochreiter, S., Bengio, Y., Frasconi, P., Schmidhuber, J.: Gradient Flow in Recurrent Nets: the Difficulty of Learning Long-Term Dependencies. In: Kolen, J., Kremer, S. (eds): Field Guide to Dynamic Recurrent Networks. Wiley-IEEE Press (2001) 237–243
5. Hochreiter, S., Schmidhuber, J.: Long Short-Term Memory. Neural Computation **9** 8 (1997) 1735–1780
6. Jaeger, H.: The "Echo State" Approach to Analysing and Training Recurrent Neural Networks. Technical Report GMD Report 148, German National Research Center for Information Technology (2001)
7. Jaeger, H.: Short Term Memory in Echo State Networks. Technical Report GMD Report 152, German National Research Center for Information Technology (2001)
8. Jaeger, H.: Tutorial on Training Recurrent Neural Networks. Available on: http://www.ais.fraunhofer.de/INDY/herbert/ESNTutorial/ (2002) release September / October, 2002
9. Kolen, J.F.: The Origin of Clusters in Recurrent Neural Network State Space. In: Proceedings from the Sixteenth Annual Conference of the Cognitive Science Society. Hillsdale, NJ: Lawrence Erlbaum Associates (1994) 508–513
10. Kolen, J.F.: Recurrent Networks: State Machines or Iterated Function Systems? In: Touretzky, D.S., Elman, J.L., Mozer, M.C., Smolensky, P., Weigend A.S. (eds): Proceedings of the 1993 Connectionist Models Summer School. Erlbaum Associates, Hillsdale, NJ (1994) 203–210
11. Tiňo, P., Čerňanský, M., Beňušková, L.: Markovian Architectural Bias of Recurrent Neural Networks. Accepted to IEEE Transactions on Neural Networks
12. Tiňo, P., Čerňanský, M., Beňušková, L.: Markovian Architectural Bias of Recurrent Neural Networks. In: Sinčák, P., et al. (eds): Intelligent Technologies – Theory and Applications. IOS Press (2002) 203–210
13. Werbos, P.J.: Backpropagation through Time; What It Does and How to Do It. Proceedings of the IEEE **78** (1990) 1550–1560
14. Williams, R.J., Zipser, D.: Gradient-Based Learning Algorithms for Recurrent Networks and Their Computational Complexity. In: Chauvin, Y., Rumelhart, D.E. (eds): Back-Propagation: Theory, Architectures and Applications. Lawrence Erlbaum Publishers, Hillsdale, N.J. (1995) 433–486

Processing XPath Expressions
in Relational Databases

Tadeusz Pankowski

Institute of Control and Information Engineering,
Poznan University of Technology, Poland,
Tadeusz.Pankowski@put.poznan.pl

Abstract. Research on processing XML documents gained much activity in recent times. XML query languages are mostly based on XPath expressions, which are used to select parts of XML documents. So, methods defining semantics for XPath expressions are of special importance. In the paper we propose a relational semantics for XPath expressions. The semantics consists of four semantic functions defined over specific categories of XPath expressions and over contexts determined by the current state of computation. The definition is all sound, complete and expressive. We show that semantic functions can be naturally encoded in SQL and used to query XML documents stored in relational database. Some relevant optimization problems are also discussed.

1 Introduction

XPath (XML Path Language) has been proposed by W3C [1] as a language for selecting parts of an XML document. XPath expressions are also used as core elements in other XML query languages such as XQuery [2], XSLT [3], XPointer [4], and in some specific applications [5], [6]. XML document, on which XPath expressions operate, is modeled as a tree of nodes of different types, including element, attribute, and text nodes. XPath expressions can identify these nodes based on their types, names, values, and positions, as well as the relationship of a node to other nodes in the document. Such a model of XML documents is referred to as Document Object Model (DOM) [7].

Two different approaches to process XPath expressions can be distinguished: (1) XML document is fully represented in a repository; (2) XML document is processed as a stream. In this paper we adopt the former approach and assume that XML documents are represented in a relational database. There is a number of papers discussing the problem of representing and processing XML documents within relational database system [5], [8], [9], [10], [11], [12], [13], [14]. The main advantage of such approach is that it is reasonable to use the mature and reliable relational technology to process queries against XML documents or other semistructured data. However, dealing with such problems as recursion, ordering and nesting, which are inherent in XML data and XPath expressions, is not natural in flat relational algebra [15]. On the other hand, highly expressive

P. Van Emde Boas et al. (Eds.): SOFSEM 2004, LNCS 2932, pp. 265–276, 2004.
© Springer-Verlag Berlin Heidelberg 2004

languages are to complex in comparison with needs for processing XPath expressions [16]. Such problems as ordering and nesting can be simulated (encoded) in flat relational algebra, others (recursion and transitive closure) require extension of flat relational operations [15].

In this paper, we propose a method for processing XPath expressions in relational databases, and show how it could be efficiently implemented using SQL programming facilities provided by commercial RDBMS. The main contributions of this paper are the following:

1. We specify XPath expressions using semantic functions defined by means of relational operations that can be easily expressed as SQL statements. The important feature of the specification is its coherence with semantics of XPath proposed in [1] and [17].
2. A special attention we paid on contexts in which semantic functions implementing XPath expressions are evaluated. We define four semantic functions: $\mathbb{E}$ – for a path expression and a given context returns a new context containing the resulting ordered set of nodes; $\mathbb{Q}$ – for a predicate and a given context returns a truth value, $\mathbb{V}$ – computes a value of a path expression in a given context, and $\mathbb{P}$ – returns a value of a position function reflecting ordering of document nodes in a given context.
3. We discuss a relational representation of XML documents as well as processing XPath queries using SQL. Some optimization techniques are also addressed – some of them apply optimization techniques developed for relational databases, some others, concerning XPath minimization and indexing, are under intensive investigations [14], [18], [19], [20], [21].

The structure of the paper is as follows. In Section 2 we review basic notions concerning XML documents as well as syntax of XPath expressions. In Section 3 we propose relational definition for XPath expressions and illustrate its usefulness be an example. In Section 4 some optimization issues are discussed. Section 5 concludes and summarizes the considerations.

2   XML Data and XPath Expressions

An XML document is a textual representation of data and consists of hierarchically nested element structure starting with a root element. The basic component in XML is an element. An element consists of start-tag, the corresponding end-tag and content, i.e. the structure between the tags, which can consists of elements and texts. With elements we can associate attributes.

In the XQuery/XPath Data Model proposed by the W3C [7], an XML document is represented by an ordered node-labeled tree (data tree) which includes a concept of node identity. A document order is defined on all the nodes, except attributes, in a document. The document node (the root) is the first node. Order of nodes is determined by their representation in the XML. A node in a data tree conforms to one of the seven node kinds: *root*, *element*, *attribute*, *text*, *namespace, processing instruction,* and *comment.* We restrict our attention to four first of them.

In Fig. 1 there is a sample XML document, that will be used as the running example, and its data tree. Note that every node of the data tree has a unique identifier, and may have a label or value associated with it. Additionally, each node, except attributes, is associated with a pair of numbers, where predecessor denotes the order of the node, and the successor indicates the number of descendent nodes of the node. Such numbering schema is called *extended preorder numbering* [21], and will be discussed later in Section 4.

```
<bib>                                    <book title="SQL" price="200">
  <book title="XML" price="100">           Very good
    <author>                               <author> Eva </author>
        <name> Bill </name>                <author>
        Nice fellow                          <name> Mary </name>
    </author>                                <address> Warsaw </address>
    <author> Eva </author>                 </author>
  </book>                                 </book>
                                        </bib>
```

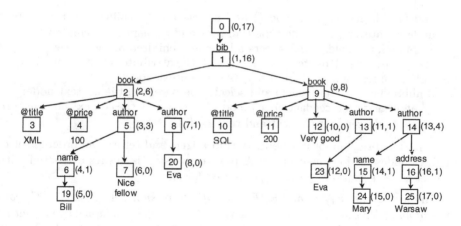

Fig. 1. A sample XML document and its data tree with extended preorder numbering

The *root node* (denoted by 0 in Fig. 1) identifies the document and does not have any label. An *element node* can have zero or more children of type element or text, and zero or more attribute nodes. The element node is the parent of each of its attributes; however, an attribute node is not a child of the element node. Label of an element node is the name specified as the tag. An *attribute node* has a string-value and a label that is preceded with "@". A *text node* cannot have any child node. The text node can appear as the child of an element node.

A text node has a string-value and does not have any label. Ordering of nodes in a data tree (the *document order*) is induced by the left-down traversing of the tree.

For selecting parts of XML documents represented by means of a data tree one can use XPath expressions [1].

Definition 1. *An XPath expression is an expression conforming to the following syntax (we consider only forward and the parent axes, and use the abbreviated syntax):*

$L ::= /E \mid //E$
$E ::= label \mid @label \mid \text{text}() \mid \text{node}() \mid * \mid @* \mid . \mid .. \mid E/E \mid E//E \mid E|E \mid E[Q]$
$Q ::= E \mid E\ \theta\ V \mid \text{position}()\ \theta\ V \mid \text{last}()\ \theta\ V \mid \text{position}()\ \theta\ \text{last}()$
$\qquad \mid Q \wedge Q \mid Q \vee Q \mid \neg Q$
$V ::= E \mid Const$
$\theta ::= < \mid \leq \mid > \mid \geq \mid = \mid \neq$ □

The meaning of abbreviations used in Definition 1 is [1]:

- *label* abbreviates child::*label* and selects the *label* element children of the context node;
- @*label* abbreviates attribute::*label* and selects the *label* attribute of the context node;
- text() abbreviates child::text() and selects all text node children of the context node;
- node() abbreviates child::node() and selects all the children of the context node, whatever their node type (i.e. text and element node children);
- * abbreviates child::* and selects all element children of the context node;
- @* abbreviates attribute::* and selects all the attributes of the context node;
- . abbreviates self::node() and selects the context node;
- .. abbreviates parent::node() and selects the parent of the context node;
- // abbreviates descendant-or-self::node() and selects the context node as well as all its descendant element and text nodes.

A path expression locates nodes within a tree, and returns an ordered set of distinct nodes in document order. A path expression is always evaluated with respect to an *evaluation context* (or *context* for short).

Definition 2. *Let E_1/E_2 and $E_1[E_2]$ be path expressions. A context for E_2 consists of an ordered set S (the context set) of distinct nodes obtained by evaluating E_1 in some context for E_1. Every node x in S is called the context node. The full context, needed for evaluating position functions* position() *and* last()*, includes also position of x in S and the cardinality of S.* □

A path expression consists of one or more steps separated by '/'. Each step selects a set of nodes. A step begins at the context node, navigates to those nodes that are reachable from the context node via a predefined *axis*, and selects some subset of the reachable nodes. A step has three parts: an *axis*, a node *test*, and zero or more *predicates*: an *axis* specifies the relationship between the nodes selected by the step and the context node; a *test* specifies the node type and label of the selected nodes; a *predicate* is a further filter for the set of selected nodes.

3   Processing Path Expressions

In this section, we specify a method for processing XPath expressions by means of relational operations. We assume that each XML document is represented in a relational database and is an instance of the database schema.

Definition 3. *A document database is an instance D over a document database schema **DSch** consisting of the following set of relational schemes:*

$$DSch = \{\text{Root}(rN),\ \text{Node}(retN,\ order,\ size),\ \text{EE}(reN,\ eChild),\ \text{EA}(eN,\ aN),$$
$$\text{ET}(eN,\ tChild),\ \text{Label}(eaN,\ label),\ \text{Value}(atN,\ value)\} \qquad \square$$

Additionally, we will use two relations, which are views over base relations: Parent(etaN, rePar), and DescOrSelf(retN, retDos).

The attribute name αN in relational schemes denotes a *node identifier*, where the prefix α indicates the kind of the node: r, e, a, t occurring in α denote *root*, *element*, *attribute*, and *text* kind of nodes, respectively; similarly for αChild, αPar and αDos.

The meaning of relations in a document database is the following:

- for $r \in \text{Root}(rN)$, r is the root node, i.e. the document identifier of an XML document represented in the document database;
- for $(n, o, s) \in \text{Node}(retN,\ order,\ size)$, o is the *order* and s is the *size* of a node n according to the *extended preorder numbering schema*(see Fig. 1);
- for $(n, e) \in \text{EE}(reN,\ eChild)$, e is an element node child of a node n;
- for $(e, a) \in \text{EA}(eN,\ aN)$, a is an attribute node of an element node e;
- for $(e, t) \in \text{ET}(eN,\ tChild)$, t is a text node child of an element node e;
- for $(n, l) \in \text{Label}(eaN,\ label)$, l is the label of a node n;
- for $(n, v) \in \text{Value}(atN,\ value)$, v is the value of a node n;
- for $(n, p) \in \text{Parent}(etaN,\ rePar)$, p is the parent node of a node n;
- for $(n, d) \in \text{DescOrSelf}(retN,\ retDos)$, d is a node descendent of a node n, or d is identical with n.

Further on, we will need an *extended context table* $\Delta(C, X)$ storing relationship between a context node and a context set obtained from this context node.

Definition 4. *Let E_1/E_2 (or $E_1[E_2]$) be a path expression, and S_c be the result of evaluating E_1 in a context (C, c), $c \in C$. An extended context table for E_2 is the set of tuples: $\Delta(C, X) = \{[C : c, X : x] \mid c \in C, x \in S_c\}$.* $\qquad \square$

In Table 1 we give definitions of semantic functions for evaluating XPath expressions in terms of relational data model, where we define meaning of four semantic functions: $\mathbb{E}$, $\mathbb{Q}$, $\mathbb{V}$, and $\mathbb{P}$ (Δ is an extended context table):

- $\mathbb{E}_{/E}()$ and $\mathbb{E}_E(\Delta)$ return extended context tables, E is a path expression;
- $\mathbb{Q}_Q(\Delta, c, x)$ returns true or false, Q is a predicate, $(c, x) \in \Delta$;
- $\mathbb{V}_V(c, x)$ returns a value, V is a path expression or a constant, the pair (c, x) is taken from some extended context table;
- $\mathbb{P}_{pfun}(\Delta, c, x)$ returns an integer, $pfun \in \{\text{position}(),\ \text{last}()\}$, $(c, x) \in \Delta$.

Table 1. Relational definition of XPath expressions

$\mathbb{E}_{/E}(root)$:= $\mathbb{E}_E(\{[C:NULL, X:root]\})$

$\mathbb{E}_{//E}(root)$:= $\mathbb{E}_{/\text{desc-or-self::node}()/E}(\{[C:NULL, X:root]\})$

$\mathbb{E}_{\text{desc-or-self::node}()}(\Delta)$:= select R.X as C, D.retDos as X
  from Δ as R, DescOrSelf as D where R.X = D.retN

$\mathbb{E}_{label}(\Delta)$:= select R.X as C, EE.eChild as X
  from Δ as R, EE, Label as L
  where R.X = EE.reN and EE.eChild = L.eaN
  and L.Label = $label$

$\mathbb{E}_{@label}(\Delta)$:= select R.X as C, EA.aN as X
  from Δ as R, EA, Label as L
  where R.X = EA.eN and EA.aN = L.eaN
  and L.Label = $label$

$\mathbb{E}_{\text{text}()}(\Delta)$:= select R.X as C, ET.tChild as X
  from Δ as R, ET where R.X = ET.eN

$\mathbb{E}_{*}(\Delta)$:= select R.X as C, EE.eChild as X
  from Δ as R, EE where R.X = EE.eN

$\mathbb{E}_{\text{node}()}(\Delta)$:= $\mathbb{E}_{\text{text}()|*}(\Delta)$

$\mathbb{E}_{@*}(\Delta)$:= select R.X as C, EA.aN as X
  from Δ as R, EA where R.X = EA.eN

$\mathbb{E}_{.}(\Delta)$:= select R.X as C, R.X as X from Δ as R

$\mathbb{E}_{..}(\Delta)$:= select R.X as C, P.rePar as X
  from Δ as R, Parent as P where R.X = P.etaN

$\mathbb{E}_{E_1/E_2}(\Delta)$:= $\mathbb{E}_{E_2}(\mathbb{E}_{E_1}(\Delta))$

$\mathbb{E}_{E_1//E_2}(\Delta)$:= $\mathbb{E}_{E_1/\text{desc-or-self::node}()/E_2}(\Delta)$

$\mathbb{E}_{E_1|E_2}(\Delta)$:= select * from $\mathbb{E}_{E_1}(\Delta)$ union select * from $\mathbb{E}_{E_2}(\Delta)$

$\mathbb{E}_{E[Q]}(\Delta)$:= select * from $\mathbb{E}_E(\Delta)$ as R where $\mathbb{Q}_Q(\mathbb{E}_E(\Delta), R.C, R.X))$

$\mathbb{Q}_{Q_1 \wedge Q_2}(\Delta, c, x)$:= $\mathbb{Q}_{Q_1}(\Delta, c, x)$ and $\mathbb{Q}_{Q_2}(\Delta, c, x)$

$\mathbb{Q}_{Q_1 \vee Q_2}(\Delta, c, x)$:= $\mathbb{Q}_{Q_1}(\Delta, c, x)$ or $\mathbb{Q}_{Q_2}(\Delta, c, x)$

$\mathbb{Q}_{\neg Q}(\Delta, c, x)$:= not $\mathbb{Q}_Q(\Delta, c, x)$

$\mathbb{Q}_E(\Delta, c, x)$:= exists(select * from $\mathbb{E}_E(\{[C:c, X:x]\}))$

$\mathbb{Q}_{E\theta V}(\Delta, c, x)$:= $\mathbb{V}_E(c, x)\ \theta\ \mathbb{V}_V(c, x)$

$\mathbb{V}_E(c, x)$:= select V.value from $\mathbb{E}_E(\{[C:c, X:x]\})$ as R, Value as V
  where R.X = V.atN

$\mathbb{V}_{Const}(c, x)$:= $Const$

$\mathbb{Q}_{\text{position}()\theta V}(\Delta, c, x)$:= $\mathbb{P}_{\text{position}()}(\Delta, c, x)\ \theta\ \mathbb{V}_V(c, x)$

$\mathbb{Q}_{\text{last}()\theta V}(\Delta, c, x)$:= $\mathbb{P}_{\text{last}()}(\Delta, c, x)\ \theta\ \mathbb{V}_V(c, x)$

$\mathbb{Q}_{\text{position}()\theta\text{last}()}(\Delta, c, x)$:= $\mathbb{P}_{\text{position}()}(\Delta, c, x)\ \theta\ \mathbb{P}_{\text{last}()}(\Delta, c, x)$

$\mathbb{P}_{\text{position}()}(\Delta, c, x)$:= select R.K from (select R1.C, R1.X, count(*) as K
  from Δ as R1, Δ as R2,
  Node as P1, Node as P2
  where R1.C=R2.C and R1.X=P1.retN
  and R2.X=P2.retN and P2.order $<=$ P1.order
  group by R1.C, R1.X) as R
  where R.X = x

$\mathbb{P}_{\text{last}()}(\Delta, c, x)$:= select R.N from (select R1.C, R1.X, count(*) as N
  from Δ as R1, Δ as R2,
  where R1.C = R2.C
  group by R1.C, R1.X) as R
  where R.X = x

Example 1. Evaluate the following XPath expression against data tree from Fig. 1:

`L=/bib/book[@price>=100]/author[position()<last() ∨ //text()='Warsaw']`

Fragments of the evaluation are shown in Table 2 and some intermediate extended context tables are depicted in Fig. 2. In Table 3 are definitions of semantic functions written in Transact-SQL (SQL programming language in MS SQL Server 2000). Answer to the query is included in the X column of Δ_6, i.e. it is the result of (see Table 3):

`select R.X from L(0) as R`

□

Table 2. Application of relational semantics to (fragments of) XPath expression from Example 1

Expression and its evaluation	*Result*
1. $\mathbb{E}_{/\text{bib}}(0) := \mathbb{E}_{\text{bib}}(\{[C:NULL, X:0]\})$	Δ_1
2. $\mathbb{E}_{/\text{bib}/\text{book}}(0) := \mathbb{E}_{\text{book}}(\Delta_1)$	Δ_2
3. $\mathbb{E}_{/\text{bib}/\text{book}[@\text{price}>=100]}(0) :=$	
$:= \text{select} * \text{from } \Delta_2 \text{ as R where } \mathbb{Q}_{@\text{price}>=100}(\Delta_2, R.C, R.X)$	Δ_3
$\mathbb{Q}_{@\text{price}>=100}(\Delta_2, 1, 2) := \mathbb{V}_{@\text{price}}(1,2) >= \mathbb{V}_{100}(1,2)$	true
$\mathbb{V}_{@\text{price}}(1,2) := \text{select V.value from } \mathbb{E}_{@\text{price}}(\{[C:1, X:2]\}) \text{ as R, Value as V}$	
$\text{where } R.X = V.\text{atN}$	T_1
$\mathbb{E}_{@\text{price}}(\{[C:1, X:2]\}) := \text{select R.X as C, EA.aN as X}$	
$\text{from } \{[C:1, X:2]\} \text{ as R, EA, Label as L where } R.X = EA.eN$	
$\text{and } EA.aN = L.eaN \text{ and } L.\text{Label} = @\text{price}$	Δ_4
$\mathbb{V}_{100}(1,2) := 100$	100
4. $\mathbb{E}_{/\text{bib}/\text{book}[@\text{price}>=100]/\text{author}}(0) := \mathbb{E}_{\text{author}}(\Delta_3)$	Δ_5
5. $\mathbb{E}_L(0) :=$	
$:= \text{select} * \text{from } \Delta_5 \text{ as R where } \mathbb{Q}_{\text{position}()<\text{last}()\vee//\text{text}()='\text{Warsaw}'}(\Delta_5, R.C, R.X)$	Δ_6
$\mathbb{Q}_{\text{position}()<\text{last}()\vee//\text{text}()='\text{Warsaw}'}(\Delta_5, 9, 14) :=$	
$:= \mathbb{Q}_{\text{position}()<\text{last}()}(\Delta_5, 9, 14) \text{ or } \mathbb{Q}_{//\text{text}()='\text{Warsaw}'}(\Delta_5, 9, 14)$	true
$\mathbb{Q}_{\text{position}()<\text{last}()}(\Delta_5, 9, 14) := \mathbb{P}_{\text{position}()}(\Delta_5, 9, 14) < \mathbb{P}_{\text{last}()}(\Delta_5, 9, 14)$	false
$\mathbb{Q}_{//\text{text}()='\text{Warsaw}'}(\Delta_5, 9, 14) := \mathbb{V}_{//\text{text}()}(9, 14) = \mathbb{V}_{'\text{Warsaw}'}(9, 14)$	true
$\mathbb{V}_{//\text{text}()}(9, 14) := \text{select V.value from } \mathbb{E}_{//}(\{[C:9, X:14]\}) \text{ as R,}$	
$\text{Value as V where } R.X = V.\text{atN}$	T_2
$\mathbb{E}_{//}(\{[C:9, X:14]\})$	Δ_7

Fig. 2. Result tables produced by evaluations from Table 2

Table 3. Implementation of semantic functions used to process XPath expression from Example 1

```
create function L(@root int)
returns table as return
  select R.C, R.X from "/bib/book[@price>=100]/author"(@root) as R
  where dbo.position(@root, R.X) < dbo.last(@root, R.X) or
    dbo."V_//text()"(R.X) = 'Warsaw'

create function "V_//text()"(@node int) returns varchar(20)
begin declare @value varchar(20)
  select @value = V.value from "T_//text()"(@node) R, Value V
  where R.X = V.atN
  return @value
end

create function "T_//text()"(@node int)
returns table as return
  select @node as C, ET.tChild as X
  from  DescOrSelf as D, ET where D.retN = @node and D.retDos = ET.eN)

create function last(@root int, @node int) returns int
begin
  declare @last int
  select @last = R.N
  from(
    select R1.C,R1.X,count(*) as N
    from "/bib/book[@price>=100]/author"(@root) as R1,
         "/bib/book[@price>=100]/author"(@root) as R2
    where R1.C = R2.C
    group by R1.C,R1.X) as R
  where R.X = @node
  return @last
end

create function position(@root int, @node int) returns int
begin
  declare @pos int
  select @pos = R.K from
  (select R1.C, R1.X, count(*) as K
   from "/bib/book[@price>=100]/author"(@root) as R1,
        "/bib/book[@price>=100]/author"(@root) as R2,
        Node as P1, Node as P2
   where R1.C = R2.C and R1.X = P1.retN and R2.X = P2.retN and
         P2.[order] <= P1.[order]
   group by R1.C, R1.X) as R where R.X = @node
  return @pos
end

create function "/bib/book[@price>=100]/author"(@root int)
returns table as return
  select R.X as C, EE.eChild as X
  from  "/bib/book[@price>=100]"(@root) as R, EE, Label as L
  where R.X = EE.reN and EE.eChild = L.eaN and L.label = 'Author'

create function "/bib/book[@price>=100]"(@root int)
returns table as return
  select * from "/bib/book"(@root) as R
  where dbo.V_price(R.X) >= 100

create function V_price(@node int)
returns money
begin
  declare @price int
  select @price = V.value from A_price(@node) R, Value V
  where R.X = V.atN
  return @price
end
```

Table 3. (cont.) Implementation of semantic functions used to process XPath expression from Example 1

```
create function A_price(@node int)
returns table as return
  select @node as C, EA.aN as X from  EA, Label as L
  where @node = EA.eN and EA.aN = L.eaN and L.Label = 'Price'

create function "/bib/book"(@root int)
returns table as return
  select R.X as C, EE.eChild as X
  from  "/bib"(@root) as R, EE, Label as L
  where R.X = EE.reN and EE.eChild = L.eaN and L.Label = 'Book'

create function "/bib"(@root int)
returns table as return
  select R.X as C, EE.eChild as X
  from  "/"(@root) as R, EE, Label as L
  where R.X = EE.reN and EE.eChild = L.eaN and L.Label = 'Bib'

create function "/"(@root int)
returns table as return
  select NULL as C, @root as X
```

4   Optimization Issues

Optimization of processing XPath expressions in relational databases should consider: (a) *minimization* of XPath queries known also as the *containment problem*, which has recently received increasing attention [18], [19], [20]; (b) *materialization* of some intermediate tables to avoid multiple computation of the same table; (c) using *conventional optimization mechanisms* supported by relational systems (indexing, optimal query plans generation etc.).

Node-descendant and node-parent relationships. One of the most time consuming operation while processing XPath queries is that of obtaining descendant-or-self relationship between nodes of a document tree. To facilitate performing this operation we use the extended preorder numbering schema. The most important advantage of this method is that node-descendant relationship can be determined in constant time. The extended preorder numbering schema associates each node x in the document tree with a pair of numbers $(order, size)$, where *order* is the *extended preorder* of x, and *size* is the *range of descendants* denoting the number of descendants of x. In particular, the extended preorder can be equal to the preorder number (see Fig. 1), but usually it should be greater to reserve extra spaces to accommodate future insertions into the document tree without global reordering. Note that deleting a node does not cause renumbering the nodes. The following property is of crucial importance for computing the set of descendents of a node [21].

Lemma 1. *For every two triples $(x, o_x, s_x), (y, o_y, s_y) \in Node(retN, order, size)$, y is a descendant of x if and only if:*

$$o_x < o_y \leq o_x + s_x.$$

□

Using the above property we can effectively obtain the relation DescOr-Self(retN,retDos). The relation Parent(etaN,rePar) is the union of three relations: EE, EA, and ET. So we have the following definitions:

```
create view DescOrSelf(retN,retDos)          create view Parent(etaN,rePar)
as                                           as
  select N.retN,D.retN                         select eChild,reN from EE
  from Node N, Node D                          union
  where N.retN=D.retN or                       select aN,eN from EA
    N.[order]<D.[order] and                    union
    D.[order]<=N.[order]+N.[size]              select tChild,eN from ET
```

Top-down vs. bottom-up processing. As was stated in [22], the optimal query plan for processing XML data depends not only on the values in the database but also on the shape of the graph containing the data, and this additional factor makes optimization of queries over XML data both important and difficult. In order to process an XPath query like

    (Q1) : /bib/book[//text()='Warsaw']

we can traverse the XML data tree in either *top-down* or *bottom-up* fashion.

In the top down approach, we start from the root and select all paths starting from a bib element. Then, for every result, we find paths with the next element being book . It is achieved by joining (using nested-loop index join) the result extended context table with the EE relation (to test element-child relationship) and the Label relation (to test label of the child node). To test the predicate, all paths leading from nodes from a result extended context table into a text node should be examined to find out whether a value of the text node is 'Warsaw' or not. This implies that it is absolutely necessary to examine every possible path starting from each node determined by /bib/book, because it is not usually known whether the path ends in a text node and whether the text node has the value we are looking for. Using top-down strategy we have to examine a large portion of data tree, sometimes the entire tree will be traversed.

The cost of tree traversal may be reduced by a *bottom-up* strategy. To answer the (Q1) query in this strategy, we first identify all text nodes that satisfy the [text()='Warsaw'] predicate by using an appropriate value index. Once we have a node satisfying the predicate, we traverse backwards the tree using the Parent relation and/or the reverse of the DescOrSelf relation, and examine whether there exist ancestor nodes with desired labels. The advantage of this approach is that we start with nodes satisfying some predicates and avoid exploring path only to find out that the final value does not satisfy the predicate. Bottom-up is not always better than top-down, and its cost might be sometimes even higher than that of top-down approach [22]. Additionally, the bottom-up strategy may not be used when position functions, position() or last(), are involved into predicate (see Example 1).

In [22] a hybrid strategy has been proposed that traverses in both top-down and bottom-up fashions, meeting in the middle of a path expression. An approach based on decomposition of a path expression has been described in [21], where a complex path expression is decomposed into several simple path expressions. Each simple expression produces an intermediate result that can be used in the subsequent stage of processing.

5 Conclusions

In the paper we have proposed a relational semantics for XPath expressions. The semantics consists of four semantic functions defined over specific categories of XPath expressions and over contexts determined by the current state of computation. The definition is all sound, complete and expressive. The presented approach assumes that processed XML documents are stored in relational database, and has the following advantages:

- It allows to define semantics of XPath expressions by means of relational operations; the definition is coherent with this suggested in the standard [2] and proposed in other works (e.g. [17], [23]). In particular, it allows for operating on ordered data trees representing XML documents.
- The semantic functions can be easy encoded in standard SQL and processed in any SQL database system.

The method discussed in the paper has been developed in the context of systems for querying and transforming semistructured data and XML documents [5], [6]. Currently, we are investigating the possibility to increase efficiency of processing. In order to do this, some optimization problems discussed in the previous section are under investigations.

References

1. XML Path Language (XPath) 2.0, W3C Working Draft. (2002) www.w3.org/TR/xpath20
2. XQuery 1.0: An XML Query Language. W3C Working Draft. (2002) www.w3.org/TR/xquery
3. XSL Transformations (XSLT) 2.0. W3C Working Draft. (2002) www.w3.org/TR/xslt20
4. XML Pointer Language (XPointer). W3C Working Draft. (2002) www.w3.org/TR/xptr
5. Pankowski, T.: XML SQL: An XML Query Language Based on SQL and Path Tables. In: XML-Based Data Management and Multimedia Engineering – EDBT 2002 Workshops. Lecture Notes in Computer Science **2490** (2002) 184–209
6. Pankowski, T.: Transformation of XML Data Using an Unranked Tree Transducer. In: E-Commerce and Web Technologies, 4th International Conference, EC-Web 2003. Lecture Notes in Computer Science **2738** (2003) 259–269
7. XQuery 1.0 and XPath 2.0 Data Model. W3C Working Draft. (2002) www.w3.org/TR/query-datamodel
8. Deutsch, A., Fernandez, M., Suciu, D.: Storing Semistructured Data with STORED. SIGMOD Record **28** (1999) 431–442

9. Florescu, D., Kossmann, D.: Storing and Querying XML Data Using an RDBMS. IEEE Data Engineering Bulletin **22** (1999) 27–34
10. Manolescu, I., Florescu, D., Kossmann, D.: Pushing XML Queries inside Relational Databases. INRIA, Rapport de recherche 4112 (2001)
11. Shanmugasundaram, J., Tufte, K., Zhang, C., He, G., DeWitt, D.J., Naughton, J.F.: Relational Databases for Querying XML Documents: Limitations and Opportunities. In: Proc. of the 25th International Conference on Very Large Data Bases, VLDB 1999, Edinburgh, Scotland. (1999) 302–314
12. Yoshikawa, M., Amagasa, T., Shimura, T., Uemura, S.: XRel: A Path-Based Approach to Storage and Retrieval of XML Documents Using Relational Databases. ACM Transactions on Internet Technology **1** (2001) 110–141
13. Harding, P.J., Li, Q., Moon, B.: XISS/R: XML Indexing and Storage System Using RDBMS. In: Proc. of the 29th International Conference on Very Large Data Bases, VLDB 2003, Berlin, Germany. (2003) 1073–1076
14. Rho, H., Hou, W.C., Che, D., Wang, C.F.: Querying Semistructured Data Efficiently. Database and Expert Systems Application, DEXA 2003, Lecture Notes in Computer Science **2736** (2003) 18–27
15. Abiteboul, S., Hull, R., Vianu, V.: Foundations of Databases. Addison-Wesley, Reading, Massachusetts (1995)
16. Abiteboul, S., Buneman, P., Suciu, D.: Data on the Web. From Relational to Semistructured Data and XML. Morgan Kaufmann, San Francisco (2000)
17. Wadler, P.: Two Semantics for XPath. www.research.avayalabs.com/user/wadler/ (2000)
18. Miklau, G., Suciu, D.: Containment and Equivalence for an XPath Fragment. In: Proc. of the 21st ACM Symposium on Principles of Database Systems (PODS-02), ACM Press (2002) 65–76
19. Flesca, S., Furfaro, F., Masciari, E.: On the Minimization of XPath Queries. In: Proc. of the 29th International Conference on Very Large Data Bases, VLDB 2003, Berlin, Germany. (2003) 153–164
20. Wood, P.T.: Minimising Simple XPath Expressions. In: Proc. of the 4th Int. Workshop on the Web and Databases, WebDB 2001. (2001) 13–18
21. Li, Q., Moon, B.: Indexing and Querying XML Data for Regular Path Expressions. In: Proc. of the 27th International Conference on Very Large Data Bases, VLDB 2001, Rome, Italy. (2001) 361–370
22. McHugh, J., Widom, J.: Query Optimization for XML. In: Proc. of the 25th International Conference on Very Large Data Bases, VLDB 1999, Edinburgh, Scotland, UK. (1999) 315–326
23. Gottlob, G., Koch, C., Pichler, R.: Efficient Algorithms for Processing XPath Queries. In: Proc. of the 28th International Conference on Very Large Data Bases, VLDB 2002, Hong Kong, China. (2002) 95–106

An Embedded Language Approach to Router Specification in Curry*

J. Guadalupe Ramos[1], Josep Silva[2], and Germán Vidal[2]

[1] Instituto Tecnológico de La Piedad
Av. Tecnológico 2000, Meseta los Laureles, La Piedad, Mich., México
guadalupe@dsic.upv.es
[2] DSIC, UPV, Camino de Vera s/n, E-46022 Valencia, Spain
{jsilva,gvidal}@dsic.upv.es

Abstract. The development of modern routers require a significant effort to be designed, built, and verified. While hardware routers are faster, they are difficult to configure and maintain. Software routers, on the other hand, are slower but much more flexible, easier to configure and maintain, less expensive, etc. Recently, a modular architecture and toolkit for building software routers and other packet processors has been introduced: the Click system. It includes a specification language with features for declaring and connecting router elements and for designing abstractions.

In this work, we introduce the domain-specific language Rose for the specification of software routers. Rose is embedded in Curry, a modern declarative multi-paradigm language. An advantage of this approach is that we have available a framework where router specifications can be transformed, optimized, verified, etc., by using a number of existing formal techniques already developed for Curry programs. Furthermore, we show that the features of Curry are particularly useful to specify router configurations with a high-level of abstraction. Our first experiments point out that the proposed methodology is both useful and practical.

1 Introduction

In heterogeneous environments, special devices to interconnect different technologies are often required. Within Internet networks, the *router* is that device. Basically, routers connect two or more networks and forward data packets between them. Thus, the primary function of a router is to determine the best path in a complex network. Originally, routers have been developed entirely as hardware components. However, there is a clear trend towards extending the set of functions that network routers should support. These new functions include, e.g., packet filtering, address translation, run proxies, performance monitoring, etc. The flexibility required to cope with all these new functions motivated the

---

* This work has been partially supported by CICYT TIC 2001-2705-C03-01, by the Generalitat Valenciana under grant CTIDIA/2002/205, and by the MCYT under grants HA2001-0059, HU2001-0019 and HI2000-0161.

P. Van Emde Boas et al. (Eds.): SOFSEM 2004, LNCS 2932, pp. 277–288, 2004.
© Springer-Verlag Berlin Heidelberg 2004

definition of so called *extensible routers* [6], which support run-time customization of router functionality.

The most important approaches to extensible routers are Scout, Router Plugins, and Click. In Scout [14], the basic abstraction unit is the *path*: a linear flow of data that starts at a source device and ends at a destination device. Each path is composed by *stages* that are instances from a specific *module*, which implements a well understood protocol (IP, TCP, etc). Scout provides tools to create, modify, schedule, and control paths. Implemented in the NetBSD operating system, Router Plugins allows users to write (limited) extensions to an IP router. These extensions can be placed at well known points—called *gates*—of the router's IP execution. Gates have been chosen to suit a wide variety of applications, like routing, packet scheduling, and security processing. Finally, Click [11], [10] is based on composing many simple *elements* to produce a system that implements the desired behavior. Each element may have multiple *ports* to connect it to other elements. These elements control every aspect of the behavior of the router, from communicating with devices to packet modification to queuing, dropping policies and packet scheduling. New configurations can be built by gluing elements together with a simple language (which is also called Click).

According to [6], Click is the most flexible of the three architectures above. Its ability to form virtually any configuration from the set of elements gives the programmer a high degree of freedom to modify routers incrementally and to add new services. On the negative side, this flexibility also implies that Click provides very little guidance on what constitutes a well-formed and meaningful configuration. For this purpose, Click already includes a set of tools which help the user to deal with complex configurations. Nevertheless, the inclusion of *semantic* aspects in Click (e.g., an abstract description of each element, with the number of input and output ports, how it modifies the passing packets, etc) would be very useful for the programmer.

In this paper we introduce Rose, a domain-specific language—which is based on Click—for router specification. Rose is *embedded* in Curry [9], a declarative multi-paradigm language which integrates features from the most popular declarative paradigms (namely, functional, logic and concurrent programming). Therefore, router configurations are first-class objects in Curry, which allows us to use the higher-level facilities of Curry, such as higher-order combinators, constraints, laziness, logical variables, etc. Moreover, there already exists a number of tools for transforming, optimizing, and verifying Curry programs—with a solid theoretical basis—that are also available to the programmer. Let us clarify that we do not intend to compete with Click. Rather, our aim is to develop a complementary approach. For instance, one can use Rose during the first design phases and, then, (automatically) translate the developed specification into Click. One can also translate an existing Click configuration into Rose to perform some transformation and analyses and, then, translate the result back into Click. In other words, we do not plan to develop software routers in Curry (as Click does), only their semantic *specification*. Consequently, Rose elements only contain high level information which is useful for analysis, simulation, verification, etc. The main advantage of our proposal is that it provides an appropriate basis to develop specific analysis and optimization tools (while only a few such tools already exists for Click and, moreover, they have not been formally verified).

This paper is organized as follows. Section 2 introduces an overview of the language Curry. In Section 3, we present our approach to router specification: Section 3.1 reviews the Click language, Section 3.2 presents the specification of Click elements in Rose, Section 3.3 defines some composition operators to build larger components, and Section 3.4 briefly describes the implementation of Rose. Finally, Section 4 discusses some related works and Section 5 concludes and presents some directions for future work.

2   The Curry Language

Curry [9] is a declarative multi-paradigm language which combines in a seamless way features from functional programming (nested expressions, higher-order functions, lazy evaluation), logic programming (logical variables, partial data structures, built-in search), and concurrent programming (concurrent evaluation of expressions with synchronization on logical variables). The development of Curry is an international initiative intended to provide a common platform for the research, teaching and application of integrated functional logic languages.

In Curry, functions are defined by a sequence of rules (or equations) of the form

$$f \quad t_1 \ldots t_n = e$$

where $t_1, \ldots, t_n$ are *constructor* terms and the right-hand side e is an *expression*. The left-hand side must not contain multiple occurrences of the same variable. Constructor terms may contain variables and constructor symbols, i.e., symbols which are not defined by the program rules. Functions can be also defined by *conditional equations* which have the form

$$f \quad t_1 \ldots t_n \,|\, c = e$$

where the condition (or *guard*) c can be either a Boolean function or a constraint. Elementary constraints are **success**, which is always satisfied, and *equational constraints* $e_1 =:= e_2$ between two expressions. The latter is satisfied if both expressions are reducible to a same ground constructor term (i.e., the so-called *strict equality* [13]). Operationally, an equational constraint $c_1 =:= c_2$ is solved by evaluating e_1 and e_2 to unifiable constructor terms.

We can define *non-deterministic* functions either by providing several rules with overlapping left-hand sides or by introducing *free variables* (i.e., variables that do not occur in the left-hand side) in the condition or in the right-hand side of the rules. For instance, the following function non-deterministically inserts an element in a list (where [] denotes the empty list and x:xs a list with first element x and tail xs):

```
insert x []     = [x]
insert x (y:ys) = x : y : ys
insert x (y:ys) = y : insert x ys
```

Local declarations can be defined by using the let or where constructs. The following Curry function splits a list into two lists containing the smaller and larger elements:

```
split e []               = ([], [])
split e (x:xs) | e >= x  = (x:l, r)
               | e < x   = (l, x:r)
               where (l,r) = split e xs
```

Higher-order features include partial function applications and lambda abstractions. Function application is denoted by juxtaposition of the function and its argument. For instance, the well-known function map is defined in Curry by

```
map f []     = []
map f (x:xs) = f x : map f xs
```

Lambda abstractions—anonymous functions—are expressions of the following form: $\x_1 \ldots x_n$ -> exp. The application of the above lambda abstraction to input arguments $e_1, \ldots, e_n$ produces the same result as the call "foo $e_1 \ldots e_n$", where foo is defined by "foo $x_1 \ldots x_n$ = exp". Curry also allows the use of functions which are not defined in the user's program, like arithmetic operators, usual higher-order functions (map, foldr, etc.), basic input/output facilities, etc.

We refer the interested reader to the report on the Curry language [9] for a detailed description of all the features of the multi-paradigm language Curry.

3   Specifying Click Routers

3.1   The Click Language

The Click programming language textually describes Click router configurations. Click has only two basic constructs which are enough to describe any configuration graph [10]: *declarations* create (instances of) elements and *connections* connect existing elements together. In order to build a router configuration, the user chooses a collection of *elements* and connects them via *ports* into a directed graph. For instance, the following graph shows several elements connected into a simple router that counts incoming packets and, then, throws them all away:

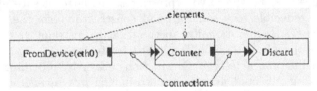

In the Click language, this router is specified as follows:

```
// Declarations              // Connections
src   :: FromDevice(eth0);    src -> ctr;
ctr   :: Counter;             ctr -> sink;
sink  :: Discard;
```

Basically, Click elements [10] fall into one of the following categories:

Packet sources. They spontaneously generate packets, either by reading them from the network, reading them from a dump file, creating them from specified data, or creating them from random data. They have one output and no inputs.

Packet sinks. They remove packets from the specified system, either by simply dropping them, sending them to the network, writing their contents to a dump file, or sending them to the Linux networking stack. They have one input and no outputs.

Packet modifiers. They are used to change packet data. They have one input and one (or two) outputs. Packets arriving on the input are modified and then emitted on the first output (the second output, if present, is for erroneous packets).

Routing elements. They choose where incoming packets should go based on a packet-independent switching algorithm, general characteristics of packet flow, or an examination of packet contents. For instance, a typical round-robin switch pushes each arriving packet to one of the outputs; the next packet will be pushed to the following output in round-robin order. They have one input and two or more outputs.

Scheduling elements. They choose packets from one of several possible packet sources. A Click packet scheduler is naturally implemented as an element with two or more inputs and one output. For instance, this element could react to requests for packets by choosing one of its inputs in turn until one produces a packet, pulling a packet from it, and returning that packet. When the next request is produced, it starts from the input after the one that last produced a packet. This amounts to a round-robin scheduler.

3.2   The Specification Language Rose: Basic Elements

Designing a new programming language implies a considerable amount of work: the definition of its syntax and semantics, the implementation of interpreters and compilers, the development of a number of useful tools for analysis, debugging, optimization, program manipulation, etc. An alternative approach is to define an *embedded* language, i.e., to develop libraries in some existing language—the *host* language—which allow us to define programs in the new language as *objects* in the host language. In this way, we can reuse the syntax, language features and tools of the host language.

In the following, we present the language Rose for the specification of Click routers. Since we do not want to define yet another specification language, we build Rose as an embedding in the multi-paradigm language Curry so that we can reuse the features and tools of a powerful declarative language. We use Curry because it has many useful properties for specification: the embedding is easy,[1] there are many features which are useful to describe routers (e.g., laziness, guarded rules, and higher-order combinators), and it allows the use of logical

---

[1] Indeed, Curry has already been used to embed other languages, e.g., a language for distributed programming [7].

features (like logical variables, non-determinism and search), which can be useful for simulation and testing (see below).

Let us summarize the main advantages of our approach and, in particular, of embedding Rose in the multi-paradigm language Curry:

Data structures and recursion. We use Curry lists to describe elements that have multiple inputs. Often such elements can be defined for any size, a property that is called *genericity* in hardware description languages like VHDL. A common way of defining and manipulating such elements is to use recursion.

Polymorphism. Some elements can accept as parameters different types in such a way that they can be reused in many parts of the router with different input data.

Higher-Order Functions. Higher-order facilities are essential in order to build a router configuration by connecting or composing existing elements. The *composition* operators that will be described in Section 3.3 make extensive use of higher-order functions.

Laziness. Curry follows a *lazy* evaluation model, which means that functions are evaluated *on demand*. This is particularly useful to deal with infinite data structures (like packet streams). For instance, we can define a router as a function which generates an infinite stream of packets; however, if the user only demands the visualization of the first 10 packets, the remaining packets are not actually built.

Type System. Curry includes a standard type inference algorithm during compilation. Type errors can be very useful to detect errors in a router configuration, e.g., to detect that two incompatible elements have been erroneously connected.

Logic Features. Current proposals, particularly Lava [3] and Hawk [12], are based on pure functional languages (i.e., Haskell). In contrast, Curry provides logical features like non-deterministic functions, logical variables, built-in search, etc. Although these features have not been exploited yet, they will be useful to perform simulations with incomplete information (where the *holes* are represented by logical variables), to define some kinds of analysis, etc. This is subject of ongoing work and justifies our choice of Curry to embed the specification language Rose.

Click elements are packet processors. Therefore, each element in the router configuration can be abstracted by a function which takes a number of packet streams and returns a number of packet streams. In particular, each input port receives a packet stream and each output port emits a packet stream. Packets and streams are specified by means of the following types:

```
type Packet = [Int]
type Stream = [Packet]
```

A packet is regarded as a (finite) list of bytes, here encoded as integers, and streams are (potentially infinite) lists of packets. Typically, a Click element has the following type:

```
element :: [Conf] -> [Stream] -> [Stream]
```

i.e., it takes some configuration parameters (if any), a list of input streams (which can be empty if the element is a packet source), and returns a list of output streams (which can be empty if the element is a packet sink). Configuration parameters contain additional information to define the particular element behaviour.

Now we show examples of the five kinds of elements we distinguished in the previous section.

Packet sources. These elements are encoded as functions with no input streams and only one output stream. For instance, the Click element `FromDevice(eth)` is a packet source, where `eth` is a network device. It is specified in Rose by

```
fromDevice :: [Conf] -> [Stream] -> [Stream]
fromDevice [eth] [] = infiniteSource [eth] []
```

where the auxiliary function `infiniteSource` is similar to `fromDevice` but *simulates* the stream of packets coming from a given network address. Clearly, there is no difference in Rose between the Click elements `fromDevice` and `infiniteSource`, since we do not implement actual connections to the network.

Packet sinks. These elements are encoded as functions that return the input streams *with no modification* (in contrast to Click packet sinks, which have no output streams). The reason for this behavior is to allow the user to *observe* the output of the router, which can be useful during the specification phase to test the router behavior. For instance, the Click element `ToDevice(eth)` sends a stream of packets to some network device. In Rose, we specify this element by[2]

```
toDevice [eth] [ps] = [aux ps]
              where aux []     = []
                    aux (p:ps) = p : aux ps
```

Here, we discard the network device in the local function `aux` since we are not interested in the network devices to which packets are sent. If more detailed information would be needed, we could easily modify the above function in order to return pairs (ethernet device, packet).

Packet modifiers. In contrast to Click, we consider packet modifiers with one input stream and one output stream (i.e., we do not consider erroneous packets). As an example of a packet modifier, we show the specification of the Click element `Strip(n)`, which deletes the first `n` bytes from each packet (e.g., to get rid of the Ethernet header). In Rose, it is encoded as follows:

```
strip [n] [ps] = [st_ n ps]
            where st_ m []     = []
                  st_ m (q:qs) = drop m q : st_ m qs
```

where `drop` is a predefined Curry function—it is part of the Curry *prelude*—which returns a suffix of a given list without the first `n` elements.

---

[2] In the following, we do not show the type of elements since it always has the form "`[Conf] -> [Stream] -> [Stream]`".

Routing elements. These elements have only one input stream and two or more output streams. As an example, in the following we consider the Click element `Classifier(pat₁,...,pat_n)` which classifies packets according to their contents. To be more precise, it takes a sequence of patterns $pat_1,...,pat_n$ which are pairs `offset/value`, compares each incoming packet data against the set of patterns, and sends the packet to an output port corresponding to the first pattern that matched. For instance, the Click declaration

```
Classifier(12/0806 20/0001,
           12/0800,
           -);
```

creates an element with three outputs intended to process Ethernet packets: ARP requests (offset 12 has the hexadecimal value 0806 and offset 20 has the hexadecimal value 0001) are sent to the first output, IP packets (offset 12 has the hexadecimal value 0800) are sent to the second output and all other packets (denoted by the special case "-") are sent to the third output.

In Rose, we denote patterns by a list of expressions "**Pat** *cons*", where *cons* is a list with an odd number of integers and such that each pair of integers n, m denotes the following condition: byte n of the packet must have value m. The last integer denotes the output stream (starting from zero). Also, the special case "-" (which matches every packet) is represented by a pattern with only one element, the output stream. In this way, the above configuration string, "12/0806 20/0001, 12/0800, -", is specified in Rose as follows:

```
[Pat [12,8,13,6,20,0,21,1,0], Pat [12,8,13,0,1], Pat [2]]
```

Here, we denote each Click pair `offset/value` by several pairs `byte,value`; for instance, the Click pattern 12/0800 is represented by the sequence $12, 8, 13, 0$.

Now, the Rose specification of the element classifier can be given as follows:

```
classifier pats [p:ps] = add n p qs
                    where n = class pats p
                          qs = classifier pats [ps]

class (Pat pat : pats) p = let n = class_ pat p
                       in if n == (-1) then class pats p
                                       else n

class_ [n] p = n
class_ (pos:val:es) p = if p!!pos == val then class_ es p
                                         else -1

add n p qs = if n==0 then (p : qs!!0) : tail qs
                     else (qs!!0) : add (n-1) p (tail qs)
```

In general, a call of the form `classifier pats (p:ps)` returns a list of streams $[qs_1, ...,p:qs_n,...,qs_k]$, where $[qs_1, ...,qs_n,...,qs_k]$ is the list returned by `classifier pats ps`. Function `classifier` proceeds by first determining the output stream n of the first input packet p—using the function `class`—

and then adding—using the function add—packet p on top of the n stream of the result of applying classifier recursively to the remaining input packets ps.

Given a call of the form "ps!!n", the predefined function !! returns the nth element of the list ps, while a call of the form "tail ps" returns the tail of ps.

Scheduling elements. These elements have one output stream and two or more input streams. They choose a packet from an input stream—according to some scheduling policy—and send it to the output stream. Here, we assume that there are always available packets in each input stream. For instance, the following Rose function implements a trivial round-robin strategy:

```
roundRobin [] ss = [rr ss]
    where rr []    = []
          rr (s:ss) = if s==[] then rr ss
                               else (s!!0) : rr (ss++[tail s])
```

Function roundRobin takes a list of input streams and no configuration parameters. It returns the packet on top of the first input stream, moves the remaining packets of this stream to the last position, and calls roundRobin recursively.

3.3   Composition Operators

Rose provides the user with a Curry library containing the specification of the main Click elements. However, this is not enough to specify a router configuration. The programmer also needs simple ways to connect single elements in order to build larger components. For this purpose, we also provide typical *composition operators*, which are defined by using the higher-order facilities of the language Curry.

The simplest composition operator is used to combine a number of elements in such a way that the output of one element is the input of the next one. This operator is defined as follows:

```
seq :: [[Stream] -> [Stream]] -> [Stream] -> [Stream]
seq []         = id
seq (elem : es) = \input -> seq es (elem input)
```

where id is the identity function. Function seq takes a list of elements and returns a new element whose input in the input of the first element in the list and whose output is the output of the last element in the list. For instance, the following function represents the router shown in Sect. 3.1:

```
simpleRouter = seq [fromDevice [Eth 0], Counter [], Discard []]
```

Another useful composition operator is mult, which is used to connect a routing element (with multiple output streams) to several packet modifiers. The specification of mult is as follows:

```
mult :: ([Stream] -> [Stream]) -> [[Stream] -> [Stream]]
          -> [Stream] -> [Stream]

mult elem es = \input -> mult_ es (elem input)
```

```
mult_ :: [[Stream] -> [Stream]] -> [Stream] -> [Stream]

mult_ es ss = concat (m es ss)
              where m [] []        = []
                    m (e:es) (s:ss) = (e [s]) : m es ss
```

where `concat` is a predefined Curry function to concatenate a list of lists. Function `mult` takes an element with n output streams and a list of elements with one input stream and connects them. It produces a new element whose input is the input of the single element and whose output streams are the output streams of the list of elements. For instance, the following function

```
classST = mult (classifier [Pat [12,8,13,6,20,0,21,1,0],
                            Pat [12,8,13,0,1],
                            Pat [2]])
               [strip [I 14], checkIPHeader [], toDevice [Eth 0]]
```

creates a new component that takes an input stream and sends ARP requests to element `strip` (which deletes the first 14 bytes from each packet), IP packets to element `checkIPHeader` (which checks that the packet length is reasonable and that the IP source address is a legal unicast address), and all other packets to the packet sink `toDevice [Eth 0]`.

There are more composition operators in Rose (e.g., to compose several packet modifiers with a scheduling element) that are not shown here.

3.4   Implementation

We have implemented a Curry library to design router specifications in Rose. This library contains

- a significant subset of the Click router elements,
- the basic composition operators, and
- some useful functions to test a router configuration.

Test functions have the following form:

```
test router n port = take n (router!!port)
```

In this way, one can obtain the first `n` packets sent to the output stream `port` by the router specification `router`, thus avoiding an infinite loop if the input stream is infinite. Predefined function `take` returns the `n` first elements of a given list. Additionally, the library contains a number of auxiliary functions, like common packet positions:

```
colAnnEth = 38             --color annotation in Ethernet packets
colAnnIP  = colAnnEth - 14 --color annotation in IP packets
ttlIP     = 8              --TTL field position in IP packets
...
```

or useful functions to manipulate packet data, like the application of a function to a given packet position. Moreover, in order to show the practicality of the ideas presented so far, we have specified a typical IP router (from [10]) in Rose.

Preliminary experiments are encouraging and point out the usefulness of our approach. More information is available at the following URL:

```
http://www.dsic.upv.es/~jsilva/routers/
```

4   Related Work

To the best of our knowledge, there is no previous approach for the specification of router configurations based on a well-established declarative language. We find, however, similar approaches for the design and verification of hardware components based on a language embedded in the lazy functional language Haskell [3], [12]. Clearly, our approach is inspired by these works in that we also define an embedded language rather than a completely new language. We think that this approach greatly simplifies the development of new domain-specific languages. There are, however, some important differences:

- The base language is different. While [3], [12] embed their specification language in the lazy functional language Haskell, we embed Rose in the multi-paradigm language Curry, which extends Haskell with logical features and concurrent constraints. We think that these additional facilities can be useful for future developments: simulation, verification, optimization, etc.
- The specified systems are different. While [3], [12] specify hardware circuits, we deal with router configurations. Although they share some similarities, the specification of routers has some particularities that are not present in the specification of hardware circuits.

5   Conclusions

We have introduced the domain-specific language Rose for the description of router configurations. It is embedded in the declarative multi-paradigm language Curry, which means that we have available all existing Curry tools for analysis, optimization, program manipulation, etc. For instance, we can use a Curry partial evaluator [1] to specialize generic router configurations, a fold/unfold transformation system [2] to manipulate router configurations in a semantics-preserving way, or use the tracing facilities of the PAKCS environment [8] to debug router specifications. We have shown how the basic Click elements are specified in Rose and how the composition operators are used to build larger configurations. In this way, Rose allows one to specify router configurations concisely, modularly and re-usably, while retaining its declarative nature.

There are many interesting topics for future work. On the one hand, we plan to extend Rose in order to cover all the existing Click elements. Also, it would be interesting to implement translators from Click into Rose and vice versa. This will facilitate the interaction with Click so that Rose can be regarded as a practical tool for the design and verification of Click router specifications. Finally, we will investigate the definition of specific analyses for Rose specifications, e.g., by using well-established abstract interpretation techniques [4], [5].

Acknowledgments. We would like to thank Eddie Kohler for useful comments and suggestions.

References

1. Albert, E., Hanus, M., Vidal, G.: A Practical Partial Evaluation Scheme for Multi-Paradigm Declarative Languages. Journal of Functional and Logic Programming **2002** (2002)
2. Alpuente, M., Falaschi, M., Moreno, G., Vidal, G.: A Transformation System for Lazy Functional Logic Programs. In: Proc. of the 4th Fuji Int'l Symp. on Functional and Logic Programming (FLOPS'99), Springer LNCS 1722 (1999) 147–162
3. Claessen, K.: Embedded Languages for Describing and Verifying Hardware. PhD Thesis, Chalmers University of Technology and Göteborg University, Department of Computing Science (2001)
4. Cousot, P., Cousot, R.: Abstract Interpretation: A Unified Lattice Model for Static Analysis of Programs by Construction or Approximation of Fixpoints. In: Proc. of 4th ACM Symp. on Principles of Programming Languages. (1977) 238–252
5. Cousot, P., Cousot, R.: Systematic Design of Program Analysis Frameworks. In: Proc. of 6th ACM Symp. on Principles of Programming Languages. (1979) 269–282
6. Gottlieb, Y., Peterson, L.: A Comparative Study of Extensible Routers. In: 2002 IEEE Open Architectures and Network Programming Proceedings. (2002) 51–62
7. Hanus, M.: Distributed Programming in a Multi-Paradigm Declarative Language. In: Proc. of the Int'l Conf. on Principles and Practice of Declarative Programming (PPDP'99), Springer LNCS 1702 (1999) 376-395
8. Hanus, M., Antoy, S., Koj, J., Sadre, R., Steiner, F.: PAKCS 1.5: The Portland Aachen Kiel Curry System User Manual. Technical report, University of Kiel, Germany (2003)
9. Hanus (ed.), M.: Curry: An Integrated Functional Logic Language. (Available at: http://www.informatik.uni-kiel.de/~mh/curry/)
10. Kohler, E.: The Click Modular Router. PhD thesis, Massachusetts Institute of Technology (2001)
11. Kohler, E., Morris, R., Chen, B., Jannotti, J., Kaashoek, M.: The Click Modular Router. ACM Transactions on Computer Systems **18** (2000) 263–297
12. Matthews, J.: Algebraic Specification and Verification of Processor Microarchitectures. PhD thesis, University of Washington (2000)
13. Moreno-Navarro, J., Rodríguez-Artalejo, M.: Logic Programming with Functions and Predicates: The language Babel. Journal of Logic Programming **12** (1992) 191-224
14. Peterson, L., Karlin, S., Li, K.: OS Support for General-Purpose Routers. In: Workshop on Hot Topics in Operating Systems (Hot-OS-VII), IEEE Computer Society Technical Committee on Operating Systems (1999) 38–43

Multi-document Automatic Text Summarization Using Entropy Estimates

G. Ravindra[1], N. Balakrishnan[1], and K.R. Ramakrishnan[2]

[1] Supercomputer Education and Research Center, Institute of Science,
Bangalore-560012, India
{ravi@mmsl.,balki@}serc.iisc.ernet.in
[2] Dept. of Electrical Engineering, Institute of Science, Bangalore-560012, India
krr@ee.iisc.ernet.in

Abstract. This paper describes a sentence ranking technique using entropy measures, in a multi-document unstructured text summarization application. The method is topic specific and makes use of a simple language independent training framework to calculate entropies of symbol units. The document set is summarized by assigning entropy-based scores to a reduced set of sentences obtained using a graph representation for sentence similarity. The performance is seen to be better than some of the common statistical techniques, when applied on the same data set. Commonly used measures like precision, recall and f-score have been modified and used as a new set of measures for comparing the performance of summarizers. The rationale behind such a modification is also presented. Experimental results are presented to illustrate the relevance of this method in cases where it is difficult to have language specific dictionaries, translators and document-summary pairs for training.

1 Introduction

The fast moving Internet age has resulted in a huge amount of digital data that has redefined paradigms in the field of data storage, data mining, information retrieval and information assimilation. Automatic text summarization is seen as an important off-shoot of this digital era. It is envisaged that machine generated summaries are going to help people assimilate relevant information quickly. It also helps in quick search and retrieval of desired information form a summary database which is a reduced version of a larger database.

Automatic extraction-based text summarization consists of a set of algorithms and mathematical operations performed on sentences/phrases in a document so that the most difficult task of identifying **relevant sentences** can be performed. Definition of relevance is subjective and measures to determine the relevance of a sentence to a summary is mathematically difficult to express. The cognitive process that takes place when humans try to summarize information is not clearly understood, yet we try to model the process of summarization using tools like decision trees, graphs, wordnets and clustering algorithms. Although

P. Van Emde Boas et al. (Eds.): SOFSEM 2004, LNCS 2932, pp. 289–300, 2004.

these pattern recognition techniques may not correctly represent the human cognitive process, these methods are popular and seem to produce reasonable if not perfect results. Techniques that attempt to understand natural language the way humans do, might help produce better summaries, but such systems might not work well for all languages. Many of the methods work well for specific sets of documents. Techniques that rely on features such as position, cue words, titles and headings perform poorly on unstructured text data. Methods that rely on word frequency counts obtained after analyzing the document collection to be summarized, perform well in cases such as multiple news reports on the same event, but fare badly when there is only one document to be summarized.

2   Related Work

In [1], Baldwin and Morton present a query-based summarizer wherein sentences are selected from the document such that all the phrases in the query are covered by these selected sentences. A sentence in the document is said to include a phrase present in the query, if the query and the sentence co-refer to the same information unit. In [2], Carbonell and Goldstein introduce a new relevance measure called the Maximal Marginal Relevance(MMR). MMR is a linear combination of "novelty" and "relevance" measured independently. They have applied this measure for ranking documents in an IR environment. They have also applied it to passage extraction as a method for query-based text summarization and in multi-document text summarization.

SUMMARIST [3], from the University of Southern California strives to create text summaries based on topic identification and document interpretation. The identification stage filters input documents to determine the most important topics. The interpretation stage clusters words and abstracts them into some encompassing concepts and this is followed by the generation stage. SUMMARIST uses traditional IR techniques augmented with semantic and statistical methods. WordNet has been used to identify synonyms and sense disambiguation algorithms have been used to select the proper word sense. Latent Semantic Analysis [4] has been used to solve the term dependency problem. Topic identification has been realized using a method called "optimal position policy (OPP)". This method tries to identify those sentences that are more likely to convey maximum information about the topic of discourse. Cue phrases such as "in conclusion", "importantly" etc have also been used for sentence selection. As reported in [5] use of location and cue phrases can give better summaries than just word frequency counts. The serious drawback with the OPP method is that location and cue phrase abstraction is dependent on the text genre.

Barzilay and Elhadad [6], present a method that creates text summaries by using lexical chains created from the document. Lexical chains are created by choosing candidate words [7] from the document , finding a related chain using relatedness criteria and introducing that word into the chain. Relatedness of words is determined in terms of the distance between their occurrences and shape of the path connecting them in the WordNet database. For summarizing the document, strong chains are selected from the lexical chain and sentences are chosen based on chain distribution.

Gong and Liu [8], present and compare sentence extraction methods using latent semantic analysis and relevance measures. The document is decomposed into sentences where each sentence is represented by a vector of words that it is composed of. The entire document itself is represented as a single vector of word frequencies. The word frequencies are weighted by local word weights and global word weights and these weighted vectors are used to determine the relevance. A sentence that has the highest relevance is selected from the document and included in the summary and then all the terms contained in this sentence are removed from the document vector. This process is continued till the number of sentences included into the summary has reached a pre-defined value. The latent semantic analysis approach uses singular value decomposition (SVD) to generate an index matrix which is used to select appropriate sentences to be included in the summary. The SVD operation is capable of capturing the interrelationships between words so that they can be semantically clustered.

MEAD summarizer [9], [10], uses a centroid-based summarization scheme for multiple document summarization. The scheme creates centroids which are pseudo-documents consisting of words with a "word count x IDF" measure greater than a threshold. Sentences containing words from these centroids are more indicative of the topic of the cluster. Scores are computed by a weighted sum of proximity to the cluster centroid, length and position values.

Our work uses an entropy measure to rank sentences in order of relevance based on "past knowledge" in the particular domain which the documents to be summarized belong to. The method works well for single document as well as multiple-documents as redundancy in information is not the only criterion used for sentence selection. Document-summary pairs have not been used for feature extraction and other statistical calculations. The principle reason for taking this approach is governed by some of the problems encountered in the context of Indian languages. There are almost as many as 45 dialects and information in the form of news articles, magazines are available in many of them. It becomes a very difficult task to generate dictionaries, have document-summarizer pairs for training and have language translators. Hence a language independent framework that can be trained with only raw (untagged,unparsed etc.) data can be used. This framework when applied to documents in English language has shown encouraging results. Further the importance of "past/background knowledge" in improving the summarizer performance has been shown. The remaining part of the paper is organized as follows: section-3 explains the sentence selection procedure using entropy estimates. Section-4 describes the measures used for comparing summaries followed by experimental results in section-5. Section-6 concludes the paper with some observations.

3   Sentence Selection Technique

Any document set to be summarized is first classified as belonging to a particular domain. We use a database of documents clustered into various domains/topics. Using an IR technique the document set to be summarized is first classified as belonging to one of these domains. Once the domain/topic has been identified, an entropy model for the various words and collocations in the identified domain is generated. Documents available in this identified domain constitute the training data set. The calculated entropy values are applied to each of the sentences in the document set to be summarized and a sentence ranking formula is computed. In the remaining part of the paper we use summary and extract interchangeably.

3.1   Redundancy Removal

The document set to be summarized is subjected to a pre-processing step aimed at removing redundant information. The entropy-based sentence selection formula cannot be used to detect if two or more sentences are similar in word composition. We use a graph representation of sentences to detect and remove redundancy before applying the entropy based ranking formula.

Every sentence is represented as a node in a directed graph. A link is established from one node to another if at least 3 non-stop-words are common to them. If the parent node represents a longer sentence than what the child node represents, then the link weight is the ratio of number of words common to both the sentences to the length(number of non-stop words) of the child node. If not, the link weight is the ratio of common words to the length of the parent node. For every parent node, those child nodes which have a link weight greater than a particular threshold and which are shorter than the parent node are excluded from the sentence ranking process. Hence, sentences that have been repeated and sentences that are almost similar in word composition are thrown away.

As a second option for removing redundancy we use latent semantic indexing (LSI). The result of this step is a collection of candidate sentences for the entropy-based method to choose from. LSI uses singular value decomposition (SVD) on a weighted term x sentence matrix to produce the right and left singular vectors and the singular values in descending order of importance. LSI-based summarizers select sentences based on the magnitude of singular values. But in reality, singular values do not indicate the strength of a topic in terms of its importance. On the other hand LSI helps to efficiently remove redundant information which may be expected in a multi-document summarization case, even in the case of synonymy and polysemy. We exploit this capability of LSI to effectively remove redundancy and use entropy-scores to compensate for its inability to choose important sentences.

3.2   Entropy Measure for Sentence Selection

Let $T = [t_1, t_2, t_3 \ldots \ldots, t_M]$ be a set of M sentences in a training set for a particular domain or topic. We define a window of length L within which word collocations are counted. We define the vocabulary $V = \{v_1, v_2, ..., v_{|V|},\}$ for this domain, as the set of all unique non-stop words that occur in the training data set. We represent any sentence t_i as a sequence of non-stop words $[w_1, w_2.........,w_n]$ where n is the length of the sentence t_i in terms of number of non-stop words. Different collocations starting with the word w_i discovered in a sentence can be written as $\{(w_i, w_{i+1}), (w_i, w_{i+2}), ..., (w_i, w_{i+L})\}$, where L is the length of the collocation window. Let $C(v_i, v_j)$ be the number of collocations with the first word v_i and the second word v_j in the collocation pair $\langle v_i, v_j \rangle$. The probability that the word v_j occurs as the second word given v_i as the first word is

$$p(v_j|v_i) = \frac{C(v_i, v_j)}{\sum_{j=1}^{j=|V_i|} C(v_i, v_j)} \tag{1}$$

where $|V_i|$ is the number of unique collocations discovered with V_i as the first word. The uncertainty in the occurrence of a word from the vocabulary in the second position of a collocation, given the first word, can be expressed using the conditional entropy relation as

$$H(v_i, x) = - \sum_{j=1}^{j=|V_I|} p(v_j|v_i) ln[p(v_j|v_i)] \tag{2}$$

where $|V_J|$ is the number of unique words from the vocabulary in the collocations with v_i as the first word. Instead of including the entire vocabulary as the word-set participating in the collocation, this method includes only that subset of the vocabulary which contributes non-zero values to the entropy score. The probability of occurrence of the collocation pair $\langle v_i, v_j \rangle$ is $p(v_i)p(v_j|v_i)$ and this is not the same as the probability for the pair $\langle v_j, v_i \rangle$ as the order has to be preserved in a collocation. Hence the uncertainty when the word v_i is encountered can be computed as

$$- \sum_{j=1}^{j=|V_J|} p(v_i)p(v_j|v_i) ln[p(v_i)p(v_j|v_i)] \tag{3}$$

which can be further expressed in terms of conditional entropy and word probability as

$$E_F(v_i) = -p(v_i)\{ln[p(v_i)] - H(v_i, x)\} \tag{4}$$

This we call the forward entropy equation. Similarly the uncertainty in the occurrence of the first word, given the second word of the collocation is given by

$$H(y, v_j) = - \sum_{i=1}^{i=|V_I|} p(v_j|v_i) ln[p(v_j|v_i)] \tag{5}$$

where $|V_I|$ is the number of unique words from the vocabulary in the collocations with v_j as the second word. This results in the backward entropy equation which can be expressed as

$$E_B(v_i) = -p(v_i)\{ln[p(v_i)] - H(y, v_j)\} \tag{6}$$

The forward and backward entropies for all the words in the training set is computed. As can be seen, the entropy computation procedure does not use language specific features and parsing techniques to determine measures for words. The basic philosophy is to consider meaningful text as just a sequence of symbols(words,phrases etc.) and see how to use such a frame work for sentence selection in summarization applications.

3.3   Sentence Ranking

Once the forward and backward entropies have been computed for a particular domain/topic the summarizer is ready to perform sentence selection tasks on the document to be summarized.

For every sentence t_i in the document set to be summarized, an entropy score is computed as

$$H(t_i) = \frac{\sum_{k=1}^{k=|t_i|} E_F(w_k) + E_B(w_k)}{|t_i|} \tag{7}$$

where $|t_i|$ is the number of non-stop words in the sentence. Estimated entropy values are not substituted if the forward and backward entropies for a particular word cannot be determined form the training data. After entropy scores have been computed for all sentences in the document(s) to be summarized, sentences are ranked in the ascending order of entropy scores. The first N sorted sentences are selected as the candidate sentences to be included into an extract or for further processing.

4   Comparing Summaries

A common approach to judge the quality of summaries is to allow human experts to score them on a scale of 0-5 or 0-10. Human judges can vary in their opinions and assigning scores is based on the extent to which the expert knows about the subject. Getting experts and taking their opinion is a laborious task and is difficult to establish consistency. Other method followed is to count the number of sentences that are common between machine generated and human summaries and then compute precision and recall scores. Exact sentence matches do not take into account slight variations in word composition. Hence we use modified precision,recall and f-score measures to compare summaries. As we use a fuzzy set paradigm, these new measures are called as fuzzy precision, recall and f-score measures.

4.1   Membership Grades

Let $H=\{h_1,h_2,h_3,...,h_{|H|}\}$ be a human generated summary that consists $|H|$ sentences. Let $M=\{m_1,m_2,.......,m_{|M|}\}$ be a machine generated extract consisting of —M— sentences. Each sentence is represented by a unit normal vector of word collocations. The dimensionality of each of these vectors is the total number of unique collocations discovered in the machine and human generated summaries, using the collocation window which was mentioned in the previous section. Let R_H and R_M be the matrices whose columns are vectors representing the human summary and machine summary respectively. Let $F = \{f_1,f_2,f_3,...,f_{|H|}\}$ be a set of fuzzy sets corresponding to each of the sentences in H. The matrix product $\Phi = R_H^T \times R_M$ gives the matrix of membership values of each sentence belonging to M in F. For example, the ith row of Φ gives the membership value of each sentence of M in the fuzzy set f_i. The human summary can be considered as union of the sets of F. If $\mu_{H_k}(m_j)$ is the membership grade in the set f_k then the membership grade in the set $H = \bigcup_{k=1}^{k=|H|} f_k$, is given by $\mu_H(m_j) = max_i[\Phi_{i,j}]$. This relation is used in computing the precision scores.

Similarly the membership grade of the sentence h_j in the machine summary becomes $\mu_M(h_j) = max_i[\Phi_{ji}]$ and this relation is used to compute the recall scores.

4.2   Fuzzy Precision, Recall, and F-Score Measures

Precision, recall and f-score have been used as one of the standard methods for evaluating summaries. Precision is defined as the ratio of number of sentences of the machine summary that has an exact match with the sentences in the human summary, to the number of sentences in the machine summary. Hence the fuzzy precision measure can be defined as

$$Fp = \frac{\sum_{j=1}^{j=|M|} \mu_H(m_j)}{|M|}$$

Recall is defined as the ratio of number of sentences of the human summary that has an exact match with the sentences in the machine summary, to the number of sentences in the human summary. Hence, fuzzy recall measure can be defined as

$$Fr = \frac{\sum_{j=1}^{j=|H|} \mu_M(h_j)}{|H|}$$

The fuzzy F-score becomes $\frac{1}{(\lambda \frac{1}{F_p} + (1-\lambda)\frac{1}{F_r})}$.

5   Results and Discussion

5.1   Experimental Conditions

MEAD, LSI-based summarizer and the entropy-based summarizer were evaluated on a summary data set consisting of 13 document clusters and their corresponding summaries. These 13 clusters were chosen from the DUC2002 data set

released by NIST. The reason for choosing particular document sets from this
data set is, because relevant information about the topics that they discuss were
available in our topic database. Each document cluster consists of two possible
human summaries compressed to 400 words. Each cluster can have between 7
and 12 documents, all of them containing information about a common topic.
The topics covered by these 13 document sets fall under the following categories:
**hurricanes, earthquakes, explosions, personalities, floods, Berlin wall
history, turmoils and scientific pursuits**

The MEAD summarizer (version-3.05) was used with the default configuration file parameters. Compression basis was "sentences" and compression percentage was varied so that each document cluster was summarized to produce
between 20 and 22 sentences. This translates to a compression varying between
6-13% for the original document set, in terms of sentence count. The LSI-based
summarizer was implemented fully in C using matlab-library functions. Full rank
SVD was computed on the word x sentence matrix for the cluster to be summarized. The columns of the right-singular vectors were sorted in the ascending
order and the sentences corresponding to first 20 largest singular values were
selected to be included into the summary. The 'word x sentence' vectors were
normalized and $ln[N/c]$ was used as the IDF weighting formula before SVD
computation.

Table 1. Number of sentences per cluster and the reduced rank after SVD

Sentences per cluster	Reduced Rank
243	134
118	80
219	133
212	127
309	172
177	112
120	84
236	146
334	194
332	191
199	124
111	76

For the method where LSI was used as a pre-processing step before entropy-
based sentence selection was used, all the unique sentences corresponding to the
largest index values were used as the reduced set of sentences. Table-1 shows the
number of sentences in the original document set and the number of sentences
selected as the output of the preprocessing step.

Word entropies were computed after stop-words were removed but word stem-
ming was not performed. The window length for collocation discovery while
computing entropy values was set to 4 non-stop words.

5.2   Experimental Results and Discussion

Precision, recall, f-score and their fuzzy variants were used as measures to evaluate the summaries produced by the summarizers. Hence forth we call the entropy-
based summarizer using graph representation for redundancy removal as "E-G"
or "Entropy" method and entropy-based summarizer with LSI for redundancy
removal as "E-LSI" or "LSI+Entropy" method. The precision and recall values
for E-G method, MEAD, LSI and E-LSI using exact sentence-match are shown
in Fig.1. Fscores corresponding to the maximum scoring summary for each document, have been listed in Table-2.

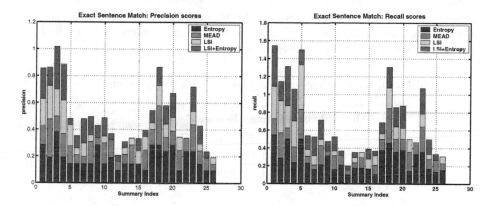

Fig. 1. Precision and Recall scores using exact sentence match

Table 2. Exact Sentence Match: Fscore

Document Type	LSI	MEAD	LSI+Entropy	Entropy
earthquake	0.2941	0.2857	0.3030	0.3750
hurricane2	0.2703	0.1765	0.3684	0.4324
johnmajor	0.2400	0.1905	0.1143	0.2222
explosion	0.1026	0.1875	0.1951	0.1714
hurricane1	0.0513	0.1579	0.1463	0.3000
kashmir	0	0.1176	0.0488	0.2000
hubble	0.0541	0.1290	0.0513	0.1579
india	0.1053	0.1250	0.1000	0.1538
wall	0.1818	0.3333	0.1714	0.3529
flashflood	0.1176	0.1212	0.2105	0.3243
aquino	0.1176	0.1765	0	0.2778
sakharov	0.1176	0.2353	0.2222	0.2857
ship	0.0606	0.1111	0.0541	0.1176

There are some cases where the increase in these scores for E-G method
is as high as 0.25 which translates to selecting 3-4 sentences more than the

other methods. At the same time there are 2 cases where the other methods have out performed E-G method by a maximum difference of 0.1 showing that this method selected 1 sentence less than the other methods. Exact sentence-match shows that on an average, E-G method selects 2 sentences more than the other methods. Sentence redundancy removal using graph-based method resulted in the same quality of summary as LSI-based removal would give. But exact sentence match with the human summary shows 3 cases where E-LSI method produced a summary in which none of the sentences matched with the human summary. This can be attributed to inaccuracy of SVD when the matrices are sparse. Another reason is that when there are more than two sentences having the same index value only one of them is chosen. Table-3 shows the average increase in precision,recall,f-score and number of sentences selected when evaluation was done using exact sentence match. This is for the case where E-G method was compared against the other three methods.

Table 3. Average improvement in scores with exact sentence match

Exact Match	Precision	Recall	F-score	Average increase in matching sentences
MEAD	0.0622	0.1196	0.0842	1.8
LSI	0.0979	0.1365	0.1131	2.15
E-LSI	0.0784	0.1078	0.0891	1.5

Exact sentence match may not be a good criterion especially if a machine has to judge a summary based on the above mentioned metrics. Sentences that are very similar in word composition but not having the same words and word sequence will not be considered as a match. For example the sentence "JAMMU-KASHMIR IS THE ONLY STATE WITH A MOSLEM MAJORITY IN PREDOMINANTLY HINDU INDIA" and the sentence "HINDU DOMINATED INDIA ACCUSES PAKISTAN OF ARMING AND TRAINING KASHMIRI MILITANTS FIGHTING FOR SECESSION OF JAMMU KASHMIR INDIA S ONLY STATE WITH A MOSLEM MAJORITY" would end up as sentences that are completely different in the case of an exact sentence match. But a fuzzy sentence match would give a partial match score which is the true picture. More over, by using word collocations as already mentioned, the above two sentences can be found similar with regard to the collocations ¡JAMMU KASHMIR> <HINDU INDIA> <MOSLEM MAJORITY>. By using word pairs we are imposing tighter bounds on information and by using the 4-word window there is flexibility in finding similarity when there are adjective words and other word modifiers. For example, the second sentence does not contain <HINDU INDIA> as consecutive words but within the window [HINDU DOMINATED INDIA ACCUSES] the word pair can be found. The Fuzzy precision,recall and fscore measures for the different summarizers is shown in Fig.2 and Table-4. The average increase in these scores over MEAD,LSI and E-LSI for E-G method is shown in Table-5. The table also shows that on an average, the E-G method chooses 3 sentences more than the other two methods.

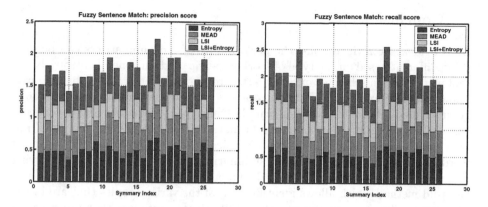

Fig. 2. Precision and Recall scores using Fuzzy sentence match

Table 4. Fuzzy Sentence Match: Fscore

Document Type	LSI	MEAD	LSI+Entropy	Entropy
earthquake	0.3839	0.3121	0.5287	0.5288
hurricane2	0.2793	0.2363	0.4629	0.5040
johnmajor	0.3262	0.2859	0.2163	0.3895
explosion	0.2119	0.3299	0.2969	0.3708
hurricane1	0.1906	0.2651	0.4421	0.5039
kashmir	0.1855	0.2423	0.2990	0.3848
hubble	0.3389	0.2339	0.1866	0.2767
india	0.2547	0.3024	0.2782	0.2507
wall	0.2547	0.4572	0.3161	0.4957
flashflood	0.2477	0.2567	0.3600	0.4499
aquino	0.2004	0.3452	0.1965	0.3658
sakharov	0.1931	0.3676	0.3853	0.4341
ship	0.1174	0.2709	0.1477	0.2719

Table 5. Average improvement in scores with Fuzzy sentence match

Fuzzy Match	Precision	Recall	F-score	Average increase in Matching Sentences
MEAD	0.0835	0.1465	0.1104	2.78
LSI	0.1423	0.1574	0.1521	3.19
E-LSI	0.0670	0.0752	0.0717	1.15

6   Conclusion

As is evident from the graphs, the performance of the summarizers can be seen to be different based on the type of scoring metric used. In general entropy-based sentence selection scheme can be expected to perform better. If the background knowledge required to compute entropies is not sufficient many sentences may go un-scored. Hence no decision can be taken as to whether such sentences can be included into the summary or not. LSI on the other hand does not require any background knowledge but relies purely on redundancy in terms of word frequencies. Hence LSI-based summarization cannot be used while trying to extract sentences from a single document. MEAD on the other hand uses centroid method which allows identification of the various topics that are in the document. This is more efficient than LSI. Hence sentences that are relevant to each of those topics are selected. As already mentioned all the topics may not be of importance when the final extract is created. There can be multiple sentences belonging to the same topic that are important. The entropy-based selection framework allows sentence extraction method suited for most languages where words are separated by definite markers. As information related to the document layout is not considered while scoring, entropy-method can be used more efficiently for summarizing un-structured text.

References

1. Baldwin, B., Morton, T.: Dynamic Co-Reference Based Summarization. In: Proc. Third Conference on Emperical Methods in Natural Language Processing. (1998) 630–632
2. Carbonell, J.G, Goldstein, J: Use of mmr Diversity-Based Re-Ranking for Recording Documents and Producing Summaries. In: Proc.ACM (SIGIR'98). (1998)
3. Hovy, E.H, Lin, C.Y.: 8. In: Automated Text Summarization in SUMMARIST. MIT. Press, Cambridge Massachusetts, London, England (1999)
4. Deerwester, S, D., et al.: Indexing by Latent Semantic Analysis. American Society for Information Science **41** (1990) 391–407
5. Paice, C.: Constructing Literature Abstracts by Computer: Techniques and Prospects. Information Processing and Management **26** (1990) 171–186
6. Barzilay, R., Elhadad, M.: Using Lexical Chains for Text Summarization. In: Proc. Workshop on Intelligent Scalable Text Summarization(Madrid-Spain). (1997)
7. Morris, J, Hirst, G: Lexical Cohesion Computed by Thesaural Relations as an Indication of the Structure of Text. Computational Linguistics **17** (1991) 21–43
8. Yihong Gong, X.L.: Generic Text Summarization Using Relevance Measure and Latent Semantic Analysis. In: Proc.ACM (SIGIR'01). (2001) 19–25
9. Radev, D., Budzikowska, M: Centroid-Based Summarization of Multiple Documents: Sentence Extaction, Utility-Based Evaluation and User Studies. In: Proc.(ANLP/NAACL'00). (2000)
10. Dragomir Radev, V.H., McKeowen, K.R.: A Description of the Cidr System as Used for tdt-2. In: Proc.DARPA Broadcast News Workshop, Herndon. (1999)

Implicit Flow Maximization by Iterative Squaring*

Daniel Sawitzki**

University of Dortmund, Computer Science 2
Baroper Str. 301, D-44221 Dortmund, Germany
daniel.sawitzki@cs.uni-dortmund.de

Abstract. Application areas like logic design and network analysis produce large graphs $G = (V, E)$ on which traditional algorithms, which work on adjacency list representations, are not practicable anymore. These large graphs often contain regular structures that enable compact implicit representations by decision diagrams like OBDDs [1], [2], [3]. To solve problems on such implicitly given graphs, specialized algorithms are needed. These are considered as heuristics with typically higher worst-case runtimes than traditional methods. In this paper, an implicit algorithm for flow maximization in 0–1 networks is presented, which works on OBDD-representations of node and edge sets. Because it belongs to the class of layered-network methods, it has to construct blocking-flows. In contrast to previous implicit methods, it avoids breadth-first searches and layer-wise proceeding, and uses iterative squaring instead. In this way, the algorithm needs to execute only $O(\log^2 |V|)$ operations on the OBDDs to obtain a layered-network or at least one augmenting path, respectively. Moreover, each OBDD-operation is efficient if the node and edge sets are represented by compact OBDDs during the flow computation. In order to investigate the algorithm's behavior on large and structured networks, it has been analyzed on grid networks, on which a maximum flow is computed in polylogarithmic time $O(\log^3 |V|)$ and space $O(\log^2 |V|)$. In contrast, previous methods need time and space $\Omega(|V|^{1/2} \log |V|)$ on grids, and are beaten also in experiments for $|V| \geq 2^{26}$.

1 Introduction

Algorithms on graphs $G = (V, E)$ typically work on adjacency lists, which contain for every node $v \in V$ the set of its adjacent nodes $\text{adj}(v) = \{w \mid (v, w) \in E\}$. This kind of representation has size $\Theta(|V| + |E|)$, and is called *explicit*.

However, there are application areas in which problems on graphs of such large size have to be solved that an explicit representation on today's computers is not possible. In the verification and synthesis of sequential circuits,

---

* An extended version of this paper can be obtained via
  http://ls2-www.cs.uni-dortmund.de/~sawitzki/IFMbIS.pdf.
** Supported by the Deutsche Forschungsgemeinschaft (DFG) as part of the Research Cluster "Algorithms on Large and Complex Networks" (1126).

P. Van Emde Boas et al. (Eds.): SOFSEM 2004, LNCS 2932, pp. 301–313, 2004.

state-transition graphs with for example 10^{27} nodes and 10^{36} edges occur. Other applications produce graphs which are representable in explicit form, but for which even runtimes of efficient polynomial algorithms are not practicable anymore. Modeling of the WWW, street, or social networks are examples of this problem scenario.

Yet we expect the large graphs occurring in application areas to contain regular structures rather than to be randomly originated. If we consider graphs as Boolean functions, we can represent them by *Ordered Binary Decision Diagrams* (*OBDDs*) [1], [2], [3], which reward regularities with good compression. In order to represent a graph $G = (V, E)$ by an OBDD, its edge set E is considered as a Boolean *characteristic function* χ_E, which maps binary encodings of E's elements to 1 and all others to 0. This representation is called *implicit*, and is not essentially larger than explicit ones. Nevertheless, we hope that advantageous properties of G lead to "small," that is sublinear OBDD-sizes. Examples are grid graphs [4], [5], which have OBDDs of size $O(\log |V|)$, and cographs [6], which have OBDDs of size $O(|V| \log |V|)$.

OBDDs offer a set of functional operations which are efficient w. r. t. the sizes of the participating OBDDs. Although each single operation is efficient, a sequence of $O(\log |V|)$ operations may generate OBDDs of exponential size. Thus, the over-all runtime of an implicit algorithm is essentially influenced by the size of both the input OBDDs and of OBDDs generated during the algorithm execution. In general, it is difficult to analyze these sizes for an interesting input subset. Sometimes, the number of OBDD-operations is bounded as a hint on the real over-all runtime [7], [8], while most papers on OBDD-algorithms contain only experimental results. Because implicit algorithms typically have a higher worst-case runtime than corresponding algorithms which work on adjacency lists, they are considered as heuristics to save time and/or space when the input graphs are heavily structured and possibly too large for an explicit representation. Hopefully, each OBDD-operation processes many edges in parallel.

Implicit OBDD-algorithms for some particular graph problems like reachability analysis have been well studied in the context of logic design [9]. Newer research tries to attack more general graph problems. The algorithm of Hachtel and Somenzi [10] represents one of the first steps in this direction. It computes a maximum s–t-flow in an implicitly given 0–1 network $N = (V, E, s, t)$. In experiments, the algorithm was able to handle very large state-transition graphs as well as dense random graphs. Anyhow, the individual processing of network layers may enforce a superlinear amount of $\Omega(|V| \log |V|)$ iterations, and destroys the possibility of sublinear runtime. This paper's algorithm circumvents this problem by using the technique of *iterative squaring* (called *IS-algorithm* in the following). Its essential idea is to construct graph paths by iteratively doubling their lengths. In this way, $O(\log^2 |V|)$ OBDD-operations suffice to compute at least one augmenting path. This enables exponential less OBDD-operations than Hachtel and Somenzi's algorithm. We pursue this approach with the focus on heavily structured networks with high diameter, on which we expect efficient over-all runtimes.

The paper is organized as follows: Section 2 introduces the principles of graph representation by OBDDs. Section 3 gives an overview of the IS-algorithm, while separate sections describe its submodules: The layered-network module in Sect. 4, the augmenting path construction in Sect. 5. In Sect. 6, we present analytical and experimental results for the case of grid networks. Finally, Sect. 7 gives conclusions, and hints to possible future research in the area of implicit graph algorithms.

2 Implicit Graph Representation by OBDDs

In the following, the class of Boolean functions $f\colon \{0,1\}^n \to \{0,1\}$ is denoted by B_n. The ith character of a binary string x is denoted by x_i, while $|x| := \sum_{i=0}^{n-1} x_i 2^i$ identifies its value.

Node resp. edge sets S handled by implicit algorithms are represented by their characteristic Boolean function χ_S, which maps binary encodings of elements $e \in S$ to 1 and all others to 0. Therefore, the nodes get numbers $|x| \in \{0, \ldots, |V| - 1\}$, whose binary encoding x is passed to characteristic functions as $n := \lceil \log |V| \rceil$ Boolean variables. Edges are passed as pairs of node numbers by $2n$ variables: $\chi_S(x, y) = 1 \Leftrightarrow (x, y) \in S$. The Boolean functions χ_S in turn are represented by OBDDs G_{χ_S} [1], [2], [3], which are graph-based data structures considered as black boxes in this paper.

Because an OBDD G_f for a function $f \in B_n$ is also a graph, its *size* $\mathrm{size}(G_f)$ is measured by the number of its nodes. In this paper, we adopt the usual assumption that all occurring OBDDs are minimized. This is reasonable since all mentioned OBDD-operations produce only minimized diagrams, which are known to be canonical. Then, it is $\mathrm{size}(G_f) = O(2^n/n)$ for every $f \in B_n$, and a graph's edge set $E \subseteq V \times V$ has an OBDD of worst-case size $O(V^2/\log |V|)$.

Whether the function f represented by G_f is satisfiable (i.e., $f \neq 0$) can be decided in time $O(1)$. The negation $\overline{f}$ as well as the replacement of a function variable x_i by a constant c (i.e., $f_{|x_i=c}$) is computable in time $O(\mathrm{size}(G_f))$. Whether two functions f and g are equivalent (i.e., $f = g$) can be decided in time $O(\mathrm{size}(G_f) + \mathrm{size}(G_g))$. These operations are considered as *cheap*. Further essential operations offered by OBDDs are the *binary synthesis* $f \otimes g$ for $f, g \in B_n$, $\otimes \in B_2$ (e.g., "$\wedge$" and "$\vee$") and the *quantification* $(Qx_i)f$ for a quantifier $Q \in \{\exists, \forall\}$. The computation of $G_{f \otimes g}$ takes time $O(\mathrm{size}(G_f) \cdot \mathrm{size}(G_g))$, and is considered as an *expensive* operation. The computation of $G_{(Qx_i)f}$ can be realized as two cheap operations and one binary synthesis.

Besides implicit node sets and edge sets, there may occur characteristic functions $\chi_S \in B_{kn}$ representing sets $S \in V^k$ during an algorithm, which consequently receive kn Boolean variables encoding k node numbers. We will denote implicit sets $S \in V^k$ by $S(x^1, \ldots, x^k)$. In this context, the *swapping* of node arguments is an important OBDD-operation possible in linear time $\mathrm{size}(G)$ (e.g., $F(x, y) := G(y, x)$).

For example, the OBDD G_{χ_E} representing a graph's edge set E will be just denoted by $E(x, y)$; a swap of x and y yields $E(y, x)$, and reverses E's edges.

Singletons $\{s\} \subseteq V$ are represented by OBDDs $s(x)$ with $s(x) = 1 \Leftrightarrow x = s$. The IS-algorithm will be described by functional assignments like "$F(x) := G(x) \wedge H(x)$." This example corresponds to the computation of a new OBDD called $F(x)$ representing the node set $F = G \cap H$. Analogously, the disjunction "$\vee$" corresponds to the set union "$\cup$." The quantification $(\exists y_{n-1} \ldots \exists y_0)\, F(x, y)$ over the n bits of a node number y will be denoted by $(\exists y)\, F(x, y)$. Although this seems to be one OBDD-operations, this corresponds to $O(n)$ operations.

3   The IS-Algorithm

This section introduces the IS-algorithm, which computes a maximum flow from a source node s to a terminal node t in a 0–1 network $N = (V, E, s, t)$, where (V, E) is an asymmetric and directed graph. "0–1" means that all edges have capacity 1. The input N is passed to the IS-algorithm as three OBDDs $E(x, y)$, $s(x)$, and $t(x)$ corresponding to the sets E, $\{s\}$, and $\{t\}$. The number n of variables encoding one node number implies $|V| = 2^n$. The algorithm outputs the implicit edges $F(x, y)$ of a maximum set of edge-disjoint s–t-paths, which particularly is a maximum s–t-flow.

Algorithm 1 shows the outline of the IS-algorithm. As Hachtel and Somenzi's method, it pursues the layered-network approach [11] (assumed to be known by the reader). That is, the algorithm improves an actual flow $F(x, y)$ (which is initially empty) during a sequence of *phases*. In each phase, the *residual network* $A(x, y)$ is obtained by reversing the actual flow edges $F(x, y)$ in $E(x, y)$. Then, the *layered-network* $U(x, y)$ is computed, which contains the edges of all shortest s–t-paths in $A(x, y)$ (called *augmenting paths*). The main loop in lines 3–12 performs phases as long as $A(x, y)$ contains such an augmenting s–t-path (i. e., $F(x, y)$ is not maximum). The layered-networks are computed by the module layeredNetwork (lines 2 and 11), described in Sect. 4. It returns the characteristic function $U(x, y)$ respectively the zero-function if no augmenting path exists.

Algorithm 1 The IS-algorithm.

1: $F(x, y) := 0$;
2: $U(x, y) := \text{layeredNetwork}(E(x, y), s(x), t(x), F(x, y))$;
3: **while** $U(x, y) \neq 0$ **do** {Phase}
4:      $B(x, y) := 0$;
5:      **repeat** {Sweep}
6:          $B^*(x, y) := \text{compPaths}(U(x, y))$;
7:          $B(x, y) := B(x, y) \vee B^*(x, y)$;
8:          $U(x, y) := U(x, y) \wedge \overline{B^*(x, y)}$;
9:      **until** $B(x, y)$ is maximal
10:     $F(x, y) := [E(x, y) \wedge B(x, y)] \vee \left[F(x, y) \wedge \overline{B(y, x)} \right]$
11:     $U(x, y) := \text{layeredNetwork}(E(x, y), s(x), t(x), F(x, y))$;
12: **end while**

At next, a maximal (not necessarily maximum) set $B(x,y)$ of edge-disjoint s–t-paths (called *blocking-flow*) is constructed in $U(x,y)$. This construction is divided into iterations called *sweeps* (lines 5–9), each containing one call to the module compPaths (see Sect. 5). The latter results in a nonempty set $B^*(x,y)$ of edge-disjoint s–t-paths, that is added to the "blocking-flow candidate" $B(x,y)$ (line 7), while it is removed from $U(x,y)$ (line 8). Starting with $B(x,y) := 0$, this is iterated until $U(x,y)$ contains no further s–t-paths because $B(x,y)$ is maximal. In order to decide this in line 9, we compute the transitive closure [12] of $U(x,y)$ using $O(n^2)$ OBDD-operations.

One step remains to finish the actual phase: The paths of $B(x,y)$ are used to improve (*augment*) the actual flow $F(x,y)$ (line 10). Edges (u,v) with the same direction in $E(x,y)$ and $B(x,y)$ (called *forward-edges*) have not been reversed, and are added to $F(x,y)$. Reversed edges (u,v) with $(u,v) \in B$ and $(v,u) \in E$ (called *backward-edges*) are subtracted from $F(x,y)$. So the augmented flow corresponds to $[E(x,y) \wedge B(x,y)] \vee \left[F(x,y) \wedge \overline{B(y,x)}\right]$.

This outline is similar to Hachtel and Somenzi's algorithm. In Sects. 4 and 5, we will incorporate the concept of iterative squaring in order to reduce the number of operations. The following theorem on the number of OBDD-operations is proven at the end of Sect. 5.

Theorem 1. *The IS-algorithm computes a maximum flow $F_{\max}$ on a network $N = (V, E, s, t)$ through $O(\log^2 |V| \cdot S) = O(\log^2 |V| \cdot val(F_{max})) = O(\log^2 |V| \cdot |V|)$ OBDD-operations, whereby S is the number of sweep iterations and $val(F_{max})$ the maximum flow value.*

4 Layered-Network Construction

Nodes x whose shortest s–x-paths have length ν in $U(x,y)$ are said to be in *node layer ν*. Accordingly, edges from node layer ν to $\nu + 1$ are said to be in *edge layer ν*. Hachtel and Somenzi's algorithm builds $U(x,y)$ layer by layer. In contrast, the IS-algorithm works component-wise. That is, we compute a partition $C_0(x,y), \ldots, C_{r-1}(x,y)$, whereby each *partition-component* $C_i(x,y)$ contains not only one but a whole sequence of 2^{k_i} successive edge layers. The exponents k_i are strictly decreasing w.r.t. i. The edge layers of C_{i-1} and C_i are neighbored in U: C_{i-1}'s last one and C_i's first one are adjacent. Their common node layer will be called *separation-layer Z_i*. All shortest residual s–Z_i-paths have length $\sum_{j=0}^{i-1} 2^{k_j}$. Therefore, the depth of U is $\ell := \sum_{j=0}^{r-1} 2^{k_j}$. Separation-layer 0 just contains the source s ($Z_0(x) := s(x)$). In addition, we define $Z_r(x) := t(x)$.

At first, the edges $A(x,y)$ of the residual network have to be computed:

$$A(x,y) := \left[E(x,y) \wedge \overline{F(x,y)}\right] \vee F(y,x) .$$

Then, we determine functions $PATH_{k}^{\leq}(x,y)$ and $SPATH_k(x,y)$ by iterative squaring. $PATH_{k}^{\leq}(x,y)$ contains node pairs (x,y) such that there is an x–y-path not longer than 2^k in the residual network $A(x,y)$. $SPATH_k(x,y)$ contains node pairs (x, y) with a shortest x–y-path of length exactly 2^k. Both functions are initialized for $k = 0$; then, the path lengths are doubled in each iteration from k to $k + 1$:

$$PATH_0^{\leq}(x, y) := (x = y) \vee A(x, y) \ ,$$

$$PATH_{k+1}^{\leq}(x, y) := (\exists z) \, [PATH_k^{\leq}(x, z) \wedge PATH_k^{\leq}(z, y)] \ .$$

A similar recursion is used to compute $SPATH_{k+1}(x, y)$ from $SPATH_k(x, y)$ starting with $SPATH_0(x, y) = A(x, y)$. Both $PATH_k^{\leq}$ and $SPATH_k$ are now computed iteratively with increasing k until for some k^* it is either $PATH_{k^*}^{\leq}(s, t) = 1$ (the terminal has been reached) or $PATH_{k^*+1}^{\leq}(x, y) = PATH_{k^*}^{\leq}(x, y)$ (no augmenting path exists; $U(x, y) = 0$ is returned). Due to the exponential growth of the path lengths, it is $k^* = \lceil \log |V| \rceil = O(n)$.

Let us consider the layered-network depth ℓ as a binary number $\ell_{k^*} \ldots \ell_0$. Each of the r set bits $\ell_j = 1$ corresponds to one partition-component i with $k_i = j$. That is, $U(x, y)$ is composed of partition-components $C_i(x, y)$ in the same way as ℓ is composed of addends 2^{k_i}. We will use $PATH_k^{\leq}(x, y)$ and $SPATH_k(x, y)$ to perform a sort of recursive binary search called findTerminal (see Algorithm 2). This subalgorithm decides for every bit ℓ_j of ℓ whether it is set, i. e., whether a partition-component with 2^j edge-layers has to be generated.

In general, we have already computed a sequence $s(x) = Z_0(x), \ldots, Z_i(x)$ of implicit separation-layers, the component length exponents $k_0, \ldots, k_{i-1}$, and the set $R(x)$ of nodes covered by the part of U considered so far. Subalgorithm findTerminal is called to compute the remaining $(Z_{i+1}(x), \ldots, Z_r(x)) =: \mathcal{Z}$ as well as $(k_i, \ldots, k_{r+1}) =: \mathcal{K}$. It receives the arguments $Z(x) := Z_i(x)$, $R(x)$, and the exponent a, which determines the search interval $]0, 2^a]$. We start the binary search with findTerminal$(s(x), s(x), k^*)$ from source node $s(x)$ with $a = k^*$, because 2^{k^*} is an upper bound for the depth ℓ of U. The result is the lists $(Z_1(x), \ldots, Z_r(x))$ and $(k_0, \ldots, k_{r-1})$. Figure 1 shows the partitioning of an example layered-network of depth $\ell = 13$.

Algorithm 2 The recursive algorithm findTerminal$(R(x), Z(x), a)$.

1: **if** $[SPATH_a(x, t) \wedge Z(x)] \neq 0$ **then** {Case 1}
2:    return $t(x)$, a;
3: **else if** $[PATH_{a-1}^{\leq}(x, t) \wedge Z(x)] \neq 0$ **then** {Case 2}
4:    return findTerminal$(R(x), Z(x), a - 1)$;
5: **else** {Case 3}
6:    $Z'(x) := (\exists y) \, [SPATH_{a-1}(y, x) \wedge Z(y)] \wedge \overline{R(x)}$;
7:    $R'(x) := R(x) \vee (\exists y) \, [PATH_{a-1}^{\leq}(y, x) \wedge Z(y)]$;
8:    $\mathcal{Z}', \mathcal{K}' :=$ findTerminal$(R'(x), Z'(x), a - 1)$;
9:    return $(Z'(x), \mathcal{Z}')$, $(a - 1, \mathcal{K}')$;
10: **end if**

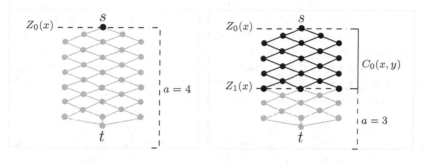

(a) Situation at the beginning
of findTerminal$(s(x), s(x), 4)$

(b) Case 3: Partition-component
$C_0(x, y)$ with $k_0 = 3$ is generated

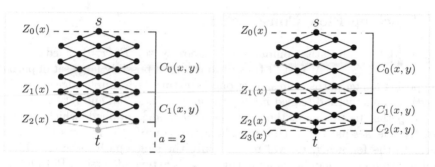

(c) Case 3: Partition-component
$C_1(x, y)$ with $k_1 = 2$ is generated

(d) After two restrictions of the
search interval (i. e. Case 2), Case 1
applies: t is found in layer 13

Fig. 1. Partitioning an example layered-network of depth 13. Black nodes/edges have already been partitioned; grey parts are unknown yet. Dashed lines indicate separation-layers. Solid brackets span partition-components, dashed brackets span search intervals

We now consider the three cases which are distinguished within Algorithm 2.

Case 1. It is $[SPATH_a(x, t) \wedge Z(x)] \neq 0$: The depth of the remaining layered-network equals 2^a. One further partition-component $i = r - 1$ with $k_i = a$ is needed. This exponent together with the final separation-layer $Z_r(x) = t(x)$ is returned (line 2).

Case 2. It is $[PATH_{a-1}^{\leq}(x, t) \wedge Z(x)] \neq 0$: There is a residual Z–t-path not longer than 2^{a-1}. Speaking in terms of a binary search, we continue in the left half $]0, 2^{a-1}]$ of the search space $]0, 2^a]$. This is achieved by the recursive call findTerminal$(R(x), Z(x), a - 1)$ in line 4.

Case 3. None of the two cases above applies: On the one hand, no partition-component of length 2^a is needed to reach t; on the other hand, none of length

2^{a-1} suffices. Thus, a further partition-component i with $k_i = a - 1$ is necessary. The nodes $Z_{i+1}(x) =: Z'(x)$ (line 6), which are reached by C_i's last edge layer, represent the starting point for the next search in $]2^{a-1}, 2^a[$. The nodes visited by paths in $C_i(x, y)$ are added to $R(x)$; the result is called $R'(x)$ (line 7).

We return $Z'(x)$ and $a - 1$ (line 9) prepended to the result lists $\mathcal{Z}'$ resp. $\mathcal{K}'$ of the remaining partitioning (done by findTerminal$(R'(x), Z'(x), a - 1)$ in line 8). The binary search continues in the right half of the search space.

With $SPATH_k(x, y)$, $k \in \{k_0, \ldots, k_{r-1}\}$, and $Z_i(x)$, $i \in \{0, \ldots, r\}$, we have all necessary information to compute the layered-network edges $U \subseteq \bigcup_{i=0}^{r-1} C_i$. For this easy step we refer to the extended version of this paper. Finally, $U(x, y)$ contains exactly those edges belonging to a shortest augmenting s–t-path in the residual network $A(x, y)$.

5   Blocking-Flow Construction

The module compPaths computes a non-empty set $B^*(x, y)$ of edge-disjoint s–t-paths in $U(x, y)$. At first, it tries to construct a possibly large set of paths by composing longer paths from shorter ones, starting with simple edges as paths of length 1. This method (called *multi-path method*) may fail and return an empty set of paths. In this case, the *single-path method* is applied, which computes exactly one s–t-path p in $U(x, y)$. Therefore, compPaths returns at least one path. In the following, we will present only the single-path method, while the multi-path method can be found in this paper's extended version. Both methods use $O(n^2)$ OBDD-operations.

5.1   Single-Path Method

All s–t-paths in $U(x, y)$ have length $\ell \leq |V| - 1$ (the layered-network depth). Although ℓ has not to be a power of two, we assume $\ell = 2^h$ for $h \in \mathbb{N}$, in order to simplify the method's description. For general depths $\ell \notin \{2^h \mid h \in \mathbb{N}\}$, the algorithm can be easily adapted.

In a preprocessing step, we compute functions $P_k(x, y, z)$, $k \in \{0, \ldots, h\}$, representing triples (x, y, z) such that an x–y-path as well as a y–z-path both of length 2^{k-1} exist in $U(x, y)$. This is done by iterative squaring similar to $PATH_k^{\leq}(x, y)$ in Sect. 4. Then, the edges $B^*(x, y)$ of an augmenting s–t-path p are obtained by computing functions $D_k(x, z)$ for $k \in \{0, \ldots, h\}$. We initialize $D_h(x, z) := s(x) \wedge t(z)$ with the pair (s, t) of p's start- and end-node. In general, $D_k(x, z)$ contains pairs (x, z) connected by paths of length 2^k in $U(x, y)$. This means that p visits x and z, while the path between these nodes is not fixed yet. Therefore, for every pair $(x, z) \in D_k$ one node y with $(x, y, z) \in P_k$ is fixed to be part of p. These resulting pairs (x, y) and (y, z), which represent subpaths of length 2^{k-1}, are united in $D_{k-1}(x, z)$.

In this way, the set $D_h(x, z)$ (which initially corresponds to all possible s–t-paths) shrinks to the set $D_0(x, z)$ whose pairs (x, z) are just edges of one augmenting path p. We now describe how $D_{k-1}(x, z)$ is computed from $D_k(x, z)$. At first, we determine all triples $(x, y, z) \in P_k$ whose start- and end-nodes x resp. z are fixed to be part of p:

$$Q_k(x, y, z) := P_k(x, y, z) \wedge D_k(x, z) .$$

$Q_k(x, y, z)$ now represents all possible subpaths $(x, \ldots, y, \ldots, z)$ of length 2^k. The middle-nodes y are selected using a *priority function* $\Pi_{x,z}$, which represents a total order $<_{x,z}$ on V depending on x and z. Hachtel and Somenzi [10] suggested two priority functions whose OBDDs have size $O(n)$.

$$\Pi_{x,z}(y', y) = 1 \Leftrightarrow y' <_{x,z} y$$
$$T_k(x, y, z) := Q_k(x, y, z) \wedge \overline{(\exists y') [Q_k(x, y', z) \wedge \Pi_{x,z}(y', y)]}$$

A triple (x, y, z) is in T_k if and only if $(x, \ldots, y, \ldots, z)$ is a possible subpath of p that respects D_k (guaranteed by Q_k) and there is no alternative $(x, y', z) \in Q_k$ whose middle-node y' is lower than y according to $\Pi_{x,z}$. That is, we choose the node y that is minimal w.r.t. $<_{x,z}$. $D_{k-1}(x, z)$ simply consists of all "upper" and "lower" parts (x, y) and (y, z) of the triples $(x, y, z) \in T_k$.

Finally, we return the edges of p as $B^*(x, y) := D_0(x, y)$. Figure 2 shows an example of a single-path construction in a layered-network of depth $\ell = 8$.

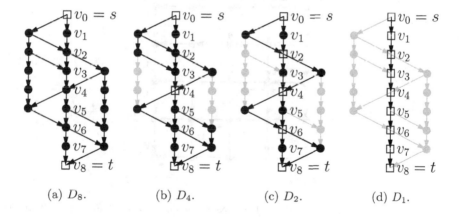

(a) D_8.   (b) D_4.   (c) D_2.   (d) D_1.

Fig. 2. Single-path construction of a path $(s = v_0, \ldots, v_8 = t)$. Boxes symbolize nodes that are already fixed in D_k. Grey nodes/edges symbolize parts of $U(x, y)$ which are already excluded from the path construction. Initially, D_8 contains the start-/end-node pair (v_0, v_8). Finally, D_1 contains p's edges and the path construction is finished

Proof (Theorem 1). Without loss of generality, we assume that a new layered-network is computed after each sweep. Each of these $O(S)$ layered-network computations contains $O(k^* + r) = O(\log |V|)$ iterations. Each iteration performs $O(n) = O(\log |V|)$ OBDD-operations (caused by quantifications over node number of length n). Each sweep calls module compPaths, which consists of $O(h) = O(\log |V|)$ iterations with $O(n)$ operations each. The maximality test of $B(x, y)$ incorporates a transitive closure computation with $O(\log^2 |V|)$ operations. The remaining steps of removing $B^*(x, y)$ from $U(x, y)$ and augmenting $F(x, y)$ by $B(x, y)$ can be done by a constant number of operations. Altogether, each sweep executes $O(\log |V|^2)$ OBDD-operations, and increases F's value.   □

6   Grid Networks

In this section, both an analytical and an experimental result for the case of quadratic $(2^k + 1) \times (2^k + 1)$-grid networks $N = (V, E, s, t)$ is presented. (For a detailed analysis the reader is referred to [5].) These grids are $(2^k+1) \times (2^k+1)$-matrices of nodes $V = \{0, \dots, 2^k\}^2$ which contain edges between horizontally as well as between vertically adjacent nodes. Edges are directed towards the higher row resp. column index. $(0, 0) =: s$ serves as the source, while $(2^k, 2^k) =: t$ serves as the terminal. Independent from k, the maximum flow value of these grids is 2 and the IS-algorithm executes two sweeps at most. In fact, it can be shown that only one sweep is necessary. Figure 3 shows such a network for $k = 2$ as well as the maximum flow constructed by the IS-algorithm.

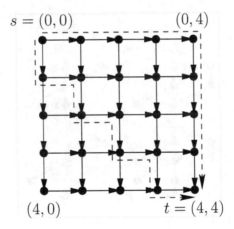

Fig. 3. The 5×5-grid network and a maximum flow. Dashed arrows indicate the constructed maximum flow

6.1   Analysis

Theorem 2. *The IS-algorithm computes a maximum flow on $(2^k+1) \times (2^k+1)$-grid networks in time $O(k^3)$ and space $O(k^2)$.*

It is $|V| = 2^{2k}+2^{k+1}+1$ and $k = \Theta(\log |V|)$. We assume that grid nodes $x \in V$ are encoded by $n := 2(k + 1)$ Boolean variables $x_{n-1} \dots x_0$, which represent the row index x^{r} and column index x^{c} of x each by $k + 1$ bits. Consider a function $F \in B_{d(k+1)}$ defined on $d = O(1)$ row or column arguments $y^1, \ldots, y^d \in \{0,1\}^{k+1}$. If there are weights $w_1, \ldots, w_d \in \{-1, 0, 1\}$ and a threshold value $T \in \mathbb{Z}$ such that

$$F(y^1, \ldots, y^d) = \left(\sum_{i=1}^{k} w_i \cdot |y^i| \geq T \right) ,$$

then F is called a *multivariate threshold function* [4]. Any constant-size formula over such multivariate threshold functions can be represented by an OBDD of size $O(k)$. Due to Woelfel [13], this still holds after the application of an arbitrary sequence $\exists y^{i_1} \ldots \exists y^{i_m}$ of m existential quantifiers, $i_1, \ldots, i_m \in \{1, \ldots, d\}$. Moreover, operations on such OBDDs take only time $O(k)$ [5].

The idea of the analysis is to prove for functions $F \in B_{dn}$ occurring during the flow maximization that they realize constant-size formulas over multivariate threshold functions. We exemplarily consider the implicit edge set $E(x, y)$:

$$E(x, y) = (x^{\mathrm{r}} \leq 2^k) \wedge (x^{\mathrm{c}} \leq 2^k) \wedge (y^{\mathrm{r}} \leq 2^k) \wedge (y^{\mathrm{c}} \leq 2^k)$$
$$\wedge \, (y^{\mathrm{r}} - x^{\mathrm{r}} + y^{\mathrm{c}} - x^{\mathrm{c}} = 1) \wedge (y^{\mathrm{r}} - x^{\mathrm{r}} \geq 0) \wedge (y^{\mathrm{c}} - x^{\mathrm{c}} \geq 0) \, .$$

Only nodes within the $(2^k + 1) \times (2^k + 1)$-square are touched by edges. There is an edge between node x and y if and only if either there horizontal or vertical distance is 1.

In the same way, it can be shown that all OBDDs during the flow maximization on $(2^k + 1) \times (2^k + 1)$-grid networks have size $O(k)$ and can also be processed in time $O(k)$. This implies a runtime $O(k)$ for each of the $O(k^2)$ operations and, therefore, the over-all runtime result. Because no more than $O(k)$ OBDDs are present at the same time during the algorithm, the space usage is $O(k^2)$. In contrast, Hachtel and Somenzi's method [10] needs $\Omega(2^k \cdot k)$ operations. These results hold if the square between s and t is embedded in a larger non-quadratic grid.

6.2   Experimental Results

Both the IS-algorithm and Hachtel and Somenzi's maximum flow method [10] have been implemented[1] in C++. In order to confirm the practical relevance of Theorem 2, both algorithms have been applied on $(2^k + 1) \times (2^k + 1)$-grids for $0 \leq k \leq 16$ on a PC with Pentium 4 2GHz processor and 512 MB of main memory. For $k > 16$, the system's memory did not suffice to apply Hachtel and Somenzi's method. In contrast, the IS-algorithm was executed up to $k = 19$, and did not reach the memory limit in the experiments. Figures 4(a) and 4(b) show the experimental results by means of runtime and space usage. Space is measured in the maximum number of nodes contained in all OBDDs at any time. It can be seen that the IS-algorithm beats the space usage of Hachtel and Somenzi's method for $k \geq 13$, while the runtime is beaten for $k \geq 16$.

---

[1] Implementation available at http://thefigaro.sourceforge.net/.

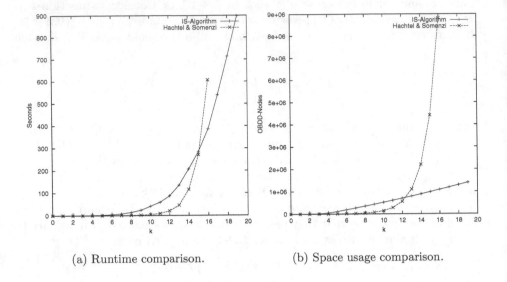

(a) Runtime comparison.   (b) Space usage comparison.

Fig. 4. Experimental results on $(2^k + 1) \times (2^k + 1)$-grid networks

7   Conclusions

An implicit algorithm for flow maximization in 0–1 networks has been presented
which uses the technique of iterative squaring. In this way, only $O(\log^2 |V|)$
OBDD-operations are needed to compute a layered-network or at least one augmenting path. At best, this amount suffices for the whole flow computation (in
particular for constant maximum flow values). The over-all runtime is influenced
also by the occurring OBDD-sizes. These have been analyzed exemplarily for grid
networks, on which the IS-algorithm beats previous methods both asymptoti-
cally and in experiments.

   At the moment, there exist only implicit flow maximization methods for the
special case of 0–1 networks. The extension to networks with arbitrary edge
capacities could be an area of future research. Moreover, it is desirable to analyze the runtime behavior of implicit max-flow algorithms on more sophisticated
network classes. Promising candidates are slightly irregular grids, decomposable
graphs, and graphs with locality properties. Furthermore, flow problems like
flow minimization or multicommodity flows as well as other important graph
problems may be attacked by implicit methods.

Acknowledgments. Thanks to Thomas Hofmeister and Ingo Wegener for
proofreading and for helpful discussions.

References

1. Bryant, R.: Symbolic Manipulation of Boolean Functions Using a Graphical Representation. In: Design Automation Conference, ACM Press (1985) 688–694
2. Bryant, R.: Graph-Based Algorithms for Boolean Function Manipulation. IEEE Transactions on Computers **35** (1986) 677–691
3. Wegener, I.: Branching Programs and Binary Decision Diagrams. SIAM, Philadelphia (2000)
4. Woelfel, P.: Symbolic Topological Sorting with OBDDs. Volume 2747. (2003) 671–680
5. Sawitzki, D.: Implicit Flow Maximization on Grid Networks. Technical Report, Universität Dortmund (2003)
6. Woelfel, P.: The OBDD-Size of Cographs. Internal Report, Universität Dortmund (2003)
7. Bloem, R., Gabow, H., Somenzi, F.: An Algorithm for Strongly Connected Component Analysis in $n \log n$ Symbolic Steps. In: Formal Methods in Computer-Aided Design. LNCS, Vol. 1954. Springer (2000) 37–54
8. Ravi, K., Bloem, R., Somenzi, F.: A Comparative Study of Symbolic Algorithms for the Computation of Fair Cycles. In: Formal Methods in Computer-Aided Design. LNCS, Vol. 1954. Springer (2000) 143–160
9. Hachtel, G., Somenzi, F.: Logic Synthesis and Verification Algorithms. Kluwer Academic Publishers, Boston (1996)
10. Hachtel, G., Somenzi, F.: A Symbolic Algorithm for Maximum Flow in 0–1 Networks. Formal Methods in System Design **10** (1997) 207–219
11. Even, S.: Graph Algorithms. Computer Science Press, Rockville (1979)
12. Hojati, R., Touati, H., Kurshan, R., Brayton, R.: Efficient ω-Regular Language Containment. In: Computer-Aided Verification. LNCS, Vol. 663. Springer (1993) 396–409
13. Woelfel, P.: Private Communication (2003)

Evolving Constructors for Infinitely Growing Sorting Networks and Medians

Lukáš Sekanina

Faculty of Information Technology, Brno University of Technology
Božetěchova 2, 612 66 Brno, Czech Republic
sekanina@fit.vutbr.cz

Abstract. An approach is presented in which the object under design can grow continually and infinitely. First, a small object (that we call the embryo) has to be prepared to solve the trivial instance of a problem. Then the evolved program (the constructor) is applied on the embryo to create a larger object (solving a larger instance of the problem). Then the same constructor is used to create a new instance of the object from the created larger object and so on. Every new instance of the object is able to perform the function of all previous instances. As an example, constructors for growing sorting and median networks are evolved and analyzed.

1 Introduction

In the past few years, evolutionary algorithms have successfully been applied to automatically design various objects including computer programs, neural networks, electronic circuits, etc. [1], [16]. However, these methods have produced interesting results only for design of relatively small objects.

For instance, the problem of scale is usually considered as a major problem of evolvable hardware. It is practically impossible to evolve really complex circuits from scratch nowadays. Complex systems require huge number of gates (inputs, outputs, etc.) to be implemented, i.e. long genotypes in the case of the evolutionary approach. Long genotypes imply large search spaces. Then it is usually difficult to design an efficient search algorithm. Miller et al. offer two ways to build large systems [17]: (1) to discover a general scalable principle of design or (2) to produce building blocks as efficient and large as possible. Three major approaches have been developed in order to overcome the scaling problem [19]: functional level evolution, incremental evolution and the embryonic approach.

The concept of development in which the entire organism is built from a mother cell was adopted from biology to allow the "growth" of objects' complexity. When such a concept is implemented, the chromosome has to contain a prescription for constructing a target object.

It is a common feature of artificial developmental systems that the object under construction is not functional during its development. In contrary, biological systems are able to perform some operations at any given time point

P. Van Emde Boas et al. (Eds.): SOFSEM 2004, LNCS 2932, pp. 314–323, 2004.

of the development. These "skills" are improved and new skills are continually created during the growth of the system. The organism does not usually forget the obtained skills.

In this paper we present an approach in which an object can grow continually and infinitely. First, a small object (that we call the embryo) has to be prepared to solve the trivial instance of a problem. Then the evolved program (the constructor) is applied on the embryo to create a larger object (solving a larger instance of the problem). Then the constructor is used to create a new instance of the object from the created larger object and so on. Every new instance of the object is able to perform the function of all previous instances.

The main objective of this research is to design the constructor automatically by means of evolutionary techniques. The constructor will consist of two basic operations: copy and modify. It is shown that such the constructor can be evolved. As examples large sorting networks and median networks will be constructed because it is difficult to evolve large instances of these objects directly.

This paper is organized as follows. In Section 2 related research is presented in which evolutionary algorithms were combined with developmental systems. Sorting networks and medians are considered as the application domain in Section 3. The evolutionary algorithm utilized to design constructors of an infinitely growing median network is described in Section 4. Section 5 summarizes and discusses the obtained results. Finally conclusions are given in Section 6.

2   Related Work

Nature approaches the problem of scale by using a complicated mapping embodied in the process of biological development. Biological genomes contain a complex process of regulated gene expression to map genotype to phenotype.

In bioinspired hardware and software systems this mapping is often implemented by means of re-writing systems. Boers and Kuiper have utilized L-systems to create the architecture of feed-forward artificial neural networks (numbers of neurons and their connections) [2]. Haddow et al. have adopted L-system in order to evolve scalable circuits [7]. Kitano have applied a matrix re-writing to develop digital circuits. Three dimensional mechanical objects have been designed by evolution that also utilized a variant of L-system [9].

John Koza has introduced an original method in which analog circuits (competitive with best human designs) have been constructed according to the instructions produced by genetic programming [16]. Koza's team employed this technique for routine duplication of fourteen patented inventions in the analog circuit domain [20].

In another approach, Gordon and Bentley have utilized the interaction of genes and proteins to model the development in digital circuits [6]. CAM Brain machine [5] and POEtic platform [21] are examples of those systems that use cellular automata-based development.

Miller and Thomson have invented a developmental method for growing graphs and circuits using Cartesian genetic programming in order to evolve similar constructors to ours (referred to as iterators in [18]). Because they worked at a very low level of abstraction (as configuration bits of a hypothetical re-configurable hardware) no general constructor has been found for even parity circuits. However, other researchers have successfully evolved completely general solutions to even-parity problems; for instance Huelsbergen, who has worked at the machine code level [10].

3   Sorting Networks and Medians

The concept of sorting networks was introduced in 1954; Knuth traced the history of this problem in his book [14].

A *compare–swap* of two elements (a, b) compares and exchanges a and b so that we obtain $a \leq b$ after the operation. A sorting network is a sequence of compare–swap operations that depends only on the number of elements to be sorted, not on the values of the elements [14].

Although a standard sorting algorithm such as quicksort usually requires a lower number of compare operations than a sorting network, the advantage of the sorting network is that the sequence of comparisons is fixed. Thus it is suitable for parallel processing and hardware implementation, especially if the number of sorted elements is small. Figure 1 shows an example of a sorting network.

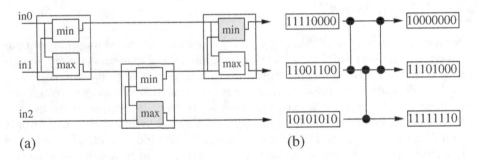

(a)   (b)

Fig. 1. (a) A 3-sorting network consists of 3 components, i.e. of 6 subcomponents (elements of maximum or minimum). A 3-median network consists of 4 subcomponents. (b) Alternative symbol. This sorting network can be tested in a single run if 2^3 bits can be stored in a single data unit

Having a sorting network for N inputs, the *median* is simply the output value at the middle position (we are interested in odd N only in this paper). For example, efficient calculation of the median value is important in signal processing where median filters are widely used with $N = 3\text{x}3$ or $5\text{x}5$ [19].

The number of compare–swap components and the delay are two crucial parameters of any sorting network. Since we will only be interested in the number of components in this paper, the following Table 1 shows the number of components of some of the best currently know sorting networks, i.e. those which require the least number of components for sorting N elements. Some of these networks ($N = 13$–16) were discovered using evolutionary techniques [3], [8], [12], [16]. However, the evolutionary approach is not scalable. For instance, we were not able to directly evolve any 25-median network up to now.

Note that the compare-swap consists of two subcomponents: maximum and minimum. Because we need the middle output value only in the case of the median implementation, we can omit some subcomponents (dead code at the output marked in gray in Fig. 1) and so to reduce implementation cost in hardware. Hence in the case of K components, we obtain $2K - K + 1$ subcomponents (Table 1, line 3). However, in addition to deriving median networks from sorting networks, specialized networks have been proposed to implement optimal median networks. Table 1 (line 2) also presents the best-known numbers of subcomponents for optimal median networks. These values are derived from the table on page 226 of Knuth's book [14] and from papers [4], [15], [22]. The space complexity of the general algorithm constructing sorting networks is $O(N(logN)^2)$ [14].

Table 1. Best known minimum-comparison sorting networks and median networks for some N. $c(N)$ denotes the number of compare–swap operations, $s(N)$ is the number of subcomponents. The last line holds for median networks derived from sorting networks

N	3	4	5	6	7	8	9	10	11	12	13	14	15	16	25
sortnet, $c(N)$	3	5	9	12	16	19	25	29	35	39	45	51	56	60	144
median, $s(N)$	4	-	10	-	20	-	30	-	42	-	52	-	66	-	174
median, $s(N)$	4	-	14	-	26	-	42	-	60	-	78	-	98	-	264

The *zero–one* principle helps with evaluating sorting networks. It states that if a sorting network with N inputs sorts all 2^N input sequences of 0's and 1's into nondecreasing order, it will sort any arbitrary sequence of N numbers into nondecreasing order [14]. Furthermore, if we use a proper encoding, on say 32 bits, and binary operators AND instead of minimum and OR instead of maximum, we can evaluate 32 test vectors in parallel and thus reduce the testing process 32 times. Figure 1 illustrates this idea for 3 bits. Note that it is usually impossible to obtain the general solution if only a subset of input vectors is utilized during the evolutionary design [11].

4   Development Using Copy and Modify

Consider that we have a 3-median network (i.e. $N = 3$ as seen in Fig. 1) and we are going to evolve a program (constructor) that will create a 5-median network from the 3-median network. The same program has to be able to create a 7-median network from the 5-median network and so on. Another available information is the number of active inputs (i.e. N) of the currently constructed network.

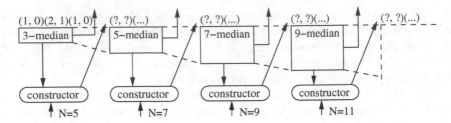

Fig. 2. Designing larger sorting networks from smaller sorting networks by means of constructor

4.1   Representation

The 3-median network is represented by the sequence of pairs $(1, 0)(2, 1)(1, 0)$ indicating the ordering of compare–swap operations over the inputs 0, 1 and 2. The constructor is also a sequence of instructions: each of which is encoded as three integers. Only three instructions are utilized: *copy*, *modify* and *skip*. Table 2 introduces their operational codes and parameters. The sequences representing sorting networks as well as constructors are implemented using variable-length arrays. A sentinel (STOP) indicates the end of the valid sequence.

Table 2. Instruction set. The pc pointer is increased to $pc \leftarrow pc + 3$ after execution of each instruction. The former sequence (a, b)(c, d)... is transcribed to new sequence (a', b')(c', d')... M denotes the number of inputs of the currently created median network

Instruction	Opcode	Op1	Op2	Description
ModifyN	0	x	y	$(a', b') \leftarrow ((a + x) \bmod M, (b + y) \bmod M)$ $pn \leftarrow pn + 2$
ModifyR	1	x	y	$(a', b') \leftarrow ((a + x) \bmod M, (b + y) \bmod M)$ $pf \leftarrow pf + 2, pn \leftarrow pn + 2$
CopyN	2	x	y	copies $M - x$ pairs from former to new sequence $pn \leftarrow pn + 2(M - x)$
CopyR	3	x	y	copies $M - x$ pairs from former to new sequence $pf \leftarrow pf + 2(M - x), pn \leftarrow pn + 2(M - x)$
Skip	4	x	y	$pf \leftarrow pf + 2$

The constructor, according to its program, sequentially reads the embryo and copies (or copies and modifies) the embryo into the next instance. Three pointers are utilized in order to indicate the current position in sequences: the embryo pointer (pf), the next instance pointer (pn) and the constructor pointer (pc). The constructor creates the next instance of the network not from the entire previous instance, but only from its newest part. The process of construction terminates when either STOP symbol is read in the sequence of "embryo" or all instructions of the constructor have been executed. The constructed median network is then tested in the process of fitness calculation.

4.2   Evolutionary Algorithm

Any chromosome consists of a sequence of integers that represents a constructor. We initially approached the problem with variable-length chromosomes. However, the approach did not produce general constructors. Hence we had to use the fixed size of chromosomes. After some experiments we learned that useful constructors consist of 5–8 instructions, i.e. 15–24 integers.

A typical setting of the evolutionary algorithm is as follows. Initial population of 320 individuals is seeded randomly using alleles of 0–4. New individuals are generated using operators of crossover ($p_c = 60\%$) and mutation (1 integer per chromosome). Tournament selection with base 2 is combined with elitism. The evolutionary algorithm is left running until a fully correct individual is found or 2000 generations are exhausted. We also increase mutation rate if no improvement is observable during the last 30 generations.

The objective is to evolve a general constructor. However, because of scalability problems only several instances of the median network can be evaluated in the fitness calculation process. Hence a candidate constructor is used to build the 5-median, 7-median, 9-median and 11-median network from the 3-median embryo. We have not been able to evolve general constructors by testing smaller networks. The fitness value is calculated as follows:

$$fitness = m_5 + m_7 + m_9 + m_{11},$$

where m_k denotes the number of median values calculated correctly from 2^k testing binary vectors of size k. Hence 32+128+512+2048=2720 is the best possible value that we could obtain.

5   Results and Discussion

If a constructor is able to create the median network for a sufficiently high value of N (N=27 in our case) then we consider the constructor as general. In our experiments, 108 of 180 runs led to the perfect fitness. However, we identified only 11 general constructors. These general constructors (listed in Table 3) consist of 5 to 8 instructions. For example, gr5-3 and gr5-4 are practically the same programs because they differ only in the last integer, which represents the second (meaningless) operand of the Modify instruction as seen in Table 2.

We were also interested in reducing the number of components in the evolved designs. Table 4 shows the size of two median networks generated using gr5-4 and gr6-1 constructors. While the gr5-4 constructor consists of six instructions, the gr6-1 utilizes only five instructions. The gr5-4 constructor – and thus also gr5-1 and gr5-3 constructors – are probably the best constructors we have ever evolved. We were not able to reduce the size of networks if only 5 instructions should be used. Furthermore, Table 4 also shows that we were not able to beat the well-known general approach for designing larger networks illustrated in Fig. 5.

Table 3. Chromosomes of eleven general constructors evolved

Constructor	Chromosome
gr3-6	0,2,2, 0,3,3, 2,2,4, 0,2,2, 3,4,4, 3,4,0, 2,1,3, 2,1,3
gr4-6	0,2,2, 0,3,2, 0,2,2, 0,3,3, 0,2,1, 3,0,4, 2,2,0
gr4-7	0,2,2, 0,3,1, 0,2,4, 0,3,3, 0,2,2, 3,0,1, 2,2,3
gr4-8	0,2,2, 0,2,3, 0,0,2, 0,3,3, 0,2,1, 3,3,4, 3,2,3
gr4-9	0,2,2, 0,1,1, 0,3,2, 0,3,3, 3,2,3, 3,1,4, 0,2,0
gr5-1	0,2,2, 0,3,2, 0,3,1, 0,3,3, 3,1,0, 2,3,2
gr5-3	0,2,2, 0,3,1, 0,3,3, 0,2,2, 3,2,3, 2,0,3
gr5-4	0,2,2, 0,3,1, 0,3,3, 0,2,2, 3,2,3, 2,0,4
gr6-1	1,2,1, 0,2,2, 0,1,1, 2,3,2, 2,1,1
gr13-8	1,2,1, 0,2,2, 0,1,1, 2,3,0, 3,1,2
gr13-9	1,2,1, 0,2,2, 0,1,1, 2,3,2, 3,1,3

Table 4. The number of compare-swap operations $c(N)$ used by two evolved constructors and the conventional approach (according to Fig. 5) to realize growing median networks

N	3	5	7	9	11	13	15	17	19	21	23	25	27
gr5-4	3	10	21	36	55	78	105	136	171	210	253	300	351
gr6-1	3	10	23	40	61	86	115	148	185	226	271	320	373
conventional	3	10	21	36	55	78	105	136	171	210	253	300	351

Figure 3 shows that the gr4-5 constructor generates regular pattern of compare–swap operations. First, new four compare–swap operations are generated in order to deal with two emerging inputs. Then the median network is copied from the previous instance. It is interesting to see that the first two comparisons can be performed in parallel.

It was surprising for us that although we wanted to evolve general constructors only to create median networks, we obtained general constructors for building sorting networks. We used all 11 general constructors to generate sorting networks and they worked! An open question is whether general constructors exist that create median networks only but they do not create sorting networks. We can observe after the analysis of growing networks that their structure is very similar to the well-known principle of building a sorting network for $N + 1$ elements from a sorting network of N elements (see [14]). Thus we rediscovered this principle by artificial evolution.

Another question is whether the created networks are of practical interest. Although a number of developmental systems have been proposed to make the evolutionary design scalable, only a few of them have been applied to design objects more complex than we can do without development. The created networks are large and fully operational; however, inefficient in terms of compare–swap operations.

The proposed algorithm produced the expected results, since a lot of problem-domain knowledge (such as the usage of copy and modify instructions) has been

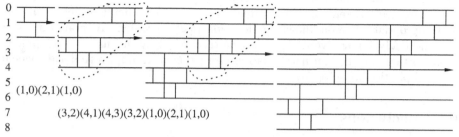

(1,0)(2,1)(1,0)

(3,2)(4,1)(4,3)(3,2)(1,0)(2,1)(1,0)

(5,4)(6,3)(6,5)(5,4)(3,2)(4,1)(4,3)(3,2)(1,0)(2,1)(1,0)

constructor:
ModifyN 2,2; ModifyN 3,1; ModifyN 3,3; ModifyN 2,2; CopyR 2,3; CopyN 0,4;

Fig. 3. Constructing larger networks using the evolved gr5-4 constructor

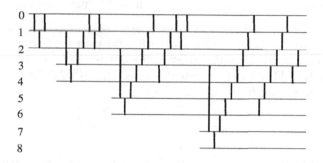

Fig. 4. Constructing larger networks using the evolved gr6-1 constructor

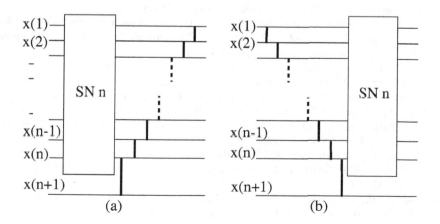

Fig. 5. Making (n+1)-sorters from n-sorters: (a) insertion, (b) selection

presented in its inductive bias. The idea of evolving constructors for infinitely growing objects is generally applicable. However, it is difficult to define embryo and appropriate domain knowledge for a particular problem. Although it seems that no really innovative designs can be discovered by means of development, large sorting and median networks represent typical examples that can benefit from inspiration in ontogeny.

6 Conclusions

A simple method with strong inductive bias was proposed for evolving constructors of infinitely growing median networks. It was not a problem to evolve general constructors for sorting network since they are the same as for growing median networks. However, the open questions are whether it is possible to evolve general constructors for creating (1) more area–efficient median networks and (2) those area–efficient networks that do not fully operate during development. These problems will be investigated in our future research.

Acknowledgment. The research was performed with the Grant Agency of the Czech Republic under No. 102/03/P004 *Evolvable hardware based application design methods* and the Research intention No. CEZ MSM 262200012 – *Research in information and control systems*.

References

1. Bentley, P.: Evolutionary Design By Computers. Morgan Kaufmann Publishers, San Francisco CA (1999)
2. Boers, E. J. W., Kuiper, H.: Biological Metaphors and the Design of Artificial Neural Networks. Master Thesis, Departments of Computer Science and Experimental and Theoretical Psychology, Leiden University (1992)
3. Choi, S. S., Moon, B. R.: More Effective Genetic Search for the Sorting Network Problem. In: Proc. of the Genetic and Evolutionary Computation Conference GECCO'02, Morgan Kaufmann (2002) 335–342
4. Devillard, N.: Fast Median Search: An ANSI C Implementation. (1998) http://ndevilla.free.fr/median/median/index.html
5. de Garis, H., et al.: ATR's Artificial Brain (CAM-Brain) Project: A Sample of What Individual "CoDi-1 Bit" Model Evolved Neural Net Modules Can Do With Digital and Analog I/O. In: Proc. of the 1st NASA/DoD Workshop on Evolvable Hardware, IEEE CS Press (1999) 102–110
6. Gordon, T.G.W., Bentley, P.: Towards Development in Evolvable Hardware. In: Proc. of the 2002 NASA/DoD Conference on Evolvable Hardware, IEEE CS Press (2002) 241–250
7. Haddow, P., Tufte, G., van Remortel, P.: Shrinking the Genotype: L-systems for EHW? In: Proc. of the 4th International Conference on Evolvable Systems: From Biology to Hardware, LNCS 2210, Springer–Verlag 128–139
8. Hillis, W.D.: Co-Evolving Parasites Improve Simulated Evolution as an Optimization Procedure. Physica D 42 (1990) 228–234

9. Hornby, G.S., Pollack, J.B.: The Advantages of Generative Grammatical Encodings for Physical Design. In: Proc. of the 2001 Congress on Evolutionary Computation CEC2001, IEEE CS Press, (2001) 600–607
10. Huelsbergen, L.: Finding General Solutions to the Parity Problem by Evolving Machine-Language Representations. In: Proc. of Conf. on Genetic Programming (1998) 158–166
11. Imamura, K., Foster, J.A., Krings, A.W.: The Test Vector Problem and Limitations to Evolving Digital Circuits. In: Proc. of the 2nd NASA/DoD Workshop on Evolvable Hardware, IEEE CS Press (2000) 75–79
12. Juillé, H.: Evolution of Non-Deterministic Incremental Algorithms as a New Approach for Search in State Spaces. In: Proc. of 6th Int. Conf. on Genetic Algorithms, Morgan Kaufmann (1995) 351–358
13. Kitano, H.: Morphogenesis for Evolvable Systems. In: Towards Evolvable Hardware: The Evolutionary Engineering Approach, LNCS 1062, Springer-Verlag (1996) 99-117
14. Knuth, D.E.: The Art of Computer Programming: Sorting and Searching (2nd ed.). Addison Wesley (1998)
15. Kolte, P., Smith, R., Su, W.: A Fast Median Filter Using AltiVec. In: Proc. of the IEEE Conf. on Computer Design, Austin, Texas, IEEE CS Press (1999) 384–391
16. Koza, J.R., Bennett III., F.H., Andre, D., Keane, M.A.: Genetic Programming III: Darwinian Invention and Problem Solving. Morgan Kaufmann (1999)
17. Miller, J., Job, D., Vassilev, V.: Principles in the Evolutionary Design of Digital Circuits – Part II. Genetic Programming and Evolvable Machines. **1** 2 (2000) 259–288
18. Miller, J., Thomson, P.: A Developmental Method for Growing Graphs and Circuits. In: Proc. of the 5th Conf. on Evolvable Systems: From Biology to Hardware ICES 2003. LNCS 2606, Springer–Verlag (2003) 93–104
19. Sekanina, L.: Evolvable Components: From Theory to Hardware Implementations. Natural Computing Series, Springer-Verlag (2003)
20. Streeter, M.J., Keane, M.A., Koza, J.R.: Routine Duplication of Post-2000 Patented Inventions by Means of Genetic Programming. In: Proc. of the 5th European Conference on Genetic Programming, Kinsale, Ireland, LNCS 2278, Springer-Verlag (2002) 26-36
21. Tempesti, G. et al.: Ontogenetic Development and Fault Tolerance in the POEtic Tissue. In: Proc. of the 5th Conf. on Evolvable Systems: From Biology to Hardware ICES 2003, LNCS 2606, Springer-Verlag (2003) 141–152
22. Zeno, R.: A Reference of the Best-Known Sorting Networks for up to 16 Inputs. 2003, http://www.angelfire.com/blog/ronz/

Fuzzy Group Models for Adaptation in Cooperative Information Retrieval Contexts

Miguel-Ángel Sicilia and Elena García

Computer Science Department, Polytechnic School, University of Alcalá
Ctra. Barcelona km. 33.6, 28871 – Alcalá de Henares, Madrid, Spain
{msicilia,elena.garciab}@uah.es

Abstract. Cooperation in information retrieval contexts can be used to share query results inside groups of individuals with common objectives, provided that all of them are aware of each other. The strength of the social relationships between group members is in most cases a matter of comparative degree, and thus relationships can be modelled through fuzzy conceptual associations. These associations can then be used to implement personalized features, aimed at improving the interaction of the user with the query tool. In this paper, an approach to modelling imprecise relationships between users in the context of information retrieval is described, along with a concrete case study implemented as a wrapper of a conventional search engine, using a fuzzy database to store the model of the group members.

Keywords. Fuzzy conceptual modelling, cooperative information retrieval, adaptive hypermedia, fuzzy databases.

1 Introduction

Research on *interactive information retrieval* (IIR) [16] is concerned with the study of human interaction issues in their process of using information retrieval (IR) systems. IIR can be considered a complementary view of the classical system-oriented view of IR (see, for example, [8]), and has given rise to specific models like the interactive feedback and search model proposed by Spink [23]. From among the diverse complex interactions that are pursued in IR contexts, cooperation[1] between users in a group have resulted in specific algorithms that exploit the history of queries (see, for example, [9]) in the process of resolving new ones. But, in addition to improved retrieval algorithms, the social context of the search activity can be exploited to improve other aspects of user's everyday's search tasks when the group is organized around common objectives. For example, in the context of a research group, users can share some of their conference bookmarks that are supposedly of interest to other people in the group.

---

[1] We use here the term cooperation: "to act or work with another or others" as a more general term than collaboration "to work jointly with others or together ", since the latter entails a common concrete desired outcome.

P. Van Emde Boas et al. (Eds.): SOFSEM 2004, LNCS 2932, pp. 324–334, 2004.

In consequence, user interfaces for IR systems that enable cooperation [17] can take advantage of some kind of *group model* — i.e. a model of the interrelation between group members — to implement adaptive features [5].

Collaborative filtering (CF) systems [11] exploit similarities between users in browsing or search processes, but they do that in a transparent manner for the user, so that people receiving recommendations are unaware of the fact that neighborhoods of users that somewhat agree with them have been computed by the CF algorithm. Thus, a system-oriented view of groups is used, that does not take into account the potential of explicit, user-initiated interactions between users that are socially aware of the others, which are known to improve cooperation, as studied in systems like [13].

In this paper, a concrete cooperative IR model is described, which provides a number of features for the explicit cooperation between users in a group with related interests (i.e. that provides functionalities for cooperative search *tactics* [2]). Two key aspects of such a cooperative setting are the modelling of the *closeness* between users and of the *perceived relevance* of certain types of communication events like user-to-user recommendations. Both kinds of social relationships between group members are inherently imprecise and uncertain, since they evolve with time and they should be measured by some form of analysis of the recorded interaction history. We describe here how these relationships can be modelled as fuzzy relationships at the conceptual level, and also how they can be stored in fuzzy relational database structures in the final implementation. In addition, relationships can be used to define fuzzy categories of users with regards to their social interaction characteristics, like the concept of "pertinent" users. Although the model only deals with fuzziness at the group model level, it could be potentially combined with existing fuzzy techniques that enhance the query resolution process — see, for example [12].

The rest of this paper is structured as follows. In Section 2, the general cooperative information retrieval setting is described. Section 3 provides the conceptual description of a concrete case study that uses fuzziness to model social relationships, along with a brief description of the implementation. Finally, conclusions and future research directions are provided in Section 4.

2   Modelling Fuzzy Social Relations in Group IR Tasks

Cooperative IR contexts are used by one or several groups of users that can be denoted by a set $G = \{g_1, \ldots, g_n\}$. Each of the groups is made up of a collection of users from a set U that can be denoted as $users(g_i)$ or $g_i = \{u_1^i, \ldots, u_m^i\}$. Communications can be initiated by users inside the same group. *Awareness* is taken for granted in this model, so that it's assumed that the group constituents know each other *a priori* or appropriate awareness tools are provided.

The information retrieval system S continuously resolves queries matching query strings against the contents of its resource base, which essentially is a set of contents C (in different, possibly multimedia, formats). The set representing the history of queries of the group g_i is denoted by s_{g_i}, and the subset of queries for a given user $x \in g_i$ is denoted by $s_{g_i}^x$.

Essentially, two basic policies can be used to improve the interaction of each user from information provided by others users of the group. *System-intentional* interactions take information from the group constituents to obtain patterns or similarity measures. Research on *collaborative filtering* is mainly focused on this kind of interaction — even when it target groups like in [15] —, in which the system elaborates recommendations by exploring relationships between items and between users [18]. *Peer-intentional* interactions are of a very different nature. In this case, the users consciously direct suggestions or indications — that they believe to be interesting or significant — to some of their colleagues. Of course, both kinds of policies can be combined.

The system provides a number of peer-intentional interactions in the form of asynchronous messages with signatures, i.e., **m**(*parameters*). A typical example of such a message is that of recommending a search result to a peer or a set of them, which could be modelled as **recommend**$(u : 2^U; \ c : C)$. This concrete type of message is central to the case study described below.

The general form of a social relationship inside a group can be denoted by a fuzzy relation with the form $R : g_i \times g_i \to [0, 1]$, so that $R(u_a^i, u_b^i)$ represents the strength of the relationship between users a and a inside group i. The model of each social relationship $R \in \mathcal{R}$ that we are concerned in this work is thus constructed from the history of message instances by some form of computation algorithm denoted by $\mathcal{C}_R$. In addition, fuzzy categories of users can be defined as fuzzy subsets of the set of users in the social group $g_i \in G$ being considered. Both forms of fuzziness are generalizations of their crisp counterparts that are found in adaptive hypermedia modelling frameworks [21].

3   Case Study Description

The generic modelling approach described in Section 2 has been used for the design of a research group-oriented cooperative IR interface called `deiSearch`, which follows a peer-intentional policy of interaction. The application is essentially a wrapper using the `Google` programming interfaces[2] to resolve queries and obtain results, while recording the search history of each group member to implement adaptive features based on simple cooperative behaviors.

3.1   Conceptual Model

The conceptual modelling elements for adaptive hypermedia applications described in [21] can be used to specify the model of `deiSearch` in term of the major architectural components usually found in adaptive hypermedia, known as user, domain and adaptation model.

Figure 1 shows the essential elements of the model and its relationships in the form of a UML [14] static diagram.

---

[2] [http://www.google.com/apis/]

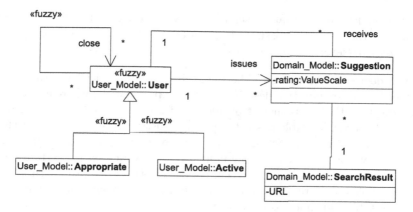

Fig. 1. Core Elements of the Case Study Model, depicted as a UML diagram

The model in Figure 1 is structured around packages corresponding to common high-level architectural components of adaptive hypermedia systems [25], namely, the user model (in our case, a group model) and the domain model (that is, the terms that are specific of the application's domain). Essentially, users interact with the IR system by issuing queries that return sets of search results, and they are allowed to share some of these results with other users, as represented by the Suggestion class in Figure 1. These suggestions are subject of rating by its receivers, using a linguistic label set (represented by the ValueScale data type) for that purpose. The following modelling notions about users have been considered for the application:

- The concept of user, embodied in the User class is considered as a fuzzy class or set (denoted by the <<fuzzy>> UML stereotype[3]). The grade of membership to this class is directly computed from the frequency of use of the application.
- Closeness between users is modelled as a fuzzy relation, represented as a <<fuzzy>> association (see [19]). This relationship is constructed from the history of recommendations, that serves as an estimator due to the fact that deeper knowledge of each other is assumed to be correlated to the quantity of interactions.
- A fuzzy subset Appropriate of the users is defined. This relationship models a form of trust — in the sense given in [1] — that is essentially a (inter-)subjective belief about the usefulness of the recommendations of a given individual. This kind of subsets are modelled by a <<fuzzy>> generalization/specialization relationship, which defines a fuzzy subset between two classifiers, so that if B is a subclass of A, $\forall x\ \mu_B(x) \leq \mu_A(x)$.
- A fuzzy subset Active of the users is also defined (again as a fuzzy specialization). This subset is a characterization of the level of communicative activity (in our case, the frequency of recommendations issued by him/her).

---

[3] Stereotypes are a way of defining virtual, specialized meta-classes in UML

It should be noted that a user may be very active, but also very unappropriate, that is, it may issue a large number of messages that are perceived grossly irrelevant by his/her peers.

The degree of belonging to the User class is obtained in a straightforward manner by the computation described by the expression (1), where a group $g \in G$ is assumed, so that s_g is the set of queries of the group and s_g^x is the subset of queries of user x. Variable t is a temporal adjustment factor to model the fact that in initial stages of the algorithm, the percentage of searches initiated by a user affects only slightly its belonging to the user class. It starts as a large number that can be adjusted to each concrete setting (e.g. 10^q with $q = 4$) so that q decreases till reaching zero and its effect disappears after a reasonable and preestablished time has elapsed.

$$\mu_{user}(x) = \min(1, \ [1 - \frac{\sum_{u \in g - \{x\}} |s_g^u|}{|s_g|} \cdot t] \cdot k) \tag{1}$$

The constant k should be somewhat dependant of the size of the group, since in bigger groups, the same percentage of participation must be considered as a larger degree of evidence about system's usage. Concretely, we have used the $\frac{|g|}{2}$ value, which provides a good heuristic for groups that are below 30 participants. For example, in a group of twenty participants, after t has reached its top, a member with a five percent of the total number of searches is considered as having a 0.5 degree of 'userness'. But with the same k definition, in a group of a hundred participants, an individual with that five percent of searches would be considered as fully belonging to the (fuzzy) set of users. Note that the expression (1) only assigns partial membership grades to users that have non-significant volumes of activity. Table 1 provides a sample of usage data. Concretely, it provides the number of queries issued by a group of ten researchers in intervals of ten days during two months.

Table 1. Example query data for a group of ten users

user	10	20	30	40	50	60
a	10	54	38	36	15	20
b	60	84	92	115	93	88
c	32	100	54	45	90	56
d	30	32	36	38	43	34
e	45	43	21	34	54	56
f	67	56	46	58	30	34
g	34	29	12	2	12	82
h	10	12	14	16	23	25
i	12	34	40	20	16	21
j	2	11	81	34	9	12
totals	302	455	434	398	385	428

Figure 2 depicts the corresponding evolution of the degree of *userness* of six of the users in Table 1 with an initial $q = 2$. It should be noted that all of them are provided initially with a full belonging to that set, which models the initial uncertainty of the system derived from the small amount of evidence available.

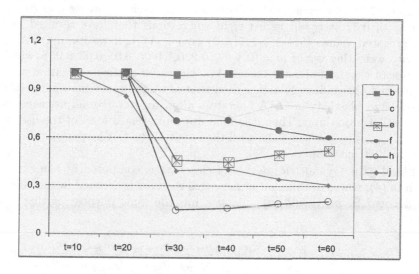

Fig. 2. Evolution of the degree of userness for six of the users

The subgroup of *active* users is computed by the number of recommendation messages issued by each individual, in a similar way to the degree of 'userness', but under the constraint that $\mu_{user}(x) \geq \mu_{active}(x)$.

The degree of appropriateness of a user is computed from his/her history of recommendations by the expression (2). The computation algorithm $\mathcal{A}_{appropriate}$ operates in two phases:

- First, each of the peer assessments v_s^u, where $u \in g - \{x\}$, of the suggestions of the user x under consideration are aggregated by an aggregation operator $\mathcal{M}_1$ (satisfying the general properties of this kind of elements described in [4]), as showed in (3).
- After that, a second aggregation operator $\mathcal{M}_2$ (2) is used to combine the assessments of all the suggestions issued by the user. In this case, the degree of *activeness* described before can be used to model the fact that not only the adequacy but the volume of suggestions are considered in our concept of 'appropriateness', since it's intended to reflect some form of utility of the individual with regards to the objectives of the entire group.

$$\mu_{appropriate}(x) = \mathcal{M}_2(v(s_1), \ldots, v(s_p)) \cdot \mu_{active}(x) \qquad (2)$$

$$\forall s \in Suggestions \quad v(s) = \mathcal{M}_1(v_s^{u_1}, \ldots, v_s^{u_r}) \qquad (3)$$

A natural choice for the operators $\mathcal{M}_1$ and $\mathcal{M}_2$ would be that of an OWA operator modelling majority [26], but other design consideration would also be considered in concrete settings, like, for example, different weights assigned to individuals depending on their *reputation*[1]. Empirical assessments can also be used for the determination of the most appropriate quantifier design (see, for example, [24]). For example, let's suppose that user f (having a degree of activeness of 0.32 at t=60) issued eight suggestions that have resulted in a set of aggregated values $\{5, 4, 5, 3, 1, 5, 4, 2\}$ (using $\mathcal{M}_1$). If we use a OWA operator with weighting vector $w = (0.3, 0.2, 0.2, 0.1, 0.05, 0.05, 0.05, 0.05)$ (which has a degree of *orness* of about 0.143) as $\mathcal{M}_2$, the result of the aggregation will yield a value of 4.4, significantly higher than that of a simple weighted mean (this *orness*-related plasticity of OWA operators allow for iterative adjustments of the aggregation procedure). Then, the final appropriateness level of the user would be $\mu_{appropriateness} = 0.88 \cdot 0.32$, with the result of the OWA operator normalized into the $[0, 1]$ interval.

Finally, the (symmetric) degree of closeness is computed by the expression given in (4), where the amount of messages received is denoted in each direction are denoted by $m_{i \to j}$ and $m_{j \to i}$, and k has the same purpose as that defined in (1).

$$\forall i \neq j \ closeness(i, j) = \min(1, \min(\frac{m_{j \to i}}{m_{i \to j}}, \frac{m_{i \to j}}{m_{j \to i}}) \cdot \frac{m_{j \to i} + m_{i \to j}}{\sum_{x, y \in g \times g} m_{x \to y}} \cdot k) \quad (4)$$

The minimum of the relation of the messages between i and j in both directions is used to filter unidirectional relations, which are not good estimators for closeness. For example, if i issues a hundred messages to j but receive only one from i, the minimum will yield a low value, while the maximum value will be obtained with the amount of messages is equal in both directions, which indicates a constant cooperation. The second part of the formula in (4) is used as an heuristic to increase closeness for the most active pairs of users, so that a pair of users with a total amount of messages interchanged. For example, if we have a total number of 178 messages interchanged in the group, and given that $m_{h \to c} = 26$ and $m_{c \to h} = 18$, we have a degree of closeness $closeness(h, c) = \min(1, 0.692307692 \cdot \frac{26+18}{178} \cdot 5) = 0.856$.

It should be noted that the computation algorithms are not intended to be general models for cooperative IR, but concrete realizations that embody specific, designer-dependent characteristics, so that other formulations are possible.

Based on the models for the social aspects just described, the computation algorithms are implemented as processes triggered in a periodical basis that updates a relational database. The f JDBC framework described in [20] was used for the logical database design derived from the conceptual model described above. This model provides direct support for the representation of fuzzy generalization relationships, fuzzy classes and fuzzy associations, and enables direct querying from JDBC[4]-like code.

---

[4] The Java API for database access: [http://java.sun.com/products/jdbc/]

3.2 Adaptive Behaviors

The overall interface of `deiSearch` is fairly similar to the basic `Google` interface. In Figure 3, a screenshot of the results of a query is shown. It should be noted that a link under each result is provided to issue a recommendation message.

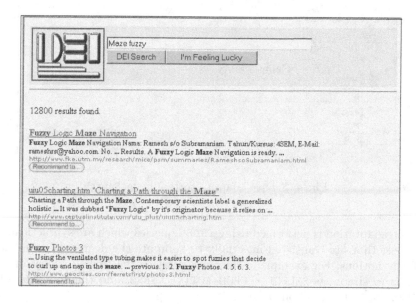

Fig. 3. Sample `deiSearch` search results interface

The following *adaptive technologies* [3] that use the above-described fuzzy categories and relationships have been implemented:

- When elaborating a recommendation, the user is presented with a list of the members of the group. The closeness relationship is used to implement adaptive sorting, as showed in Figure 4 (note that the grades are showed only for illustration and they're normally hidden to the user). This entails that the user would more likely find the intended receivers without a need to scroll or read the entire list.
- When a user is receiving new recommendations (by traversing a link in the principal interface), an adaptive sorting process is used again, but this time using the overall appropriateness degree of the issues, so that the most 'trustworthy' individuals are considered first.
- In the case that a user receives a recommendation that comes from a highly relevant user that, simultaneously, has a high degree of closeness to him, a *direct navigation* adaptive feature is used, so that a link to the recommendation is put directly in the principal interface, so that it would very likely be read immediately by the receiver.

Figure 4 shows an example of how adaptive sorting based on the degree of closeness between the current user and the rest of the users.

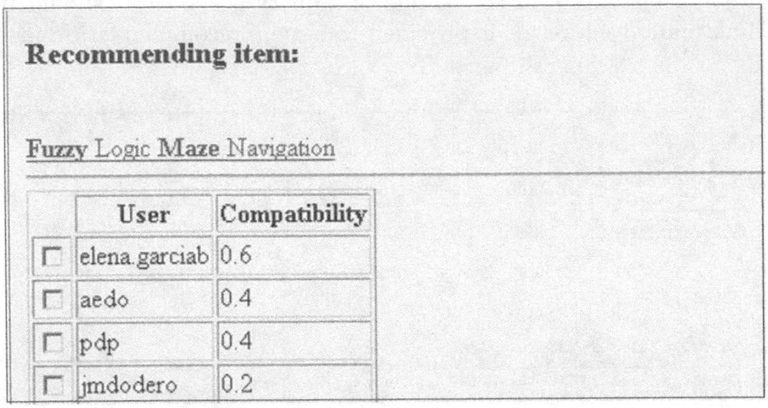

Recommending item:

Fuzzy Logic Maze Navigation

	User	Compatibility
☐	elena.garciab	0.6
☐	aedo	0.4
☐	pdp	0.4
☐	jmdodero	0.2

Fig. 4. Sample adaptive sorting in deiSearch

The adaptation is performed using f JDBC queries which are syntactically SQL sentences that are translated internally to compute the degrees of membership to fuzzy notions. For example, a query to retrieve the (fuzzy) subset of active users is as simple as SELECT * FROM ACTIVE_USERS, and the definition of the ACTIVE_USERS table is done as described in [20]:

```
<fuzzy:fuzzy-relation name="ACTIVE_USERS" type="subclass">
        <fuzzy:relation   name="users"/>
        <fuzzy:oidField   name="userid"/>
        <fuzzy:membField name="Muser"/>
   </fuzzy:fuzzy-relation>
```

The Tomcat[5] Java-enabled Web server was used to implement the just described case study.

Initial evaluations of the prototype in a group with ten participants for two months pointed out that a significant increment (about 15%) in query results considered as relevant for the task (i.e. searching for information about a specific research theme oriented toward writing a project proposal). Nonetheless, further methodological and experimental work is required in evaluating the effects of the cooperation-oriented and adaptive features.

4   Conclusions and Future Work

Social relationships in cooperative IR settings can be modelled by fuzzy associations and fuzzy categories constructed from the history of communications

---

[5] http://jakarta.apache.org/tomcat/

between users. A concrete case study has been described that models the notion of closeness and of relevance of recommendations. These kind of relationships enable the development of adaptive features that enhance explicit cooperation tactics between users. In addition, an underlying fuzzy relational schema has been used for the implementation.

Future work should carry out additional inquiries about which kind of relationship are the most appropriate for specific work contexts, in order to customize the overall framework described here to concrete objectives. In addition, the use of fuzzy relationships in user collaboration mechanisms for specific tasks [6] will be considered. These improvements should take into account cross-cultural studies like [7], and also long-term realistic revision mechanisms [22] for the group model.

The interpretation given to imprecision and uncertainty of social relationships in the described case study has been chosen by its simplicity and according to design heuristics, but it may be approached from more elaborated viewpoints with regards to uncertainty, e.g. from belief-theory or other related frameworks [10].

References

1. Abdul-Rahman, A., Hailes, S.: Relying on Trust to Find Reliable Information. In: Proceedings of the 1999 International Symposium on Database, Web and Cooperative Systems (DWACOS'99), Baden-Baden, Germany (1999)
2. Bates, M.J.: Where Should the Person Stop and the Information Search Interface Start? Information Processing & Management **26** (1990) 575-591
3. Brusilovsky, P.: Adaptive Hypermedia. User Modeling and User Adapted Interaction **11** 1/2 (2001) 87-110
4. Calvo, T., et al.: Aggregation Operators: Basic Concepts, Issues and Properties. In: Calvo, T., Mayor, G., Mesiar, R. (eds.): Aggregation Operators: New Trends and Applications. Studies in Fuzziness and Soft Computing **97** (2002) 3-106
5. Davis, A., Bueno, D.: User Modeling and Cooperative Information Retrieval in Information Retrieval Systems. International Journal of Knowledge Organization **26** 1 (1999) 30-45
6. Dodero, J.M., Aedo, I., Díaz, P.: Participative Knowledge Production of Learning Objects for e-Books. Electronic Library, **20** 4, (2002) 296-305
7. Duncker, E: Cross-Cultural Usability of the Library Metaphor. In: Proceedings of the ACM/IEEE Joint Conference on Digital Libraries (2002) 223-230
8. Grossman, D.A., Frieder, O.: Information Retrieval: Algorithms and Heuristics. Kluwer (1998)
9. Hust, A., Klink, S., Junker, M., Dengel, A.: Towards Collaborative Information Retrieval: Three Approaches. In: Franke, Nakhaeizade, Renz (eds.): Text Mining - Theoretical Aspects and Applications, Springer-Verlag (2002)
10. Klir, G.J., Wiermann, M.J.: Uncertainty-Based Information. Elements of Generalized Information Theory. Physica-Verlag, Heidelberg (1998)
11. Konstan, J., Miller, B., Maltz, D., Herlocker, J., Gordon, L., Riedl, J.: GroupLens: Applying Collaborative Filtering to Usenet News. Communications of the ACM **40** 3 (1997) 77-87

12. Kraft, D.H., Bordogna, G., Pasi, G.: Fuzzy Set Techniques in Information Retrieval. In: Bezdek, J.C., Didier, D., Prade, H. (eds.): Fuzzy Sets in Approximate Reasoning and Information Systems, Vol. 3, The Handbook of Fuzzy Sets Series, Norwell, MA: Kluwer Academic Publishers (1999) 469-500

13. Liechti, O., Sifer, M.J., Ichikawa, T.: A Non-obtrusive User Interface for Enabling Social Awareness on the World Wide Web. Personal Technologies **3** (3) (1999) 22-32

14. Object Management Group (OMG): The Unified Modelling Language Specification. Version 1.4, September 2001

15. O'Connor, M., Cosley, D., Konstan, J. A., Riedl, J.: PolyLens: A Recommender System for Groups of Users. In: Proceedings of the Seventh European Conference on Computer Supported Cooperative Work (2001) 199-218

16. Robins, D.: Interactive Information Retrieval: Context and Basic Notions. Informing Science Journal **3** 2 (2000)

17. Romano, N., Roussinov, D., Nunamaker, J.F., Chen, H.: Collaborative Information Retrieval Environment: Integration of Information Retrieval with Group Support Systems. In: Proceedings of the 32nd Hawaii International Conference on System Sciences (HICSS-32) (1999)

18. Sarwar, B. M., Karypis, G., Konstan, J.A., Riedl, J.: Item-Based Collaborative Filtering Recommendation Algorithms. In: Proceedings of the 10th International World Wide Web Conference (2001) 285-295

19. Sicilia, M.A., Gutiérrez, J.A., García, E.: Designing Fuzzy Relations in Orthogonal Persistence Object-Oriented Database Engines. In: Proceedings of the 8th Ibero-American Conference on AI IBERAMIA'02, Springer Lecture Notes in Computer Science 2527 (2002) 243-253

20. Sicilia, M.A., García, E., Díaz, P., Aedo, I.: Extending Relational Data Access Programming Libraries for Fuzziness: The fJDBC Framework. In: Proceedings of the 5th International Conference on Flexible Query Answering Systems. Lecture Notes in Computer Science 2522, Springer (2002) 314-328

21. Sicilia, M.A., García, E., Díaz, P., Aedo, I.: Fuzziness in Adaptive Hypermedia Models. In: Proceedings of the North American Fuzzy Information Processing Society (2002) 268-273

22. Sicilia, M.A. Observing Web Users: Conjecturing and Refutation on Partial Evidence. In: Proceedings of the North American Fuzzy Information Processing Society (2003) 530-535

23. Spink, A., Saracevic, T.: Human Computer Interaction in Information Retrieval: Nature and Manifestations of Feedback. Interacting with Computers: The International Journal of Human Computer Interaction, **10** 3 (1998) 249-267

24. Torra, V.: Empirical Analysis to Determine Weighted OWA Orness. In: Proceedings of the 5th Intl. Conference on Information Fusion (Fusion 2001), Montreal, Quebec, Canada (2001)

25. Wu, H., De Kort, E., De Bra, P.: Design Issues for General-Purpose Adaptive Hypermedia Systems. In: Proceedings of the ACM Conference on Hypertext and Hypermedia (2001) 141-150

26. Yager, R.R.: Quantifier Guided Aggregation Using OWA Operators. International Journal of Intelligent Systems, **11** (1996) 49-73

Theory of One Tape Linear
Time Turing Machines

Kohtaro Tadaki*[1], Tomoyuki Yamakami[2], and Jack C.H. Lin[2]

[1] ERATO Quantum Computation and Information Project
Japan Science and Technology Corporation, Tokyo, Japan
[2] School of Information Technology and Engineering
University of Ottawa, Ottawa, Ontario, Canada

Abstract. A theory of one-tape linear-time Turing machines is quite different from its polynomial-time counterpart. This paper discusses the computational complexity of one-tape Turing machines of various machine types (deterministic, nondeterministic, reversible, alternating, probabilistic, counting, and quantum Turing machines) that halt in time $O(n)$, where the running time of a machine is defined as the height of its computation tree. We also address a close connection between one-tape linear-time Turing machines and finite state automata.

1 Model of Computation: Turing Machines

We use a standard definition of an off-line Turing machine. Of special interest is a *one-tape Turing machine* (abbreviated 1TM) $M = (Q, \Sigma, \Gamma, \delta, q_0, q_{acc}, q_{rej})$, where Q is a finite set of (internal) states, Σ is a nonempty finite input alphabet[1], Γ is a finite tape alphabet including Σ, q_0 in Q is an initial state, q_{acc} and q_{rej} in Q are an accepting state and a rejecting state, respectively, and δ is a transition function. Different transition functions δ give rise to various types of 1TMs described in later sections. A *halting state* is either q_{acc} or q_{rej}. Our 1TM is equipped only with one input/work tape such that (i) the tape stretches infinitely to both ends, (ii) the tape is sectioned by cells, and (iii) all cells in the tape are indexed with integers. The tape head starts at the cell indexed 0 (called the *start cell*) and either moves to the right (R) or moves to the left (L), or stays still (N).

In general, a computation of a 1TM forms a tree (called a *computation tree*) whose nodes are configurations. We say that a TM *halts* on input x if *every* computation path of M on input x reaches a certain halting state. An *accepting* (*rejecting*, resp.) *computation path* is a path terminating in an accepting (rejecting, resp.) state. A 1TM is said to be *synchronized* if all computation paths terminate at the same time on each input.

---

* Present address: 21st Century COE Program: Research on Security and Reliability in Electronic Society, Chuo University, Tokyo, Japan. This work was partly done while he was visiting the University of Ottawa in November 2001.
[1] Throughout this paper, we use the notation Σ to denote an arbitrary nonempty finite alphabet. For a string x over Σ, $|x|$ denotes the *length* of x.

P. Van Emde Boas et al. (Eds.): SOFSEM 2004, LNCS 2932, pp. 335–348, 2004.
© Springer-Verlag Berlin Heidelberg 2004

Unlike polynomial-time computation, one-tape linear-time computation is sensitive to the definition of the machine's running time. Such sensitivity is also observed in average-case complexity theory [20]. Michel [15] took the *weak definition* for the running time of a nondeterministic Turing machine (that is, the shortest accepting path) and showed that linear-time nondeterministic 1TMs can recognize non-regular languages. This weak definition therefore gives an enormous power to one-tape nondeterministic machines. From a more realistic point of view, we rather take a *strong definition* (in Michel's term), which defines the running time to be the length of the longest computation path. Throughout this paper, we use the term *"running time"* $\text{Time}_M(x)$ of a 1TM M on input x to mean the height of the computation tree produced by the execution of M on input x; in other words, the length of the longest computation path of M on x. We often use $T(n)$ to denote a time-bounding function of a given 1TM that maps from the set[2] $\mathbb{N}$ to $\mathbb{N}$. Furthermore, a "linear function" means a function of the form $cx + d$ for a certain constant $c, d \in \mathbb{R}^{\geq 0}$ $(= \{r \in \mathbb{R} \mid r \geq 0\})$. A 1TM M is said to run in *linear time* if its running time $\text{Time}_M(x)$ is bounded above by a certain linear function $f(|x|)$, where x is any input.

Although our machine has only one input/work tape, the tape can be split into a constant number of *tracks*. To describe such tracks, we use the following notation. For any pair of symbols $a, b \in \Sigma$, $\left[\begin{smallmatrix} a \\ b \end{smallmatrix}\right]$ denotes the special tape symbol for which a is written in the upper track and b is written in the lower track of the same cell. For any strings $x, y \in \Sigma^*$ with $|x| = |y|$, $\left[\begin{smallmatrix} x \\ y \end{smallmatrix}\right]$ denotes the concatenation $\left[\begin{smallmatrix} x_1 \\ y_1 \end{smallmatrix}\right]\left[\begin{smallmatrix} x_2 \\ y_2 \end{smallmatrix}\right] \cdots \left[\begin{smallmatrix} x_n \\ y_n \end{smallmatrix}\right]$ if $x = x_1 x_2 \cdots x_n$ and $y = y_1 y_2 \cdots y_n$.

For any 1TM, certain *acceptance criteria* are imposed to define the set of accepted input strings. In general, a language A is said to be *recognized* by a 1TM M of certain machine type if, for every string x, $x \in A$ iff M eventually halts on input x and satisfies the given acceptance criteria.

A *language* (or simply a "set") *over alphabet* Σ is a subset of Σ^*, and a *complexity class* is a collection of certain languages. The *complement* of A is $\Sigma^* - A$ and often denoted $\overline{A}$ if Σ is clear from the context. For any complexity class $\mathcal{C}$, the notation co-$\mathcal{C}$ denotes the *complement* of $\mathcal{C}$; that is, the collection of all languages whose c omplements belong to $\mathcal{C}$.

The non-regularity plays an important role. For any pair x and y of strings and any integer $n \in \mathbb{N}$, we say that x and y are *n-dissimilar* with respect to a given language L if there exists a string z such that (i) $|xz| \leq n$ and $|yz| \leq n$ and (ii) $xz \in L \iff yz \notin L$. For each $n \in \mathbb{N}$, define $N_L(n)$ (the *non-regularity* of L at n) to be the maximal cardinality of the set in which any distinct pair is n-dissimilar with respect to L [6]. It is immediate from the Myhill-Nerode theorem [9] that a language L is regular iff $N_L(n) = O(1)$. This is further improved by the results of Karp [10] and Kaneps and Freivalds [11] as follows: a language L is regular iff $N_L(n) \leq \frac{n}{2} + 1$ for all but finitely-many numbers n in $\mathbb{N}$.

---

[2] Let $\mathbb{N}$ be the set of all natural numbers (i.e., non-negative integers) and set $\mathbb{N}^+ = \mathbb{N} - \{0\}$.

We assume the reader's familiarity with the notion of *finite (state) automata* (see, e.g., [9]). The class of all *regular* languages is denoted REG. The classes CSL and CFL consist of all *context-sensitive* languages and of all *context-free* languages, respectively.

A *rational (one-head one-way) generalized probabilistic finite automaton* (rational 1GPFA) [17,19] is a 5-tuple $N = (n, \Sigma, \pi, \{M(\sigma) \mid \sigma \in \Sigma\}, F)$, where (i) $n \in \mathbb{N}^+$ is the number of states, (ii) Σ is an alphabet, (iii) π is a row vector which has n rational components, (iv) for each $\sigma \in \Sigma$, $M(\sigma)$ is an $n \times n$ matrix whose elements are rational numbers, and (v) $F \subseteq \{1, \ldots, n\}$ is the set of accepting states. A *word matrix* $M(x)$ ($x \in \Sigma^*$) of N is defined as $M(\lambda) = I_n$ for the *empty string* λ, where I_n is the identity matrix of order n and $M(x_1 \ldots x_k) = M(x_1) \ldots M(x_k)$ for $x_1, \ldots, x_k \in \Sigma$. For each $x \in \Sigma^*$, the *acceptance function* $p_N(x)$ is defined as $\pi M(x) \eta^F$, where η^F is the column vector whose i-th component is equal to 1 or 0 depending on whether $i \subset F$ or not. By 1GAF$_{rat}$, we denote the set of all acceptance functions of rational 1GPFAs. For each $\varepsilon \in [0,1]$, let $T(N, \varepsilon) = \{x \in \Sigma^* \mid p_N(x) > \varepsilon\}$ and $T^=(N, \varepsilon) = \{x \in \Sigma^* \mid p_N(x) = \varepsilon\}$. Moreover, a *rational (one-head one-way) probabilistic finite automaton* (rational 1PFA) [16] is a rational 1GPFA $(n, \Sigma, \pi, \{M(\sigma) \mid \sigma \in \Sigma\}, F)$ such that (i) all components of π are in $[0,1]$ and their sum is 1, and (ii) for each $\sigma \in \Sigma$, all elements of $M(\sigma)$ are in $[0,1]$ and the sum of all the elements of each row of $M(\sigma)$ is 1. For any rational 1PFA N, since $p_N(x)$ equals the probability that N accepts x, $p_N(x)$ is called the *acceptance probability* of N on input x. Let GSL$_{rat}$ and SL$_{rat}$ be the collections of all sets $T(N, 1/2)$ for certain rational 1GPFAs N and for certain rational 1PFAs, respectively. Similarly, GSL$_{rat}^=$ and SL$_{rat}^=$ are defined by substituting $T^=(N, 1/2)$ for $T(N, 1/2)$. Turakainen [19] showed that the equivalence of GSL$_{rat}$ and SL$_{rat}$. With a similar idea, we can show that GSL$_{rat}^= =$ SL$_{rat}^=$.

Finally, all logarithms in this paper are to the base two.

2   Deterministic and Reversible Computation

This section establishes a basic collapse result of linear-time deterministic reversible 1TMs. Since the notation DLIN is widely used for the model of multiple-tape linear-time Turing machines, we use the following new notations to emphasize our one-tape model. The notation 1-DTime($T(n)$) denotes the collection of all languages recognized by $T(n)$-time deterministic[3] 1TMs. Given a set $\mathcal{T}$ of time-bounding functions, 1-DTime($\mathcal{T}$) is the union of 1-DTime($T(n)$) for every function T in $\mathcal{T}$. The *one-tape deterministic linear-time* complexity class 1-DLIN is then defined to be 1-DTime($O(n)$).

Earlier, Hennie [8] proved that REG $=$ 1-DLIN. Elaborating Hennie's argument, Kobayashi [12] improved his result by showing REG $=$ 1-DTime($o(n \log n)$). This bound $o(n \log n)$ is optimal because 1-DTime($O(n \log n)$) contains non-regular languages, e.g., $\{a^n b^n \mid n \in \mathbb{N}\}$ and $\{a^{2^n} \mid n \in \mathbb{N}\}$.

---

[3] Its transition function δ is a map from $(Q - \{q_{acc}, q_{rej}\}) \times \Gamma$ to $Q \times \Gamma \times \{L, N, R\}$.

Proposition 1. [8], [12] $REG = 1\text{-DTime}(o(n \log n)) \neq 1\text{-DTime}(O(n \log n))$.

For later use, we define the functional version of 1-DLIN. A function from Σ^* to Σ^* is in 1-FLIN if there exists a deterministic 1TM M satisfying that, on any input x, (i) M halts by entering *any* halting state in time linear in $|x|$ and (ii) when M halts, the tape consists only of $f(x)$ (surrounded by the blank symbols) with the leftmost symbol of $f(x)$ written in the start cell.

Damm and Holzer [5] considered Karp-Lipton type advice for automata. To make most of advice, we take a slightly different formulation for 1TMs. In general, for any complexity class $\mathcal{C}$ based on 1TMs, the notation $\mathcal{C}/n$ represents the collection of all languages A such that there exist an alphabet Σ, a set B in $\mathcal{C}$, and a length-preserving[4] function h from $\mathbb{N}$ to Σ^* (called an *advice function*) such that, for every $x \in \Sigma^*$, $x \in A$ iff $\left[{x \atop h(|x|)} \right] \in B$. For instance, any language A whose density $|A \cap \Sigma^n|$ is always at most 1 clearly belongs to REG/n. However, the set $L_{num} = \{ x \in \{0,1\}^* \mid \#_0(x) = \#_1(x) \}$, where $\#_i(x)$ denotes the number of symbol i in x, does not belong to REG/n.

Lemma 1. *The language L_{num} is not in REG/n.*

Proof.   Let $\Sigma = \{0,1\}$. Assuming that $L_{num} \in REG/n$, choose a deterministic finite automaton $M = (Q, \Sigma, q_0, F)$ and an advice function h from $\mathbb{N}$ to Σ^* such that, for every $x \in \Sigma^*$, $x \in L_{num}$ iff $tr_h(x) \in B$, where $tr_h(x)$ denotes $\left[{x \atop h(|x|)} \right]$. Take the minimal integer n satisfying $n + 1 > |Q|$. For each $k \in \{0,1,\dots,n\}$, define y_k to be any string of length n satisfying $\#_0(y_k) = k$. Hereafter, we focus on strings yz's of length $2n$.

There exist two distinct $k, l \in \{0,1,\dots,n\}$ such that (i) $y_k z_k, y_l z_l \in L_{num}$ for some $z_k, z_l \in \Sigma^n$ and (ii) M enters the same internal state after reading y_k as well as y_l (since $n + 1 > |Q|$). It follows from these conditions that M also accepts input $tr_h(y_k z_l)$. However, we have $\#_0(y_k z_l) \neq \#_1(y_k z_l)$, a contradiction. Therefore, $L_{num} \notin REG/n$.   □

In the early 1970s, Bennett [2] initiated a study of reversible computation. We take the definition given in [3] in connection to quantum Turing machines in Section 7. A *reversible 1TM* is a deterministic 1TM of which each configuration has at most one predecessor configuration. We use the notation $1\text{-revDTime}(T(n))$ to denote the collection of all languages recognized by $T(n)$-time reversible 1TMs and let $1\text{-revDTime}(\mathcal{T})$ be $\bigcup_{T \in \mathcal{T}} 1\text{-revDTime}(T(n))$. Finally, let $1\text{-revDLIN} = 1\text{-revDTime}(O(n))$. Obviously, $1\text{-revDLIN} \subseteq 1\text{-DLIN}$.

Kondacs and Watrous [13] recently demonstrated that any one-head one-way deterministic finite automaton can be simulated in linear time by a certain one-head two-way reversible finite automaton. Since any one-head two-way reversible finite automaton is indeed a reversible 1TM, we obtain that $REG \subseteq 1\text{-revDLIN}$. Proposition 1 thus concludes:

Proposition 2. $REG = 1\text{-revDLIN} = 1\text{-revDTime}(o(n \log n))$.

---

[4] A function from $\mathbb{N}$ to Σ^* is called *length-preserving* if $|f(n)| = n$ for all $n \in \mathbb{N}$.

3   Nondeterministic Computation

Nondeterminism has been widely studied in the literature since many problems naturally arising in computer science have nondeterministic traits.

Similar to the deterministic case, let 1-NTime($T(n)$) denote the collection of all languages recognized by $T(n)$-time nondeterministic[5] 1TMs and let $1 - \mathrm{NTime}(\mathcal{T})$ be the union of all $1 - \mathrm{NTime}(T(n))$ for all $T \in \mathcal{T}$. We define the *one-tape nondeterministic linear-time* class 1-NLIN to be 1-NTime($O(n)$).

We expand Kobayashi's collapse result on 1-DTime($o(n \log n)$) and show the following theorem.

Theorem 1.   REG = 1-NTime($o(n \log n)$) $\neq$ 1-NTime($O(n \log n)$).

The proof of Theorem 1 consists of two technical lemmas: Lemmas 2 and 3. The first lemma is a core of Kobayashi's argument in [12, Theorem 3.3] and the second lemma is due to Hennie [8, Theorem 2].

Now, we introduce the key terminology for the lemmas. Let M be any 1TM. Any boundary that separates two adjacent cells in M's tape is called an *inter-cell boundary*. The *crossing sequence* at intercell boundary b along computation path s of M is the sequence of inner states of M at the time when the tape head crosses b, first from left to right, and then alternately in both directions. Assume that an input/work tape contains a string x, which may be surrounded by non-blank symbols. The *right-boundary* of x is the intercell boundary between the rightmost symbol of x and its right-adjacent symbol. Similarly, the *left-boundary* of x is defined as the intercell boundary between the leftmost symbol of x and its left-adjacent symbol. Any intercell boundary between the right-boundary and the left-boundary of x (including both ends) is called a *critical-boundary* of x.

Lemma 2 comes from the close observation of Kobayashi's argument that (i) the acceptance criteria of nondeterministic 1TMs are irrelevant and (ii) the argument is applicable to any other models of 1TMs dealt with in this paper.

Lemma 2.   *Assume that $T(n) = o(n \log n)$. For any $T(n)$-time nondeterministic 1TM M, there exists a constant $c \in \mathbb{N}$ such that, for each string x, any crossing sequence at every intercell boundary in every computation path of M on input x has length at most c. In addition, no acceptance criteria of the machine are necessary.*

In essence, Hennie [8] proved that any deterministic computation with short crossing sequences has non-regularity bounded above by a certain constant. We generalize his result to the nondeterministic case in the following lemma. Different from the previous lemma, Lemma 3 relies on the acceptance criteria of nondeterministic 1TMs. Nonetheless, Lemma 3 does not refer to rejecting computation paths.

---

[5] Its transition function δ is a map from $(Q - \{q_{acc}, q_{rej}\}) \times \Gamma$ to $2^{Q \times \Gamma \times \{L, N, R\}}$, where 2^A denotes the power set of A.

Lemma 3. *Let L be any language and let M be any nondeterministic 1TM that recognizes L. For each $n \in \mathbb{N}$, let S_n be the set of all crossing sequences at any critical-boundary along any accepting computation path of M on any input of length $\leq n$. Then, $N_L(n) \leq 2^{|S_n|}$ for all $n \in \mathbb{N}$, where $|S_n|$ denotes the cardinality of S_n.*

Since REG is closed under complementation, so is 1-NTime($o(n \log n)$). In contrast, a simple crossing sequence argument proves that 1-NTime($O(n \log n)$) does not contain the set of palindromes $L_{pal} = \{x \in \{0,1\}^* \mid x = x^R\}$, where x^R is the reverse of x. Since $\overline{L_{pal}} \in$ 1-NTime($O(n \log n)$), 1-NTime($O(n \log n)$) is different from co-1-NTime($O(n \log n)$).

Corollary 1. *The class 1-NTime($o(n \log n)$) is closed under complementation whereas 1-NTime($O(n \log n)$) is not closed under complementation.*

The reducibility has played a central role in the theory of NP-completeness. Similarly, we can introduce the following restricted reducibility. Let $\mathcal{T}$ be any set of time-bounding functions. A set A over alphabet Σ_1 is *many-one 1-NTime(\mathcal{T})-reducible to* another set B over alphabet Σ_2 (notationally, $A \leq_m^{\text{1-NTime}(\mathcal{T})} B$) if there exist a function $T \in \mathcal{T}$ and a nondeterministic 1TM M such that, for every string x in Σ_1^*, (i) M on input x halts within time $T(|x|)$ with the tape consisting only of one block of non-blank symbols, say y_p, on each computation path p, provided that the first symbol of y_p must be in the start cell, (ii) when M halts, the tape head returns to the start cell along each computation path, and (iii) $x \in A$ iff $y_p \in B$ for a certain computation path p of M on input x. We use the notation 1-NTime($\mathcal{T}$)$_m^B$ to denote the collection of all languages A that are many-one 1-NTime($\mathcal{T}$)-reducible to B.

A straightforward simulation shows that 1-NTime($o(n \log n)$)$_m^{\text{REG}}$ is included in 1-NTime($o(n \log n)$). Since REG = 1-NLIN, 1-NLIN is closed under many-one 1-NTime($o(n \log n)$) reductions. This result will be used in Section 4.

Proposition 3. *The class 1-NLIN is closed under many-one 1-NTime($o(n \log n)$)-reductions.*

As a special case, we say that A is *many-one 1-NLIN-reducible to* B if A is many-one 1-NTime($O(n)$)-reducible to B and we then define the relativized complexity class 1-NLIN$_m^B$. Similarly, we can define the "many-one 1-DLIN-reducibility" and its corresponding relativized class 1-DLIN$_m^B$. The oracle separation is possible between 1-DLIN$_m^B$ and 1-NLIN$_m^B$.

Proposition 4. *There exists an oracle B such that 1-DLIN$_m^B \neq$ 1-NLIN$_m^B$.*

4   Alternating Computation

Chandra, Kozen, and Stockmeyer introduced the concept of alternating Turing machines as a natural extension of nondeterministic Turing machines. An *alternating 1TM* is similar to a nondeterministic 1TM except that its internal states are labeled[6] either $\exists$ (existential) or $\forall$ (universal). The *k-alternation* means that the number of the times when states change between $\exists$ and $\forall$ equals k. Let k and T be any functions from $\mathbb{N}$ to $\mathbb{N}$. The notation $1\text{-}\Sigma_{k(n)}\text{Time}(T(n))$ denotes the collection of all languages recognized by certain $T(n)$-time alternating 1TMs with at most $k(n)$-alternation starting with an $\exists$-state. In particular, we write $1\text{-}\Sigma_{k(n)}^{\text{LIN}}$ for $1\text{-}\Sigma_{k(n)}\text{Time}(O(n))$. In contrast, let 1-ALIN be the collection of all languages recognized by linear-time alternating 1TMs with unbounded alternation.

Here, we consider the case of constant alternation. Clearly, REG $\subseteq 1\text{-}\Sigma_k^{\text{LIN}} \subseteq$ 1-ALIN for any $k \in \mathbb{N}^+$. In what follows, we prove that $1\text{-}\Sigma_k^{\text{LIN}}$ collapses to REG.

Theorem 2. REG $= \bigcup_{k \in \mathbb{N}^+} 1\text{-}\Sigma_k^{\text{LIN}}$.

The proof of Theorem 2 proceeds by induction on k. The base case $k = 1$ is already shown in Theorem 1 since an alternating 1TM with 1-alternation starting with an $\exists$-state is identical to a nondeterministic 1TM. The induction step $k > 1$ follows from Proposition 3 and Lemma 4. In Lemma 4, we show that alternation can be viewed as an application of many-one 1-NLIN-reductions.

Lemma 4. *Let* $k \in \mathbb{N}$. *A set* A *is in* $1\text{-}\Sigma_{k+1}^{\text{LIN}}$ *iff* A *is many-one 1-NLIN-reducible to* $\overline{B}$ *for a certain set* B *in* $1\text{-}\Sigma_k^{\text{LIN}}$.

Proof.   (Only If – part) Take any linear-time alternating 1TM M with at most k-alternation that recognizes a given set A over alphabet Σ_1. Without loss of generality, we can assume that M never visits the cell indexed -1 since, otherwise, we can "fold" a computation into two tracks, in which the first track simulates the tape region of nonnegative indices, and the second track simulates the tape region of negative indices.

First, we define the linear-time nondeterministic 1TM M' as follows. On input x, M' marks the start cell and then simulates M. Whenever M writes a blank symbol, replace it with a new symbol not in Σ_1, say $\#$. If M enters the first $\forall$-state p, M' marks the cell (by changing its tape symbol a to the new symbol $\left[\begin{smallmatrix} a \\ p \end{smallmatrix}\right]$), moves the head back to the start cell, and erases the mark. It is important to note that M' has at least $|x|$ non-blank symbols in its tape when it halts. Let Σ consist of all symbols of the form $\left[\begin{smallmatrix} a \\ p \end{smallmatrix}\right]$ for any symbol $a \in \Sigma_1$ and any $\forall$-state p.

Next, we define N as follows. Let $\Sigma_2 = \Sigma_1 \cup \Sigma \cup \{\#\}$. On input y in Σ_2^*, N changes all $\#$s to the blank symbol, finds in the tape the first symbol from Σ, say $\left[\begin{smallmatrix} a \\ p \end{smallmatrix}\right]$, and changes it back to a. Recover the state p as well. By starting with this $\forall$-state p, N simulates M. The desired set B consists of all input strings rejected by N. Obviously, B is in $1\text{-}\Sigma_{k-1}^{\text{LIN}}$. It is also not difficult to show that A is many-one 1-NLIN-reducible to $\overline{B}$ via M'.

(If – part) The proof is done by induction on $k \in \mathbb{N}$. Assume that A is many-one 1-NLIN-reducible to $\overline{B}$ via a reduction machine N, where B is in $1\text{-}\Sigma_k^{\text{LIN}}$. Choose a linear-time alternating 1TM M that recognizes B with k-alternation

---

[6] This labeling is done by the function g that maps Q to $\{\exists, \forall\}$.

starting with an $\exists$-state. Define $\overline{M}$ to be the one obtained from M by exchanging $\forall$-states and $\exists$-states and swapping an accepting state and a rejecting state. Now, we define N' as follows: on input x, run N, and, when it halts, run $\overline{M}$. Clearly, N' runs in linear time. It is also easy to show that N' recognizes A with $(k+1)$-alternation. Thus, A belongs to $1\text{-}\Sigma_{k+1}^{\mathrm{LIN}}$.   □

5   Probabilistic Computation

Probabilistic (or randomized) computation has been proven to be essential to many applications in computer science. Probabilistic extensions of deterministic Turing machines have been studied since as early as the 1950s. For simplicity, we use Gill's notion of probabilistic Turing machines with *fair coin* flips. Formally, a *probabilistic 1TM* is defined as a nondeterministic 1TM that has *at most* two nondeterministic choices at each step, which is often called a *coin toss* (or *coin flip*) if there are exactly two choices. Each coin toss is made with probability $1/2$. Instead of taking an expected running time, we define a probabilistic 1TM M to be $T(n)$-*time bounded* if, for every x, any computation path of M on input x has length at most $T(|x|)$. The probability associated with computation path s equals 2^{-m}, where m is the number of coin tosses along path s. The *acceptance probability* of M on input x, denoted $p_M(x)$, is the sum of all probabilities of any accepting computation paths. We say that M *recognizes L with error probability at most* ε if, for every x, (i) if $x \in L$, then $1 - p_M(x) \leq \varepsilon$; and (ii) if $x \notin L$, then $p_M(x) \leq \varepsilon$.

We begin with a key lemma, which is a probabilistic version of Lemma 3. Kaneps and Freivalds [11], following Rabin's [16] result, proved a similar result for probabilistic finite automata.

Lemma 5. *Let L be any language and let M be any probabilistic 1TM that recognizes L with error probability at most $\varepsilon(n)$, where $0 \leq \varepsilon(n) < 1/2$ for all $n \in \mathbb{N}$. For each $n \in \mathbb{N}$, let S_n be the set of all crossing sequences at any critical-boundary of x along any accepting computation path of M on every input x of length $\leq n$. Then, $N_L(n) \leq 2^{|S_n|\lceil|S_n|/\delta(n)\rceil}$ for all $n \in \mathbb{N}$, where $\delta(n) = 1/2 - \varepsilon(n)$.*

Proof.   Fix $n \in \mathbb{N}$ arbitrarily. For every string $x \in \Sigma^{\leq n}$ and every crossing sequence $v \in S_n$, let $w_l(x|v)$ ($w_r(v|z)$, resp.) be the sum, over all z (all x, resp.) with $|xz| \leq n$, of all probabilities of the coin tosses made during the head staying in the left-side region of the right-boundary of x (the right-side region of the left-boundary of z, resp.) along any accepting computation path of M on input xz. By their definitions, we have $0 \leq w_l(x|v), w_r(v|z) \leq 1$. The key observation is that the acceptance probability of M on input xz with $|xz| \leq n$ equals $\sum_{v \in S_n} w_l(x|v)w_r(v|z)$.

Now, we say that x n-*supports* (i, v) if $|x| \leq n$, $i \in \{0, 1, \ldots, \lceil|S_n|/\delta(n)\rceil - 1\}$, $v \in S_n$, and $i \cdot \delta(n)/|S_n| \leq w_l(x|v) \leq (i+1)\delta(n)/|S_n|$. Define the set $\mathrm{Supp}_n(x) = \{(i, v) \mid x \text{ } n\text{-supports } (i, v)\}$. We first show that, for every x, y, z with $|xz| \leq n$

and $|yz| \leq n$, if $xz \in L$ and $\text{Supp}_n(x) = \text{Supp}_n(y)$, then $yz \in L$. This is shown as follows. Since $\text{Supp}_n(x) = \text{Supp}_n(y)$, $|w_l(x|v) - w_l(y|v)| \leq \delta(n)/|S_n|$ for all $v \in S_n$. Thus, $|p_M(xz) - p_M(yz)| = |\sum_{v \in S_n}(w_l(x|v) - w_l(y|v)) \cdot w_r(v|z)| \leq \sum_{v \in S_n}|w_l(x|v) - w_l(y|v)| \leq \sum_{v \in S_n}\delta(n)/|S_n| = \delta(n)$. Since $xz \in L$, we obtain $p_M(xz) \geq 1 - \varepsilon(n)$, which yields $p_M(yz) > \varepsilon(n)$. Therefore, $yz \in L$.

Note that $N_L(n)$ is bounded above by the number of distinct $\text{Supp}_n(x)$'s for all $x \in \Sigma^{\leq n}$. Therefore, $N_L(n)$ is at most $2^{|S_n|\lceil|S_n|/\delta(n)\rceil}$. □

For any language L, we say that M *recognizes L with bounded-error probability* if there exists a constant $\varepsilon > 0$ such that M recognizes L with error probability at most $\frac{1}{2} - \varepsilon$. We define 1-BPTime$(T(n))$ as the collection of all languages recognized by $T(n)$-time probabilistic 1TM with bounded error probability. We also define 1-BPTime$(\mathcal{T})$ similar to the nondeterministic case. The *one-tape bounded-error probabilistic linear-time* class 1-BPLIN is 1-BPTime$(O(n))$.

Let L be any language recognized by a probabilistic 1TM M with bounded-error probability in time $o(n \log n)$. Lemmas 2 and 5 guarantee that $N_L(n) = O(1)$. Therefore, we obtain the following theorem.

Theorem 3. REG $=$ 1-BPTime$(o(n \log n)) \neq$ 1-BPTime$(O(n \log n))$.

Next, we consider unbounded-error probabilistic computation. We define 1-PLIN to be the collection of all languages of the form $\{x \in \Sigma^* \mid p_M(x) > 1/2\}$ for certain linear-time probabilistic 1TMs M. It is easy to show that 1-PLIN is closed under complementation and symmetric difference[7].

The following theorem establishes an automaton-characterization of 1-PLIN. We write 1-synPLIN for the subset of 1-PLIN defined by linear-time probabilistic 1TMs that are particularly *synchronized*.

Theorem 4. 1-PLIN $=$ 1-synPLIN $=$ SL$_{rat}$.

Theorem 4 follows from Lemmas 6 and 7. We begin with Lemma 6.

Lemma 6. SL$_{rat} \subseteq$ 1-synPLIN.

Proof. Given a rational 1PFA N, assume that the set of all transition probabilities of N is of the form $\{r_1/m, r_2/m, \ldots, r_k/m\}$ for certain positive integers $m, r_1, r_2, \ldots, r_k$. A new probabilistic 1TM M simulates each step of N by first generating $2^{\lceil \log m \rceil}$ branches without moving its head. The first $2^{\lceil \log m \rceil} - m$ branches are referred to as *marked* and the rest is used for simulating N's step. When N finishes scanning the entire input, M makes one more coin flip and enters N's last states (in case where they are not final states, we force M to enter q_{rej}) except that, if M's computation path includes at least one marked branch, M accepts and rejects with the equal probability. This simulation makes M's computation paths not only terminate all at once but also toss the equal number of coins. □

The following lemma complements Lemma 6 since 1-synPLIN $\subseteq$ 1-PLIN.

---

[7] The *symmetric difference* between two sets A and B is $(A - B) \cup (B - A)$.

Lemma 7. 1-PLIN $\subseteq$ SL$_{rat}$.

Proof.   Assume that L is any set in 1-PLIN. First, we build a linear-time probabilistic 1TM $M = (Q, \Sigma, \Gamma, \delta, q_0, q_{acc}, q_{rej})$ with the following five conditions: (i) M recognizes L with unbounded-error probability, (ii) M never visits the cell indexed -1, (iii) M modifies tape symbols only in the *input area* (i.e., the block of cells that initially consists of an input string), (iv) M does not enter q_0 from any other states, and (v) M finally crosses the right-boundary of input x by entering a halting state. For simplicity, we can assume that, when the input is the empty string λ, M immediately enters a halting state without moving its head. The construction of such a restrictive machine is done by first marking the right and left end of the input area and then by "folding" the computation into a constant number of tracks of the tape. To help the later description, we assume that M first moves its head to the right to find the first blank symbol in state q_1 and steps back to mark the right-end marker by entering state q_2. After this marking process, M's head never scans the right-side region of the right-end marker except for the final step (at which the machine enters a halting state). Thus, the crossing sequence at the right-boundary of x can be assumed to be (q_1, q_2, q), where $q \in \{q_{acc}, q_{rej}\}$.

The goal is to construct the rational 1GPFA N for which $L = T(N, 1/2)$. Let S be the set of all crossing sequences of M. For convenience, we assume that S includes the sequence (q_0). By Lemma 2, all such crossing sequences have their length bounded above by a certain constant. Let σ be any symbol in Σ. For any pair (u, v) of elements in S, we define $P(u; \sigma; v)$ as the *probability* of the following event: for a certain pair of strings y and z, the following holds. Consider the computation where M starts on input $y\sigma z$ with the head initially scanning σ in state q, which is the first entry of u. In this computation, (i) if $u \neq (q_0)$, then u coincides with the crossing sequence at the left-boundary of σ, (ii) if $u = (q_0)$, then M never crosses the left-boundary of σ, and (iii) v coincides with the crossing sequence at the right-boundary of σ. Obviously, $P(u; \sigma; v)$ is a rational number. It follows that, for each $x = \sigma_1 \cdots \sigma_m \in \Sigma^*$ where $m \geq 1$ and each σ_i is in Σ, $p_M(x) = \sum_v \prod_{i=1}^m P(v_{i-1}; \sigma_i; v_i)$, where the summation is taken over all sequences $v = (v_1, \ldots, v_{m-1})$ of S with $v_0 = (q_0)$ and $v_m = (q_1, q_2, q_{acc})$.

The desired rational 1GPFA $N = (|S|, \Sigma, \pi, \{M'(\sigma) \mid \sigma \in \Sigma\}, F)$ is defined as follows. Let f be any bijection from S to $\{1, \ldots, |S|\}$. For each $\sigma \in \Sigma$, let $M'(\sigma)$ be the $|S| \times |S|$ matrix whose (i, j)-element is $P(f^{-1}(i); \sigma; f^{-1}(j))$ for any $i, j \in \{1, \ldots, |S|\}$. Let π be the row vector whose i-th component is equal to 1 (0, resp.) if $i = f(q_0)$ ($i \neq f(q_0)$, resp.). We set $F = \{f(q_0)\}$ if $\lambda \in L$ and $F = \{f(q_1 q_2 q_{acc})\}$ otherwise. It is easy to verify that, for every input $x \neq \lambda$, $p_N(x) = \pi M'(x) \eta^F = p_M(x)$. Hence, we have $L = T(N, 1/2)$; and therefore, $L \in \text{GSL}_{rat} = \text{SL}_{rat}$. $\square$

Dwork and Stockmeyer [7] demonstrated that the set $L_{cent} = \{x1y \mid x, y \in \{0,1\}^*, |x| = |y|\}$ is in CFL $-$ SL$_{rat}$. Note that L_{cent} is also in REG$/n$. Moreover, Macarie [14] showed the proper containment SL$_{rat} \subsetneq$ L, where L is the class of all languages recognized by multiple-tape deterministic Turing machines, with a read-only input tape and read/write work-tapes, that uses $O(\log n)$ tape-space in all tapes except for the input tape. We thus conclude the following corollary of Theorem 4.

Corollary 2. CFL $\cap$ REG$/n \not\subseteq$ 1-PLIN *and* 1-PLIN $\subsetneq$ L.

6   Counting Computation

Any decision problem of asking whether there exists a "solution" naturally induces the problem of counting the number of such solutions. A *counting 1TM* is a variant of a nondeterministic 1TM, which behaves like a nondeterministic 1TM except that, when it halts, it outputs the number of its accepting computation paths. Let $\#M(x)$ denote the outcome of a counting 1TM M on input x.

Similar to Valiant's $\#$P, we use the notation 1-$\#$LIN (pronounced "one sharp lin") for the collection of all functions f, from Σ^* to $\mathbb{N}$, which are computed by certain linear-time counting 1TMs. This class 1-$\#$LIN naturally includes 1-FLIN by identifying any natural number n with the nth string over alphabet Σ (in the standard order). Another useful function class is 1-GapLIN, which is defined as the class of all functions whose values are the difference between the number of accepting paths and the number of rejecting paths of linear-time nondeterministic 1TMs. Such functions are conventionally called *gap functions*. It is easy to show the following closure properties: for any functions f and g in 1-GapLIN, the functions $f \cdot g$, $f+g$, and $f-g$ all belong to 1-GapLIN. Moreover, 1-GapLIN is a proper subset of 1GAF$_{rat}$.

Lemma 8. 1-GapLIN $\subsetneq$ 1GAF$_{rat}$.

Proof. The lemma is proven in two steps. Firstly, the proof technique of Lemma 7 allows us to prove the containment 1-$\#$LIN $\subseteq$ 1GAF$_{rat}$ by defining $P(u; \sigma; v)$ to be the number of computation paths instead of probabilities. Secondly, since 1-GapLIN $\subseteq \{f-g \mid f, g \in$ 1-$\#$LIN$\}$, the lemma is immediate from the following closure property of 1GAF$_{rat}$: for any $f_1, f_2 \in$ 1GAF$_{rat}$ and any $c_1, c_2 \in \mathbb{Q}$, $c_1 f_1 + c_2 f_2$ is in 1GAF$_{rat}$. The inequality is trivial. □

Lemmas 6 and 8 build a bridge between counting computation and unbounded-error probabilistic computation.

Proposition 5. 1-PLIN $= \{A \mid \exists f \in$ 1-GapLIN $[A = \{x \mid f(x) > 0\}]\}$.

We introduce the counting class 1-SPLIN as the collection of all languages whose characteristic functions[8] belong to 1-GapLIN. Moreover, the class 1-$\oplus$LIN (pronounced "one parity lin") consists of all languages of the form $\{x \in \Sigma^* \mid f(x) \equiv 1 \mod 2\}$ for certain functions f in 1-$\#$LIN. It follows that REG $\subseteq$ 1-SPLIN $\subseteq$ 1-$\oplus$LIN. We prove that these classes collapse to REG.

---

[8] The *characteristic function* χ_A of a set A is defined as $\chi_A(x) = 1$ if $x \in A$ and $\chi_A(x) = 0$ otherwise.

Theorem 5. REG = 1-SPLIN = 1-⊕LIN.

Proof.   It suffices to show that 1-⊕LIN ⊆ REG. This can be shown by modifying the proof of Lemma 5. Here, we define $w_l(x|v)$ and $w_r(v|z)$ to denote the number of accepting computation paths instead of probabilities. We also define $\text{Supp}_n(x)$ to be the set $\{v \in S_n \mid w_l(x|v) \equiv 0 \mod 2\}$. For any x, y with $|xz| \leq n$ and $|yz| \leq n$, we can prove that, if $xz \in L$ and $\text{Supp}_n(x) = \text{Supp}_n(y)$, then $\#M(xz) - \#M(yz) \equiv 0 \pmod 2$, which implies $yz \in L$. Hence, $N_L(n)$ is bounded above by a certain absolute constant.   □

The notion of many-one 1-NLIN reducibility can be expanded into other complexity classes (such a complexity class is called *relativizable*). A language A is called *many-one low* for a relativizable complexity class $\mathcal{C}$ of languages or of functions if $\mathcal{C}_m^A \subseteq \mathcal{C}$. A class $\mathcal{D}$ is *many-one low* for $\mathcal{C}$ if every set in $\mathcal{D}$ is many-one low for $\mathcal{C}$. The notation $\text{low}_m\mathcal{C}$ denotes the collection of all languages that are many-one low for $\mathcal{C}$. For instance, Proposition 3 implies $\text{low}_m 1\text{-NLIN} = \text{REG}$. The following corollary is a direct consequence of Theorem 5.

Corollary 3. REG = $\text{low}_m 1\text{-}\#\text{LIN} = \text{low}_m 1\text{-GapLIN}$.

Proof.   To prove the corollary, we first note that REG $\subseteq \text{low}_m 1\text{-}\#\text{LIN}$. Conversely, for any set A in $\text{low}_m 1\text{-GapLIN}$, since $\chi_A \in 1\text{-FLIN}_m^A \subseteq 1\text{-GapLIN}_m^A$, it follows that $\chi_A \in 1\text{-GapLIN}$. Thus, A is in 1-SPLIN, which equals REG.   □

We further introduce another counting class 1-C$_=$LIN (pronounced "one C equal lin") as the collection of all languages of the form $\{x \mid f(x) = 0\}$ for certain functions f in 1-GapLIN. The language $L_{eq} = \{a^n b^n | n \geq 0\}$, for instance, belongs to 1-C$_=$LIN. The class 1-synC$_=$LIN is the subset of 1-C$_=$LIN defined only by linear-time synchronized counting 1TMs.
Proposition 5 leads to the following relationship between 1-C$_=$LIN and 1-PLIN.

Lemma 9. 1-C$_=$LIN $\subseteq$ 1-PLIN $\subseteq$ 1-NLIN$_m^{1\text{-C}_=\text{LIN}}$.

Similar to Lemma 6, we can prove that $\text{SL}_{rat}^= \subseteq$ 1-synC$_=$LIN. Moreover, by Lemma 8, we can show that 1-C$_=$LIN $\subseteq \text{SL}_{rat}^=$. Therefore, the following theorem holds.

Theorem 6. 1-C$_=$LIN = 1-synC$_=$LIN = $\text{SL}_{rat}^=$

Since $\text{SL}_{rat}^=$, co-$\text{SL}_{rat}^=$, and SL_{rat} are all different classes [18], we immediately obtain the following corollary.

Corollary 4. 1-C$_=$LIN $\neq$ co-1-C$_=$LIN $\neq$ 1-PLIN.

Recall from Lemma 1 that the set L_{num} is not in REG/n. Obviously, this set belongs to 1-C$_=$LIN. We can also prove that the non-context-free language $L_{abc} = \{a^n b^n c^n \mid n \in \mathbb{N}^+\}$ is in 1-C$_=$LIN $\cap$ REG/n. Thus, we have the following separation.

Proposition 6. 1-C$_=$LIN $\not\subseteq$ REG/n *and* 1-C$_=$LIN $\cap$ REG/$n \not\subseteq$ CFL.

7   Quantum Computation

The notion of a quantum Turing machine was introduced by Deutsch and reformulated by Bernstein and Vazirani [3]. In accordance with our definition of 1TMs, we use a slightly more general model of one-tape quantum Turing machines with a tape head allowed to stay still. A *one-tape quantum Turing machine* (abbreviated 1QTM) is similar to the classical 1TM except that its transition function δ is a map from $Q \times \Gamma$ to the vector space $\mathbb{C}^{Q \times \Gamma \times \{L,N,R\}}$. For more detail, the reader refers to [3], [21], [22].

Let K be any nonempty subset of $\mathbb{C}$. A language L is in 1-BQLIN$_K$ if there exist a linear-time[9] well-formed[10] stationary[11] 1QTM M with K-amplitudes[12] and an error bound $\varepsilon > 0$ such that, for every string x, (i) if $x \in L$, then M accepts input x with probability $\geq 1/2 + \varepsilon$ and (ii) if $x \notin L$, then M accepts input x with probability $\leq 1/2 - \varepsilon$.

Note that every reversible 1TM can be viewed as a well-formed stationary 1QTM with $\mathbb{Q}$-amplitudes. Proposition 2 therefore implies REG $\subseteq$ 1-BQLIN$_{\mathbb{Q}}$. By applying the argument used in [1] for the containment BQP $\subseteq$ PP, we can show that 1-BQLIN$_{\mathbb{Q}} \subseteq$ 1-PLIN because the amplitude set is restricted to $\mathbb{Q}$.

Proposition 7. REG $\subseteq$ 1-BQLIN$_{\mathbb{Q}} \subseteq$ 1-PLIN.

A variant of quantum Turing machine, so-called a "nondeterministic" quantum Turing machine, which is considered as a quantum analogue of a nondeterministic Turing machine, was introduced by Adleman et al. [1]. Let K be any nonempty subset of $\mathbb{C}$. A language L is in 1-NQLIN$_K$ if there exist a linear-time well-formed stationary 1QTM M with K-amplitudes such that, for every x, $x \in L$ iff M accepts input x with positive probability.

Brodsky and Pippenger [4] presented a measurement-once model of one-way quantum finite automaton that recognizes L_{eq} with unbounded-error probability. By a slight modification of their algorithm, we can show that $\overline{L_{eq}}$ belongs to 1-NQLIN$_{\mathbb{Q}}$.

Theorem 7. REG $\subsetneq$ 1-NQLIN$_{\mathbb{Q}}$.

Acknowledgments. The first author is grateful to the Japan Science and Technology Corporation and the 21st Century COE Security Program of Chuo University for the financial support. He also thanks Masahiro Hachimori for valuable

---

[9] The *running time* of M on input x is the minimal number t such that, at time t, all configurations of M on input x become configurations with halting states for the first time. Thus, any time-bounded 1QTM can be considered as synchronized 1TMs.

[10] A 1QTM M is *well-formed* if its time-evolution operator preserves the ℓ_2-norm (Euclidean norm), where the *time-evolution operator* for M is the operator that maps a configuration to the next configuration resulted by the transition function δ of M.

[11] A time-bounded 1QTM M is called *stationary* if, when M halts, the tape head halts in the same cell (not necessarily the start cell).

[12] For any subset K of $\mathbb{C}$, a 1QTM is said to have K-*amplitudes* if all amplitudes in δ are drawn from K.

suggestions on probabilistic computations. The second author thanks Harumichi Nishimura and Raymond H. Putra for discussions on Turing machines.

References

1. Adleman, L.M, DeMarrais, J., Huang, M.A.: Quantum Computability. SIAM J. Comput., **26** (1997) 1524–1540
2. Bennett, C.H.: Logical Reversibility of Computation. IBM J. Res. Develop., **17** (1973) 525–532
3. Bernstein, E., Vazirani, U.: Quantum Complexity Theory. SIAM J. Comput., **26** (1997), 1411–1473.
4. Brodsky, A., Pippenger, N.: Characterizations of 1-Way Quantum Finite Automata. SIAM J. Comput., **31** (2002), 1456–1478
5. Damm, C., Holzer, M.: Automata that Take Advice. Proc. 20th MFCS, LNCS Vol. 969. Springer (1995) 149–158
6. Dwork, C., Stockmeyer, L.J.: A Time Complexity Gap for Two-Way Probabilistic Finite State Automata. SIAM J. Comput., **19** (1990) 1011–1023
7. Dwork, C., Stockmeyer, L.: Finite State Verifiers I: The Power of Interaction. J. ACM, **39** (1992) 800–828
8. Hennie, F.C.: One-Tape, Off-Line Turing Machine Computations. Inform. Control, **8** (1965) 553–578
9. Hopcroft, J.E., Ullman, J.D.: Introduction to Automata Theory, Languages, and Computation. Addison-Wesley (1979)
10. Karp, R.M.: Some Bounds on the Storage Requirements of Sequential Machines and Turing Machines. J. ACM **14** (1967), 478–489
11. Kaneps, J., Freivalds, R.: Minimal Nontrivial Space Complexity of Probabilistic One-Way Turing Machines. Proc. 19th MFCS, LNCS Vol. 452. Springer (1990) 355–361
12. Kobayashi, K.: On the Structure of One-Tape Nondeterministic Turing Machine Time Hierarchy. Theor. Comput. Sci. **40** (1985) 175–193
13. Kondacs, A., Watrous, J.: On the Power of Quantum Finite State Automata. Proc. 38th FOCS (1997) 66–75
14. Macarie, I.I.: Space-Efficient Deterministic Simulation of Probabilistic Automata. SIAM J. Comput., **27** (1998) 448–465
15. Michel, P.: An NP-Complete Language Accepted in Linear Time by a One-Tape Turing Machine. Theor. Comput. Sci. **85** (1991) 205–212
16. Rabin, M.O.: Probabilistic Automata. Inform. Control **6** (1963) 230–245
17. Turakainen, P.: On Stochastic Languages. Inform. Control **12** (1968) 304–313
18. Turakainen, P.: On Languages Representable in Rational Probabilistic Automata. Annales Academiae Scientiarum Fennicae, Ser. A **439** (1969) 4–10
19. Turakainen, P.: Generalized Automata and Stochastic Languages. Proc. Amer. Math. Soc. **21** (1969) 303–309
20. Yamakami, T.: Average Case Complexity Theory. Ph.D. Dissertation, University of Toronto. Technical Report 307/97, University of Toronto. See also ECCC Thesis Listings (1997)
21. Yamakami, T.: A Foundation of Programming a Multi-Tape Quantum Turing Machine. Proc. 24th MFCS, LNCS Vol. 1672. Springer (1999) 430–441
22. Yamakami, T.: Analysis of Quantum Functions. To appear in: International Journal of Foundations of Computer Science. A preliminary version appeared in: Proc. 19th FST&TCS. LNCS Vol. 1738, Springer (1999) 407–419

Avoiding Forbidden Submatrices by Row Deletions*

Sebastian Wernicke, Jochen Alber, Jens Gramm, Jiong Guo, and
Rolf Niedermeier

Wilhelm-Schickard-Institut für Informatik, Universität Tübingen,
Sand 13, D-72076 Tübingen, Fed. Rep. of Germany
{wernicke,alber,gramm,guo,niedermr}@informatik.uni-tuebingen.de

Abstract. We initiate a systematic study of the Row Deletion(B)
problem on matrices: For a fixed "forbidden submatrix" B, the question
is, given an input matrix A (both A and B have entries chosen from
a finite-size alphabet), to remove a minimum number of rows such that
A has no submatrix which is equivalent to a row or column permutation
of B. An application of this question can be found, e.g., in the construction of perfect phylogenies. Establishing a strong connection to variants
of the NP-complete Hitting Set problem, we show that for most matrices B Row Deletion(B) is NP-complete. On the positive side, the
relation with Hitting Set problems yields constant-factor approximation algorithms and fixed-parameter tractability results.

1 Introduction

Forbidden subgraph problems play an important role in graph theory and algorithms (cf., e.g., [1, Chapter 7]). For instance, in an application concerned with
graph-modeled clustering of biological data [9] one is interested in modifying
a given graph by as few edge deletions as possible such that the resulting graph
consists of a disjoint union of cliques (a so-called *cluster graph*). Exact (fixed-
parameter) algorithms to solve this NP-complete problem make use of the fact
that a graph is a cluster graph iff it contains no vertex-induced path of three
vertices as a subgraph [3], [4]. There is a rich literature dealing with such "graph
modification problems," cf., e.g., [6]—many problems here being NP-complete.

By way of contrast, in this paper we start the so far seemingly widely neglected investigation of forbidden submatrix problems from an algorithmic point
of view. Here, given an input matrix A and a fixed matrix B, the basic question
is whether B is *induced* by A. This means that a *permutation* B' of B—that is,
B can be transformed into B' by a finite series of row and column swappings—
can be obtained from A by row and column deletions. This work studies corresponding "matrix modification problems" where, given A and a fixed B, we

---

* Supported by the Deutsche Forschungsgemeinschaft (DFG), project PEAL (parameterized complexity and exact algorithms), NI 369/1; project OPAL (optimal solutions for hard problems in computational biology), NI 369/2; junior research group
"PIAF" (fixed-parameter algorithms), NI 369/4.

P. Van Emde Boas et al. (Eds.): SOFSEM 2004, LNCS 2932, pp. 349–360, 2004.
© Springer-Verlag Berlin Heidelberg 2004

are asked to remove as few rows from A as possible such that the resulting matrix no longer induces B. Forbidden submatrix problems, e.g., are motivated by questions of computational biology concerning the construction of "perfect phylogenies" [8], [10]. Here, a binary input matrix A allows for a perfect phylogeny iff A does not induce the submatrix B consisting of the rows $(1, 1)$, $(1, 0)$, and $(0, 1)$ (see [8], [10] for details).

We initiate a systematic study of matrix modification problems concerning the complexity of row deletion for forbidden submatrices. Our main result is to establish a very close link between many of these problems and restricted versions of the NP-complete HITTING SET problem [2]. We describe and analyze structures of the forbidden submatrix B which make the corresponding row deletion problem "equivalent" to particular versions of HITTING SET. On the negative side, this implies NP-completeness for most row deletion matrix modification problems, holding already for binary alphabet. On the positive side, we can also show that approximation and fixed-parameter tractability results for HITTING SET carry over to the corresponding row deletion problems. To the best of our knowledge, no such systematic study has been undertaken so far. We are only aware of the related work of Klinz et al. [5] dealing with the permutation of matrices (without considering row deletions) in order to avoid forbidden submatrices. There, however, they consider the case of permuting rows and columns of the "big" matrix A to obtain a matrix A' such that A' cannot be transformed into a fixed matrix B by row and column deletions. Among other things, they show NP-completeness for the general decision problem.

The paper is structured as follows. In Section 2, we start with the basic definitions and some easy observations. After that, in Section 3, the main results of the work are presented, giving (or sketching) several "parameter-preserving reductions" (the core tool of this paper) from HITTING SET problems to ROW DELETION(B) for various types of the forbidden submatrix B. Then, in Section 4 we show how ROW DELETION(B) can be solved using algorithms for HITTING SET problems, again using a parameter-preserving reduction. Finally, we end with some concluding remarks and open problems in Section 5.

Due to the lack of space, several proofs have been omitted or shortened in this article, more details can be found in [11].

2   Definitions and Preliminaries

All matrices in this work have entries from an alphabet Σ of fixed size ℓ; we call these matrices ℓ-ary. Note, however, that all computational hardness results already hold for binary alphabet. The central problem ROW DELETION(B) for a fixed matrix B is defined as follows.

  Input: A matrix A and a nonnegative integer k.
  Question: Using at most k row deletions, can A be transformed into a matrix A' such that A' does not induce B?

Herein, A' *induces* B if there exists a B' obtained from B through a finite series of row and column swappings such that B' can be obtained from A by row and column removal. The remaining rows and columns of A resulting in B' are called *occurrence* of B in A. A matrix A is *B-free* if B is not induced by A.

This work establishes strong links between ROW DELETION(B) and the d-HITTING SET problem for constant d, which is defined as follows.

> **Input:** A collection $\mathcal{C}$ of subsets of size at most d of a finite set $\mathcal{S}$ and a nonnegative integer k.
>
> **Question:** Is there a subset $S' \subseteq \mathcal{S}$ with $|S'| \leq k$ such that S' contains at least one element from each subset in $\mathcal{C}$?

Already for $d = 2$, d-HITTING SET is NP-complete [2].

To express the closeness between variants of ROW DELETION(B) and d-HITTING SET for various d, we need the following strong notion of reducibility. Let $(\mathcal{S}, \mathcal{C}, k)$ be an instance of d-HITTING SET. We say that there is a *parameter-preserving reduction* from d-HITTING SET to ROW DELETION(B) if there is a polynomial time algorithm that transforms $(\mathcal{S}, \mathcal{C})$ into a matrix A and $(\mathcal{S}, \mathcal{C}, k)$ is a true-instance of d-HITTING SET iff (A, k) is a true-instance of ROW DELETION(B). The important observation here is that the "objective value parameter" k remains unchanged. This makes it possible to link approximation and exact (fixed-parameter) algorithms for both problems.

Finally, for actually performing row deletions in the input matrix A of ROW DELETION(B), it is necessary to find the set of rows in A that induce B. A straightforward algorithm yields the following.

Proposition 1 *Given an $n \times m$ matrix A and a fixed $r \times s$ matrix B (where $1 \leq r \leq n$ and $1 \leq s \leq m$), we can find all size-r sets of rows in A that induce B in $O(n^r \cdot m \cdot s \cdot r!)$ worst-case time.* $\square$

Observe that Proposition 1 gives a pure worst-case estimation not making use, e.g., of the special structure of the respective B. In any case, however, for constant values of r and s the running time is polynomial.

3   Computational Hardness

In this section, we explore the relative computational hardness of ROW DELETION(B) by studying its relationship to d-HITTING SET. We point out many cases concerning the structure of B for which ROW DELETION(B) is at least as hard as d-HITTING SET for some d depending only on B.

Summary of Results

The key idea behind all reductions from d-HITTING SET to ROW DELETION(B) is to choose a symbol σ from the alphabet Σ and to decompose B—in a certain manner—into four submatrices, one of them consisting only of σ's and one of them which does not contain σ. We can then use the latter submatrix to encode a given d-HITTING SET instance into an instance of ROW DELETION(B) (i.e., a matrix A) and use σ as a "fill-in" symbol to prevent unwanted occurrences of B in A.

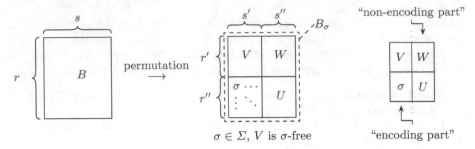

Fig. 1. General scheme for the σ-decomposition of a matrix B over the alphabet σ

We call this special decomposition of the forbidden submatrix B a σ-*decomposition*, illustrated in Fig. 1 and formally defined as follows:

Definition 1. (σ-DECOMPOSITION) *Given an ℓ-ary $r \times s$ matrix $B = (b_{ij})$ over the alphabet Σ. A permutation B_σ of B is called a σ-decomposition of B if there exists a $\sigma \in \Sigma$ and there exist r', r'', s', s'' with $r' + r'' = r, s' + s'' = s$ such that*
(1) $r' > 0$ and $s' > 0$,
(2) $\forall\, 1 \leq i \leq r', 1 \leq j \leq s'$: $b_{ij} \neq \sigma$ (call this upper left submatrix V) and
(3) $\forall\, r' < i \leq r, 1 \leq j \leq s'$: $b_{ij} = \sigma$.
The upper right $r' \times s''$ submatrix $(b_{ij})_{1 \leq i \leq r', s' < j \leq s}$ of B_σ is called W, the lower right $r'' \times s''$ submatrix $(b_{ij})_{r' < i \leq r, s' < j \leq s}$ is referred to as U.
 The left part $(b_{ij})_{1 \leq i \leq r, 1 \leq j \leq s'}$ of B_σ (the one containing V) is called the encoding part *of B_σ. The right part $(b_{ij})_{1 \leq i \leq r, s' < j \leq s}$ of B_σ (the one consisting of W and U) is called the* non-encoding part *of B_σ.*

For a given $\sigma \in \Sigma$, a corresponding σ-decomposition can be easily computed in time linearly depending on the size of B (details omitted). In the following hardness proofs, the height of V plays a crucial role.

Our main hardness results then are the following.

Theorem 1. *Let B be a forbidden submatrix of size $r \times s$ with a σ-decomposition B_σ where the submatrix V (of height r') of B_σ is not induced in the non-encoding part of B_σ. Then there exists a parameter-preserving reduction from r'-HITTING SET to ROW DELETION(B). Hence, if $r' \geq 2$, ROW DELETION(B) is NP-complete.*

Clearly, it is possible that V *is* induced in the non-encoding part of B_σ. In particular, then each column vector of V is induced at least once in the non-encoding part. If we can find one column vector of V which is induced *at most once* in the non-encoding part, we again are able to achieve a hardness result for ROW DELETION(B):[1]

---

[1] Observe that it is possible to construct a submatrix B which fulfills the prerequisites of Theorem 1, but does not fulfill the prerequisites of Theorem 2, and vice versa.

Theorem 2. *If the $r \times s$ submatrix B has a σ-decomposition B_σ where the submatrix V of height r' has a column vector v that is induced at most once in the non-encoding part of B_σ, then r'-*HITTING SET *is parameter-preserving reducible to* ROW DELETION(B).*

If the submatrix B does not fulfill any of the two prerequisites from Theorems 1 or 2, we can determine two further subcases for which a hardness result can be established:

Theorem 3. *Let B be a forbidden $r \times s$ submatrix with a σ-decomposition B_σ where all entries of U are equal to σ and V contains r' rows. Then r'-*HITTING SET *is parameter-preserving reducible to* ROW DELETION(B).*

Theorem 4. *Let B be a forbidden $r \times s$ submatrix with a σ-decomposition B_σ where all entries of W are equal to σ and V contains r' rows. Then r'-*HITTING SET *is parameter-preserving reducible to* ROW DELETION(B).*

For all other cases, i.e., if B does not fulfill any of the prerequisites from Theorems 1–4, we are not aware of a general statement on the complexity of ROW DELETION(B). As an example of such a matrix consider $B = \left(\begin{smallmatrix} 1 & 0 & 0 \\ 0 & 1 & 0 \\ 0 & 0 & 1 \end{smallmatrix}\right)$ over the alphabet $\Sigma = \{0, 1\}$.

It is also clear that ROW DELETION(B) is not NP-hard for all B. For example, ROW DELETION(B) is solvable in polynomial time if B is a 1×1-matrix. Besides, there are also non-trivial examples for which ROW DELETION(B) is solvable in polynomial time, as the matrix $B = \left(\begin{smallmatrix} 1 \\ 0 \end{smallmatrix}\right)$ over the alphabet $\Sigma = \{0, 1\}$ shows: Observe that a B-free matrix A has the property that all its columns consist either solely of 1's or solely of 0's, i.e., all rows of A are identical. This implies that the minimum number of rows that need to be deleted in order to make an $n \times m$ matrix B-free is equal to $n - x$, where x denotes the size of the largest set of identical rows in A, which can be determined efficiently.

Observe, however, that ROW DELETION(B) for $B = \left(\begin{smallmatrix} 1 \\ 1 \end{smallmatrix}\right)$ over the alphabet $\Sigma = \{0, 1\}$ already is NP-complete by Theorem 1, since B trivially has a σ-decomposition with $\sigma = 0$, $V = B$, and $W = U = \emptyset$.

Outline of Hardness Proofs

As mentioned above, all hardness results are proven by encoding an instance $(\mathcal{S}, \mathcal{C}, k)$ of d-HITTING SET—where the value of d is determined by the forbidden submatrix B—as an instance (A, k) of ROW DELETION(B). The key idea concerning how to use a given σ-decomposition of B to encode a d-HITTING SET instance is illustrated by the following proof of Theorem 3. Subsequently, we indicate how this construction can be extended to prove, in ascending involvedness of the construction, Theorem 4, Theorem 1, and Theorem 2. Note that due to lack of space and for a better understandability of the key ideas involved, parts of some proofs are only sketched; for their details, refer to [11].

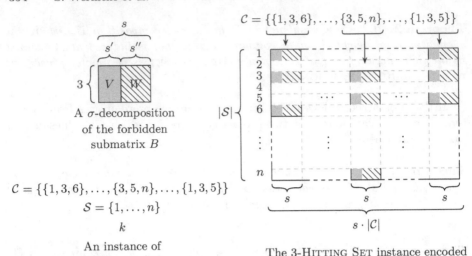

Fig. 2. An example reduction from 3-HITTING SET to ROW DELETION(B) following from the proof of Theorem 3 (illustrated for the case where $r' = r$)

Proof (Theorem 3). Given an instance $(\mathcal{S}, \mathcal{C}, k)$ of r'-HITTING SET and a σ-decomposition B_σ of the forbidden $r \times s$ submatrix B. Let $\mathcal{S} = \{1, \ldots, n\}$ and $\mathcal{C} = \{C_1, \ldots, C_m\}$. For now, assume that $r' = r \Rightarrow r'' = 0$ (i.e., B consists only of V and W). We generate a matrix A of size $n \times (s \cdot m)$. Each row of A corresponds to an element in $\mathcal{S}$. For each set $C \in \mathcal{C}$, one occurrence of B is encoded into s consecutive columns of A, using the rows that correspond to the elements in C. For example, consider $C_h \in \mathcal{C}$, $1 \leq h \leq m$, with $C_h = \{z_1, \ldots, z_r\}$ and $z_1, \ldots, z_r \in \{1, \ldots, n\}$. Then, we generate the submatrix $(a_{ij})_{1 \leq i \leq n, (h-1) \cdot s < j \leq h \cdot s}$ of A such that the z_ith row of this submatrix equals the ith row of B, for all $i = 1, \ldots, r$, and all other rows of this submatrix are set equal to σ (an illustration for this is provided in Fig. 2). In this way, A contains m blocks of s consecutive columns where each block induces B exactly once. These are the only occurrences of B, since two columns from two different blocks cannot have r rows containing no σ. Observe how the property of A that B is only induced within each block and, furthermore, exactly once in each block, is due to using σ as a "fill-in" symbol: Since σ is not contained in V, we ensure that, by using σ as the "default-entry" for A, no additional occurrences of V (and therefore B) are induced in the rows of a block other than the ones intended. The outlined reduction can be performed in $O(n \cdot m \cdot s)$ time.

The construction is easily generalized for the case where $r' < r$, i.e., $r'' > 0$, by adding $r'' + k$ rows containing only σ at the bottom of A. Note that by this construction, although B is induced multiple times in each block, V is induced only once in each block.

It can easily be shown that solutions to the original instance of r'-HITTING SET have a "1:1-correspondence" with solutions to ROW DELETION(B) on A:

"$\Rightarrow$" Assume that we have a solution S' to the original instance of r'-HITTING SET with $|S'| = k$. Then, delete those rows in A that correspond to the elements in S', thus obtaining A'. Note that then, from the submatrix V of each B that was encoded into A, at least one row has been deleted. Every column in A' contains less than r' symbols different from σ. This directly implies that V does not occur in A', and therefore A' is B-free. We have a solution for the ROW DELETION(B) instance with k row deletions.

"$\Leftarrow$" Assume that by deleting at most k rows in A we can make A B-free. Note that we cannot destroy any of the induced B in A by deleting at most k of the bottom $r'' + k$ rows of A. Therefore, it must be possible to delete at most k of the top n rows of A to make A B-free. Furthermore, from each induced B in A, at least one row must have been deleted. Thus, choosing the elements in S that correspond to the deleted rows into a set S' yields a solution of size k to the original r'-HITTING SET problem. $\square$

The idea of the above proof—using the submatrix V of B_σ to encode an instance of d-HITTING SET—is employed in all of the following proofs. In order to show the "1:1-correspondence" of the original d-HITTING SET problem and the generated ROW DELETION(B) instance, mainly two conditions need to be fulfilled:

> **Condition (1):** If the optimal solution to the d-HITTING SET instance has size k, there are no "cheaper" solutions for the generated ROW DELETION(B) instance.
>
> **Condition (2):** If there is a solution of size k to the original d-HITTING SET instance, deleting the corresponding rows in A destroys all occurrences of B in A.

Whilst Condition (1) is rather straightforward to meet by extending the idea of the above proof, Condition (2) is quite intricate to fulfill in general, because it must be ensured that parts of Bs encoded into A due to different sets in C do not induce additional occurrences of B.

Proof (Theorem 4). Given an instance of r-HITTING SET and a σ-decomposition for the forbidden submatrix B, the resulting matrix A of this proof's reduction is composed of four submatrices: The upper left submatrix is generated by the encoding scheme presented in the proof of Theorem 3 using V as the forbidden submatrix, the upper right and lower left submatrices are filled with σ's. Two cases are distinguished for writing U into the lower right submatrix of A: If U does not induce V (Case I), the lower right submatrix has size $(k+1)r'' \times (k+1)s''$ and contains $k + 1$ times the matrix U in a diagonal scheme. If U induces V (Case II), the lower right submatrix has size $(k + 1)r'' \times s''$ and contains $k + 1$ copies of U—the two cases are illustrated by Fig. 3.

Observe that the reduction for Case I keeps the right part of A V-free. Recall that a single U by itself cannot induce V according to the prerequisite of Case I. However, if we would encode occurrences of U one upon the other as for Case II, on the one hand, V could be induced by rows from different encodings of U in the lower right part of A. On the other hand, U could be induced

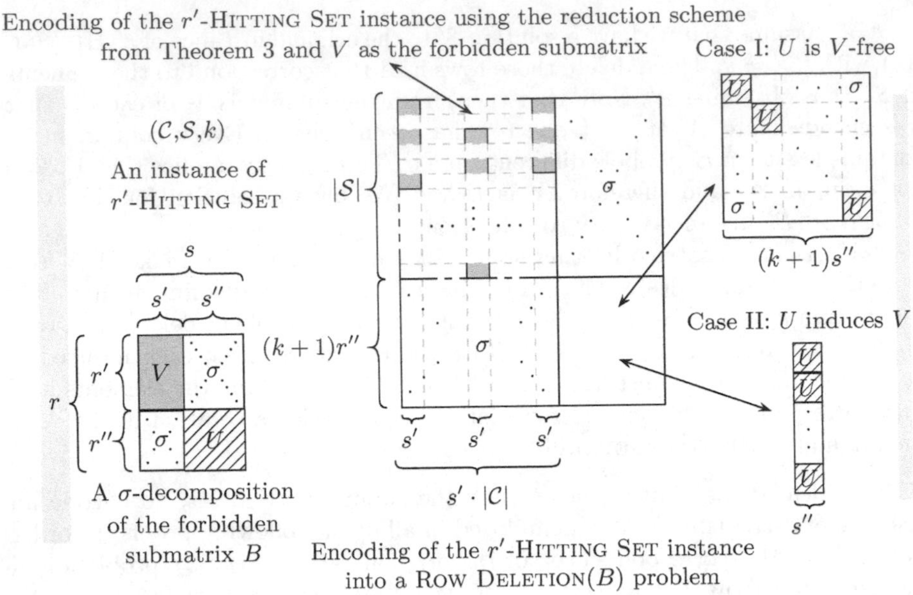

Fig. 3. Illustration of the reduction in the proof of Theorem 4

by several encodings of V in the upper left part of A. Consequently, we would have unwanted occurrences of B. The diagonal scheme avoids these unwanted occurrences of V and keeps in particular the right part of A B-free. In Case II, the reduction cannot keep the right part of A V-free because already a single occurrence of U induces V. However, B cannot be induced there because the reduction does not provide enough columns for an occurrence of B. Therefore, if we destroy all induced Vs in the upper left part of A , then U cannot be induced in the left part of A due to the prerequisite of Case II. Then, the matrix A can be made B-free, even if there are some occurrences of V in the right part of A.

Now, we show the "1:1-correspondence" of the solutions:

"$\Rightarrow$" Assume that we have a solution $\mathcal{S}'$ to the encoded r'-HITTING SET instance. Then, delete those of the n topmost rows in A that correspond to the elements in $\mathcal{S}'$, obtaining A'. Note that this destroys all occurrences of V in the left part of A (ensuring Condition (2)). For Case I, this directly implies that A' is V-free and therefore B-free. For Case II, recall that B is not induced in the right part of A since we can find no sufficiently large set of columns such that both U and V are induced there. But recall that since V is not induced in the left part of A', this also means that U is not induced there. Hence, A' is B-free.

"$\Leftarrow$" Assume that by deleting k rows, we can make A B-free. Note that by deleting one of the $(k+1)r''$ bottommost rows in A, we can destroy at most one induced B in A. Therefore, there is an optimal solution to ROW DELETION(B) that involves only the deletion of k of the n topmost rows of A. The rest of the argument follows from the proof of Theorem 3: If, by deleting k of the n

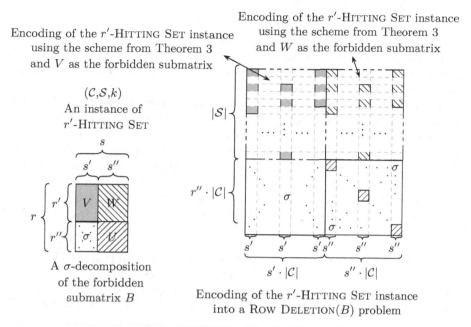

Fig. 4. Reduction from r'-HITTING SET to ROW DELETION(B) used in the proof of Theorem 1

topmost rows of A, we can make A B-free, then from each V encoded into the left part of A, at least one row must have been deleted (ensuring Condition (1)). Since each encoded V corresponds directly to a set in C, choosing the elements in S that correspond to the deleted rows in A yields a solution to the original r'-HITTING SET instance.   □

Proof (Theorem 1). [Sketch] As illustrated in Fig. 4, this reduction is similar to the one used in the proof for Case I of Theorem 4. The resulting matrix A is again composed of four submatrices, the reduction only differs in the construction of the upper right submatrix of A. In the upper right submatrix of A, the given r'-HITTING SET instance is encoded using the scheme from the proof of Theorem 3 and W as the forbidden submatrix. As in the previous two proofs, the parameter k is preserved and the encoding can be carried out in polynomial time with respect to the input size.

As in the proof of Theorem 4, the encoding process ensures that B is not induced in the right part of A. This is due to the following observation: Assume that B is induced in the right part of A. Then, V is induced there as well. By the prerequisites of the theorem, the non-encoding part of B does not induce V. Therefore, an occurrence of V involves columns from at least two different encodings of U. However, note that any two such columns of A can—due to the encoding scheme—only have less than r' rows that do not contain a σ. But V has r' rows with no symbol equal to σ, a contradiction.

Now note that by deleting one of the $r'' \cdot |\mathcal{C}|$ bottom rows in A, we can destroy at most one induced submatrix B in A—this could always be achieved by deleting one of the $|\mathcal{S}|$ topmost rows of A. Therefore, every solution of the produced ROW DELETION(B) instance can be translated to one deleting only rows from the topmost $|\mathcal{S}|$ rows.

From the second observation it is clear that an optimal solution of ROW DELETION(B) can only consist of the n topmost rows of A. The elements of $\mathcal{S}$ that correspond to the deleted rows form a solution for the original r'-HITTING SET instance, using the same argument as in the previous proofs. Conversely, if we have a solution of size at most k to the original r'-HITTING SET instance, deleting the corresponding rows in A destroys all occurrences of V in A due to the first observation and makes A B-free. Hence, every solution to the r'-HITTING SET instance $(\mathcal{S}, \mathcal{C}, k)$ implies a solution to the ROW DELETION(B) instance (A, k) and vice versa. □

The scheme and ideas of the above proof are also used in proving Theorem 2. The details of the proof are rather involved, firstly establishing the result for $r \times 2$ matrices and then extending this result to obtain Theorem 2. We shall only present the main idea for the reduction involved, referring to [11] for details.

Proof (Theorem 2). [Reduction scheme for $r \times 2$ matrices, key ideas] For $r \times 2$ matrices that fulfill the prerequisites of the theorem, the reduction is performed as follows: Given an instance of r'-HITTING SET, the matrix A is constructed just as in the proof of Theorem 1. Then, the following algorithm is performed: As long as there are two columns in the right part of A whose upper n entries are identical to each other, remove one of the two columns from A. It is possible to show that after this "merging" of columns in A, the right part of A is B-free.

An extension of this scheme from $r \times 2$ matrices to all matrices that fulfill the prerequisites of this theorem is performed by arguing that by being able to avoid the occurrence of an $r \times 2$ submatrix of B in the right part of A, we are also able to avoid the occurrence of B there altogether. □

4   Algorithmic Tractability

This section points out an algorithmic approach to solve ROW DELETION(B). To this end, we give a parameterized reduction to r-HITTING SET where r is the number of rows in B.

Theorem 5. *Given a fixed $r \times s$ submatrix B, ROW DELETION(B) is parameter-preserving reducible to r-HITTING SET in $O(n^r \cdot m \cdot s \cdot r!)$ time.*

Proof. Given an instance (A, k) of ROW DELETION(B) (where A is an $n \times m$ matrix), we construct an instance $(\mathcal{S}, \mathcal{C}, k)$ of r-HITTING SET as follows: (1) We construct a set $\mathcal{S} = \{r_0, \ldots, r_{n-1}\}$ containing one element for every row in A. (2) We compute a set $\mathcal{C}$ of subsets of $\mathcal{S}$: For every set $R \subseteq \{r_0, \ldots, r_{n-1}\}$ with $|R| = r$ corresponding to r rows in A that induce B, we add R to $\mathcal{C}$. (3) The

	c_0	c_1	c_2	c_3	c_4	c_5	c_6	c_7	c_8	c_9
r_0	0	1	1	0	0	0	1	0	0	0
r_1	0	0	0	0	0	0	0	0	0	1
r_2	0	0	0	1	0	0	0	0	1	1
r_3	0	0	0	0	0	0	1	1	1	1
r_4	0	0	0	0	0	0	1	1	0	0
r_5	0	1	0	0	1	1	0	0	0	0

$$\mathcal{C} = \{\{r_0, r_1, r_3\}, \{r_0, r_2, r_3\},$$
$$\{r_0, r_3, r_5\}, \{r_0, r_4, r_5\},$$
$$\{r_1, r_3, r_4\}, \{r_2, r_3, r_4\}\}$$

Fig. 5. Illustrating the reduction from Row Deletion(B) to r-Hitting Set. Let B be the matrix consisting of rows $(1,1)$, $(0,1)$, and $(1,0)$. Given an input matrix A as shown, we generate an r-Hitting Set instance consisting of a set $\mathcal{S} = \{r_0, r_1, \ldots, r_5\}$ and the set $\mathcal{C}$ as shown. The gray underlay shows, as an example, how B is induced by rows r_0, r_3, and r_5 in columns c_1 and c_6 of A, leading to the the subset $\{r_0, r_3, r_5\}$ in $\mathcal{C}$

parameter k is directly preserved. Then, $(\mathcal{S}, \mathcal{C}, k)$ is the resulting r-Hitting Set instance. An example for the reduction is illustrated in Fig. 5.

The direct "1:1-correspondence" between the solutions of the r-Hitting Set instance and the Row Deletion(B) instance can be shown as follows: Let $\mathcal{S}' \subseteq \mathcal{S}$ be a solution of size k to the r-Hitting Set instance $(\mathcal{S}, \mathcal{C}, k)$. We delete the rows in A that correspond to the elements in $\mathcal{S}'$, yielding A'. Assume that B were still induced in A' by a set I of rows. Then, the rows in I did induce B in A, meaning a set containing the elements corresponding to these rows was put into $\mathcal{C}$. But one row of I must then have been deleted since $\mathcal{S}'$ is a valid solution to $(\mathcal{S}, \mathcal{C}, k)$, a contradiction. Therefore, B cannot be induced by A' anymore.

If, on the other hand, A can be made B-free by deleting k rows, then for each occurrence of B in A by some rows, at least one of these rows must have been deleted. By choosing the elements corresponding to the deleted rows as a solution $\mathcal{S}' \subseteq \mathcal{S}$ to the generated r-Hitting Set instance, we have chosen at least one element from every set in $\mathcal{C}$, making $\mathcal{S}'$ a valid solution of size k.

The running time follows with Proposition 1.   □

Theorem 5 directly implies the following two positive results:

— The best known polynomial-time approximation algorithm for r-Hitting Set, which currently has approximation factor r, can be used to obtain a factor-r approximation for the corresponding Row Deletion(B).
— r-Hitting Set can be trivially solved in $O(r^k \cdot n^r)$ time, where k denotes the size of the solution. This means that for constant r Row Deletion(B) is fixed-parameter tractable with respect to parameter k. See [7] for the currently best fixed-parameter algorithms for r-Hitting Set—for instance, the best exponential term for 3-Hitting Set is known to be 2.27^k instead of only 3^k.

5 Conclusion

In this work, we have started a systematic study on complexity of and algorithms for ROW DELETION(B). Among others, we were able to show NP-completeness for a number of natural cases of forbidden submatrices B. It remains open to generalize all special cases treated in this work, e.g., by proving or disproving the following conjecture: For every forbidden submatrix B with at least three rows, ROW DELETION(B) is NP-complete.

Our work was partially motivated by constructing perfect phylogenies from binary matrices [8], [10]. For this special case, where we have to consider a forbidden submatrix B consisting of the rows $(1,1)$, $(1,0)$, and $(0,1)$, our results yield that ROW DELETION(B) is at least as hard as 2-HITTING SET (which is the same as the well-known VERTEX COVER problem) and that it always can be solved by transforming it into an instance of 3-HITTING SET.

Note that there remains a "gap" between the results of this work: Let an $r \times s$ forbidden submatrix B have a σ-decomposition with height-r' submatrix V. Then, if $r > r'$, we showed, on the one hand, that in certain cases ROW DELETION(B) is at least as hard to solve as r'-HITTING SET and, on the other hand, that it is not harder to solve than r-HITTING SET.

References

1. Brandstädt, A., Le, V.B., Spinrad, J.P.: Graph Classes: A Survey. SIAM Monographs on Discrete Mathematics and Applications (1999)
2. Garey, M.R., Johnson, D.S.: Computers and Intractability: A Guide to the Theory of NP-Completeness. W. H. Freeman (1979)
3. Gramm, J., Guo, J., Hüffner, F., Niedermeier, R.: Graph-Modeled Data Clustering: Fixed-Parameter Algorithms for Clique Generation. In: Proc. of 5th CIAC. LNCS Vol. 2653. Springer (2003) 108–119
4. Gramm, J., Guo, J., Hüffner, F., Niedermeier, R.: Automated Generation of Search Tree Algorithms for Graph Modification Problems. In: Proc. of 11th ESA. LNCS Vol. 2832. Springer (2003) 642–653
5. Klinz, B., Rudolf, R., Woeginger, G.J.: Permuting Matrices to Avoid Forbidden Submatrices. Discrete Applied Mathematics **60** (1995) 223–248
6. Natanzon, A., Shamir, R., Sharan, R.: Complexity Classification of Some Edge Modification Problems. Discrete Applied Mathematics **113** (2001) 109–128
7. Niedermeier, R., Rossmanith, P.: An Efficient Fixed-Parameter Algorithm for 3-Hitting Set. Journal of Discrete Algorithms **1** (2003) 89–102
8. Pe'er, I., Shamir, R., Sharan, R.: On the Generality of Phylogenies from Incomplete Directed Characters. In: Proc. of 8th SWAT. LNCS Vol. 2368. Springer (2002) 358–367
9. Shamir, R., Sharan, R., Tsur, D.: Cluster Graph Modification Problems. In: Proc. of 28th WG. LNCS Vol. 2573. Springer (2002) 379–390
10. Sharan, R.: Graph Modification Problems and Their Applications to Genomic Research. Ph.D. Thesis, School of Computer Science, Tel-Aviv University (2002)
11. Wernicke, S.: On the Algorithmic Tractability of Single Nucleotide Polymorphism (SNP) Analysis and Related Problems. Diploma Thesis, WSI für Informatik, Universität Tübingen, September 2003

Building a Bridge between Mirror Neurons and Theory of Embodied Cognition*

Jiří Wiedermann

Institute of Computer Science, Academy of Sciences of the Czech Republic,
Pod Vodárenskou věží 2, 182 07 Prague 8, Czech Republic
jiri.wiedermann@cs.cas.cz

Motto: *"The discovery of mirror neurons in the frontal lobes of monkeys, and their potential relevance to human brain evolution ... is the single most important "unreported" (or at least, unpublicized) story of the decade. I predict that mirror neurons will do for psychology what DNA did for biology: they will provide a unifying framework and help explain a host of mental abilities that have hitherto remained mysterious and inaccessible to experiments"*

V.S. Ramachandran, [12]

Abstract. Mirror neurons are specialized neurons recently discovered in the brains of primates. In experiments mirror neurons showed activity both when a subject performed an action and when it observed the same action performed by self or another (possibly conspecific) subject. We formulate and study possible computational consequences of the hypothesis in which the experimentally observed properties of mirror neurons are generalized to other perceptive modalities and the underlying mechanism for coupling sensory and motor information is extended by an associative mechanism serving for completion of cross-modal information composed of perception and motor information. Depending on of what kind of information is completed, the hypothesis opens the door for understanding the mechanisms for sensorimotor coordination, imitation learning, and thinking and is inspiring for the design of such mechanisms in the case of artificial agents. Our results justify the hopes generally related to the discovery of mirror neurons.

1 Introduction

Until recently, the mechanism behind the ability of humans to infer the intentions and emotions of other people, entirely based on observation, has not been satisfactorily explained. The recent discovery of mirror neurons in the brains of primates (cf. [13]) have brought a breakthrough in this respect. Roughly speaking, the mirror neurons are neurons that fire if their owner performs a certain action as well if it observes the same species performing the same action. This can be interpreted as mirror neurons being a mechanism for "mind reading" of

---

* This research was partially supported by GA ČR grant No. 201/02/1456.

P. Van Emde Boas et al. (Eds.): SOFSEM 2004, LNCS 2932, pp. 361–372, 2004.
© Springer-Verlag Berlin Heidelberg 2004

other subjects. Other researchers have speculated on the existence of similar neurons also in primates and developed far-reaching conjectures on the importance of mirror neurons for understanding the intentions of other people, empathy, imitation learning and even for the language readiness (cf. [1], [8], [12]). Currently we are witnessing an explosion of interest in (readily) incorporating the artificial mirror neurons into the architecture of embodied cognitive agents, mainly for visual–motor coordination in humanoid robots (to mention but one recent representative paper, cf. [6]). The prevailing approach is based on so–called synthetic modelling (cf. [11]), stressing the idea of "understanding by building". In fact this is a manifestation of the central paradigm of embodied cognition that cognition cannot be studied without a proper embodiment(cf. [2]). Note that for imitation learning embodiment is a sine qua non condition because the elementary goal in imitation learning is the ability to imitate an observed bodily movement.

Looking for the place and role of mirror neurons in embodied cognition presents the main framework of our paper. In our approach we abstain from studying concrete physical embodiments of agents. This is because we aim at the discovery of algorithmic mechanisms that are behind more complicated cognitive tasks, especially behind imitation learning and derived cognitive abilities, such as sign communication, empathy, language evolution and thinking which up to now have resisted to a formal and uniform algorithmic approach. We believe that the respective algorithmic principles cannot depend much on the concrete physical embodiment — rather they must depend on the cooperation of principal sensory and motor abilities of the agent. Thus, we will aim at a "body independent" definition of a cognitive agent and of its actions. Therefore, central to our approach will be a computational model of a cognitive agent and a definition, what it means that an agent is embodied for a realization of a given cognitive task and situated in a given environment. *We further conjecture and we also bring a plausible evidence that the key to all mental tasks mentioned before is offered by a net of mirror neurons which serves not only as a mean for a coordination but, moreover, under some well defined circumstances, also for completion of the perceptive–motor information.* This seems to be a new hypothesis that offers a uniform explanation of cognitive activities in cases when either perceptive or motor information is missing. Thanks to the associative ability of a mirror neural net, missing information can be supplied resulting again into a complete situatedness of the agent. This time, however, the situatedness is virtual, not based on on-line data. As a result, the same cognitive mechanisms can be invoked for imitation learning, and even for thinking, as in the standard case of sensori–motor coordination when no information is missing. The hypothesis opens the way both for understanding the cognitive phenomena that hitherto remained poorly understood, and for their algorithmic realization in embodied agents.

In Section 2 we mention the basic notions needed for further explanation: a definition of a finite cognitive agent, followed by a definition of a cognitive task, embodiment and situatedness. Next we give an overview of the results achieved under assumptions of our hypothesis on the role of mirror neurons. In Section 3 we sketch the mechanisms underlying the sensori–motor coordination, imitation learning and thinking. A brief schema of an evolutionary development of cognitive abilities is in Section 4. Finally, in the closing section we summarize and comment our achievements.

Because the respective research is still in its beginning the paper is mainly of an introductory and explanatory nature: it focuses to the existence of algorithmic principles offered by our hypothesis on the role of mirror neurons by which the cognitive abilities could be explained, without considering the respective mechanisms in more detail. The preliminary and in some parts more elaborated version of this paper can be found in [17].

2   Basic Notions

In our setting a finite cognitive agent (FCA) consists of a finite set of perceptional–motor units (PMUs) and of a finite state transducer. This transducer translates a potentially infinite stream of sensory and proprioceptive data as delivered by the perceptional parts of agents' PMUs into a potentially infinite stream of motor data that are sent back to the motor parts of agents' PMUs. A finite state transducer represents the "brain", or the "mind" of a FCA whereas the PMUs represent its "body". As its name suggests each PMU is a combination of a perceptional and motor unit (similar to Turing machine's read/write head). This unit sends perceptive information obtained from the unit's sensory organs to the transducer and receives from the transducer *motor instructions* for the moves of the PMU (and thereby, of the entire agent). The perceptional information is twofold. The first kind is *sensory (or exteroceptive) information* from the PMU's external sensors reacting to the properties of the external world, delivering data (visual, auditory, haptic, electromagnetic, etc.) on the environment. The second kind is *proprioceptive information* obtained from the PMU's internal sensors delivering data related to the PMU's internal state, such as muscle tonus, status information such as a feeling of pain, hunger, voltage level, etc. Thus, proprioception also corresponds to internal feelings that are related to agents' motor action performed at that time. All three kinds of information — motoric, sensory and proprioceptive — will be jointly termed as *multimodal information*. Note that within each PMU, proprioceptive information provides a feedback — so-called *internal feedback* — for the corresponding motor instruction. A scheme of an FCA is in Fig. 1.

An FCA can move in the environment with the help of its PMUs (such as wheels, legs, wings, etc.) specialized for locomotion and can modify the environment with the help of other PMUs (hands, arms, tentacles, etc.). The environment itself is not a subject of our modelling. A PMU can provide a feedback to another PMU. A typical example is a hand–eye system. If the agents' eye "observes" its own hand we say that there is an *external feedback* between the respective PMUs. We also say that both PMUs are coordinated.

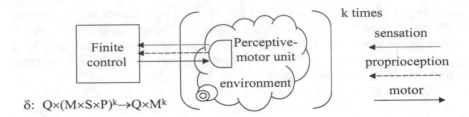

Fig. 1. The schema of a finite cognitive agent

The activity of an FCA is defined with the help of a *transition function* that, given the current state, currently issued motor instructions for the motor parts of all PMUs and current information from perceptional parts of all PMUs assigns a new state and a new set of instructions for motor parts of all PMUs.

An FCA as a whole does not compute in the classical sense of this word: neither its input nor its output are data. The agents' "input" is the external world that is perceived by the agent via its sensory units. It is the task of these units to produce data. The "quality" of this data depend on the kind and resolution of the agents' sensors. The agents' "output" is the agents' behavior by which the agent changes its environment (either by modifying it, or by moving in it) or itself (by moving parts of its body, or modifying its finite control). Behavior's appropriateness and effectiveness depend, in addition to the agents' control, on the quality of the agents' effectors. Thus, the "mapping" capturing agents' activity cannot be characterized mathematically as long as we do not have a mathematical description of the environment and a mapping realized by agents' PMUs. That is why in general the notion of a cognitive task cannot be defined formally. Informally, a cognitive task is defined from the observer's point of view. In a given environment a *cognitive task* for an FCA calls for performing a sequence of interactions by which, in the eye of the observer, the FCA "passes" the test related to the task at hand. For instance, the Turing test is a test for a cognitive task called "intelligence".

We say that an FCA $\mathcal{A}$ is *embodied* in environment E w.r.t. a cognitive task τ if and only if $\mathcal{A}$ is equipped by such PMUs that provide $\mathcal{A}$'s control unit with enough perceptive information and sufficient motor abilities to perform task τ in environment E. In this case we say that $\mathcal{A}$'s control is *situated* in E through agents' PMUs, or we simply say that $\mathcal{A}$ is situated in E.

3   The Role of Mirror Neurons

No doubt that the finite control of a cognitive agent can be realized with the help of neural nets (cf. [16]). An important part in this net will be played by mirror neurons. We will consider the activity of mirror neurons in two basic modes: in a *standard* (or learning) mode, and in an *associative* mode. In a standard mode the mirror neurons serve for learning and checking coordination of multimodal information. During all agent's life, the sensori–motor coordination is built and enhanced. That is, the association among the perceptive, proprioceptive, and motor parts of information is reinforced each time the agent performs a "standard" elementary action (cf. [14]). What is "standard" is in the simplest case decided by a built-in mechanism of emotions, or affects: after performing a correct action pertinent to a given cognitive task, a "good feeling" is automatically invoked (e.g. after tasting a nutrition). In advanced cases there is a teacher issuing a reward to the agent. In the mentally most developed agents a result of a mental activity itself can lead to a feeling of satisfaction. In all cases the reward leads to a strengthening of the association among the parts of current multimodal information. Performing sequences of elementary actions also leads to a strengthening of the respective chains linking the respective "clusters" of multimodal information (cf. [15]). Note that in this way an agent learns a proper "syntax" of the multimodal information. Since "feelings" (proprioception), sensation (sensory information), and motor actions corresponding to an elementary activity are bound together (by mirror neurons), the agent has information available "what it is like" to perform that activity. Stated otherwise, agent's activities are grounded in its sensory, proprioceptive, and motor experience (cf. [7], [6]).

It may happen that in some situation a current multimodal information does not correspond to a previously acquired information. Especially this may happen when agent A observes agent B performing an action familiar to A. "Familiar to A" means that A has already learned how to perform the same action, but A "knows" this action only from its own "inner perspective". That is, A knows "how it is like" to perform this action by itself (that is, A has acquired the necessary multimodal information), but does not know (yet) how this action looks like when performed by B and observed by A. In that case A receives a sensory information that is familiar to it[1] (its eyes report a movement of "some" hand, say, that might as well be its own hand), but neither A's proprioception nor its motor orders correspond to that observation. Now we turn to our hypothesis on mirror neurons: we assume that the corresponding mirror neurons work in an associative mode, resulting into correction of the current "mismatch" in multimodal information. By virtue of assumed associative ability of mirror neurons, the sensory information of A is complemented by the correct (namely from A's experience) proprioceptive and motor information; the information that the resulting multimodal information has been reconstructed is also available to A. In this way, A has the same information that B has available at this very moment: A has "read the mind" of B! This observation has profound consequences. First, A can repeat an action, or a sequence of actions, of B. This is the basis for *imitation learning*. Second, by observing B, A can infer B's "mental state", e.g. B's feelings (such as fear, joy, etc.) or intentions (attack, escape, etc.) and react to it "on distance". Of course, this is a basis for a *communication*. Apparently

---

[1] The observation of a movement by somebody else is always quite different from the visual observation of performing the same movement yourself; therefore the "discovery" of the similarity of both movements' observation requires an additional processing.

a communication starts at the level of body movements and depending on the architecture and mental development of the agent at hand it can develop up to a gesture or spoken language (cf. [3]).

Now we can show that the properties of "our" mirror neurons match the properties of mirror neurons described in the literature (see their description in the introductory part of this paper). Assume that the control sends a motor instruction both to the arm and the eye of an FCA in the standard mode. In the respective mirror neuron m these instructions will meet the signals from the arm's and eye's perceptive sensors and assuming that all this happens under the standard mode m will fire. This means that m is active if the agent performs a movement and "checks" (watches) it via the external sensory–motor feedback. Consider now the situation when agent $\mathcal{A}$ observes an arm of agent $\mathcal{B}$ performing the same movement. The completing mechanism described above corrects the mismatched multimodal information to a correct one which mirror neuron m will react to.

A primitive form of conversation can also be seen as a result of interactively invoking sequences of multimodal information from a mirror net in which motor actions (namely those of speaking organs) are coupled with sounds, with everything grounded in the respective proprioception. Now imagine "speaking to itself": an agent interacts with itself. Obviously, in such a case a loud pronouncing of words is loosing its original meaning (namely a communication at a distance), since the motor instructions for speaking organs already contain the same information (albeit in a different form) that is "heard" by agents' ears. Moreover, the missing acoustic information is provided automatically by mirror neurons. Thus, the necessity of pronouncing sentences decays and what remains from speaking to itself is *thinking* in its rudimentary form (cf. [5]). A summary of various modes of completion of missing multimodal information is given in Table 1.

It is worth to note that in the case of thinking, there is no on-line sensory and no on-line perceptive information taken into account; only motor instructions (realization of which is suppressed, however) for speaking organs are issued. According to our hypothesis, this motor information is continuously complemented by the corresponding perceptive information. As a result, a thinking agent becomes situated again, albeit not in a real world, but only in agent's internal world representation that is implicitly captured by the mirror neural net. The "syntax" of this world is represented by the set of all multimodal information

Table 1. Completing multimodal information

Motor	Sensation	Proprio-ception	Completed by	Mode
Yes	Yes	Yes	No completion needed	Standard
No	Yes	No	Motor&Proprioception	Imitation
Yes	No	No	Sensation&Proprioception	Thinking

kept in the mirror neurons. That is, the agent has at its disposal a schema describing the world as perceived by its senses and proprioception and as explored by its motor activities. This is where the agents' mechanism for situatedness is rooted. Should a part of the world in this schema be missing then the agent either has not entered this part of the world or simply it has not been able to explore it via its perceptive or motor abilities. In [4] a similar conclusion of the existence of an implicit world model in the cognitive agents that is also realized with the help of a neural net, was also reached.

The neural architecture of a cognitive embodied agent according to our ideas is depicted in Fig. 2. Here, the cogitoid denotes a part of neural network that takes care of the learning and computation of the transition function of the finite transducer that controls the activity of the agent. In other words, the cogitoid's task is to generate a stream of motor instructions based on the stream of multimodal information completed and delivered by the mirror net. Note that when compared to the cogitoid's task, the mirror net realizes a relatively simple and straightforward task. What a mirror net does is in fact learning patterns of complete multimodal data (in the standard mode) and recognition of the learned patterns from incomplete multimodal data (in the associative mode). Thus, the essence of an agent's "intelligence" is hidden in its cogitoid. In the next section we therefore concentrate to the evolutionary development of agent's mind in which the cogitoid plays an important role.

4   A Sketch of the Evolutionary Development of the Agent's Mind

Consider now a hypothetical, highly speculative evolutionary development of a cognitive agent which would lead to the formation of its control abilities that would resemble the mind. Doing so it is natural to assume a development passing through a number of evolutionary stages in which mechanisms taking care of the agents' activities aiming at its survival in a corresponding ecological niche will be formed. Clearly, the agents' physical development should go hand in hand with its mental development, both developments also corresponding to possible changes in the agents' living environment. Both developments must be in the

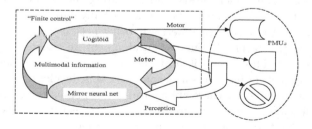

Fig. 2. The schema of the neural architecture of a finite cognitive agent

so–called *ecological balance*: it does not make sense for an agent to have PMUs delivering more information than its brain can handle, or vice versa, to have a more efficient brain than the one that is sufficient to process the data delivered by the agents' PMUs (cf. [11]).

- *Grounding of elementary actions in sensory-motor coordination*
- *Formation of the "self" concept, imitation of elementary actions*
- *Imitation of sequences of actions with the help of learning*
- *Communication via gestures, sign language, "mind reading" (i.e., intention discovering by observation), empathy*
- *Adding vocalization to gestures and its association with gesture motor system instructions, later with speech organs instructions*
- *Development of the "vocabulary of understanding" belonging to gestures and words and a development of the respective access mechanism by means of words; development of the corresponding proprioception*
- *Keeping of evolutionary balance between the increase of a number of word stimuli and the size of the brain*
- *Direct concept activation via words, development of abstract concepts*
- *The dawn of thinking: starting with a laud speaking to oneself, later gradually replacing speaking by mere movements of speech organs; while thinking the vocalization subsequently looses its merit; speech instructions get associated directly with the "meaning" of words*
- *Subjective experience as a proprioception of abstract concept activation*
- *Thinking as virtually situated damped sensory-motor actions*

Fig. 3. The process of evolutionary development of mental abilities of an FCA

The so-called *grounding* of an agent in the environment is the basic assumption of the cognition (cf. [7]). This means that an agent must have information available how to handle the environment by means of its actions; this information is obtained via its PMUs. Technically this information is represented as multimodal information stored in the agents' mirror neural net. Grounding thus takes care about agents' elementary understanding the world. Note that at the level of elementary actions an agent cannot do any but "reasonable" actions, since others are not a part of its repertoire, other actions than "useful" ones are not acquired by the agent. For further development an agent needs a faculty of imitation learning. This ability is provided by the self-control and multimodal information completing mechanism. Apparently this developmental stage differs from the previous one since there are creatures not possessing even rudimentary imitation abilities (e.g. such creatures do not have sensory organs enabling them to "see", in order to mirror the movements of other creatures). The ability of mirroring leads to the emergence of the self-concept that is necessary in order to distinguish between the actions observed by one's own sensors on one's own body and the actions of other agents. What develops next is the ability to learn sequences of actions, still with the help of imitation. The mechanism that takes care of these and other abilities, such as learning by analogy, Pavlovian reflexes, operant conditioning, emotion processing, etc., is denoted as a cogitoid in Fig. 2. Note that the cogitoid is not directly connected to any peripheral input device — in fact it is a classical information processing device that has been considered in the computational paradigm of the classical AI. The input into a cogitiod is formed by a stream of preprocessed, corrected or completed multimodal information streaming from a mirror neural net. This data reflects the outer world and causes that a cogitoid is specialized solely to process situated data. What a cogitoid does is "computing" the transition function, i.e. the "next move", given the current state and multimodal information. A cogitoid is designed so as to be able to learn from experience, in various modes (in a supervised or unsupervised mode, by trial and error, positive or negative reinforcement, etc.) and their combinations. In its most developed form a cogitoid learns with the help of thinking — by "mentally" simulating possible scenarios of future situation development based on experience. This simulation consists of steps, each step realizing one transition of δ which is technically realized as one circulation of multimodal information between the mirror net and the cogitoid. Hence, in the thinking mode the multimodal information circulates in the network without any external interference. The cogitiod's mode of work is modulated by emotions. For more details on cogitoid see [15]. Going hand in hand with the evolution of learning mechanisms is the evolution of communication abilities and empathy. Communication is very simple initially, based on visual signaling via gestures, in some cases perhaps based on olfactory signals, and is related to emotion or specific context transfer. The signalling repertoire gradually builds up and new communication channels, especially the acoustic ones, enter the game. By this the limbs used for gestures are freed again to other bodily activities. A multimodal combination of all signals is always built with the key role played by the motor activities. The importance of visual communication decays and the main role is taken over by a vocal communication. The role of motor activities shifts from the gesture and body language towards the organs of speech (cf. [3]). The vocabulary of notions keeps developing while keeping them grounded in the perceptive-motor multimodal information. The notions (concepts) and emotions can be activated by hearing the corresponding word(s), not only with the help of sensors. It could be the case that there is also a proprioception caused by word activation and that this proprioception gets associated with further multimodal information related to the words. The spoken language enables a further discrimination of objects, a further structuring of the world since an agent distinguishes more object categories. It is as though the perception organs started to deliver more distinguishable information then before making use of the same channels. What follows is a further evolution of the brain that has to cope with this blow up of information. Agents are now able to communicate among themselves and also one with itself by speaking to oneself. An agent speaking to itself starts to "think loudly". In the further evolution the vocalization accompanying thinking is slowly loosing its importance, the movements of the speech organs decay until only motor signals (especially those for the speech organs) prevail that, however, are no longer realized but are still associated with perceptive and proprioceptive information in which the motoric is grounded. From the viewpoint of its perception an agent finds itself in a virtual environment mediated this time not by its senses but by its completion mechanism (which was formed by the agents' senses in the standard mode). The information on its virtual situatedness has the agent to its disposal and maybe that here are the roots of the agents' consciousness. Namely, it can happen then that an agent becomes a subject of its own observation: in the observational mode the agent is informed about its being in a thinking mode. Could it be the case that the respective proprioceptive information could give rise to the agents' feeling of consciousness? The entire process of evolutionary mind development is summarized in Fig. 3.

The hypothetical evolution of agents' mental abilities sketched above roughly corresponds to similar ideas of other authors, especially those of philosophers of mind (cf. [5]). The difference is that in our case our ideas are less (albeit still quite) speculative since they are supported by concrete mechanisms that are taking care of individual evolutionary stages of the mental development of cognitive agents within a single model of an FCA.

5   Conclusion

The opinions on the mechanisms of thinking in embodied agents presented in this paper originate from a single conjecture. It is a hypothesis that the mirror neurons are a part of a mechanism that serves for learning, self-control (verification) and eventually completion of multimodal information. This mechanism was extended to a mechanism also profiting from proprioceptive information. Proprioceptive information serves here not only as an additional mean for multimodal information grounding and for increasing the robustness of multimodal information against its possible incompleteness, but also as a basis of internal sensation. The mechanism of multimodal information completing, further enabled bringing a seemingly unrelated perception-motor (i.e., standard) and thinking modes onto a common basis. In our model thinking takes a form of suppressed motor actions which are from the agents' viewpoint accompanied by virtual sensations provided by the completion mechanism. A proprioception of this state of the mind could open the door to consciousness.

Our "body independent" model of an FCA, our treatment of cognitive agents and the ideas on the agent's mental development with formation of concepts strongly grounded in interaction with other agents support recent beliefs of some scientists — notably those of Luc Steels [10] — that technology is no constraint and that focusing on the individual behavior is not the key for achieving a fully-fledged computational intelligence. What is needed is not only the ability to learn new increasingly more complex behaviors, but also the ability to form concepts that can be shared and exchanged with other agents, thereby developing their own "minds", just as humans do.

Our ideas on the role of mirror neurons go beyond those concerning the importance of the sensory–motor information for the classification of objects, summarized e.g. in [11], because we have pointed to a concrete and experimentally verifiable real mechanism (namely mirror neurons) on which such a model can be based. Our views on the development of language abilities and thinking in embodied cognitive agents are well in line with current theories (cf. [1], [3], [5], [8], [9], [10], [15]). The main contribution of our hypothesis is that it gives a plausible algorithmic framework for the development of cognitive abilities, inclusively the thinking, building consistently on the principles of embodied cognition and making use of the same mechanism — viz. mirror neurons.

The theory emerging in our paper aims at an algorithmic theory of thinking. The principles presented here have been, to a various extent, described and envisaged by many philosophers, psychologists and people from the field of artificial intelligence and cognitive science. Until now a plausible computational framework enabling a consistent explanation of cognitive mechanisms behind thinking has been missing. The hypothesis concerning the role of mirror neurons in embodied cognitive agents proposed in this paper presents a possible computational framework for the theory of cognition we are after. However, the validity of our hypothesis remains to be verified by more evidence both from psychology, neuroscience and experimental robotics. The ideas presented in this paper could serve as a preliminary research plan for such an endeavor.

References

1. Arbib, M. A.: The Evolving Mirror System: A Neural Basis for Language Readiness. In: Christiansen, M.H., Kirby, S. (eds): Language Evolution: The States of the Art. Oxford University Press (2003)
2. Brooks, R.: Cambrian Intelligence: The Early History of the New AI. MIT Press (A Bradford Book) (1999)
3. Corballis, M.C.: The Gestural Origins of Language. American Scientist On–line, March–April 1999, http://www.americanscientist.org
4. Cruse, H.: The Evolution of Cognition — a Hypothesis. Cognitive Science **27** Elsevier (2003) 135–155
5. Dennett, D.C.: Consciousness Explained. Penguin Books (1991) 511 p.
6. Fitzpatrick, P., Metta, G.: Grounding Vision through Experimental Manipulation. Accepted for publication in the Philosophical Transactions of the Royal Society: Mathematical, Physical, and Engineering Sciences (2003) (see draft pdf at http://www.ai.mit.edu/people/paulfitz/publications.shtml)
7. Harnad, S.: The Symbol Grounding Problem. Physica D **42** (1990) 335–346
8. Hurford, J.R.: Language Beyond Our Grasp: What Mirror Neurons Can, and Cannot, Do for Language Evolution. In: Kimbrough, O., Griebel, U., Plunkett, K. (eds.): The Evolution of Communication systems: A Comparative Approach. The Viennna Series in Theoretical Biology, MIT Press Cambridge, MA, (2002)
9. Morrison, C.T., Cannon, E.N., Cohen, P.R., Bogartz, R.S., Beal, C.R.: When Push Comes to Shove: A Preliminary Study of the Relation Between Interaction Dynamics and Young Children's Verb Use. Submitted to 25 Annual Meeting of the Cognitive Science Society (2003)

10. Manuel, T.L.: Creating a Robot Culture: An Interview with Luc Steels. http://www.computer.org/intelligent/ex2003/x3059.pdf, (2003)
11. Pfeifer, R., Scheier, Ch.: Understanding Intelligence. The MIT Press, Cambridge, Massachusetts, London, England (1999) 697 p.
12. Ramachandran, V.S.: Mirror Neurons and Imitation as the Driving Force behind "the Great Leap Forward" in Human Evolution. EDGE: The third culture, http://www.edge.org/3rd_culture/ramachandran/ramachandran_p1.html
13. Rizzolatti, G., Fadiga, L., Gallese, V., Fogassi, I.: Premotor Cortex and the Recognition of Motor Actions. Cognitive Brain Research **3** (1996) 131–141
14. Sutton, R., Barto, A.G.: Reinforcement Learning: An Introduction. Press, Cambridge, MA (1998)
15. Wiedermann, J.: Towards Algorithmic Explanation of Mind Evolution and Functioning (Invited Talk). In: Proc. of the 23-rd International Symposium on Mathematical Foundations of Computer Science. LNCS Vol. 1450. Springer Verlag Berlin (1998), 152–166
16. Wiedermann, J.: The Computational Limits to the Cognitive Power of the Neuroidal Tabula Rasa. Journal of Experimental and Theoretical Artificial Intelligence (JETAI), **15** 3 (2003) 267–279
17. Wiedermann, J.: Mirror Neurons, Embodied Cognitive Agents and Imitation Learning. Technical Report V-894, ICS AS CR, Prague 2003 (cf. http://www.cs.cas.cz and the respective pages in section Research)

Fully Truthful Mechanisms*

Ning Chen and Hong Zhu

Department of Computer Science, Fudan University, P. R. China
{nchen, hzhu}@fudan.edu.cn

Abstract. In this paper, we consider that in mechanism design, the mechanism itself has a reservation value to the result of the output. Based on this extended model, we define a more general definition of truthfulness, fully truthfulness. Unfortunately, the ordinary VCG mechanism is not fully truthful in our new model. Therefore we extend VCG mechanism and discuss the fully truthfulness of the new mechanisms.

1 Introduction

With the emergence of the Internet as a platform for communications and connections among enormous numbers of computers and humans, game theory [14] has become more and more widely applied to the study of computer science [15], communication networks [1], [4]. In the traditional sense, inputs for a problem are explicitly given at the beginning of the algorithm, and the goal is to find out the corresponding desired output. In a distributed environment such as the Internet, however, participants are not centrally controlled so that protocol designers may have to take their reactions into consideration.

Mechanism design, a classic economic concept [9], [14], deals with algorithmic design problems involving in such human factors, as in task allocation problems [4], [13], and combinatorial auctions [3], [8], [11]. Intuitively, mechanism design can be described as the design of protocols that realize a given target (objective function) under the assumption that the participants (agents) are all self-interested and rational ones who aim to optimize their own goals. One of the most important issues in mechanism design is that of truthfulness (incentive compatibility), i.e., a protocol that motivates agents to tell their private preferences (valuations) truthfully.

One important design problem is the optimal mechanism that maximizes the expected revenue of the mechanism itself. Myerson [10] partially solved this problem when the valuations of agents are independent and the probability distributions obey some conditions. Unfortunately, most results recently are negative, e.g., [1], [5], [16], [17].

Another central design problem, which we will mainly discuss in this paper, is the utilitarian mechanism. The goal of a utilitarian mechanism is to maximize the total valuations of agents. Such mechanisms (and specifically, VCG mechanism

* This work was supported by grants from China National Natural Science Fund [60273045], and the Ministry of Science and Technology [2001CCA03000].

[2], [7], [18]) have been discussed, e.g., in [6], [7], [9], extensively. Nisan and Ronen [12], [13] studied this problem from the point of view of algorithmic design. We observe that in reality, the mechanism may have its own requirement (besides the goal of the optimization of objective function) to the result of objective function. That is, when the optimal solution of objective function is not up to the reservation value c of the mechanism, which is determined by the mechanism in advance, the mechanism may choose to output nothing.

For example, in the 1-item Vickrey auction in which an auctioneer sells one item good to n agents, with bids $b_1 \geq b_2 \geq \cdots \geq b_n$, respectively. The agent who bids b_1 wins the item at price b_2. For this outcome, the value of objective function is b_1. Thus, if the reservation value c is less than b_1, the auctioneer won't sell the good to any agent. Intuitively, reservation value c is the mechanism's utility (evaluation) for the objective function. That is, if the optimal solution of objective function is not worse than the reservation value c, the mechanism is guaranteed to preform this output.

Note that the traditional concept of truthfulness is specified to the case that $c \leq 0$, whereas for other different values of c, agents' strategies will be changed accordingly. Therefore we introduce the concept of *fully truthfulness* in which for all possible reservation values, the mechanism is truthful. Unfortunately, the ordinary VCG mechanism that solves utilitarian problems perfectly is not fully truthful even under a relatively relaxed condition (Theorem 2). Therefore we extend VCG mechanism and demonstrate the fully truthfulness for the extended mechanism, c-verified VCG mechanism. Specifically, we prove that a special kind of c-verified VCG mechanisms is fully truthful (Theorem 4), which is a sufficient and necessary condition under mild assumptions.

In Section 2, we briefly review some basic concepts of mechanism design and VCG mechanism. In Section 3.1, we introduce our new notion of fully truthfulness based on the extended mechanism model. The ordinary VCG mechanism is not fully truthful is demonstrated in Section 3.2. In Section 3.3, we extend the ordinary VCG mechanism and discuss its property of fully truthfulness. In Section 3.4, we extend the mechanism further and show the same property as above. We conclude our work in Section 4 with remarks and discussions on further research.

2   Preliminaries

In this section, we present the formal definition of mechanism and review the classic VCG mechanism. More details are referred to [13].

2.1   The Model

Assume there are n agents desiring possible outcome $o \in O$, where O is a finite set of outcomes. Each agent $i \in \{1, \ldots, n\}$ has a privately known real function $v^i(o)$, for all $o \in O$, termed as *type*, representing his benefit from the possible outcome

o in terms of some common currency. We denote $(a^1, \ldots, a^{i-1}, a^{i+1}, \ldots, a^n)$ by a^{-i}, and let $(a^i, a^{-i}) = (a^1, \ldots, a^n)$.

Intuitively, a mechanism is a protocol that solves a given problem by assuring the required outcome occurs. Formally,

Definition 1 (Mechanism) ([12,13]) *A (direct revelation) mechanism $m = (o, p)$, on input vector $w = (w^1, \ldots, w^n)$ of the declarations of agents, is composed of two parts:*

1. *An outcome function $o(w) \in O$.*
2. *A payment function $p(w) = (p^1, \ldots, p^n)$. This is the payment handed by the mechanism to each agent (e.g., if $p^i = -2$, agent i pays two units of currency to the mechanism).*

Remark 1. In the above definition, the declaration w^i of agent i is not necessarily equal to v^i, since he may not tell the truth to the mechanism. His strategy is determined in terms of how to maximize his *utility* value $u^i = v^i(o) + p^i$, where o is the outcome of the mechanism.

Remark 2. A mechanism is called *truthful* (or *incentive compatible*) if truth-telling is a dominant strategy for each agent. That is, for any agent i and declarations w^{-i} of other agents, agent i's utility is maximized by reporting his true type v^i. Truthfulness is one of the most important concepts in the mechanism design, and we will discuss it in detail in the following.

Remark 3. We may define various outcome functions in different models. In this paper, we only discuss *utilitarian problems*, in which the outcome function of the mechanism is to select an optimal outcome $o \in O$ that maximizes the *objective function* $g(o, v) = \sum_{i=1}^{n} v^i(o)$, which is termed as *social utility*.

2.2 VCG Mechanism

One of the most important results in mechanism design is that of Vickrey-Clarke-Groves (VCG) mechanism (or Generalized Vickrey Auction (GVA)) [18], [2], [7]. Specifically, VCG mechanism provides a good solution for all utilitarian problems.

Definition 2 (VCG Mechanism) *A mechanism $m = (o, p)$ belongs to VCG family if:*

1. *$o(w) \in \arg\max_{o \in O} \sum_{i=1}^{n} w^i(o)$.*
2. *The payment is calculated according to the VCG formula*

$$p^i(w) = \sum_{j \neq i} w^j(o(w)) + h^i(w^{-i}),$$

where h^i is an arbitrary function of w^{-i}.

Theorem 1 ([7]) *VCG Mechanism is truthful.*

Note that because of truthfulness, each agent indeed reports his true type v^i in VCG mechanism, i.e., $w^i = v^i$. Hence, for any $1 \leq k \leq n$, the utility value of agent k is

$$
\begin{aligned}
u^k &= v^k(o) + p^k \\
&= v^k(o) + \sum_{j \neq k} v^j(o) + h^k(v^{-k}) \\
&= \sum_{i=1}^{n} v^i(o) + h^k(v^{-k}),
\end{aligned}
$$

where o is optimal solution of the outcome function.

3   Fully Truthful Mechanisms

In this section, we extend the ordinary mechanisms and introduce the concept of fully truthfulness. Then we discuss the property of fully truthfulness on the extended model of mechanism.

3.1   Definitions

Note that in Discussion 1, the mechanism as a whole do not have any utility or target, and its function is just to choose an outcome $o \in O$ that serves best for all agents. Sometimes, however, none of the outcomes is a good selection. Therefore, the mechanism should prevent each outcome from being selected in such situation.

Definition 3 (c-Verified Mechanism) *Given constant c, c-verified mechanism $m = (o, p)$ is same as the ordinary mechanism (Definition 1) except that after executing the protocol, the mechanism verifies that whether the value of objective function $g(o, v)$ is higher or [1] equal to c. If it is, c-verified mechanism outputs as the ordinary mechanism. Otherwise, it outputs nothing.*

In this paper, we assume without loss of generality that the real c is determined by the mechanism in advance and all agents do not know its value. In utilitarian problems, if $\max_{o \in O} \sum_{i=1}^{n} v^i(o) \geq c$, the mechanism selects this optimal outcome o and computes the corresponding payment function. But if the social utility of all possible outcomes is less than c, then none of them will be selected and the mechanism outputs nothing.

There are several ways to get the meaning of c. For example, we may regard c as the minimal welfare of the mechanism required when performing the optimal outcome. In the economic terminology, such c is usually denoted by *reservation value*.

---

[1] Here the criterion of goodness is in terms of various mechanism design models.

Similar to the above section, we can define the concept of truthfulness for c-verified mechanism similarly, but such definition is meaningless when c is sufficiently small. Fiat et al. [5] presented a kind of truthful auctions where they named as *cancelable auction*. Here we apply this idea to the following definition.

Definition 4 (Fully Truthful Mechanism) *A c-verified mechanism* $m = (o, p)$ *is called* fully truthful *if for any reservation value c, c-verified mechanism is truthful. That is, no matter what the value c is, the utility of each agent is maximized by reporting his true type.*

3.2 VCG Mechanism Is Not Fully Truthful

A natural question is what kind of mechanisms is fully truthful. Trivially,

Proposition 1 *1-item Vickrey auction is not fully truthful.*

Proof. It's easy to see that 1-item Vickrey auction belongs to VCG mechanism family, and each agent bid his type truthfully. Here, we only consider the agent i with the highest bid v^i. When executing c-verified mechanism, the auctioneer compares v^i with c. If $c > v^i$, no agent gets the good; otherwise agent i wins at the price of the second highest bid. Thus when $c > v^i$, agent i may bid w^i sufficiently large such that $c \leq w^i$, and wins the good at the same price (assume the bids of other agents do not change). That means agent i's utility is not maximized by bidding his true type for some value c, i.e., 1-item Vickrey auction is not fully truthful. □

If we require all agents to be limited to *participation constraints*, that is, the utility value of truthful agent is guaranteed to be non-negative, we have the following theorem.

Theorem 2 *Assume the type of each agent with participation constraints is finite, then any VCG mechanism, in which (1) $\sum_{j \neq i} v^j + h^i$ is the payment function for agent i and (2) there exists k, $1 \leq k \leq n$, such that h^k is independent of c, is not fully truthful under c-verified sense.*

Proof. The proof idea is similar to Proposition 1. We only need to show that for certain agents (with their true types), there exists $i \in \{1, \ldots, n\}$ such that agent i's utility is not maximized by reporting his true type.

Given true types $v^1, \ldots, v^n$ of all agents, the ordinary VCG mechanism selects an outcome $o \in O$ that maximizes the social utility $\sum_{i=1}^{n} v^i(o)$. Due to participation constraints, we know that for any agent j, his utility value should satisfy

$$\sum_{i=1}^{n} v^i(o) + h^j(v^{-j}) \geq 0.$$

For the given k in which h^k is independent of c, we consider the utility of agent k in the following two cases:

Case 1. Agent k's utility is strictly larger than zero, i.e.,

$$\sum_{i=1}^{n} v^i(o) + h^k(v^{-k}) \; > \; 0.$$

For a sufficiently large constant c, we must have $\sum_{i=1}^{n} v^i(o) < c$, and according to Definition 3, the mechanism outputs nothing. But if agent k reports $w^k(o)$ sufficiently large such that

$$w^k(o) + \sum_{j \neq k} v^j(o) \; \geq \; c,$$

his utility value, $\sum_{i=1}^{n} v^i(o) + h^k(v^{-k})$, would still be positive, assuming other agents still report their true types. (Since $h^k(\cdot)$ is independent of c, agent k's utility value does not change, regardless of $v^i(o)$ or $w^i(o)$ that he reports.)

Case 2. Agent k's utility is equal to zero, i.e.,

$$\sum_{i=1}^{n} v^i(o) + h^k(v^{-k}) \; = \; 0.$$

In this case we define another agent k' taking place of agent k in the mechanism. The true type of k' satisfies $v^{k'}(o) = v^k(o) + 1$ for the above outcome o and $v^{k'}(o') = v^k(o')$ for all $o' \in O \setminus \{o\}$. Then o is still the optimal solution for the mechanism to maximize the total utility. And it's easy to see that at this time, we have

$$v^{k'}(o) + \sum_{j \neq k'} v^j(o) + h^{k'}(v^{-k}) \; > \; 0,$$

where $h^{k'} = h^k$. That is, the utility value of agent k' is strictly larger than zero, which is equivalent to case 1. Thus the theorem follows. □

Some comments are in place. Note that the theorem is also correct even if we remove participation constraints (the proof is similar). In addition, if there exists an agent with infinite type value, c-verified mechanism is degenerated to the ordinary case.

3.3 c-Verified VCG Mechanism

As we have shown above, ordinary VCG mechanism is good enough for the traditional sense of truthfulness, but under the fully truthful sense, it does not work well.

Note that in the proof of Theorem 2, the main point is that h^i is independent of c. Thus we may extend VCG mechanism by assuming that for any i, h^i is not independent of c, i.e., c is one of variables in function h^i. In the following parts of this paper, all VCG mechanisms and VCG formulae are specified to this extended case.

Definition 5 (c-Verified h-VCG Mechanism) *Given constant c and collection of functions* $h = (h^1, \ldots, h^n)$, *where* h^i *is an arbitrary function of* v^{-i} *and c, a mechanism* $m = (o, p)$ *(on input vector w) is called c-verified h-VCG mechanism if*

1. $o(w) \in \arg\max_{o \in O} \sum_{i=1}^{n} w^i(o)$ *(as ordinary VCG mechanism). If*

$$\max_{o \in O} \sum_{i=1}^{n} w^i(o) \geq c,$$

   the mechanism performs next step. Otherwise, the mechanism stops and outputs nothing.
2. *The payment is calculated according to h-VCG formula*

$$p^i(w) = \sum_{j \neq i} w^j(o(w)) + h^i(w^{-i}, c).$$

Unless stated otherwise, c-verified h-VCG mechanism is denoted by h-VCG mechanism. Let $-h = (-h^1, \ldots, -h^n)$. In the following we mainly discuss the property of fully truthfulness of $(-h)$-VCG mechanism.

Theorem 3 *For any collection of functions* $h = (h^1, \ldots, h^n)$, *if there exist* $i \in \{1, \ldots, n\}$, *c and* w^{-i} *such that* $h^i(w^{-i}, c) < c$, *then* $(-h)$-VCG *mechanism is not fully truthful.*

Proof. In the proof, we do not mention the optimal outcome $o \in O$ of the mechanism explicitly, but all relations are according on this outcome. We consider two cases as follows.

Case 1. For the above i, c and w^{-i}, we have $\sum_{j \neq i} w^j < c$.

It's easy to see that there exists a non-negative real r such that

$$h^i(w^{-i}, c) < r + \sum_{j \neq i} w^j < c.$$

Let $v^i = r$, that is, the true type of agent i (on outcome o) is r. Thus we can see clearly that if agent i reports v^i truthfully, his utility value is zero. But if he reports a sufficiently large real w^i, his utility would be

$$v^i + \sum_{j \neq i} w^j - h^i(w^{-i}, c) > 0.$$

Case 2. For the above i, c and w^{-i}, we have $\sum_{j \neq i} w^j \geq c$.

Similarly, there exists a negative real r' such that

$$h^i(w^{-i}, c) < r' + \sum_{j \neq i} w^j < c.$$

Let $v^i = r'$ and the following part is same to case 1.

Therefore agent i's utility is not maximized by bidding his true type, and the theorem follows.   □

Intuitively, a mechanism is fully truthful if agent's utility is in consistence with the social utility. That is, when the utility of each agent is maximized by reporting his true type, the social utility should also be optimized (or at least not less than the given constant c). As we will see following, many other formulae, which belong to VCG formulae family, can define fully truthful mechanisms.

Theorem 4 *Assume all agents are restricted to participation constraints. If the collection of functions $h = (h^1, \ldots, h^n)$ satisfies that for any $i \in \{1, \ldots, n\}$, c and w^{-i}, we have $h^i(w^{-i}, c) \geq c$, then $(-h)$-VCG mechanism is fully truthful.*

Proof. Assume the true type of agent i is v^i. For all possible values of i, c and w^{-i}, the utility of agent i is non-negative if

$$v^i + \sum_{j \neq i} w^j - h^i(w^{-i}, c) \geq 0.$$

Thus we must have

$$v^i + \sum_{j \neq i} w^j \geq c, \quad \text{since } h^i(w^{-i}, c) \geq c.$$

That is, if agent i gets non-negative utility when reporting his true type, the declarations of agents can always pass the verification of the mechanism in Definition 5.

On the other hand, if $v^i + \sum_{j \neq i} w^j < c$, even if agent i may report a sufficiently large value w^i to pass the verification, his utility value is still negative since

$$v^i + \sum_{j \neq i} w^j < c \leq h^i(w^{-i}, c).$$

Note that there is another possible case,

$$c \leq v^i + \sum_{j \neq i} w^j < h^i(w^{-i}, c),$$

which can not happen because of the participation constraints.   □

From the above two theorems, we divide VCG formulae into two subsets completely, in which one defines fully truthful mechanism and the other does not. Note that if removing participation constraints from Theorem 4, similar as the above proof, we can show that only $(-c)$-VCG mechanism, in which the function h^i is equal to constant $-c$, is fully truthful. Another great advantage of $(-c)$-VCG mechanism is that the time complexity of computing the objective and payment function is linear to the number of agents and cardinality of the outcome set.

Since it's known that VCG is the only truthful mechanism for utilitarian problems under mild assumptions [6], it follows that only those VCG formulae in Theorem 4 define fully truthful mechanisms.

Definition 6 (Fully Truthful VCG Formula Family) *A collection of functions* $h = (h^1, \ldots, h^n)$ *belongs to* fully truthful VCG formula family *if* h-VCG *mechanism is fully truthful under participation constraints. That is, for all* $i \in \{1, \ldots, n\}$, c *and* w^{-i}, *we have* $h^i(w^{-i}, c) \geq c$.

3.4   Extension of c-Verified Mechanism

In Definition 3, c-verified mechanism is defined in terms of a fixed constant c. More generally, for any element o_i in the outcome set O, there exists a corresponding reservation parameter c_i. That is, if the outcome of the mechanism is o_i, then the value of objective function should be higher or equal to c_i.

Definition 7 (C-Verified Mechanism) *Given outcome set* $O = \{o_1, \ldots, o_k\}$, *and real vector* $C = \{c_1, \ldots, c_k\}$, *let* $O' = \emptyset$, C-*verified mechanism* $m = (o, p)$ *performs in the following way (on input vector w):*

1. *For any* $o_i \in O$, *the mechanism verifies that whether objective function is higher or*[2] *equal to* c_i, *when selecting* o_i *as an outcome. If it is, let* $O' = O' \cup \{o_i\}$, *where* o_i *is called a* valid outcome.
2. *If* $O' = \emptyset$, *the mechanism stops and outputs nothing. Otherwise, for all* $o_i \in O'$, *the mechanism chooses one to optimize the objective function.*
3. *Payment function is calculated, as the ordinary mechanism, according to the outcome selected in the above step.*

Intuitively, C-verified mechanism chooses a valid outcome, which has been passed the verification, to optimize the objective function. In utilitarian problems, o_j is a valid outcome if $\sum_{i=1}^{n} v^i(o_j) \geq c_j$. One may argue what's the motivation of the above definition. Let's look at the following example.

Example 1 A government plans to build a railway from x to y. Each vertex i of the graph is an agent and its type v^i represents the convenience that he may get from the railway. ($v^i < 0$ means that agent i doesn't want the railway passing his position since it may bring about, e.g., noises). What the government concerns about is the total valuations (i.e., social utility) of agents. There're two possible choices for the government, o_1 and o_2. Although the total valuations of outcome o_1, 100, may be higher than that of o_2, 80, but since the cost of constructing o_1 is much higher than o_2, the reservation value of o_1 and o_2 is 120 and 60 respectively. In this situation, the government will select o_2 rather than o_1 according to the above definition. Note that in the ordinary utilitarian mechanism, o_1 will be selected as an outcome because of its higher total valuations.

Similar to Definition 4, we call C-verified mechanism is *fully truthful* if for any real vector C, C-verified mechanism is truthful.

The key point in fully truthful C-verified mechanism is to motivate all agents revealing their types truthfully in the first step of the mechanism. In step 2, 3,

---

[2] Similarly, the criterion of goodness is in terms of different mechanism models.

any ordinary VCG formulae applies. But the truthful behavior of agents in the first step is related to the payment function in step 3. Thus our arguments in the above subsections is helpful here.

Definition 8 (C-Verified VCG Mechanism) *Given any vector C, a mechanism $m = (o, p)$ is called C-verified VCG mechanism if it's a C-verified one and*

1. *The outcome function is same as the ordinary VCG mechanism except that the outcome is selected from the valid outcome set.*
2. *The payment function is $p^i = \sum_{j \neq i} w^j + h^i$ for agent i, where $h = (h^1, \ldots, h^n)$ belongs to fully truthful VCG formula family.*

Theorem 5 *C-verified VCG mechanism is fully truthful for any vector C under participation constraints.*

Proof. For any vector C and $h(\cdot)$ that belongs to fully truthful VCG formula family, we need to prove that the mechanism is truthful when using $\sum_{j \neq i} w^j + h^i$ as the payment function for agent i.

For any agent i, assume his true type is $v^i(o_j)$ for any $o_j \in O$. Suppose truthtelling is not a dominant strategy for him. Then there exists $w = \{w^1, \ldots, w^n\}$ such that

$$u^i(w^{-i}, w^i) > u^i(w^{-i}, v^i),$$

according to the outcome and payment function.

Assume o_l is the outcome of the mechanism upon receiving input $w = (w^{-i}, w^i)$, which implies that $\sum_{i=1}^{n} w^i(o_l) \geq c_l$. Note that we have

$$\sum_{j \neq i} w^j(o_l) + v^i(o_l) < c_l. \tag{1}$$

That is, o_l is not a valid outcome when input vector of the mechanism is (w^{-i}, v^i). Otherwise, there must be $u^i(w^{-i}, w^i) \leq u^i(w^{-i}, v^i)$, which contradicts to our assumption.

Then we may construct an extreme case in which for all agents, the true type of the outcome o_l is same as the above, and the type of all other outcomes is $-\infty$. Now consider c_l-verified VCG mechanism for this extreme case. It's trivial to see that o_l is the only possible valid outcome. When agent i reveals true type v^i, his utility is zero according to (1). But if he reports w^i instead of v^i to the mechanism, o_l passes the verification and agent i gets positive utility since

$$u^i(w^{-i}, w^i) > u^i(w^{-i}, v^i) = 0.$$

That is, agent i's utility is not maximized by reporting his true type, which contradicts the fact that $h(\cdot)$ belongs to fully truthful VCG formula family. □

4   Conclusion

Recently, a great deal of work have been done on mechanism design and related issues. A more general concept of truthfulness, fully truthfulness, is studied in this paper. Specifically, fully truthful mechanism concerns not only the objective function, but also the expected utility itself. That is, the mechanism selects one possible outcome from the valid outcome set to optimize the given target, which ensures the expected return. Note that the concept of fully truthfulness we introduced in this paper is based on utilitarian problems, but it can be generalized to other mechanism design models and objective functions.

Fully truthful mechanism is a more general concept in mechanism design and has many applications, especially when considering the target of the mechanism itself. Hence, the mechanism we think about here is not by far the robotistic one, but like our human beings that have utilities, i.e., selecting an output "he/she" prefers. We argue that this notion of mechanism is more practical. On one hand, it does guarantee the target (objective function) to be happened; on the other hand, it ensures the required utility of the mechanism.

In addition, as we have seen in this paper and many other works, the implementation of truthfulness is on the cost of decreasing the revenue of the mechanism. Thus can we find a weaker feasible notion of truthfulness (such as approximation or average case) is a very meaningful direction in the future work.

Acknowledgments. We thank Wolfram Conen, Xiaotie Deng for many fruitful discussions. We thank Mingming Lu, Yunlei Zhao for their careful clarifications on this paper. We also thank the anonymous reviews for their suggestions for improving this paper.

References

1. Archer, A., Tardos, E.: Frugal Path Mechanisms, SODA (2002) 991–999
2. Clarke, E.H.: Multipart Pricing of Public Goods. Public Choice **11** (1971) 17–33
3. de Vries, S., Vohra, R.: Combinatorial Auctions: A Survry. INFORMS Journal on Computing, forthcoming
4. Feigebaum, J., Papadimitriou, C.H., Shenker, S.: Sharing the Cost of Multicast Transmissions. STOC (2000) 218–227
5. Fiat, A., Goldberg, A.V., Hartline, J.D., Karlin, A.R.: Competitive Generalized Auctions. STOC (2002) 72–81
6. Green, J., Laffont, J.J.: Characterization of Satisfactory Mechanism for the Revelation of Preferences for Public Goods. Econometrica (1977) 427–438
7. Groves, T.: Incentives in Teams. Econometrica **41** (1973) 617–631
8. Lehmann, D., O'Callaghan, L., Shoham, Y.: Truth Revelation in Rapid, Approximately Efficient Combinatorial Auctions. ACM Conference on E-Commerce (EC) (1999) 96–102
9. Mas-Collel, A., Whinston, W., Green, J.: Microeconomic Theory. Oxford University Press (1995)
10. Myerson, R.B.: Optimal Auction Design. Mathematics of Operation Research **6** (1981) 58–73

11. Nisan, N.: Bidding and Allocation in Combinatorial Auctions. ACM Conference on E-Commerce (EC) (2000) 1–12
12. Nisan, N.: Algorithms for Selfish Agents. STACS (1999) 1–15
13. Nisan, N., Ronen, A.: Algorithmic Mechanism Design (Extended Abstract). STOC (1999) 129–140. Full version appeared in Game and Economic Behavior **35** (2001) 166–196
14. Osborne, M.J., Rubistein, A.: A Course in Game Theory. MIT Press (1994)
15. Papadimitriou, C.H.: Algorithms, Games, and the Internet. STOC (2001) 749–753
16. Ronen, A., Saberi, A.: Optimal Auctions are Hard. FOCS (2002) 396–405
17. Segal, I.R.: Optimal Pricing Mechanisms with Unknown Demand. Working paper (2002)
18. Vickrey, W.: Counterspeculation, Auctions and Competitive Sealed Tenders. Journal of Finance **16** (1961) 8–37

Author Index